D1030853

Liberty Tree

Liberty Tree

Ordinary People and the American Revolution

Alfred F. Young

CONSULTING EDITOR, HARVEY J. KAYE

New York University Press

NEW YORK AND LONDON

NEW YORK UNIVERSITY PRESS
New York and London
www.nyupress.org

Library of Congress Cataloging–in–Publication Data
Young, Alfred Fabian, 1925–
Liberty tree : ordinary people and the American
Revolution / Alfred F. Young.
p. cm.
Includes bibliographical references and index.
ISBN–13: 978–0–8147–9685–6 (cloth : alk. paper)
ISBN–10: 0–8147–9685–0 (cloth : alk. paper)
ISBN–13: 978–0–8147–9686–3 (pbk. : alk. paper)
ISBN–10: 0–8147–9686–9 (pbk. : alk. paper)
1. United States—History—Revolution, 1775–1783—Social
aspects. 2. Radicalism—United States—History—18th
century. I. Title.
E.209.Y68   2006
973.3—dc22   2006008340

New York University Press books are printed on acid-free paper,
and their binding materials are chosen for strength and durability.

Manufactured in the United States of America

c 10 9 8 7 6 5 4 3 2 1
p 10 9 8 7 6 5 4 3 2 1

For my grandchildren:
Davia, Noah, Isabel, and Ruby

Contents

List of Illustrations   ix

Introduction: Why Write the History of Ordinary People?   1

PART I. The People Out of Doors

1. The Mechanics of the Revolution: "By Hammer and
    Hand All Arts Do Stand"   27

2. "Persons of Consequence": The Women of Boston and
    the Making of the American Revolution, 1765–1776   100

3. Tar and Feathers and the Ghost of Oliver Cromwell:
    English Plebeian Culture and American Radicalism   144

PART II. Accommodations

4. Conservatives, the Constitution, and the
    "Genius of the People"   183

5. How Radical Was the American Revolution?   215

PART III. Memory: Lost and Found

6. The Celebration and Damnation of Thomas Paine   265

7. The Freedom Trail: Walking the Revolution in Boston   296

8.   Liberty Tree: Made in America, Lost in America   325

      Index   395
      About the Author   419

List of Illustrations

1. Liberty tree, James Pike's powderhorn, 1776 — 2
2. *Pat Lyon at the Forge*, oil painting by John Neagle, 1827 — 28
3. Poor Richard Illustrated, engraving, c.1796 — 38
4. General Society of Mechanics and Tradesmen of New York certificate — 55
5. Society of Master Sailmakers certificate — 57
6. The death of Christopher Seider, broadside, 1770 — 101
7. "A New Method of Macarony Making," engraving, 1774 — 145
8. Oliver Cromwell, engraving, Nathaneal Low's *Almanack for 1774* — 157
9. Society of Pewterers of New York, flag, 1788 — 184
10. "Gen. Daniel Shays and Col. Job Shattuck," engraving, 1787 — 193
11. "The World Turned Upside Down," engraving, 1783 — 216
12. Thomas Paine, engraving, London, c.1792 — 266
13. "Mad Tom in a Rage," engraving, c.1800 — 283
14. Map of the Freedom Trail — 297
15. Liberty tree, engraving by Paul Revere, 1765 — 326
16. "The True-Born Sons of Liberty," broadside, Boston, 1765 — 332
17. Liberty pole, New York City, engraving by P. E. DuSimitiere, c.1770 — 350
18. "Defence of the Liberty Pole in New York," by Felix Darley — 352

Introduction
Why Write the History of Ordinary People?

Joseph Plumb Martin was a Connecticut farm boy who enlisted in the Continental Army in 1777 when he was sixteen and served until 1783, the length of the Revolutionary war. He was a private, then a sergeant, in the Corps of Miners and Sappers who conducted sieges of enemy fortifications, a dangerous service. In 1830, when he was seventy, Martin published his memoir, *A Narrative of the Adventures, Dangers and Sufferings of a Revolutionary Soldier*, which has to be the best autobiography that has survived for a rank-and-file soldier: pungent, humorous, and always irreverent.

After describing a particularly hard-fought battle he had taken part in, Martin wrote, "but there has been little notice taken of it, the reason for which is, there was no Washington, Putnam, or Wayne there. Had there been the affair would have been extolled to the skies." He was naming three of the most famous generals of the war: Israel Putnam, Anthony Wayne, and, of course, the commander in chief George Washington, under whom he had served from Valley Forge to Yorktown. "Great men get great praise; little men, nothing," wrote Martin. He conceded that "every private soldier in the army thinks his service is essential to carry on the war he is engaged in," but he asked, "What could officers do without such men? Nothing at all. Alexander never could have conquered the world without private soldiers."

Martin remembered the army in the terrible winter of 1777, when soldiers were "not only starved but naked. The greatest part were not only shirtless and barefoot but destitute of all other clothing, especially blankets." And he remembered joining his fellow soldiers, "exasperated beyond endurance," by such conditions, who resorted to mutiny in 1780. To Martin his comrades in arms were "a family of brothers," but a half century after the war he was bitter. When soldiers enlisted, he wrote, "they were

The liberty tree is at the center of a scene carved on James Pike's powderhorn. To the left are British soldiers labeled "REGULARS the AGGRESSORS, April 19, 1775," and to the right, "PROVINCIALS DEFENDING." The scene represents the patriot version not only of the Battle of Lexington but of the Revolutionary war. Pike was a Massachusetts militia man who served at the Battle of Bunker Hill. Soldiers stored their gunpowder in powderhorns. Photograph courtesy of the Chicago Historical Society.

promised a hundred acres of land.... When the country had drained the last drop of blood it could screw out of the poor soldiers, they were turned adrift like old worn-out horses, and nothing said about land to pasture them upon.... Such things ought not to be."[1]

After the war, Martin, the landless veteran, "squatted" on land on the Maine frontier confiscated from Loyalists and bought by General Henry Knox, one of the "Great Proprietors" who acquired legal title to hundreds of thousands of acres for a pittance. Together with other settlers in Maine, Martin fought for years for the right to the land he farmed, believing with the Liberty Men, as they called themselves, that "Who can have better rights to the land than we who have fought for it, subdued it & made it valuable ... God gave the earth to the children?" In 1801, settlers won the right to buy the land they farmed, but Martin was never able to pay for his and eventually lost it. In 1818, when he applied for a pension under the first general pension law passed by Congress for veterans "in reduced circumstances," he testified, "I have no real or personal estate, nor any income whatever.... I am a laborer, and by reason of my age and infirmity, I am unable to work. My wife is sickly and rheumatic. I have five children....

Without my pension I am unable to support myself and my family." Martin eked out a living and died in 1850. The epitaph on his gravestone reads, "A Soldier of the Revolution."[2]

Martin's poignant life story opens a window to a side of American history almost totally lost in the master narrative of the Revolution when it is told as a success story led by "great men." Martin was not unusual, save for his ability as a writer. He was one of more than one hundred thousand young men, most of them landless, who saw military service in the Continental Army over the seven years of the war. Another one hundred thousand served in the militia, and several tens of thousands at sea. He was among the tens of thousands of veterans who applied for a pension in 1818, or in 1832. And he was like several thousand farmers in other states who for several decades after the war faced struggles to acquire or to hold on to land: the Green Mountain Boys in Vermont, the debt-ridden, tax-plagued rebels in western Massachusetts (among them Daniel Shays), Down-Renters in the Hudson Valley, the misnamed Whiskey rebels in Pennsylvania. Many would have shared a sense of the Revolution as not fulfilling its promises, as expressed by Herman Husband, leader of two backcountry rebellions in North Carolina in the 1770s and in western Pennsylvania in the 1790s that were both put down with force: "In Every Revolution, the People at Large are called upon to assist true Liberty," but when "the foreign oppressor is thrown off, learned and designing men" assume power to the detriment of the "laboring people."[3]

As Martin's words testify, ordinary people in the revolutionary era were far from being inarticulate or passive. Quite the contrary, they could be eloquent. As the participant-historian Dr. David Ramsay of South Carolina wrote in 1789, "When the war began, the Americans were a mass of husbandmen [farmers], merchants, mechanics and fishermen, but the necessities of the country gave a spring to the active powers of the inhabitants and set them on thinking, speaking, and acting in a line far beyond that to which they had been accustomed.... It seemed as if the war not only required but created talents." One can say the same thing about ordinary people in the Revolution that the historian Ira Berlin said of freed African American men and women in the era of the Civil War and Reconstruction after reading thousands of their letters: "under the pressure of unprecedented events, ordinary men and women can become extraordinarily perceptive and articulate."[4]

Martin was one of more than five hundred Revolutionary war soldiers who kept diaries or wrote their memoirs or collaborated with others in "as told to" accounts. Some tens of thousands told their wartime experiences in their pension applications. Collective activity by ordinary people was the hallmark of the American Revolution: the Sons of Liberty, Committees of Correspondence, Committees of Inspection, Committees of Safety, town meetings, caucuses, county conventions, militia organizations. And for these there are bodies of scattered documents: petitions, resolutions, newspaper accounts, speeches, court testimony, legal records. If, over the past half century, a fraction of the resources that have poured into the projects publishing the papers of the leaders of the Revolution went into assembling the full record of popular participation, we might have a more proportionate sense of the role of ordinary people in the Revolution.[5]

The essays in this volume grow out of my long-standing interest in exploring "history from the bottom up" in the long era of the American Revolution. I have been interested in exploring successively three large questions: What part did ordinary people play in the making of the Revolution? What impact did they have on the results, and what impact did the Revolution in turn have on them? And how have they fared in the public memory of the Revolution? I have grouped the essays in this volume in historical sequence, which allows the reader who so chooses to follow strands of the Revolution as they unfolded and passed into public memory.

As it happens, the arrangement of the essays is also more or less in the sequence in which they were published between 1980 and 2004. They are reprinted as they originally appeared, save for some changes to avoid repetition. Two essays, written for this volume, appear in print for the first time: "The Mechanics of the Revolution: By Hammer and Hand All Arts Do Stand," originally presented at an international conference in Milan and published in an Italian historical journal in 1982, is much expanded on the basis of two decades of new scholarship—my own and others. "Liberty Tree: Made in America, Lost in America," the most recent essay, is entirely new. In these two new essays I take up all three of the questions about popular movements of the Revolution that have engaged me: their origins, their impact, and public memory.

For readers interested in where these pieces fit in with my other, more familiar books on the Revolution, most of them were published after *The American Revolution: Explorations in American Radicalism* appeared in 1976, with groundbreaking scholarship by other historians focused for the most part on the origins of popular movements, and before its sequel in 1993, *Beyond the American Revolution: Explorations in the History of American*

Radicalism, in which scholars focused on results. The essays in this volume were written while I was also trying to get at the questions I posed about groups by exploring the lives of little-known individuals. My study of George Robert Twelves Hewes, the Boston shoemaker active in the Boston Massacre and the Boston Tea Party who told his life story while he was in his nineties, was an attempt to get at the consciousness of artisans by exploring one artisan's memory of the Revolution. My biography of Deborah Sampson, a twenty-one-year-old weaver and former indentured servant in a Massachusetts farm town who disguised herself as a man and served in the Continental Army for seventeen months, was an attempt to understand what the Revolution meant to women of her social class, who had limited life options.[6]

"The People Out of Doors," the title of part 1 of the book, is a phrase commonly used at the time of the Revolution to refer to people outside the political system or on its edges who made demands on legislators and officials who ruled "within doors." My focus in the three essays in this part is on city people: the "mechanics" in the major seaboard cities (Boston, New York, Philadelphia, and Charleston) and the women of the "middling" and "lower sort" in one city, Boston. "Mechanics" is the term adopted by artisans (master workmen employing journeymen and apprentices) as they became conscious of their power as active citizens and a presence in political life. I follow them through the making of the Revolution into the postwar era and the years of the young nation (1788–1815), when their influence in public life peaked, after which the traditional artisan system eroded.

The women of Boston called "Daughters of Liberty" by the "Sons of Liberty" thought of themselves, as one of them put it, as "persons of consequence," as they assumed one role after another in the conflict with Britain: spectators, boycotters, manufacturers, rioters, mourners, exhorters, and military supporters. In the third essay I examine the ritualized activities which appeared for the first time in America in the revolutionary era: tar-and-feathering, summoning up the ghost of Oliver Cromwell, and artisans marching en masse in parades with symbols of their crafts. I look for the origins of these activities in English plebeian culture, leaving the door open for what has been called the "invention of tradition." In the "Liberty Tree" essay in part 3 I return to this puzzle of where political symbols came from, as well as how they were lost in public memory.

The popular movements of the revolutionary era of the cities and countryside have often been dismissed as short-lived, localized, and of little consequence. The essays in part 2, called "Accommodations," examine the influence of the movements "from below" and "from the middle" by measuring their impact on those "on top." I am interested in the would-be ruling classes who tried to create a "political system" (as James Madison called it) that would put the genie of popular radicalism back in the bottle. I focus (in essay 4) on the political results of the Revolution at the point of drafting and ratifying the federal Constitution in 1787–88. I see the framers essentially as a conservative elite trying to fence in agrarian majorities that threatened "moneyed men" with "the excess of democracy," as many of them put it in the Constitutional convention in Philadelphia. The framers were forced to grant democratic concessions both to create a government that would survive in an increasingly democratic society and in order to secure the popular approval necessary for ratification—especially from city mechanics.

In essay 5, I broaden the discussion of results to ask, "How radical was the American Revolution?" and pull the camera back to attempt a panoramic view of the country as a whole. I see would-be rulers forced to make accommodations of all sorts, not only with people of the "middling sort" who were pushing their way into the political system—yeoman farmers and artisans—but also with those not in the system: enslaved African Americans on the "bottom," and with the "outsiders" to the system: women and Native Americans. Looking at this process of ongoing negotiations in the private sphere as well as the public sphere, the Revolution seems at once more radical and more deeply conservative than the conventional master narrative has allowed.

The history of the American Revolution, like most history, was passed down in two kinds of memory: the private memories of individuals and in public memory managed by keepers of the past. These were the people who in the fifty years after the Revolution erected statues and decided what holidays should be observed, whose papers historical societies should collect, and what should go into children's textbooks. Public memory is made up of what a leading scholar calls "dominant memories (or mainstream collective consciousness)" and "alternative (usually subordinate) memories," held by those outside the mainstream. The study of public memory is especially important in recovering ordinary people because history is usually written by the winners, and what happened to the losers often is passed down with the winners' class bias, or it is willfully forgotten.[7]

In part 3, "Memory: Lost and Found," I explore how three famous icons of the Revolution have fared in public memory: Thomas Paine, Boston's

Freedom Trail, and the liberty tree. Paine, commonly regarded as the quintessential radical of the Revolution, was the author of *Common Sense* and *The Rights of Man*, the two most influential pamphlets of the revolutionary era. The Freedom Trail, initiated in the 1950s, links the historic sites of some of the most celebrated popular events of the Revolution. The liberty tree at the time of the Revolution was a major site of popular resistance in Boston (conducted literally out of doors), as were liberty trees and liberty poles throughout the colonies. As it turns out, each essay in this part is an exploration of lost public memory. When Paine returned to the United States from France in 1802, he was reviled in many quarters as was no other major figure of the era, the beginning of two centuries of remarkable ups and down in historic memory.[8] On Boston's Freedom Trail, visitors can follow the red brick line in the streets to buildings that have been restored with loving care, but they are left to themselves to piece together where ordinary people fit into the picture. As for the liberty tree in Boston, the site is not even on maps of the Freedom Trail, nor are liberty trees and liberty poles marked in most other places.

I chose *Liberty Tree* as the title for this book after I discovered—actually very recently and very much to my surprise—that the liberty tree was the principal symbol of popular opposition to British measures and at the same time the site of the efforts of the Sons of Liberty leaders to control popular resistance. During the war it became a major symbol of the Revolution, and it became a metaphor to later generations, especially African Americans, seeking to fulfill the unfulfilled promise of the Revolution. That so important a symbol should be lost in historical amnesia in a country that demands so much reverence for its patriotic symbols is astonishing.

Why write the history of ordinary people in the American Revolution? I use the term "ordinary" not as the opposite of "extraordinary" but in opposition to "elites," the people in a society with wealth, power, and status. I prefer the term "common people," which, unlike "ordinary people," was much used at the time, except that when used today too often it smacks of condescension. Actually, the most common term at the time was simply "the people," which emerged as part of the changing language of the Revolution. In Boston, leaders called meetings of "the whole body of the people" when they wanted to broaden participation at public rallies beyond those eligible to vote in official town meetings. John Adams referred to "the whole people," James Madison to "the genius of the people," others to "the people at large." And, of course, the Declaration of Independence spoke of "the right of the people to alter or abolish" governments that per-sistently violated their rights.[9]

Such common usage alone should make us wonder: do we even have to ask why write the history of "ordinary people"? They were there. They were actors and players: they made history happen, as individuals and especially collectively. They were hardly marginal or peripheral—indeed they were often indispensable. And they have not received the recognition they sought at the time. But much more is at stake than giving credit, as important as that is. And it is more than a matter of expressing a humane compassion, not that that isn't much needed in the United States in the twenty-first century. The simple truth is that we cannot understand the American Rev-olution without taking into account the part played by the "people at large." Consider briefly three famous "moments" in the Revolution in 1765, 1776, and 1787, which essays in this volume take up.

1. *Sometimes the presence of "the little men," to use Sergeant Martin's words, casts the "great men" in a new light. The ideas and actions of the lead-ers take on new dimensions when set alongside the aspirations and actions of ordinary people.* The Revolution in Boston is often interpreted as the work of the famous leaders Samuel Adams, John Hancock, and John Adams. In the best-known biography of Samuel Adams, subtitled *Pioneer in Propa-ganda,* Adams is treated as the puppeteer who manipulated all the mari-onettes of the city. Examine the political explosion that set off the era, the resistance to the Stamp Act in Boston in 1765, when the Tree of Liberty made its first appearance (see essay 8), and the three leaders look different when set alongside the little-known Ebenezer Mackintosh, who was called "Captain General of the Liberty Tree." He was a poor shoemaker previ-ously known only as the head of one of the two rival "companies" that every November 5 managed the raucous ritual of Pope's Day (Guy Fawkes Day in England). In the campaign against the Stamp Act in 1765, Mackin-tosh was the visible leader of the five major crowd actions, ranging from the peaceful self-disciplined parade of two thousand Bostonians that in effect nullified the Act, to the violent crowd that gutted Lieutenant Gover-nor Thomas Hutchinson's mansion. The Sons of Liberty leaders courted Mackintosh, collaborated with him, and then shunted him aside. From 1765 on they waged a war on two fronts: against British measures and to control the crowd. The liberty tree is an apt symbol of these two sides of the Revolution.

The political leaders who came out on top in this internal tug-of-war were men who followed the advice that Robert R. Livingston Jr., a landed aristocrat of the Hudson Valley in New York, gave to the fellow members of his class who were confronted with rebellious tenants, politically awakened yeoman farmers, and urban mechanics with leaders of their own. Convinced of "the propriety of Swimming with a Stream which it is impossible to stem," he warned them that "they should yield to the torrent if they hoped to direct its course."[10] In Massachusetts, the leaders who survived learned to navigate through the torrent of democratic politics, each in different ways. Samuel Adams became a "tribune of the people," one of America's first professional politicians. John Hancock, the wealthiest merchant in New England, became a master of an aristocratic paternalism, using his fortune to buy popularity. And John Adams, a lawyer steeped in political philosophy, began a long career trying to balance the "democratic" and the "aristocratic." The American political leaders who set themselves against the torrent generally did not survive.

2. *Sometimes ordinary people have enough influence to shape the outcome of events. Add "the people at large" to the picture and time and again the conventional picture changes.* Take a very famous moment in July 1776 which many Americans feel is familiar: the day when the delegates to the Continental Congress from the thirteen colonies meeting in Philadelphia adopted a Declaration of Independence. *Whose moment was it?* We feel we know it from visiting the faithfully restored Independence Hall in Philadelphia or from looking at John Trumbull's endlessly reproduced painting of the delegates now displayed in the rotunda of the United States Capitol building in Washington. We also feel we know the event from the familiar facsimile of the handwritten version of the Declaration on parchment on which John Hancock's signature is sprawled across the page and leads us to the signatures of the "signers" below.

The painting invariably misnamed "The Signing of the Declaration of Independence," represents a "top-down" version of the event. It actually portrays not the signing but the five members of the drafting committee presenting the document to Congress: Thomas Jefferson, John Adams, Benjamin Franklin, Roger Sherman and—"Swimming with the Stream"— Robert R. Livingston. The delegates only look on. The signing actually took place later over many months. Trumbull, who worked on the painting for some three decades, took great pains to make sure he rendered an accurate likeness of each "eminent statesman" but he perpetuated the myth of an American consensus for independence. There was no such scene when all the delegates were gathered. Trumbull included men who voted *against* declaring independence, men who were absent at the time of the vote, and many who opposed a break with England. The painting delivers the message that the "signers" within doors led the way to independence.[11]

You would never know from the painting that the well-dressed gentlemen Trumbull portrayed—the "men in suits" of that day—had been brought to abandon reconciliation and declare American independence by a groundswell of opinion publicly expressed "out of doors" by the "plough joggers" of the countryside, who wore homespun clothes, and the mechanics of the cities, known as "leather apron men" (see essay 1). Nor would you know that war had begun and people were debating options for the country and for themselves as never before. In January 1776, *Common Sense* appeared, written by a former English artisan recently arrived in Philadelphia who made the case for independence in language that stirred ordinary people to a sense of their own capacity to effect change. "We have it in our power to begin the world over again," wrote Thomas Paine. By July 1776, more than one hundred thousand people had read his pamphlet or had had it read to them in army camps, taverns, and meeting houses. It was "greedily bought up and read by all ranks of people," said the delegate from New Hampshire (see essay 6).

In the spring of 1776, while Congress dithered, some eighty local meetings adopted resolutions instructing their representatives to support independence: town meetings, county conventions, militia companies. Nine state conventions did the same thing. The delegates knew it: on May 20, John Adams wrote that "Every post and every day rolls in upon us independence like a torrent." On July 3, the day after Congress voted for independence, he spelled out the process: "Time has been given for the whole people maturely to consider the great question of independence ... by discussing it in newspapers and pamphlets, by debating it in assemblies, conventions, committees of safety and inspection, in town and county meetings as well as in private conversations, so that the whole people in every colony of the thirteen, have now adopted it as their own." But Trumbull portrayed the men within the Pennsylvania State House as if they alone were responsible for the decision. In reality, "the whole people" were ahead of Trumbull's "eminent statesmen." A recent biographer of Adams could not have been more off the mark in writing, "It was John Adams, more than anyone who made it happen." Trumbull, who excelled at painting stirring historical panoramas, of course would have needed another canvas to portray the "people out of doors."[12]

3. *Sometimes there is a complex interplay of the people and the leaders, and the political decisions of men at the top can be explained only by taking*

into account the movements from below of which they were intensely aware.
Witness the drafting of the Constitution at the Philadelphia convention
and the process of ratification in 1787–88 (see essay 4), as well as the
response to it among mechanics (see essay 1). James Madison, James Wilson, and the other framers make sense not as "geniuses" who wrought "a
miracle in Philadelphia," as they are often portrayed, but as astute political
leaders who knew they had to accommodate "the genius of the people," a
phrase that meant their values or spirit. As George Mason, a respected Virginia delegate put it, "Notwithstanding the oppression & injustice experienced among us from democracy, the genius of the people is in favor of it,
and the genius of the people must be consulted."[13]

The delegates were drawn from the elites: they were more well-to-do,
more educated, more politically experienced than the average man—and
they were far more conservative. Such democratic spokesmen as Thomas
Paine, Daniel Shays, and Abraham Yates were not present at the convention, yet they were a distinct presence. They were the ghosts of the popular
movements of the preceding two decades who haunted the delegates.
Paine was so popular because he was the champion not only of independence but of simple democratic government based on a broad suffrage.
Shays was one of several leaders of a rebellion of angry, overtaxed, debt-
ridden farmers in western Massachusetts in the 1780s which set off a tremor
of alarm among conservatives everywhere. Yates was a stormy petrel in the
New York Senate, a man who began life as a shoemaker, a foe of all "high
flyers," as he called Alexander Hamilton. (Hamilton put him down as the
"late cobbler of laws and old shoes.") He was typical of state legislators
elsewhere who had "an itch for paper money" (Madison's phrase) and for
laws preventing foreclosures on farm mortgages, both measures opposed
by "moneyed men."

The new Constitution vested the new national government with the
power to "suppress insurrections" (so much for the ghost of Daniel Shays)
and erected specific curbs on the states' ability to "emit" paper money or
pass "laws impairing the obligation of contracts" (which presumably laid
the ghost of Abraham Yates). It also provided for the return to their
owners of future fugitive slaves—a giant "ghost" that loomed over southern slaveholders, who had experienced a massive loss of runaway slaves
during the war. (George Washington, presiding officer at the Convention,
lost seventeen slaves from his Mount Vernon plantation alone.) But to
accomplish these goals the framers knew they had to create a government
that would "last for the ages" and, more immediately, that could be ratified

by conventions in the states in which the delegates had to be elected by popular vote. In the big cities this meant by democratic-minded mechanics.

As these three moments suggest, would-be rulers were very much aware that they were living through a time of tumults, rebellions, democratic upheavals, and popular awakenings that challenged the status quo. One of the charges in the Declaration of Independence was that the king had "excited domestic insurrections," a reference to the appeal to slaves by the British general in Virginia to flee their masters. Another charge was that the king had made the colonies subject to "convulsions within," a reference to the democratic upsurges in the political vacuum of 1774–76. Still another was that he had encouraged the "merciless Indian savages" on the frontier, which was hardly the way the many tribes of Native Americans viewed their choice to defend their own independence from the colonists. The American Revolution was not a proletarian revolution, but it was a revolution with strong plebeian currents, some of which flowed into the mainstream and many of which ran as crosscurrents to it. Viewing this storm-tossed history solely from the conventional vantage point of the "top down" simply fails to come to grips with the history seen from the "bottom up" (African Americans) or from the "middle" (yeoman farmers and artisans), let alone seen from the vantage point of outsiders (Native Americans) or of women. My objective in these essays is a more inclusive history that brings these perspectives together and illuminates the whole.

Years ago in an undergraduate literature course on Emerson, Thoreau, and Whitman, I was taken by Ralph Waldo Emerson's advice to scholars in his famous "The American Scholar" address, delivered at Harvard in 1837, to explore "the near, the low [and] the common." And I was introduced to "mechanics" by Whitman's "I Hear America Singing." The themes of a democratic history of the Revolution are not new to Americans or to historians. They are hardly the result of some recent fashion for "political correctness," a red herring dragged across the trail. I encountered the themes in graduate school more than half a century ago when I became a historian. And I have since written at length about the way historians throughout the twentieth century responded to the challenge posed by the so-called progressive historians who dealt with them. J. Franklin Jameson, a historian at the peak of the historical profession, asked scholars to consider *The American Revolution as a Social Movement*: "But who can say to the waves of Revolution: Thus far shall we go and no farther.... The stream of revolution, once started, could not be confined within narrow banks, but spread abroad upon the land. Many economic desires, many social aspirations were set free by the political struggle." Carl Becker, focusing on the political, framed the double character of the Revolution as not only a war for "home rule" but "a war for who shall rule at home." And Charles Beard, the most influential and widely read American historian through the 1940s posited the Constitution as the triumph of a small group of leaders trying to curb "the excess of democracy."

These interpretations by the progressives were common among historians, as well as in many textbooks, until the end of World War II. They moved our understanding of the Revolution away from a rather arid constitutional interpretation. They were insightful and provocative in the best sense, yet in many ways limited. (My exploration of the mechanics was inspired in part by a desire to explain a class Beard could not account for, and my book on the Democratic Republicans by a desire to understand Jeffersonians who could not be explained solely as "agrarians.")[14]

In the decade and a half after World War II well into the 1960s, however, the very questions the progressives raised were eclipsed among all but a handful of scholars. "At the height of the cold war," the historian Peter Novick concludes after examining the writings and private correspondence of a host of leading historians, "a sense of urgent crisis and impending Armageddon was widespread" in the historical profession. The focus of American historians "shifted from the conflict of classes to a consensual culture," Novick writes. Radicalism outside the consensus, suspect in the age of McCarthyism, was out of fashion in the study of the past.[15]

From the point of view of ruling circles, the American Revolution had to be sanitized and made into a safe revolution for export. The cold war, framed as an apocalyptic struggle between "democracy" and "communism," was also a time when colonies and former colonies in the third world were undergoing revolutions of their own, some taking inspiration from the Russian Revolution, some from the American. It would not do to portray the American revolutionary era, as had the progressives, as rife with social transformations, internal strife, and leaders who represented class interests. Nor would it do to probe its failures: celebration was in and iconoclasm out. I can remember a president of the American Historical Association, a leading colonialist, warning young historians against "robbing the people of their heroes ... insulting their folk memory of great figures they admired." He called for "a sanely conservative history of the United States."[16]

The events of the mid-1960s and 1970s punctured this balloon. The debacle of the Vietnam War (which Americans might have understood if they had a better grasp of their own successful seven-year colonial struggle that toppled the greatest imperial power of the eighteenth century) and the corruption epitomized by Watergate put a big dent in the hero worship of national leaders. The successes in the broadly based struggles for racial and gender equality made Americans—historians among them— more aware that there was a long past to such struggles and enormous gaps in our historical knowledge. As the historical profession expanded amidst a boom in higher education and reflected more of the diversity in American life, and as a changed atmosphere in academic life encouraged a more questioning attitude, new approaches to history were entertained and new fields of history came into being. The agency of movements bringing about contemporary change made it impossible to ignore the agency of their predecessors. "Agency" is a word that became popular among historians as it was expressed in a memorable turn of phrase by E. P. Thompson, the widely read English historian, who said that he was "seeking to rescue … from the enormous condescension of posterity" the "agency of working people, the degree to which they contributed, by conscious efforts, to the making of history."[17]

As a result of these changes, subjects long regarded as closed (and considered "uninteresting" by most senior historians) were reopened, and historians began to rediscover the popular side of the Revolution, including a range of subjects the progressives had paid scant attention to, like the ideologies they had dismissed as "propaganda" or the histories of African Americans and Native Americans left out of the conventional narrative. The new scholarship, as the historian Linda Kerber summed up the achievements of the first generation of historians as of 1990, tended "to restore *rebellion* to histories of the American Revolution," stressing the ways various groups "shaped the revolution and were in turn affected by it." By 2005, Gary Nash, another leading pathbreaker, summing up two generations of scholarship, could write, "in the last few decades, a remarkable flowering of an American history sensitive to gender, race, religion and class, which is to say a democratized history, is giving us an alternative, long forgotten American Revolution."[18]

"How radical was the American Revolution?" (the subject of essay 5) is a question that would have been dismissed several decades earlier with the response, "not very," and would have been difficult to answer as long as historians focused on a very small cast of leaders and were preoccupied with the "origins" and "causes" of the Revolution to the exclusion of revolutionary processes and outcomes. It is a sign of the enormous shift in scholarship that in 1994 the National Standards for History could set as a requirement for students that they be able "to confront the central issue of how revolutionary the Revolution actually was." And to accomplish this, students "necessarily will have to see the Revolution through different eyes—enslaved and free African Americans, Native Americans, white men and women of different social classes, religions, ideological dispositions, regions and occupations." The Standards were drafted after several years of discussion by hundreds of historians, teachers, and educators at all levels delegated by some thirty national educational organizations.[19]

In truth, the volume and quality of scholarship has so expanded that trying to grasp the Revolution as a whole has become challenging and exhilarating. The study of African American history has moved both the agency of the enslaved and slavery as a public issue from the periphery to the center of the Revolution, forcing a long overdue reexamination of the policies of the "great men."[20] Research on farmers has shown that rebellions were common and widespread, while research on the working people of the cities has revealed a tenacious "mechanic presence." A rich new social history dealing with long-range trends in private life has made it possible, among other things, to compare American society before and after the Revolution. Women's history has revealed not only the active role of women in different classes and the emergence of American advocates for the rights of women but also how restrictive were the notions of gender embedded in the ideology of the founders. The new Indian history shows how catastrophic the expanding American empire looked from the vantage point of those in its path and how varied was their response.

If you imagine the revolutionary era as a dramatic play, you could say that historians have been successful in peopling the stage with a much larger cast of characters, who in the past were treated as extras in a crowd scene or given no more than bit parts. The famous "great men" are still very much there, but they are no longer the only actors on the stage, they don't have all the lines, and they interact with players they confronted at the time. The play now has to accommodate a host of people who in various ways made a difference either as leaders of popular movements or as exemplars of a trend: leaders of agrarian movements (Herman Husband, William Prendergast, Ethan Allen, Samuel Ely, Daniel Shays, John Fries); urban radicals (Thomas Paine, Dr. Thomas Young, James Cannon, Alexander McDougall, Isaac Sears); activist artisans (Ebenezer Mackintosh, Paul Revere, George Robert Twelves Hewes, Samuel Simpson, Timothy Bigelow, George Warner, James Cox); legislators risen from humble origins (Abraham

Yates, William Findley, Matthew Lyon, Melancton Smith); articulate women (Abigail Smith Adams, Mercy Otis Warren, Judith Sargent Murray, Deborah Sampson Gannett, Phillis Wheatley); African Americans (Richard Allen, Absalom Jones, Prince Hall, Elizabeth "Mumbet" Freeman, Thomas Peters, Boston King); soldiers and seamen who were hard-core veterans who recorded their experiences (Joseph Plumb Martin, Jeremiah Greenman, James Collins, William Widger, Andrew Sherburne); radicals of various persuasions (John Woolman, Rezin Hammond, Abraham Clark, Philip Freneau, Joel Barlow, William Manning); crusaders for First Amendment freedoms (Isaac Backus, Jemima Wilkinson, Tunis Wortman, Jedediah Peck); and, of course, Native American chieftains (Dragging Canoe, Joseph Brant, Cornplanter, Red Jacket, Alexander McGillivray, Daniel Nimham).

If the names of the players in this vastly expanded cast of characters send readers to libraries, it is a sign of the times that readers are likely to find a good many of them written up in the new multivolume collections of biography which are changing the "who's who" of American history.[21]

Historians have added so many characters in so many subplots that how the play should end is subject to differing interpretations: the play seems to cry out for multiple endings at different times because lots of these histories are not confined by the dates of the political American Revolution. The Constitution of 1787 may have been the consummation of the Revolution for some but hardly for others. And the many groups on the stage were decidedly not in harmony with one another: the cast did not all assemble at the finale to sing a chorus of "Yankee Doodle," the national anthem of the Revolution. The Revolution was more multisided and multicolored than has been allowed, which is why it could be at the same time more radical and yet more conservative. If we in the audience two hundred years later allow ourselves to respond emotionally to the drama, we may see that the Revolution was more inspiring and more heartbreaking than most Americans ever imagined.

As I look back on the past half century or so, I am struck not only by how much the research of historians has changed the contours of the American Revolution but also by the ways in which the institutions responsible for scholarship about early American history have changed. Study in what in 1945 was called "a neglected field" has expanded and become decentralized and democratized. The training of historians is no longer confined to a handful of elite graduate schools. Major bodies of original sources, once available only in a small number of libraries and archives in the East, have been made more accessible, first through microcopy and more recently through electronic dissemination. (In 1950, for my dissertation on the Democratic Republicans of New York, in order to read the newspapers and pamphlets published in the state I had to travel in a 1937 Ford to a dozen libraries.) The Institute of Early American History, founded in 1945 and long clubbish and stuffy, has become a path breaker in broadening the boundaries of scholarship and making way for young scholars.

Disseminators of historical knowledge have responded. Decades ago, when Colonial Williamsburg Inc. restored the capital of colonial Virginia as a living museum in an age of segregation, tourists would never have known that half the colonial town was African American. Today it sponsors "the other half" tours and reenacts stark scenes from slave life, like the capture of a runaway. The Chicago Historical Society mounted an exhibit, "We the People" (1987–2005), for which I served as guest co-curator, devoted to the question, what was the role of ordinary people in shaping the nation? The National Park Service has been open to revising interpretations at many of its sites of the Revolution. The multiauthored college textbooks in American history usually include historians who have contributed to the new scholarship. The National Standards for History, mentioned earlier, have been welcomed by high school teachers. All of this suggests that there are many publics ready to welcome the new scholarship about the Revolution.[22]

But in spite of such very substantial gains—indeed, probably because of them—many gatekeepers of the past have resisted change. Publishers of elementary school textbooks throw in token images of the groups left out but seem all too ready to cave in to pressure groups that threaten the boards which grant approval for school adoptions. Television, which gave us a moving documentary about ordinary people in Ken Burns's *The Civil War* and a riveting series dramatizing slavery in *Roots*, cannot seem to break out of a reverential narrative dominated by the founding fathers. Hollywood is yet to produce a first-rate movie on the Revolution. In *The Patriot*, Mel Gibson created a fantasy world in which a South Carolina planter's happy slaves join with him to fight on the American side, when in reality they were more likely to have run away to join the British. The National Endowment for Humanities (NEH), long a major source of funding for innovative research and public history, now "flags" proposals dealing with sexuality, race, and gender for special review. A former chairman of the NEH rails against the National Standards for History (which the NEH funded and which she earlier sponsored) on the misleading charge that George Washington "makes only a fleeting appearance in them."[23]

It has long been common in the United States for self-appointed guardians of the past to take potshots at history professors and school textbooks. (Charles Beard lost his job at Columbia in World War I.) In the late 1940s and the 1950s, the cold war inquisition into political opinions, followed in the 1960s by the intolerant backlash against nonconformists, took a toll on college faculties, historians among them. In 1970–73, I served on a committee of the American Historical Association that reported on the wreckage of these decades. As a result of that report, the AHA adopted an Academic Bill of Rights for Historians.[24] I am struck by the extent to which in the 1980s and 1990s the radical right made history and historians a target in their "culture wars." Their campaigns are well funded, orchestrated, and sustained. In the 1990s, one year it was the National Standards, one year the curators at the Smithsonian museum, the next year the NEH itself, in one state a campaign for a school curriculum that eliminates slavery as a subject of study, in other states laws legislating "diversity" in state university faculties. There is a steady drumbeat demonizing historians and humanities faculties for "political correctness," "relativism," and "multiculturalism" as caricatured by the right.[25]

The self-appointed guardians of the past seem intent on policing the founding era in particular. They would have us look upon the founders as demigods, the Constitution as the "Miracle at Philadelphia," and the original copies of the Declaration, the Constitution, and the Bill of Rights as sacred texts, enshrined for public display in Washington. They parse the words of the Constitution to discover the "original intent" of the framers, as if those very pragmatic men wanted to keep government frozen for two centuries. How reluctant the guardians are to allow historical issues to become central to the Revolution that might detract from the "founding fathers." How narrow their conception of who were "founders." They want a history of the United States taught in the spirit of triumphalism.[26]

The success of the new scholarship accounts in part for the guardians embracing the celebratory biographies of the "great men" of the era that have appeared in such profusion: they see them as an antidote to the new scholarship, books that bring the country back to the comforting heroic master narrative of the Revolution.[27] The new biographers have drawn on the new scholarship embodied in the richly edited multivolume publication projects of the "Papers" of the greats, yet have refused to accept the challenge of the massive new scholarship that arguably puts the leaders in a new light—with the exception of one subject: the biographers have found it more and more difficult to avoid the issue of slavery in the revolutionary era on which the new scholarship confronts the founders at their Achilles heel.[28]

As I listen to the din from the right-wing guardians of the past, they seem unwilling to recognize the historical method itself. They cling to the notion that there is some finite, unchanging body of facts about history in general and the American Revolution in particular. The reality is that historians, whatever their subject, have no choice but to select from among a vast array of facts to present a narrative or an analysis. This means that as new facts are discovered, the narrative or analysis is revised. A president sneers at "revisionist historians" as if "revisionist" is a dirty word.[29] But that, of course, is what historians do: revise interpretations of the past found wanting. Historical revisions often have political implications, but sometimes they cut one way, sometimes another. The business of historians is to examine previous versions of history: to look at familiar subjects from a new vantage point or with original sources that have been newly discovered or little appreciated. Above all, the business of the historian is to ask new questions of the past in the light of new interests that sometimes arise from perceived gaps in historical knowledge and often arise out of the world we live in. The essays in this book flow from all of the above.

Joseph Plumb Martin, the irreverent sergeant in the Continental Army who wrote, "Great men get praise; little men, nothing," was unduly pessimistic when he added, "But it was always so and always will be." Martin would be excited to know that his memoir of 1830 was reprinted several times in the twentieth century and that historians make use of it to recover the experiences of rank-and-file soldiers and probe the meaning of the Revolution for those who felt its promises were unfulfilled. We can take heart in the knowledge that one generation's "revisionism" is very often accepted as the next generation's wisdom.

I express my scholarly debts for each essay in this volume at the end of each essay. For the book as a whole it is a pleasure to acknowledge my debts: to Harvey J. Kaye, who first had the idea of publishing a collection of my essays; to Niko Pfund, then editor of New York University Press, who was enthusiastic about the idea; and to the team at NYU Press: Eric Zinner, Editorial Director; Deborah Gershenowitz, whose perceptive criticism, patience, and support as editor was indispensable; Andrew Katz, a superb copyeditor; and Despina P. Gimbel, Managing Editor, a true expediter.

NOTES

I wish to express my appreciation to the scholars who have offered insightful criticism of several drafts of this introduction: Woody Holton, Harvey Kaye, Ray Raphael, David Waldstreicher, and especially Gary B. Nash, whose successful battles in the history wars give heart to scholars everywhere.

1. Joseph Plumb Martin, *A Narrative of Some of the Adventures, Dangers and Sufferings of a Revolutionary Soldier, Interspersed with Anecdotes of Incidents That Occurred within His Own Observation* (Hallowell, Maine, 1830), reprinted as *Private Yankee Doodle: Being a Narrative of Some of the Adventures, Dangers and Sufferings of a Revolutionary Soldier* by Joseph Plumb Martin, ed. George E. Schneer (Boston, 1962, reprinted 1992), 95 (great men); 101 (naked); 182 (mutiny); 280 (brothers); 283 (land).

2. Alan Taylor, *Liberty Men and Great Proprietors: The Revolutionary Settlement on the Maine Frontier, 1760–1820* (Chapel Hill, N.C., 1990), 103 (rights); 247–49 (petition).

3. Herman Husband, "Manuscript Sermons," 48–49, cited in Mark Jones, "The Western New Jerusalem: Herman Husband's Utopian Vision" (unpublished manuscript). For scholarship on agrarian movements, see essay 4 in this volume and Alan Kulikoff, *The Agrarian Origins of American Capitalism* (Charlottesville, Va., 1992), chap. 5 and bibliography, 273–329.

4. David Ramsay, *The History of the American Revolution*, 2 vols. (Philadelphia, 1789; repr., Indianapolis, 1990), 1:315–16; Ira Berlin et al., eds., *Free at Last: A Documentary History of Slavery, Freedom, and the Civil War* (New York, 1992), xiv.

5. J. Todd White and Charles H. Lesser, eds., *Fighters for Independence: A Guide to Sources of Biographical Information on Soldiers and Sailors of the American Revolution* (Chicago, 1977); and see John Dann, ed., *The Revolution Remembered: Eyewitness Accounts of the War for Independence* (Chicago, 1980), for a sample of pension applications.

6. Alfred F. Young, ed., *The American Revolution: Explorations in the History of American Radicalism* (DeKalb, Ill., 1976); Alfred F. Young, ed., *Beyond the American Revolution: Explorations in the History of American Radicalism* (DeKalb, Ill., 1993); Alfred F. Young, "George Robert Twelves Hewes (1742–1840): A Boston Shoemaker and the Memory of the American Revolution," *William and Mary Quarterly*, 3rd ser., 38 (1981): 561–623, also reprinted in Alfred F. Young, *The Shoemaker and the Tea Party: Memory and the American Revolution* (Boston, 1999); Alfred F. Young,

Masquerade: The Life and Times of Deborah Sampson, Continental Soldier (New York, 2004).

7. Michael Kammen, *Mystic Chords of Memory: The Transformation of Tradition in American Culture* (New York, 1991), 9–10; Young, *Shoemaker and the Tea Party*, part 2.

8. See Harvey Kaye, *Thomas Paine and the Promise of American Life* (New York, 2005), both a biography and an analysis of Paine in public memory.

9. For Boston, see essay 8 in this volume; for Madison, see essay 4; for a discussion of the language of class, see essay 5.

10. Robert R Livingston Jr. to William Duer, June 12, 1777, R. R. Livingston Papers, New-York Historical Society, cited in Alfred F. Young, *The Democratic Republicans of New York: The Origins, 1765–1797* (Chapel Hill, N.C., 1967), 15.

11. For the painting, see Alfred F Young, Terry Fife, and Mary Janzen, *We the People: Voices and Images of the New Nation* (Philadelphia, 1993), xi–xii; David Fischer, *Liberty and Freedom: A Visual History of America's Founding Ideas* (New York, 2005), 190–94; Irma B. Jaffe, *John Trumbull: Patriot-Artist of the American Revolution* (Boston, 1975), chap. 7.

12. For the political context, see Pauline Maier, *American Scripture: Making the Declaration of Independence* (New York, 1997), chap. 2, 33–34 (Bartlett of New Hampshire); Ray Raphael, *Founding Myths: Stories That Hide Our Patriotic Past* (New York, 2004), chaps. 6, 7, and pp. 248–251; John Adams to Abigail Adams, July 3, 1776, in C. F. Adams, ed., *Familiar Letters of John Adams to His Wife Abigail Adams, during the Revolution* (Boston, 1875), 193; David McCullough, *John Adams* (New York, 2002), 129.

13. Max Farrand, ed., *The Records of the Federal Convention of 1787*, 4 vols. (New Haven, Conn., 1937), 1:101 (George Mason). There are ten other places in the debates in Farrand, ed., *Records*, where the framers use the phrase "genius of the people."

14. Ralph Waldo Emerson, "The American Scholar," in Brooks Atkinson, ed., *The Complete Essays and Other Writings of Ralph Waldo Emerson* (New York, 1940), 61; for twentieth-century trends in historical scholarship, see Alfred F. Young, "American Historians Confront 'The Transforming Hand of Revolution,'" in Ronald Hoffman and Peter J. Albert, eds., *The Transforming Hand of Revolution: Reconsidering the American Revolution as a Social Movement* (Charlottesville, Va., 1995), 346–492; Alfred F. Young, "The Mechanics and the Jeffersonians: New York, 1789–1801," *Labor History* 5 (1964): 247–76; and Young, *Democratic Republicans*.

15. For the climate of opinion, see Peter Novick, *That Noble Dream: The "Objectivity Question" and the American Historical Profession* (Cambridge, U.K., 1988), 332–33 (consensus).

16. Samuel Eliot Morison, cited in Novick, *That Noble Dream*, 332–33.

17. Edward P. Thompson, *The Making of the English Working Class* (New York, 1963), 12; for his other influential essays, see Thompson, *Customs in Common*

(New York, 1993), chap. 4, "The Moral Economy of the English Crowd in the Eighteenth Century," and chap. 6, "Time, Work-Discipline and Industrial Capitalism."

18. Linda Kerber, "The Revolutionary Generation," in Eric Funer, ed., *The New American History*, for the American Historical Association (Philadelphia, 1990), 26; Gary B. Nash, *The Unknown American Revolution: The Unruly Birth of Democracy and the Struggle to Create America* (New York, 2005), xxix; for another outstanding synthesis, see Edward Countryman, *The American Revolution* (New York, 1985; 2nd ed., 2003), with a commanding bibliographical essay, 237–63.

19. *National Standards for History: Basic Edition* (National Center for History in the Schools, Los Angeles, Calif., 1996), 85; for the origin and controversy over the standards told by its principal directors, Gary Nash and Charlotte Crabtree, see Gary B. Nash, Charlotte Crabtree, and Ross E. Dunn, *History on Trial: Culture Wars and the Teaching of the Past* (New York, 1998).

20. For a summa of the scholarship on African American history, see Ira Berlin, *Many Thousands Gone: The First Two Centuries of Slavery in North America* (Cambridge, Mass., 1998); and Ira Berlin, *Generations of Captivity: A History of African-American Slaves* (Cambridge, Mass., 2003).

21. Compare John A. Garraty and Mark C. Carnes, eds., *American National Biography*, 24 vols. (New York, 1999), with Allen Johnson and Dumas Malone, eds., *Dictionary of National Biography*, 20 vols. (New York, 1928–1937); for an analysis of the *American National Biography*, see Edmund S. Morgan and Marie Morgan, "Who's Really Who," *New York Review of Books* 47 (March 9, 2001): 38–43; see also Edward James et al., eds., *Notable American Women*, 3 vols. (Cambridge, Mass., 1971); Henry Louis Gates and Evelyn Brooks Higginbotham, eds., *African American Lives* (New York, 2004); Darlene Clark Hine, *Black Women in America: An Historical Encyclopedia*, 2 vols. (Brooklyn, N.Y., 1993); Richard L. Blanco, ed., *The American Revolution, 1775–1783: An Encyclopedia*, 2 vols. (New York, 1993).

22. For changes in the academic institutions, see Novick, *That Noble Dream*, chap. 12; for changes in one bellwether museum, see Richard Handler and Eric Gamble, *The New History in an Old Museum: Creating the Past at Colonial Williamsburg* (Durham, N.C., 1997); for changes in one city's historical institutions, see Gary B. Nash, *First City: Philadelphia and the Forging of Historical Memory* (Philadelphia, 2002); for changing historic sites, see James W. Loewen, *Lies across America: What Our Historic Sites Get Wrong* (New York, 1999), and Gary B. Nash, *Landmarks of the American Revolution* (Oxford, U.K., 2003); for the campaign over the National Park Service's interpretation of the Liberty Bell, see www.ushistory.org/presidentshouse.

23. For NEH, see Lynne Cheney, cited in Nash, *History on Trial*, 3, and Anne Marie Borrego, "Humanities Endowment Returns to 'Flagging' Non-Traditional Projects," *Chronicle of Higher Education* (January 16, 2004): 1, 20–21; for the attack on the Smithsonian, see Edward T. Linenthal and Tom Engelhardt, eds., *History Wars: The Enola Gay and Other Battles for the American Past* (New York, 1996),

Alfred Young, "S.O.S.: Storm Warning for American Museums," *OAH Newsletter* (Organization of American Historians) (November 1994): 1, 6–7, and Alfred F. Young, "A Modest Proposal: A Bill of Rights for American Museums," *Public Historian* 14 (1992): 67–75.

24. Ad Hoc Committee on the Rights of Historians, American Historical Association, *Final Report* (March 1974); "The Rights of Historians: An AHA Report," *AHA Newsletter* 12 (1974): 9–12; Ellen Schrecker, *No Ivory Tower: McCarthyism and the Universities* (New York, 1986); Ellen Schrecker, *Many Are the Crimes: McCarthyism in America* (Princeton, N.J., 1998).

25. For the war against history, see Harvey J. Kaye, *The Powers of the Past: Reflections on the Crisis and Promise of History* (Minneapolis, 1991); Lawrence W. Levine, *The Opening of the American Mind: Canons, Culture and History* (Boston, 1996); Nash et al., *History Wars*; John K. Wilson, *The Myth of Political Correctness: the Conservative Attack on Higher Education* (Durham, N.C., 1995).

26. Frances Fitzgerald, *America Revised: History Schoolbooks in the Twentieth Century* (New York, 1979); for a follow-up, see James W. Loewen, *Lies My Teacher Told Me: Everything Your American History Textbook Got Wrong* (New York, 1995).

27. For responses to the new wave of biographies from a range of scholars, see T. H. Breen, "Ordinary Founders—The Forgotten Men and Women of the American Revolution," (*London*) *Times Literary Supplement* (May 28, 2004): 14–15; Sean Wilentz, "America Made Easy: McCullough, Adams and the Decline of Popular History," *New Republic* (July 2, 2001); Alan Taylor, *Writing Early American History* (Philadelphia, 2005); Jeffrey Pasley, Andrew Robertson, and David Waldstreicher, eds., *Beyond the Founders: New Approaches to the Political History of the Early Republic* (Chapel Hill, N.C., 2004), introduction; David Waldstreicher, "Founders Chic as Cultural War," *Radical History Review* 84 (2002): 185–92; Ray Raphael, *Founding Myths: Stories That Hide Our Patriotic Past* (New York, 2004).

28. For recent works devoted to the leaders and slavery, see Henry Wiencek, *An Imperfect God: George Washington, His Slaves, and the Creation of the Nation* (New York, 2003); David Waldstreicher, *Runaway America: Benjamin Franklin, Slavery, and the American Revolution* (New York, 2004). See also Cassandra Pybus, *Epic Journeys of Freedom: Runaway Slaves of the American Revolution and Their Global Quest for Liberty* (Boston, 2005).

29. George W. Bush, cited in James McPherson, "Revisionist Historians," *Perspectives* (American Historical Association), (September 2003); "President's Column."

The People Out of Doors

The Mechanics of the Revolution
"By Hammer and Hand All Arts Do Stand"

In the 1790s, when Paul Revere put down an account of his since famous ride of April 19, 1775, to warn the countryside that a British army was en route from Boston to Lexington, he began with, "I was one of upwards of thirty who formed ourselves into a Committee for the purposes of watching the movements of the British soldiers." After he completed the sentence, he went back, inserted a caret mark after "upwards of thirty," and added "chiefly mechanics." It was a wonderful marker of the way Revere, a silversmith before the war, thought of himself as engaged not in an act of solitary heroism but as part of a collective effort with his fellow mechanics. In 1795, Revere became the first president of the Massachusetts Mechanics Association.[1]

Had he written his account in 1775, Revere might have referred to himself and his fellow artisans as "tradesmen," the most common term in colonial Boston. In 1783, he spoke of himself as "very well off for a Tradesman." Through the colonial era in most American cites, "mechanic" was a term laden with condescension when used by the "better sort." The change in Revere's choice of words measures the way in which artisans had taken a term of derision and worn it as a badge of honor, in much the same way that others would take back words like "Jacobin" or "democrat" or "black" and use them with pride. The old usage was not abandoned: in 1788 Revere was a member of a committee that issued a call to "tradesmen, mechanics and artizans" to assemble. Including "mechanics" was an indicator of a shift in consciousness between the 1760s and the 1790s that symbolized the arrival of mechanics as a presence in public life in the era of American Revolution. This essay explores this process.[2]

The long era of the Revolution, as historians now think of it, extended beyond the period of political conflict with Britain from 1765 to 1775. It included the war waged from 1775 to 1783 and the period of nation-building,

Pat Lyon at the Forge epitomizes a proud, independent working artisan who lived by "the sweat of his brow" as he wanted to be portrayed. Lyon, a successful Philadelphia manufacturer of fire engines, asked the painter, John Neagle, to depict him at work as a blacksmith, the way he started out. He wears the crafts-man's leather apron, his tools around him, a young apprentice in the background. The view out the window is the jail in which Lyon was falsely imprisoned, a reminder of the injustice he successfully fought as a citizen. Courtesy of the Penn-sylvania Academy of the Fine Arts, Philadelphia.

1783 to 1815, during which internal conflict was renewed over the fruits of the Revolution—in all, almost half a century. This essay focuses on artisans in this long era in the three major seaports of the north—Boston, New York, Philadelphia—with an excursion to Charleston, the largest southern city, and glances at Baltimore and other cities. It addresses these questions: First, who were the mechanics and what were their aspirations? Second, what was their "agency" in public life over this half century? Third, how did artisans' consciousness change as a result of their experience? Fourth, can we measure their impact on American public life? Lastly, what was the artisan legacy and how was it appropriated by later generations?

My argument is that mechanics played a major role in the shaping of events in the revolutionary era. Their aspirations for personal independence became entwined with American aspirations for national independence. As artisans became a presence in political life, their traditional consciousness of themselves as craftsmen and producers broadened to include a keen awareness of themselves as citizens and a "mechanic interest." Taken as a whole, the four strands of consciousness can be called artisan republicanism. The impact of artisans on American politics in the new nation was measurable: they were the urban counterpart to the yeomanry deemed essential to a democracy by Thomas Jefferson, but how much they were recognized as such is open to examination. In the first quarter of the nineteenth century, as a developing capitalist economy began to transform the country, the artisan system eroded, rent by a conflict between journeymen and master mechanics. Later generations of workers losing their independence, as well as aspiring entrepreneurs, reached back to appropriate the artisan heritage.[3]

1. Who Were the Mechanics? Distinctions and Dependencies

Two artisans, Paul Revere and Benjamin Franklin, dominate the popular memory of the artisans of early America, yet the common images by which they are known misrepresent the reality that historians have uncovered. Revere is popularly known as the intrepid courier glorified by Henry Wadsworth Longfellow's poem, "The Midnight Ride of Paul Revere" (1861), or as the skilled silversmith in John Singleton Copley's portrait. Franklin is known from his *Autobiography* as the apprentice printer who went from Boston to Philadelphia and from rags to riches or is known from his almanac as the author of the maxims of the American gospel of success, like "Early to bed, early to rise makes a man healthy, wealthy and wise." But the American way of glorifying the individual at the expense of the group he was part of is at work here: Revere was nothing if not a leader of the mechanics of Boston's North End, and in Philadelphia the young printer Franklin swam in a sea of artisan culture: the club of artisans he organized was first called "The Leather Apron," after the common garment of working artisans.[4]

The surviving artifacts of skilled craftsmen can also be misleading. Revere's silver bowls and Duncan Phyfe's chairs grace museums, but most museumgoers have never seen a leather apron. And the cozy restorations of craftsmen's shops in outdoor museums like Colonial Williamsburg and Old Sturbridge Village, for all their authenticity, mislead in a larger way. Unintentionally, they convey a sense of a secure, prosperous artisan world, free from hard times and the tumultuous political activity that was the hallmark of city artisans.[5]

Words also get in the way. Artisan and craftsman, the common terms today, were infrequently used in colonial America, while today "mechanic" has been narrowed to refer to an automobile mechanic. Americans are uncomfortable with "tradesman" because it carries some of the snobbery of its English origins. But in the colonies, "tradesman" seems to have been the most common term: a tradesman was a man who followed a skilled trade, which he learned as an apprentice and usually practiced as a journeyman before he became a master. He may have pursued his trade in a workshop, from which he sold the products that he made, but he did not think of himself as a "shopkeeper," a word for a retailer who sold merchandize made by others. "Manufacturer" could mean an artisan or the owner of a large-scale enterprise like an iron forge or a ropewalk, or the merchant investor in a would-be "manufactory." In the 1770s, when men in the trades became active in politics, they might address a call to a meeting to "mechanics, manufacturers and tradesmen" (as they did in Philadelphia) to make sure they were inclusive. In the revolutionary era the terms were in flux—a clue to the way the artisans' collective sense of themselves was changing.[6]

Artisans were the largest proportion of the population in the colonial cities, and although cities were not a very large segment of the overall colonial population, they were important in public life out of proportion to their size. In the decade before 1776, in a total population of about 2,500,000, which included 500,000 slaves, about 100,000 people lived in the largest cities on the Atlantic seaboard: Philadelphia, the largest, with 33,000 people; New York, 25,000; Boston, 15,000; Charleston, 12,000; Baltimore, 6,700. By 1800, the population of these cities had more than doubled to about 200,000 in a total population of 4,000,000. Within the three largest cities, easily two-thirds of the free adult males were in the laboring classes as a whole, and about 45% of the total population were artisans. In Boston in 1790, when occupations can be counted with some precision, there were 1,271 skilled artisans out of 2,754 adult males, almost half.[7]

About 20% of the free adult males were workers outside the skilled hierarchy of tradesmen: merchant seamen (highly skilled in the ways of ships and the sea but not by formal apprenticeship); common laborers such as sawyers, ditch diggers, and dockworkers; itinerant workers such as chimney sweeps, peddlers, and hawkers; and cartmen (or truckmen or draymen), who owned their own horse-drawn carts and hauled cargo about town. Close to the bottom in New York and Philadelphia before the Revolution were indentured servants, almost all migrants from the British Isles or northern Europe.

At the very bottom in the cities were African Americans, almost all enslaved, a small number free. While they were a declining proportion of the total labor force, in the pre-revolutionary era there were about 5,000 slaves in the three major northern cities: 750 in Boston, 670 in Philadelphia, 3,000 in New York. In Charleston, a city in a slave society, there were about 6,000 slaves—half the population. Master artisans might own slaves: they made up about a third of all slave owners in Philadelphia and an even larger share in New York. Some slaves became artisans: in Charleston, white artisans constantly petitioned to exclude or limit skilled slaves hired out by their masters.[8]

To refer to this heterogeneous group as a "class" or to use the nineteenth-century term "working class" seems anachronistic, whatever one's concept of class. People spoke of "sorts" (lower, middling, and better) and "ranks." "Class," however, came into use in the late 1780s and 1790s. "Laboring classes" (in the plural), which I use in this essay, avoids this double anachronism. "Petty bourgeois," while theoretically accurate for property-holding urban artisans, is not especially helpful as an analytical category. A master artisan, as Karl Marx pointed out with some acuity, had a double character: he was a capitalist who "does indeed own the conditions of production—tools, materials, etc. ... and he owns the product. To that extent he is a *capitalist*." But "within the process of production he appears as an artisan, like his journeymen, and it is he who initiates his apprentices into the mysteries of the craft."[9]

In the 1760s and 1770s, most artisans were native born and of English ancestry. The migration of indentured servants from Europe and the British Isles to the middle-Atlantic colonies was heavy in the decade before the Revolution, adding to the numerous Scots, Scotch Irish, Irish, and Germans already in Philadelphia. New York was polyglot in a different way; Boston was considered a very "English" town. (Paul Revere's father changed the spelling of his name from the French "Rivoire" because the bumpkins could not pronounce it.) In an overwhelmingly Protestant society, all but a handful of artisans were Protestant. And the trades were male. In the big towns one might encounter many women in a score of skilled "female" trades, for example, the needle trades or the care-giving trades, but only a sprinkling of women in "male" trades, invariably inherited from their husbands. In a typical small craft workshop located in a home, women worked as "help-meets" to artisan husbands who assumed the prerogatives of patriarchy.[10]

The big cities were seaports. Their well-being rose or fell with "navigation"—the ocean-going import-export trade conducted in each city by from one to two hundred merchants who owned the ships, wharves, and warehouses. You almost always knew you were in a port: you saw the tall masts of ocean-going vessels at the end of the streets that ran to the docks and you heard the din of shipyards. In these commercial centers, one can distinguish roughly four major "branches" of tradesmen based on the market for their labor: (1) the maritime trades: workers in shipyards, rope-walks, sailcloth lofts, and a score of trades that built and outfitted ocean-going ships; (2) the building trades: house carpenters, masons, and the like who thrived when the cities were expanding; (3) trades producing consumer goods for the local, naturally protected market like the proverbial "the butcher, the baker, and the candlestick maker"; and (4) trades producing consumer goods in competition with manufactures imported from Britain, which included both the "luxury trades" (fine furniture makers, carriage makers, etc.) and trades selling to a broader consumer market (metal smiths and leather workers).[11]

Artisans were very conscious of a range of economic and social distinctions both within "the trade," among trades, and between the trades and other classes. First, of course, came rank within the trade hierarchy: master, journeyman, apprentice. A typical master was a small-scale producer who owned and worked in his own shop. He usually had an apprentice or two who lived under his roof and worked for "keep" for the customary seven years of a formal indenture while learning the "arts and mysteries of the trade," in the words of an indenture so common that printers sold a stock form, the names to be filled in. A master may have employed a journeyman (a man who had completed his apprenticeship) who worked for wages. Or he himself might work for wages in a large-scale work site: a shipyard employing from half a dozen to a score of men; a ropewalk with perhaps ten men; or an iron forge (almost all in the countryside close to water power), with as many a dozen full-time craftsmen. Before the Revolution, in most city trades there were more masters than journeymen. This was especially true in Boston but less so in Philadelphia. The line between master and journeyman, however, could be blurred: in the building trades, a house carpenter might be his own "boss" on one job, employing others, yet work for someone else on another job. Within this skilled hierarchy, apprentices were the largest single category of workers in the cities (Charleston aside), and apprenticeship was the education most city boys got.[12]

How much mobility was there within this system? The ideal was expressed in the slogan, "Today's journeyman, tomorrow's master." When an aged Philadelphian reminisced early in the nineteenth century that when he was a boy "no masters were seen exempted from personal labour in any branch of business—living on the profits derived from many hired journeymen," and "every shoemaker and tailor was a man for himself; thus was every tinman, blacksmith, hatter, wheelwright [and] weaver," he was misled by his nostalgia for the ideal. In the first half of the eighteenth century there was enough mobility to give the ideal some reality. But from 1750 to 1770, far fewer journeymen became masters. It was hardly a golden age: in Philadelphia a large proportion of the numerous journeymen shoemakers and tailors never acquired their own shops.[13]

Artisans were also very conscious of the distinctions of wealth within and among the trades. A minority of tradesmen became as successful as Franklin, able to retire on his investments at forty-two, or as prosperous as Revere, who late in life became the owner of a brass foundry and a copper mill. Artisans may have run the gamut from the rich to the very poor, but there were only a few trades in which they might rise to wealth; in most trades they were "middling sort" or "lower sort." Contemporaries spoke of "substantial" tradesmen and "inferior" tradesmen. The house carpenters of Philadelphia who built the magnificent Carpenters Hall, which still stands, shipwrights, and men in the "luxury" trades were often "substantial."

But in four "inferior" occupations—shoemakers, tailors, sailors, and laborers—the historian Billy Smith has found that "the specter of poverty and deprivation haunted their lives" and that life for them was "nasty, short, and brutish." In the major colonial cities, a good number of "middling" artisans were perched precariously on the margins of poverty and might land in debtor's prison or on poor relief. The ups and downs of commercial life in the seaports meant that many trades "knew 'broken days,' slack spells and dull seasons," as the historian Gary Nash writes, or as they themselves might have put it, they knew "cucumber times" or times of living on "buttermilk and potatoes." In other words, a sizeable proportion of city artisans normally lived with anxiety about downward mobility—a fear of falling.[14]

Boston's economy was the most depressed of the major cities. In the two decades before 1750, artisans deserted the city in droves, the number of "rateable" persons on the tax rolls actually declining by one thousand. "The Middling Sort of People are daily decreasing," wrote one observer, and "many of them are sinking into extream Poverty … many honest Tradesmen are without Employ." In 1750, it was possible for a pamphleteer to contrast the poor with "the rich" who profited from the recent war with France and "build ships, Houses, buy Farms, set up their Coaches, Chariots, live very splendidly, purchase Fame, Posts of Honour." In the 1760s and 1770s this gap between rich and poor remained a very visible part of the urban social landscape: you saw it in houses, which ranged from lavishly furnished mansions to hovels; you saw it on the streets, where some rode in carriages, others were on horseback, and some pushed wheelbarrows with heavy loads; and you saw it in the "seating" of meeting houses according to wealth. In the political conflict that began in the mid-1760s (in the midst of a postwar depression), class resentments were never far below the surface.[15]

Artisans, whatever their wealth, were also especially conscious of their social status, the distinctions between themselves and the "lower sort" below them and their "betters" above them. The status of all but a handful of masters was low. Ladies and gentlemen who regarded themselves of the "better sort" located tradesmen as the "middling" or "lower sort" or spoke of themselves as "well born" and others as "base born." They would have agreed with the pejorative definition of "mechanic" in Samuel Johnson's English dictionary (1756) as a "manufacturer; a low workman" and, as an adjective, as "Mean; servile, of mean occupation." ("Mean" had the connotation of contemptible or unworthy.) The seven colonial colleges taught their small enrollments of would-be gentlemen scholars that the liberal arts were superior to the mechanic arts. A Harvard student dismissed a printer as a "meer mechanic in the art of setting and blacking type" who was "below the notice of a freshman." A thriving artist like John Singleton Copley, whose flattering portraits transformed scores of Boston's nouveaux riches into aristocrats, complained that his clients saw painting as "no more than any other useful trade, as they sometimes term it, like that of a Carpenter, tailor or shoemaker." Even a respected artisan like Revere was introduced by a patriot leader of Boston with a distinct note of condescension as "my worthy friend, Revere ... no man of his rank and opportunities in life deserves better of the community."[16]

Many artisans internalized such ranking. In Boston, a newspaper correspondent mused about the "whimsical degrees of distinction which are kept up between tradesmen and tradesmen." As he saw it, "the woolen-draper speaks of the tailor as a low fellow; and this worthy wight thinks himself equally indifferent to the shoemaker." In New York, a printer apologized for overstepping his "station in life." Even the successful Franklin, in promoting useful public projects in Philadelphia, in print assumed the persona of "a poor ordinary mechanic."[17]

Whatever their status, in these commercial economies, almost all in the laboring classes were enmeshed in webs of dependency. Journeymen and apprentices were dependent on masters for work, and masters on merchants for business (for "custom" they would say). Masters who worked out of a shop usually did "bespoke work," making a product to the order of a customer. Luxury tradesmen like coach makers and fashionable tailors were often in a client-patron relationship, beholden to "the carriage trade." Shoemakers, blacksmiths, and bakers, on the other hand, who made only small transactions with an everyday public, served people like themselves. Mechanics in need of capital were dependent on private money lenders (there were no banks until after the Revolution), and laboring people who rented (as did a large proportion of them) were at the mercy of their landlords. The dense skein of mercantilist regulations of the city governments established a set of dependencies on municipal rulers: cartmen for licenses, butchers for market stalls, and bakers for favorable decisions on the assize of bread. To receive relief, an impoverished working man or widow had to deal with an "overseer of the poor," who literally was just that. As a result of "an inequality of wealth," wrote John Adams, no mean observer of American society, "It will easily be conceived that all the rich men will have many of the poor in the various trades, manufactures, and other occupations in life, dependent upon them in their daily bread." Such dependencies and such social distinctions shaped aspirations and came into play in politics. The revolutionary era was a time when artisans would have to overcome both the dependencies and distinctions to act together to achieve their aspirations.[18]

2. Aspirations: To Become "A Man for Himself"

It is possible to distinguish aspirations of three sorts among artisans. First, most strived to achieve what the English called a "competency" ("a sufficiency of means for a comfortable living, an estate," according to the *Oxford English Dictionary*) and what colonial artisans might have called "independence," "independency," a "maintenance," or "an honest livelihood." An artisan wanted to become "a man for himself" or "his own master," phrases common at the time. This meant he would rise within his trade, but not out of it. A 1779 petition of Philadelphia's tanners, curriers, and cordwainers (all leather trades) illustrates how common this assumption was. It was a "circumstance well known to everybody," they wrote, that "no person of either of these trades, however industrious and attentive to his business, however frugal in his manner of living had been able to rise to a fortune rapidly … the far greater part of us have been contented to live decently without acquiring wealth, nor are the few among us possessed of more than moderate estates." What were their goals? "Our professions rendered us useful and necessary members of the community, proud of that rank, we aspired no higher." Most tradesmen probably thought of themselves this way. In Boston in 1788 when 380 of "the most respectable real tradesmen of this town" met to lobby for the Constitution, they defined themselves as "men who obtain their support from the sweat of their brow and the labor of their hands, men who are constantly employed in the hive of the common wealth for their subsistence and the dignity of the state." These two remarkable epitomes of artisan values expressed an adherence to a labor theory of value and a moral economy. The traditional artisan made his living by the "sweat of his brow" and was content to remain a "respectable tradesman."[19]

Second, some men aspired to rise out of their trade to wealth. "Shoemaking, I suppose was too mean and diminutive an occupation for Mr. Thomas Hollis," the Massachusetts lawyer John Adams observed in 1760, "as wig making was to Mr. Nat Green, or house building to Mr. Daniel

Willard." All attempted "sudden transitions," he said, "in order to rise in the world," which led to their destruction. Others made it: an artisan might reap a windfall profit by outfitting the British army or navy in one of several wars with France, investing his savings in a share of a voyage of a merchant ship, or by speculating in city real estate. One in four men listed as merchants in Boston's directory of 1789 was the son of an artisan. But during the eighteenth century not one of the ten most wealthy occupations in Boston belonged to an artisan.[20]

Third, some in the laboring classes, including many in the "inferior" trades, could hope to do no more than survive. These were the poor, who, as a merchant explained, "always lived from hand to mouth, i.e., who depended on one day's labour to supply the wants of another." These included the working poor, not only the poor already dependent on city charity. Mounds of evidence sifted by historians attest to how common urban poverty was from midcentury on: the bulging records of newly built alms houses and work houses and for "out" relief distributed at home; the "warning out" notices towns served on newcomers they feared might become charity wards (which turned them into the "strolling poor" of the New England coastal areas); the ease in the colonial wars with which the British recruited city men for their American armies and with which sea captains lured men to join the crews of privateers; and not least, the wills at probate which reveal the pitiful estates left by men in the lower trades after a lifetime of toil. All such records included artisans, their widows, and their children.[21]

The popularity of Benjamin Franklin's maxims shows how widely held were the middle-level aspirations. Issued in a yearly almanac from 1737 on and as a separate pamphlet in thirty-six editions from 1758 to 1800, *Poor Richard's Almanac* was one of the most favorite pieces of literature in city as well as countryside. Franklin made a point of addressing artisans. He glorified a trade: "he that hath a trade hath an estate, and he that hath a calling hath an office of profit and honour." He also clearly spoke as one employer to another: "the eye of a master will do more work than both his hands." But he took it for granted that artisan employers worked with their hands. "Handle your tools without mittens; remember that the cat in gloves catches no mice."[22]

We know the principal virtues Franklin advocated: sobriety, industry, frugality. But practice these towards what end? One had to "avoid, above all, else debt." "Think what you do when you run to debt. You give to another power over your liberty." "The Borrower is a slave to the lender,

Benjamin Franklin's advice in the maxims of "Poor Richard" were taken to heart by artisans of all ranks. In this London engraving, "He that hath a trade hath an estate" is illustrated by a blacksmith stoking his fire and his wife hammering a horseshoe at the forge, not an unusual scene. The beehives in the background are symbols of "industry," advocated in another maxim. From "Bowles Moral Pictures or Poor Richard Illustrated," broadside, London, c.1790–1800. Courtesy of the American Philosophical Society.

and the debtor to the creditor, disdain the chain, preserve your freedom, and maintain your independency, be industrious and free, be frugal and free." "The Way to Wealth," the title Franklin attached to the essay assembling these maxims, can be misread. The goal was a decent middling living permitting a man to hold up his head, raise a family in comfort, and provide for his children and for himself in old age.

What has also been lost to modern readers is that these individualistic virtues created a sense of collective identity and pride among artisans. Observe the way they were invoked in a broadside calling "mechanics, manufacturers and tradesmen" to a political meeting in Philadelphia in 1773: "Corruption, extravagance, luxury are seldom found in the habitations of tradesmen"; on the contrary, "Industry, economy, prudence and fortitude generally inhabit there." Latter-day Americans, by imposing the nineteenth-century individualism of "the self-made man" on "Poor Richard," have missed what Franklin's advice meant to his artisan readers: the values bonded them, giving them an awareness of their distinctions from the ostentatious rich above them and the wretched poor below them, both of whom presumably did not live by the values. To become "a man for himself" did not mean it was "every man for himself and the devil take the hindmost." There was a sense of mutuality and fellow-feeling among artisans. They commonly referred to the "brethren in the trade."[23]

Other elements of a shared culture bonded the middling sort of artisans. Historians know a good deal about the Franklins and the Reveres, a world of prosperous masters, literate and self-educated, patrons of bookstores and subscription libraries, readers of newspapers, keepers of account books, and writers of letters. It was a world of the Enlightenment, whose artisan tinkerers in the "mechanical arts" (Revere in metallurgy, Franklin with his numerous inventions) contributed to the practical arts and sciences. They belonged to Congregationalist and Quaker meeting houses, Masonic lodges, fraternal societies, militia companies, fire-fighting companies, fishing societies, and drinking clubs, in all of which they might mix with others of the middling sort. These in sum were the "respectable" tradesmen.[24]

Historians have only begun to excavate the darker world of the men of the "inferior" trades and men and women of the "lower sort," who may have had more in common with seamen and laborers (and sometimes slaves) than with "respectable" tradesmen. Their intellectual world seems less touched by the Enlightenment. They were readers of broadsides with bawdy verses hawked through the streets and of English chapbook adventures imported by American booksellers by the thousands. They might have been members of the militia or fire companies. They spent time in the numerous waterfront or neighborhood taverns of the cities, and their recreations (south of New England) included such blood sports as cock fighting and animal baiting. They very likely attended the spectacle of a public hanging (to which the whole town might turn out). In Philadelphia, they could have been members of the crowd that stoned a "witch" to death in 1776 and again in 1787 or of the crowd in New York City that in 1788 rioted for three days against medical students who stole cadavers for anatomy classes from the paupers' graves. With fewer prospects of rising, they were lured to sea on privateers with the recruiter's cry to "serve your country and make your fortune." Less rooted in the community, some may have become part of a footloose seafaring proletariat circulating in the North Atlantic world.[25]

At times, these two worlds overlapped. Laboring men and women of all sorts shared the "enthusiastic religion" of the great evangelical preachers, George Whitfield foremost among them, with their message of salvation open to all regardless of wealth or status. On his four tours of the colonies between 1740 and 1770, the English evangelist focused on the "populous towns," where he might draw open-air crowds of ten thousand and pack the largest meeting houses day after day. In Boston, his favorite city, he often preached at 6:00 a.m., attended by working men and women before they set out on their day's work. Although Whitfield's message was not radical, orthodox ministers were enraged that he, and especially the American evangelists who followed in his wake, encouraged "Every low-bred illiterate Person" to believe that he "can resolve Cases of Conscience, and settle the most difficult Points of Divinity, better than the most learned Divines." When Whitfield died at Newburyport, Massachusetts, in 1770, Boston's printers issued more broadside eulogies for him than for anyone else in the eighteenth century (one by the African American poet Phillis Wheatley), and in 1776, when the militia of Newburyport marched off to war, they stopped at his tomb and tore shreds from his shroud to carry into battle as a talisman. In the late colonial era, Whitfield, no less than Franklin, was a cultural icon to several generations in the laboring classes.[26]

3. *Custom: The Trade, the Workplace, and the Community*

There is a clear record of collective action by master artisans in colonial America. Masters sustained only a few organizations like the Carpenters Company of Philadelphia. They might form a "Friendly Society" or a "Fellowship Club" to provide benefits for members, but it was common for masters in a single trade in a city to join together on an ad hoc basis to deal with mutual needs. Masters in many trades would have been on familiar terms with most of "the brethren" in their own trades. House carpenters met to set prices, bakers to cope with city regulations, and a host of trades to petition government to keep out interlopers or assist them in one way or another. In Massachusetts, over the course of 150 years, 39 trades sent 258 petitions to the colonial assembly. There was similar petitioning in other colonies. Among journeymen, however, although collective action against masters was infrequent, strikes were not unheard of. But to say that there was no labor movement until wage workers struck in 1827, as did the pioneer American labor historian John R. Commons, is to project later criteria for trade unionism onto the past.[27]

Apprentices and indentured servants expressed "a fondness for freedom," as Reverend Cotton Mather of Boston put it in 1720, by running away or taking their masters to court to enforce the terms of their indentures. You can scarcely open an issue of a colonial newspaper in the North that does not have advertisements from masters desperate to recover labor that had taken flight: runaway apprentices, runaway indentured servants (women as well as men), or runaway slaves. Or there might be a notice from an irate husband about his runaway wife, for whose debts he would not be responsible because she had "left my bed and board." Among runaways of both sexes, who usually headed for the cities, these notices reveal a hidden world of plebeian ingenuity: of assumed identities, cross-dressing, and living by one's wits.[28]

An absence of formal organization among workers did not mean an absence of protection: artisan workshops were ruled by custom, inherent in the craft process. The apprentice learned the skills of the craft from his master, who told him this was the way things were done "from time immemorial." In the traditional small shop, master, journeyman, and apprentice worked side by side with a sense of reciprocal obligations. Craftsmen paced themselves by the task and not by the clock, turning out the whole product or, if in a shipyard, taking pride in their collective product. The rhythm of work undoubtedly differed from work in England. It did not follow the pattern so vividly portrayed by the historian E. P. Thompson: a work week marked by "bouts of intense labor and of idleness," the observance of "Saint Monday" at the pub as a second day of leisure after Sunday, and a work year punctuated by frequent festivals and holidays. American artisan labor was more regular, few observed "Saint Monday," and festive days were sparse. Yet there were many signs of the carryover of the work culture of the "old country." After all, Franklin's underlying assumption was that as "Poor Richard," he had to conduct an unending battle with older task-oriented and recreation-oriented ways of working people to convince them that "TIME is money."[29]

In work sites with a fairly large number of workers, old-world customs surfaced. Drink breaks were common on the job, as well as at the end of the day's work. We have tantalizing glimpses of workplace rituals: of shipyard workers in Boston in the 1760s stopping for drink and food promptly at 11:00 a.m. and 4:00 p.m. and elsewhere of celebrating with rum after completing each stage in constructing a ship from laying the keel to launching the vessel; of ropewalk workers in Salem in the 1790s celebrating November 25 as Saint Catherine's day "with uncommon shew & noise, guns firing, flags displayed, &c." In the late 1780s, had the aged Franklin visited the large printing workshops in Philadelphia or New York, he might have seen journeymen and apprentices practicing hazing customs he had endured as a printer's devil sixty years before in London. Sailors lived by a thick array of customs governing their collective work at sea, out of the sheer need for self-protection in a dangerous job. But a shoemaker did not have to work in a large workshop to know that St. Crispin was the patron "saint" of his craft.[30]

The laboring classes also exercised customary rights in crowd actions in which trades and ranks were mixed, demonstrating horizontal solidarities.[31] Boston in particular had a reputation as a "mobbish" town: before 1750 there were four grain riots, two market riots, and in 1747 an anti-impressment riot that brought the city to a standstill for days—expressions of a commitment to the norms of a "moral economy." "Rough music," rituals of punishment in which crowds dispensed popular justice to offenders of the community's sexual mores, was in vogue in New England and other areas to which the region's culture was diffused. In Boston, for more than a generation before the Revolution, November 5 was Pope's Day, a festivity in which plebeians and young people ruled Boston for a day. New Yorkers also observed Pope's Day, and Philadelphians observed May 1 as King Tammany's Day. During the Revolutionary war, in thirty places there would be price-control actions by crowds in which women were prominent.[32]

The point of this recital of customs and traditions is that from the 1760s on, when resistance to British measures politicized the urban laboring classes, they had a repertoire of popular culture they could draw upon—of the trade, the workplace, and the community.

4. Politics: "This we have tamely submitted to so long"

Prior to the first major crisis with Britain in 1765, artisans had not found their voice in politics. As property holders, most "middling" masters were within the political system, qualified to vote in elections for members of the colonial assemblies. In New England they would have been voters in the town meetings which each year elected delegates to the assembly as well as town selectmen. In New York City and Philadelphia the franchise was more restrictive and elections were held at infrequent intervals. Procedures made elections less than free: in New York a person voted by voice in public before the sheriff; in the Boston town meeting (where business was arranged by a caucus), decisions were usually by a show of hands. In Boston where there were about 2,000 adult white males, the turnout at official meetings between 1763 and 1774 averaged 555 and at its height was about 1,000. Faneuil Hall, the site of the meetings, could hold 1,200 people. But when patriot leaders called protest meetings of "the whole body of the people," eliminating property qualifications, they had to hold them in the Old South Meeting House, where in 1773, 5,000 and more were said to have attended the overflow meetings that deliberated action against the landing of tea.[33]

Did mechanics show deference to elite political leadership? Take what seems to be a classic example of deference in colonial Maryland, a society dominated by large plantation owners. The great planters, observed a Philadelphian (possibly Benjamin Franklin), "treat the poor Planter [i.e., the yeoman or tenant farmer] with Haughtiness, and the artificer [i.e., the artisan] with Contempt; while both must stand Cap-in-hand when they speak to the Lordlings, and *your Honor* begins or ends every sentence." Displaying hat courtesy and addressing a person with an honorific title were quintessential signs of deference. But how much of this deference was the product of economic dependence, and how much was internalized, has been something of a puzzle to historians. Much of what was perceived as deference in colonial America arguably was more like role-playing: enslaved African Americans were especially adept in putting on the mask of servility that their masters expected. In the cities, the endless dependencies of the laboring classes would have contributed to an outward acquiescence to their betters.[34]

Going into the 1760s, politics in the colonies remained by and large a competition among elites: the Livingston family versus the Delancys in New York, the proprietary versus the assembly party in Pennsylvania, the "court" versus the "popular" party in Massachusetts. When the fighting got rough, gentlemen might organize a "Leather Apron Club," as they did in Philadelphia in the 1730s, or appeal for artisan votes by masquerading in print under mechanic names, as they did in New York. Artisans seem to have been more acted upon than acting. Master artisans, who were perfectly capable of meeting with members of their own trade to draft a petition or set prices, were not accustomed to meeting for electoral purposes. They rarely put up one of their own for elective office; in Boston they might have spoken in town meetings and they clearly filled most of the minor appointive offices, but they elected selectmen and assemblymen of the "better sort." What tradesman could afford to take time off from his work? And what self-educated artisan was willing to face ridicule by the "better sort" for his unpolished speech or rough demeanor?[35]

Support from below, however, had to be bought or negotiated, even from dependents, a sign of the erosion of deference. We get a glimpse of this process from a Bostonian writing in 1765, as if he were a merchant running for office:

> I can ... tell you some of the steps I take two or three weeks before an election comes on. I send to the cooper and get all my casks put in order. ... I send to the mason and have some job done to my hearths or chimney; I have the carpenter to make some repairs on the roof or the wood house; I often go down to the ship yards about eleven o'clock when they break off to take their drink, and enter into conversation with them. They all vote for me.

A Philadelphian gives us a glimpse of another way "gentlemen" played this game: "How many poor men, common men, and mechanics have been made happy within this fortnight [of an election] by a shake of a hand, a pleasing smile and a little familiar chat with a gentleman who have not for the seven years past condescended to look at them."[36]

The best evidence for the persistence of what might better be called acquiescence than deference is that whoever tried to mobilize mechanics at the polls assumed that they had to free them from it. Take the language used by a committee of tradesmen in an election in Boston in 1760. Tradesmen, they said, should "put on their Sabbath Cloathes ... wash their hands and faces that they may appear neat and cleanly," and turn out to vote. Or consider these appeals in Philadelphia newspapers. In 1739, "Constant Trueman" had to plead with mechanics not to be "frightened by the Threats or Frowns of great Men from speaking their minds." Three decades later, "Brother Chip," addressing his "brethren the tradesmen, mechanics, &c.," lamented that "It has been customary for a certain company of leading men to nominate persons" and assume that tradesmen will "give sanction" to the ticket:

> This we have tamely submitted to so long that those gentlemen make no scruple to say that the mechanics (though by far the most numerous, especially in the county) have no right to be consulted, that is, have no right to speak or think for themselves.[37]

The response to an incident in Charleston in 1774 that was widely reported in the newspapers included a similar confession of submission. After an Anglican clergyman derided "every silly clown and illiterate mechanic" for presuming to censure his rulers, he faced an uproar. "Crispin Heeltap" replied in the local paper that "a good Cobbler is better entitled to Respect than a bad Preacher," and his congregation dismissed him. A correspondent in a Rhode Island paper held that "all such divines should be taught to know that mechanics and country clowns" were "the real absolute masters of kings, lords, commons and priests." But, he added revealingly, "though (with shame it be spoken) they too often suffer their servants to get upon their backs and ride them most barbarously."[38]

Perhaps evidence of this sort allows us to say of such behavior among mechanics in late colonial America what E. P. Thompson said of it among the plebeian classes in England in the same period: "that deference could be very brittle indeed ... made up of one part of self-interest, one part of dissimulation, and only one part of the awe of authority." In America, in the hothouse of the conflict of the decade that led to independence, it would crack.[39]

5. *Agency: Crowds, Committees, Coalitions*

From 1765 to 1776, in the major seaboard cities the entry of mechanics into the public arena changed the character of politics. Mechanics and the laboring classes as a whole came alive politically for reasons they shared with other classes as well as for reasons of their own.

First, whatever affected the rights of the colonists to self-government, such as the imposition of taxes by Parliament without their consent, affected mechanics. "Liberty and Property," the common Whig patriot slogan after 1765, was not confined to large property holders. As small property holders with a stake in the system, mechanics and farmers could respond to it. But so might others in the laboring classes with little or no property. In Philadelphia in 1773, "A Mechanic" argued that the Tea Act was oppressive "whether we have Property of our own, or not." A principle was at stake: the act was the "breach" by which the British ministry would "enter the Bulwark of our sacred Liberties, and not desist, until they have made a conquest of the whole." At issue was "whether our property, and the dear earned fruits of our own labour are at our own disposal."[40]

It was also possible to argue, as a Bostonian did in 1770 when meetings of "the whole body of the people" let in journeymen, apprentices, and seamen, that "if they had no property they had liberty, and their posterity might have property." Even more fundamental, it was a truism among artisans that labor itself was property. Masters and journeymen looked on their skill acquired from the "arts and mysteries" of their craft as their property. "Labour at that time," argued a petition of 1792 signed by no less than twelve hundred Connecticut mechanics, referring to the years before the Revolution, "was the principal property the citizen possessed."[41]

The right of all who labored by "the sweat of our brows" to "the fruits of our labor" became a mantra in the 1760s and 1770s. This was already a given among English political thinkers like John Locke, as well as among American evangelical preachers. The other side of this coin was a condemnation of the unproductive classes. This explains why Americans damned Stamp Act distributors, customs commissioners, and their employees as people who "live in idleness, affluence and luxury, on the labors of the honest and industrious." They were parasites or, in the words that appeared in Massachusetts almanacs, "pensioners," "placemen," "pimps," "panders," "prostitutes and whores." Or they were "leeches" and "cankerworms." The labor theory of value was the link between the Whig ideology of rights expounded by lawyers, ministers, merchants, and planters, who did not live by the "sweat of their brows," with plebeians of countryside and city, who did.[42]

Second, an array of British actions affected the interests of some laboring people directly. For seafaring men and others who worked around the docks, the renewal in the 1760s of the dreaded impressment by the British navy literally threatened their liberty. Strict enforcement of the customs laws touched sailors smuggling no more than a few bottles of rum, a traditional custom of the sea. The regiments of British soldiers stationed in Boston and New York from the late 1760s were an abrasive presence, especially because they were allowed to moonlight, taking civilian jobs and depressing wages for American workers.[43]

Third, manufacturing became an issue. The restrictions that the British Parliament imposed on particular manufactures by colonial Americans (finished iron, hats, and woolen textiles) do not seem to have been a major grievance. But after royal authority vetoed laws by colonial legislatures to encourage manufactures, British opposition to American manufactures in general became an issue. "It is sincerely to be lamented," wrote a Philadelphian in 1771, "that the mechanic arts and manufactures cannot be encouraged by our legislature with the same propriety that they promote the liberal arts and sciences; but it happens somehow that our Mother Country apprehends she has a right to manufacture every article we consume, except Bread and Meat." The enormous increase in the American consumption of manufactured goods of all sorts in the eighteenth century—the "consumer revolution"—was a mixed blessing for artisans because it led to a heavy flow of imports from Britain—"the Baubles of Britain," Samuel Adams called them. "Made in London" had more cachet than "Made in Philadelphia" or "Made in Boston." But in the 1760s when the patriot movement adopted the tactic of the nonimportation of British goods, the corollary, "Buy American," aroused a vision of the potential for American manufactures. And when merchants who relied on British imports grew cool to the boycott, mechanics became aware that their own interests were distinct from "mercantile dons," as the New Yorkers called them. What began as a tactic became a goal, feeding an artisan sense of distinct class interests.[44]

The traditional aspirations of individual artisans for personal "independence" thus became entwined with a movement to make the country independent of British manufactures. A resolve of the Massachusetts Provincial Congress of 1774, for example, moved from the premise that "the more independent" a family, "the happier they are" to the need "to encourage agriculture, manufactures and economy, so as to render this state as independent of every other state as the nature of our country will admit." It then listed a long catalog of products made in Massachusetts worthy of public support. This vision of American manufactures making for an independent nation was a red thread that would run through artisan banners for half a century.[45]

Crowd action was the most spectacular way the laboring classes expressed themselves. The targets of city crowds were royal officials, customs informers, occupying troops, American Tories, and not least, merchants who refused to go along with the boycotts. Crowds were of many sorts and many minds: multiclass crowds organized by Whig gentlemen or the middling sort of Sons of Liberty leaders; crowds of the lower sort led by their own, often venting raw class antagonisms; and crowds that got out of hand, starting out one way and ending up another.[46]

Crowds that hung effigies—an action that required a plan of action, printed notices calling people to the event, stuffing the dummies with straw—were often led by the middling sort. Spur-of-the-moment crowds, on the other hand, like those that tarred and feathered customs officers or harassed British soldiers, were usually a mix of apprentices, journeymen, "inferior" artisans, seamen, young people, and Negroes. Early in 1770 such crowds were responsible in New York for the skirmishes over the liberty pole that led to the "Battle of Golden Hill" and in Boston for the taunting of troops that led to the "Boston Massacre." Crowd action was a major source of conflict within the patriot coalition. "No violence or you will hurt the cause" was literally a slogan of Boston's Sons of Liberty leaders, who for a decade were engaged in a battle to control the crowd while resisting Britain. In such conflicts, mechanics could be found on both sides.[47]

In striking ways, crowd actions drew on familiar traditions of popular customs. In Boston, resistance to the Stamp Act was built on the leadership, symbolism, and constituency of the annual Pope's Day festivity (see essay 8 in this volume). Everywhere, tarring and feathering drew on rough music as well as official public rituals of shaming criminals. Huge public protest meetings, with flamboyant oratory and verbal responses from audiences, echoed the forms of enthusiasm popularized by evangelical preachers like Whitfield.

The direction of mechanic politics was to bring the people "out of doors" indoors. Mechanics took part in committees, electoral politics, and formal associations and, in New England, in town meetings and county conventions. In Philadelphia, where radicals articulated a political agenda in 1775–76, there was relatively little prior crowd action. In Boston, where there was a great deal of it, on the other hand, mechanics did not develop their own agenda or organizations until after the war. There was no single pattern save increased involvement. In Boston, substantial mechanics took part in patriot organizations like the Loyal Nine and the North End Caucus. In Charleston, mechanics who already had their own benevolent Fellowship Society formed the political John Wilkes Club. By 1774, in Charleston, Philadelphia, and New York, distinct mechanics committees emerged which called meetings of "mechanics and tradesmen," passed resolutions, chose delegates to joint committees with merchants, and ran mechanics for office. In these three cities, mechanics won from a quarter to a half of the places on the citywide revolutionary committees.[48]

In Philadelphia, after the formation of a volunteer militia in 1775, a Committee of Privates with delegates from some thirty militia companies composed mostly of mechanics of the "lower sort" voiced demands on behalf of their own interests. Joined by radicals of the middling sort, they became the engine for an equalitarian political radicalism—debating politics, planning strategy, issuing manifestos—all resonant of soldiers in Oliver Cromwell's army in England a century before.[49]

As political resistance turned into military rebellion, city mechanics often took the lead. In 1774, when a British army occupied Boston, house carpenters refused to build barracks for the troops, and the town's Committee of Correspondence sent Paul Revere to New York to ask the Sons of Liberty there to urge the city's mechanics not to respond to the British appeal for strikebreakers. (The New York mechanics did not succumb.) In 1775, about thirty Boston mechanics formed the underground committee to spy on British troop movements that gave Revere, the silversmith, and William Dawes, a tanner, the intelligence they relayed to patriots in Lexington. An artillery militia company well known to be "composed principally if not altogether of mechanics" smuggled out of the city the brass cannon that proved indispensable to General Washington.[50]

In this wide range of activity, mechanics responded to a range of leaders. First, they supported the middling sort of Sons of Liberty men who often had some natural point of contact with working people: in Boston, Samuel Adams, one of the town's tax collectors who easily rubbed shoulders with leather aprons, and Thomas Young, a doctor with a practice among the poor; in New York, Alexander McDougall and Isaac Sears, captains of privateering vessels experienced in winning the assent of their crews; in Philadelphia, Timothy Matlack, a brewer well known for sponsoring cock-fighting, bull-baiting, and horse-racing, James Cannon, a professor, Benjamin Rush, a doctor, and Thomas Paine, a former artisan recently arrived from England. All such leaders were a new kind of politician, dependent on and at home with a mechanic constituency.[51]

Second, mechanics supported men of wealth who proved their patriotism, patricians like Christopher Gadsden of Charleston or John Hancock, Boston's wealthiest merchant. Hancock's popularity may be explained partly by patronage—John Adams thought that more than one thousand New England families depended on him for "their daily bread." But Hancock's political career was very much an exercise in a paternalistic public theater: donating a bell to a church or a fire engine to the town, ordering the construction of a ship or a wharf to employ out-of-work artisans, buying uniforms for the officers of the Pope's Day companies. As a rich man, he had to prove his virtue as a republican; economic dependency alone would not work. John Singleton Copley painted him not as he did other would-be aristocrats displaying their lavish wealth but as a merchant at his desk holding a ledger, his pen in hand—handsomely dressed to be sure, but a man at his trade.[52]

Third, leaders emerged from the laboring classes. In the Stamp Act Crisis of 1765–66, street actions were often led by the lower sort: in Boston, by Ebenezer Mackintosh, a shoemaker; in New York, by "Tony and Daly," identified by a British army captain as "two ship carpenters who it seems … can raise or suppress a Mob instantly"; in Newport, by John Weber, called by the local newspaper a "deserted convict aged about 20 or 21" but just as likely a sailor recently arrived from England. Such men were shunted aside. In 1770, "out landish jack tarrs," as John Adams called them, like the seaman Crispus Attucks in Boston, took the lead in actions against soldiers. In the final crisis of 1774–76 in Philadelphia, New York, and Charleston, "substantial" mechanics from a range of trades provided a continuity to leadership on committees, while in Philadelphia "inferior" artisans emerged in the Committee of Privates.[53]

As the political issue became war in '75, and independence in '76, mechanics were predominantly patriot. During the war, the proportion of Loyalists among them was extremely low in Boston and Charleston, higher in Philadelphia, and highest in New York (occupied by a British army for the length of the war). Very likely, a larger proportion of mechanics was patriot than was true of any other class. There was little sign in the cities of the kind of inverted class feeling that led poor farmers long at war with their own landed gentry to reject the patriot cause because it was supported by their class enemies.

What can we say about the impact of all this energy on the course of events? Mechanic influence within the patriot coalition was usually in inverse proportion to the degree of Whiggery or patriotism among merchants. It was strongest in Philadelphia, where the traditional ruling classes abdicated or hung back in neutralism and mechanics rushed into the void. In Boston, by contrast, where at least two-thirds of the merchants were Whig and where the Sons of Liberty depended on "those worthy members of society, the tradesmen" on "carrying all before them," as Dr. Young put it, mechanics apparently felt no need for their own committees. In New York and Charleston, where mechanics organized on their own and a wing of the merchant-landlord aristocracy took an active part in popular politics, mechanic influence was somewhere in between that in Philadelphia and Boston.[54]

It is hard not to exaggerate the influence of urban mechanics. In the major cities they nullified the Stamp Act (1765–66), provided the physical coercion to enforce the boycotts (1768–70), took the initiative in direct action against British troops (from 1768 on), and provided the muscle for the tea actions (1773–74). The specter of upheavals, urban and rural, what the Declaration of Independence called "convulsions within," frightened men of wealth, driving many of them into Loyalism and pushing Whigs to try to dominate the coalitions with those below. The radicalism of the cities and countryside pushed would-be rulers to shape a sophisticated conservatism. Robert R. Livingston, head of a leading aristocratic merchant-landlord family in New York, advised his class to learn the "propriety of Swimming with a Stream which it is impossible to stem"; they had to "yield to the torrent if they hoped to direct its course." Mechanics were a major part of the torrent.[55]

From early in 1774 to mid-1776, when the issue became independence versus reconciliation with the mother country, mechanics were indispensable. That the push for independence in Philadelphia came from the politicized Committee of Privates shows the impact of the "lower sort." That the carpenters offered their hall to the first Continental Congress as a meeting place is a sign of the conversion of the substantial mechanics to the cause. Thomas Paine's *Common Sense* (1776), an ardent plea for a democratic republicanism to accompany independence written by a former artisan recently arrived from England, signaled the arrival on the American political scene of a writer with artisan sensibilities. It was the most influential pamphlet of the revolutionary era. Mechanics and farmers, in sum, exerted the pressures from below that moved reluctant elites toward independence.[56]

6. *The Mechanic Presence: "Leathern Aprons" in "Mechanics Hall"*

As mechanics participated in one crowd action after another, as crowds became meetings, as meetings formed committees and backed candidates for office, they recognized their capacity to shape events. As independence loomed, the prospect of new state governments confronted patriots with the issue of who should rule at home. Gouverneur Morris, the young scion of a landed aristocratic family of New York, captured a moment of polarization in this process in New York City. In 1774, as he "stood on the balcony" observing a huge outdoor mass meeting, he was struck by the divisions of class. "On my right hand were ranged all the people of property, with some few poor dependents," he wrote, "and on the other all the tradesmen etc., who thought it worth while to leave their daily labour for the good of the country." He had an alarming sense of a political awakening of "the tradesmen, etc.": "The mob begins to think and reason. Poor reptiles! It is with them a vernal morning; they are struggling to cast off their winter's slough, they bask in the sunshine, and ere noon they will bite, depend on it. The gentry begin to fear this." The issue was no longer whether and how to oppose British measures: "they fairly contended about the future forms of our Government, whether it should be founded upon aristocratic or democratic principles."[57]

Every effort by "people of property" to put mechanics down only heightened their consciousness. They defiantly turned around expressions of contempt. For example, in Philadelphia in 1774, after mechanics nominated their own candidates and conservatives questioned the capacity of "leather aprons" to govern, a newspaper correspondent asked indignantly, "Do not mechanicks and farmers constitute ninety-nine out of a hundred of the people of America?" and "Is not one half of the property of the city of Philadelphia owned by men who wear LEATHERN APRONS?" This was hyperbole (the top 10 percent of property holders owned 72 percent of the city's wealth), but it was a way of rallying mechanics to a sense of their importance.[58]

A similar process was at work in the major southern cities. By 1775, the lieutenant governor of South Carolina was convinced that the Charleston mechanics "have discovered their own strength and importance" and would not be "so easily governed by their former leaders." The governor of Georgia was shocked that Savannah's revolutionary committee was "a Parcel of the Lowest People, chiefly carpenters, shoemakers, blacksmiths etc, with a Jew at their head." Their "insolence and pertness would raise any Englishman's indignation," another wrote. Gentlemen had long subscribed to the motto "Shoemaker, stick to thy last" to epitomize their contempt for manual workers in politics. They now seemed outraged that men who never knew more than "to cobble an old shoe in the neatest manner, or build a necessary house" had the audacity to offer opinions on affairs of state.[59]

Such expressions of class contempt brought out in mechanics and the laboring classes their distrust of men of great wealth, which had its roots in the values articulated by Benjamin Franklin, George Whitfield, and Thomas Paine, the three most definable influences on mechanics of the late colonial era. The distrust was fed by Franklin's valorizing of the middling ideal, Whitfield's evangelical Protestant antipathy to luxury and display, and Paine's infusing ordinary people with confidence in their capacity to make decisions on the basis of their own "common sense."

In the final crisis of 1774–76 this distrust led mechanics to demand direct class representation. In Philadelphia, the Committee of Privates asked militia members to elect "Men of like Passions and Interests with ourselves," warning against "great and over-grown rich Men" and "gentlemen of the learned Professions." In New York, mechanics now held their meetings in a building they had bought and christened "Mechanicks Hall," a sign that they intended to remain a political presence.[60] With the drafting of a state constitution in the offing, they demanded that it be submitted to them for approval. "The Mechanics in Union" resolved that the "right which God has given them, with all men, to judge whether it [the proposed form of government] be consistent with their interest to accept or reject." Where the political system thwarted mechanics, as it did in New York, they asked for reforms: newspapers teemed with demands for a secret ballot, annual elections, and rotation in office. In Philadelphia, radicals pressed not only for a broad suffrage but also for laws to curb "an enormous proportion of property vested in a few individuals" because it was "destructive to the common happiness of mankind." Where the political system already accommodated the middling sort, as it did in Boston, they were not advocates of reform; indeed, most mechanics defended the turbulent direct democracy of the town meeting when elites renewed old schemes to replace it with an elected mayor and aldermen.[61]

In general, in the states with the large cities, the greater the mechanics' influence within the patriot alliance, the more democratic the state constitution. Pennsylvania's was the most radical, South Carolina's was one of the most conservative, and Massachusetts's and New York's were in between. The new Pennsylvania government came closest to the democratic ideal of that era: a one-house legislature with a weak executive, annual elections with a franchise open to all taxpayers, no property qualifications for public office, and rotation in office. (The proposed radical curb on great wealth was rejected.) But the New York constitution, which a conservative called "a perfect balance between the democratic and the aristocratic," was not a bone of contention with mechanics. In Massachusetts, where two constitutions were submitted for public debate, 968 Bostonians in a town meeting unanimously rejected the undemocratic 1778 constitution but then acquiesced in 1780 to support a revised conservative version.[62]

The clue to mechanic thinking may lie in Paine's *Common Sense*. The thrust of the pamphlet was against monarchy and in favor of "republican government," but Paine did no more than "threw out a few thoughts" on the specifics of a constitution: frequent elections, "a large and equal representation," and the protection of rights. Paine himself was a champion of the Pennsylvania model, but given no more than his sparse "hints," it is not hard to see how his mechanic readers elsewhere might settle for middle-of-the-road state constitutions with bicameral legislatures and strong executives, provided they were based on frequent elections, equal representation, and a suffrage that enfranchised small property holders. "Freedom of election is the most valuable jewel that can be possessed by men," the New York mechanics had resolved, and the state's constitution enhanced it by annual assembly elections and the promise of a future secret ballot. In New York, where democrats feared the influence that Hudson Valley landlords exerted on several thousand tenant farmers, universal male suffrage was not an issue for several decades. This stance is a clue to the support mechanics later gave the federal Constitution of 1787.[63]

The long war from 1775 to 1783 halted the momentum of mechanic movements. British armies occupied New York City for the length of the war and Boston, Philadelphia, and Charleston for shorter periods. Laboring people enlisted in the American army in numbers disproportionate to their share of the population and went to war at sea in privateering vessels,

The strong raised arm of a workman clenching a hammer was the central motif on the membership certificate of the General Society of Mechanics and Tradesmen of New York, formed in 1785. The hammer was the most common tool used in the crafts. The motto "By Hammer & Hand all Arts do Stand" was a proud assertion of the superiority of the mechanic arts over the liberal arts. Courtesy of the General Society of Mechanics and Tradesmen of the City of New York.

where they had a prospect of sharing in captured booty. The war disrupted the urban economies, bringing special hardship to the poor. The inequities of the war, the profiteering of merchants, and the failure of price controls increased class antagonisms but also pitted mechanics against one another. With victory in 1783 and the reopening of foreign trade, a wave of British manufactured imports threatened to swamp American mechanics. The result was a heightened sense of a mechanic interest.[64]

7. Consciousness: Craft, Producer, Mechanic Interest

Follow mechanics from the end of the war in 1783 to about 1815, and it is possible to distinguish four strands of consciousness among them: a craft consciousness, a producer consciousness, a mechanic interest consciousness, and a citizen consciousness. Their sense of themselves as craftsmen and producers was very old, but their sense of a collective mechanic interest and their sense of their common capacity as citizens was new. All were intertwined, although at times one consciousness took priority over another or displaced it.

CRAFT CONSCIOUSNESS. This, the oldest and most natural kind of consciousness among artisans, can be measured in the growth of associations in one trade after another late in the eighteenth century: cabinetmakers, house carpenters, chairmakers, coopers, cordwainers, pewterers, printers, shipwrights, sailmakers—the roll call could go on. Primarily among masters (later among journeymen), these were self-interest groups setting prices for their labor or "friendly" societies providing benefits for members in the event of sickness or death. Although the records of only a few of them have survived, they seem to have been formal associations with constitutions, certificates of membership, elected officers, and minute books, unlike the ad hoc coming together of men in a trade in colonial years.[65]

Three membership certificates of New York societies exhibit this expanded craft pride. The Society of Master Sailmakers of the City of New York depicted every stage of making sails: from weaving the tough sailcloth to stitching it to rigging the sails on ocean-going vessels docked at the water's edge. (It also depicted a member distributing benefits to a widow and a female "Liberty" emancipating a slave.) The Coopers Society depicted its craft process: making staves, hooping them together to make a barrel, rolling the barrels on board a ship. The "True Assistant Society" of hatmakers, very likely composed of journeymen, featured an American eagle holding a hat in its beak, with a leather-aproned craftsman below shaking hands with a man in gentleman's clothes (either a master hatter or a customer). This small certificate mounted on stiff cardboard might have been carried by a journeyman hatter "tramping" for work to attest to an employer that he had completed his apprenticeship.[66]

Craft pride is also vivid in the portraits in which successful artisans had themselves portrayed with emblems of their trade. In colonial times, the rare artisan who had his portrait painted usually masked his origins. When Benjamin Franklin retired in the late 1740s he had himself painted as a would-be gentleman: in Robert Fekes's portrait he is poised wearing a wig and a velvet coat with ruffles at the sleeves. You would never know that he had recently been a printer. In the late 1760s, however, Copley

In its membership certificate, the Society of Master Sailmakers of New York celebrated each stage of production in its trade: weaving the sailcloth, sewing the cloth into a sail, mounting the sail on a ship. A member bestows charity to the widow of a member (upper right) and a female "Liberty," holding a staff with the liberty cap, emancipates a slave (upper left). Courtesy of the Collection of the New-York Historical Society.

painted Paul Revere at his workbench proudly displaying a silver teapot of his own making with a tool before him. He wears a linen shirt and his natural hair is combed back. Early in the nineteenth century, Duncan Phyfe, whose name was then synonymous with fine furniture in New York, was painted by an unknown artist wearing a Scot's cap and holding a carpenter's saw. This tradition would grow.[67]

PRODUCER AND MECHANIC INTEREST CONSCIOUSNESS. When political thinkers discussed "interests," a "manufacturing interest" might refer either to owners of large-scale "manufactories" or artisans or both. In the 1780s and 1790s, mechanics often spoke of themselves as a "mechanic interest": a body of small producers with their own economic needs. They demonstrated this awareness in two ways: in the campaign for protection for American manufactures and in the formation of citywide associations.

The driving force that created the mechanic interest was a double need: protecting American artisans from British manufactures that were flooding the American market and arresting the decline in "navigation," which depressed shipping and, with it, the maritime trades. A product of the boycotts of the 1760s and 1770s, which were quiescent during the war, the movement was revived with a vengeance in the 1780s. Led by trades with a direct stake in keeping out competing British wares and by the maritime trades, mechanics joined with export-import merchants who sought the promotion of ocean-going commerce in an age of closed empires. In the words of the New York mechanics in 1789, which they repeated verbatim in 1800, "foreign importations were highly unfavorable to mechanical improvement, nourishing a spirit of dependence, defeating in a degree the purpose of our Revolution." Their cry for protective tariffs was met by the state governments of Massachusetts, New York, and Pennsylvania, but the inability of the separate states to dam the flood propelled mechanics toward strengthening the national government.[68]

Two kinds of mechanic organizations made their appearance after the war. The protection campaign led immediately to the formation of committees composed of delegates selected by each branch of trade, in Boston called the Association of Tradesmen and Manufacturers. The goal, the Boston organizers explained, was that "each man becomes interested not only in his own branch but in those of his brethren." The Boston committee, writing to its counterparts in New York, Philadelphia, and Baltimore, also hoped that "a general harmony will prevail throughout the whole manufacturing interest of this country." But this delegated body, which lasted only about two years, was a road not taken. For the second type of organization mechanics in Boston and New York formed multipurpose membership societies whose names suggested a desire to embrace artisans however they identified themselves: in Boston, the Massachusetts Mechanics Association (later renamed the Massachusetts Charitable Mechanics Association); in New York, the Mechanics Society (later the General Society of Mechanics and Tradesmen); in Charleston, the Charleston Mechanics Society, open to "free white Mechanics, Manufacturers and Handicraftsmen."

Over the 1790s and the early 1800s, the general mechanic societies proliferated; in New England in Portland, Portsmouth, Newburyport, Worcester, Salem, and Providence; in New York in Albany, Lansingburgh, Hudson, Catskill (Hudson Valley towns), as well as in Kings County and in the south in Savannah and Norfolk (joining Baltimore and Charlestown, the prewar groups). Undoubtedly there were others: they were a contagious phenomenon. To join such societies, a man usually had to have completed an apprenticeship, which meant the societies were composed overwhelmingly of masters. Who qualified as a mechanic could be a subject of debate: the Boston and Providence societies admitted factory owners and superintendents.[69]

In New York and Boston, the societies were chartered by state governments only after protracted struggles with elites frightened by their potential economic and political influence: the New Yorkers had to wait seven years, until 1792, for their charter and the Bostonians had to wait until 1806. The Boston society, with about 125 members, remained small and unrepresentative, never including more than a tenth of the masters in the city, but the New York society flourished, with about 600 members by 1798. The societies assumed a variety of functions: upholding apprenticeship, dispensing benefits, arbitrating disputes, promoting manufactures, and occasionally lending capital. In later decades, they would sponsor libraries for apprentices, schools for the children of members, banks, and exhibits promoting the mechanic arts. They would also erect their own buildings. Their importance lay, above all, in establishing a presence in the city for the "respectable mechanics and tradesmen." When the issue of protection for American manufactures came up, the ad hoc committees with delegates from the trades rained petitions on Congress.[70]

The certificates of the general societies are vivid expressions of mechanic producer consciousness, a visual tribute to an array of trades. The engraving of the New York group had insets, each portraying a man who clearly lived by "the sweat of his brow": a carpenter turning a lathe, a housewright putting up a building, shipwrights at work in a shipyard, a blacksmith at his forge, and a farmer behind his plow. The central symbol (also adopted in Charleston and Providence) was the raised muscular arm of a working man, his hand gripping a hammer under the motto "By Hammer & Hand all Arts Do Stand." (In Charleston it was "Industry Produceth All Wealth.") Here was a proud assertion of the primacy of "the useful and mechanic arts" to society—a bold challenge to the traditional claim of gentlemen for the superiority of the liberal arts. The symbol caught the imagination of artisans and would appear on parade banners.[71]

Even when the symbolism was less defiant and emphasized a harmony of interests of mechanics and merchants, it staked out new ground. The central emblem on the Boston certificate (adopted in Salem and Portsmouth) was a set of scales beneath an eagle with outstretched wings, with the slogan "Be Just, Fear Not." From the right balance, bales were suspended, the society's minutes explained, "to represent the commercial"; from the left balance were "numerous implements of handicrafts to designate the *Mechanic* interests of the community": the lever, the screw, the wedge, the pulley, the wheel. If the scales were "equally balanced the merchant and the mechanic, in being Just may Fear Not."[72]

In this producer consciousness, mechanic symbolism paid only lip service to farmers: in 1788 the committee of Boston mechanics spoke of "the respectable real tradesmen and the yeomanry as the democratic part of the community," but in the 1780s they never formed a political alliance with farmers. Quite the contrary: city mechanics, often creditors, shared the opposition of merchants to agrarian pleas for debtor relief in state legislatures. Boston's mechanics were hostile to Shays's Rebellion (but also to harsh punishment for the rebels). By 1785–86, in one city after another mechanics joined a coalition with merchants who sought a stronger national government not only to promote their own commercial needs but also to thwart radical agrarian majorities in the states. As early proponents of national independence, mechanics were predisposed to champion a stronger central government: in *Common Sense*, Paine had written that "the continental belt" was "too loosely buckled." Mechanics thus entered an alliance with the "mercantile dons" they had long distrusted to support the drafting and ratification of the federal Constitution.[73]

8. *Citizen Consciousness: Mechanics on Parade*

From 1765 to 1776, mechanics were awakened to citizenship in response to issues initiated by the Whig patriot leaders and over time acquired a sense of their own interests. In the 1780s mechanics began with a sense of their own interests, launched their own campaigns, and formed their own organizations. While they clearly responded to issues raised by others—Federalists in the late 1780s and Republicans in the mid-1790s—these political movements responded to them.

No activity registered mechanics' citizen consciousness more than their marching in parades, and no parades expressed their outlook more clearly than those that celebrated ratification of the Constitution in 1788. The "grand processions" took place in every major American city, with a massive outpouring of citizens of all ranks: Boston (4,000 people), New York (5,000), Philadelphia (5,000–6,000), Baltimore (3,000), and Charleston (2,800). Parades were also held in many lesser cities, among them Portsmouth, Albany, New Haven, Trenton, and Savannah, as well as in country towns. The parades were festive civic events in which mechanics were the most numerous and prominent marchers—in effect the first "labor" parades in American history.[74]

Mechanics were a presence even if they were not present in the convention that met in Philadelphia in the summer of 1787 to draft a federal constitution. Delegates became aware that if the constitution was to be ratified in each state by conventions elected by popular vote, mechanic voters in the cities had to be reckoned with. The convention's solution to the issue of the qualifications for suffrage in the House of Representatives (taken up in essay 4 in this volume) illustrates the way in which the framers accommodated mechanics, defeating a proposal to limit the vote to landholders. For mechanics, as we have seen, the franchise was the sine qua non of popular government.[75]

In the popular debate on ratification, more people were involved than in any other debate of the revolutionary era. In the cities, debates raged in taverns, workplaces, barbershops, and not only in pamphlets and newspapers. Both sides appealed to mechanics, but the appeals by anti-Federalists to class, which won enthusiastic support among the yeomanry, fell on deaf ears in the cities. Melancton Smith, New York's most articulate anti-Federalist and a city merchant, took the pen name "Plebeian" but clearly defined the "middling classes" and the "common people" he spoke for as the "substantial yeomanry." In a biting "Address of John Humble" on behalf of "the *low born* of the United States of America," a Philadelphia writer laid into the "well born" for constructing a government of "kings, lords and commons" which would be ruled by six hundred rich men and result in a new "royal government [supported] by the sweat and toil of our bodies." The appeal, which struck every note that mechanics had responded to for years in Philadelphia, got nowhere.

Federalists were successful by dwelling not on the lofty political theory of *The Federalist* but on harsh bread-and-butter realities. In Boston, one writer pointed to "a long train of industrious tradesmen who are now spending their past earnings, or selling their tools for a subsistence." Another said that the mechanic "stands idle half his time, or gets nothing for his work but truck [i.e., payment in kind], half our sailors are out of business—the laborer can find no employ." Both protection from British manufactures and support for American ocean-going commerce were at stake. Samuel Bryan, a perceptive anti-Federalist leader in Philadelphia, recognized what had happened: "The numerous Classes of Tradesmen who depend on Commerce & particularly those who depend on Navigation [i.e., overseas trade] were distressed" and favored the Constitution, while other mechanics "divided according to their former attachments to the Revolution"—Whig or Tory—and to the radical Pennsylvania Constitution. In other words, among city mechanics desperate for employment, economic interest trumped traditional class allegiances.[76]

In the elections for delegates to the state ratifying conventions, city mechanics voted overwhelmingly Federalist. In Philadelphia, anti-Federalists polled only 150 votes out of 1,400 cast; in New York, with universal male suffrage prevailing, the vote was 150 anti-Federalist, 2,700 Federalist. In Boston, mechanics backed a predominantly Federalist slate that made room for their old political friends, Samuel Adams and John Hancock, both of whom were noncommittal. It was when Adams wavered at the state convention that 380 "respectable" tradesmen met in the Green Dragon tavern and sent a delegation to him (Paul Revere among them) that convinced Adams to withdraw his opposition. Thus, when the Constitution was ratified, mechanics could feel that they had played a part in the process.[77]

The parades were a magnificent summa of the four strands of artisan consciousness. Citizen consciousness lay in the very fact that mechanics marched, almost everywhere grouped by trades. The parades were celebratory but were also political, aimed at bringing pressure for ratification on three holdout states. The first parade, held in Boston in February, hailed ratification by Massachusetts; the others were held in the spring and on July 4 while some states still teetered on the brink of a decision. Only in Boston did a Committee of Tradesmen make the arrangements; elsewhere, civic leaders organized the day, with each trade in charge of preparing its own contingent. This meant that in each trade, masters had to meet and make decisions on the emblems to be carried and the slogans on the banners, whether to sponsor a float, and if so, how to construct it in a matter of days. Mechanics marched of their own volition and with enthusiasm: these were festive affairs, new to America (see essay 3 in this volume).

The sheer number of artisans of all ranks who turned out was unprecedented. Mechanics marched by trade, arranged "promiscuously" in Philadelphia, elsewhere by lot, often grouped with kindred trades—the building trades, the maritime trades, and so forth. The newspapers usually reported the number in each contingent. In Boston, the smallest of the three big cities, on a snowy day in midwinter almost all of the city's twelve hundred artisans turned out, a sleigh with the Committee of Tradesmen (including Colonel Paul Revere) bringing up the rear. In Philadelphia, the major contingents were huge: 450 architects and house carpenters, 350 ship carpenters "wearing sprigs of white oak," 300 cordwainers, "six abreast each wearing a white leathern apron," 80 victuallers (the butchers) "all drest in white." Some forty to fifty trades marched.[78]

Craft pride and producer consciousness suffused the artisan divisions. Within each trade the conventional hierarchy was honored: typically, in the contingent of one hundred cabinet and chair makers in Philadelphia, masters, headed by "four of the oldest masters," marched first, six abreast, followed by their float, behind which the journeymen and apprentices marched, "six abreast wearing linen aprons and buck'd tails in their hats." (Linen aprons were more common than leather work aprons.) In Boston, where the parade was hastily improvised, tradesmen carried a tool or product of their trade. In Philadelphia (and less so in New York), there were large floats with rolling workshops on which artisans performed their craft, a sight never before seen in an American procession. There were model workshops of cordwainers, blacksmiths, boatbuilders, gunmakers, saddlers, cabinet makers, potters, wheelwrights, printers, and bakers. Where workers did not act out their trade, they displayed a finished product, dubbed with an appropriate name; the bakers, for example, carried a huge "Federal Loaf" that they distributed to spectators.

The most striking display in Philadelphia was the "Grand Federal Edifice or The New Roof," constructed by the house carpenters and drawn by ten white horses. Its dome was "supported by thirteen Corinthian columns ... with ten columns complete," standing for the ratifying states as of July 4, 1788, and three "left unfinished." On top of the dome was the Goddess of Plenty with a cornucopia. The hit of the parade in the major cities was a large ship, symbolic of the "ship of state" (in Philadelphia, thirty feet long with twenty-four guns), mounted on wheels and drawn by teams of horses. Built by shipwrights and manned by seamen miming ship-board tasks at the command of their captain, it was called variously "The Federal Ship Union," "The Ship of State," "The Constitution," and in New York, "The Hamilton."

On their banners some trades but no more than the traditional emblem of the craft (the shoemakers, for example, presenting "St. Crispin"), while others offered slogans that spoke to their political economy. All of the slogans expressed the hope that the new government would support each craft's economic interests, the slogans varying with the market for their products. The shipjoiners spoke for commerce, their lifeline:

> This Federal ship will our commerce revive
> And the merchants and shipwrights and joiners shall thrive.

Blacksmiths and nailers wanted protection from imports:

> While industry prevails
> We need no foreign nails.

Chairmakers wanted to export to foreign markets:

> The Federal States in union bound
> O'er all the world our chairs are bound.

The leather workers summed up the general mood:

> Americans encourage your own manufactures.

Finally, banners voiced artisan variants of republican citizenship. In Philadelphia, the smiths proclaimed, "By Hammer and Hand all Arts Do Stand," and the brick-layers, "Both buildings and rulers are the work of our hands," a bold double entendre. The printers, carrying a portrait of Franklin, offered, "Where Liberty dwells there is my country," which the tallow chandlers turned around to say, "The stars of America a light to the world." The upholsterers of New York (all thirteen of them) carried an elegant "Federal Chair of State," flanked by two "comely lads" carrying either a staff topped by the cap of liberty or a "sword of justice."

The processions were the first in which mechanics (masters, journey-men, and apprentices) marched on masse by trades—and in this sense they were the first American "labor" parades—but they were hardly exclusive. In Boston, the account emphasized "150 of the principal merchants"; in Philadelphia and New York, there were separate contingents for merchants, doctors, lawyers, the clergy, teachers, students, and so on. Officials—city, state, and national—marched. In New York and Philadelphia, military companies were interspersed among the divisions. As the processions as a whole testify, mechanics saw their own interest linked with that of others in the community. The agricultural interest was represented by token farmers, and large-scale manufacturers by the Manufacturing Society in Philadelphia, which sponsored a float replicating a textile "manufactory," the investors marching in front.

In the eyes of the planners, the "Grand Federal Procession" was intended to be the people and not merely represent them. And after the processions were over, at the giant open-air banquets, or "collations," mechanics sat down to eat and drink with other classes in the community (in New York, at thirteen tables radiating from a center). The rituals of the day thus gave mechanics what they had been seeking in the revolutionary era: recognition, respect, a voice. The parades were exhilarating: in Boston, a cry went up to build a "Mechanics Hall" as a permanent meeting place; in Philadelphia, a tavern keeper saved the "Federal Ship Union" and the "Federal Edifice" for use in future parades.[79]

The grand processions, of course, presented an idealized version of "the trade." Picture the magnificent flag carried by the New York Society of Pewterers, today mounted at the New-York Historical Society. On the upper left is the U.S. flag with the stars and stripes; below it, the pewterers' emblem, adapted from the London guild, flanked by two properly clothed American pewterers bearing kettles of their own making, their motto: "Solid and Pure." At the upper right is a large image of a pewterer's workshop, with a master, a journeyman, and two young apprentices working side by side, all in shirtsleeves. Above it, a verse expresses ideals most artisans would have shared:[80]

> The federal plan most solid & secure
> Americans their freedom will ensure
> All arts shall flourish in Columbia's land
> And all her sons join as one social band

"One social band": the verse spoke of a harmony that would pass within the lifetime of the younger marchers, the apprentices and journeymen, and of a moral economy in which the trades were recognized as useful contributors to the commonwealth. The processions masked a range of latent conflicts that would emerge within a few years: between merchants dependent on importing British manufactures and mechanics seeking to wall them out; between democratic-minded mechanics and conservative elites frightened by the political threat they posed; between masters becoming capitalist entrepreneurs and the journeymen they squeezed; and between apprentices imbued with notions of equality and masters insisting on their subordination. Describing the Philadelphia procession, an enthusiastic Benjamin Rush could say, no more than, "Rank *for a while* forgot all its claims."[81]

The processions were also an exercise in exclusion. All the trades marched, the "inferior" with the high status trades, but save for seamen and cartmen, no contingents were designated for the lower sort outside the artisan system: day laborers, dock workers, fishermen, street peddlers, household servants, chimney sweeps, much less for residents of the alms house. Nor were there women in skilled trades, who, had they been invited, in the big cities might easily have formed a dozen contingents: spinners and weavers, seamstresses, tailoresses, makers of gloves, lace, and mantuas, nurses, teachers of "dame schools," washer women. In Philadelphia, the float of the textile factory, with several women spinners, was a harbinger of the future. Women of all classes and their children would have been the principal spectators, in Philadelphia crowding the "footways, the windows, and roofs of the houses." As republican mothers, they would have been responsible for instructing their children in the symbolism of the day, no small role. But who, may we ask, sewed the craft banners and stitched the linen aprons? Who cooked the food for the banquets?[82]

And if we ask whether African American artisans, sailors, or servants were in any processions, we are reduced to reading the silences in the descriptions. It is more likely that the absence of mention of Negroes in the numerous accounts signifies their absence in the processions rather than color blindness by the reporters. (Slaves had been freed in Philadelphia and Boston but were still numerous in New York and were still half the population of Charleston). It is hard to believe that in Boston the leather dressers would have turned away Prince Hall, a free black leather worker who kept a shop at the sign of the Golden Fleece, a war veteran and the master of the African Masonic Lodge. But then again, Hall, an angry petitioner against postwar Boston's denial of the rights of free blacks, may have chosen not to celebrate a Constitution that locked in slavery. In 1788, no mechanic banner carried a hint about emancipation, but neither did anyone else's. Northern city dwellers were party to the framers' accommodation of slaveholders in the Constitution.[83]

In the years that followed, parades became the expression of choice among the laboring classes. In 1789, when President Washington in his grand tour of the northern states made his appearance in Boston, he saw forty-six contingents of tradesmen in a procession organized by the city (arranged in alphabetical order from bakers to wheelwrights), each contingent carrying a newly made white banner bearing a traditional emblem of its trade. On the president's arrival, the marchers were asked to divide ranks and face inward, so that Washington rode on horseback through a sea of mechanic faces—a republican "royal entry." In the 1790s, in the face of a shrill upper-class scorn for "greasy caps" and the "swinish multitude," marching became a very visible way for working people to assert their equal rights. In 1794, when the fear of a British naval attack led to a demand to strengthen the fortifications on Governor's Island in New York Harbor, each trade volunteered a day's work gratis, marching through the streets to the Battery, fife and drums playing, to take boats to the island. For the next two decades on the Fourth of July, trade and fraternal societies paraded to a church, where the Declaration of Independence was read and a Republican delivered an oration.[84]

Mechanics seized every opportunity to march en masse in civic processions. They paraded to mourn the death of a patriot hero (Franklin in 1790, Washington in 1800), to celebrate the opening of a public enterprise they helped build (the Charles River bridge in Boston in 1786, the Erie Canal in New York in 1825), and in 1824–25 to receive the hero of two revolutions, the Marquis de Lafayette.[85] Parading became a way for trades of low status to claim a place in the civic sun. In Boston this was epitomized by the truckmen parading to Cambridge on Harvard College's commencement day, a traditional day of public celebration. On Boston's crowded streets, truckmen driving their horse-drawn carts surrendered the right-of-way to no one, prompting an English visitor to observe wryly that they "seem so conscious that all men are created equal, that they take pride in shewing their knowledge of this principle on every occasion." Normally grimy from their work, they rode out on their horses to Cambridge, dressed in white smocks and blue pants. In Philadelphia the "victuallers," the name by which butchers elevated their trade, conducted their own parade through the city streets. Their aprons were normally bloody from their trade, but on this occasion they were dressed in white smocks, riding on white horses and carrying a banner that read "We Feed the Hungry," with the ship saved from the 1788 parade bringing up the rear. It is not surprising that when journeymen conducted their first strikes, they often paraded through the streets, banners aloft, fife and drums playing. Nor should it surprise us that free African Americans in the three big northern cities paraded, often amidst the derision of whites. After Congress abolished the slave trade in 1807, African Americans created their own annual holiday on July 14, a day that both acknowledged and defied the Fourth of July. In short, parades were a major measure of the impact of mechanics on American public life.[86]

9. The Mechanic Presence: "The yeomanry of the city"?

There were other measures of the mechanics presence. In 1785 in *Notes on the State of Virginia*, Thomas Jefferson spoke of "those who labour in the earth" as "the chosen people of God, if ever he had a chosen people." They alone were free from "a corruption of morals.... Dependence begets subservience and venality" and "suffocates the germ of virtue." Jefferson was unequivocally opposed to manufactures and especially to cities: "While we have land to labor then, let us never wish to see our citizens occupied at a work-bench or twirling a distaff ... for the general operations of our manufacture, let our workshops remain in Europe." In 1793, as Jefferson watched the emergence of an urban opposition to Federalist policy in Philadelphia, in a flash of insight he recognized tradesmen as among "the *yeomanry* of the city (not the fashionable people nor paper men)." By 1794 the honeymoon of mechanics and Federalists was over: mechanic voters in New York, Philadelphia, and Baltimore helped send Republicans to Congress. And by 1800, besides these three cities, Republicans carried Newport, Wilmington, and Norfolk and were closing in on Boston. The major seaboard cities (Charleston and Providence excepted) helped make Jefferson president and then became mainstays of Republican rule from 1801 to 1825. What was the impact of this mechanic presence in public life in the new nation on American policy and thought? Did Jefferson ever find a place for the virtuous mechanic alongside the virtuous yeoman?[87]

The mechanic presence was most apparent of course in political life. Urban artisans contributed to the downfall of the Federalists, the triumph of the Democratic-Republicans, and the democratization of American politics. Artisan republicanism shaped political party Republicanism, especially in the middle-Atlantic cities, where it is hard to distinguish the two. Although Republicans never became a "labor" party, the laboring classes were a wing of the party, and in the cities of the North they were the most numerous voters in a coalition that included merchant Republicans and large-scale manufacturing Republicans. In New England artisan federalism also influenced the Federalist Party.[88]

From the 1790s on, mechanics were visible in almost every facet of the Republican movement. They joined multiclass associations led by merchants and lawyers: the explicitly political Democratic-Republican societies which flourished in Boston, New York, Philadelphia, Baltimore, and Charleston, as well as in the smaller cities like Portland, New Haven, Norwalk, Newark, New Castle, Norfolk, and a host of country towns—more than forty groups in all. In Philadelphia, about a third of the members were mechanics. A hostile cartoonist depicted their meetings as filled with demonic lower-class figures, including blacks. The New Yorkers granted a Federalist charge that their meetings were attended by "the lowest order of mechanics, laborers and draymen," explaining that working men could only meet in the evening after their day's work. Artisans were an even larger proportion of republican fraternal orders like the Sons of Saint Tammany.[89]

Mechanic readers were a mainstay of Republican newspapers. In the 1770s, the patriot Boston printer Isaiah Thomas was unique in making a success of the *Massachusetts Spy*, which, he wrote, was "calculated to obtain subscriptions from mechanics and other classes of people who had not much time to spare from business." As the number of newspapers grew from 91 in 1790 to 234 in 1800 (24 of them dailies), there were many papers like Thomas's, a majority of them Republican. The men who served in the combined role of publisher, editor, compositor, and pressman often thought of themselves as working mechanics. A score of radical émigrés from political persecution in Great Britain who became urban Republican editors were especially successful in reaching out to new immigrants.[90]

As they did in 1776, artisans once again consumed political pamphlets. (Between 1790 and 1800 the number of imprints from American printers doubled to twenty-six hundred). And once again, Thomas Paine's pamphlets—*Rights of Man* (1791–92) and *Agrarian Justice* (1795–96)—resonated with American artisans and farmers. He indicted governments whose taxes took "the fruits of their labor" from men who lived "by the sweat of their brow," the artisan mantras.[91] More artisans were also book literate, able to borrow books from subscription or mechanic society libraries. In some larger workplaces artisans read aloud to one another. The New York sailmaker Stephen Allen remembered as an apprentice hearing long recitations from *Hamlet* and *Romeo and Juliet* from "the best scholar in the [sail] loft."[92]

Some plebeians, rural and urban, became writers of lengthy disquisitions. "The Mechanick on Taxation" was William Brewster, a twenty-eight-year-old shoemaker whose series of eleven articles led to a petition signed by twelve hundred artisans against an inequitable Connecticut tax. We also have glimpses of autodidacts who went unpublished, like William Manning, a Massachusetts yeoman and tavern keeper who took the pen name "A Laborer." He wrote a lengthy address "To the Republicans, Farmers, Mechanics and Laborers in America," explaining why they needed a nationwide "Laboring Society" to protect "the Many" from "the Few." David Brown, self-described as a "labouring man," was an agitator said to have tramped through eighty Massachusetts towns reading aloud from a sheaf of his own manuscripts (plus Paine's *Age of Reason*). Federalists had him jailed under the Sedition Act. Mechanics also wrote the orations they gave before their own societies and at Fourth of July observances.[93]

Mechanics elected their own to public office, the fulfillment of long-standing aspirations. In the cities in the early nineteenth century it was common to see mechanics on the Republican ticket, often identified by trade. In New York nineteen of the twenty-five officers of the General Society of Mechanics before 1820 were elected either to the city council or state assembly. Stephen Allen, a prosperous master sailmaker and ardent Republican, became the first artisan mayor of New York City, elected three times from 1821 to 1824. And after Boston did away with the town meeting in 1822, Charles Wells, a master builder, was the third elected mayor.

For Congress, mechanics might support professionals. In New York they sent the lawyer Edward Livingston to Congress three times and the Columbia professor Samuel L. Mitchell five times, and they did not elect an artisan—the sailmaker Peter Hercules Wendover—until 1816. Baltimore elected a watchmaker to that body. Mechanic voters had no compunctions about electing merchant Republicans to Congress (which they did in Philadelphia, Baltimore, and later Salem). Mechanics in effect were in a new coalition with Republican merchants who were breaking away from trade connections with England and opening up trade to France, Asia, and South America.[94]

The thrust of artisan republicans into electoral politics had an effect on street politics. Crowd action did not disappear, but Republicans seemed able to channel class antagonisms into the political system. A cause célèbre in New York in 1795–97, growing out of an act of class injustice, measures the change since the 1760s. After two poor Irish ferrymen verbally abused an alderman who was impatient to be taken from Brooklyn to Manhattan, a haughty Federalist mayor sentenced the ferrymen to be whipped and imprisoned for the crime of "insulting an official." One of the two escaped and died. When William Keteltas, a young Democratic-Republican lawyer, pleaded their cause before the state assembly, which quickly found him in contempt, several thousand people escorted him to jail on a chair, shouting, "The Spirit of '76." In prison, Keteltas pleaded his case in Republican papers for a legal redress of grievances, and upon his release, another restrained crowd pulled him through the streets in an open carriage decorated with a picture of a man being whipped and the inscription, "What, you rascal, insult your superiors." In the election of 1796, Republicans put Keteltas on their assembly slate. They lost by a margin of 2,250 to 1,775 votes, but it was the highest voter turnout in the city's history. Republicans went on to champion the interests of such lower trades as tallow chandlers, cartmen, and cordwainers and to carry the city by the election of 1800.[95]

Before the Revolution, crowds brimming with such class feeling might have attempted to pull down the house of the mayor, hung the alderman in effigy, or forced resignations from both with the threat of tar and feathers. They could not have expressed their rage in infrequent elections with voice voting and with a restricted suffrage. In the big cities, the outer wards and neighborhoods in which the laboring classes were concentrated became Republican strongholds.

Thus, it is not hard to explain why Federalists lost their near universal support of 1788 among artisans. In *The Federalist*, Alexander Hamilton was convinced that "mechanics and manufacturers will always be inclined with few exceptions to give their votes to merchants, in preference to persons of their own professions and trades." But as long as Hamilton kept a hand in New York politics, his party was sure to run one or more mechanics on its assembly slate. By 1794, as the tide began to turn, Hamilton paid homage to "the body of useful mechanics now rising to a well-earned importance in society." But in 1796 he was dumbfounded that the "vile affair" of whipping the Irish ferrymen had made the election, "in the view of the common people, a question between the Rich and the Poor." In 1800, Hamilton attempted a Federalist comeback in New York City by running virtually an entire slate of little-known mechanics for the assembly that would chose presidential electors, but by then it was too late. And the populism that Federalists espoused after their defeat never made serious inroads among mechanics.[96]

Federalists lost the artisans because they were hostile to the democratizing process of the era and never delivered on the promise to promote manufactures. Wedded politically to merchants who imported British manufactures and therefore opposed protective tariffs, Federalists also required a tariff for revenue to pay for Hamilton's program of funding the public debt. Hamilton's vaunted program for manufactures, which had in mind investors in large-scale "manufactories," not artisan workshops, actually did little for either.[97]

In New England, where artisans remained predominantly Federalist through the 1790s, they shaped a kind of artisan Federalism not far removed from artisan Republicanism. In Boston, Federalist mechanics paraded, turned out en masse to town meetings, signed petitions, and were a mainstay of the *Columbian Centinel*, the city's major Federalist paper. Arguably, Boston experienced less growth than the middle Atlantic cities, it drew few immigrants, and its traditional artisan system remained in tact longer, allowing for more harmony between merchant and mechanic. Paul Revere would not have been the only prosperous native-born conservative Federalist artisan who said of himself, "I was allways a warm *Republican*; I allways deprecated Democracy; as much as I did Aristocracy."[98]

Artisan Republican leaders enhanced the citizen consciousness of mechanics. The litany of the 1790s against "purse proud aristocrats," "great and overgrown rich men," and "the haughty well-born" was directed at Federalist elites who attempted to coerce voters, an old refrain. "The freedom and rights of election" was the indispensable "means for the preservation of liberty," said George James Warner, a Republican sailmaker in his Fourth of July oration in New York in 1797. "Wherever the wealthy by the influence of riches, are enabled to direct the choice of public offices, there the downfall of liberty cannot be very remote." This happens because "tradesmen, mechanics, and the industrious classes of society consider themselves of TOO LITTLE CONSEQUENCE to the body politic." This distinct echo of the appeals to mechanics two decades earlier suggests that the struggle to free dependent working people from acquiescence to men who held economic power over them had to be renewed in each generation. What made Warner's appeal successful was that he was speaking to an audience composed of mechanic members of four societies. An artisan might now be a member of a society in his own trade, of the General Society of Mechanics, of a fraternal order, of a Democratic-Republican club, and perhaps of a Republican Party caucus. He was also a subscriber to a Republican newspaper, a voter, and a man who paraded.[99]

We have begun to answer the question, what was the mechanic impact on American life? Artisan republicanism in the middle-Atlantic cities was equalitarian, civil libertarian, and humanitarian. The Tammany Society at one dinner toasted "a speedy abolition of every species of slavery," "a happy melioration of our Penal Laws," and "the establishment of public schools." Within "the trade," however, masters did not expand the boundaries of equalitarianism. They were of no mind to open the skilled trades to free African Americans or to accept the rising insubordination of apprentices. And reading Paine's *Rights of Man* did not necessarily lead an artisan to read Mary Wollstonecraft's *Vindication of the Rights of Women*.[100]

The self-styled "respectable mechanics" were winning the respect they had long sought. In the first quarter of the nineteenth century, the term "mechanic" seems to have lost the stigma of low status that it had in Samuel Johnson's English dictionary of 1756. In the first American dictionary in 1806, Noah Webster, a Federalist who believed that the English language should accommodate popular American usage, defined "mechanic" as "an artificer, a handicraftsman," somewhat archaic terms, yet free from pejorative values. In his second edition in 1828 he defined a mechanic by what he did: "a person whose occupation is to construct machines, or goods, wares, instruments, furniture and the like."[101]

There are also hints of the visibility of mechanics among novelists and artists. In William Hill Brown's *The Power of Sympathy* (1789), the first American novel, a male character rebukes a social gathering for "scornfully" dismissing an accomplished young woman as "a mechanick's daughter." In *Modern Chivalry* (1792–1815), a picaresque novel by Hugh Henry Brackenridge, "Teague Oregano," an insubordinate Irish-born servant, usually gets the best of his master, Captain Farrago. The two men witness an election at which the voters explain to them why they prefer a "common weaver" to a wealthy "man of education." Artists now put artisans into city scenes. Before the Revolution, drawings of American urban landscapes were devoid of people. In the early 1800s, the New York artist William Chappel portrayed housewrights and firemen at work in street scenes and Tammany on parade in full regalia. John Lewis Krimmel, a gifted German immigrant, could be called the artist laureate of Philadelphia artisans. He painted an election scene in front of the state house in which a "leather apron" harangues several well-clothed gentlemen on behalf of his candidate; a Fourth of July celebration in which citizens of all ranks mingle in a public park; and a panorama of the butchers on parade. His genre painting of two leather-aproned workers in a tavern portrayed them as respectable artisans observing their customary drink break.[102]

The term "mechanic" had political cachet, so much so that it was appropriated by businessmen. The names on new banks—the Mechanics Bank in New York, the Farmers and Mechanics Bank of Philadelphia, the Manufacturers and Mechanics Bank of Boston—were camouflage for investor manufacturers and merchants who eventually dominated their boards. In the national debates over government support for manufactures, Republicans valorized the artisan workshop as well as "domestic," that is, "household," manufactures by farmers. Although some Republican editors supported factories, rank-and-file Republicans were suspicious of "corporations," "capitalists," and "monopolists" who might replicate the wretchedness of English factory towns. By 1816 artisan societies had dropped out of the movement for tariff protection, leaving it in the hands of factory owners.[103]

The Republican Party, in power nationally from 1801 on and with a northern urban wing of merchants and manufacturers influential in Congress and the cabinet, never acted on Jefferson's purist agrarian principles. The "Report on Manufactures" (1810) by Albert Gallatin, Secretary of the Treasury to both Jefferson and Madison (and himself a manufacturer), proposed realistic support for manufactures. Arguably, over the presidencies of Jefferson, Madison, and Monroe, Republicans did more for American manufactures, consciously as well as inadvertently by the embargo of British imports, than Hamilton had ever done.[104]

How did Jefferson respond to this expanded recognition of manufacturing and mechanics? Jefferson clearly changed his mind about manufacturing. In response to urgent pleas from his urban political supporters handicapped by his earlier agrarianism, he made any number of public statements recognizing that "To be independent, for the comforts of life, we must fabricate them ourselves—we must now place the Manufacturer by the side of the Agriculturalist." As to what kind of manufactures, he was equivocal. He could be rhapsodic about "household" manufactures that would make "every family in the country a manufactory within itself." He made gestures towards large-scale manufacturing, for example, publicizing a suit made with cloth woven in a Connecticut factory. But Jefferson was ambivalent about urban artisans. Privately, he acknowledged that "as yet our manufacturers"—by which he here meant tradesmen—"are as much at their ease, as independent & moral as our agricultural inhabitants"—a remarkable admission—"and they will continue so as long as there are vacant lands for them to resort to: because whenever it shall be attempted by the other classes to reduce them to the minimum of subsistence, they will quit their trades and go to laboring in the earth." Thus, his recognition was based on a mythical safety valve in vacant lands to which oppressed city artisans might migrate: the skills of an artisan and a farmer were not interchangeable. Publicly, moreover, for all his rhetoric about manufactures, Jefferson never seemed to have found a place for the "independent & moral" city tradesman alongside the virtuous farmer.[105]

Nor did most Americans. Republican orators in the cities hailed mechanics as "the sinews and muscle" of the nation. But artisans had to celebrate themselves—which after all was why they paraded and formed their own societies. But the artisan with "hammer in hand" never became the symbolic equal of the husbandman behind the plow. There is of course an irony here. The large-scale manufacturing that took root late in the ascendancy of the Republican presidents was the fruit of a campaign that mechanics had initiated before the Revolution and sustained for almost half a century. But the factories on the rural landscape and the large-scale artisan workshops in the cities were harbingers of the erosion of the traditional artisan way of life.

10. Legacy: "Labor is the Source of All Wealth"

Over the first quarter of the nineteenth century a rapidly expanding capitalist economy began to undermine the artisan mode of production. Artisans in the big cities were by no means a dying breed, but the pressures of the commercial marketplace challenged the old ways of masters, journeymen, and apprentices.

Among masters in one trade after another, the entrepreneurial strain, a recessive trait under the restraints of a moral economy and face-to-face relationships within the trade, became dominant. Or, as Marx might have put it, the master who was both capitalist and artisan became more of a capitalist and less of a working artisan. Again, symbols reveal changing values. Recall the central emblem of the 1786 membership certificate of New York's General Society of Mechanics and Tradesmen: the raised muscular arm of a craftsman clenching a hefty hammer. The Society became the sponsor of the Mechanics Bank, which rapidly became the largest in the city. In an "illumination" at the bank celebrating the American victory in the War of 1812, the hammer in hand was still there, but the background was filled with ships sailing in and out of the harbor, representing commerce, and a cornucopia graced the foreground "as an emblem of plenty discharging eagles and dollars." A decade later in 1825, on a certificate of the Society's apprentice library, the illustrations of the craftsmen at work on the earlier certificate had disappeared, replaced by two well-dressed gentlemen tradesmen, one bestowing charity to a widow and the other pointing her son to the Society's school. In the distance, a very faint raised arm, hammer in hand, recedes into the clouds, an apt symbol for masters who had ceased to be sweat-of-the-brow artisans. In the 1840s in New York, the symbol appeared as a commercial trademark on the box of "Arm and Hammer" baking soda, where it remains to this day.[106]

In these years the proportion of journeymen to masters shifted dramatically. In New York, Duncan Phyfe, who acquired fame as a craftsman of fine furniture, actually supervised three shops with as many as one hundred workers. In Philadelphia, more and more masters, as the journeymen cordwainers said of theirs in 1805, were "only the retailers of our labor ... who in truth live upon the work of our hands." Apprenticeship decayed as more masters turned their boys into "half way journeymen."[107]

At the same time, the equalitarianism of the revolutionary era unglued the deference that journeymen and apprentices were supposed to show to their masters. The term "master" went out of fashion with working people (much as "lord and master" did with many wives). European travelers were struck by the way household servants, who refused to be called "servant," denied that they had a "master" and insisted on being called "help" or "helps," which made their employment an act of volition. The journeymen "working shoemakers" of Philadelphia objected to the use of "master" as aping "the slavish style of Europe." As master mechanics were winning their long battle for respect from their "betters," they were losing it from their "inferiors"—another irony.[108]

"Turnouts" or "walkouts" became familiar in several "sweated" trades. Journeymen cordwainers conducted strikes in four cities, strife which put Republicans to a test. When master cordwainers hauled their journeymen into court for forming "combinations" in restraint of trade, Republicans divided. In the Philadelphia and New York trials eminent Republicans could be found on the legal side of both defense and prosecution. But when journeymen shoemakers were found guilty, Philadelphia's Republican editor alone took up their cause, and there was no public outcry.[109]

It was left to hard-pressed journeymen to push into new terrain the artisan republicanism they had imbibed. Witness the strike declaration of the New York Journeymen House Carpenters in 1809. They began with the words of the Declaration of Independence: "Among the unalienable rights of man are life, liberty and the pursuit of happiness." Then, they borrowed from Thomas Paine, probably from *Agrarian Justice*: "By the social compact every class in society ought to be entitled to benefit in proportion to its usefulness." While individuals had duties to society, society owed individuals "compensation for services sufficient not only for the current expenses of livelihood, but to the formation of a fund for the support of that time of life when nature requires a cessation of labor."[110]

Confronted by these sea changes, many older artisans tried to perpetuate the ideals they had lived by, often poignantly so. When Benjamin Franklin (1706–1790), in the last years of his life, returned to his unfinished memoir, he took the story of his life only through the 1750s and never got to the Revolution, the time of his greatest fame. The result was that he left as the heart of his autobiography his rise from apprentice to master printer and his rules for success as a tradesman, which meant that this is how he would be remembered. In the year before his death, he wrote a long codicil to his will setting aside £1,000 each for the cities of Boston and Philadelphia to make loans to "assist young married artificers in setting up their business" because "among artisans, good apprentices are most likely to make good citizens." After his death, New York's General Society toasted "the memory of our late brother mechanic," and through the incomplete autobiography Franklin lived on for a long time in the persona of an artisan.[111]

Paul Revere (1734–1816), in his old age the owner of a brass foundry in Boston's old North End, as well as of a sheet-copper rolling mill in rural Canton, was steadfast to his values as a young silversmith. He was rich and famous, but he did not put on airs. In the 1800s, Revere still dressed in the "small clothes" of the colonial era: knee breeches and a tricorn hat. In his copper mill in the countryside, where he employed as many as a dozen "hands" under the direction of a superintendent, Revere deplored their pre-industrial work habits: they came to work when they pleased, and as soon as "they began to know something of the Business, they leave us." He wanted factory workers to behave as if they were in the old artisan hierarchy. After Revere died in 1816, the people who knew him remembered him as "a Prosperous North End Mechanic" who was "a born leader of the people" and whose "influence was pervading, especially among the mechanics and workingmen of Boston, with whom his popularity was immense."[112]

In 1826, Patrick Lyon (1768[?]–1829), a successful Philadelphia engineer and manufacturer of fire engines, sought to perpetuate himself visually as the blacksmith and locksmith he was in the 1790s, when he started out in America. A Scottish immigrant and a Republican, Lyon was falsely imprisoned in 1798 as a suspect in the robbery of the Bank of Pennsylvania. He successfully defended himself in print as an "ingenious mechanic" and "a useful citizen" who was the victim of injustice. Eventually vindicated, he prospered and rose. In 1826, he instructed the painter John Neagle how to portray him in a portrait: "I wish you sir to paint me at full length, the size of life, representing me at the smithery, with my bellows-blower, hammers and all the etceteras of the shop around me." And he was emphatic: "I wish you to understand, clearly, Mr. Neagle, that I do not desire to be represented in the picture as a gentleman—to which character I have no pretention. I want you to paint me at work at my anvil with my sleeves rolled up and my apron on." Lyon got his wish. He appears at his forge in his shirtsleeves holding a hammer, his apprentice nearby, and through the window in the background is a vista of the Walnut Street jail in which he was imprisoned. *Pat Lyon at the Forge* (1826–27) depicts the quintessential artisan republican: a craftsman proud of his trade celebrating his productive labor and a citizen's triumph over injustice. In 1832, two hundred Philadelphia blacksmiths marched in a procession honoring the centennial of Washington's birth, displaying an enlarged copy of Neagle's painting.[113]

As these men of the revolutionary era faded, their world did not disappear. The traditional forms of artisan production continued in many trades in the big cities, thrived in smaller eastern cities, and as the population spread across the continent, reemerged in western cities, which is why one can encounter today in San Francisco a Mechanics Institute and a mechanics monument. Artisan republican values rooted among small producers, the "man for himself" kind of artisan who lived by the "sweat of his brow," were appropriated by Americans high and low. Benjamin Franklin's ideals became an inspiration to rise up out of one's class that was celebrated by "self-made" entrepreneurs like the Carnegies and Rockefellers.[114]

Artisan republican ideals were especially meaningful to laboring people losing their independence: to "workingmen" and "the working classes," confronting "capitalists," terms that now entered common usage. By the late 1820s and 1830s, wherever the new labor movement emerged—journeymen trade unions, labor parties, and labor reformers—the Fourth of July became a day for kindling the "spirit of '76" among wage workers. In fact, the Fourth was the first American civic holiday that was also a day off from work. In Boston in 1835, the Trades Union of Boston held the city's first exclusively journeymen's parade on the Fourth, the masons marching under a banner proclaiming, "Labor is the Property of Those who Produce it," and the coopers avowing, "All Men are Born Free and Equal."[115]

Workers now reached back to claim the American Revolution as a whole as their own. The shoemakers of Lynn, Massachusetts, caught up in the merchants' putting-out system, reprinted the Declaration of Independence in the first issue of their newspaper, *The Awl*, and in the second compared their "bosses" to King George III. In 1835, after a Massachusetts judge outlawed "combinations," the carpenter Seth Luther, son of a veteran of the Revolution, delivered an oration all over the East in which he asked, "Was there no combination when the leather aprons of farmer and mechanic were seen mingling with the shining uniforms of British Regulars" at Bunker Hill? The destruction of the tea in Boston and the Declaration of Independence were "the work of a combination." In Philadelphia, in the midst of the city's first general strike, an artisan offered a toast to "our forefathers: theirs was a glorious strike for liberty."[116]

Industrial workers made the same appropriation. When eight hundred women factory workers in a Lowell textile mill turned out against a wage slash, they marched to hear "one of their leaders [make] a flaming Wollstonecraft speech on the rights of women" and the inequities of "the *monied* aristocracy."[117] When Lynn became a factory town of men and women shoeworkers, they began their strike of 1860 on Washington's birthday. In the great railroad upheaval of 1877, striking railroad workers emulated the tableau of Archibald Willard's recent painting, *The Spirit of '76*, marching as the patriotic bloodstained soldiers of three generations, one playing a fife, one a drum, the third carrying the flag. And in 1882, in the first Labor Day parade in New York City, a leading banner which proclaimed, "Labor is the Source of All Wealth," could easily have come down from eighteenth-century artisans.[118]

In the twentieth century, as the business-oriented restrictive craft unions of the old American Federation of Labor became known as the "aristocracy of labor," this rich artisan legacy was erased and the new industrial unions turned to other radical traditions. Recovering the lost democratic legacy of the "leather aprons" who had a fellow feeling for their "brethren" puts our imagination to a test. Today, it is difficult to attach the dimension of their collective struggles to the craftsmen at work in idyllic restored colonial workshops, just as it is difficult to break through the stereotyped images of Revere and Franklin to recapture their artisan loyalties. Yet artisans warrant a place as the first American labor movement and as shapers of the nation and its democratic ideals. They, too, were founders.

NOTES

This essay was revised for this volume from earlier versions. It was originally presented at the conference of the Milan Group in Early American History (1978) and at the Organization of American Historians Convention (1980) and was published as "Sul Martello e Sulla Si Fondano Tute le Arti: Gil Artigiani e la Rivoluzione," in *Revista di Storia Contemporanea* (Turin) 1 (1982): 1–32. An abbreviated version, "Revolutionary Mechanics," appeared in *In These Times* 4:32 (August 1980) and was reprinted in Paul Buhle and Alan Dawley, eds., *Working for Democracy: American Workers from the Revolution to the Present* (Urbana, Ill., 1985), 1–9. I have also drawn on my own articles, "The Mechanics and the Jeffersonians, 1789–1801," *Labor History* 5 (1964): 247–76, and "After Carl Becker: The Mechanics and New York City Politics, 1774–1801," in the same journal, 216–24 (jointly written with Staughton Lynd).

For rigorous criticisms of drafts of the current version of the article I am especially indebted to Gary Kornblith and Edward Countryman. My thanks to scholars who offered criticism of early versions, made suggestions, or answered my queries: J. L. Bell, Alan Dawley, Paul Gilje, Vincent Golden, John Kaminski, Bruce Laurie, Patrick Leehey, Jesse Lemisch, Lisa Lubow, Staughton Lynd, Loretta Mannucci, Simon Middleton, Simon Newman, Gregory Nobles, Elaine Weber Pascu, William Pretzer, Marcus Rediker, Howard Rock, Steven Rosswurm, Jeffrey Slansky, Barbara Clark Smith, Richard Twomey, and Shane White. I owe a heavy debt to the scholarship of Gary B. Nash, which will be apparent in the early sections of the essay, as will be my intellectual debt to Edward P. Thompson and Herbert Gutman, who opened up the study of artisans for me. I alone am responsible for whatever errors remain.

1. Paul Revere to Jeremy Belknap, undated but published in 1798, in Edmund S. Morgan, ed., *Paul Revere's Three Accounts of His Famous Ride* (Boston, 1968), unpaged; Jayne E. Triber, *A True Republican: The Life of Paul Revere* (Amherst, Mass., 1998), 156–58; E. H. Goss, *The Life of Colonel Paul Revere*, 2 vols. (Boston, 1891), 610–11.

2. Triber, *True Republican*, 141; *Massachusetts Centinel*, January 9, 1788.

3. Richard B. Morris, *Government and Labor in Early America* (New York, 1946), is still unsurpassed for its analysis and rich documentation of the many types of labor; Carl Bridenbaugh, *The Colonial Craftsman* (Chicago, 1950), was the

first synthesis of the subject which grew out of his two works that provided a context for the urban craftsman: *Cities in the Wilderness: The First Century of Urban Life in America, 1625–1742* (New York, 1938) and *Cities in Revolt: Urban Life in America, 1743–1776* (New York, 1955). Bridenbaugh's scholarship was overtaken by Gary Nash, *The Urban Crucible: Social Change, Political Consciousness, and the Origins of the Revolution* (Cambridge, Mass., 1979), which provides acute analysis based on quantitative sources within a narrative history. Many of his articles on artisan themes are collected in Nash, *Race, Class, and Politics: Essays on American and Colonial and Revolutionary Society* (Urbana, Ill., 1986).

For surveys of historiography about American artisans, see Sean Wilentz, "The Rise of the American Working Class, 1776–1877," in J. Carroll Moody and Alice Kessler-Harris, eds., *Perspectives on American Labor History: The Problem of Synthesis* (DeKalb, Ill., 1989), 83–152; Bruce Laurie, *Artisans into Workers: Labor in Nineteenth-Century America* (New York, 1989), 221–40; Richard S. Dunn, "Servants and Slaves: The Recruitment and Employment of Labor," in Jack P. Greene and J. R. Pole, eds., *Colonial British America: Essays in the New History of the Early Modern Era* (Baltimore, 1984), 157–94; Thomas J. Schlereth, "Artisans and Craftsmen: A Historical Perspective," in Ian M. G. Quimby, ed., *The Craftsman in Early America* (New York, 1984), 31–61. For surveys of labor history in an economic context, see John J. McCusker and Russell R. Menard, *The Economy of British America, 1607–1789* (Chapel Hill, N.C., 1985), part 3, and in the context of technology, Judith A. McGaw, ed., *Early American Technology: Making and Doing Things from the Colonial Era to 1850* (Chapel Hill, N.C., 1994), 358–460.

4. For the historical reputations of Revere and Franklin, see David Hackett Fischer, *Paul Revere's Ride* (New York, 1994), 327–44; *Benjamin's Franklin's Autobiography*, ed. J. A. Leo Lemay and P. M. Zall (New York, 1986), which includes essays about popular opinion of Franklin over the years; and David Waldstreicher, *Runaway America: Benjamin Franklin and the American Revolution* (New York, 2004).

5. For museums that deal with artisans in their exhibits, see Barbara Clark Smith, *After the Revolution: Everyday Life in America* (New York, 1985), about the Smithsonian; Alfred F. Young, Terry J. Fife, and Mary E. Janzen, *We the People: Voices and Images of the New Nation* (Philadelphia, 1993), viii–xxi, about the Chicago Historical Society; Gary Nash, *First City: Philadelphia and the Forging of Historical Memory* (Philadelphia, 2002), intro. and chaps. 1–3, about the Historical Society of Pennsylvania. For critiques of Colonial Williamsburg, see Mike Wallace, *Mickey Mouse History and Other Essays on American History* (Philadelphia, 1996), 3–32, 177–246; Richard Handler and Eric Gable, *The New History in an Old Museum: Creating the Past at Colonial Williamsburg* (Durham, N.C., 1997).

6. The subject of language cries out for its historian: see Alan Kulikoff, "The Language of Class in Rural America," in Kulikoff, *The Agrarian Origins of American Capitalism* (Charlottesville, Va., 1992), 60–95. Usage varied from city to city: "mechanic" was common before the war in Charleston and Baltimore, where there

were mechanic societies; see Richard Walsh, *Charleston's Sons of Liberty: A Study of the Artisans, 1763–1789* (Columbia, S.C., 1959), and Charles G. Steffen, *The Mechanics of Baltimore: Workers and Politics in the Age of Revolution, 1763–1812* (Urbana, Ill., 1984). If members of a particular trade met, they might refer to the meeting as "a meeting of the trade," but in the commercial cities a newspaper report of "a meeting of the trade" usually referred to merchants. See, for example, a report from Boston in the *Pennsylvania Gazette*, September 27, 1770. For eighteenth-century identities of labor in England, see E. P. Thompson, *Customs in Common* (London, 1991; New York, 1993), passim; R. W. Malcolmson, *Life and Labor in England, 1700–1780* (London, 1981), chaps. 1 and 4; John Rule, *The Experience of Labour in Eighteenth-Century Industry* (London, 1981), chaps. 1, 6, and 8.

7. For demographic trends, see Nash, *Urban Crucible*, esp. chaps. 9 and 12 and the appendix; John J. McCusker and Russell Menard, *The Economy of British America, 1607–1789* (Chapel Hill, N.C, 1985), chap. 10; for the "lower sort," see Billy G. Smith, *The "Lower Sort": Philadelphia's Laboring People, 1750–1800* (Ithaca, N.Y., 1990); Howard Rock and Paul Gilje, "'Sweep O! Sweep O' African American Chimney Sweeps and Citizenship in the New Nation," *William and Mary Quarterly*, 3rd ser., 51 (1994): 507–38; Paul A. Gilje and Howard B. Rock, eds., *Keepers of the Revolution: New Yorkers at Work in the Early Republic* (Ithaca, N.Y., 1992).

8. Gary Nash, "Forging Freedom: The Emancipation Experience in the Northern Seaports, 1775–1820," in Nash, *Race, Class, and Politics*, 285; Ira Berlin, *Many Thousands Gone: The First Two Centuries of Slavery in North America* (Cambridge, Mass., 1998), chap. 7.

9. Karl Marx, *Capital*, trans. Ben Fowkes (London, 1976), I: 1029, cited in Sean Wilentz, *Chants Democratic: New York City and the Rise of the American Working Class, 1788–1850* (New York, 1984), 4–5.

10. For immigration, see Bernard Bailyn, *Voyagers to the West: A Passage in the Peopling of America on the Eve of the Revolution* (New York, 1986); for women, see references in essay 2 in this volume. For a breakdown of proportions within the labor force, see Gary Nash, Billy G. Smith, and Dirk Hoerder, "Laboring Americans and the American Revolution," in *Labor History* 24 (1983); appendix, table 1, 434–39; for a breakdown of Boston workers by occupation, see Alan Kulikoff, "Progress of Inequality in Revolutionary Boston," *William and Mary Quarterly* 28 (1971): 375–412, appendix at 411–12.

11. On occupational categories in the cities, see Nash, *Urban Crucible*, appendix, table 1; Jacob Price, "Economic Function and the Growth of the American Port Towns in the Eighteenth Century," *Perspectives in American History* 8 (1974): 123–86.

12. On the proportion of groups within the artisan hierarchy, see Gary Nash, "A Historical Perspective on Early American Artisans," in Francis J. Puig and Michael Conforti, eds., *The American Craftsman and the European Tradition, 1620–1820* (Hanover, N.H., 1989), 1–13; Smith, "*Lower Sort*," chap. 4; for apprentices, see W. J. Rorabaugh, *The Craft Apprentice: From Franklin to the Machine Age in*

America (New York, 1986), and Lawrence W. Towner, *A Good Master Well Served: A Social History of Servitude in Massachusetts, 1620–1750* (New York, 1998); for indentured servants, see Sharon V. Sallinger, *"To Serve Well and Faithfully": Labor and Indentured Servants in Pennsylvania, 1682–1800* (Philadelphia, 1987).

13. John Fanning Watson, *Annals of Philadelphia, and Pennsylvania, in the Olden Time …*, 3 vols. (Philadelphia, 1887), 1:220–21 (reminiscences); Gary Nash, "Up from the Bottom in Franklin's Philadelphia," *Past and Present* 77 (1977); Jackson T. Main, *The Social Structure of Revolutionary America* (Princeton, 1965), passim; Nash, *Urban Crucible*, chaps. 9 and 12; Paul Revere Memorial Association, *Paul Revere—Artisan, Businessman, Patriot: Man behind the Myth* (Boston, 1988), 95–115; Triber, *True Republican*, chaps. 10 and 11. For ship carpenters, see James Hutson, "An Investigation of the Inarticulate: Philadelphia's White Oaks," *William and Mary Quarterly*, 3rd ser., 27 (1971): 3–25, with a rebuttal by Jesse Lemisch and John K. Alexander and a note by Simeon Crowther, *William and Mary Quarterly*, 3rd ser., 29 (1972): 109–42.

14. Smith, *"Lower Sort,"* 124–25, 199. The pioneering scholarship is James Henretta, "Economic Development and Social Structure in Colonial Boston," *William and Mary Quarterly*, 3rd ser., 22 (1965): 75–92, and Kulikoff, "Progress of Inequality." For a scholarly exchange on the distribution of wealth, see Gary Nash, "Urban Wealth and Poverty in Pre-Revolutionary America," *Journal of Interdisciplinary History* 6 (1976): 545–84, with rejoinders by G. B. Warden and Jacob Price. For a second exchange, see Herman Wellenreuther, "Labor in the Era of the American Revolution: A Discussion of Recent Concepts and Theories," *Labor History* 22 (1981): 573–600, with a rejoinder by Gary Nash, Billy G. Smith, and Dirk Hoerder and a reply by Wellenreuther, *Labor History* 24 (1983): 414–454.

15. For the depressed status of Boston artisans, see Robert Blair St. George, *Conversing by Signs: Poetics of Implication in Colonial New England Culture* (Chapel Hill, N.C., 1998), 205–95, esp. 238–42, quotation at 239; Gary Nash, "Urban Wealth and Poverty," in Nash, *Race, Class, and Politics*, 199.

16. Samuel Johnson, *A Dictionary of the English Language*, 2 vols. (London, 1756); Main, *Social Structure*, chap. 6; Stephen Botein, "'Meer Mechanics' and an Open Press: The Business and Political Strategies of Colonial American Printers," *Perspectives in American History* 9 (1975): 127–228, citation at 158 ("meer mechanic"); Paul Staiti, "Accounting for Copley," in Carrie Rebora, Paul Staiti, et al., *John Singleton Copley in America* (New York, 1995), 25–51; Dr. Thomas Young to John Lamb, May 13, 1774, in Isaac Q. Leake, *Memoirs of the Life of General John Lamb* (Albany, N.Y., 1850), 85–86.

17. *The American Journal and Suffolk Intelligencer*, March 29, 1785 ("whimsical degrees"), cited in Myron F. Wehtje, "A Town in the Confederation: Boston, 1783–1787" (Ph.D. diss., University of Virginia, 1973), 43–44; Gordon S. Wood, *The Americanization of Benjamin Franklin* (New York, 2004), 35–49, 41 ("station in life"), 47 ("poor ordinary mechanic").

18. John Adams, *Defence of the Constitutions of Government of the United States* (1787), in Charles F. Adams, ed., *Works of John Adams*, 10 vols. (Boston, 1850–56), 4:391–95. For analysis, see Richard L. Bushman, *King and People in Provincial Massachusetts* (Chapel Hill, N.C., 1985), chap. 2, "Dependence"; Richard L. Bushman, "'This New Man': Dependence and Independence, 1776," in Bushman et al., eds., *Uprooted Americans: Essays to Honor Oscar Handlin* (Boston, 1979), 79–96. For the licensed trades, see Morris, *Government and Labor*, intro.; Simon Middleton, "'How It Came That the Bakers Bake No Bread': A Struggle for Trade Privileges in Seventeenth-Century New Amsterdam," *William and Mary Quarterly*, 3rd ser., 58 (2001): 347–72; Graham R. Hodges, *New York City Cartmen, 1667–1850* (New York, 1986).

19. *To the Inhabitants of Pennsylvania in General, and Particularly Those of the City and Neighborhood of Pennsylvania* (Philadelphia, 1779); *Massachusetts Centinel*, January 9, 1788. The Philadelphia petition is discussed in Gary Nash, "Artisans and Politics in Eighteenth-Century Philadelphia," in Nash, *Race, Class, and Politics*, 245–47, and in the books by Steven Rosswurm and Ronald Schultz cited in notes 25 and 49, respectively. For comparable ideals of a London artisan, see Iorwerth Prothero, *Artisans and Politics in Early Nineteenth-Century London: John Gast and His Times* (Baton Rouge, La., 1979), chap. 2.

20. John Adams, June 17, 1760, in L. H. Butterfield et al., eds., *Diary and Autobiography of John Adams*, 4 vols. (Cambridge, Mass., 1961), 1:135; Main, *Social Structure*, chap. 5, citation at 190.

21. "Letter of John Andrews" (1774), in *Massachusetts Historical Society Proceedings*, series 8 (1864–65): 344; St. George, *Conversing by Signs*, chap. 3; Douglas Lamar Jones, *Village and Seaport: Migration and Society in Eighteenth-Century Society* (Hanover, N.H., 1981) (strolling poor); Nash, *Urban Crucible*, appendix, tables 5 and 10; Ruth Wallis Herndon, *Unwelcome Americans: Living on the Margin in Early New England* (Philadelphia, 2001) (warning out); Smith, *"Lower Sort,"* chap. 4; and Billy G. Smith, "The Vicissitudes of Fortune: The Careers of Laboring Men in Philadelphia, 1750–1800," in Stephen Innes, ed., *Work and Labor in Early America* (Chapel Hill, N.C., 1988), 221–51; Simon Newman, *Embodied History: The Lives of the Poor in Early Philadelphia* (Philadelphia, 2003). For a collection of recent essays, see Billy G. Smith, ed., *Down and Out in Early America* (University Park, Pa., 2005), with an introduction by Gary Nash analyzing the causes of poverty.

22. Richard Saunders, *Poor Richard Improved: Being an Almanac and Ephemeris . . .* (Philadelphia, 1758), which also appeared as *Father Abraham's Speech . . .* (Boston, 1758, 1760), reprinted in *The Papers of Benjamin Franklin*, ed. Leonard Labaree (New Haven, Conn., 1963), 7:326ff.; J. E. Crowley, *This Sheba Self: The Conceptualization of Economic Life in Eighteenth-Century America* (Baltimore, 1974), 84.

23. "To the Tradesmen, Mechanics &c. of the Province of Pennsylvania," broadside (Philadelphia, December 3, 1773).

24. For studies applicable to both groups, see for reading, Elizabeth C. Reilly and David Hall, "Customers and the Marketplace of Modalities of Reading" and "The Colonial Book in the Transatlantic Worlds," in Hugh Amory and David Hall, eds., *A History of the Book in America*, 5 vols. (Cambridge, U.K., 1999), 1: chap. 11; for fire-fighting clubs, see Benjamin L. Carp, "Fire of Liberty: Firefighters, Urban Voluntary Culture, and the Revolutionary Movement," *William and Mary Quarterly*, 3rd ser., 58 (2001): 781–818; for taverns, see David W. Conroy, *In Public Houses: Drink and the Revolution of Authority in Colonial Massachusetts* (Chapel Hill, N.C., 1995), Sharon Salinger, *Taverns and Drinking in Early America* (Baltimore, 2002), and Peter Thompson, *Rum, Punch, and Revolution: Taverngoing and Public Life in Eighteenth-Century Philadelphia* (Philadelphia, 1999); Steven C. Bulock, "The Revolutionary Transformation of American Freemasonry, 1752–1792," *William and Mary Quarterly*, 3rd ser., 47 (1990): 347–69.

25. Marcus Rediker, "Good Hands, Stout Heart and Fast Feet: The History and Culture of Working People in Early America," in Geoff Ely and William Hunt, eds., *Reviving the English Revolution: Reflections and Elaborations on the Work of Christopher Hill* (London, 1988), 221–49; Peter Linebaugh and Marcus Rediker, *The Many-Headed Hydra: Sailors, Slaves, Commoners, and the Hidden History of the Revolutionary Atlantic* (Boston, 2000), chaps. 2 and 6; Fred Anderson, *A People's Army: Massachusetts Soldiers and Society in the Seven Years' War* (Chapel Hill, N.C., 1984), chap. 2 (recruiting); Steven Rosswurm, *Arms, Country, and Class: The Philadelphia Militia and the "Lower Sort" during the American Revolution* (New Brunswick, N.J., 1987), 11–39; for hangings, see Lawrence W. Towner, "True Confessions and Dying Warnings in Colonial New England," in Towner, *Past Imperfect: Essays on History, Libraries, and the Humanities*, ed. Alfred Young (Chicago, 1993), 56–81; for London's laboring classes through the prism of hangings, see Peter Linebaugh, *The London Hanged: Crime and Civil Society in the Eighteenth Century* (London, 1991).

26. Nash, *Urban Crucible*, chap. 8, 216 ("low-bred illiterate Person"). My calculation of broadsides for Whitfield is based on the imprint files arranged by date in the catalogs of the New York Public Library Rare Book Room and the American Antiquarian Society.

27. Morris, *Government and Labor*, chap. 3. In a densely documented seventy-one-page chapter on "Concerted Action" in colonial America, Morris devoted twenty-eight pages to action by masters and fourteen pages to journeymen; Mary Roys Baker, "Anglo-Massachusetts Trade Union Roots, 1130–1790," *Labor History* 14 (1973): 352–96. John R. Commons et al., *History of Labor in the United States*, 4 vols. (New York, 1918), 1:25 (traditional view).

28. Lawrence W. Towner, "A Fondness for Freedom: Servant Protest in Puritan Society," *William and Mary Quarterly*, 3rd ser., 19 (1962): 201–19; David Waldstreicher, "Reading the Runaways: Self-Fashioning, Print Culture and Confidence in Slavery in the Eighteenth-Century Mid-Atlantic," *William and Mary Quarterly* 56

(1999): 241–72, cites recent collections of runaway documents; Jonathan Prude, "'To Look Upon the Lower Sort': Runaway Ads and the Appearance of Unfree Laborers in America, 1750–1800," *Journal of American History* 78 (1991–92): 124–60; for evocative drawings based on runaway notices, see Bailyn, *Voyagers to the West*, 352ff.; for women in flight, see Alfred F. Young, *Masquerade: The Life and Times of Deborah Sampson, Continental Soldier* (New York, 2004), 6–12.

29. The classic articles are E. P. Thompson, "Time, Work-Discipline, and Industrial Capitalism," *Past and Present* 38 (1967): 56–97, reprinted in Thompson, *Customs in Common*, 352–403, and Herbert Gutman, "Work, Culture, and Society in Industrializing America, 1815–1918," *American Historical Review* 78 (1973): 531–88, reprinted in a book by Gutman with the same title (New York, 1976). Paul B. Hensley, "Time, Work and Social Context in New England," *New England Quarterly* 45 (1992): 531–59; David R. Roediger and Philip S. Foner, *Our Own Times: A History of American Labor and the Working Day* (London, 1989), chap. 1; David Brody, "Time and Work during Early American Industrialism," *Labor History* 30 (1989): 5–46, barely touches on eighteenth-century customs. This subject awaits further inquiry.

30. William Bentley, *Diary*, 4 vols. (Salem, Mass., 1907; Gloucester, Mass., 1962), 2:75, 247 (ropewalk workers); for shipyards, see *The Conversation of Two Persons under a Window* (Boston, 1765), cited in Nash, *Urban Crucible*, 278; Joseph Goldenberg, *Shipbuilding in Colonial America* (Charlottesville, Va., 1976), 68–71; Gutman, "Work, Culture, and Society," 544–45, 556–57. For printers, see William Pretzer, "Tramp Printers, Craft Culture, Trade Unions and Technology," *Printing History* 6 (1984): 3–16, and William Pretzer, "'Of the Paper Cap and Inky Apron': The Labor History of Journeymen Printers," in Robert A. Gross and Mary Kelley, eds., *An Extensive Republic: Print, Culture, and Society in the New Nation, 1790–1840*, vol. 2 of *A History of the Book in America* (New York, forthcoming). For seamen, see Marcus Rediker, *Between the Devil and the Deep Blue Sea: Merchant Seamen, Pirates, and the Anglo-American Maritime World, 1700–1750* (Cambridge, U.K., 1987), and Marcus Rediker, "The Anglo-American Seaman as Collective Worker, 1700–1750," in Stephen Innes, ed., *Work and Labor in Early America* (Chapel Hill, N.C., 1988), 252–86. For craft culture in general, see Bryan D. Palmer, "Most Uncommon Common Men: Craft and Culture in Historical Perspective," *Labour/Le Travailleur* 1 (1976): 5–31.

31. For English crowd traditions, see E. P. Thompson, "The Moral Economy of the English Crowd in the Eighteenth Century," *Past and Present* 50 (1971): 76–136, reprinted in Thompson, *Customs in Common*, 185–258, with "The Moral Economy Reviewed," 259–351.

32. Barbara Clark Smith, "Food Rioters and the American Revolution," *William and Mary Quarterly*, 3rd ser., 51 (1994): 3–38, offers a new perspective. For American crowds, see Pauline Maier, "Popular Uprisings and Civil Authority in Eighteenth-Century America," *William and Mary Quarterly*, 3rd ser., 27 (1970):

3–35; Gordon Wood, "A Note on the Mobs in the American Revolution," *William and Mary Quarterly,* 3rd ser., 23 (1966): 635–42; Dirk Hoerder, *Crowd Action in Revolutionary Massachusetts, 1765–1780* (New York, 1977), chap. 1; Paul A. Gilje, *The Road to Mobocracy: Popular Disorders in New York City, 1763–1834* (Chapel Hill, N.C., 1987), chap. 1. For "rough music", see essay 3 in this volume and the groundbreaking essays in William Pencak, Matthew Dennis, and Simon Newman, eds., *Riot and Revelry in Early America* (University Park, Pa., 2002), by Steven J. Stewart, Brendan McConville, Thomas J. Humphrey, William Pencak, and Susan E. Klepp.

33. For voting practices, see Chilton Williamson, *American Suffrage: From Property to Democracy, 1760–1860* (Princeton, N.J., 1960); chaps. 1–4. For comparative changes in voting in the new state constitutions, see Willi Paul Adams, *The First American Constitutions* (Chapel Hill, N.C., 1980), chap. 9 and appendixes; Edward Countryman, *A People in Revolution: The American Revolution and Political Society in New York, 1760–1790* (Baltimore, 1981), chap. 3; Charles S. Olton, *Artisans for Independence: Philadelphia Mechanics and the American Revolution* (Syracuse, N.Y., 1975), chap. 4. For lucid overviews of mechanics in public life in the colonial and revolutionary eras, see Gary Nash, "A Historical Perspective on Early American Artisans," in Puig and Conforti, eds., *American Craftsman,* 1–13; and for Philadelphia, see Gary Nash, "Artisans and Politics in Eighteenth-Century Philadelphia," in Margaret C. Jacob and James R. Jacob, eds., *The Origins of Anglo-American Radicalism* (London, 1984), 162–182.

34. "Pennsylvanus," "A True State of the Dispute Now Subsisting in the Province of Pennsylvania," *Pennsylvania Journal,* March 26, 1756, supplement, attributed to Franklin by Ralph Ketcham, ed., *The Political Thought of Benjamin Franklin* (Indianapolis and New York, 1965), 134. Ketcham was associate editor of the Papers of Benjamin Franklin. The editors write of Franklin that they "do not believe that he wrote it," although it is possible that he "had a direct hand in it." *The Papers of Benjamin Franklin,* Leonard Labaree et al., eds. (New Haven, Conn., 1963), 5:421–22n. My thanks to Gary Nash, Vincent Golden, and Elaine Pascu in tracking this article. For discussion of class, see the Symposia in *Journal of American History* 85 (1998): 93–98, and *Early American Studies: An Interdisciplinary Journal* 3, no. 2 (2005); and Gregory H. Nobles, "Class," in Daniel Vickers, ed., *A Companion to Colonial America* (Oxford, U.K., 2003), 259–87.

35. See Nash, *Urban Crucible,* part 1, esp. chaps. 2 and 4, for an overview of pre-Revolutionary politics.

36. *The Conversation of Two Persons under a Window* (Boston, 1765), cited in Nash, *Urban Crucible,* 278; *Philadelphia Evening Post,* April 27, 1776.

37. *Boston Gazette,* May 5, May 12, 1760, cited in Nash, *Urban Crucible,* 274; Constant Trueman, *Advice to the Free-Holders and Electors of Pennsylvania* (Philadelphia, 1739), 1–2, cited in Nash, "Artisans and Politics in Philadelphia," in Quimby, ed., *Craftsman,* 78; "A Brother Chip," *Pennsylvania Gazette,* September 27, 1770.

38. "Crispin Heeltap," *South Carolina Gazette and Country Journal,* August 14, 1774; Walsh, *Charleston's Sons of Liberty,* 70–71; *Virginia Gazette,* October 13, 1774, copied from a Rhode Island paper, cited in Merrill Jensen, "The American People and the American Revolution," *Journal of American History* 57 (1970): 22.

39. E. P. Thompson, "The Patricians and the Plebs," in *Customs in Common,* 16–96 at 67, an essay reprising "Patrician Society, Plebeian Culture," *Journal of Social History* 7 (1974): 382–405, and "Eighteenth-Century English Society: Class Struggle without Class," *Social History* 3 (1978): 133–66.

40. "To the Tradesmen, Mechanics &c."

41. Unnamed Boston speaker, cited in John C. Miller, *Sam Adams: Pioneer in Propaganda* (Boston, 1936), 207; James P. Walsh, "Mechanics and Citizens: The Connecticut Artisan Protest of 1792," *William and Mary Quarterly,* 3rd ser., 42 (1985):66–89; for the English tradition, see John Rule, "The Property of Skill in the Period of Manufacture," in Patrick Joyce, ed., *The Historical Meaning of Work* (New York, 1987), 99–118.

42. For the almanacs, see Scott McIntosh, "Liberty and Property, Arms and God: The Political Culture of the Crowds in Boston, 1765–1775" (senior thesis, Princeton University, 1979), 60–63; for analogous trends in farmers' thought, see Richard Bushman, *King and People in Provincial Massachusetts* (Chapel Hill, N.C., 1985), chap. 5, a work that deserves attention.

43. For seamen, the classic article is Jesse Lemisch, "Jack Tar in the Streets: Merchant Seamen in the Politics of Revolutionary America," *William and Mary Quarterly,* 3rd ser., 25 (1968): 371–407; for prior opposition to impressment, see John Lax and William Pencak, "The Knowles Riot and the Crisis of the 1740's in Massachusetts," *Perspectives in American History* 10 (1976): 163–214, and Linebaugh and Rediker, *Many-Headed Hydra,* chap. 7.

44. "A Pennsylvania Planter," *Pennsylvania Gazette,* August 1, 1771, cited in Olton, *Artisans for Independence,* 19–20, and chaps. 2 and 3; Joseph Ernst, "Ideology and an Economic Interpretation of the Revolution," in Alfred F. Young, ed., *The American Revolution: Explorations in the History of American Radicalism* (DeKalb, Ill., 1976), 159–85; Dana Frank, *Buy American: The Untold Story of Economic Nationalism* (Boston, 1999), chap. 1; T. H. Breen, *The Marketplace of Revolution: How Consumer Politics Shaped American Independence* (New York, 2004), part 2; and T. H. Breen, "'Baubles of Britain': The American and the Consumer Revolutions in the Eighteenth Century," in Cary Carson et al., eds., *Of Consuming Interest: The Style of Life in the Eighteenth Century* (Charlottesville, Va., 1994), 444–82.

45. "Resolution of the Massachusetts Provincial Congress, December 8, 1774," in Merrill Jensen, ed., *English Historical Documents: American Colonial Documents to 1776* (New York, 1955), 823–24; Lawrence Peskin, *Manufacturing Revolution: The Intellectual Origins of American Industry* (Baltimore, 2003), chaps. 2 and 3.

46. For an analytical overview of the Revolution, see Gary B. Nash, *The Unknown American Revolution: The Unruly Birth of Democracy and the Struggle to*

Create America (New York, 2005); for the classic Tory view of the "mob," see Peter Oliver, *Peter Oliver's Origin & Progress of the American Rebellion: A Tory View*, ed. Douglas Adair and John A. Schutz (Stanford, Calif., 1961), 68; for interpretations of crowd actions in the era, see the works cited in this essay by Edward Countryman, Paul A. Gilje, Dirk Hoerder, Jesse Lemisch, Pauline Maier, Barbara Clark Smith, and Robert St. George.

47. For the slogans, see Pauline Maier, *From Resistance to Revolution: Colonial Radicals and the Development of American Opposition to Britain, 1765–1776* (New York, 1972), passim. For divisions among artisans in Philadelphia, see Olton, *Artisans for Independence*; for divisions around liberty trees and liberty poles, see essay 8 in this volume.

48. For New York, see Staughton Lynd, "The Mechanics in New York Politics, 1774–1785," in Lynd, *Slavery, Class Conflict, and the United States Constitution: Ten Essays* (Indianapolis, 1967), 79–108; Countryman, *People in Revolution*, chap. 5. For Philadelphia, see Richard Ryerson, *The Revolution Is Now Begun: The Radical Committees of Philadelphia, 1765–1776* (Philadelphia, 1978). For Charleston, see Walsh, *Charleston's Sons of Liberty*, chap. 3; and Pauline Maier, "The Charleston Mob and the Evolution of Popular Politics, in Revolutionary South Carolina," *Perspectives in American History* 4 (1970): 173–96.

49. Rosswurm, *Arms, Country, and Class*, chaps. 2 and 3; Ronald Schultz, *The Republic of Labor: Philadelphia Artisans and the Politics of Class, 1720–1830* (New York, 1993), chaps. 1 and 2.

50. Fischer, *Paul Revere's Ride*, 93–112 ("The Midnight Ride as a Collective Effort"); J. L. Bell, *Behold, the Guns Were Gone: Four Brass Cannons and the Start of the American Revolution* (Boston, 2006).

51. Pauline Maier, *The Old Revolutionaries: Political Lives in the Age of Samuel Adams* (New York, 1980), chaps. on Adams, Young, and Sears; John Alexander, *Samuel Adams: America's Revolutionary Politician* (Lanham, Md., 2002); Roger J. Champagne, *Alexander McDougall and the American Revolution in New York* (Schenectady, N.Y., 1975), chaps. 1–5; for Philadelphia, see Rosswurm, *Arms, Country, and Class*, chaps. 1–3.

52. William Fowler, *The Baron of Beacon Hill: A Biography of John Hancock* (Boston, 1979); Charles W. Akers, *The Divine Politician: Samuel Cooper and the American Revolution in Boston* (Boston, 1982), passim (on Hancock); Gregory H. Nobles, "'Yet the Old Republicans Still Persevere': Samuel Adams, John Hancock, and the Crisis of Popular Leadership in Revolutionary Massachusetts, 1775–1790," in Ronald Hoffman and Peter Albert, eds., *The Transforming Hand of Revolution: Reconsidering the American Revolution as a Social Movement* (Charlottesville, Va., 1995), 258–85; Paul Staiti, "Character and Class," in Rebora, Staiti, et al., *John Singleton Copley*, 53–78 (for the context) and 211–14 (portrait).

53. Jesse Lemisch, *Jack Tar versus John Bull: The Role of New York's Seamen in Precipitating the Revolution* (New York, 1997), 101 (Tony and Dale); Countryman,

People in Revolution, 62–63; Edmund Morgan and Helen Morgan, *The Stamp Act Crisis: Prologue to Revolution* (New York, 1962), 245–48 (Newport); Steffen, *Mechanics of Baltimore*, 75–77.

54. Rosswurm, *Arms, Country, and Class*, 250; Thomas Young to John Lamb, June 19, 1774, John Leake, *Life of John Lamb*, 89–90; for lower-class hostility in the countryside to upper-class Whigs, see Lynd, *Slavery, Class Conflict*, chap. 2; Edward Countryman, "'Out of the Bounds of Law': Northern Land Rioters in the Eighteenth Century," in Young, ed., *American Revolution*, 37–69; Countryman, *People in Revolution*, chaps. 4 and 5; Ronald Hoffman, "The 'Disaffected' in the Revolutionary South," and Marvin L. Michael Kay, "The North Carolina Regulation, 1766–1776: A Class Conflict," both in Young, ed., *American Revolution*, 73–123, 275–316.

55. Robert R. Livingston to William Duer, June 12, 1777, R. R. Livingston Papers, New-York Historical Society.

56. Eric Foner, *Tom Paine and Revolutionary America* (New York, 1976), chap. 3; Eric Foner, "Tom Paine's Republic: Radical Ideology and Social Change," in Young, ed., *American Revolution*, 188–232; John Keane, *Tom Paine: A Political Life* (New York, 1995), chap. 4.

57. Gouverneur Morris to Mr. [John] Penn, May 24, 1774, in Peter Force, comp., *American Archives*, 9 vols. (Washington, D.C., 1837–53), 1:343.

58. "Queries Addressed to the Writer Who Signs Himself Cato," *Pennsylvania Evening Post*, March 14, 1774; Nash, *Race, Class, and Politics*, 176, table 1 (wealth distribution).

59. Walsh, *Charleston's Sons of Liberty*, 67–68 (lieutenant governor); for Savannah, see Governor James Wright to Lord Dartmouth, December 19, 1775, *Georgia Historical Society Collections* 3 (1873): 228, cited in Philip Foner, *Labor and the American Revolution* (Westport, Conn., 1976), 146, and "Extract of a Letter from Savannah, December 26, 1775," in Margaret Willard, ed., *Letters on the American Revolution, 1774–76* (Boston, 1925), 245.

60. "To the Several Battalions of Military Associators in the Province of Pennsylvania," June 26, 1776, cited in Rosswurm, *Arms, Country, and Class*, 101–2.

61. "The Respectful Address of the Mechanicks in Union, Malcolm McUen, Chairman," *New York Gazette*, June 17, 1776; Wehtje, "A Town in the Confederation," chap. 6 (Boston town meeting).

62. Elisha Douglass, *Rebels and Democrats: The Struggle for Equal Political Rights and Majority Rule during the American Revolution* (Chapel Hill, N.C., 1955); Jackson T. Main, *Sovereign States, 1775–1783* (New York, 1973), chaps. 5 and 6; Gordon Wood, *The Creation of the American Republic, 1776–1787* (Chapel Hill, N.C., 1969), chaps. 4–6; Nash *Unknown American Revolution*, chap. 6 (states as a whole) and 290–305 (Boston). For the Boston town meeting's response to the drafts of the Massachusetts constitutions, see Oscar and Mary F. Handlin, eds., *The Popular Sources of Political Authority* (Cambridge, Mass., 1966), 307–10, 749–69; and

Stephen Patterson, *Political Parties in Revolutionary Massachusetts* (Madison, Wis., 1973), chaps. 6–9. For New York, see Alfred F. Young, *The Democratic Republicans of New York, 1788–1797* (Chapel Hill, N.C., 1968), 21 (balance). For Pennsylvania, see Schultz, *Republic of Labor*, chap. 2.

63. For Paine, see essay 6 in this volume; "The Respectful Address of the Mechanics in Union," *New York Gazette*, June 17, 1776.

64. The history of artisans in the war remains to be written. Philip Foner, *Labor in the American Revolution* (Westport, Conn., 1976), chap. 10, touches on the subject. Charles Neimeyer, *America Goes to War: A Social History of the Continental Army* (New York, 1996), chaps. 1 and 6, deals with the composition of the army, and Holly A. Mayer, *Belonging to the Army: Camp Followers and Community in the American Revolution* (Columbia, S.C., 1996), deals with workers in army camps. For the disproportionate number of Boston working people in the army, see Philip Swain, "Who Fought? Boston Soldiers in the Revolutionary War" (honors thesis, Tufts University, 1981), based on an analysis of 1895 enlistments. For conflict at home, see Rosswurm, *Arms, Country, and Class*, chaps. 5 and 6; Barbara Smith, "Food Rioters"; John K. Alexander, "The Fort Wilson Incident of 1779: A Case Study of the Revolutionary Crowd," *William and Mary Quarterly*, 3rd. ser., 31 (1974): 589–612.

65. Morris, *Government and Labor*, 139–56; for two rich collection of documents, see Howard B. Rock, ed., *The New York City Artisan, 1789–1825: A Documentary History* (Albany, N.Y., 1989), part 4, and Rock and Gilje, eds., *Keepers of the Revolution*, chaps. 2 and 3; Steffen, *Mechanics of Baltimore*, chap. 5; Philip S. Foner, *History of the Labor Movement in the United States: From Colonial Times to the Founding of the American Federation of Labor* (New York, 1947), chap. 5.

66. For the certificates, see Rock, ed., *New York City Artisan*, 25 (coopers), 204 (hatmakers); Howard B. Rock, *Artisans of the New Republic: The Tradesmen of New York in the Age of Jefferson* (New York, 1979), 133 (sailmakers).

67. Harry Rubenstein, "With Hammer in Hand: Working-Class Occupational Portraits," in Howard B. Rock, Paul A. Gilje, and Robert Asher, eds., *American Artisans: Crafting Social Identity, 1750–1850* (Baltimore, 1995), 176–98; for Revere, see Rebora, Staiti, et al., *John Singleton Copley*, 246–49, cf. Nathaniel Hurd, an engraver not depicted as an artisan, 208–11. The Revere portrait is in the Boston Museum of Fine Arts, and the Phyfe portrait is reproduced without a source in *American Collector* (May 1942) and reprinted in Rock, ed., *New York City Artisan*, 230.

68. For New York, see Lynd, "Mechanics in New York Politics," and Alfred F. Young, "Mechanics and the Jeffersonians," *Labor History* 5 (1964): 225–76; Peskin, *Manufacturing Revolution*, chaps. 4 and 5; Minutes of the General Society, January 28, 1799, cited in Rock, *Artisans of the New Republic*, 172.

69. My enumeration of the societies is based on imprints of addresses, constitutions, and the like in the card catalogs arranged by city and date in the New York

Public Library and American Antiquarian Society. My analysis of the New York and Boston societies is based on their manuscript minutes. For New England, the indispensable work is Gary Kornblith, "From Artisans to Businessmen: Master Mechanics in New England, 1789–1850" (Ph.D. diss., Princeton University, 1983), chaps. 1–4 (Boston); for New York, see especially Rock, *Artisans of the New Republic*, 129–32 and passim, and Young, *Democratic Republicans*, passim. In Philadelphia, it seems, there was no general society, which is a puzzle. Schultz, *Republic of Labor*, 101, 228, reports a proposal for a citywide association (1785), which was apparently never formed.

70. The petitions are in Walter Lowrie and Matthew Clarke, eds., *American State Papers: Finance*, 38 vols. (Washington, D.C., 1832–61), 1:5–11. For a listing of petitions for the first four congresses, see *Petitions, Memorials and Other Documents Submitted for the Consideration of Congress, March 4, 1789 to December 14, 1795 (House Committee on Energy and Commerce)*, 99th Cong., 2nd sess., April 1986.

71. Howard B. Rock, "'All Her Sons Join as One Social Band': New York City Artisanal Societies in the Early Republic," in Rock, Gilje, and Asher, eds., *American Artisans*, 156–75; Thomas Schlereth, "Artisans in the New Republic: A Portrait from Visual Evidence," in Schlereth, *Cultural History and Material Culture: Everyday Life, Landscapes, Museums* (Charlottesville, Va., 1990), 114–43; Charles F. Hummel, *With Hammer in Hand: The Dominy Craftsmen of East Hampton, New York* (Charlottesville, Va., 1968) (carpenter). A membership certificate is in Winterthur Museum; a blank certificate is in the GSMT Library, New York.

72. Joseph Buckingham, comp., *Annals of the Massachusetts Charitable Mechanics Association* (Boston, 1853), 71–72.

73. Peskin, *Manufacturing Revolution*, chap. 4; for the formation of the merchant-artisan alliance in Pennsylvania, see Eric Foner, *Tom Paine*, chap. 6; for New York, see Lynd, "Mechanics in New York Politics," and Young, *Democratic Republicans*, chaps. 3 and 4; for the conflict of interests within Massachusetts, see Robert A. Gross, ed., *In Debt to Shays: The Bicentennial of an Agrarian Rebellion* (Charlottesville, Va., 1993), essays in parts 1 and 2; Van Beck Hall, *Politics without Parties: Massachusetts, 1780–1791* (Pittsburgh, 1972), chaps. 6 and 7.

74. For historians' accounts of the parades, see Whitfield Bell Jr., "The Federal Processions of 1788," *New-York Historical Society Quarterly* 46 (1962): 5–39; Kenneth Silverman, *A Cultural History of the American Revolution* (New York, 1976), 570–87; Loretta Valtz Mannucci, "The Look of Revolution: Presentation and Representation in the American Revolution," in Mannucci, ed., *The Languages of Revolution* (Quaderno 2; Milan: Milan Group in Early United States History, 1989), 25–36; David Waldstreicher, *In the Midst of Perpetual Fetes: The Making of American Nationalism; 1776–1820* (Chapel Hill, N.C., 1997), 103–7; Len Travers, *Celebrating the Fourth: Independence Day and the Rites of Nationalism in the Early Republic* (Amherst, Mass., 1997), chap. 3; Laura Rigal, *The American Manufactory: Art, Labor, and the World of Things in the Early Republic* (Princeton, N.J., 1998), chap. 1.

75. For my analysis of the convention, see essay 4 in this volume.

76. "The Address of John Humble," in Herbert Storing, ed., *The Anti-Federalist*, 5 vols. (Chicago, 1981), 3:89–90; for essays published in New York, see ibid., vols. 2 and 6, and for Massachusetts, see ibid., vol. 4. For the fullest record of the debate in the newspapers, see Merrill Jensen, John P. Kaminski, and Gaspare Saladino, eds., *The Documentary History of the Ratification of the Constitution* (Madison, Wis., 1976–), *Ratification of the Constitution by States: Pennsylvania*, vol. 2, and *Commentaries on the Constitution Public and Private*, vol. 4. For Massachusetts, I read the documents collected by the Ratification of the Constitution Project, Madison, Wisconsin, then in loose-leaf notebooks, for which I am indebted to the project's director, John Kaminski; for Philadelphia, see Saul Cornell, ed., "Reflections on 'The Late Remarkable Revolution in Government': Aedanus Burke and Samuel Bryan's Unpublished History of the *Ratification of the Federal Constitution*," *Pennsylvania Magazine of History & Biography* 101 (1988): 103–30. For anti-Federalist thought, see Jackson T. Main, *The Anti-Federalists* (Chapel Hill, N.C., 1961), chaps. 6–8; and Saul Cornell, *The Other Founders: Anti-Federalism and the Dissenting Tradition in America, 1788–1828* (Chapel Hill, N.C., 1999), part 1. Cornell identifies very few anti-Federalist appeals to mechanics.

77. For the votes on ratification, see Roland Baumann, "Democratic Republicans of Philadelphia: The Origins, 1776–1797" (Ph.D. diss., Pennsylvania State University, 1970), chap. 3 and 607 (vote); Young, *Democratic Republicans*, chap. 4, 89–90 (vote).

78. I have drawn on the historians' accounts cited in note 74 and the following contemporary accounts: *(Boston) Massachusetts Centinel*, February 9, 1788; *New York Journal*, July 23, 1788, and *New York Packet*, August 5, 1788; Francis Hopkinson, *An Account of the Grand Federal Procession* ... (Philadelphia, 1788), reprinted in *The American Museum* (1788), 57–88, and in *Old South Leaflets*, Nos. 230–31 (Boston, 1961); *(Baltimore) Maryland Journal*, May 6, 1788; John P. Kaminski and Gaspare Saladino, eds., *Documentary History of the Ratification of the Constitution* (Madison, Wis., 1995), *Commentaries on the Constitution Public and Private*, vol. 6, 221–311 for the celebrations.

79. For interpretations of the parades that stress elite sponsorship and values, see Paul A. Gilje, "The Common People and the Constitution: Popular Culture in New York City in the Late Eighteenth Century," in Paul A. Gilje and William Pencak, eds., *New York in the Age of the Constitution, 1775–1800* (Rutherford, N.J., 1992), 48–73; and Susan Davis, *Parades and Power: Street Theatre in Nineteenth-Century Philadelphia* (Philadelphia, 1986), 117–26.

80. The pewterers' flag is on display at the New-York Historical Society (Item No. 1903.12, Henry Luce Center for the Study of American Culture), reproduced in Rock, Gilje, and Asher, eds., *American Artisans*, 161. For Philadelphia, in Carpenter's Hall the Carpenters Company displays its own flag, which was carried in the 1788 parade, and the Library Company of Philadelphia has the flag of the

tobacconists. The Bostonian Society has four artisan flags that were carried for the first time in the 1789 Boston procession that welcomed President Washington.

81. Benjamin Rush, "Observations on the Fourth of July Procession," in Kaminski and Salidino, eds., *Documentary History of Ratification*, 6:263 (emphasis added).

82. Susan Branson, *These Fiery Frenchified Dames: Women and Political Culture in Early National Philadelphia* (Philadelphia, 2001), 16–18 (the Hewsons); for women's occupations, see essay 2 in this volume.

83. Charles Wesley, *Prince Hall: Life and Legacy* (Washington, D.C., 1977), passim.

84. Alfred F. Young, "Artisans and the Constitution" (Merrill Jensen Lecture, University of Wisconsin, 1996) (1789 parade); Young, *Democratic Republicans*, 386–88.

85. For parades in general in 1788 and the following years, see Sean Wilentz, "Artisan Republican Festivals and the Rise of Class Conflict in New York City, 1788–1837," in Michael H. Frisch and Daniel J. Walkowitz, eds., *Working-Class America: Essays on Labor, Community, and American Society* (Urbana, Ill., 1983), 37–77; Waldstreicher, *In the Midst of Perpetual Fetes*, chaps. 1–4; Davis, *Parades and Power*.

86. For Boston truckmen, see John Drayton, *Letters Written during a Tour through the Northern and Eastern States of America* (1794), in Warren S. Tyron, ed., *A Mirror for Americans*, 3 vols. (Chicago, 1952), 1:12; *Boston Independent Chronicle*, July 19, 1795; for Philadelphia victuallers, see Anelise Harding, *John Lewis Krimmel: Genre Artist in the Early Republic* (Winterthur, Del., 1996), figs. 339, 344; for African American parades, see Shane White, "It Was a Proud Day: African Americans, Festivals and Parades in the North, 1741–1834," *Journal of American History* 81 (1994–95), 13–50; and Waldstreicher, *In the Midst of Perpetual Fetes*, chap. 6.

87. Thomas Jefferson, *Notes on Virginia*, in Merrill D. Peterson, ed., *The Portable Thomas Jefferson* (New York, 1975), query 19.

88. Alfred Young, "The Mechanics and the Jeffersonians, 1789–1801," *Labor History* 5 (1964): 247–76; Young, *Democratic Republicans*; Steffen, *Mechanics of Baltimore*, part 2; Rock, *Artisans of the New Republic*, chap. 1; Baumann, "Democratic Republicans of Philadelphia"; Schultz, *Republic of Labor*, chaps. 4 and 5; Paul Goodman, *The Democratic-Republicans of Massachusetts: Politics in a Young Republic* (Cambridge, Mass., 1964), chap. 5, "The Urban Interest"; William Bruce Wheeler, "Urban Politics in Nature's Republic: The Development of Political Parties in the Seaport Cities in the Federalist Era" (Ph.D. diss., University of Virginia, 1967), has chapters on Philadelphia, Baltimore, New York, and Boston (p. 400 lists seaports carried by Republican candidates in 1800).

89. Eugene P. Link, *The Democratic Republican Societies, 1790–1800* (New York, 1942); Philip S. Foner, ed., *The Democratic-Republican Societies, 1790–1800* (Westport, Conn., 1976): 3–53; Young, *Democratic Republicans*, chap. 18, 395 (evening meetings); Baumann, "Democratic Republicans of Philadelphia," chap. 9; Albert

Koschnik, "The Democratic Societies of Philadelphia and the Limits of the Public Sphere," *William and Mary Quarterly* 58 (2001): 615–36.

90. Isaiah Thomas, *The History of Printing in America* (1810; New York, 1960), 265 (Thomas); Donald H. Stewart, *The Opposition Press of the Federalist Period* (Albany, 1969), 15, 630, 856 n. 72; Jeffrey L. Pasley, *The Tyranny of the Printers: Newspaper Politics in the Early American Republic* (Charlottesville, Va., 2001), chaps. 1 and 2 (printers as mechanics); Michael Durey, "Thomas Paine's Apostles: Radical Emigres and the Triumph of Jeffersonian Republicanism," *William and Mary Quarterly* 44 (1987): 682.

91. Thomas Paine, *Rights of Man, Part Second* (1792), chap. 5, 398–454, and *Agrarian Justice* (1795–96), 606–23, both in P. Foner, ed., *Complete Works of Thomas Paine*, 2 vols. (New York, 1945), vol. 1.

92. Cathy N. Davidson, *Revolution and the Word: The Rise of the Novel in America* (New York, 1986), chaps. 2 and 4; David D. Hall, *Cultures of Print: Essays in the History of the Book* (Amherst, Mass., 1996), 36–78; "Memoirs of Stephen Allen," ed. John C. Travis, typescript, New-York Historical Society, excerpts from which are reprinted in Gilje and Rock, eds., *Keepers of the Revolution*.

93. J. Walsh, "Mechanics and Citizens," 66–89; William Manning, *The Key of Liberty*, ed. Sean Wilentz and Michael Merrill (Cambridge, Mass., 1993); for Brown, see James M. Smith, *Freedom's Fetters: The Alien and Sedition Laws and American Civil Liberties* (Ithaca, N.Y., 1956), 257–70; for orations to and by mechanics, see Rock, *Artisans of the New Republic*, chap. 5; for Tunis Wortman, a learned New York Republican who spoke to mechanic audiences, see Young, *Democratic Republicans*, 520–23.

94. For the general downward social shift of officeholders, see Jackson T. Main, "The American Revolution and the Democratization of the Legislatures," *William and Mary Quarterly*, 3rd ser., 23 (1966): 354–67; Jackson T. Main, *Political Parties before the Constitution* (Chapel Hill, N.C., 1973); Young, *Democratic Republicans*, chap. 4; Gordon S. Wood, *The Radicalism of the American Revolution* (New York, 1991), chap. 16. For mechanic support of nonmechanic candidates in congressional elections, see Young, *Democratic Republicans*, chaps. 19 and 26; Roland Baumann, "John Swanwick: Spokesman for Merchant Republicanism," *Pennsylvania Magazine of History and Biography* 97 (1973): 248–56; Steffen, *Mechanics of Baltimore*, chaps. 7 and 8; Rock, *Artisans of the New Republic*, chaps. 2–4; Goodman, *Democratic-Republicans of Massachusetts*, chaps. 5 and 6; William Whitney Jr., "The Crowninshields of Salem, 1800–1818: A Study in the Politics of Commercial Growth," *Essex Institute Historical Collections* 94 (1958): 1–36, 79–118; Frank A. Cassell, *Merchant Congressman in the Young Republic: Samuel Smith of Maryland, 1752–1839* (Madison, Wis., 1971).

95. Young, *Democratic Republicans*, chap. 22; Hodges, *New York City Cartmen*, chap. 8.

96. Alexander Hamilton, *The Federalist*, essay 35, "Hamilton Ms. 1794, last

sheet in vol XV," cited in Charles Beard, *Economic Origins of Jeffersonian Democracy* (New York, 1915), 246–47 (I have not been able to located this document); Hamilton to Rufus King, May 4, 1796, in Harold Syrett et al., eds., *Papers of Alexander Hamilton*, 27 vols. (New York, 1961–1987), 20:158.

97. John R. Nelson, *Liberty and Property: Political Economy and Policy Making in the New Nation, 1789–1812* (Baltimore, 1987), chaps. 2, 4, 6; John R. Nelson, "Alexander Hamilton and American Manufacturing: A Reexamination," *Journal of American History* 45 (1979): 971–95; Peskin, *Manufacturing Revolution*, chap. 4; Roland M. Baumann, "Philadelphia's Manufacturers and the Excise Taxes of 1794: The Forging of the Jeffersonian Coalition," *Pennsylvania Magazine of History and Biography* 106 (1982): 3–39.

98. Gary Kornblith, "Artisan Federalism: New England Mechanics and the Political Economy of the 1790s," in Ronald Hoffman and Peter J. Albert, eds., *Launching the "Extended Republic": The Federalist Era* (Charlottesville, Va., 1996), 249–72; Kornblith, "From Artisans to Businessmen," chap. 1; Triber, *True Republican*, 185.

99. George Warner, *Means for the Preservation of Liberty* (New York, 1797), 9–13, 15; for Philadelphia artisan republicanism, see the articles by William Duane in *The Aurora*, January 1807, discussed in Schultz, *Republic of Labor*, 156; for Baltimore, see Steffen, *Mechanics of Baltimore*, chaps. 6, 7, 11.

100. Young, *Democratic Republicans*, chap. 24, 520–21 (reform toasts); Richard J. Twomey, *Jacobins and Jeffersonians: Anglo-American Radicalism in the United States, 1790–1820* (New York, 1989), chap. 4; Elaine Weber Pascu, "From the Philanthropic Tradition to the Common School Ideal: Schooling in New York City, 1815–1832" (Ph.D. diss., Northern Illinois University, 1979); for Republican documents on reform themes, see Irving Mark and Eugene L. Schwaab, eds., *The Faith of Our Fathers* (New York, 1952), passim; for artisan slaveholders, see Shane White, *Somewhat More Independent: The End of Slavery in New York City, 1770–1810* (Athens, Ga., 1991), 10–13.

101. Noah Webster, *A Compendious Dictionary of the English Language* (New Haven, Conn., 1806), S.V. "mechanic"; and Webster, *An American Dictionary of the English Language*, 2 vols. (New York, 1829).

102. Davidson, *Revolution and the Word*, 105, 173–78 (novelists); for William Chappel, see Rock, ed., *New York City Artisan*, xxii, 5, 34, 171; Harding, *John Lewis Krimmel*, figs. 101, 110, 127, 338–39; Richard R. John and Thomas C. Leonard, "The Illusion of the Ordinary: John Lewis Krimmel's *Village Tavern* and the Democratization of Public Life in the Early Republic," *Pennsylvania History* 65 (1998): 87–96.

103. Nelson, *Liberty and Property*, chap. 10; Schultz, *Republic of Labor*, chaps. 5 and 6.

104. Albert Gallatin, "Report on Manufactures," in James Ferguson, ed., *Selected Writings of Albert Gallatin* (Indianapolis, 1967), 240–64; Nelson, *Liberty and Property*, chap. 10; Peskin, *Manufacturing Revolution*, part 3.

105. The quotation on manufacturing is from Jefferson to Benjamin Austin, January 6, 1816, printed in "National Utility in Opposition to Political Controversy: Addressed to the Friends of American Manufactures" (broadside, Boston, 1816), in response to Austin to Jefferson, December 9, 1815; for a similar letter, see Jefferson to the Society of Tammany, February 29, 1808, printed in *American Citizen*, April 9, 1808. The quotation on tradesmen is from Jefferson to John Lithgow, January 4, 1805 (self-identified in a letter to Jefferson, December 24, 1804, as the author of "the Essay on the Manufacturing Interest" and "Of Equality a Political Romance"). My thanks to Elaine Weber Pascu, associate editor of the Jefferson Papers, for providing manuscript copies of these exchanges. For the symbolism of clothing, see David Waldstreicher, "Why Thomas Jefferson and African Americans Wore Their Politics on Their Sleeves: Dress and Mobilization between American Revolutions," in Jeffrey Pasley, Andrew Robertson, and David Waldstreicher, eds., *Beyond the Founders* (Chapel Hill, N.C., 2004), 79–103 at 84–87. For discussions of Jefferson's political economy, see Drew McCoy, *The Elusive Republic: Political Economy in Jeffersonian America* (Chapel Hill, N.C., 1980), chap. 8; Joyce Appleby, *Capitalism and a New Social Order: The Republican Vision of the 1790s* (New York, 1994), chap. 4. For Republicans and manufacturing, see Schultz, *Republic of Labor*, chaps. 5 and 6; Peskin, *Manufacturing Revolution*, part 3; for Republican manufacturers, see John A. Munroe, *Federalist Delaware, 1775–1815* (New Brunswick, N.J., 1954), 220–27.

106. *New York Evening Post*, February 28, 1815; Rock, ed., *New York City Artisan*, 12–13 (the two certificates, mistakenly reversed in the printing).

107. On the economic changes, see Wilentz, *Chants Democratic*, chap. 1, 36–37 (Duncan Phyfe); Gary Kornblith, "Artisan Response to Capitalist Transformation," *Journal of the Early Republic* 10 (1990): 315–21; Laurie, *Artisans into Workers*, chap. 1; David Montgomery, "The Working Classes of the Pre-Industrial Cities, 1790–1830," *Labor History* 9 (1968): 3–22; Christopher Tomlins, *Law, Labor, and Ideology in the Early Republic* (Cambridge, V.K., 1993), chap. 4; Rock, *Artisans of the New Republic*, part 3; Lisa Lubow, "Artisans in Transition: Early Capitalist Development and the Carpenters of Boston, 1787–1837" (Ph.D. diss., University of California, Los Angeles, 1987); "To the Public," by Journeymen House Carpenters, April 10, 1809, in Rock, ed., *New York City Artisan*, 233–34; "Address of the Working Shoemakers of Philadelphia" (1805), in Mark and Schwaab, eds., *Faith of Our Fathers*, 334–35.

108. For language, see Albert Matthews, "Hired Man and Help," *Publications of the Colonial Society of Massachusetts* 5 (1897–98): 225–56, a classic article. The observations of European travelers on the terms for servants are almost all from the post–Revolutionary war period. For conditions, see Sharon V. Sallinger, "Artisans, Journeymen and the Transformation of Labor in Late Eighteenth-Century Philadelphia," *William and Mary Quarterly* 40 (1983): 62–84; Robert J. Steinfeld, *The Invention of Free Labor: The Employment Relation in English and American*

Law and Culture, 1350–1870 (Chapel Hill, N.C., 1991), chap. 5; Rorabaugh, "Apprentices, Masters and the Revolution," in Alfred F. Young, ed., *Beyond the American Revolution: Explorations in the History of American Radicalism,* (Dekalb, Ill., 1993), 185–217, quotations at 200, 207.

109. On the legal constraints on journeymen's combinations, see Tomlins, *Law, Labor, and Ideology,* part 2; on the response to the cases, Richard J. Twomey, "Jacobins and Jeffersonians: Anglo-American Radical Ideology, 1790–1810," in Margaret Jacob and James Jacob, eds., *The Origins of Anglo-American Radicalism* (London, 1984), 284–99; Twomey, *Jacobins and Jeffersonians,* chap. 6; Schultz, *Republic of Labor,* 160–64.

110. Journeymen House Carpenters, "To the Public," *American Citizen,* April 10, 1809, in Rock and Gilje, eds., *Keepers of the Revolution,* 101–4.

111. Benjamin Franklin, "Last Will and Testament," in Carl Van Doren, ed., *Benjamin Franklin's Autobiographical Writings* (New York, 1945), 688–98; Wood, *Americanization of Benjamin Franklin,* chap. 5.

112. Triber, *True Republican,* chap. 11, 187 (factory "hands"); Esther Forbes, *Paul Revere and the World He Lived In* (Boston, 1942), chap. 10; Patrick Leehey, "Reconstructing Paul Revere," in Paul Revere Memorial Association, *Paul Revere,* 33 ("prosperous North End mechanic").

113. Rigal, *American Manufactory,* 179–98; Patrick Lyon, *The Narrative of Patrick Lyon* ... (Philadelphia, 1799). The two versions of the portrait are in the Boston Athenaeum and the Pennsylvania Academy of Fine Arts.

114. Dixon Wecter, *The Hero in America* (New York, 1941), chap. 4; John William Ward, "Who Was Benjamin Franklin?" and J. A. Leo Lemay, "Franklin's Autobiography and the American Dream," both reprinted in Lemay and Zall, eds., *Benjamin Franklin's Autobiography,* 325–35, 349–60.

115. Wilentz, "Artisan Republican Festivals" (New York); Davis, *Parades and Power,* 125–32; (Philadelphia); Alfred F. Young, *The Shoemaker and the Tea Party: Memory and the American Revolution* (Boston, 1999), 147–50 (Boston); Michael Kammen, *Season of Youth: The American Revolution and the Historical Imagination* (New York, 1978), 44–45, 120, 198–200; Len Travers, *Celebrating the Fourth: Independence Day and the Rites of Nationalism in the Early Republic* (Amherst, Mass., 1997), chap. 4; Simon Newman, *Parades and the Politics of the Street: Festive Culture in the Early Republic* (Philadelphia, 1997), chap. 3; Waldstreicher, *In the Midst of Perpetual Fetes,* chap. 4.

116. Gutman, "Work, Culture, and Society," 550–53, 568–69; Alan Dawley, *Class and Community: The Industrial Revolution in Lynn* (Cambridge, Mass., 1976), 70–71; Paul G. Faler, *Mechanics and Manufacturers in the Early Industrial Revolution, 1780–1860* (Albany, N.Y., 1981); Seth Luther, *An Address to the Workingmen of New England* ..., 2nd ed. (New York, 1833); Philip S. Foner, ed., *We the Other People: Alternative Declarations of Independence* (Urbana, Ill., 1976), 1–40, 47–70.

117. Gutman, "Work, Culture, and Society," 568; see also Vera Shlakman,

Economic History of a Factory Town: A Study of Chicopee, Massachusetts (Northampton, Mass., 1934–35), chap. 5.

118. Kammen, *Season of Youth*, 83–84 (Willard); Bruce Nelson, *Beyond the Martyrs: A Social History of Chicago's Anarchists* (New Brunswick, N.J., 1988), chap. 6 (parades); William Cahn, *A Pictorial History of American Labor* (New York, 1972), 145 (engraving of a New York City parade, September 5, 1882).

2

"Persons of Consequence"

The Women of Boston and the Making of the American Revolution, 1765–1776

On March 31, 1776, three months before the Continental Congress adopted the Declaration of Independence, Abigail Adams, writing from the family farm she was managing in Braintree, Massachusetts, to her husband, John, a delegate to the Congress in Philadelphia, closed her long report on local affairs with a comment that has won a deserved notoriety as the opening manifesto of American feminism. "I long to hear that you have declared an independency—and by the way in the new Code of Laws which I suppose it will be necessary for you to make I desire you would Remember the Ladies, and be more generous and favourable to them than your ancestors. Do not put such unlimited power into the hands of the Husbands. Remember all Men would be tyrants if they could." Half-joking, as if to cushion the radical thrust of her demands, she added, "If perticular care and attention is not paid to the Ladies we are determined to foment a Rebelion, and will not hold ourselves bound by any Laws in which we have no voice or Representation."[1]

In a prompt reply, John Adams put down his wife. "As to your extraordinary Code of Laws, I cannot but laugh"—and he immediately made clear that the "Spirit of '76" included an upsurge of insubordination he was determined to suppress as much as it included a sentiment for independence he welcomed. "We have been told that our Struggle has loosened the bands of Government every where. That Children and Apprentices were disobedient—that schools and Colledges were grown turbulent—that Indians slighted their Guardians and Negroes grew insolent to their Masters. But your Letter was the first intimation that another Tribe more numerous and powerfull than all the rest were grown discontented."[2]

Abigail was serious enough about her proposal to turn for support to her friend Mercy Otis Warren, who had already won eminence for her

A woman on a Boston street stands aghast at the body of her son, Christopher Seider, who has been shot and killed by a customs official, seen firing from the upper
window of his house to the right. The event occurred in February 1770, when
patriot leaders organized boys to picket the shop of T. Lillie (sign to the left), an
importer who was violating the boycott of British manufactures. The cutout of a
head on a pole was to remind Lillie of the dire fate of a state criminal. From a
broadside, "The Life and Humble Confession of Richardson, the Informer." Courtesy of the Historical Society of Pennsylvania.

public writings in the patriot cause. Petulant because John "is very sausy
to me in return for a List of Female Grievances," she thought, "I will get
you to join me in a petition to Congress," thus defining the form that
"fomenting a Rebellion" would take. Summarizing her letter and his reply,
she clearly thought of her action as speaking for more than herself: "So I
have help'd the Sex abundantly."[3]

A week later she closed the issue with John for the time being. "I cannot
say I think you very generous to the Ladies for whilst you are proclaiming
peace and good will to Men, Emancipating all Nations, you insist upon
retaining an absolute power over Wives." She had lost, but she issued a

defiant warning: "Arbitrary power is like most other things which are very hard, very liable to be broken." Then she retreated, falling back on the perennial male claim for ultimate female power: "notwithstanding all your wise Laws and Maxims, we have it in our power not only to free ourselves but to subdue our Masters, and without violence throw both your natural and legal authority at our feet—

> Charm by accepting, by submitting sway
> Yet have our Humour most when we obey."[4]

This was a remarkable exchange, actually the first of several, the implications of which scholars of feminism and the American Revolution have only begun to probe.[5] What prompted so extravagant and passionate a threat? What made Abigail Adams think, even half-seriously, that it was possible in the spring of 1776 to "foment a Rebelion" among women? What activities had women engaged in during the momentous decade since the Stamp Act protests of 1765? What roles had they played? What was the relative importance of these activities? And, finally, had these led, in any way, to a change in women's consciousness? Did others have a "List of Female Grievances"?

To answer these questions, we will focus on the women of Boston from 1765 to 1776, first, because Boston was indisputably one of the most important centers of the political resistance to Britain, and, second, because the activities of the women of Boston are recoverable. The evidence, however fragmentary and frustrating, permits us to track in bold outlines women's activities and to speculate about their consciousness.[6]

Abigail Adams knew Boston well. Since her marriage in 1764, she had lived in Braintree, a town close enough to Boston for her to watch the Battle of Bunker Hill in 1776 from the town's highest hilltop. But she had also lived in Boston for three years, from the spring of 1768 through the spring of 1771, at a time when patriot activity—female as well as male—was at its height. And what she did not know from her own acute observations, she learned from the reports her husband and friends shared with her. John Adams absorbed every nuance of popular activity as he traveled on legal or political business in and out of Boston and through eastern New England.[7]

We direct our attention first to the status and conditions of women in Boston on the eve of the Revolution, second, to the institutions and traditions Bostonians, male and female, drew upon as resources, and third, to the character of the revolutionary movement in Boston. Next we turn to the activities of women within that movement from 1765 through 1775, and finally to the question of consciousness among women, returning to the special moment at which Abigail Adams threatened to "foment a Rebelion" in the spring of 1776.

I

No scholar as yet has attempted to construct a social profile of the women of Boston, but the broad outlines have been suggested by recent analysis of the social structure as a whole, especially by Gary Nash. At this stage in our knowledge this much can be said of the women of Boston at the end of the colonial era: There was a disproportionate number of women compared to other cities; they included a very large number of widows, most of whom were poor; the range of occupations open to women, whether single, widows, or spinsters, was narrow; and women lived in a society in which inequality was the norm and a large proportion of the town was either impoverished or bordered on the brink of poverty.[8]

Women outnumbered men in Boston by 700 or more. In a population of 15,220 counted in 1765, there were 3,612 adult white females and 2,941 males. Among white children under sixteen, the distribution of males and females was approximately equal—4,109 and 4,010, respectively. The town had a large number of widows: 1,200 in 1742; 1,153 in 1751; perhaps 700 in 1765. All seaport cities had more widows than inland country towns; a large number of men made their living by the sea, and the sea took its toll. But Boston's widows were primarily the heritage of the wars England fought against Spain and France from 1740 to 1763 in which Massachusetts men—and Boston men in particular—did a disproportionate share of the fighting and the dying.[9] Boston was also a magnet for the "strolling poor" of eastern Massachusetts, a good number of whom were single women.[10]

The number of female-headed households in Boston was large, perhaps a fourth, or about 500 of the 2,069 families in the 1765 census. As may be surmised, most of these female heads of household were poor. Of 1,153 widows counted by the tax assessors in 1748, one-half were called "very poor." Of 1,200 widows estimated in 1751, 1,000 were "in low circumstances." Only a fraction of women heads of households were taxpayers. The 1771 tax list, an incomplete list that was the only one to survive, enumerates 186 women out of 2,106 taxpayers, only 9 percent of the total. Data from the wills of probate from 1685 to 1775 examined by Nash point to the same conclusion. Of 2,767 wills, 334 (12.08 percent) were left by widows and 93 (3.365 percent) by spinsters. For the late colonial period, 1775, 53.2 percent of all widows died with less than £50 worth of property, which made them poor; only 2.8 percent held over £400; and another 10.1 percent held from £201 to £400, which made them well-to-do. There were few rich widows in Boston.[11]

How did women make a living—whether they were widows or spinsters who were heads of households, or housewives and daughters in male-headed households of the laboring classes? The range of occupations open to women was narrow. Boston was a seaport and capital city, a commercial entrepôt where prosperity depended on the export-import trade and where wealth lay in ships, wharves, warehouses, inventories, and real estate. Manufacturing was in the artisan stage. The major branches of trade were the maritime trades, building and outfitting ships, the building trades, and trades catering to the local consumer's market. In 1765, moreover, Boston's once prosperous economy had been ailing for over a generation. Alone among the major cities, its population declined in the middle decades of the eighteenth century.[12]

A handful of women were in male trades, but, as elsewhere, only as wives or daughters who had taken over after a husband's or father's death. In those trades that were worked at out of a shop at home, women often were "meet help"—helpmates—to their husbands. But this clearly was not possible for the wives of men in the maritime or building trades. The newspaper advertisements, which in Philadelphia demonstrate widows succeeding their husbands in a rich variety of crafts, are sparse for Boston.[13] Craftswomen in Boston seem clustered in exclusively female trades, in particular in the needle trades, where they worked as seamstresses, mantua makers (i.e., fine clothing), milliners, and glovers. The occupations of spinster and weaver were rare in the cities; unlike their rural counterparts, city women did not normally engage in household production of textiles. Women were numerous in the nurturing professions, working as nurses, midwives, wet nurses, and schoolmistresses and running "dame" schools in their homes in which preschool boys and girls learned their ABCs. A fairly large number of women sold goods and services. They were shopkeepers, petty retailers who could set up shop in their own homes with small capital and inventories, keepers of inns and taverns licensed by the town, and hucksters who either worked in market stalls or hawked their wares about town. At the bottom of the female occupational ladder were household servants, laundresses, and common laborers. With only three hundred female slaves in the town and almost no indentured servants, the largest number of household servants probably were daughters of the poor. Beyond the pale of respectability were prostitutes, who grew in number when their regular seafaring and apprentice clientele of the port was swelled by the presence of several regiments of British troops.[14]

A large number of Boston families survived, as Nash points out, only by taking in boarders. The number of people living in single household units in Boston was 50 percent higher than in New York or Philadelphia. Boston had 9.26 persons per household (1765), compared to 6.26 for Philadelphia (1760) and 6.52 for New York (1753). Many women would have echoed the comments of Sarah Osborn, a schoolmistress, that the only "means that Holds up our Heads above water at all is a couple of boarders."[15]

Few self-employed females achieved "a competence" or the "independency" to which male artisans, shopkeepers, and merchants aspired. Patricia Cleary, who has tracked down the "she-merchants" of Boston—the retailers who ran shops selling a variety of commodities that were imported from England and purchased on credit from British or American wholesale merchants—has identified forty-one between 1745 and 1759 and sixty-four from 1760 to the Revolution. Doubtless there were more. Most were widows and many were successful, in business for more than ten years.[16] But even among these, probably only a handful could write, as did Elizabeth Murray, the most prosperous among them, that she was able "to live & act as I please."

Elizabeth Murray was a self-made woman. A Scottish immigrant who migrated with a stock of dry goods, she became successful as a retailer in Boston, married a merchant/sea captain, was soon widowed, and entered her second marriage with a rare prenuptial agreement; this agreement guaranteed her both the right to manage the property she brought to the marriage and a large settlement instead of the customary dower rights. On this basis she achieved a small fortune. John Copley's portrait of her in the silk and velvet finery of her class portrays her (as a young woman remembered her), with a "stately air and manner," "vigorous mind," and "high spirit."[17]

Murray helped other women to achieve independence. She set up Anne and Betsy Cummings, two young orphaned women, in a small retail shop. They were effusive in their thanks to their "kind advisor," who had "made us independent of every one but your self." She helped Jannette Day Barclay, born illegitimately, to set up a school. "Helpless Friendless almost reduced to want," Barclay wrote, "so Sunk in my Opinion" that "I had nothing to support me," Murray's act "seemed to give me a Merit in my own Eyes, and in those of the World." Childless herself, Murray mother-henned her nieces, promoting "an usefull education." "I prefer a usefull member of society to all the fine delecate creatures of the age." If writing and accountancy were indispensable in trade, "how many families are ruined by the women not understanding accounts"? A niece thanked her for "that spirit of independence you cherished in me [which] is not yet extinct." Few women, single or widowed in Boston, could make that claim.[18]

In stark contrast was the dependence of probably the vast majority of female heads of households on poor relief. The numbers of poor, male and female, requiring relief had long staggered the town fathers. In 1757, the Overseers of the Poor reported that "the Poor supported either wholly or in part by the Town in the Almshouse and out of it will amount to the number of about 1000." Admissions to the Almshouse—indoor relief originally intended for the sick and the aged and crippled—climbed from 93 per year from 1759 to 1763 to 149 a year from 1770 to 1775 (with a winter total near 275–300). Most of the poor on relief—and most of the women— lived at home and received out-relief. The records of one Overseer for 1769 to 1772 show that about 15 percent of the householders in two wards were on relief, which projected for the city as a whole would mean five hundred to six hundred families.[19]

What is remarkable about these numerous poor dependent women of Boston is their dogged resistance to forms of poor relief that would degrade them. Impoverished women had a clear notion that relief at home was a right. A visitor to Boston caught the values that underlay resistance: the Overseers of the Poor were "very tender of exposing those that had lived in a handsome manner and therefore give them good relief in so private a manner, that it is seldom known to any of their neighbors." Women in general held to the conviction that they should not have to work either in a workhouse or a manufactory for relief. A large brick workhouse, opened in 1739, in which adults and children were employed in picking oakum, carding, and spinning under a strict regime, never had more than fifty inmates. A manufactory to produce linen set up by a company of private investors early in the 1750s fared only a little better. The sponsoring society had to set up spinning schools to teach the skill. In 1753 they staged a spinning exhibition on the Boston Common at which "Near 300 spinsters, some of them 7 or 8 years old and several of them Daughters of the best families among us ... made a Handsome appearance." The sponsors imported male weavers from abroad and built a large brick building. By

1758, the operation was over, a failure. Why? "Much of the answer," Gary Nash writes, "lies with the majority of women and children [who] were reluctant to toil in the manufactory. They would spin at home ... but removal to an institutional setting, even for daytime labor, involved a new kind of labor discipline and separation of productive and reproductive responsibilities that challenged deeply rooted values."[20] Thus, on the eve of resistance to Great Britain there was a large class of women in Boston who, dependent as they may have been, held fast to values of a moral economy and to aspirations for personal independence.

II

John Adams boasted of the institutions that made New England distinctive: the town meeting, the Congregational meetinghouse, the militia, and the public schools.[21] And well he might, for romanticized as they may have become, these institutions became the basis of the male resistance movement that made the Revolution in Boston no less than in the small country towns. Save in Boston, one could add, resistance was also built on traditions of collective crowd action that John Adams cared not to boast about, traditions that gave Boston the reputation of being the most "mobbish" town in America.

Women who participated in activities that ended in Revolution could draw on only one of these institutions: the church. But they could also draw on roles that were by custom theirs in the domestic sphere, their roles as consumers and producers in the household economy, and on rituals of the life cycle, such as the funeral procession and rituals of community punishment and shaming. And they were heirs to traditions of war.

Political institutions in Boston were the most democratic of the large colonial cities. All men with a certain amount of property were qualified to vote in the town meeting, take part in its deliberations, and elect the selectmen who administered the laws and chose delegates to the provincial assembly. In the 1760s, out of about 3,000 adult males (of whom about 2,100 were on the tax roll), 600 to 700 men usually voted; the highest turnout at a hotly contested election was 1,100.[22] Perhaps 50 percent of the adult males qualified to vote; Faneuil Hall, the usual site for the town meeting, seated 1,500. After 1770, patriot leaders called meetings of "the whole Body of the People" at which property qualifications were let down and poor artisans, journeymen, apprentices, and seamen appeared; such meetings, ranging from 3,000 to 5,000 men, had to be adjourned to the largest church in the city, the capacity of which was about 5,000.[23] The rulers of the town meeting, on the other hand, the selectmen and Overseers of the Poor, were drawn from the well-to-do classes, and the 150 or so petty officeholders from the middling sort.[24] Women neither attended, voted for, nor held office in the town meeting.

Nor were they part of the male network of associations: the political caucuses for the three parts of town (north, south, central) that prearranged town meeting affairs; a merchant's chamber of commerce; three Masonic lodges; or the array of eating and social and fire-fighting clubs.[25] Artisans sustained no permanent organizations, although specific trades met on an ad hoc basis to deal with the business of the trade—house carpenters to set prices, bakers to deal with the selectmen on the assize of bread, and tanners and a dozen others to petition the colonial government—all male trades.[26]

Boston's much vaunted public schools were also exclusively male. The town supported five schools: three writing schools (north, south, and central) and two grammar schools (north and south). For boys only, they educated no more than half of the two thousand or so school-age boys. Girls, like boys, were sent to "dame" schools to learn their ABCs, but after that, parents had to pay private tutors.[27] In 1773, "Clio" contended that "but few of the Fair Sex have been sufficiently instructed in their own language to write it with propriety and elegance," and a decade later a would-be reformer claimed that in all of Boston so few women could keep accounts, there were only "about a dozen capable of being shopkeepers."[28]

Notwithstanding this gap in formal education, the women of Boston were more literate than country women, and the proportion of the literate among them seems to have been rising.[29] Women helped sustain the city's bookstores (there were thirty-one in all between 1761 and 1776). Some read newspapers—there were five in the 1760s—even though they ran little by, for, or about women. There were no magazines aimed at female readers, as there would be after the war. Yet there are many signs of the growth of a female reading public: the popularity of imported English novels, steady sellers in a religious vein, and cheap books and broadside ballads aimed at readers at lower levels of literacy.[30]

The church very likely was the most important institution to the women of late colonial Boston. There were seventeen churches in Boston to which, in 1761, one minister estimated 2,000 families belonged, all save a quarter of the town's families. There were eleven Congregational meetinghouses, two Baptist, and one Presbyterian (these fourteen "dissenting" churches with about 1,500 families among them), and three Anglican Episcopal churches (with from 350 to 500 families altogether). The five largest Congregational churches had from 150 to 350 families, the smaller ones 100 and fewer. They were distributed throughout the city, which meant that for most families attendance was probably on a neighborhood basis.[31] In social class, the Congregationalist churches were mixed: the Brattle Street meetinghouse on the fashionable west side had the men of "more Weight and Consequence," John Adams observed, while others in the north end of town had more of an artisan flavor.[32] At the lower extreme was the First Baptist Church, a small congregation, which drew poorer artisans, Negroes, and sailors to its services.[33] The parishioners of the Anglican churches ranged from the very rich to the poor. Anglican priests were Loyalist, while the Congregationalist ministers by and large were what the Loyalist Peter Oliver called them: a "black regiment" supporting "pulpits of sedition."[34]

The dissenting churches clearly were centers for women. By midcentury, twice as many women as men were being admitted to membership; in most congregations they very likely formed a majority.[35] Men governed, as ministers, deacons, elders, and vestrymen. But for women, the congregation provided a natural form of association with their sisters. It was here, of course, that the sacraments of the life cycle were performed. It was to the church that women brought their babies to be christened, their sons and daughters to be married, and where they began the funeral processions in which all mourners walked to the burial ground behind the coffin. Funerals were ceremonies in which women, apparently of all classes, wore expensive mourning clothes—long the subject of unsuccessful regulation.

Women attended services—often twice on Sunday—and went to midweek lectures. Women were members of church choirs that flourished in the 1770s under the inspiration of Boston's William Billings, hymnist of the Revolution, a tanner-turned-choir-leader whose vigorous hymns expressed an enthusiastic religion.[36] Women read the Bible at home, sometimes aloud to each other. Women formed informal networks. The letters exchanged between Sarah Prince of Boston and Esther Edwards Burr testify to this. Sarah belonged to a female prayer group, and she humorously called her circle of woman friends a "Freemasons Club." Esther referred frequently to "the Sisterhood" she had known in Boston, a term rich with connotations.[37] And for Boston's poor widows, the churches of all denominations were a source of charity as well as sisterhood.

Women's participation in the churches had been invigorated by the evangelical preaching of the Great Awakening that in Boston began in the 1740s. George Whitfield, foremost among the itinerants, visited Boston not only in the first Great Awakening in 1740, but again in 1745, 1754, 1765, and before his death in 1770. In no major city, Nash observes, "was the awakening experienced as strongly, as enduringly, or as messianically as in Boston."[38] Nor as much by women. Whitfield "generally moved the passions of the younger people, and the Females among them," Rev. Charles Chauncy wrote. In 1745, when Whitfield lectured regularly at 6 a.m. (to reach working people before they began their day), he was overjoyed to see "so many hundreds of both sexes, neatly dressed, walking or riding so early along the streets to get food for their souls."[39] Boston was his favorite American city.

The effects of evangelism on women were striking. More women than men were among the converts, consistent with the pattern established years before. The first wave of enthusiasm had the effect of "encouraging WOMEN, yea GIRLS to speak in the assemblies for religious worship"; "for men, women, children, servants are now become as they phrase it exhorters." Critics also complained of "censoriousness," by which they meant "Husbands [condemning] their Wives, and Wives Their Husbands, Masters their Servants and Servants their Masters."[40]

Whitfield's thirty-year affair with Boston, even after the ministers tamed such enthusiasms, undoubtedly had an equalitarian impact on women. Whitfield preached a salvation open to all without regard to station, race, or gender. He was clearly Boston's most popular cultural hero of the pre-revolutionary era; when he died in 1770 at nearby Newburyport, Boston printers issued at least fourteen commemorative broadsides, more than for any other person in the eighteenth century.[41] The full measure of his impact is yet to be taken.

The revolutionary movement for men and women also drew on traditions of public ritual. In holiday rituals men were the active participants and women the spectators. The Puritans had suppressed the traditional Catholic calendar holidays; the colony's official holidays were "training day," in which the militia paraded and each town celebrated; "election day," at which the members of the legislature were installed in Boston amidst pomp and ceremony; and Harvard commencement at nearby Cambridge, a popular carnival-like festivity reduced to a genteel affair by the 1750s. In the countryside, young women took an equal part in such fall harvest festivals as cornhusking; in the city, there was no holiday in which women participated as more than spectators.[42]

Pope's Day, Boston's "red-letter day" for young people in the laboring classes, was predominantly but not exclusively male. Celebrated in England as Guy Fawkes Day, in Boston, for at least twenty-five years before the Revolution, every November 5 was a raucous ritual of reversal in which apprentices, young journeymen, and poorer artisans took over the town. In the daytime, boys and girls of all ages begged for money from householders, while two male "companies" paraded giant effigies of the Pope, the Devil, and the Pretender on large wagons. In the evening, the two "companies" representing the North End and the South End of town engaged in a bone-breaking battle to destroy the other's effigies. Women were spectators throughout the day and very likely at night, egging on their heroes. The first resistance to England, the Stamp Act riots, drew heavily on the leaders and rituals of the Pope's Day "companies."[43]

Women took a more active and equal part in rituals of public punishment. Boston, capital of the county and province, was at intervals the scene of public hangings of criminals. These followed a ritualized procedure organized by minister and magistrate: broadsides were hawked through the streets with the "True Confessions and Dying Warnings" of the convicted; there was a procession of the criminal to the gallows on Boston neck at the outskirts of town; and at the gallows a sermon was delivered to the victim before concourses that often numbered in the thousands and that included men and women of all ages and conditions, who as often as not pelted or jeered the victim. In 1773, for example, Levi Ames, a young man convicted of murder, on several Sabbaths was "carried through the streets with chains about his ankles and handcuffs ... attended by innumerable companies of boys, women, and men."[44] There are also hints of women in Boston taking part in rough music, known in New England as skimmingtons—community-organized rituals punishing male adulterers. Tar-and-feathering would draw on these rituals of public and private punishment.[45]

Women were also heirs to Boston's rich mob traditions. Boston fits the pattern Eric Hobsbawm found for the "classical" mob of the pre-industrial city that "did not merely riot as a protest but because it expected to achieve something by its riot."[46] In Boston there were grain riots (1709, 1713, 1729, and 1741) directed against merchants who exported corn for profit in time of dearth. There were market riots and actions pulling down buildings for public purposes (1734, 1737, and 1743). At intervals, brothels were pulled down and prostitutes ceremoniously driven out of town. Women, it is safe to say, sanctioned all such riots but so far as we know participated infrequently. In 1747 they very likely took part in the massive Knowles riot, the largest crowd action up to then, in which the "lower orders" held the town for three days to secure the return of men pressed into the navy.[47]

In time of war, there was in Boston, as for time immemorial, a tradition of women as exhorters of men to patriotism and as shamers of soldiers who were cowards. New England's frequent wars against the Indians and the four wars against the French gave full play to this tradition.[48] We see women, for example, in a striking female mob action in Queen Anne's War in 1707, when Boston's soldiers returned from a stunning defeat that inhabitants assumed to be of their own making. A contemporary described the shaming ritual vividly:

> They [the soldiers] landed at Scarlet's wharfe, where they were met by sever-all women, who saluted ym after his manner: 'Welcome, souldiers!' & pre-sented ym a great wooden sword & said with all 'Fie, for shame! pull off those iron spits wch hang by yor sides; for wooden ones is all ye fashion now'. At wchy one of ye officers said, 'Peace, sille woman, etc.' wch irritated ye female tribe so much ye more, yt they cal'd out to one another as they past along the streets, 'Is yor piss-pot charg'd neighbor? Is yor piss-pot charg'd neighbor? So-ho, souse ye cowards. Salute Port-Royal. Holloo, neighbor, holloww'; with a drove of children & servants with wooden swords in their hands, following ym with ye repeated salutations 'Port-Royal! Port-Royal.'[49]

Thus, on the eve of the public resistance to Britain the women of Boston were heirs to some traditions they shared with men in the public sphere: attending evangelistic mass meetings, walking in funeral proces-sions, and shaming criminals in execution rituals. As Bostonians, they were hardly strangers to mob action or to exhorting men in time of war. By custom they had a role as decision makers in the domestic sphere as consumers and household producers. From 1765 to 1775 decisions that were personal and private would become political and public.

III

As one looks anew on the famous events of Boston that have assumed a near epic quality in the memory of the making of the American Revolu-tion—the Stamp Act Riots (1765), the Boston Massacre (1770), the Boston Tea Party (1773), and the Siege of Boston (1775–76)—they are like scenes from an old familiar movie. But if one freezes the frames or, more accurately, if one focuses the camera more sharply and shifts it to unphotographed scenes, it is possible not only to detect women as faces in the crowd, but to see large numbers of them in motion on a scale that has been little appreciated.

The percentage of Loyalists in Boston was the smallest of any in the major seaboard cities, perhaps 10 percent of the total population and 15 percent of the merchants. But patriots were themselves divided. Moderate patriots drew their strength from the merchants; the popular leaders (called by some historians the radicals), who were themselves of the middling sort, opened the doors to groups unqualified to participate in the normal body politic. Or perhaps one should say that the hitherto excluded groups pushed open the doors, inviting themselves into the process. The result was a tug-of-war for control of the resistance.

The male patriot movement in Boston drew from all classes: merchants, doctors, lawyers, and ministers (the "better sort"); artisans and shopkeepers (the "middling sort"); and journeymen, apprentices, sailors, and laborers (the "meaner sort"). There were leaders on each level and distinct, if sometimes shadowy, organizations: the Chamber of Commerce for the merchants; the political caucuses and an ad hoc directing caucus, "The Loyal Nine," at the middling level; and the Pope's Day "companies" at the lower level. Ministers preached from their pulpits, and printers spread the word in newspapers, pamphlets, and broadsides.[50]

As one searches for women in this picture, they can be found from 1765 to 1774 in several distinct (although overlapping) roles: (1) as spectators, (2) as enforcers of consumer boycotts, (3) as manufacturers, (4) as rioters, (5) as mourners in politicized funeral processions and memorial meetings, and (6) as exhorters of men to direct action. Then, in 1775 and 1776, as resistance turned to armed rebellion, women can be found (7) as military supporters and (8) as political refugees. The trend of women's activities is from the genteel to the militant, from small private decisions to large-scale public activities, and from the more moderate to the more radical.

Women as Spectators

In the first wave of resistance to Britain—the Stamp Act protests of 1765–66—all patriot elements united in coordinated activities. Popular resistance was built on the cooperation of the upper- and middle-class leaders with the two Pope's Day "companies," who overcame their rivalry and converted the rituals of Pope's Day to patriotic use. There were seven major actions: a ritual hanging of the effigies of British ministers followed by the destruction of the stamp collector's office (August 14); the gutting of Lieutenant Governor Thomas Hutchinson's house (August 26); two massive military-like parades on the day the Stamp Act was to go into effect (November 1) and on the annual Pope's Day (November 5); a forced public renunciation of his commission by Andrew Oliver, the Stamp Act commissioner-designate (December 1765); and a mock public trial of the Stamp Act (February 1766), followed by a massive community celebration of the act's repeal (May 1766).[51]

Women were a presence at most of these events, primarily as spectators sought by male patriots to demonstrate the solidarity of the community. They observed the hanging and processions of August 14; they did not take part in the physical assault on the Lieutenant Governor's house, which patriot leaders repudiated, but the week before "a great number of inhabitants of both sexes surrounded his honor's dwelling house at the N. end with loud acclamations for Liberty and Property."[52] "Multitudes of Gentlemen and Ladies" joined the celebration of repeal, and at each subsequent anniversary of the resistance of August 14, "the windows of the neighbouring houses" near the Liberty Tree, as a newspaper put it, "were adorned with a brilliant appearance of the fair Daughters of Liberty who testified their Approbation by Smiles of satisfaction."[53]

In attacking the Stamp Act, patriot leaders harped on a theme they would pick up again: the alleged effect of the act on widows. The British law required stamped duties on legal papers as well as on newspapers and all printed matter. In the doggerel verse forecasting the horrors of the act, the bonds and writs "spoke":

> The probate papers next, with many a sigh
> Must we be st——pt?: with tender accent cry:
> We who our life and breath, freely spend,
> The fatherless and widow to defend.[54]

Then in the mock trial the motto on the stamped paper was "For the oppression of the WIDOW and the FATHERLESS."[55] While the intent of such a claim may have been to dramatize the effects of the act for a male audience, its appeal to women, married or widowed, was obvious.

Women as Boycotters

In the second phase of resistance, from 1767 through 1774, women were central to the key patriot tactic: the boycott of imports from Great Britain and the manufacture of American textiles as a substitute.

In Boston the bulk of the merchants signed a nonimportation agreement. Patriot committees policed nonconforming retailers—some of whom were women. For the first time male patriots appealed directly to women not to patronize shopkeepers who violated the agreement: "It is desired that the Sons and Daughters of LIBERTY refuse to buy from William Jackson," read one broadside that was posted prominently throughout the town and also reprinted in the newspapers.[56]

The town government appealed to the citizenry to boycott a long list of British-manufactured goods and to buy the same from Americans. Women as well as men were asked to sign agreements to this effect. Late in 1767 women took action of their own, pledging nonconsumption—the first exclusively female action of the decade. The *Boston News-Letter* reported this as, "in a large circle of very agreeable ladies in this town, it was unanimously agreed" not to use "ribbons & c & c," implying a meeting, discussion, and a resolution.[57] In 1770 tea became a major target. "Philagius" issued a call in the *Boston Evening Post* for "the ladies" to abstain from imported tea. In response to such appeals "upwards of 300 mistresses of Families, in which Number the Ladies of the highest rank and influence that could be waited upon in so short a time are included," signed a petition pledging, "we join with the very respectable body of Merchants and other inhabitants of this town who met in Faneuil Hall ... totally to abstain from the Use of Tea."[58] The *Boston Gazette* reported a second, separate action of "upwards of one hundred ladies at the north part of town"—the artisan center—who "have of their own free will and accord come into and signed an agreement." This "young ladies" agreement began, "We the daughters of those patriots who have and do now appear for the public interest."[59]

In general the boycotts were effective. At the same time it is not surprising that there was opposition from some female shopkeepers, who with small capital and small inventories could hardly ride out a boycott as easily as large-scale wholesale importers. Anne and Betsy Cummings, the shopkeepers set up by Elizabeth Murray, refused to go along and were the only females publicly listed with seven males as "Enemies to their country." "We have never antred into eney agreement," Betsy told the merchant's committee; their business was "verry trifling," and she was furious that they would "try to inger two industrious Girls who ware striving in an honest way to Get there bread." They assured Mrs. Murray that being listed "has not hurt us at all in our Business," because it "Spirits up our Friends to purchas from us" and therefore "we have mor custom then before."[60]

Women as Manufacturers

Using American-made manufactures—the other side of the coin of boycotting British imports—made the cooperation of women as household manufacturers indispensable. A doggerel verse set to a popular tune from *The Beggar's Opera* made an explicit "Address to the Ladies":

> Young ladies in town, and those that live round,
> Let a friend at this season advise you:
> Since money's so scarce, and times growing worse
> Strange things may soon hap and surprize you:
> First then, throw aside your high top knots of pride
> Wear none but your own country linnen;
> Of Oeconomy boast, let your pride be the most
> To show cloaths of your own make and spinning.[61]

By late 1768 in the rural areas, where spinning for household consumption was normal, although not universal, patriots were able to boast, "almost every house in the country is now a manufactory; some towns have more *looms* therein than *houses*."[62] But in the commercial cities, where spinning by women was the exception rather than the rule, spinning would have had to be taught.

Patriots sponsored spinning activities in Boston at two distinct class levels: middle and lower. The activities among the former followed the pattern that Laurel Thatcher Ulrich has found elsewhere. Of the forty-six spinning meetings in New England that she could identify for 1768–70, thirty-one were in the homes of ministers. Usually about fifty women met for the day, reported in the papers as "young ladies," "the fair sex," and occasionally as "The Daughters of Liberty." Each woman sat at a wheel spinning wool. Sometimes there was a sermon; occasionally there were songs. The skeins of wool were then donated to the minister, putting the event in the tradition of charitable work by the women of the congregation. These spinning bees were occasional, not continuous, although there is evidence that the volume of spinning by individual women picked up during these years. In Boston, Ulrich identified six such meetings: one in 1768, five in 1770. Four took place in ministers' homes; two were under lay auspices, one at the home of a known patriot. Perhaps two hundred to three hundred women in all were involved.[63]

For women of the laboring classes, on the other hand, spinning activities were sponsored by the town via a radical patriot entrepreneur, William Molineaux. In late 1767, the town government was seized again with its perennial problem of employment for the poor. A plan to manufacture sail cloth was abortive. Early in 1769, the town proposed to set aside money to hire school mistresses to teach spinning to women and children. Molineaux, the organizer, was a merchant in the Samuel Adams group and one of their two principal crowd leaders. Investing his own money as well as the town's, he had artisans build four hundred spinning wheels, and within a year claimed to have three hundred women and children spinning on a putting-out basis in their own homes. The popular leaders clearly had learned a lesson from the experience of the 1750s: Boston women could not be forced to work for relief within the walls of a manufactory. To finish the textiles, Molineaux organized a "manufacturing house" that included weaving, pressing, and dying operations and that employed skilled male laborers recently arrived from England. The operation survived an effort by the British army to take over the building, and spinning among the poor was sustained through 1775.[64]

Women as Rioters

Boston's crowd actions from 1765 to 1774 were predominantly male events in which women assumed a role in certain kinds of actions.

The history of the crowd in Boston cannot be reduced to a single pattern. In 1765–66, the merchant and middle-class popular leaders worked hand in hand with the artisan leaders of the annual Pope's Day celebrations. But Ebenezer Mackintosh, the shoemaker captain of the South End Pope's Day company who became "Captain General of the Liberty Tree," raised a specter of "Masaniello" to popular as well as conservative patriot leaders. "Masaniello," as Thomas Anielo, the fisherman who led a revolt in Naples in 1647, was known, was the archetype of disorder in revolution. After 1766, the official, Samuel Adams leadership always put forward one of their own, either Dr. Thomas Young, a physician, or Molineaux, the entrepreneur, as a street leader, shunting Mackintosh to the sidelines. Through 1775, they were as much concerned with controlling the mob as in protesting British measures. "No violence or you will hurt the cause" was literally their motto.[65]

After 1766, crowd actions in Boston were of three types. One type was sponsored by the popular leaders, whose targets usually were retailers in violation of the nonimportation agreements and later the tea merchants. Second, there were spontaneous actions, led from within, that were composed overwhelmingly of men from the laboring classes, such as the riot against the combined seizure of John Hancock's ship, *Liberty*, and the threat of naval impressment in 1768. It was especially characteristic of the tar-and-feathering mobs who punished customs informers. Third, there were crowd actions that got out of hand, beginning one way and ending another, with unplanned violence and large-scale participation, like the Lillie-Richardson affair and the Boston Massacre, both early in 1770.

Women were not invited to take part in crowd actions sponsored by the self-appointed male popular leaders. They were more likely to appear at a spontaneous event like a tar and feathering or at an unauthorized event. Early in 1768, for example, one such action was directed at the customs commissioners. Effigies hung in the Liberty Tree were cut down by members of the "Loyal Nine," the Samuel Adams group. In the evening, nonetheless, eight hundred people paraded through the town to the house of a commissioner, "Drums beating and colours flying." Adams, whose political interest dictated disassociation, dismissed the crowd as "a few disorderly persons, mostly boys," but Governor Francis Bernard, whose self-interest dictated accuracy, reported the event to London as "the assembling of a great number of people of all kinds sexes and ages, many of which showed a great disposition to the utmost disorder."[66]

After mid-1768, the presence of soldiers in Boston politicized many women as well as men. To enforce their unpopular customs laws, the British stationed at the height four thousand troops, which, even when reduced by half, meant a lot of soldiers for a town of fifteen thousand. They were a daily source of abrasive incidents. Patriot leaders exploited every incident in their zeal to oust the "standing army"; yet it is likely from the allegations of some twenty-one cases of rape and assault that women had their own gender-based grievances against the soldiers.[67] Women of the "better sort" at first took part in dancing assemblies with the officers, but later they withdrew. Among artisans, a special grievance was the practice of soldiers moonlighting, depriving them of jobs in hard times. The catalyst of the massacre in March 1770 was a fight in a ropewalk where an off-duty soldier sought work, and a brawl ensued in which soldiers were defeated by the workers and vowed vengeance. Seven women later gave depositions about violent threats they heard from soldiers in the days before the shooting. Some women responded in kind. When the wife of a British officer told Susanne Cathcart that "many of their arses would be laid low before morning," she retorted, "I hope your husband will be killed."[68]

On the night of the massacre, when apprentices precipitated the calling of a squad of soldiers by taunting a sentry, a few women were present in the small crowd confronting the soldiers, one widow, we know, trying to get her son from harm's way. After the soldiers fired pellmell into the unarmed crowd, killing five and wounding six others, several thousand men and women poured out of their homes into the square. A second disaster was narrowly averted when patriot leaders, rushing to an event they had not planned, negotiated successfully for the withdrawal of the troops.

Women as Mourners

Women played a major role in the massive rituals of community mourning for the victims of the British. In February 1770, two weeks before the massacre, there was another chilling event in which a customs official killed an eleven-year-old boy, Christopher Seider. The occasion was the peaceful picketing of the shop of T. Lillie, an importer, by a group of about 150 "boys" organized by the popular leaders. "Boys" was a term that could apply either to children or to sturdy apprentices, aged fourteen to twenty-one; in this case, it meant school-age, pre-teenage boys, which suggests they had the approval of their mothers or fathers. The picketing was uneventful until the appearance of Ebenezer Richardson, an employee of the customs service with an odious reputation as an informer. Richardson tried to break up the crowd, then retreated to the second floor of his house next door and fired wildly into the crowd below, killing Seider. The funeral for the martyr was "the largest perhaps ever known in America." Beginning at the liberty tree, from four hundred to five hundred "lads and children" marched in front of the coffin carried by six boys; two thousand men and women followed on foot, followed by the "better sort" in thirty carriages. "My eyes never beheld such a funeral," wrote John Adams.[69]

After the massacre, less than three weeks later, the funeral for the victims of the soldiers—four young single men of the laboring classes and one Crispus Attucks, an older black sailor—outdid this. "Such a concourse of people I never saw Before," a merchant recorded in his diary, "I believe ten or twelve thousand." Church bells tolled, ships flew their flags at half-mast, shops closed, and virtually the entire town—women included—marched six abreast. "The distress and sorrow visible in every countenance ... the peculiar solemnity ... surpass description."[70]

In the contemporary patriot iconography of both events, women were central figures. Paul Revere's engraving of the massacre placed a woman in black widow's weeds in the center of the crowd of hapless civilian victims of the soldiers, their red blood streaming across the cobble stones.[71] Isaiah Thomas's broadside on the Seider killing featured a crude, dramatic engraving with a distraught woman in the center of the street scene: in her arm, a pitchfork; at her feet, a dead boy, presumably her son; around her, a dozen wide-eyed boys; in the background, a smoking gun protruding from an upstairs window.[72]

Every year thereafter from 1771 until 1775 women attended the anniversary commemoration of the massacre, at which five thousand or so people jammed the town's largest meetinghouse, Old South, to hear a doleful oration on the baneful effects of standing armies. In 1773, John Adams reported, "that large church was filled and crowded in every pew, Seat, Alley and Gallery by an audience of several thousands of people of all ages and Characters and of both sexes." In 1775, when British officers mocked the annual speaker with cries of "Fie, Fie," which some heard as "fire," there was a near-panic as "women jumped out of the windows."[73]

The killings of Seider and the massacre victims probably did more to mobilize women in Boston than any other event of the decade.

Women as Exhorters

In Boston's climactic mass action of the era, the Tea Party in December 1773, women assumed a new role. They did not attend the mass meetings of "the body of the people," the largest of the decade. Nor were they among the crews that boarded the three ships to destroy the chests of tea. Women very likely were among the large assembly of silent observers on the docks who watched the dramatic events in solemn silence in the moonlight.

More important, if one follows the public debate over the tea issue in the newspapers, there are suggestions that women were playing another role, seemingly for the first time: as exhorters of men to action. The vehicle was letters to the *Massachusetts Spy*, Isaiah Thomas's patriot paper catering to a mechanic audience. "Hannah Hopeful, Sarah Faithful, Mary Truth and Abigail Trust" signed a short letter that they began with "We the daughters of liberty." They thanked the "prerogative men" for arousing resentment in "our fathers, husbands, brothers and children."[74] The *Spy* also ran a short poem from "an aged and very zealous Daughter of Liberty, Mrs. M——s," identified as "a taylor by trade":

> Look out poor Boston make a stand
> Dont suffer any tea to land
> For if on it once gets footing here
> Then farewell Liberty most dear.[75]

A Boston seamstress also took her side with "the libe[r]ty boys" against "the tyranny [that] rides in our harbour and insults us in our fields and streets."[76]

IV

After the Tea Party, the popular leaders showed the importance they attached to women by their persistent, conscious efforts to mobilize them. Nowhere was this more apparent than in the spring of 1774 in the climactic political contest of the era in Boston—the contest between popular leaders and moderates for control of the Revolution.

In the wake of the radical destruction of property in the Tea Party and the punitive British response, there was a conservative backlash among merchants, including many who earlier were part of the patriot coalition. To outflank the conservatives, the popular leaders turned to "those worthy members of society," the "tradesmen," that is, the artisans, and the "yeomanry."[77] At the same time they also turned consciously to women.

Their tactic—working through the Boston Committee of Correspondence, an extralegal body—was to mobilize the country towns to adopt a boycott of British imports, presenting Boston's reluctant merchants with a fait accompli. They secretly distributed a petition, called the Solemn League and Covenant, to the towns with a specific request that it was "to be subscribed by all adult persons of both sexes."[78] The action was radical, not only in recognizing women as members of the political community. The initiating body was extralegal, not the official town meeting. It pledged the subscribers not only to boycott British imports, but to refuse to do business with anyone who did not sign the Covenant and to "publish their names to the world"—in effect, a secondary boycott and a ritual of shunning. Finally, in harking back to the English Solemn League and Covenant of 1643, patriots were donning the revolutionary mantle of their Cromwellian forebears.

Women responded. The Covenant, one Boston merchant reported, "went through whole towns with great avidity, every adult of both sexes putting their name to it, saving a few." Another heard that in some towns the clergy put the document on the communion table, telling congregants that "they who refused to sign were not worthy to come to that table." In Worcester, in the western part of the state, which was rapidly becoming more radical than the seaboard, a self-created American Political Society circulated a separate covenant "for all the women of adult age ... to sign."[79] How widely the Covenant circulated is not clear; General Thomas Gage, assuming powers as governor, immediately declared it illegal. A few signed documents that have survived show some signatures of women next to their kin and others without the names of male kin—fairly clear evidence of a separate political will.[80]

V

From the spring of 1774, when Boston became a British garrison town and an occupied city, through the outbreak of hostilities in the spring of 1775, until March 1776, when Boston became a city under siege by the patriots, women gave further testimony to their patriot allegiances. They assumed the roles first of military providers and then of refugees.

Women as Military Supporters

In response to the defiance of the Tea Act and the refusal to make restitution, the British closed the port of Boston, moved in a large occupying army, and replaced the crumbling British political establishment with military rule. If the aim of the Port Act was to turn the population against their leaders, it was a failure. Women suffered, as did the poor as a whole.[81] With the port closed, most work at a standstill, and even the flow of food interdicted, the town depended on donations that soon poured in from surrounding villages and distant cities. The official town Committee on Donations chose work relief rather than outright grants to the destitute, putting men to work making bricks and repairing roads and distributing wool, flax, and cotton "to the spinners and knitters of the town," that is, to women. The program was set up, Samuel Adams conceded, "to keep the poor from murmuring." As another put it, "some few among them mumble that they are obliged to work hard for that which they esteem as their right without work."[82] Even in the midst of crisis, destitute women and men attempted to maintain their traditional moral economy of relief as a right.

As tension with the British soldiers mounted in Boston and the countryside, women assumed a bellicose stance. In the fall of 1774, at a false alarm of a British attack on the militia at nearby Cambridge, women, according to one observer, "surpassed the Men for Eagerness & Spirit in the Defence of Liberty by Arms." In March 1775, when British troops attempted to cross over the river from Boston to the mainland in search of hidden arms, "large crowds of men, women & children assembled on both sides, some armed with guns" to prevent them from passing.[83]

In fact, as a Loyalist observed the scene near Boston, he was convinced that "a certain epidemical phrenzy runs through our fair country women which outdoes all the pretended patriotic virtue of the more robustic males:—these little mischief making devils have entered into an almost unanimous association that any man who shall basely and cowardly give up the public cause of freedom, shall from that moment on be discarded [from] their assemblies, and no further contrition shall be able to atone for the crime."[84] If in 1765 men had mobilized women, then by 1775 women were mobilizing men.

Women as Refugees

After April 1775, when war finally broke out at nearby Lexington, until the British army left in March 1776, Boston was a city under siege by the patriot militia and army. Patriots deserted the city and Loyalists stayed, joined by other Loyalists flocking in for British protection. During the siege, Boston's civilian population of about 15,000 fell to 3,500, at least two-thirds of whom it is estimated were Loyalists. Thus, easily 12,000–13,000 Bostonians fled their city, inundating the towns of eastern Massachusetts as refugees.[85]

Women, we know, left en masse. To stay in Boston or to move into Boston clearly was a political choice indicating Loyalism, save for a small number of merchants who stayed to guard their property. To leave, it could be argued, was less a political decision than an act of self-preservation. To stay meant risking life and limb in the event of a patriot attack and, at the least, the prospect of extreme privation, if not starvation. That so many men and women left Boston for dangers unknown, especially poor women without families to turn to or resources to fall back on, should be taken as a testimony to their political convictions. These departures did not happen on the same scale when the British occupied New York City and Philadelphia.

The Quakers who came up from Philadelphia to distribute relief to these destitute refugees have left us a Domesday Book of the poor women of Boston. For each recipient, the Quaker keepers of the books methodically listed the name of the head of family and others in the family, the city of origin, church denomination, and, about half the time, the occupation. They did not calculate the number in each category, nor did they always make clear where the refugee was from; but they put the total number of widows at eight hundred. Widows with occupations were a minority, and a Quaker wrote revealingly, "Those women who have no Occupations Usually got their Living by their Hand Labour of various kinds, now obstructed & stopt by the present troubles & c." Most of the single women, on the other hand, seem to have been listed with occupations. Women in trades were in the needle trades only (seamstress, tailoress, mantua maker, weaver), and the largest single listing was spinster (which, in this context, meant an occupation, not single status). Only a few were retailers (shopkeeper, huckster, innkeeper); a large number were in nurturing professions (schoolmistress, nurse). All in all, women refugees clearly were predominantly of the laboring classes.[86] The same could not be said of women Loyalists who later left the city with the British; they were distributed more evenly among the middling and upper classes.[87]

VI

Patriot women thus played many roles. What was their importance? It is always difficult to analyze the relative weight of one group among many in popular movements. Clearly the resistance movement shaped events in Boston, and clearly women were an important part of the configuration. At times they were mobilized by males; at times they mobilized themselves; sometimes they helped mobilize males. Unmistakably, they broadened the base of support of the popular leaders; arguably they helped push resistance in a more radical direction.

The male contemporary who has left the fullest account of the impact of the women of Boston was the Loyalist Peter Oliver. It is not surprising;

he was also the most sensitive and hostile recorder of the popular movement as a whole. His manuscript, *The Origin and Progress of the American Rebellion*, completed in 1781 and unpublished until 1961, is the fullest account of events in Boston by any contemporary. Peter Oliver—Chief Justice of the colony's Superior Court; brother of Andrew Oliver, the Stamp Act Commissioner; and brother-in-law to Lieutenant Governor Thomas Hutchinson, all major targets of patriot wrath—clearly was not an impartial witness. He dipped his pen in bile. His understanding of the reasons for popular participation was, to say the least, limited by his class bias: "the People," he wrote, "in general they were like the Mobility of all Countries, perfect Machines, wound up by any Hand who might first take the Winch."[88] He was a haughty, frightened, and misogynist Tory. But he was a close observer of events in the city, and when he arrived as a refugee in England, he set down his recollections while they were still fresh.

As he narrated events chronologically, Oliver took account of the activities of women in Boston with regularity and contempt. He was amused at women from the laboring classes taking part in the boycott. "A Subscription Paper was handed about," he wrote, listing among the articles they would not purchase, "Silks, Velvets, Clocks, Watches, Coaches & Chariots." It was "highly diverting to see the names & marks, to the Subscription of Porters & Washing Women."[89] He also poked malicious fun at women who attempted to reduce English imports by forgoing the "custom of wearing expensive mourning at Funerals." "A Funeral now seemed more like a Procession to a *MayFair*, and Processions were lengthened especially by the Ladies, who figured a way, in order to exhibit their Share of Spite, & their Silk Gowns."[90] Oliver also branded the women's boycott of tea as hypocritical:

> The ladies too were so zealous for the Good of their Country, that they agreed to drink no Tea, except the Stock of it which they had by them; or in Case of Sickness. Indeed they were cautious enough to lay in large Stocks before they promised; & they could be sick just as it suited their Convenience or Inclination.[91]

Of all women's activities, spinning drew the lengthiest and most caustic description from Oliver, suggesting the importance it had for women. As he often did, he saw the Congregational clergy as the instigators:

> Mr. [James] Otis's black Regiment, the dissenting Clergy were also set to Work to preach up Manufactures instead of Gospel. They preached about it & about it, untill the Women & Children, both within Doors & without, set their Spinning Wheels a whirling in Defiance of Great Britain. The female

spinners kept on spinning for 6 Days of the Week; & on the seventh, the
Parsons took their Turns, & spun out their Prayers & Sermons to a long
Thread of Politicks; & to much better Profit than the other Spinners; for
they generally cloathed the Parson and his Family with the Produce of their
Labor: This was a new Species of Enthusiasm & might be justly termed, the
Enthusiasm of the Spinning Wheel.[92]

Of all activities by women, joining in tar-and-feathering crowds shocked
Oliver the most.

In the year 1772, they [the male patriots] continued their laudible Custom of
Tar & Feathers; even the fair Sex threw off their delicacy, and adopted this
new fashion ... one of those Ladys of Fashion was so complaisant; as to throw
her Pillows out of Window, as the mob passed by with their Criminal, in
order to help forwards the diversion.

This prompted him to his most blatant assertion of patriarchal values:
"When a Woman throws aside her Modesty, Virtue drops a tear."[93]

As Oliver reviewed these years of upheaval in Boston, his account was
dominated by his sense of outrage at the insubordination of all those
orders who had stepped out of the sphere that hierarchy and patriarchy
assigned them. That the activities of women registered on him so strongly
is ample evidence of their importance.

VII

The evidence, biased and fragmentary as it is, is adequate to establish this
broad panorama of what women did in Boston from 1765 to 1776. It is far
more scarce when we try to probe the last of the questions we have posed:
was there any change in the way women thought?

A long letter to the *Boston Gazette* under three female pseudonyms,
"Aspatia," "Belinda," and "Corinna," suggests the way in which as early as
1767 participation in patriotic activities contributed to an assertion of
female pride. The occasion was a number of letters to the paper by men
who lectured women in a patronizing tone as to precisely what they
should be doing for the cause. "Squibo" proposed that instead of drinking
tea, they drink only rum and support New England's most important
manufactured product. "Henry Flynt" hectored women "to lay aside all
superfluous ornaments for a season" and then buy a new set of American-
made clothes. Worst of all, "A Young American" in a supercilious way

asked women to "Scorn such trifling subjects as Dress, Scandal, and Detraction," stereotyping all women for such conversations.[94]

The tone of the women's reply—which the printers of the patriot *Gazette* considered important enough to publish as a supplement—combined anger, indignation, and pride. Their assumption in their opening words was that "the ladies of America" had "been divers times addressed as persons of consequence in the present oeconomical regulations." They felt "scandalously insulted" by the proposal of "Squibo" that they drink rum; they would replace Bohea and Tyson teas with what they saw fit, and the herbal teas from Labrador or their own gardens would be their choice. Their reaction to the advice of "Henry Flynt" as to what to wear was similar: "We will judge." It might be "practicable or prudent to wear out our old clothes as long as by good housekeeping we can make them look decent," and "when they are worn out," then they would replace them with "the produce of our American manufactories." As to "A Young American," he was beneath contempt because he "groundlessly insinuates" "characteristics of the sex." They concluded as they began, with an assertion of pride in "the ladies of Boston who for modesty of apparel, purity and delicacy of manners, improvement of mind and virtuous characters, are excelled by none."

The only surviving diary by a female from this period gives clues to the process of politicization. Anna Green Winslow was a girl of twelve and thirteen when she kept a diary from late November 1771 through May 1773.[95] Fortunately for us, she was a perfect mirror of a middle-class female youth in Boston, and fortunately she wrote at a point when the resistance movement among men and women was in full flower.

Anna was the daughter of an American-born British army officer stationed in Halifax and a mother from an old Massachusetts family, who sent her to Boston to live with Sarah and John Deming, her aunt and uncle, to acquire an education. The Demings were middle-class patriots. He was a deacon at Old South, a leading Congregational church; she kept a school for girls. Anna's diary took the form of letters dutifully sent to her parents. She went to several private schools (a reading school, writing school, and sewing school); she read novels (*Pilgrim's Progress* and *Gulliver's Travels* among them). She attended Old South meetinghouse, dutifully taking down sermons, and she read the Bible aloud to her aunt every day. She delighted in genteel assemblies at which she danced "cleverly"; she mastered the art of embroidery and apologized to her mother for her extravagance in clothes.

A sponge of middle-class culture, she absorbed its politics as well. Her family instructed her. Colonel Gridley, a relative, "brought in the talk of Whigs & Tories & taught me the difference between them." Her Uncle John explained the nuances of religion and politics. The Revs. Pemberton and Cooper, she reported, "had on gowns In the form of the Episcopal cassock we hear," and this "at a time when the good people of N[ew] E[ngland] are threatened with & dreading the comeing of an episcopal bishop.... Unkle says, they all have popes in their bellys."[96]

The spinning movement, her diary makes clear, politicized her. On February 8, 1772, at her aunt's suggestion, she resolved "to perfect myself in learning to spin flax. I am pleased with the proposal & am at this present, exerting myself for this purpose." She hoped "when two, or at most three months are past" to give a demonstration of "my proficiency in *this art.*" Ten days later she recorded, "Another ten knot skane of my yarn was reel'd off today."[97] And in March, after two weeks of spinning, she defined herself politically for the first time: "As I am (as we say) a daughter of liberty I chuse to wear as much of our own manufactory as pocible." At the end of May, when she visited "the factory" set up by Molineaux "to see a peace of cloth cousin Sally spun for a summer suit for unkle," she clearly was aware of the political implications of the site. "After viewing the work we recollected the room we sat down in was Liberty Assembly Hall, otherwise called factory hall, so Miss Gridley & I did ourselves the Honour of dancing a minuet in it."[98]

If Anna Winslow was typical, we may say that by 1772 middle-class females in Boston had a sense of female patriotism. If we turn to the writings of the most publicly articulate Massachusetts woman of the prewar period, Mercy Otis Warren, we can analyze its parameters.

Mrs. Warren's model was Catherine Macaulay, the English historian hailed by patriots for her multivolume account of the struggle for liberty in seventeenth-century England. Boston's Sons of Liberty toasted Mrs. Macaulay at their dinners; a Boston printer printed her engraving in his almanac; and patriots permitted her book into Boston when English books were under the nonimportation ban. Mrs. Macaulay was a republican, but in her historical writings women were absent and she never wrote as an advocate of women. Mrs. Warren and Abigail Adams corresponded with her and admired her.[99]

Mercy Otis Warren lived in Plymouth but moved in a circle of Boston's leaders and published in Boston. She could hardly have been from a more prominent patriot family: her brother, James Otis, one of the province's leading lawyers, was a stellar if erratic figure in the patriot movement; her husband, James Warren, was a leader in Plymouth County as well as the colonial legislature. Her house was always abuzz with politics, and she corresponded with male patriot leaders such as John Adams.[100] From 1772 through 1775 she wrote poems and verse plays that appeared serially in the Boston papers and then in pamphlet form. "Dramatic sketches," as she called them, written in a florid neoclassical style, were meant to be read rather than performed. In *The Adulateur* (1772), the arch-villain was Thomas Hutchinson, satirized as Rapatio, ruler of the mythical country of Servia, who was trying to crush the "ardent love of liberty in Servia's freeborn sons." Hutchinson's brother and his relatives Andrew and Peter Oliver were co-conspirators; "Brutus" and "Cassius," the heroes, could be taken for James Otis and John Adams. In *The Defeat* (1773), she continued to flay Hutchinson as a satanic creature. In *The Group* (1775), her targets were the Massachusetts men who accepted royal appointment to the military governor's council, acerbically portrayed as sycophants and "hungry harpies."[101]

Mrs. Warren's plays and poems appeared anonymously, and she was known and admired as the author only in inner circles of patriot men and women. In these prewar plays she offered no female characters. Her poems, on the other hand, introduced allegorical women and spoke to women. In one lengthy poem she chided middle-class women to lay aside imported "female ornaments" to support the boycott. She contrasted "Clarissa" and "Lamira" to the "Cornelias and Arrias fair," who joined the cause. She celebrated the Tea Party in a poem in which Neptune's wives "Amphytrite" and "Salacia" debated the issue. Another poem of 1775 was a clarion to patriotism, female as well as male.[102]

Privately, Mercy Otis Warren was at the center of a network of female correspondents, wives of political leaders—Hannah Lincoln, Hannah Winthrop, and Abigail Adams foremost among them—whom she encouraged to express their opinions. But she did not go beyond encouraging women to patriotism. After the war, in her plays of the 1780s, women appeared for the first time as central characters, as heroines in the struggle for freedom in other times and countries. And one woman scolds men for preferring in women "the fading short lived perishable trifling beauty" to their "noble exalted mental accomplishments."[103] But not until 1790 did she publish her plays and collected poems under her own name. And when she completed her three-volume history of the American Revolution in 1805, she had hardly a word to say about women. She defined female patriotism, one might say, as selfless.[104]

VIII

Our exploration over, it is now possible to return to the questions that framed it: what led Abigail Adams to raise the question of women's inequality, and what made it possible in the spring of 1776 for her to entertain the thought of "fomenting a Rebellion"? Were there other women who would have responded to her? My answer is yes, but in later years. By probing the combination of experiences that brought Abigail Adams to voice her "List of Female Grievances"—by examining her at the historic moment of the spring of 1776—we can gain insight into a process that would bring other women to do likewise.

What, we might ask first, were her "female grievances," and what did she intend by "the new Code of Laws"? She wanted to curb "unlimited powers" in "the hands of husbands." Her enemy was William Blackstone's *Commentaries on the Laws of England*, which codified the English common law under which a husband "controlled his wife's property, directing her labor and provided for her subsistence."[105] What prompted Abigail Adams to raise this particular aspect of women's unequal status? No one else seems to have raised the issue in public in Massachusetts in this decade. Probably, it was something she had already discussed privately with her lawyer husband, and that is why she did not have to spell out the reforms. (She often signed her letters to him "Portia." Was she assuming the persona of the woman lawyer in *The Merchant of Venice*?) Possibly she had thumbed through Blackstone's book or other law books in John's study, identifying the odious laws—as a young Elizabeth Cady Stanton would do in her father's law office a few decades later, so infuriated she wanted to cut out the offending passages from the books.[106]

What Abigail was doing was to make a leap from the Whig political language her husband had expressed so eloquently since 1765 and apply it to women's condition. His rhetoric was of "tyranny" and "slavery" and especially of the danger of New England's yeomen becoming "vassals" to "lords." She leaped from the relation of subjects and rulers to wives and husbands. There should be "no unlimited power" in husbands. "Your sex are naturally tyrannical"; women should not be "vassals of your sex" was her language.[107]

But why did she make the leap at this particular moment? First, she had a strong sense of the contributions of women to the patriot cause, and especially of her own contributions. She had not only supported her husband in all of his political activities but she had also become a "politician"—her word. She referred to Elizabeth Adams, Samuel's wife, as a "sister delegate" to the Philadelphia convention and asked John, "Why should we not assume your titles when we give you up our names?"[108] She had seen other women express themselves in public, Mercy Otis Warren foremost among them. And she had witnessed the suffering of the "distressed women" of Boston and since 1775 had done her best to succor the patriot refugees swarming through Braintree.

Second, she had a growing sense of empowerment as a result of the responsibilities she had assumed in her household in the eighteen months her husband had been away. John had been in Philadelphia since September 1774, returning only for short intervals. She had managed the farm business, which meant the tenants and laborers. "I shall be quite a farmeriss in another year," she ended a recital of her accomplishments in farm management. Before long she would be writing of "our" farm.[109]

Third, she had become keenly aware of the limitations, including her own, of the education of women. In John's absence she also took on the burden of being "school mistress" to their four children, all under the age of ten. Educated by her own father beyond the level of most women, and confronted by John's ceaseless admonitions as to how she should instruct the children, she still felt inadequate to the task. She took up the issue with John with unmasked belligerence:

> If you complain of neglect of Education in sons, what shall I say with regard to daughters who every day experience the want of it. With regard to the Education of my own children, I find myself soon out of my debth and destitute and deficient in every part of Education.
>
> I most sincerely wish that some more liberal plan might be laid down for the Benefit of the rising Generation, and that our new constitution may be distinguished for Learning and Virtue, if we mean to have Heroes, Statesmen and Philosophers, we should have learned women.[110]

It was an issue on which John could readily agree and that they would both return to, forging the accommodation Linda Kerber has named "Republican Motherhood."[111]

Fourth, the spring of 1776 was an extraordinary moment of radicalism in the American Revolution. Like tens of thousands of others, Abigail Adams and the women in her circle had read Thomas Paine's pamphlet *Common Sense*, she in late February. In arguing for independence and a Republican government, Paine shattered the bonds of deference to more than monarchy, breathed a sense of equality and a confidence in the capacity of ordinary people to shape their future, and ended with the millennialist appeal, "we have it in our power to begin the world over again.... The Birthday of a new world is at hand."[112] John Adams was not joking in his letter to Abigail when he listed the subordinate, dependent classes who were casting off deference to their betters. John was wary but Abigail was sympathetic to others making the leap from political liberty to personal liberty, most close at hand the slaves of Massachusetts who had petitioned the legislature for their freedom each year since 1773.[113]

Finally, it was also a moment that inspired optimism. The British army had evacuated Boston on March 17, the largest fleet ever assembled in America, seventy to one hundred vessels, sailing away with troops defeated by the strategic maneuvers of the upstart American army. Boston, the siege of a year lifted, was in "a better state than we expected"; the immediate military threat was over. Abigail wrote on March 31 in her since famous letter, "I feel very differently at the approach of spring to what I did a month ago. I feel a gaiety de Coar [i.e., a lightness of heart] to which I was a stranger. I think the Sun looks brighter, the Birds sing more melodiously and nature puts on a more chearfull countenance." And from these words, she launched her "by the way ... Remember the Ladies." It was hardly "by the way"—assertions of rights bloomed in a time of possibilities.

Other women, I would argue, would have to undergo some combination of Abigail Adams's experiences to bring them to the point where they were willing to raise female grievances either privately or publicly: the experience of participating in the making of the Revolution, the experience of war, a sense of personal empowerment in assuming male roles, a sense of exhilaration from the challenge to traditional authority, a sense of optimism as to the future.

In 1776, for most of the women returning to Boston, it was spring but not yet springtime. Women were straggling back by cart, on horse, and on foot, trying to reconstruct their lives from the chaos of war; many others would never return but attempt a new life elsewhere. Survival took priority. Boston would soon be smitten by a smallpox epidemic and then be overwhelmed with shortages and runaway inflation. Men were going off to war, and women had to cope with making a living. In Massachusetts, framing a state constitution was put off until 1777. The war took priority. Wartime was hardly the time to raise the issue of "repealing masculine systems."

Were there other women, prepared by their experiences as female patriots from 1765 to 1776, who were ready to make the same leap that Abigail had made in asking to "Remember the Ladies" in writing a new code of laws? I think so. It is possible, of course, to argue that almost everything

women had done in Boston in the decade gone by was in keeping with traditions of behavior long acceptable to a patriarchal society, that women in
all of these roles had never left the domestic sphere and therefore would
not have thought of themselves any differently.

Spinning was a traditional female domain, however atrophied in the
cities. For churchgoing women to attend spinning bees and donate the
yarn to their ministers was in the Congregational tradition. For women on
poor relief to spin in the 1770s was to return to a method of work relief
attempted in Boston in the 1750s. Decisions over consumption lay within
women's sphere. The nonconsumption of luxury goods was a theme of
Puritan ministers as old as the colony, and the campaign to curb extravagant displays in funerals predated the anti-British campaign by decades,
albeit unsuccessfully. Women had always walked in funeral processions,
and broadsides mourning children and youth cut down by death were the
prototype of the Seider and Boston Massacre broadsides. For women to
attend memorial services was equally time-honored. Large religious gath-
erings in which men, women, and youth jammed the churches to hear
Whitfield preach were a feature of his five visits to Boston from 1740 to
1770; indeed, the annual Boston Massacre commemorations were resonant
of such meetings. As to women exhorting their men to battle, this was
their experience in the many wars New England fought against the Indians
and the French.

Yet it is equally arguable that much in this decade was a departure from
tradition in women's activities. It was new for women to be asked to come
forward as a patriotic duty. It was certainly new for women to be recognized as equals in a public cause—the unmistakable implication of the
phrase "Daughters of Liberty" paralleling "Sons of Liberty." It was new for
women alone to come together to sign secular agreements to boycott
imports. It was not unusual for men and women to sign church covenants,
but it was to ask adults of both sexes to sign the Solemn League and
Covenant in 1774, an overtly political pledge cloaked in the language of the
seventeenth-century Puritan revolution. Taken together, the totality of
these experiences over a decade was new. And women who expressed their
opinions on politics, whether in private in conversation or a letter, or in
public in print or at a meeting or demonstration, were marking off new
territory.

By the early 1770s, women who had taken part in such activities—who
by 1775 would have been the overwhelming majority of the women of the
city—developed a consciousness of themselves as female patriots. How a

more explicitly feminist consciousness evolved is beyond the scope of this essay. The postwar decade, from 1784 on, would be the point at which a full investigation would be rewarding. For it is impossible to scan the newspapers, magazines, and printed matter that appeared in Boston after the war without feeling that a dam had burst and that there was an outpouring of public writing by and about women. What Abigail Adams had taken up from 1776 on only in the privacy of her letters to her husband was now a matter of public discourse.

If one thumbs through the *Massachusetts Centinel*, for example, there were articles on "Conjugal Love" and "The Causes of Unhappiness in Marriage" resonant of Abigail Adams's concerns with the domestic tyranny of husbands.[114] Education for girls was the subject of a major debate, in which women took part, that began in 1785 and led to the opening of the public schools to girls in 1789.[115] And in 1784 Judith Sargent Murray published "On the Inequality of the Sexes," the first of a series of newspaper essays, which when assembled in three volumes in 1798 constituted the first American body of feminist theory.[116]

Just as a diary of a schoolgirl suggested the process of change in the 1770s, the oration of a schoolgirl in 1791, very likely one of the first female graduates of the public schools, suggests the process at work after the Revolution. "With children of both sexes" acquiring an education, she had a sense of a new age dawning in which "the mists of superstition and bigotry are vanishing." Pointing to the achievements of women in Europe, she then proclaimed that "here on our own western shore we can justly boast of a WARREN, a MORTON, and ADAMS whose talents and virtues ornament their sex and excite emulation." And "may we not indulge in honest pride that this metropolis has been one of the foremost in exertions to promote female improvement."[117] She had a perception that we are still exploring the ways in which "female patriotism" opened a path to "female improvement."

NOTES

This essay was prepared for a conference, "Gender and Political Culture in the Age of the Democratic Revolution" (Bellagio, Italy, 1985) and appeared in Harriet B. Applewhite and Darline G. Levy, eds., *Women and Politics in the Age of the Democratic Revolution* (Ann Arbor: University of Michigan Press, 1990). Reprinted by permission of the University of Michigan Press.

I would like to express my appreciation to the members of the conference for their comment, to Linda Kerber for her insightful criticism, to Darline Levy and

Harriet Applewhite for their wise editorial counsel, and to Laurel Thatcher Ulrich, Lucy Eldersveld Murphy, Patricia Cleary, and Elizabeth Reilly, who shared their own scholarship in progress.

1. Abigail Adams to John Adams, March 31, 1776, *Adams Family Correspondence*, ed. L. H. Butterfield (Cambridge, Mass.: Harvard University Press, 1963), 1:369–71.

2. John Adams to Abigail Adams, April 17, 1776, ibid., 381–83.

3. Abigail Adams to Mercy Otis Warren, April 27, 1776, ibid., 396–98.

4. Abigail Adams to John Adams, May 7, 1776, ibid., 401–3.

5. For the pathbreaking institutional analysis, Joan Hoff Wilson, "The Illusion of Change: Women and the American Revolution," in *The American Revolution: Explorations in the History of American Radicalism*, ed. Alfred F. Young (DeKalb, Ill.: Northern Illinois University Press, 1976), 383–445; for the fullest exploration of women's activities and consciousness, Mary Beth Norton, *Liberty's Daughters: The Revolutionary Experience of American Women, 1750–1800* (Boston: Little, Brown and Co., 1980), and Linda K. Kerber, *Women of the Republic: Intellect and Ideology in Revolutionary America* (Chapel Hill: University of North Carolina Press, 1980).

6. This essay is based on evidence assembled for a forthcoming book, "In the Streets of Boston: The Common People in the Making of the American Revolution, 1745–1789." Some of the themes of this book are suggested in Alfred Young, "George Robert Twelves Hewes (1742–1840): A Boston Shoemaker and the Memory of the American Revolution," *William and Mary Quarterly*, 3d ser., 38 (October 1981): 561–623, and in essays 3 and 8 in this volume.

7. Charles Akers, *Abigail Adams: An American Woman* (Boston: Little, Brown and Co., 1980), is by the biographer most adept in the history of Boston during the Revolution. I have relied on Butterfield, ed., *Adams Family Correspondence*, vol. 1, and Butterfield, Marc Friedlander, and Mary Jo Kline, eds., *The Book of Abigail and John: Selected Letters of the Adams Family, 1762–1784* (Cambridge, Mass.: Harvard University Press, 1975).

8. Gary Nash, *The Urban Crucible: Social Change, Political Consciousness, and the Origin of the American Revolution* (Cambridge, Mass.: Harvard University Press, 1979), chaps. 7, 9, 11, and the appendix; Nash, "Urban Wealth and Poverty in Pre-Revolutionary America," *Journal of Interdisciplinary History* 6 (1976): 545–84, reprinted in Nash, *Race, Class, and Politics: Essays on American Colonial and Revolutionary Society* (Urbana: University of Illinois Press, 1986), chap. 7. The pioneer essays are James Henretta, "Economic Development and Structure in Colonial Boston," *William and Mary Quarterly*, 3d ser., 22 (1965): 75–92, and Allan Kulikoff, "The Progress of Inequality in Revolutionary Boston," *William and Mary Quarterly* 28 (1971): 375–412.

9. Nash, *Urban Crucible*, 172–73, 188–89, 253–54; Alex Keyssar, "Widowhood in Eastern Massachusetts: A Problem in the History of the Family," *Perspectives in American History* 7 (1974): 83–119, touches neither on Boston nor on the underlying political causes of the growth of widowhood.

10. Douglas Lamar Jones, *Village and Seaport: Migration and Society in Eighteenth-Century Massachusetts* (Hanover, N.H.: University Press of New England, 1981).

11. William Pencak, "The Social Structure of Revolutionary Boston: Evidence from the Great Fire of 1760," *Journal of Interdisciplinary History* 10 (1979): 274–75; Nash, *Urban Crucible*, appendix, table 5, 398; Alice Hanson Jones, *Wealth of a Nation to Be: The American Colonies on the Eve of the Revolution* (New York: Columbia University Press, 1980), 198–200, 322–25, 332.

12. For occupational breakdowns: Jacob Price, "Economic Function and the Growth of American Port Towns in the Eighteenth Century," *Perspectives in American History* 8 (1974): 171–86, and Kulikoff, "Progress of Inequality," appendix, 411–12.

13. Frances May Manges, "Women Shopkeepers, Tavernkeepers and Artisans in Colonial Philadelphia" (Ph.D. diss., University of Pennsylvania, 1958). For the year 1774 Lucy Murphy counted the following female advertisers in the *Boston Gazette*: nine retail shopkeepers (four of seeds, two of groceries, one of fabrics, one of cheese), one in the needle trades (a milliner), two school teachers, thirty-six wet nurses, and three women who might be regarded as in male trades (one baker, one wholesale/retail merchant, and one farmer [who advertised for a lost horse]) (seminar paper, Northern Illinois University, 1985). The standard earlier work is Elizabeth A. Dexter, *Colonial Women of Affairs, Women in Business and the Professions in America before 1776*, 2d rev. ed. (Boston: Houghton Mifflin, 1931). For suggestive analysis of Philadelphia, see Carole Shammas, "The Female Social Structure of Philadelphia in 1775," *Pennsylvania Magazine of History and Biography* 107 (January 1983): 69–83.

14. The primary sources that might be used for an occupational analysis of the women of Boston are Bettye H. Pruitt, ed., *The Massachusetts Tax Valuation List of 1771* (Boston: G. K. Hall and Co., 1978), 2–46 (unfortunately incomplete and with few occupations given); the Quaker records of relief distributed in 1775–76, referred to in n. 86; and the "Assessors 'Taking Books' of the Twelve Wards of the Town of Boston, 1780," in *Bostonian Society Publications*, 1st ser., 9 (1912): 15–59 (with occupations listed but in wartime and incomplete).

15. Nash, *Urban Crucible*, 194–95.

16. Patricia Cleary, "'She Merchants' of Boston: Women of Business on the Eve of the Revolution, 1745–1775" (Ms. Newberry Library Seminar in Early American History, Chicago, January, 1988); see also Cleary, *Elizabeth Murray; A Woman's Pursuit of Independence in Eighteenth-Century America* (Amherst, Mass.: University of Massachusetts Press, 2000).

17. Mary Beth Norton, "A Cherished Spirit of Independence: The Life of an Eighteenth-Century Boston Businesswoman," in *Women of America: A History*, ed. Mary Beth Norton and Carol Ruth Berkin (Boston: Houghton Mifflin, 1979), 48–60.

18. All citations, ibid.

19. Nash, *Urban Crucible*, chap. 9, passim.

20. Gary Nash, "The Failure of Female Factory Labor in Colonial Boston," *Labor History* 20 (1979): 165–88, reprinted in Nash, *Race, Class, and Politics*, 119–41.

21. L. H. Butterfield, ed., *Diary and Autobiography of John Adams*, 4 vols. (Cambridge, Mass.: Harvard University Press, 1961), 3:195.

22. Alan Day and Catherine Day, "Another Look at the Boston Caucus," *Journal of American Studies* 5 (1971): 27–28.

23. Samuel Adams to Arthur Lee, December 17, 1773, *The Writings of Samuel Adams*, 4 vols., ed. Harry A. Cushing (New York: G. P. Putnam's Sons, 1904–8), 3:73–74.

24. Dirk Hoerder, *Crowd Action in Revolutionary Massachusetts, 1765–1780* (New York: Harcourt Brace Jovanovich, 1977), 24–36, developed with statistical proof in Hoerder, *Society and Government 1760–1780: The Power Structure in Massachusetts Townships* (Berlin: John F. Kennedy Institut, 1972), 41–49; Edward M. Cook Jr., *The Fathers of the Towns: Leadership and Community Structure in Eighteenth-Century New England* (Baltimore: Johns Hopkins University Press, 1976), 167, 172–74.

25. Richard D. Brown, "Emergence of Voluntary Associations in Massachusetts, 1760–1830," *Journal of Voluntary Action Research* 2 (1973): 64–73.

26. Mary Roys Baker, "Anglo-Massachusetts Trade Union Roots, 1130–1790," *Labor History* 14 (1973): 352–96. Baker offers no trace of petitioning in the Massachusetts Archives by women in trades.

27. Richard Dufour, "The Exclusion of Female Students from the Public Secondary Schools of Boston, 1820–1920" (Ed.D. diss., Northern Illinois University, 1981), chap. 1.

28. Clio, "Thoughts on Female Education," *Royal American Magazine*, January 1774, 9–10; "Tanterbogas," *Massachusetts Centinel*, March 30, 1785.

29. Kenneth Lockridge, *Literacy in Colonial New England: An Inquiry into the Social Context of Literacy in the Early Modern West* (New York: W. W. Norton and Co., 1974), 21; Linda K. Kerber, "'Nothing Useless or Absurd or Fantastical': The Education of Women in the Early Republic," in *Educating Men and Women Together*, ed. Carol Lasser (Urbana: University of Illinois Press, 1987), 37–48.

30. Cathy Davidson, *Revolution and the Word: The Rise of the Novel in America* (New York: Oxford University Press, 1986), chap. 4; Elizabeth Reilly, "Demography and Reading in Mid-Eighteenth-Century New England," and "Cheap and Popular Print in Mid-Eighteenth-Century New England," unpublished ms. that Ms. Reilly generously shared with me.

31. Franklin Bowditch Dexter, ed., *Extracts from the Itineraries and Other Miscellanies of Ezra Stiles ...* (New Haven, Conn.: Yale University Press, 1916), 100–101.

32. Cited in Charles Akers, *The Divine Politician: Samuel Cooper and the American Revolution in Boston* (Boston: Northwestern University Press, 1982), 26.

33. Isaac Backus, *History of New England with Particular Reference to the ... Baptists* (Boston, 1796), 3:125–26.

34. Peter Oliver, *Peter Oliver's Origin and Progress of the American Rebellion: A Tory View*, ed. Douglass Adair and John A. Schutz (San Marino, Calif.: Huntington Library, 1961), 42–45.

35. Richard D. Shiels, "The Feminization of American Congregationalism, 1730–1835," *American Quarterly* 33 (1981): 46–62, which includes data for three Boston churches.

36. Kenneth Silverman, *A Cultural History of the American Revolution* (New York: Thomas Y. Crowell Co., 1976), 198–209.

37. Lucia Bergamasco, "Amitié, amour et spiritualité dans la Nouvelle-Angleterre du XVII Siècle: L'Expérience d'Esther Burr et Sarah Prince," in *Autre temps autre espaces: Etudes sur L'Amérique pré-Industrielle*, ed. Elise Marienstras and Barbara Karsky (Nancy, France: University of Nancy Press, 1986), 91–109; *The Journal of Esther Edwards Burr, 1754–1757*, ed. Carol F. Karlsen and Laurie Crumpacker (New Haven, Conn.: Yale University Press, 1986), introduction, 34.

38. Nash, *Urban Crucible*, chap. 8, citation at 219. See also Edwin Scott Gaustad, *The Great Awakening in New England* (New York: Harper and Brothers, 1957); and John William Raimo, "Spiritual Harvest: The Anglo American Revival in Boston, Massachusetts, and Bristol, England, 1739–1742" (Ph.D. diss., University of Wisconsin, 1975).

39. Charles Chauncy, *Seasonable Thoughts on the State of Religion in New England* … (Boston, 1742); George Whitfield, February 16, 1745, in Luke Tyerman, *The Life of the Reverend George Whitfield*, 2 vols. (London: Hodder, 1876–77), 2:73–74.

40. Citations from Nash, *Urban Crucible*, 204–19.

41. Clifford K. Shipton and James E. Mooney, comps., *National Index of American Imprints through 1800* (Worcester, Mass.: American Antiquarian Society, 1969), entries under George Whitfield dated 1770–71.

42. Young, "In the Streets of Boston," pt. I. For older studies, see W. deLoss Love, *The Fast and Thanksgiving Days of New England* (Boston: Houghton Mifflin, 1895); Alice Morse Earle, *Customs and Fashions in Old New England* (New York: Macmillan, 1893), chap. 9; George Kittridge, *The Old Farmer and His Almanack* (Boston: W. W. Ware, 1904), 168–83.

43. Young, "In the Streets of Boston," chaps. 1–3.

44. Lawrence W. Towner, "True Confessions and Dying Warnings in Colonial New England," in *Sibley's Heir: A Volume in Memory of Clifford Kenyon Shipton, Publications of the Colonial Society of Massachusetts* 59 (1982): 523–39.

45. Alfred Young, "English Plebeian Culture and Eighteenth-Century American Radicalism," in *Origins of Anglo-American Radicalism*, ed. Margaret Jacob and James Jacob (London: Allen and Unwin, 1983), 189–94.

46. Eric Hobsbawm, *Primitive Rebels: Studies in Archaic Forms of Social Movements in the 19th and 20th Centuries* (New York: W. W. Norton and Co., 1965), chap. 7 at 111.

47. Hoerder, *Crowd Action*, chap. 1; Nash, *Urban Crucible*, passim; Jesse Lemisch,

"Jack Tar in the Streets: Merchant Seamen in the Politics of Revolutionary America," *William and Mary Quarterly*, 3d ser., 15 (1968): 371–407; Joel Shufro, "Boston in Massachusetts Politics, 1730–1760" (Ph.D. diss., University of Wisconsin, 1976), chap. 5; Pauline Maier, *From Resistance to Revolution: Colonial Radicals and the Development of American Opposition to Britain, 1765–1776* (New York: Alfred A. Knopf, 1972), chap. 1.

48. Laurel Thatcher Ulrich, *Good Wives: Image and Reality in the Lives of Women in Northern New England, 1650–1750* (New York: Oxford University Press, 1982), chap. 10, "Viragoes."

49. Cited in George Rawlyk, *Nova Scotia's Massachusetts: A Study of Massachusetts–Nova Scotia Relations, 1680–1784* (Montreal: McGill-Queens University Press, 1973), 105, brought to my attention by Bryan Palmer.

50. Young, "In the Streets of Boston," pt. II; G. B. Warden, *Boston, 1689–1776* (Boston: Little, Brown and Co., 1970), chaps. 8–15; for the crowd, Hoerder, *Crowd Action*, chaps. 2–11; for the popular leaders, Maier, *From Resistance to Revolution*, chaps. 3–8; for merchants, Arthur M. Schlesinger, *The Colonial Merchants and the American Revolution, 1763–1776* (1918; reprint, New York: Atheneum, 1968), and John W. Tyler, *Smugglers and Patriots: Boston Merchants and the Advent of the American Revolution* (Boston: Northeastern University Press, 1986).

51. Hoerder, *Crowd Action*, chaps. 2–3; Edmund S. Morgan and Helen M. Morgan, *The Stamp Act Crisis: Prologue to Revolution*, 2d rev. ed. (New York: W. W. Norton, 1963), chap. 8.

52. *Boston Gazette*, August 19, 1765; *Boston News-Letter*, August 22, 1765.

53. *Boston Gazette*, May 26, 1766; August 22, 1768; *Boston News-Letter Extraordinary*, May 22, 1766.

54. "A Stamp Dream," *Boston Gazette*, October 14, 1765.

55. *Boston Gazette*, February 24, 1766.

56. "William Jackson, an Importer at the Brazen Head ..." (Boston, 1769–70[?], Broadside).

57. *Boston News-Letter*, November 5, 1767.

58. "Philagius," *Boston Evening Post*, February 5, 12, 1770.

59. *Boston Gazette*, February 12, 1770.

60. "A List of the Names ...," (Boston, 1770, Broadside), also in *Boston Gazette*, Supplement, March 12, 1770; Betsy and Anne Cuming, cited in Norton, "A Cherished Spirit of Independence," 55.

61. *Boston Post-Boy*, November 16, 1767.

62. Cited in Oliver M. Dickerson, ed., *Boston under Military Rule, 1768–69 as Revealed in a Journal of the Times* (Boston: Chapman and Grimes, 1936), 33.

63. Laurel Thatcher Ulrich, "'Daughters of Liberty': Religious Women in Revolutionary New England," in *Women in the Age of the American Revolution*, ed. Ronald Hoffman and Peter J. Albert (Charlottesville: University of Virginia Press, 1989), 211–43. I am indebted to Ms. Ulrich for sharing the ms. version with me.

64. Norton, *Liberty's Daughters*, 164–70. The *Boston Evening Post* reported twenty-seven incidents of spinning in New England, May–December 1769.

65. Cited in Hiller Zobel, *The Boston Massacre* (New York: W. W. Norton and Co., 1970), 151; the theme is developed in Maier, *From Resistance to Revolution*, chap. 5 and passim.

66. Samuel Adams, *Writings* 1:241–47; Governor Francis Bernard to Earl of Hillsborough, March 19, 1768, in *English Historical Documents: American Colonial Documents to 1776*, ed. Merrill Jensen (New York: Oxford University Press, 1955), 736–39.

67. Dickerson, ed., *Boston under Military Rule*, passim; Melinda Munger, "Women's Activities in Boston, 1765–1776" (seminar paper, Northern Illinois University, 1975), analyzes the entries Dickerson assembled in *Boston under Military Rule*, originally published in newspapers outside of Boston.

68. *A Short Narrative of the Horrid Massacre in Boston ... to Which Is Added an Appendix ...* (Boston, 1770), depositions nos. 2, 11, 12, 17, 20, 86, 90.

69. Young, "In the Streets of Boston," chaps. 11, 12; Zobel, *The Boston Massacre*, chap. 15; John Adams, *Diary and Autobiography* 1:349–50.

70. *Letters and Diary of John Rowe, Boston Merchant, 1759–1762, 1764–1779*, ed. Anne Rowe Cunningham (Boston: W. B. Clarke, 1903), March 8, 1770, 199.

71. Paul Revere, "The Bloody Massacre Perpetrated in King Street" (Boston, 1770, Broadside), reproduced and discussed in Clarence S. Brigham, *Paul Revere's Engravings* (New York: Atheneum, 1969), 52–78. The woman stands out especially in the prints Christian Remick colored in watercolors, less so in the several black-and-white versions.

72. "The Life and Humble Confessions of Richardson, the Informer" (Boston, 1770, Broadside). The cut is reproduced in Elizabeth Carroll Reilly, *A Dictionary of Colonial American Printer's Ornaments and Illustrations* (Worcester, Mass.: American Antiquarian Society, 1975), no. 1008. After consultation with Elizabeth Reilly, I attribute the engraving to Isaiah Thomas on the basis of Thomas's style and known political activities as a printer for this period.

73. John Adams, March 5, 1773, *Diary and Autobiography* 2:70.

74. *Massachusetts Spy*, December 2, 1773.

75. Ibid.

76. Mary Salisbury to Susanna Shaw, August 2, 1774, cited in Norton, *Liberty's Daughters*, 172; see also the exchange over the effects of tea in *Massachusetts Spy*: "A Woman," December 23, 1773; Dr. Thomas Young, December 30, 1773; "A Woman," January 6, 1774.

77. Thomas Young to John Lamb, June 19, 1774, in *Memoirs of General John Lamb*, ed. Isaac Q. Leake (Albany, N.Y.: J. Munsell, 1850), 89–91.

78. Letter of the Boston Committee of Correspondence to the People of Every Town, June 8, 1774, and the Covenant, in Peter Force, comp., *American Archives*, 4th ser., 6 vols. (Washington, D.C.: M. St. Clair and Peter Force, 1837–46), 1:397–98.

79. Harrison Gray, cited in Tyler, *Smugglers and Patriots*, 219; John Andrews to

William Barrell, July 22, 1774, in Winthrop Sargent, ed., "Letters of John Andrews, Esq. of Boston, 1772–1776," *Proceedings of the Massachusetts Historical Society* 8 (1864–65): 329; for the Worcester reference, I am indebted to Edward Countryman.

80. "We the subscribers, inhabitants of the District of Charlton ..." (Boston, June 1774, Broadside), with 132 signatures, "unusual because of the number of women represented among the signers," in *Massachusetts Broadsides of the American Revolution*, ed. Mason I. Lowance Jr., and Georgia Bumgardner (Amherst: University of Massachusetts Press, 1976), 42–43.

81. Hoerder, *Crowd Action*, 278–80; citation of Adams, ibid., 279.

82. John Andrews to William Barrell, "Letters of John Andrews," *Proceedings of the Massachusetts Historical Society* 8 (1864–65): 337.

83. *Boston News-Letter*, March 2, 1775.

84. *Middlesex Journal* (England), November 22–24, 1774, "An Extract from a Letter from Boston Dated October 25th," reprinted in R. T. H. Halsey, *The Boston Port Bill as Pictured by a Contemporary London Cartoonist* (New York: Grolier Club, 1904), 310–11.

85. Richard Frothingham, *History of the Siege of Boston* (Boston: C. C. Little and J. Brown, 1849).

86. Henry C. Cadbury, "Quaker Relief during the Siege of Boston," *Colonial Society of Massachusetts Transactions* 34 (1943): 39–149, a transcript of the manuscript records. The comment is at p. 63. My analysis is impressionistic.

87. Norton, *Liberty's Daughters*, 138; Norton, "Eighteenth-Century American Women in Peace and War: The Case of the Loyalists," *William and Mary Quarterly*, 3d ser., 33 (1976): 393–95.

88. Oliver, *Origin and Progress*, 65.

89. Ibid., 61.

90. Ibid., 62.

91. Ibid., 73.

92. Ibid., 63–64.

93. Ibid., 97.

94. The letter is in *Boston Gazette*, Supplement, December 20, 1767, reprinted in *Providence Gazette*, January 9, 1768; for "Henry Flynt," *Boston Gazette*, November 2, 1767; "A Young American," ibid., December 21, 1767. "Squibo" is reprinted in *Providence Gazette*, January 2, 1768.

95. Alice M. Earle, ed., *Diary of Anna Green Winslow, a Boston School Girl of 1771* (Boston: Houghton Mifflin, 1894); introduction by Mrs. Earle is the source of biographical detail.

96. Ibid., 14, 59.

97. Ibid., 20, 25, 27.

98. Ibid., 32, 72.

99. Lucy Martin Donnelly, "The Celebrated Mrs. Macaulay," *William and Mary Quarterly*, 3d ser., 6 (1949): 173–207.

100. Robert A. Feer, "Mercy Otis Warren," in *Notable American Women 1607–1950*, 3 vols., ed. Janet and Edward James (Cambridge, Mass.: Harvard University Press, 1971), 3:45–56; Katherine Anthony, *First Lady of the Revolution: The Life of Mercy Otis Warren* (New York: Doubleday and Co., 1958); Maud M. Hutcheson, "Mercy Warren, 1728–1814," *William and Mary Quarterly*, 3d ser., 10 (1953): 378–402.

101. Silverman, *Cultural History of the American Revolution*, 212–13, 255–56; Bernard Bailyn, *The Ordeal of Thomas Hutchinson* (Cambridge, Mass.: Harvard University Press, 1974), 202, 244.

102. Mercy Warren, *Poems Dramatic and Miscellaneous* (Boston: Thomas, 1790).

103. "The Sack of Rome" and "Ladies of Castille," in ibid.; the line about women is from *The Motley Assembly* (1779).

104. Mercy Otis Warren, *The History of the Rise, Progress and Termination of the American Revolution*, 3 vols. (Boston: Manning and Loring, 1805); Lester Cohen, "Explaining the Revolution: Ideology and Ethics in Mercy Warren's Historical Theory," *William and Mary Quarterly*, 3d ser., 37 (1980): 200–218.

105. Akers, *Abigail Adams*, 31–47. For details, see Phyllis Lee Levin, *Abigail Adams* (New York: St. Martin's, 1987); for a variant interpretation, Edith B. Gelles, "Abigail Adams: Domesticity and the American Revolution," *New England Quarterly* 52 (1979): 500–521, and Gelles, "The Abigail Industry," *William and Mary Quarterly*, 3d. ser., 45 (1988): 656–83.

106. Elizabeth Cady Stanton, *Eighty Years and More: Reminiscences, 1815–1897* (New York: T. Fisher Unwin, 1898), 31–34.

107. Abigail Adams to John Adams, March 31, 1776, *Adams Family Correspondence*, 1:369–71; for John Adams on this theme, see Richard L. Bushman, *King and People in Provincial Massachusetts* (Chapel Hill: University of North Carolina Press, 1985), chap. 5.

108. Abigail Adams to John Adams, July 25, 1775, May 9, 1776, *Adams Family Correspondence*, 1:263, 404.

109. Cited in Akers, *Abigail Adams*, 46.

110. Abigail Adams to John Adams, August 14, 1776, *Adams Family Correspondence* 2:94.

111. Kerber, *Women of the Republic*, chap. 9.

112. Thomas Paine, *Common Sense* (Philadelphia, 1776); for evidence of Adams and her female friends reading *Common Sense*, see *Warren-Adams Letters*, Massachusetts Historical Society Collections, vols. 72–73, 2 vols. (Boston, 1917–25), 1:204, 208–9.

113. Abigail Adams to John Adams, September 22, 1775, *Adams Family Correspondence*; for the petitions, Herbert Aptheker, ed., *Documentary History of the Negro People*, 2 vols. (New York: Citadel Press, 1951), 1:5–9.

114. For examples, see the (Boston) *Massachusetts Centinel*: "Clarissa," April 7, 1784; "Conjugal Love," July 7, 1784; "Some Cases of Unhappy Marriages," January 26, 1785.

115. See in the 1785 *Massachussetts Centinel*: "Humanus," February 19; "Daphne," February 26; "The Force of Education," March 2; "Humanus," March 9; "Mechanick," March 12; "Tantarbogas," March 30; "Lorenzo," April 6; "Semiramis," April 16.

116. Judith Sargent Murray, *The Gleaner*, 3 vols. (Boston, 1798); for discussion, see Norton, *Liberty's Daughters*, chap. 8, and Kerber, *Women of the Republic*, 204–6.

117. "An Oration upon Female Education Pronounced by a Member of the Public Schools of Boston, September, 1791," in Caleb Bingham, *The Columbian Orator*, 9th ed. (Boston, 1801), 47–51. Morton was Sarah Wentworth Morton of Boston, who wrote poetry as "Philenia" and to whom some attributed (falsely) *The Power of Sympathy* (Boston, 1788), the first American novel. See Davidson, *Revolution and the Word*, 85, 287n.

3

Tar and Feathers and the Ghost of Oliver Cromwell
English Plebeian Culture and American Radicalism

English plebeian culture—the customs, traditions, and rituals rooted in the laboring classes of countryside and city—has received increasing attention from scholars on both sides of the Atlantic. This essay addresses the transmission of English plebeian culture to America in the eighteenth century, its retention, transformation, and function in popular movements in the era of the American Revolution. Four tableaux, a century apart, set the stage for our discussion.

In Boston in 1675 nine ship's carpenters took John Langworthy, a carpenter, and carried him "upon a pole and by violence" from the north end of town to the town dock in the center. This "occasioned a great tumult of people, meeting there with the Constable who did rescue him." The carpenters were brought to trial and pleaded guilty, explaining that Langworthy "was an interloper and had never served his time to the trade of a ship carpenter," that is, he had not completed a seven-year apprenticeship. The magistrates fined them ten shillings each. "They understood such things were usual in England," the carpenters explained. Or, in other words, they were not usual in America.[1]

In 1768 the *Essex Gazette* of Salem ran the following account of an event in town. On 7 September a custom-house "waiter," that is, a watchman, named Ross, who had informed his superior that a ship in the harbor was in violation of the customs laws, "engaged the attention of a number of inhabitants," who were "determined to distinguish him in a conscious manner for his conduct."

He was taken from one of the wharves, and conducted to the common, where his head, body and limbs were covered with warm Tar, and then a large quantity of feathers were applied to all Parts. The poor waiter was then

In this caricature of the tar-and-feathering of John Malcolm, a customs informer, in Boston in January 1774, the London artist has telescoped the event with the Boston Tea Party in the background to the right. Sailors wearing striped trousers are prominent in the crowd, which is about to cart Malcolm through town. "A New Method of Macarony Making as Practised at Boston in North America," engraving, Carrington Bowles publisher, London, 1774. Courtesy of the Carnegie Museum of Art, Pittsburgh, Eavenson Fund.

exalted to a Seat in front of a Cart, and in this manner, led into the Main
Street, where a paper with the word *Informer* thereon, in large letters was
affixed to his Breast, and another paper with the same words to his Back.
The scene drew together within a few minutes several Hundred people, who
proceeded with Huzzas and loud Acclamations through the town.

The crowd took this "confused subject of their ridicule" to the edge of
town, warned him he should "receive higher marks of distinction" should
he ever return, and let him go.[2]

This seems to have been New England's first tar-and-feathering of the
revolutionary era. The assumption underlying the rich detail is clear: it
would not have been enough to say simply that an informer had been
tarred and feathered; no one would have known what it meant.

In 1774 an anonymous pamphlet appeared, *The American Chronicle of
the Times*, published serially in several cities in six "books" into the spring
of 1775.[3] It was written in numbered chapters and verses, in biblical diction
with the political characters of 1775 cast in biblical roles. By the end of the
third book, the priest Jedidiah, recounting the woes of Boston, was convinced that "The word shall be the sword of the Lord and of Oliver," and
cried out, "Bring me up Oliver Cromwell." In book four, Cromwell appeared. Accepting the challenge against "Thomas, surnamed the Gagite,"
the "usurper" (General Gage), Cromwell issued a proclamation as "Lord
Protector of the Commonwealth of Massachusetts Bay in New England"
and summoned his lieutenants. "Awake and rouse up my faithful Fairfax,
Lambert, and the rest of my brave warriors."

Like tar-and-feathering, Cromwell's appearance was sudden, un-
announced, and seemingly unaccountable. Cromwell had not previously
been popular with leaders of the Revolution; he was not part of their
political tradition, yet the pamphlet was "enormously popular."[4] Where
did he come from?

In 1788, from February to July in every major American city, there were
massive community parades in celebration of the new Constitution of the
United States. In every city artisans marched by trades, either with the
tools of their craft or with floats depicting themselves at work at their
trade. They carried banners with the emblems of London guilds or other
trade symbols blended with images and slogans in support of the Constitution.[5] They were the first such banners and parades in American history.
There had never been anything like them in the colonies; indeed, there
was nothing *quite* like them in contemporary England. Where, then, did
they come from?

I have chosen these four episodes because they illustrate in different ways the processes by which custom, ritual, and tradition get not only from one generation to another, but also from one country to another and from one century to another, and how in their reappearance they often change.

I make a number of assumptions about the underlying context in which the processes were at work.

First, I assume a massive carryover of popular culture from Britain to the colonies, and that the major carriers were the migrants themselves. There was not one transmission in the seventeenth century alone but many, particularly in the eighteenth century. Migration was strong in the period before and after the Revolution, bringing a good many others like Thomas Paine, one suspects, out of the Wilkesite political culture. And there were temporary migrants, bearers of culture, like the evangelist George Whitefield, who, it should be recalled, made six great tours of America over the thirty years before his death in Newburyport in 1770.[6]

This assumption of a transfer of English culture has long been explicit in major fields of colonial scholarship. It is taken for granted in intellectual history that one "begins in England," whether studying seventeenth-century Puritanism à la Perry Miller or Edmund S. Morgan, or eighteenth-century "country party" political ideology à la Bernard Bailyn. It is a theme of the older New England town studies (especially those that dwelt on town planning, architecture, or agricultural systems)[7] to which some scholars are returning to explore what one calls "the remarkable extent to which diversity in New England local institutions was directly imitative of regional differences in the mother country."[8] Among students of folk culture, retention and variation are a stock-in-trade—one thinks of such diverse subjects as witchcraft, Anglo-American ballads, material folk culture, and children's lore. "Indeed most English nursery rhymes," the leading authorities point out, "are better known in the states and in the case of the older ones, often known in versions nearer the original, than they are in the home country"—a thesis also argued for other fields.[9]

Second, a number of conditions in America, we are now learning, fostered the retention of this transmitted heritage. To the extent that plebeian culture was transmitted orally, one thinks of recent findings on literacy in colonial America. New Englanders, Kenneth Lockridge writes, "once lived closer than we have imagined to the credulous word of mouth world of the peasant, closer to its absorbing localism, closer to its dependency on tradition and on the informed few." To the extent that English customs grew out of a context of social stratification which perpetuated rituals of status reversal, one has only to point to Gary B. Nash's abundant evidence of class polarities in the cities by the mid-eighteenth century.[10] Print culture, which was flourishing in urban places in America, as Peter Burke suggests, probably acted to "preserve or even diffuse popular culture [rather] than destroy it."[11] The newspaper carried the news of tar-and-feathering from one American town to another; the pamphlet "summoned up" Cromwell; an almanac printed his picture in battle armor on its cover.

Third, other often emphasized conditions militated against the retention of English ways. People moved up; people moved away. Puritan authority suppressed the holidays which were the occasion for the rituals necessary to renew culture. Artisan institutions, like guilds which perpetuate ceremony and symbol, did not form or, if formed, did not survive.[12] A custom out of its social context loses its meaning and withers. Things get lost; the words and tunes get muddled.

Given both continuities and discontinuities, it seems important to direct our attention to the *degree* of retention of English culture. We can profit from the heuristic concepts of Melville Herskovits, the anthropologist who more than any other scholar opened up the field of Afro-American culture. Herskovits's concern was African survivals in the New World, and his emphasis was on the "tenacity" of culture and the "continuities." But he knew African culture in its variations from the "bush" in Africa through the West Indies and Latin America into the United States, south and north, rural and urban. He posited a "scale of intensity of New World Africanisms" ranging from "very African" and "quite" to "somewhat" down to "trace of African customs or absent" (no quantification, poor man!), and he distinguished the degree of retention in different categories—technology, magic, art, language, etc. On this scale he came up with the concept of a "*continuum*" of African retentions, dependent upon a host of variables.[13] He also popularized the concept of *syncretism.* Among New World African converts to Catholicism, for example, saints corresponded to African gods; in New England, blacks observed "Negro election day," using the official political observance to replicate African rituals of king, court, and Saturnalia.[14]

Herskovits's approach was contested bitterly at the time: E. Franklin Frazier, for example, was convinced that North American blacks had been "completely stripped of their social heritage."[15] Recently scholars warmly respectful of Herskovits have argued with him sharply on particulars. Herbert Gutman has criticized his "failure to study the changing history of enslaved Afro-Americans [which] has led him to emphasize direct continuities between discontinuous experience."[16] Eugene Genovese has questioned whether the slaves' preference for the Baptist religion reflected the continued strength of west African religion.[17] We could use so fruitful a controversy over the transmission and retention of English plebeian culture.

Fourth, while there was retention, I assume there was also innovation. The scholars on whom we draw for theoretical frameworks all place emphasis on a process in which there is choice: Sidney Mintz, on whom Gutman has drawn, on "culture as a kind of resource" in which there are "sets of historically available alternatives" and "choices are made and pursued";[18] Charles Tilly on "repertoires of collective action";[19] Peter Burke on "a stock of genres."[20] In all these metaphors people exercise choice, but from within a range of given alternatives. I would push this a step further to emphasize what E. P. Thompson, focusing on the eighteenth century, has called "the creative culture forming process from below,"[21] and what Eric Hobsbawm, dealing with a more self-conscious process at higher levels of society in the nineteenth century, has called "the invention of tradition."[22] These processes, I am suggesting, require special attention.

Finally, in exploring plebeian culture, I make certain assumptions as to what constitutes proof. A major part of this culture was transmitted orally. A good part of it was also out of the sight of those who wrote things down, and when the literate "discovered" the "people" their values often tainted the sources.[23] It is a field, therefore, in which the sources can be unrecorded, isolated, fragmentary, fortuitous, or biased. We need standards of proof—and craft skills—appropriate to eras of scarce records, a condition to which most scholars of American history are not accustomed.

We often have no choice but to make the most of isolated instances. At the same time, I assume there is a risk in extrapolating from a single piece of evidence. The example of the shipyard workers in 1675 may not be taken as proof that riding a man on a pole ("riding the stang" it was called in England) was common in the colonies before or after. Nor does the fact that tar-and-feathering broke out in New England about 1768 necessarily mean it was practiced earlier. The timing of things—when they *appear*, when they catch on, when they are *widely practiced*, when they *disappear*—should be of major concern if we are to analyze the *function* of custom and tradition and the *role* they play in popular consciousness and popular movements.

Our tableaux have introduced plebeian culture in three areas: the rituals of popular punishment, the traditions of popular politics, and the symbolism and ceremonial of artisan culture. In these areas I see several underlying processes at work acting in different combinations: first, a rather straightforward carryover, retention, and usage; second, a kind of holding pattern process in which customs and traditions migrate, are "stored," and not put into practice until they are functional (perhaps better put as a "thawing" process in which something "frozen" in an earlier era comes to life later); third, a process of recovery in which a newly felt need impels a group to reach over to the old country and back into the past; and, finally, a process of borrowing and amalgamation, the end product of which constitutes innovation.

I

The rituals of popular punishment—"riding the stang" and tar-and-feathering—illustrate three of these processes. There is a strong line of continuity at the level of official punishment, where authority has a special stake in maintaining traditional rituals of punishment. At the level of popular punishment, there seems to be discontinuity—a process of delayed adoption; customs widely practiced in England do not become widespread in New England until much later. And tar-and-feathering represents a process of amalgamation from contemporary official ritual, contemporary popular ritual with a seemingly very old form, long out of sight to most plebeians as well as to the better sort.

Let me try to work from the "riding the stang" episode at Boston in 1675 to the tar-and-feathering of 1768 in Salem. "Rough music" is the generic English name for the ritual of punishment in which a person violating the community's norms of morality was paraded on a horse or donkey, a wooden horse, or a poll or staff. It had many local names in England; in the northern colonies in the eighteenth century it was commonly called a "skimmington." E. P. Thompson has reopened the study of the subject for England.[24] Bryan Palmer has made clear how widespread it was in the United States and Canada during the nineteenth century.[25] For the eighteenth century we have as yet much less to go on; Steven Stewart has described nine midcentury episodes in rich detail,[26] and I know of a number of others. At this precarious stage in our knowledge we can risk only a few generalizations.

The skimmington was very much here on the eve of the revolutionary crisis—that is clear. "Oh but there was a riot which pulled down an

House," exclaimed John Adams posing as "Clarendon" writing to "Pym," mocking Tory anxieties about the events of 1765:

> So there have been an hundred riots, an hundred skimmingtons Ridings, in which some of his majesty's subjects have received damage, some by riding a Rail, and some a Bull, some for one Misdemeanor, and some for another. Nay there have been such ridings in which some of his Majestys subjects have been slain, some in which the Kings officers sheriffs have been killed in the execution of his office. Pray was that an overt act of high Treason.[27]

The reported evidence for the 1750s and 1760s suggests a location primarily in southeastern New England, the lower Hudson Valley of New York, New Jersey, and Long Island areas with English settlers. An account from southern New England in 1764 says that "skimmington rioters have late been very frequent in this part of the Country."[28] The scant evidence for earlier episodes suggests they were novel and discontinuous. The language alone of the shipwrights in 1675 points to this. The fact that they had to plead that "they understood such things were usual in England" means, as we have already noted, they were not usual in New England. In the first decade of the eighteenth century Judge Samuel Sewall recorded two episodes in which the ritual elements common in England were missing. In 1707, for example, Sewall tried a case in which seven or eight women— so it seems—"join'd together, called the man out of his house, guilefully praying him to show them the way; then by the help of a Negro youth, tore off his cloaths and whip'd him with Rods to chastise him for carrying it harshly to his wife." Sewall was furious, sentencing the woman who apparently was the leader to be whipped, for "a woman that had lost her modesty was like Salt that had lost its savor."[29]

Meanwhile, riding the wooden horse was a common official punishment in the military, and this may have kept the form alive. The British army used it in the wars against the French, but American recruits do not seem to have taken well to it. In 1746 at Louisbourg, after one private "was ordered to ride the wooden horse," that night "the wooden horse [was] torn in pieces."[30] The colonial militia took over the punishment. But if an episode on the Boston Common in 1764 is typical, it was not popular there either. When a private "behaved saucily to his Captain" and was made "to Ride the Wooden Horse, the mob got foul of the horse and broke it so that the Fellow escaped."[31]

The targets of popular punishment, in the cases thus far found, were almost always males guilty of either adultery or wife-beating. The participants were usually men (only occasionally identified as young men) who we may infer from scattered evidence were drawn from the commonality of their communities. The better sort, from Judge Sewall to lawyer Adams, were shrill in their hostility to this kind of punishment, although on occasion they gave it sanction.

Finally, the ritual element in America seems much thinner than in England. Granted that Hogarth's graphic depiction of a charivari in the *Hudibras* series is a composite, in America it seems hard to find as much symbolism, ceremonial, or raucous noise. To be sure, Americans could carry out the charivari with *éclat;* witness this description from New Jersey:

> We hear from Elizabeth-Town that an odd Sect of People have lately appeared there, who go under the Denomination of Regulars; there are near a Dozen of them, who dress themselves in Woman's Cloaths, and painting their Faces, go in the Evening to the Houses of such as are reported to beat their Wives; where one of them entering in first, seizes the Delinquent, while the rest follow, strip him, turn up his Posteriors, and flog him with Rods most severely, crying out all the Time, Wo To the Men that Beat their Wives.[32]

And we have a few examples from southern New England which suggest rough musickers experienced in the nuances of the ritual: self-restrained; interested in shaming, not violence; parading a man through town; producing a confession of wrongdoing, a promise of contrition, and a thank-you for the mob that treated him so generously. But more commonly we sense people straining to get on with the physical chastisement, quick to resort to violence—riding a man on a rail was the favored form—with resulting loss of life to victim or rioters. Perhaps this weakness of ritual, which, after all, channels aggressive action with some safety, if all play by the rules, is another clue to the pervasiveness of violence in the American past.

Why, if this pattern of evidence holds up, was there a delay in adopting the skimmington in New England? Broadly speaking, because the community could depend on the state or church to enforce its moral norms. In seventeenth-century Massachusetts adultery was a capital crime. Even under the liberalized law of 1684, however, adulterers had to sit on the gallows with a rope around their neck for an hour, receive forty lashes, and wear a letter A for the rest of their lives. Wife-beating was also a crime. A 1660 law provided that "everie married woeman shall be free from bodilie correction or stripes by her husband, unless it be in his defense upon her assalt," and an early eighteenth-century law declared that "No man shall strike his wife, nor any woman her husband, on penalty of such fine not exceeding ten pounds for one offense."[33] Law is one thing, practice another, yet there is enough evidence from the local courts to suggest male magistrates did protect females in the seventeenth century. May we not argue, then, that popular punishment became more rife when magistrate and minister ceased to perform their traditional role?[34] The community, or a segment of it, did what the law used to do, or what the law could not or would not do.

The rituals of popular punishment—especially tar-and-feathering—drew heavily upon the formalities of official punishment. Public executions in New England followed closely what Burke has described as common in early modern Europe: "a dramatic performance carefully managed by authorities to show the people that crime did not pay." Most of the European elements were there: the procession of the condemned man in a cart, mounting the scaffold, the clergy in attendance, possibly an address to the crowd, the selling of ballads recounting the alleged dying words drawing the lessons of the sin.[35] We know the ritual well for New England through Lawrence W. Towner's analysis of the "True Confessions and Dying Warning" pamphlets and broadsides.[36]

In social context, however, hangings in Boston and the county-seat towns of New England were different from those at Tyburn in the eighteenth century so vividly described by Peter Linebaugh. "The efficacy of public punishment," he writes, "depends upon a rough agreement between those who wield the law and those ruled by it." At Tyburn, "order rested less upon community consensus" than on "the force of arms and the spectacular terror in the panoply of a state hanging."[37] In Boston the execution ritual usually had enthusiastic popular support, which seemed to increase with the revolutionary fervor.[38]

There were occasional rescue riots: for example, the freeing of the militiaman on the wooden horse. Country people sprang debtors from jail, quite apart from Shays's Rebellion, but we seem to have no reports of hanging rescues. Nor is this to imply there was not strong moral sentiment against the dissection of the cadavers of the poor, the issue prompting the Tyburn riots. In 1788, New York City was racked by three days of rioting when medical students were rumoured to be snatching bodies from the graves of paupers.[39]

The execution ritual shared elements common to lesser colonial punishments. The first was public identification of the criminal. Hester Prynne's *A* for adultery and *I* for incest were still meted out in the mid-eighteenth century. Branding was practiced—*B* for burglary, *R* ("rogue") for counterfeiter—as well as cropping the ears. Identification might be temporary: in 1763 a Bedford man and woman guilty of fraud were set in a pillory for an hour "with a Paper on each of their breasts with the words, A CHEAT wrote in capitol letters thereon." Another element was painful punishment in public, commonly whipping, the stocks, and the pillory.[40] A third was humiliation; a fourth was confession and repentance. It was common to sit someone convicted of a lesser offense under the gallows with a rope around the neck to remind him or her of the fate that awaited on a second offense. Finally, implicit in all these elements was active participation by the public. When John and Ann Richardson were put on the gallows in Boston in 1764 for starving their baby to death, "the man behaved in the most audacious manner," wrote the genteel merchant John Rowe, "so that the mob pelted him which was what he deserved."[41]

The sources of tar-and-feathering in New England should now be clearer. As the tableau at Salem suggests, it owed a large debt to official punishment: public display via carting; severe punishment; and confession or a promise of repentance (elsewhere the victim might be taken to the gallows with a halter around his neck). The difference, of course, was that the sentence, instead of death, was banishment or ostracism—a throwback to the seventeenth century.

The debt to the second source, the skimmington, was not as large. In New England the first reported episodes of tar-and-feathering in 1768–9 were all in seaports: Salem, Newburyport, Gloucester, Boston, Newport, and Portsmouth (as was the first known episode of the revolutionary era, in Norfolk, Virginia, in 1766). Skimmingtons were not common to all these towns, and prior to 1765 occurred most often in the rural areas of southern New England. Tar-and-feathering in New England was north and south. Newport was the only tar-and-feathering port town with a prior history of skimmingtons. Elsewhere, however, one ritual seems to have shaded into the other. In 1769 in Boston, for example, the first victim was an American who had lured a country girl into British soldiers' barracks, where presumably an assault was attempted. There were also similarities of tone, including loud, terrifying shouting, restrained violence, and a mocking, derisive spirit. Though the action drew upon the ceremonies of public punishment, it was far less solemn—indeed, it sometimes satirized them. Where the community felt secure and unchallenged in its action, the mood of the crowd might even be playful. In Trumbull's mock epic poem, *M'Fingal* (1775), the tarred village squire is carted by a jolly procession headed by three musicians.[42]

But where did the third element, tar-and-feathering itself, come from? It drew on a very ancient British practice. In 1189, Richard I, en route to a crusade, decreed that anyone committing a crime on board ship would be tarred and feathered and put off at the nearest landfall. Tar-and-feathering appears in Hakluyt's *Voyages* and Holinshed's *Chronicles*.[43] But all such lineage-tracing is beside the point, for by the mid-eighteenth century the practice had passed out of the ken of elites; there are only a few signs of it in England proper.[44] Indeed, among laboring men, "riding the stang," "horsing on a staff," or "coolstaffing" seem to have been favored as the ritualized punishments of masters or "Blacklegs."[45] The American seaports are the best clue. Tarring and feathering seems to have been maintained as a custom among sailors, and it is possible that this is what Richard I was drawing upon. Sailors probably carried it to the colonies, and they were involved in two cases we know of prior to the revolutionary era, one involving a prostitute who boarded a ship in New York port and the other a woman detected masquerading as a seaman.[46]

On land, in New England, the only other way common people were familiar with the practice, as the Loyalist judge Peter Oliver astutely pointed out, was from the annual Pope's Day festivities in Boston and several port towns, where giant effigies of the Devil and his imps, played by young boys, were tarred. This is "the only clue I can find," wrote Oliver. As historian, Oliver was perceptive in two other observations. He sensed that tar-and-feathering was new. "About this time," he wrote caustically, "was invented the art of Tarring and Feathering," an invention "reserved for the Genius of New England ... the town of Salem hath the Honor." And he also caught its class character: tar-and-feathering was "the modern punishment by the rabble of their state criminals."[47]

An analysis of the three full-scale tar-and-featherings in Boston in the revolutionary era bears him out.[48] All three, like the episode in Salem, were (a) against customs informers, (b) the work of predominantly lower-class crowds, (c) led from within, and (d) spur-of-the-moment events. They are in sharp contrast to crowds we know were led by Whig leaders, for example, against merchants in violation of the anti-importation agreements. In these the Boston crowds were (a) more mixed in composition, (b) led from without, and the actions were (c) planned in advance and well organized. The Whig pattern is recognizable through written records: a "town meeting" or one "of the body of the people," public notices warning the targets to desist, articles in the paper, a formal delegation or committee, recognizable leaders, speeches, the whole thing clothed with the trappings of legitimacy.[49]

In Boston, Whig leaders invariably were hostile to tar-and-feathering;[50] they tried to rescue the victims. Once, in 1770, they resorted to a carefully orchestrated *threat* of tar-and-feathering to banish a merchant. But by 1774, after they failed to prevent the spectacular tar-and-feathering of John Malcolm, they moved to take control by announcing a Committee for Tar-and-Feathering, whose chairman was "Joyce, Jun.," an evocation of the bold cornet who captured Charles I in 1647.[51] In 1774, John Adams held the same attitude towards tar-and-featherings that he had expressed towards skimmingtons a decade before: "These tarrings and featherings, this breaking open Houses by rude and insolent Rabbles ... must be discountenanced."[52]

Contemporaries on both sides of the Atlantic identified tar-and-feathering as new and American. It was the "modern dress," "the American mode," "a New England jacket," and in caricature prints that made the practice known throughout England it was "a new method of macaroni making as practised at Boston."[53] In a literal sense contemporaries were wrong; in the larger sense they were right. The fusing of the three ritual elements—of the skimmington, the public execution, and the maritime punishment—entitles us to call tar-and-feathering an American invention, and the inventor, in New England at least, the laboring classes.

II

What was the process, in our second tableau, by which Cromwell got from seventeenth-century England to a 1775 American pamphlet? Perhaps, as follows. At the time of the English Revolution, New England, high and low, shared an identification with Cromwell. In defeat, Cromwell entered popular tradition, where he was stored in folklore—in legend and place lore—for more than a century. By the mid-eighteenth century the high political culture had come to reject the tradition, or at best to bury it; meanwhile the revival of enthusiastic religion invigorated it in popular culture. Beginning in 1765, a time of deep political crisis replicating the dramatis personae and plot of the seventeenth-century drama, the old political tradition was recovered. The tradition was not equally shared, its home being nonelite culture. High political culture borrowed from it or played upon it.

To say New England Puritans supported their brethren in the English Revolution puts it mildly. They prayed for them. "There were twelve special

An ASTRONOMICAL DIARY; Or,
ALMANACK
For the Year of Christian Æra,
1 7 7 4.
Being the second YEAR after BISSEXTILE or LEAP YEAR.
And the 14th Year of the Reign of K. GEORGE IIId.
Containing, besides the usual Astronomical Calculations,
&c. many curious, useful and entertaining Particulars.

By NATHANAEL LOW.

UNgrateful those, who would no Tears allow
To him, who gave them Peace and Empire too !
Princes who fear'd him, griev'd ; concern'd to see
No Pitch of Glory from the Grave is free.

BOSTON : Printed and Sold by J. KNEELAND, in Milk.
Street :—Sold also by the Printers & Bookfellers. 1774.

Oliver Cromwell, leader of the English Revolution of the seventeenth century, in armor ready to do battle, as he appeared on the front page of a Boston almanac for 1774. Paul Revere made the original of this engraving on a billhead for Cromwell's Head Tavern in Boston. The line "Princes who fear'd him, griev'd" was an unsubtle reminder of the beheading of the Stuart king Charles I by Cromwell's followers in 1647. Nathanael Low, *Astronomical Diary; or, Almanack for … 1774* (Boston, 1774), Library of Congress.

fast days observed by Massachusetts in 1644 alone," Francis Bremer writes. They banned support for the royalist cause. They went back to aid the cause. And many New Englanders "reached positions of importance: ten rose to the rank of major or above in the Parliamentary army; others sat in Parliament."[54] "Nearly half of the highly trained ministers and university men returned," Harry Stout points out.[55] Oliver Cromwell, according to Bremer, was seen by New Englanders "as a friend and disciple," whose reign seemed to usher in the new Congregational English Church. The Reverend Hugh Peter of Salem, who preached Charles's execution, was only one of several New Englanders close to Cromwell. The Reverend John Cotton's comment in a letter to Cromwell in 1651—"I am fully satisfied that you have all the while fought the Lord's battles"—was very likely the verdict of his generation and the next.[56]

To have fought in Cromwell's army remained a badge of honor for generations. In 1712, Cotton Mather was happy to offer assistance to an old man of eighty-eight "who was a souldier in the Army of my admirable *Cromwel,* and actually present in the Battel of *Dunbar.*"[57] And in 1749 Susanna Mason, who married Isaac Backus, soon New England's foremost Baptist, knew she was the great-granddaughter of "a soldier who fought with Crummel."[58]

The Puritan party-line on Cromwell changed sometime around 1700, probably when the memoirs of the republican Edmund Ludlow began to take hold, with their theme of Cromwell the usurper made urgent by Whig fears of a standing army.[59] In the Commonwealth political tradition, which New England's leaders of the revolutionary era adopted, Cromwell was anathema. To "Cato" (Trenchard and Gordon), their favorite political philosopher, he was little more than a tyrant. Mrs. Catherine Macaulay, their favorite historian, told them that "no rational and consistent friend to civil freedom" could ever "be an applauder" of Cromwell.[60] When John Adams heard a country parson praise Cromwell—there was the old tradition asserting itself—he was emphatic in his diary: "Oliver was successful but not prudent nor honest nor lawdable [*sic*] nor imitable."[61] The British army in Boston was the reminder of Cromwell's greatest sin. Josiah "Wilkes" Quincy gave Caesar and Cromwell as examples of tyrants who had enslaved their countries with armies "stationed in the very bowels of the land."[62]

To be sure, some Whig leaders—James Otis for one, and, one suspects, Samuel Adams—had a sneaking admiration for Cromwell. The Reverend Jonathan Mayhew dissociated himself from Cromwell's "maladministration" in his famous defense of the principle of regicide, yet came to his defense when he was personally impugned.[63] Even John Adams, when pressed, described Cromwell's government as "infinitely more glorious and happy than that of his Stuart Predecessor." In 1786, when Adams was minister to England, he made a pilgrimage to the battlefields at Edge Hill and Worcester, where he lectured seemingly indifferent people of the neighborhood that this was "holy Ground."[64] There was thus a kind of recessive strain in the Whig political inheritance which might come to the fore.

In England as well as in New England the popular memory preserved Cromwell more fondly in two other streams—enthusiastic religion and a subterranean folk tradition that saw Cromwell as an avenging savior—themes suggested by Christopher Hill and Alan Smith and since developed with impressive proof by Peter Karsten.[65]

In England the Cromwellian era remained central to religious dissenters. During the seventeenth century Bristol's Baptists looked back to "those halcyon days of prosperity, liberty and peace ... those Oliverian days of liberty." Two of the most popular sympathetic biographies of Cromwell were by Baptist ministers, Isaac Kimber (1725) and John Banks (1739), each in at least five editions. During the nineteenth century, "The development of non-conformist self confidence ... was in part a function of their frequent recollection of the Cromwellian era; his day was their golden past, his success their beacon."[66]

It is not clear to what extent New England Baptists embraced Cromwell. Evangelical religion, as a whole, from the Great Awakening in the 1740s through its successive waves into the Revolution, invigorated the memory of Cromwell, holding him up as a model Christian. Jonathan Edwards was quite explicit. "Zeal and resolution," he argued, were responsible for "most of the great things that have been done in this world," and they were responsible for "the great things that Oliver Cromwell did," as well as "the great things Mr. Whitfield has done everywhere."[67] In 1774 a Connecticut evangelical preached that "England was never more happy before, nor much since, than after the head of the first Stuart was severed from his body, and while it was under the protection of Oliver Cromwell." Alan Heimert is doubtless right in claiming that this minister "openly proclaimed a sentiment, that one suspects nearly every pietist in New England had secretly shared since the Great Awakening."[68]

In England, Cromwell clearly entered folklore. No less an authority than Katherine Briggs informs us that legends of Cromwell are "especially conspicuous." There are tales galore of the Cromwell-was-here genre. He is one of the changing figures in mummers' plays. Doggerel verses and nonsense rhymes indicate that he became part of children's lore. The overall image, Alan Smith suggests, is one of a furious destroyer, a desecrator of sacred places, or at best "a mighty man of valour." And for children Cromwell was invoked as a bogeyman ("old Crummell'll have 'em").[69]

Yet there is clearly another tradition in which Cromwell reappears to right the wrongs suffered by the common people. There is an amazing continuity of this notion, from the late seventeenth to the mid-nineteenth century. One line of evidence is in published appeals during times of political crisis. In the Succession Crisis of the 1670s and 1680s, when Whigs fought to keep Charles II from the throne, there appeared a pamphlet, *Oliver Cromwell's Ghost, or Old Noll Revived* (1679). It was followed by *Oliver Cromwell's Ghost Dropt from the Clouds* (1681), in which Cromwell speaks: "Oh that I could pick up the crumbs of my mangled body again ... Oh that I might be suffered to do as much for King Charles the Second as I did against King Charles the First." In a milder vein a 1755 pamphlet, *Oliver Cromwell's Ghost*, followed by similar broadsides in 1756 and 1759, "attacked the ministry for its incompetent handling of the war with France."[70]

Here are the ghostly ancestors of the 1775 *American Chronicle* pamphlet. Such political appeals in the Whig tradition drew their strength from a folk tradition. Why else would the writers make them? The evidence for a warm memory of Cromwell among common people is hidden. When we get a glimmer of it early in the nineteenth century, we seem to be in the presence of a much older cast of mind. In 1812 an anonymous worker angrily swears "vengeance" on the rulers for ignoring the "distresses of the people" and promises that "a second Oliver" would "make his appearance to cleanse the Augean stable." In 1817, Samuel Bamford, the artisan republican, declares on visiting the House of Commons, "O for the stamp of stern old Oliver on this floor." In the 1830s a labouring man tells Thomas Carlyle, as he inspects the battlefield at Worcester, he wishes to God "we had another Oliver, sir, times is dreadful bad."[71]

In New England, Cromwell survived in a folk tradition devoid of the negative features in English lore. Common American experience suggests a few fairly good indicators of the memory of an individual becoming the property of large masses of people: when he is known by his first name alone (if a contemporary African American speaks of "Martin" or "Malcolm," is there any question who he means?); when parents name their children after him; or when places lay claim to his presence ("George Washington slept here").

People did all these things to Cromwell in colonial New England. People referred to him as Oliver (even John Adams called him Oliver), and the name could only have meant Cromwell.[72] People named their children after him. Edward Cook, after searching the tax lists of a representative sample of New England towns, has "the impression that the name became noticeably more popular in the later eighteenth century." By contrast, in a number of English parish registers, "usually there are no Olivers at all, and where there were any, I was lucky to find one or two over a three-hundred-year period."[73] Peter Karsten, "after having scanned hundreds of thousands of names" in the U.S. census returns of 1800, has the "distinct impression" that Oliver was "far more common in New England than in Pennsylvania or South Carolina."[74] Such impressions can hardly be dismissed. Where Cromwell was associated with a place, the hold was tenacious. Cromwell, Hampden, and Pym were supposed to have made preparations to emigrate to Saybrook, Connecticut. The issue was so important that a long line of historians from Cotton Mather to Thomas Hutchinson felt they had to take a stand on it. Even more extraordinary, as late as 1864 the author of a memoir of a sailor in the Revolution could say that "the building lots assigned to them by colonists are still pointed out."[75] Connecticut also named a town Cromwell.

In Boston the memory of Cromwell was kept alive by the Cromwell's Head inn. Near the center of town, it seems to have catered to the middling sort, judging by its printed billhead with the head of Cromwell at the top, engraved by Paul Revere. Out in front the same face was on a sign "hung so low that all who passed by were compelled to make an involuntary reverence," that is, to bow their head before the Protector. Its owner, Joshua Brackett, was known as a Son of Liberty, and during the siege of Boston, British soldiers took it down. Brackett, "in whose eyes this circumstance gave it additional value, replaced it after the evacuation."[76]

Throughout New England the memory of Cromwell was also implicit in the rich lore of the three regicide judges. Goffe, Whalley, and Dixwell found havens, first in Boston, then in New Haven, and Goffe in Hadley in western Massachusetts. The lore of Goffe and Whalley was resonant of Cromwell as deliverer. Both had been generals in Cromwell's army. Goffe entered into legend as the guardian angel of Hadley, who came out of his place of hiding in King Philip's War to rally the citizens and deliver them from a near-fatal Indian raid. The story was widely known—Hutchinson told it in his *History of Massachusetts*—and it passed into literature, first in Sir Walter Scott's *Peveril of the Peak* (1829), and best known in Nathaniel

Hawthorne's "The Gray Champion" (1835). In folk tales Goffe and Whalley also became invincible swordsmen.[77]

New Haven, like Hadley, nursed the place lore of the regicides, as the present names of Dixwell and Whalley avenues suggest. John Dixwell lived out his life there (under an alias) and was buried on the town green. His true identity was so well known that in 1775 British officers went out of their way to desecrate the grave. In the 1780s, when Ezra Stiles, president of Yale, compiled his *History of the Three Judges of Charles I*—America's first oral history—he spoke to residents, who passed on the most detailed stories of the regicides' flight.[78] Dixwell's son, also John (1680–1725), came to Boston, lived in good repute, and became a ruling church elder, as Hutchinson wrote in 1764.[79] New Englanders thus had green memories of the regicides, which ironically the Anglican Church kept alive by commemorating the anniversary of the execution of Charles I, every 30 January.[80]

The efforts of the Pretenders to regain the throne in 1715 and then in 1745 made the seventeenth-century struggle a continuing one for the New World, confronted as it was with a papist enemy on its borders. From about 1745, every 5 November was celebrated in Boston and other New England seaports as Pope's Day. Giant effigies of the devil prompting the pope prompting the Pretender were paraded through town. It was a "gala day" in Boston on which apprentices, young journeymen, sailors, and youth of all classes took over the town. In the evening there was a battle royal between North End and South End Pope's Day gangs, which ended in the burning of the effigies. What in England remained Guy Fawkes Day or Gunpowder Plot Day, commemorating the saving of a Stuart king from destruction, was transformed in New England into a ritual of detestation of the Stuarts and a constant reminder of their pretensions to power and, by implication, of the heroes who fought them.[81]

With Cromwell thus in popular memory, and the memory invigorated by evangelical enthusiasm, it should not be surprising that he appeared as a savior early in the revolutionary crisis. In 1765, in Connecticut, a strongly New Light colony, when the Anglican Church refused to go along with a fast day on the Stamp Act, "a new religious comic liturgy" was printed and "acted out in many towns by the young people on evenings by way of spirit and amusement. ... Instead of 'We beseech thee to hear us, good Lord,' was substituted. 'We beseech thee, O Cromwell to hear [our prayers]' ... 'From plague pestilence & famine,' &c was followed by 'O, Cromwell, deliver us.'" The Episcopal clergy fumed; a grand jury brought an indictment for blasphemy, but a magistrate refused to issue a warrant. Although the grand jury then indicted the magistrate for high treason, no other magistrate would grant a warrant. Cromwell was worth standing up for.[82]

As the crisis deepened, thoughts of a savior went with thoughts of regicide. In Boston in 1769 a paid informer, the innkeeper Richard Sylvester, reported eight "Sentiments of the Sons of Liberty," which began with "That the King was a tyrant, a Rascal and a Fool, and deserv'd to have his head cut off, as much as Charles the first," and ended with "That Oliver Cromwell was a glorious fellow, and what a pitty it was that they had not such another to espouse their cause at present." This informer was not entirely reliable. Authorities were fishing for evidence of a patriot conspiracy for direct action, and it is not at all clear which Sons of Liberty he was reporting on. But in the light of the distinct pattern of turning to Cromwell as a savior, especially among enthusiasts, such sentiments can hardly be dismissed as "wild ravings."[83]

They were soon out in the open. Late in 1769 a paragraph appeared in the *Boston Gazette* signed "Goffe and Whalley," the writer adding the knowing postscript, "Springfield the 30th of October. We almost said the 30th of January." Early in 1771 "Oliver Cromwell" appeared in an article to inform "all the Freeborn Sons of America" he had long watched "the many injuries and insults" they had borne from "tyrannical ministers and their infamous tools (the genuine offspring of my ancient enemies and the Popish Stuarts)." He promised, "I will soon point out a way of relief," a way to make it impossible for such men "ever to oppress you.... I am with peculiar affection your assured friend, Oliver Cromwell."[84] Here was the deliverer on the way. In March 1772, Bostonians were abuzz with the brazen symbol of regicide: "a queer Feast ... in a certain Court [i.e., inn] of this town for the entertainment of a number of Tories—perhaps seventeen. One [dish] contain'd three calves heads (skin off) with their appurtinences anciently call'd pluck." This was a replica of the ceremony of the Calves' Head Club of London (1693–1735), whose members met every 30 January to feast on calves' heads and drink to "the patriots who killed the tyrant."[85]

In Boston, as patriots moved from words to deeds, Cromwell became a central symbol. In November 1773 letters and handbills threatening the tea consignees with violence, unless they resigned their commissions, were signed "O.C." and "O.C. Secy"—initials which could have but one meaning.[86] In January 1774, "Joyce, Jun." appeared as "Captain" of the "Committee for Tarring and Feathering"—a name meant to invoke the symbolism of Cornet George Joyce of Cromwell's army, who in 1647 seized Charles I and in 1649 was rumored to be one of the masked men at his execution. His image in 1774, in broadsides and newspapers, was of an all-powerful figure who would mobilize the people against their enemies but would not countenance mob action.[87] From Joyce it was only a jump in 1775 to Cromwell, the military savior dressed in full battle armor, in *The American Chronicle of the Times.*

As resistance turned to rebellion, Tories portrayed New England leaders as Cromwellians. A caustic satirist, searching for the most damning jibes he could make about a Boston committee of 1775, said Edward Proctor was "a retailer of Lemons and an Oliverian in principle"; Herman Brimmer was "a candidate for deacon in Dr. Chauncey's, alias Hugh Peter's meeting house"; Joshua Brackett was a "publican well known under Cromwell's head," and John Winthrop Jr. was "alias, Joyce, Junior."[88] Peter Oliver was convinced of "too great a Sympathy of Soul between the Brethren of Old & of New England ... their Principles so perfectly coincided."[89]

The Tories, of course, were only half right. Samuel Adams was not the "would-be Cromwell" of America.[90] The "Sympathy of Soul" lay in the folk traditions and enthusiastic religion. The leaders drew upon this popular tradition, assuming a persona in Cromwell or Joyce. They fit a pattern Peter Karsten has identified: the "efforts of elites to capitalize on what they perceived to be existing popular veneration of a particular patriot symbol."[91]

III

Where did the artisan parades of 1788 come from? Artisan culture migrated to the New World—Boston shipbuilders, shoemakers, and coopers attempted guilds in the 1640s. But how much of it was retained? The guilds, after all, did not survive.[92] Where on Herskovits's "scale of intensity" was artisan culture, say, in the mid-eighteenth century? Not flourishing, our limited evidence suggests. The evidence is thicker during and after the Revolution, in particular among urban mechanics. As they took collective action, especially in politics, they acquired a greater consciousness of themselves as citizens, as producers, and as a "mechanic interest," and in doing so they reached back and over to retrieve traditions. In the case of Cromwell, New Englanders were recovering what had always been theirs and had lain dormant. Artisans were recovering what they had lost and belonged to their predecessors in an earlier time.

The process by which urban artisans and laborers entered the political arena after 1765 and emerged in the 1780s with a new sense of awareness and a new set of unmet needs has been established by a number of scholars; we need not go over it here.[93] If, however, we examine the Constitution paradcs closely, we get a vivid picture of the point in the process that had been reached by 1788 (see essay 1 in this volume).

The floats, the banners, the slogans were a magnificent *summa* of the mechanic consciousness that had welled up in the Revolutionary era: pride of craft, producer consciousness, awareness of mechanic interest, above all pride of citizenship—together constituting artisan republicanism.

Everywhere mechanics stressed their craft. In Boston blacksmiths and carpenters marched "with tools of every sort decorated"; each ropemaker marched with a knot of hemp around his waist. Elsewhere workers accompanied a stage with their craft product as a political symbol: bakers with a huge "Federal Loaf"; upholsterers with an oversized "Chair of State"; the carpenters, in Philadelphia, with a "Grand Federal Edifice." Shipwrights invariably sponsored a small ship fully manned, outfitted, and rigged, mounted on wheels and pulled by a huge team of horses. Other artisans plied their trades on the floats: the coopers making a new barrel, hooping thirteen states together; or the blacksmiths at a forge, beating swords into ploughshares; the printers turning out an ode for the occasion on their press.

Peale, the painter, counseled against a slavish imitation of English patterns. Some trades, however, reached back to antiquity, like the Baltimore coopers who bore a golden figure of Bacchus sitting on a cask, or the painters and glaziers who carried a likeness of Michelangelo. In New York and Philadelphia the banners blended English and American symbols. The tailors' banner depicted Adam and Eve and the slogan "And they sewed fig leaves together"—this was the emblem of the London tailors' guild—but they added a chain of ten links in the center, the word "majority," and a sun beaming its rays on the ratifying states. Over all, a huge figure of George Washington held a parchment, the federal Constitution, and a federal eagle with expanded wings soared towards the sun.

Where did all this—the symbolism, the configurations of the marching—come from? In late-colonial America it was common for self-employed artisans in a single trade in one city to join together on an ad hoc basis to set prices (the building trades), to cope with city fathers over mercantilist regulations (for example, the bakers), and especially to petition colonial assemblies for aid or relief. But masters sustained only a few organizations, except for the carpenters, and there were very few friendly societies. And journeymen rarely took collective action; the first strikes in different trades occurred in 1779, 1786, or more likely the 1790s.[94]

Colonial artisans do not seem to have made much of traditional trade emblems. The well-organized house carpenters used their symbol—three calipers and a square—on their publications.[95] Here and there a craftsman put a London symbol on his shop sign or trade card.[96] But it is revealing that in 1789, when forty-six Boston trades were asked to march with emblems of the trade (to welcome President Washington) they had to make flags for the occasion.[97]

It would seem, therefore, that not until after the Revolution did craftsmen begin to search out symbols. The pewterers, with an elaborate flag in the New York parade, had already formed a society. The committee responsible for the membership certificate of the General Society of Mechanics and Tradesmen of New York, in 1786, also knew London arms. The central motif was the strong right arm of a workman holding aloft a hammer, above it the slogan "By hammer and hand all arts do stand." The slogan came from the blacksmiths, but the arm could be found on the emblem of the farriers, feltmakers, pavoirs (street-pavers), and wheelwrights. In founding a society that was unprecedented—a citywide membership society open to all trades—New Yorkers picked a symbolic common denominator.[98]

But where did the civic procession of the trades come from? There were no precedents on the American side of the Atlantic. In the colonies, laboring men paraded in the militia. The Pope's Day processions were by apprentices, youths, and the lower sort. Masonic processions had a sprinkling of artisans of the higher trades. In the revolutionary agitation plebeians joined pellmell in all sorts of crowd actions which might include marches. But when the "mechanics, tradesmen and manufacturers" assembled, as in Philadelphia, it was at a mass meeting or, in Boston, at a town meeting.

There were precedents in England. During the medieval period ceremonial processions of the guilds marked the religious calendar.[99] In London from the mid-sixteenth to the very early eighteenth century the livery company of the incoming Lord Mayor sponsored an inauguration parade. Initially rich with trade symbolism, at their height the Lord Mayor's shows were steeped in classical and pastoral allegory and produced by playwrights. A diarist of about 1700 writes of "a sort of stages carried by men and on ye top many men and boys acting ye respective trades or Employ[ments] of each company."[100] But, never strictly trade processions, they faded early in the eighteenth century, were revived about 1760, to atrophy once again. In Bristol, on the other hand, a port with important transatlantic connections, Nicholas Rogers has found evidence of trade processions on official anniversaries: for example, Coronation Day in 1760.[101]

For parades by English workers in individual crafts there is more abundant evidence in recent scholarship. Workers often presented their grievances by marching in processions, "with colours flying, drums beating and fifes playing."[102] Some trades paraded on their patron saint's day (if only to the local tavern): the shoemakers on St. Crispin's Day, the ropeworkers for St. Catherine, the woolcombers for Bishop Blaze.[103] And craftsmen who formed friendly societies often displayed banners, like the weavers of Taunton who met "with ensigns and Flags hung out at the door of their meeting."[104]

Some American mechanics might have drawn on such experiences or the memories of them, but most would have had to reach very far back to traditions they could have been only dimly aware of. In any case, the American parades, taken as a whole, were innovations, just as the Constitution and popular participation in the ratification process were innovations. Though mechanics reached back and over to retrieve symbols and forms of action, they put all these together in a way that made them new.

When British craftsmen formed trade unions in the 1820s after they were legal, they did the same thing. "Practically all of the craft unions," writes John Gorman, who has assembled their banners, "made at least some use of traditional mottoes, emblems and symbols of the guilds, borrowing in part if not in entirety. They sought to trace the origins of their craft, if not their organisation in order to justify their claims to represent the best interests of the trade and not only the welfare of the men." The first banner Gorman could locate was in 1820.[105] American usage dates at least thirty years before. Perhaps we should entertain the hypothesis that there was a transit of plebeian culture eastwards across the Atlantic.

IV

What happened to the customs and traditions we have been discussing? What was the process in the nineteenth century? The rituals of popular punishment flourished. Tar-and-feathering rejoined the rough-music family in New England as a ritual for the enforcement of sexual morality.

In the Boston area, for example, the first postwar victim was a man who moved into the royal governor Shirley's estate at Roxbury and was accused of maltreating his wife.[106] As it spread it was used on many targets, left and right, from tax collectors in the Whiskey Rebellion in the 1790s to Mississippi River con men in Mark Twain's *Huckleberry Finn* to CIO labor organizers in the South. The skimmington became a "vital presence" across the United States and Canada, put to a variety of plebeian purposes, as Bryan Palmer has made clear,[107] before it ended up as the benign shivaree community send-off for newlyweds.

Seventeenth-century political traditions did not entirely disappear. In 1794, President Ezra Stiles of Yale published his *History of the Three Judges of Charles I*, to justify the execution of the French king. "There must and would arise new Cromwells," he wrote, "to resume the work which Oliver and the Judges once achieved."[108] In New England, Cromwell entered into the marrow of nineteenth-century crusaders like Wendell Phillips, who wrote in his commonplace book as a young man, "Wendell Phillips, born November 29, in 1811. I love the Puritans, honor Cromwell, idolize Chatham & huray for [Daniel] Webster."[109]

In Boston, not Cromwell, but "Joyce Jun." lived on as an apocryphal avenging figure ready to come to the aid of the laboring classes. In 1777 he made a personal appearance on horseback at the head of a mob punishing merchants who were violating wartime price controls. In 1785 he threatened dire action against "British agents, British factors and British merchants" who were swamping American manufacturers, and urged "tradesmen" to form their own "association." In 1805 he appeared in a broadside warning "money changers," "sharpers," "usurers," and "bank directors" to reduce rents and interest rates, "otherwise he shall be obliged to mount his Jack Ass" once again. Thereafter he was in folk memory.[110]

American artisans continued to parade in precisely the style of 1788. Sean Wilentz has made this vivid for New York parades celebrating victory after the War of 1812, Lafayette's visit, the opening of the Erie Canal in the 1820s, and the French Revolution of 1830. By 1834, in fact, New York boasted a "standard and banner painter and society supplier," perhaps a good deal earlier than London.[111] The workman's raised arm, hammer in hand, made its way on to countless nineteenth-century emblems. The motto "By hammer and hand all arts do stand," the proud assertion of producer consciousness, was expressed in New York in 1882 on the placards of the first Labor Day parade as "Labor creates all wealth."[112] Or was there perhaps a discontinuity, and did the idea have to migrate once again from Europe?

Finally, what do these examples of plebeian culture have to do with eighteenth-century American radicalism? Our judgments depend upon how we define radicalism in a revolution of colonial liberation fought by a coalition in which there was, after all, the same "dialectical dance" of classes Eric Hobsbawm has spoken of for European revolutions.[113]

Tar-and-feathering, as the major instrument of establishing revolutionary justice, until its function was taken over by formal committees for detecting conspiracies, was radical. Anyone who doubts the capacity of a tar-and-feathering crowd, composed of the laboring sort, to articulate their sense of justice might eavesdrop on the dialogue in the streets of Boston in January 1774, at the action against John Malcolm. "Several gentlemen endeavored to divert the populace of their intention," arguing that Malcolm was "open to the laws of the land which would undoubtedly award a reasonable satisfaction to the parties he had abused." The crowd, heavy with sailors, replied that Malcolm "had been an old impudent and mischevious offender—he had joined in the murders at North Carolina [i.e., he had fought against the Regulators]—he had seized vessels on account of sailors' having a bottle or two of gin on board; he had in other words behaved in the most capricious, insulting and daringly abusive manner." The "gentlemen" pleaded again to allow the law to "have its course with him." Members of the crowd then asked,

> what course had the law taken with [Captain] Preston on his soldiers [in the Boston Massacre], with Captain Wilson [alleged to have provoked slaves], or Richardson [who had been found guilty of killing an eleven-year-old boy, Christopher Seider, sentenced, and pardoned by the Crown]? And for their parts, they had seen so much partiality to the soldiers and customhouse officers by the present judges, that while things remained as they were, they would, on all such occasions, take satisfaction their own way, and let them take it off.[114]

Cromwell's ghost enabled common people and their betters to take up arms—surely a radical action in 1775—fortified with the memory of a successful revolution that had toppled a king. The "Yankee Doodles," who became the first American army, did indeed have something of the spirit of the New Model Army. A British surgeon visiting a patriot military camp near Boston in 1775 found an army that was "truly nothing but a drunken, canting, lying, praying, hypocritical rabble.... they are congregationalists, divided and subdivided into a variety of distinctions, the descendants of

Oliver Cromwell's army who truly inherit the spirit which was the occasion of so much bloodshed ... from 1642 till the Restoration."[115]

As to the artisans on parade, the Constitution they celebrated, I argue in essay 4 in this volume preserved the essential gains that the mechanic classes had made the sine qua non of democratic government: a suffrage to which most of them were eligible, the right to participate in the process of government; and it set up a government strong enough to speak to the needs of their political economy. We might argue with the bricklayers of Philadelphia who carried the banner "Buildings and rulers are the work of our hands," but we may not say they were fools.

In England, plebeian culture, E. P. Thompson has argued, "was not, to be sure, a revolutionary nor even a proto-revolutionary culture—but one should not describe it as a deferential culture, either. It bred riots, but not rebellions; direct actions but not democratic organisations."[116] In America, plebeian culture seems to have carried people farther. Ordinary people went through riots to revolution, from direct action to democratic organization. New movements invented traditions. If we would understand the outcome, we need more attention to the processes of the transmission, retention, recovery, and transformation.

NOTES

This essay was given at a conference, "The Origins of Anglo-American Radicalism" (New York, 1980) and published in Margaret Jacob and James Jacob, eds., *The Origins of Anglo-American Radicalism* (London: Allen & Unwin, 1984; Atlantic Highlands, N.J.: Humanities Press, 1991). Reprinted with the permission of Humanities Press International, Inc.

I am indebted to Pauline Maier, Jesse Lemisch, and the late Herbert Gutman for comment and to Robert W. Malcomson and Nicholas Rogers for suggestions.

1. Cited in Richard B. Morris, *Government and Labor in Early America* (New York: Columbia University Press, 1946), p. 147.

2. *Essex Gazette*, 13 September 1768.

3. *The First Book of the American Chronicle of the Times*, chs. 1–4 (Boston/Philadelphia, 1774–5). It was also published in New Bern, S.C., and Norwich, Conn. See J. R. Bowman, "A bibliography of *The First Book* ...," *American Literature*, vol. 1 (1929–30), pp. 69–74.

4. Bernard Bailyn, *The Ideological Origins of the American Revolution* (Cambridge, Mass.: Harvard University Press, 1967), p. 10.

5. See sources in section III below.

6. Mildred Campbell, "English emigration on the eve of the American Revolution," *American Historical Review*, vol. 61 (1955–6), pp. 1–20; George Mellor, "Emigration from the British Isles to the New World, 1765–1775," *History*, vol. 40 (1955), pp. 68–83; John Bumsted and Charles Clark, "New England's Tom Paine: John Allen and the Spirit of Liberty," *William and Mary Quarterly*, vol. 21 (1964), pp. 561ff.; Joseph Belcher, *George Whitefield: A Biography, with Special Reference to His Labours in America* (New York: American Tract Society, 1857).

7. See Sumner Chilton Powell, *Puritan Village: The Formation of a New England Town* (Middleton, Conn.: Wesleyan University Press, 1963); Anthony N. B. Garvan, *Architecture and Town Planning in Colonial Connecticut* (New Haven, Conn.: Yale University Press, 1951); and, of the more recent studies, Kenneth Lockridge, *A New England Town, the First Hundred Years: Dedham, Massachusetts, 1636–1736* (New York: Norton, 1970), pp. 18–9.

8. David Grayson Allen, *In English Ways: The Movement of Societies and the Transferral of English Law and Custom to Massachusetts Bay in the Seventeenth Century* (Chapel Hill: University of North Carolina Press, 1981); Timothy Breen and Stephen Foster, "Moving to the New World: The character of early Massachusetts migration," *William and Mary Quarterly*, vol. 30 (1973), pp. 189–222; Timothy Breen, "Persistent localism: English social change and the shaping of New England institutions," *William and Mary Quarterly*, vol. 32 (1975), pp. 3–28.

9. Iona Opie and Peter Opie, *The Oxford Dictionary of Nursery Rhymes* (London: Oxford University Press, 1951; reprinted 1973), p. 42; George Lyman Kittredge, *Witchcraft in Old and New England* (Cambridge, Mass.: Harvard University Press, 1929), and Jon Butler, "Magic, astrology, and the early American religious heritage," *American Historical Review*, vol. 84 (1979), pp. 317–46; Henry Glassie, *Pattern in the Material Folk Culture of the Eastern United States* (Philadelphia: University of Pennsylvania Press, 1968), pp. 47, 124–5, 133–4, 142, 184, 187, 209.

10. Lockridge, *New England Town*, ch. 1; Kenneth Lockridge, *Literacy in Colonial New England* (New York: Norton, 1974); James A. Henretta, "Families and farms: mentalité in pre-industrial America," *William and Mary Quarterly*, vol. 35 (1978), pp. 3–32; Gary B. Nash, *The Urban Crucible: Social Change, Political Consciousness and the Origins of the American Revolution* (Cambridge, Mass.: Harvard University Press, 1979), chs. 9, 11; James A. Henretta, *The Evolution of American Society, 1700–1815: An Interdisciplinary Analysis* (Lexington, Ky.: Heath, 1973).

11. Peter Burke, *Popular Culture in Early Modern Europe* (New York: Harpers, 1978), p. 257; E. P. Thompson, "Eighteenth-century English society: Class struggle without class?" *Social History*, vol. 3 (1978), p. 153.

12. Morris, *Government and Labor*, pp. 139–56.

13. Melville J. Herskovits, *The Myth of the Negro Past* (New York: Harper, 1941; reprinted Boston: Beacon Press, 1958), and "Problem, method and theory in Afroamerican studies" (1945), in his *The New World Negro* (Bloomington: Indiana

University Press, 1966), pp. 43–61; George E. Simpson, *Melville J. Herskovits* (New York: Columbia University Press, 1973), esp. pp. 25–42.

14. Joseph Reidy, "Negro election day and the New England black community, 1750–1850," *Marxist Perspectives*, vol. 3 (1979), pp. 102–17.

15. E. Franklin Frazier, *The Negro Family in the United States* (Chicago: University of Chicago Press, 1939).

16. Herbert Gutman, *The Black Family in Slavery and Freedom, 1750–1925* (New York: Pantheon, 1976), pp. 211–2.

17. Eugene Genovese, *Roll Jordan Roll: The World the Slaves Made* (New York: Pantheon, 1974), pp. 232–3.

18. Sidney Mintz, Foreword to Norman E. Whitten and John F. Szwed (eds.), *Afro-American Anthropology: Contemporary Perspectives* (New York: Free Press, 1970), pp. 1–16; Herbert Gutman, "Work, culture and society in industrializing America, 1815–1919," *American Historical Review*, vol. 78 (1973), pp. 541–53.

19. Charles R. Tilly, *From Mobilization to Revolution* (Reading, Mass.: Addison Wesley, 1978), pp. 151–9.

20. Burke, *Popular Culture*, pp. 116, 124.

21. E. P. Thompson, "Patrician society, plebeian culture," *Journal of Social History*, vol. 7 (1974), pp. 393–4.

22. Eric J. Hobsbawm and Tenance Ranger (eds.), *The Invention of Tradition* (Cambridge: Cambridge University Press, 1983).

23. Burke, *Popular Culture*, ch. 1.

24. E. P. Thompson, "Rough music: The charivari anglaise," *Annales*, vol. 27 (March–April 1972), pp. 285–312; E. P. Thompson, "Rough music and charivari: Some further reflections," unpublished paper, Le Charivari dans l'Europe Préindustrielle Conference, Paris, April 1977, since published in Thompson, *Customs in Common* (London: Merlin, 1991), 467–533.

25. Bryan Palmer, "Discordant music: Charivari and white capping in North America," *Labor/Le Traveilleur*, vol. 1 (September 1978), pp. 5–62.

26. Steven J. Stewart, "Skimmington riots: A means of enforcing social behaviour," unpublished paper, 1975; and "Skimmington," unpublished manuscript, 1981, which Mr. Stewart, kindly allowed me to read. Stewart also identifies half a dozen "antecedents to skimmingtons"; he finds the first use of the term "skimmington ride" in a 1751 episode at Poughkeepsie, New York. Paper since published in William Pencak, Matthew Dennis, and Simon P. Newman (eds.), *Riot and Revelry in Early America* (University Park: Pennsylvania State University Press, 2002), 41–86.

27. "Clarendon to Pym," 11 January 1766, in *Diary and Autobiography of John Adams*, ed. L. H. Butterfield, 4 vols. (Cambridge, Mass.: Harvard University Press, 1961), vol. 1, p. 291.

28. *Newport Mercury*, 9 and 12 November 1764, reporting the episode at Attleborough, Mass., brought to my attention by Edmund Morgan.

29. *The Diary of Samuel Sewall, 1674–1729*, ed. M. Halsey Thomas, 2 vols. (New York: Farrar, Straus & Giroux, 1973), vol. 1, p. 572 (10 September 1707), and p. 520 (3 March 1705), for an earlier incident in Boston.

30. James Green (ed.), *Three Military Diaries Kept by Groton Soldiers in Different Wars* (Groton, N.Y., 1901), pp. 3–39, cited in John A. Murrin, "Anglicizing an American colony: The transformation of provincial Massachusetts," Ph.D. dissertation, Yale University, 1966, pp. 105–6.

31. *Letters and Diary of John Rowe*, ed. Anne Rowe Cunningham (Boston: Clarke, 1903), p. 61 (11 September 1764).

32. James E. Cutler, *Lynch-Law* (New York: Longmans, Green, 1903), pp. 46–7.

33. Edwin Powers, *Crime and Punishments in Early Massachusetts, 1620–1692* (Boston: Beacon Press, 1966), esp. chs. 6, 7; George E. Howard, *A History of Matrimonial Institutions*, 3 vols. (Chicago: University of Chicago Press, 1904), vol. 2, pp. 175–7, 188–97.

34. John Demos, *A Little Commonwealth: Family Life in Plymouth Colony* (New York: Oxford University Press, 1970), ch. 5; David Flaherty, "Law and the enforcement of morals in early America," *Perspectives in American History*, vol. 5 (1971), pp. 203–53, at 225–45.

35. Burke, *Popular Culture*, p. 197.

36. Lawrence W. Towner, "True confessions and dying warnings in colonial New England," in Frederick S. Allis (ed.), *Sibley's Heir: A Volume in Memory of Clifford Kenyon Shipton* (Boston: Colonial Society of Massachusetts, 1972), pp. 523–39.

37. Peter Linebaugh, "The Tyburn riot against the surgeons," in Douglas Hay et al., *Albion's Fatal Tree: Crime and Society in Eighteenth-Century England* (New York: Pantheon, 1975), pp. 65–117, at 67.

38. See, for example, the case of Levi Ames, Boston, 1773, in Justin Winsor (ed.), *The Memorial History of Boston*, 4 vols. (Boston, 1881), vol. 2, pp. 486–7.

39. Dirk Hoerder, *Crowd Action in Revolutionary Massachusetts, 1765–1780* (New York: Academic Press, 1977); Jules Calvin Landenheim, "'The Doctors' Mob' of 1788," *Journal of the History of Medicine*, vol. 5 (Winter 1950), pp. 23–43.

40. Alice Morse Earle, *Curious Punishments of Bygone Days* (Chicago, 1896); George Francis Dow, *Everyday Life in the Massachusetts Bay Colony* (Boston: Society for the Preservation of New England Antiquities, 1935), pp. 213–4.

41. *Diary of John Rowe*, p. 65 (4 October 1764).

42. John Trumbull, *M'Fingall: A Modern Epic Poem in Four Cantos* (Boston, 1799).

43. *Oxford English Dictionary*, vol. 11, p. 89. A British officer in Boston quoted Rymer's *Foedera* (1704) as his source for Richard I introducing the practice: *Diary of Frederick MacKenzie*, ed. Allen French (Cambridge, Mass.: Harvard University Press, 1930), pp. 10–1 (8 March 1775).

44. For a tar-and-feathering of monks in 1623, see James Howell, *Familiar Letters* (London, 1645), p. 81; for an episode in 1696 in London in which the "rabble" tar-and-feathered a bailiff attempting to imprison a debtor, see John

H. Jesse, *London and Its Celebrities*, 2 vols. (London, 1850), vol. 2, p. 343, both cases also in *Notes and Queries*, 4th ser., vol. 5 (29 January 1870), p. 116. Peter Linebaugh reports the threat of shipwrights in Woolwich in 1775 to seize their master and "rowl him in Tar and Feathers," in "The Passage from workers' power in the period of manufacture: Samuel Bentham, technological repression, and the eighteenth-century British shipyards," unpublished paper, 1978.

45. C. R. Dobson, *Masters and Journeymen: A Prehistory of Industrial Relations, 1717–1800* (London: Croom Helm, 1980), pp. 17–8, 90; John Rule, *The Experience of Labour in Eighteenth-Century Industry* (London: Croom Helm, 1981), p. 187; John Stevenson, *Popular Disturbances in England, 1700–1870* (London: Longmans, 1979), pp. 47–50; Robert W. Malcolmson, *Life and Labour in England 1700–1780* (London: Hutchinson, 1981), pp. 105, 126. None of these detailed studies reports tar-and-feathering.

46. Earle, *Curious Punishments*, p. 126; Carl Bridenbaugh, *Cities in Revolt: Urban Life in America, 1743–1776* (New York: Knopf, 1955), p. 121. For British sailors' parading in Boston in 1775 on the twelfth day of Christmas with a "he devil" "completely tarr'd and feather'd," see "Letters of John Andrews," *Proceedings of Massachusetts Historical Society*, vol. 8, p. 393.

47. Douglass Adair and John Schutz (eds.), *Peter Oliver's Origin and Progress of the American Rebellion: A Tory View* (San Marino, Calif.: Huntington Library, 1961), p. 94. On earlier tar-and-feathering, R. S. Longley, "Mob activities in Revolutionary Massachusetts," *New England Quarterly*, vol. 6 (1933), p. 115, n. 54, writes, "Mr Leonard London informs me that there was a tarring and feathering in Essex County [Mass.] between 1670 and 1680." Steven Stewart informs me of a case in New York in 1762, preserved in the John Tabor Kemp Papers, New-York Historical Society.

48. The Boston episodes were George Gailer (28 October 1769), Owen Richards (18 May 1770), and John Malcolm (25 January 1774). There was also a small-scale affair, in Charlestown across the Bay (November 1769), involving a man who enticed a woman into the soldiers' barracks in Boston. The abortive Whig affair, led by Dr. Thomas Young, was against Patrick McMaster (June 1770); British soldiers conducted an action in Boston against Thomas Ditson (8 March 1775). For the Malcolm affair, see Alfred F. Young, "George Robert Twelves Hewes, 1742–1840: A Boston shoemaker and the memory of the American Revolution," *William and Mary Quarterly*, vol. 38 (October 1981), pp. 592–6; for my earlier analysis, see Alfred F. Young, "Pope's Day, tar and feathers and Cornet Joyce, Jun.: From ritual to rebellion in Boston, 1745–1775," unpublished paper, Anglo-American Historians' Conference, Rutgers University, 1973.

49. Types of crowd action are best delineated in Hoerder, *Crowd Action*, passim.

50. Pauline Maier, *From Resistance to Revolution: Colonial Radicals and the Development of American Opposition to Britain, 1765–1776* (New York: Knopf, 1972), pp. 128–9, 272–3. For mobs in which leading citizens participated, ibid.,

pp. 12–3; for tar-and-featherings in which leaders took part, see Pauline Maier, "The Charleston mob and the evolution of popular politics in Revolutionary South Carolina, 1765–1784," *Perspectives in American History*, vol. 4 (1970), pp. 184–5; and for Norfolk, Virginia, Merrill Jensen, *The Founding of a Nation* (New York: Oxford University Press, 1968), pp. 301–2.

51. See below, section II.

52. John Adams to Abigail Adams, 7 July 1774, cited in Maier, *Resistance to Revolution*, p. 274.

53. For English references, see Francis Grose, *A Classical Dictionary of the Vulgar Tongue* (London, 1785), "Tar and feathering," and the captions to a series of caricatures published in 1775 in M. Dorothy George (ed.), *Catalogue of Political and Personal Satires … in the British Museum*, vol. 5 (London: British Museum, 1935), no. 5232, pp. 168–89.

54. Francis J. Bremer, *The Puritan Experiment: New England Society from Bradford to Edwards* (New York: St. Martin's Press, 1976), pp. 108–12.

55. Harry Stout, "The morphology of remigration: New England university men and their return to England, 1640–1660," *Journal of American Studies*, vol. 10 (1976), pp. 151–72.

56. Bremer, *Puritan Experiment*, p. 112; Cromwell to Rev. John Cotton, 2 October 1651, in Thomas Hutchinson, *A Collection of Original Papers Relative to the History of the Colony of Massachusetts Bay* (Boston, 1769), pp. 233–7.

57. Cited in Barrett Wendell, *Cotton Mather: The Puritan Priest* (New York: Harcourt, Brace, 1891; reprinted 1963), p. 179.

58. William G. McLoughlin, *New England Dissent 1630–1833: The Baptists and the Separation of Church and State*, 2 vols. (Cambridge, Mass.: Harvard University Press, 1971), vol. 1, p. 432.

59. Edmund Ludlow, *A Voyce from the Watch Tower, Part 5: 1660–62*, ed. A. B. Worden, Camden Society, 4th ser., vol. 21 (London, 1978), brought to my attention and its importance explained by my colleague Stephen Foster.

60. David L. Jacobson (ed.), *The English Libertarian Heritage from the Writings of John Trenchard and Thomas Gordon* (New York: Bobbs-Merrill, 1965), pp. xxxv, 72, 206–7, 221, 223; Lucy M. Donnelly, "The celebrated Mrs. Macaulay," *William and Mary Quarterly*, vol. 6 (1949), pp. 191, 193–4, 202; Trevor Colbourn, *The Lamp of Experience: Whig History and the Intellectual Origins of the American Revolution* (Chapel Hill: University of North Carolina Press, 1965), ch. 4, esp. pp. 200, 223.

61. *Diary of John Adams*, vol. 1, p. 220 (10 September 1761).

62. Colbourn, *Lamp of Experience*, p. 79.

63. John J. Waters Jr, *The Otis Family in Provincial and Revolutionary Massachusetts* (Chapel Hill: University of North Carolina Press, 1968), p. 11; Pauline Maier, "Coming to terms with Samuel Adams," *American Historical Review*, vol. 81 (1976), esp. pp. 34–7; Charles Akers, *Called unto Liberty: A Life of Jonathan Mayhew, 1720–1776* (Cambridge, Mass.: Harvard University Press, 1964), p. 159.

64. *Diary of John Adams*, vol. 3, p. 185 (4–10 April 1786).

65. Christopher Hill, *God's Englishman: Oliver Cromwell and the English Revolution* (New York: Dial Press, 1970), ch. 10; Alan Smith, "The image of Cromwell in folklore and tradition," *Folklore*, vol. 79 (1968), pp. 17–39, and "Nineteenth-century Cromwell," *Past and Present*, no. 40 (1968), pp. 187–90; Peter Karsten, *Patriot Heroes in England and America: Political Symbolism and Changing Values over Three Centuries* (Madison: University of Wisconsin Press, 1979).

66. Hill, *God's Englishman*, pp. 266, 271; Smith, "Cromwell in folklore"; Karsten, *Patriot Heroes*, pp. 30–1.

67. Jonathan Edwards, *Works*, 10th ed. (London, 1865), vol. 1, p. 424.

68. Alan Heimert, *Religion and the American Mind from the Great Awakening to the Revolution* (Cambridge, Mass.: Harvard University Press, 1966), p. 357.

69. Katherine M. Briggs, *A Dictionary of British Folk-Tales*, 4 vols. (Bloomington: University of Indiana Press, 1971), pt. B, vol. 2, pp. 3, 25–7, 52–3; Smith, "The image of Cromwell," p. 39.

70. Karsten, *Patriot Heroes*, pp. 21–2.

71. Hill, *God's Englishman*, pp. 273–4.

72. Comment of Edmund Morgan to the author, 1974.

73. Edward Cook to the author, 24 June 1981. Cook scanned lists he used in his book *The Fathers of the Towns: Leadership and Community Structure in Eighteenth-Century New England* (Baltimore: Johns Hopkins University Press, 1976). Twenty-six lists had no "Oliver"; thirty had from one to five. Examples of high incidence: Billerica (1771), 5 out of 290 taxpayers; Dedham (1771), 5 out of about 250; Hadley (1771), 5 out of 145; Sudbury (1770), 4 out of 438. I am indebted to Prof. Cook for making this search.

74. Peter Karsten to the author, 23 July 1974, generously sharing information not in *Patriot Heroes*.

75. John W. Dean, "The reported embarkation of Cromwell, and his friends for New England," *New England Historical and Genealogical Register*, vol. 20 (1866), pp. 113–21; Charles I. Bushnell (ed.), *Adventures of Christopher Hawkins* (New York, 1864), p. 305, brought to my attention by Jesse Lemisch.

76. Samuel Adams Drake, *Old Landmarks and Historic Personages of Boston* (Boston: Little, Brown, 1900), pp. 61–2.

77. Thomas Hutchinson, *History of the Province of Massachusetts-Bay*, 2 vols. (Boston, 1764–7), vol. 1, pp. 185–7; John Warner Barber, *Massachusetts Historical Collections* (Worcester, Mass., 1839), pp. 325–6; Noah Warner, "Further reminiscences of the valley of the Pawtucket River and its branches," *Narragansett Historical Register* (1889), p. 238.

78. Ezra Stiles, *A History of the Three Judges of King Charles I* (Hartford, Conn., 1794); *The Literary Diary of Ezra Stiles*, ed. Franklin B. Dexter, 3 vols. (New York: Scribner, 1901), vol., 3, pp. 168–71.

79. Hutchinson, *History of Massachusetts-Bay*, vol. 1, pp. 183–5, 186–7 n.

80. Jonathan Mayhew, *A Discourse Concerning Unlimited Submission and Non-resistance to the Higher Powers with Some Reflections on the Resistance Made to King Charles I on the Anniversary of His Death ... the 30th of January, 1749–50* (Boston, 1750); Bernard Bailyn (ed.), *Pamphlets of the American Revolution, 1750–1776* (Cambridge, Mass.: Harvard University Press, 1765), vol. 1, pp. 204–11, introduction.

81. Young, "Pope's Day, tar and feathers," secs. I, II, III.

82. Rev. Samuel Peters, *General History of Connecticut ...* (1781; reprinted New York, 1877), pp. 231–2.

83. "Sentiments of the Sons of Liberty February 1769," in Jared Sparks, *New England Papers*, vol. 10, no. 2, p. 18 (Houghton Library, Harvard University); Bailyn, *Thomas Hutchinson*, pp. 127–8.

84. *Boston Gazette*, 29 November 1769, 25 February 1771.

85. *Diary of Anna Green Winslow*, ed. Alice Morse Earle (Boston, 1894), pp. 44–5 (14 March 1772); Karsten, *Patriot Heroes*, p. 22.

86. Benjamin W. Labaree, *The Boston Tea Party* (New York: Oxford University Press, 1964), pp. 109–11; see also "Oliver Cromwell," *Boston Gazette*, 19 October 1772.

87. Young, "Pope's Day, tar and feathers," sec. VI: Albert Matthews, "Joyce, Jun.," *Colonial Society of Massachusetts Publications*, vol. 8 (1903), pp. 89–104, and "Joyce, Jun., once more," ibid., vol. 9, pp. 280–94.

88. *Massachusetts Historical Society Proceedings*, 2nd ser., vol. 12 (1897–8), pp. 139–42, and in manuscript in James Bowdoin Papers, Massachusetts Historical Society.

89. Oliver, *Origin and Progress*, p. 22.

90. Cited in John C. Miller, *Sam Adams: Pioneer in Propaganda* (Boston: Little, Brown, 1936), p. 343.

91. Karsten, *Patriot Heroes*, p. 7.

92. Morris, *Government and Labor*, pp. 139–56.

93. Ibid., ch. 3; Nash, *Urban Crucible*, chs. 11, 12; Eric Foner, *Tom Paine and Revolutionary America* (New York: Oxford University Press, 1976); Philip Foner, *Labor and the American Revolution* (Westport, Conn.: Greenwood Press, 1976); Alfred F. Young, *Democratic Republicans of New York: The Origins, 1763–1797* (Chapel Hill: University of North Carolina Press, 1968), chs. 4, 5; Staughton Lynd, "The mechanics in New York politics, 1774–1788," *Labor History*, vol. 5 (1968), pp. 225–46; Charles Olton, *Artisans for Independence: Philadelphia Mechanics and the American Revolution* (Syracuse, N.Y.: Syracuse University Press, 1975), ch. 9; Richard Walsh, *Charleston's Sons of Liberty: A Study of the Artisans, 1763–1789* (Columbia: University of South Carolina Press, 1959), ch. 5.

94. Mary Roys Baker, "Anglo-Massachusetts trade union roots, 1730–1790," *Labor History*, vol. 14 (1973), pp. 352–96; Morris, *Government and Labor*, pp. 193–207; Philip Foner, *History of the Labor Movement in the United States* (New

York: International, 1941), vol. 1, ch. 5; John R. Commons et al., *History of Labor in the United States*, 4 vols. (New York: Macmillan, 1918), vol. 1, pt. 1.

95. Roger Moss, "The origins of the Carpenters Company of Philadelphia," in Charles E. Peterson (ed.), *Building Early America* (Radnor, Pa.: Chilton, 1976), pp. 35–53; see also "Articles and regulations of the Friendly Society of Tradesmen House Carpenters in the City of New York, 1767" (Broadside) and *Articles of the Carpenters Company of Philadelphia and Their Rules for Measuring and Valuing House Carpenters Work* (Philadelphia, 1786).

96. See, for example, Harriet Ropes Cabot, *Handbook of the Bostonian Society* (Boston: Boston Society, 1979), pp. 4–5; for collections of trade cards, see Clarence Brigham, *Paul Revere's Engravings* (New York: Atheneum, 1969), pp. 167–75, and Bella C. Landauer, *Early American Trade Cards* (New York: Rudge, 1927), and Trade Card Collection, American Antiquarian Society, Worcester, Mass.

97. "Procession, Boston, October 19, 1789" (Broadside).

98. "Certificate of the General Society of Mechanics and Tradesmen of the City of New York," New-York Historical Society and elsewhere; cf. John Bromley and Heather Child, *The Armorial Bearings of the Guilds of London* (London: Warne, 1960), illustrations facing pp. 15, 79, 86, 262.

99. Charles Phythian-Adams, "Ceremony and the citizen: the communal year at Coventry, 1450–1550," in Peter Clark and Peter Slack (eds.), *Crisis and Order in English Towns, 1500–1700* (London: Routledge & Kegan Paul, 1972), pp. 57–85.

100. Robert Withington, *English Pageantry: An Historical Outline*, 2 vols. (Cambridge, Mass.: Harvard University Press, 1926), vol. 2, ch. 6, esp. pp. 67, 94–5; Frederick W. Fairholt (ed.), *Lord Mayor's Pageants* (London: Percy Society, 1843–4), esp. pp. 133–59.

101. Nicholas Rogers to the author, 5 January 1982, citing Avon Reference Library, Bristol, Jeffries MSS, xii, 27, and *Annals of Bristol* (10154). Prof. Rogers also clarified the Lord Mayor's processions for me.

102. Dobson, *Masters and Journeymen*, pp. 82, 123.

103. Robert W. Malcolmson, *Popular Recreations in English Society, 1700–1850* (Cambridge: Cambridge University Press, 1973), pp. 52–3; Rule, *Experience of Labour*, pp. 206–7; the basic source is William Hone, *Everyday Life*, 2 vols. (London, 1826–7).

104. Malcolmson, "Workers' combinations in eighteenth-century England," p. 192.

105. John Gorman, *Banner Bright: An Illustrated History of the Banners of the British Trade Union Movement* (London: Allen Lane, 1973), p. 30.

106. Esther Forbes, *Paul Revere: The World He Lived In* (Boston: Houghton Mifflin, 1942), pp. 212–13.

107. Palmer, "Discordant music," p. 22.

108. Stiles, *Three Judges*, pp. 29, 77, 114.

109. Cited in Irving H. Bartlett, *Wendell Phillips, Brahmin Radical* (Boston: Beacon Press, 1961), p. 31.

110. Baker, "Anglo-Massachusetts trade union roots," pp. 389–90; [Boston] *Massachusetts Centinel*, 13, 27 April, 5, 25 May 1785; "Miserable times! Miserable times! … Joyce Junior" (Broadside) (Boston, n.d. 1805[?]), Houghton Library, Harvard University; Matthews, "Joyce, Jun., once more," pp. 280–94.

111. Sean Wilentz, *Chants Democratic: New York City and the Rise of the American Working Class, 1790–1850* (Oxford: Oxford University Press, 1984), chs. 2, 6; and Sean Wilentz, "Artisan republican festivals and the rise of class conflict in New York City, 1788–1837," in Michael Frisch and Daniel Walkowitz (eds.), *Working-Class America* (Urbana: University of Illinois Press, 1983).

112. *Leslie's Illustrated Weekly*, 16 September 1882, reproduced in M. B. Schnapper, *American Labour: A Pictorial Social History* (Washington, D.C.: Public Affairs Press, 1972), p. 172.

113. Eric Hobsbawm, *The Age of Revolution, 1789–1848* (New York: World Publishing, 1962).

114. *Massachusetts Gazette and Boston Weekly Newsletter*, 27 January, 3 February 1774; Young, "George Robert Twelves Hewes," pp. 592–6.

115. Letter from a surgeon of one of His Majesty's ships at Boston, 25 May 1775, in Henry S. Commager and Richard B. Morris (eds.), *The Spirit of '76* (1958; reprinted New York: Harpers, 1967), p. 153.

116. Thompson, "Patrician society, plebeian culture," p. 397.

Part II

Accommodations

4

Conservatives, the Constitution, and the "Genius of the People"

On June 18, 1787, a very hot Monday in Philadelphia, Alexander Hamilton delivered a five- to six-hour address at the Constitutional Convention, easily the longest and very likely the most curious speech made to the convention. From the premise that "all communities divide themselves ... into the rich and the well-born," adding the corollary that "the mass of people ... seldom judge or determine right," the delegate from New York moved to his ideal for an American government. He proposed a president and senate elected for life ("to serve during good behavior") and a house popularly elected for a three-year term. The president would have an absolute "negative" over the congress and the power to appoint the governors of each state, who in turn could veto any state law. If others quickly saw a resemblance to a king, House of Lords, and House of Commons, they were not mistaken; the British constitution, in Hamilton's opinion, was "the best model the world has ever produced."[1]

As important as the speech was, so too was the delegates' reaction. There was no discussion; the session adjourned. Gouverneur Morris called the speech "the most able and impressive he had ever heard." Three days later, William Samuel Johnson was more or less accurate in saying that Hamilton's proposals "had been praised by everybody [but] he has been supported by none." A few days later, Hamilton absented himself for a month. He was not exactly a pariah; George Washington pleaded with him to return. He did, to play a part in the final deliberations and then sign the finished document claiming "no plan was more remote from his own."[2]

The paths not taken in history often shed light on the paths taken. Douglass Adair has argued with his usual cogency that "we mistake the significance of Hamilton's proposal of an elective monarch as a solution of the crisis of 1787 if we think of his plan as either *original* or *unrepresentative* of the thought of important segments of American opinion in 1787."[3]

The banner that the Society of Pewterers carried in the parade celebrating the Constitution in 1788 in New York was a summa of artisan ideals: support for the Constitution and the nation, symbolized by the flag (upper left) and the verse (upper right); the traditional artisan workshop, with a master laboring alongside a journeyman and apprentices (to the right); the traditions of their craft in the coat of arms of the English pewterers (lower left); and their pride as producers who display their manufactures (the pewter ware). Courtesy of the Collection of the New-York Historical Society

To understand not so much why Hamilton brought forth his plan but why the convention rejected it is an avenue into the heart of the Constitution.

In this essay I will argue that the Constitution was the work of accommodating conservatives who drafted an essentially middle-of-the-road document that, by its very nature, produced different responses among contemporaries of a democratic bent. To develop this argument, we will need to explore the political experiences of the revolutionary generation. We will turn, first, to the democratic movement and thought that emerged with popular mass resistance to Britain after 1765 and, second, to the variant conservative responses to this threat. We will then return to the Constitutional Convention to probe the way conservatives were impelled in democratic directions. Finally, we will examine the responses to the Constitution in the controversy over ratification of men who might be considered democratic: those who were hostile, those who gave it qualified support, and those who gave it an enthusiastic endorsement. Taken together, this exploration may contribute toward answering the question, How democratic is the Constitution? by answering the question, How democratic was it in 1787?

The Democratic Threat

By the spring of 1774, the democratic threat once implicit in mass participation in the resistance to Great Britain was explicit. As Gouverneur Morris, son of the owner of Morrisania, a large tenanted estate in Westchester County, observed a huge mass meeting in New York City, he wrote "with fear and trembling" that ... "The mob begin to think and reason. Poor reptiles.... They fairly contended about the future forms of our Government, whether it should be founded upon aristocratic or democratic principles."[4]

What Morris captured was a moment in a process. A popular movement that had begun with "mob" actions in 1765 was transforming itself. Sons of Liberty organizations led by lawyers, sea captains, lesser merchants, and prosperous artisans were giving way to self-led Committees of Mechanics (the term for skilled craftsmen); crowd actions were giving way to public meetings; formerly deferential mechanics were insisting on direct representation on committees. By the spring of 1776, with independence a prospect and a state constitution to be drafted, in New York City a Committee of Mechanics insisted it was "a right which God has given them in common with all men, to judge whether it be consistent with their interest to accept or reject a constitution." The process was to continue with the transfer of power into the hands of endless committees: committees to enforce boycotts, committees to represent the militia, committees of safety, committees to detect conspiracies.[5]

In 1776, Thomas Paine's *Common Sense* registered still another moment in the process: the flowering of a democratic ideology. Paine offered much more than an argument for independence. He began with the section "Of the origin and design of government in general" and moved to "Of monarchy and hereditary succession" before he reached "Thoughts on the present state of American Affairs" and concluded with further thoughts on a "Continental Charter."[6]

Paine rejected not only King George III but also monarchy in principle, not only British policies but also "the so much boasted Constitution of England," attacking the underlying assumptions of hierarchy, hereditary rulers, and mixed or balanced government. The pamphlet precipitated not only a debate with Tories over independence but with conservative advocates of independence. John Adams, for example, who thought *Common Sense* "so democratical, without any restraint or even an attempt at equilibrium or Counterpoise, that it must produce confusion and every Evil work," rushed into print with *Thoughts on Government* to tutor America's novice constitution makers.[7]

Paine's creed stressed simple government: "The more simple a thing is, the less liable it is to be disordered, and the easier repaired when disordered." Direct democracy was the ideal, but, that being impossible, elected representatives should mirror their constituents and be elected from convenient districts, at frequent intervals, "because … the *elected* might by that means return and mix again with the general body of the electors in a few months." "Let the [state] assemblies be annual, with a President only. The representation more equal," ran an afterthought.[8]

In his vision of a "continental" government, Paine's central principle was "a large and equal representation." A congress should be elected directly by the voters, with the states divided into districts, each sending "at least thirty" representatives, for a total of at least 390. A president would be elected by the congress on a rotating basis, from among the states, with decisions made by a three-fifths majority. He also proposed a separate body, "a Continental Conference," to draft a "Continental Charter answering to what is called the Magna Charta of England." This conference would be chosen indirectly by a combination of congressmen, state assemblymen, and "representatives of the people at large" assembled "from all parts of the province for that purpose." And it would secure "freedom and property to all men and above all things the free exercise of religion ... with such other matters as is necessary for a charter to contain."⁹

These hints guided a great many men as they confronted the task of erecting constitutions in their independent states in 1776 and, it is not too much to claim, as they confronted the federal Constitution in 1787–1788. Paine said relatively little about structures, however.

The Pennsylvania constitution, a victory of radical democrats, may be taken as the democratic creed fulfilled at its extreme. A Declaration of Rights preceded it. The structure was simple: a one-house legislature with a weak, plural executive. Representation was from districts newly apportioned by population (to be reapportioned at seven-year intervals). Elections were annual and rotation required; no one could serve more than four years in seven. There were no property qualifications for any office (only an oath of allegiance to the new state). Suffrage was open to all taxpayers. Popular participation in the legislative process was the goal: The assembly was to be open; the votes and proceedings were to be published. More important, a bill could not become a law until, after the first reading, it was publicized throughout the colony, discussed, and voted upon at the following session. The executive was to carry out the will of the assembly (it was a twelve-person council, elected for three-year terms, with one-third rotating every year). A Council of Censors, popularly elected, was to review the constitutionality of laws at seven-year intervals. Supreme Court judges were to be appointed by the executive council for seven-year terms, subject to removal by the assembly for misbehavior. Other court officials, for example, justices of the peace and sheriffs, were to be selected by the council from candidates elected by popular vote each year. Finally, under the Pennsylvania constitution, even militia officers were to be popularly elected.¹⁰

In only one important respect did the Pennsylvania constitution fall short of a widely held democratic ideal. Its architects introduced, but later withdrew, what contemporaries called an "agrarian" clause:

> That [since] an enormous Proportion of Property vested in a few individuals is dangerous to the Rights, and destructive of the common happiness of Mankind ... therefore every free state hath a Right by its laws to discourage the Possession of such Property.¹¹

One should be wary, however, of making the Pennsylvania constitution the exclusive litmus test for democratic political thought. Relatively few democrats seem to have argued for a unicameral legislature (only Pennsylvania, Vermont, and Georgia adopted it). As for suffrage, a good many democrats were wary of venturing beyond a small-freehold property qualification, especially where there were large dependent populations like the Hudson Valley tenants. More important, it was a time when ideas were in flux. Many ordinary men awakening to political consciousness had to find their own minds. As John Jay said of the committee drafting New York's constitution, "Our politicians are like some guests at a feast, are perplexed and undetermined which dish to prefer." We need also to remind ourselves that there was a war on and a need to preserve a coalition.[12]

The war intensified the democratizing process. David Ramsay, the South Carolina physician who in 1789 wrote one of the first histories of the Revolution, caught this moment in the process:

> When the war began, the Americans were a mass of husbandmen, merchants, mechanics and fishermen, but the necessities of the country gave a spring to the active powers of the inhabitants and set them on thinking, speaking and acting in a line far beyond that to which they had been accustomed. ... It seemed as if the war not only required but created talents.[13]

One consequence, particularly after the war, was an increase in participation in the political process: more people voting, more seeking public office.[14]

As a major result of all this ferment, the social composition of the state legislatures shifted downward a notch, and sometimes more. Contemporaries spoke of the "new men," "the raw new hands," and the "better sort" sniffed at "men unimproved by education and unrefined by honor" who now framed laws. The New York legislature, dominated before the war by Livingstons, Schuylers, Van Rensselaers, Delanceys, and Beekmans, "gentlemen" all, did not try, after the war, to raise a quorum at harvest time; too many members were plain farmers.[15] Jackson Turner Main, the scholar who has given the subject the most assiduous attention, has provided elaborate quantitative proof of this shift. What is striking is that it occurred in the senates, designed to be the protectors of large property, as well as in assemblies.[16] This point, at which the democratic movement of the revolutionary era had perhaps its greatest impact, the state legislatures, had the most threatening potential to conservatives.

Conservative Responses

The democratic political movement was a pervasive force in the revolutionary era, helping to shape the response of every major political group: popular patriot leaders, loyalists, and conservative patriots. The "mob" was a problem to popular leaders no less than to Gouverneur Morris. The recent scholarship of Pauline Maier has made clear that, for over a decade, Sons of Liberty leaders like Samuel Adams were waging a war on two fronts: to pressure Britain and to control the movements from below. In 1775, Adams was informed by his ally Elbridge Gerry, a merchant, that a government had to be established as quickly as possible to replace the British because "the people are fully possessed of their dignity from the frequent delineation of their rights.... They now feel rather too much their own importance, and it requires great skill to produce such subordination as is necessary." Adams agreed. Men like Samuel Adams and Patrick Henry were not "radicals," if that term is defined as favoring internal political democracy; both followed John Adams's lead on balanced constitutions and a due "subordination." They were radical only toward Britain. They might have agreed "vox populi, vox dei," but they retained their following (which included men in their "establishments" as well as among the commonality) on the basis of their effective, militant leadership in the cause against Britain.[17]

Loyalist men of wealth, it might be argued, were victims of the mob. Many became Loyalists in good part from the Gouverneur Morris syndrome, from a fear of their total inability to cope with the mob, especially when transformed into a democratic movement. A number of misleading stereotypes about Loyalists have been corrected in recent years. Not all rich men became Tories; on the contrary, the dominant wealth of Massachusetts, including Boston, and Virginia, the two centers of the Revolution, was patriot. Not all Tories were rich men; a strain of loyalism and "disaffection" existed among poor white farmers and black slaves who, with a kind of inverted class feeling, took the opposite stand from their patriot masters or landlords. A large number of the rich, however, especially in the middle colonies, were Loyalist. Aristocratic, ridden with the prejudices of their class toward the "meaner sort," unequipped to take part in the hurly-burly of politics, they lacked any models for coping with a popular movement save that of repression or coercion. Accordingly, they abdicated political responsibility (as in Philadelphia), became political and military collaborators with the British (as in New York), or went into exile (as did one hundred thousand during and after the war).[18]

Conservative patriots were drawn from the same social sources as Loyalists: merchant elites of the cities, landlord estate holders of the Hudson Valley, prosperous slaveholders in the South. Why some men raised with a certain set of conservative social values should turn Tory and others Whig remains a mystery and a matter of general interest, because the split seems to recur in America's history. The experience of the revolutionary era suggests it may have something to do with the degree of confidence men of wealth had in their ability to deal with democratic movements.

The New York elite offers a case study. Gouverneur Morris's metaphor for the mob was a reptile that might bite. One had to scotch a snake; it was impossible to tame it. He also referred to the mob as a horse that had to be whipped. Robert R. Livingston, his associate, had a metaphor more apropos for the tactic he and his fellow conservatives adopted. He was convinced of "the propriety of Swimming with a Stream which it is impossible to stem." On the completion of New York's constitution in 1777, he contrasted the success of his friends with the failure of their counterparts in Pennsylvania: "I long ago advised that they should yield to the torrent if they hoped to direct its course—you know nothing but welltimed delays, indefatigable circumstance could have prevented our being exactly in their situation."[19]

The New Yorkers had begun years before—Livingston, John Jay, James Duane, and Philip Schuyler foremost among them—teaching themselves the tactic of "swimming with the stream" in committee sessions, in electoral politics, and at public meetings. Their task was formidable, facing as they did rivals in the Sons of Liberty and politically conscious mechanics, a merchant landlord elite that was probably more than half Tory, their own tenantry ready to take to arms, and yeomanry who would have nothing to do with "great men."

The New York constitution of 1777 was their handiwork. The provisions for voting typify the compromise written into the entire document. Governor and senators would be elected by voters with one hundred-pound freeholds; members of the assembly by voters with twenty-pound freeholds or men who paid forty shillings rent. The governor would be elected by written ballot, the other officials by voice voting (which might be discontinued after the war). The governor, elected for a three-year term, would have veto power over legislation, exercised jointly with a Council of Revision composed of the high judges, and appointive power, exercised with a Council of Appointment composed of four senators. The concessions to democracy were annual assembly elections, a written ballot, larger representation, and compulsory reapportionment. Had extreme conservatives prevailed, there would have been elections at four-year intervals by voice voting and an upper house and governor chosen indirectly. Had the democrats won, there might have been taxpayer suffrage, a written ballot in all elections, annual election for all offices, and no executive veto. A contemporary said of the result that it "preserved a proper line between Aristocracy on the one hand and Democracy on the other." It was so delicately balanced, said John Jay, that "another turn of the winch would have cracked the cord."[20]

The machinery, however, did not work quite as intended. In the first election, Philip Schuyler was defeated for governor by George Clinton, whose "family and connections," said Schuyler, "do not entitle him to so distinguished a predominance." The conservatives, having lost, then formed a coalition with Clinton. He appointed them to high positions, and he quelled the tenant rebellion that threatened their estates. They supported him politically until the mid-1780s. On the other hand, they could neither control nor influence the "new men" in the New York state legislature. Once this was clear, they turned to national power to curb the state power that had eluded them. Then they broke with Clinton. Years later, after Livingston broke with the Federalists to rejoin Clinton, he spoke of returning to a "close union of the Livingston family with the democratic interests of the state."[21]

The New York experience of 1777—so rich in implications for 1787—may have been more typical than historians have allowed. As Jackson Main writes, after subjecting the state constitutions to exhaustive scrutiny, "Whig thought seldom appeared in pure form, and when put into practice the pull of democratic ideology distorted the blessed symmetry of a balanced government. In the same fashion, adherents of democracy, confronting both practical circumstances and a determined opposition, diluted their ideal with Whig accretions." In most states, the two ideologies "compromised and the resultant moderate constitutions reflected therefore a kind of consensus, genuinely accepted by many Americans, incorporating ideas shared by Whigs and democrats alike."[22]

The gentry in Maryland offer a different case study: They consolidated their power by an ultraconservative constitution first, then they appeased the underclasses to maintain their authority. In Maryland, in addition to a large class of poor whites, tenants, and freeholders, slaves composed 25 percent of the population (40 to 50 percent in some areas). Ten percent of the whites controlled 50 percent of the wealth; 20 percent controlled 75 percent of the wealth.[23]

Charles Carroll of Carrollton enables us to follow the attitudes of this elite. Enthusiastic in 1773 for resistance to Britain, by 1776 he was fearful the colonies "would be ruined" by the "bad governments" that would be "simple democracies." He joined his fellow men of large property to draft a constitution in which property alone ruled. To be a member of the lower house, a man had to own a minimum of five hundred pounds' worth of real or personal property; to be a member of the upper house or the governor's council, or sheriff, a minimum of one thousand pounds'; and to be governor, five thousand pounds' or more. Voters elected only members of the lower house, the sheriffs, and members of an electoral college; the electors would select the senators, who, in turn (with the members of the house), would select the governor. Under these provisions, only 10.9 percent of all adult white males in Maryland were qualified to serve in the house and only 7.4 percent in the senate.[24]

The consolidation of elite control only worsened the enormous disaffection from the patriot cause within Maryland, leading to outright Loyalist resistance, refusal to do military service, insubordination in the militia, unrest among the slaves, and the threat of poor-white support for slave insurrection. The elite was patriot, and, as the most recent scholar of Maryland politics has explained, in 1777 they "anxiously sought to save both their class and the Revolution by popularizing the movement for independence." Their solution, writes Roland Hoffman, was a fiscal program "aimed at subduing the class antagonisms that underlay much of the internal protest": a tax system under which the planter elite assumed a greater burden and a tender law that in effect "voided the bulk of all internal credit obligations," severely affecting them as creditors.[25]

Charles Carroll of Annapolis, father of the Carrollton Carroll and a large moneylender, was enraged; if the lawmakers went so far, what was to stop them from saying, "No man shall hold above 500 acres of land"? His son explained the need of conciliation: "The law suits the multitudes, individuals must submit to partial losses; no great revolutions can happen in a state without revolutions or mutations of private property." He was candid: "I have long considered our personal estate, I mean the monied part of it, to be in jeopardy," he explained. "If we can save a third of that and all our lands and Negroes I shall think ourselves well off." "There is a time when it is wisdom to yield to injustice and to popular heresies and delusions." The alternative was worse: "violence and greater injustice."[26]

Thus, in variant ways, the gentry in New York and Maryland weathered the storm of the Revolution. From the mid-1780s on, it could be argued

"Gen. Daniel Shays and Col. Job Shattuck," in the uniforms of Continental soldiers, identified with exaggerated mock titles in this cut from a Boston almanac. "Shays's Rebellion" was a misnomer for the insurgency of debt-ridden, tax-plagued farmers of western Massachusetts which had many leaders. Farmers in arms terrified the men who drafted the Constitution, which in turn was bitterly opposed by these farmer rebels. From Bickerstaff's *Boston Almanack for 1787*, Courtesy of the National Portrait Gallery, Smithsonian Institution.

that the gentry, north and south, faced another storm, if not in their own states, in their neighbors'. There was a general crisis in the "system"—a word in common usage—a new threat that was difficult to accommodate.

Scholars traditionally have emphasized Shays's Rebellion in Massachusetts in 1786 as a catalyst to conservatives. They are not wrong. There were "combustibles in every State, which a spark might set fire to," as Washington stated and as recent scholarship has verified.[27] One of James Madison's principal complaints in 1787 was the "want of guaranty to the states of their constitutions and laws against internal violence." But there was, in a sense, a danger worse than rebellion. The defeated Shaysites were turning to state elections, said Madison, "by endeavoring to give the elections such a turn as may promote their views under the auspices of Constitutional forms." What, he asked, if they succeeded? This then would be legal Shaysism: a danger for which there seemingly was no remedy.[28]

In state after state, the "new men" were able to pass, or threatened to pass, paper currency laws, mortgage stay laws, and tax laws shifting burdens to the rich. As Madison stated,

> Debtors have defrauded their creditors. The landed interest has borne hard on the mercantile interest. The Holders of one species of property have thrown a disproportion of taxes on the holders of another species.

These were the "Vices of the Political System of the United States" Madison had in mind on the eve of the Constitutional Convention in 1787, in the memorandum to himself that became the basis of several speeches at the convention and later of the equally important *Federalist* No. 10.[29]

The vices of the state governments as a major factor impelling conservatives to stronger national government is a theme that has found its historian in Gordon Wood. As Madison summarized it for Jefferson in 1787, these vices "contributed more to that uneasiness which produced the Convention and prepared the public mind for a general reform, than those which accrued to our national character and interest from the inadequacy of the Confederation to its immediate objectives."[30] Hamilton, in his private "conjectures," said the same thing; he counted among the "circumstances" in favor of the Constitution "the good will of most men of property in the several states who wish a government of the union able to protect them against domestic violence and the depredations which the democratic spirit is apt to make on property."[31]

As Madison reflected on these vices in the state governments, he was impelled to generalize about their causes, an analysis he made famous in *Federalist* No. 10.

> All civilized societies are divided into different interests and factions, as they happen to be creditors or debtors—rich or poor—husbandmen, merchants or manufacturers—members of different religious sects—followers of different political leaders—inhabitants of different districts—owners of different kinds of property &c &c.

The problem was that

> in republican government the majority however composed, ultimately give the law. Whenever therefore an apparent or common passion unites a majority what is to restrain them from unjust violations of the rights and interests of the minority, or of individuals?[32]

The notion "honesty is the best policy," "a respect for character," and "religion" were inadequate. One solution lay in "an enlargement of the sphere" of government,

> not because the impulse of a common interest or passion is less predominant in this case with the majority; but because a common interest or passion is less apt to be felt and the requisite combinations less easy to be formed by a great than a small number. The Society becomes broken into a greater variety of interests, of pursuits of passions, which check each other, whilst those who may feel a common sentiment have less opportunity of communication and concert.

An "extensive republic" was therefore one remedy to the "vices" of "a small republic." A second remedy, which Madison developed elsewhere, was a national "negative" or veto of state legislation.[33]

Thus, as conservatives became Founding Fathers, their priority was to counter the powers of the states with national power. On this score, they were not in any "spirit of accommodation." To achieve this priority, however, they were ready to practice the accommodation they had mastered in the decade and more gone by.

The Constitutional Convention and Accommodation

At the Philadelphia Convention in 1787, the chief architects of the Constitution were conservatives, either of an accommodating cast of mind (like Madison and James Wilson) or of an "ultra" cast of mind (like Gouverneur Morris). The delegates, if analyzed according to their experience with the political conflicts we have been describing, either (1) had direct experience within their own states with the threat of democratic movements, (2) like James Madison, were attuned to these threats by virtue of their position as national leaders in the Congress, or (3) were tutored at the convention by those who had such experiences. If they were not accommodating—and many were not—they nonetheless took part in a process of accommodation in which a middle-of-the-road constitution was the end-product.

The delegations from the three states we have dwelt on are in themselves suggestive. Six of Pennsylvania's eight delegates were members of the "Republican Constitutionalist" faction, fighting since 1777 to overturn their state's radical constitution (they did succeed in 1790). These included its leaders, James Wilson, Robert Morris, and Gouverneur Morris, then transient in Philadelphia. New York's delegation was composed of foes; on the one side, Hamilton, who had married into the New York landlord-commercial aristocracy (joining John Jay, James Duane, Robert R. Livingston and his father-in-law, Philip Schuyler), and, on the other side, John Lansing and Robert Yates, supporters of the Clintonian holders of state power that Hamilton despised. Maryland elected Charles Carroll, the younger, who was too preoccupied with internal state politics, it was said, to come; his cousin, Daniel Carroll, came, as did other members of the Carroll faction.[34]

Personal experience with democratic opponents did not automatically turn a conservative to the path of accommodation. The contrast is clear if one takes the two men who, next to Madison, are acknowledged as major shapers of the Constitution, Gouverneur Morris and Wilson. Morris never got over thinking about popular movements as animals requiring restraint. At the convention, he seems to have spoken consistently and often for the conservative solution to problems. Not only did he admire Hamilton's speech, he agreed with it: "We must have monarch sooner or later ... and the sooner we take him, while we are able to make a bargain with him, the better."[35]

Wilson, on the other hand, although he had the searing experience in 1779 of having his house the target of an attack by the radical militia, was, as Robert McCloskey argues,

> more consistent than anyone else, including Madison, in advocating political democracy. He favored direct popular election of both Senate and House, and he joined with Madison in urging that the proposed Constitution be submitted to popularly elected conventions in each state.... But when Madison supported a freehold qualification for voting, Wilson opposed it, and Wilson was practically alone in arguing that the president too should be elected directly by the people.... Wilson stands forth as one of the most consistent democrats of his era.[36]

The accommodating cast of mind showed itself in the first week in the debate over a resolution on the Virginia plan "that the members of the first Branch of the national legislature ought to be elected by the people of the several states" and not the state legislatures.[37] Elbridge Gerry of Massachusetts, the memory of Shays's Rebellion fresh in his mind, is often quoted for his remark:

> The evils we experience flow from an excess of democracy.... He had been
> too republican heretofore; He was still however republican, but had been
> taught by experience the danger of the levelling spirit.

The responses of George Mason of Virginia, Wilson, and Madison were
more typical:

> Mr. Mason argued strongly for an election of the larger branch by the
> people. It was to be the grand depository of the democratic principle of the
> Government. It was, so to speak, to be our House of Commons—It ought
> to know and sympathize with every part of the community. He admitted
> that we had been too democratic but was afraid we sd. incautiously run
> into the opposite extreme. We ought to attend to rights of every class of
> the people.

Wilson "contended strenuously for drawing the most numerous branch of
the Legislature immediately from the people," revealing his underlying
assumptions:

> He was for raising the federal pyramid to a considerable altitude and for
> that reason wished to give it as broad a basis as possible. No government
> could long subsist without the confidence of the people.

Second,

> he also thought it wrong to increase the weight of the State Legislatures by
> making them the electors of the national Legislature.... On examination it
> would be found that the opposition of States to federal measures had
> proceeded much more from the Offices of the States than from the people
> at large.

Madison used a different metaphor: "The great fabric to be raised would
be more stable and durable if it should rest on the solid foundation of the
people themselves" than if it rested "merely on the pillars of the Legislatures." The problem was that in some states one branch was already
elected indirectly; if the house were elected by such legislatures, "the peo
ple would be lost sight of altogether and the necessary sympathy between
them and their rulers and officers, too little felt." He was, he made clear,

> an advocate for the policy of refining the popular appointments by succes-
> sive filtrations, but thought it might be pushed too far. He wished the expe-
> dient to be resorted to only in the appointment of the second branch of the
> Legislature, and in the executive and judiciary branch of the Government.

Gerry then backtracked:

> Mr. Gerry did not like the election by the people.... Experience he said had shown that the State legislatures drawn immediately from the people did not always possess their confidence. He had no objection however to an election by the people if it were so qualified that men of honor and character might not be unwilling to be joined in the appointments. He seemed to think the people might nominate a certain number out of which the state legislatures should be bound to choose.

As one focuses on such a debate, as one probes for the assumptions underlying the debate as a whole, it seems one can differentiate five factors impelling the delegates in a democratic direction.

First, the underlying political theory to which the delegates subscribed dictated that, to survive in the long run, governments had to be adjusted to the mores and customs of the people to be governed (this was Montesquieu). The delegates were erecting a government "intended to last for ages," said Madison. "The British government cannot be our model," explained Wilson. "We have no materials for a similar one. Our manners, our laws, the abolition of entails and of primogeniture, the whole genius of the people, are opposed to it." Mason used the same term: "The genius of the people must be consulted."[38]

Second, one of the theoretical solutions to curbing the "vices" of democratic majorities in the states, an "extended republic," clearly led in a democratic direction. This aspect of Madison's thought is so familiar there is no need to develop it here. At one point in presenting this theory, Madison even abandoned the term "republican" to argue that to "enlarge the sphere" was "the only defense against the inconvenience of *democracy* consistent with the democratic form of Government."[39] The immediate application of this theory was a house of representatives elected by popular vote. The long-range implication was the admission of new states to the union on a basis of equality that would "enlarge the sphere" still further. The argument needs no elaboration.

The second theoretical solution to the vices of the states, a national veto of state legislation, was equally undemocratic. Perhaps it is significant that Madison never achieved this in the form he wanted.

Third, the delegates recognized a short-term political reality. If the Constitution were to be adopted, it had to meet with popular approval. The convention could not submit it to the state legislatures—they were part of the problem. It therefore had to go to conventions whose delegates would be elected for the sole purpose of voting on the Constitution. Delegates were extremely sensitive to the "people out of doors." Pierce Butler, the South Carolina planter, put it well, in a response to a proposal to extend a federal judiciary into the states:

> The people will not bear such innovations. The states will revolt at such encroachments. Supposing such an establishment to be useful, we must not venture on it. We must follow the example of Solon who gave the Athenians not the best Government he could devise but the best they would receive.[40]

Fourth, there was an even more immediate political need to conciliate delegates "within doors." The delegates were hardly of one mind. Benjamin Franklin, for example, the nation's ornament, second in popularity only to Washington, was long a sympathizer with Pennsylvania's democratic constitution. As Clinton Rossiter has pointed out,

> [Franklin] would have preferred a constitution with these radically different arrangements: a plural executive, unsalaried and probably elected by the legislature; a unicameral legislature, with representation proportioned to population; annual elections for all holders of public office, including officers of the militia; universal manhood suffrage, with no bow to property; a straightforward, unqualified bill of rights; and an easy method of formal amendment.[41]

George Mason, the author of his state's bill of rights, was no less a sage in the eyes of Virginians. Yates and Lansing walked out; Mason, Randolph, Gerry, and Luther Martin stayed to the end but refused to sign. The chief architects labored to avoid such setbacks. They also had to placate a group of moderate nationalist delegates, in particular from New England.[42]

Nothing is more revealing of this self-imposed pressure to conciliate than Washington's action literally in the closing hour of the convention. Nathaniel Gorham of Massachusetts, "for the purpose of lessening objections to the constitution," moved to alter the number of representatives in the House from one for forty thousand inhabitants to one for thirty thousand; the number of representatives was a sore point with the democratic-minded. Washington left the chair—he had not spoken through the entire convention—"yet he could not forebear expressing his wish that the alteration proposed might take place. It was much to be desired that the objections to the plan recommended might be as few as possible."[43]

The fifth factor contributing to democratic results at the convention was the force of circumstance: diversity. Diversity led to bitter contention that almost rent the convention: the differences between the large and small states, between slaveholding and nonslaveholding states, cutting across the differences between agricultural and commercial interests. These differences led to the since classic compromises of the Constitution. At the same time, with issues affecting democracy such as qualifications for voting and officeholding, the diversity of political practice in the states produced a stalemate in which the delegates fell back on the solution of allowing each state to go its own way. The result in both the short run and long run was a democratic plus.

The debate on the suffrage may be taken as an example of how these several factors came into play, often explicitly, sometimes implicitly. This debate, late in the convention, was on the drafting committee's proposal for the election of members of the House by whomever each state allowed to vote for its "most numerous branch," that is, the lower house. Gouverneur Morris characteristically moved to amend it, limiting the vote to freeholders, that is, men who owned land of a certain value or acreage and explicitly requiring the national legislature rather than the states to determine the qualifications.[44] Morris, still trying to destroy the reptile, still discerning, sounded the traditional maxim that property was essential for an "independent" vote:

> Give the votes to people who have no property and they will sell them to the rich who will be able to buy them. We should not confine our attention to the present moment. The time is not distant when this Country will abound with mechanics and manufacturers who will receive their bread from their employers.... The man who does not give a vote freely is not represented. It is the man who dictates his vote.

Madison expressed a similar fear, pointing to the cities as historic sources of corruption.

The opposition to Morris's amendment was broad and vigorous. Mason feared the short-term political consequences: "Eight or nine states have extended the right of suffrage beyond the freeholders, what will the people there say, if they should be disfranchised[?]" Oliver Ellsworth, chief justice of Connecticut, dwelt on the problem of diversity:

> How shall the freehold be defined? Ought not every man who pays a tax to vote for the representative who is to levy and dispose of his money? Shall the wealthy merchants and manufacturers, who will bear a full share of the public burdens be not allowed a voice in the imposition of them?

The warmest opposition stemmed from delegates sensitive to urban constituencies in which the mass of mechanics already voted. Franklin, a man who had to be placated, made this one of the rare occasions at the convention when he spoke, paying a glowing tribute to "the lower class of Freemen" who would be disfranchised by a freehold requirement. "This class have hardy virtues and [great] integrity—the late war is a glorious testimony in favor of plebeian virtue." Wilson of Philadelphia dealt with realities:

> It was difficult to form any uniform rule of qualifications for all the States.... It would be very hard and disagreeable for the same persons at the same time, to vote for representatives in the State Legislature and to be excluded from a vote for those in the National Legislature.

Nathaniel Gorham, a Boston merchant, pointedly answered Madison's claim that elections in the cities are unsafe. "The elections in Phila[delphia] N[ew] York and Boston where the Merchants and Mechanics vote are at least as good as those made by freeholders only." As to the English experience, "the cities and large towns are not the seat of crown influence and corruption." Moreover, in America "the people" "will never allow [this right] to be abridged. We must consult their rooted prejudices if we expect their concurrence in our propositions."

Madison clearly was torn. He had no doubt that the issue should be resolved by the Constitution; "the right of suffrage is certainly one of the fundamental articles of republican Government, and ought not to be left to be regulated by the Legislature." But how? On the one hand was the short-term reality:

> Whether the Constitutional qualification ought to be a freehold, would with him depend much on the probable reception such a change would meet with in States where the right was now exercised by every description of people. In several of the States a freehold was now the qualification.

On the other hand was the problem of long-run stability:

> Viewing the subject in its merits alone, the freeholders of the Country would be the safest depositories of Republican liberty. In future times a great majority of the people will not only be without landed, but any other sort of, property. These will either combine under the influence of their common situation; in which case, the rights of property and the public liberty will not be secure in their hands; or which is more probable, they will become the tools of opulence and ambition, in which case there will be equal danger on another side.

In this speech he left his thought dangling; the thrust of it was clearly sympathetic to Morris, and that is how others recorded it. In the balloting, Virginia voted against Morris's freehold amendment, and Madison's biographers presume he voted with his delegation. More than likely, the practical—"the probable reception" of such a proposal—overrode the theoretical—"viewing the subject in its merits alone."[45]

The freehold requirement was overwhelmingly defeated—seven states against, one in favor (Delaware), one divided (Maryland), one absent (Georgia). Not only would the suffrage remain fairly broad (and varied) as it was in 1787, but there would be nothing in the Constitution to prevent the states from broadening it. Three days later, a proposal to require property qualifications for members of the House and Senate "was rejected by so general a 'no' that the States were not called."[46] In such ways, diversity combined with political theory and political reality to produce a democratic result.

In looking at the Constitution as a whole, in measuring it on a spectrum of the revolutionary era in which Pennsylvania's constitution of 1776 stood at one end and Hamilton's proposal of June 1787 at the other, the federal end product was in the middle of the road. The argument has focused not on intentions but on a process by which the Founding Fathers did things "in spite of themselves," so to speak. They made democratic concessions to achieve conservative ends. They wanted a "broad basis" of popular support, because they intended to "raise the federal pyramid" so high. They wanted to "extend the sphere" to disperse the threat of democratic majorities.

They obviously got a good deal of what they wanted, but they also got less than they wanted. In a long letter to Jefferson shortly after the convention, Madison expressed what can only be called bitter disappointment at failing to achieve a federal veto of state legislation. "The restraints against paper emissions and violations of contracts" were "not sufficient" and were "short of the mark"; judicial review would only catch "mischiefs" after the fact. On the other hand, James Wilson, pointing to the same two curbs on the states, thought that "if only the following lines were inserted in this new constitution I think it would be worth our adoption." The chief architects themselves were divided—or of one opinion privately and another publicly. This, too, may be considered further testimony to the middle-of-the-road character of what they had wrought.[47]

Democratic Responses

Among those with a claim to being called democrats, the response to the Constitution in 1787–88 was divided. Some opposed it; some gave it modified approval; some were enthusiastic supporters. Such division was what might be expected in response to a middle-of-the-road document.

Democrats who opposed the Constitution were to be found among the Antifederalists. Not all Antifederalists were democrats, a fact forcefully clarified by Cecilia Kenyon. In fact, in a very important way, the ideological tables of 1776 were turned. Men who in 1776 stressed a Paineite simple government, epitomized by a one-house legislature in which majorities would rule unchecked, now found the checks and balances in the national government inadequate. They did not take the ground that the progressive J. Allen Smith would take in 1906 and Charles Beard would repeat, namely that checks and balances were a means of thwarting democratic majorities. Indeed, they asked for more of them.[48]

The reversal was not all that inconsistent. Many democrats—if not most—had come around to accepting both bicameralism and the separation of powers. The New York Antifederalists, for example, probably agreed with their governor, George Clinton, that theirs was "our excellent state constitution." In 1790, many Pennsylvania democrats were to go along with the conservative restructuring of their state constitution.[49]

In 1787–88, many democrats were convinced that a "consolidated" national government had been created by a few men of wealth whose excessive powers threatened the states. The starting point in their thinking about the Constitution among ordinary Antifederalists was a raw, gut feeling that the drafters and proponents of the new government were their class enemies. "An apprehension that the liberties of the people are in danger," said Rufus King of Massachusetts, "and a distrust of men of property and education have a more powerful effect upon the mind of our opponents than any specific objections against the Constitution."[50]

That frame of mind was summarized in one speech at the Massachusetts convention by Amos Singletary (a countryman from Worcester County, a self-taught man of whom it was said he "never attended school a day in his life" and who had served in the provincial congress and the assembly):

These lawyers, and men of learning, and moneyed men, that talk so finely, and gloss over matters so smoothly, to make us poor illiterate people swallow down the pill, expect to get into congress themselves; they expect to be managers of this Constitution and get all the power and all the money into their own hands, and then they will swallow up all us little folks, like the great Leviathan, Mr. President; yes just as the whale swallowed up *Jonah.* This is what I am afraid of.[51]

The political theory of such democratic Antifederalists was articulated well by Melancton Smith, the leading Antifederalist debater at New York's ratifying convention.[52] Smith developed his democratic assumptions in a clash over the number of representatives in the house, the issue that had led conservatives to a last-minute accommodation of one congressman for thirty thousand instead of forty thousand voters. Smith moved one for twenty thousand. His concept of representation harked back to Paine:

> The idea that naturally suggests itself to our minds, when we speak of repre-
> sentatives, is, that they resemble those they represent. They should be a true
> picture of the people, possess a knowledge of their circumstances and their
> wants, sympathize in all their distresses, and be disposed to seek their true
> interests. The knowledge necessary for the representative of a free people
> not only comprehends extensive political and commercial information,
> such as is acquired by men of refined education, who have leisure to attain
> to high degrees of improvement, but it should also comprehend that kind
> of acquaintance with the common concerns and occupations of the people,
> which men of the middling class of life are, in general, more competent to
> than those of a superior class.[53]

Smith's underlying fear was that "the influence of the great will generally enable them to succeed in elections." They "easily form associations; the poor and middling class form them with great difficulty" and usually divide among themselves. As a result, "a substantial yeoman of sense and discernment will hardly ever be chosen," and the "government will fall into the hands of the few and the great."

An increase in the size of the house thus was crucial to permit democratic representation. In turning to the senate, Smith sought reforms to meet both his democratic assumptions of representation and his fears for the state governments. He argued for the rotation and recall of senators; they should be eligible to serve only six years in any twelve-year period. Recall was necessary because senators were "the representatives of state legislatures. ... When a state sends an agent commissioned to transact any business, or perform any services, it certainly ought to have a power to recall." He spoke for an amendment to limit the president to one term, which he was willing to lengthen to seven years. He also wanted the president's military powers and powers of appointment curbed. To restrain the federal judicial power, Smith favored a series of curtailing amendments.[54]

The New York convention, under Smith's leadership, adopted a long series of amendments that would have seriously altered the structure of the federal government. Later, when the Bill of Rights amendments alone were passed, Abraham Yates, the stormy petrel of New York Antifederalism, pronounced them "unimportant or trivial" compared to what was sought.[55]

We may let Thomas Jefferson speak for those moderate democrats who gave the Constitution qualified support and rapidly swallowed their objections. This generation is sanguine about the limitations of Jefferson's aristocratic liberalism: the darker side of his record on civil liberties, his failures on slavery and racial equality, his own insistence that the practical must control the theoretical. On reflection, he still qualifies as a democrat, albeit a moderate one compared to, say, a Philadelphia militia man. A Whig, an advocate of balanced government and the separation of powers, he was nonetheless a severe critic of the gross inequality of representation in Virginia. However much he hedged his faith in the people, he had an uncommon confidence in popular majorities.[56]

Throughout the convention, Jefferson was in Paris as America's minister to France. Predisposed to a stronger government, he was surprisingly hostile in his initial reactions to the Constitution. There were "things in it which stagger all my dispositions to subscribe to it." "All the good," he wrote John Adams, "might have been couched in three or four new articles to be added to the good, old and venerable fabric, the Articles of Confederation, which should even have been preserved as a religious relic." "I find myself nearly a neutral," he wrote another. "There is a great mass of good in it, in a very desirable form; but there is also to be a bitter pill or two." When Paine arrived in Paris, he, Jefferson, and the Marquis de Lafayette debated the document "in a convention of our own as earnestly as if we were to decide upon it," Lafayette said.[57]

Gradually Jefferson softened. To Madison, he couched his thoughts as "what I like" and "what I do not like." He liked the idea of the central government "which should go on of itself peaceably, without needing continual recurrence to the state legislatures," the three branches in the federal government, the power of the House to vote taxes, and "the negative given to the executive with a third of either house," although he would have liked the judiciary to be involved. In short, the moderate democrat did not balk at a national government, at separation of powers, presidential veto, or even judicial review.

What he did not like was, "first, the omission of a bill of rights," a point on which he belabored Madison at length and with passion. "A second feature" he "greatly disliked" "is the abandonment of the necessity of rotation in office, and most particularly in the case of the President." He was convinced that "the first magistrate will always be reelected. ... He is then an officer for life." He feared this especially because of the danger of the influence of foreign nations. "An incapacity to be elected a second time" was "the only effectual preventative." These were his likes and dislikes.[58]

It was characteristic of Jefferson that in the same letter to Madison he turned from the Constitution to Shays's Rebellion, giving another admonition against repression that might smother the spirit of liberty: "I own I am not a friend to very energetic government. It is always oppressive." It was especially characteristic of his political thinking that he concluded by saying he would agree with the majority on the Constitution. "After all it is my principle that the will of the majority should always prevail. If they should approve the proposed Constitution in all its parts, I shall concur in it cheerfully, in hopes that they will amend it whenever they shall find it works wrong." In effect, he saw no obstacle to a majority in the amending process.

To force a bill of rights, Jefferson would have preferred ratification by less than the required states, but, once ratification occurred, he shifted rapidly. Soon the Constitution was "unquestionably the wisest ever yet presented to men" and *The Federalist* the "best commentary on the principles on government, which was ever written."[59] The fact that Jefferson could change, and change so rapidly, and the fact that so many Antifederalists could also learn to live with the Constitution may well be considered testimony to the powerful pull of the democratic features of the document.

The democrats who gave the Constitution enthusiastic backing—the third type of democrat of the period—were the artisans of the major cities. Support was overwhelming from all but a small minority of the mechanic classes. (see essay 1).[60] In 1776, artisans had supported democratic constitutional reform. On what basis did they support the Constitution of 1787? Paine gives us some clues. He came as close as any man to being a spokesman for urban artisans and a hero to them. Paine was unquestionably a democrat; he defended the beleaguered Pennsylvania constitution as "good for a poor man." From the outset of the Revolution he was also a nationalist. *Common Sense* had called for a nationally elected assembly, and Paine, at the center of the effort to mobilize support for the war, was always keenly aware of the inadequacies of the confederation. "The continental belt is too loosely buckled," he put it. Postwar experiences only strengthened this conviction. As Britain dumped manufactures in America, as commerce stagnated, keeping shipbuilding at a low ebb, artisans promoted vigorous demands for tariff protection and the promotion of commerce. Meanwhile, nationalist business leaders like Robert Morris sought support for bank charters; all nationalists sought a source of independent revenue for the federal government. In Paine, all these movements converged. By 1786, in most cities an alliance of artisans and merchants was a reality.[61]

In France, Paine's response to the Constitution was similar to Jefferson's. There was a compelling need for national union. "Thirteen staves and ne'er a hoop will not make a barrel," he later wrote; "any kind of hooping the barrel, however defectively executed would be better than none." Paine boasted that as early as 1776 *Common Sense* called for "a convention to form a continental association" and that, in 1782, he had made the same proposal in a letter to Robert R. Livingston, then minister of foreign affairs. He was not ashamed to admit that he had a meeting to discuss it with Livingston, Robert Morris, and Gouverneur Morris—all of whom, we might add, found the constitution of Pennsylvania "bad for a rich man."[62]

Paine's criticism of the Constitution resembled Jefferson's only in the absence of a bill of rights. He objected to the presidency. He had "always been opposed," he explained, "to a single executive." "A plurality is far better. It combines the mass of a nation better together. And besides this, it is necessary to the manly mind of a republic that it loses the debasing idea of obeying an individual." He objected also to "the long duration of the Senate," and he seems to have had misgivings, not explained, as to the general framework of the federal government. The Constitution was "a copy, though not quite so base as the original, of the form of the British Government."

The saving grace in the Constitution, for Paine as for Jefferson, was the possibility of amending it:

> It was only the absolute necessity of establishing some Federal authority extending equally over all the States, that an instrument so inconsistent as the present Federal Constitution is, obtained a suffrage. I would have voted for it myself, had I been in America, or even for a worse, rather than have none, provided it contained the means of remedying its defects by the same appeal to the people by which it was to be established. It is always a better policy to leave removable errors to expose themselves than to hazard too much in contending against them theoretically.[63]

If artisans had any of Paine's misgivings about the Constitution, they left no record of them. They made their political thought clear in a form not usually "read" by students of political thought—the massive parades celebrating ratification in 1788, the largest parades in American history to that time.[64]

Clearly, to all these marching artisans, the Constitution was the fulfillment of the spirit of 1776, not its negation. Protection for American manufactures was a leitmotif of the mechanics movement from the first boycotts of British goods in the 1760s. The right to participate in political life—a voice, recognition, respect—was the *sine qua non* of their democratic aspirations. The Constitution guaranteed the suffrage advances of the Revolutionary era. Moreover, there was something in the very process by which the Constitution had been adopted—a convention, submission to the people, discussion, the election of delegates—that ran very close to the conception advanced in 1776 by Paine in *Common Sense* and by the New York mechanics. They must have seen in the Constitution itself an opportunity for the continued expression of their aspirations.[65]

If we return, after this long excursion into the Revolutionary era, to Hamilton's proposal at the Philadelphia Convention, it is not at all hard to see why it was rejected. It went too far: too far in "extinguishing" the states; too far toward a king, House of Lords, House of Commons. Hamilton was too astute not to realize it. He later said he knew it "went beyond the ideas of most members," but "it was brought forward to make it the subject of discussion," "not as a thing attainable by us, but as a model which we ought to approach as near as possible."[66]

A month later, Hamilton was back with a second plan, somewhat less "high-toned." At the end, he signed the document, insisting with some accuracy that it was "remote" from his own.[67] He then joined Madison to write *The Federalist Papers*, putting the Constitution in its most republican light. At the New York convention, he fought for ratification on the same basis; "he is quite a republican," said an Antifederalist ("but he is known").[68] There he pleaded for the same "spirit of accommodation" that had "governed the convention" in Philadelphia.[69] Thus, in his own way, it could be argued, Hamilton's actions proved that he too was an accommodating conservative or, at the least, that he was part of a process of accommodation to democratic pressures that was the legacy of the Founding Fathers to subsequent generations of conservatives.

NOTES

This essay was originally presented at the conference "How Democratic Is the Constitution?" sponsored by the American Enterprise Institute, and appeared in Robert A. Goldwin and William A. Schambra, eds., *How Democratic Is the Constitution?* (Washington, D.C.: American Enterprise Institute for Public Policy Research, 1980). It is reprinted with permission of the Institute.

An abbreviated version, "The Framers of the Constitution and the Genius of the People," was given as the Gilbert Osofsky Lecture at the University of Illinois, Chicago (1987) and at the Milan Group in Early American History (1988). It was published in *In These Times* (September 9–15, 1987) and *Radical History Review* 42 (1988) 7–47, with commentary by Barbara Clark Smith, Linda Kerber, James Henretta, Peter Dimock, Michael Merrill, and William Forbath.

My thanks to Morton J. Frisch, the late Jackson T. Main, a masterful historian of the politics of the 1780s, and Richard Young for comments on an early draft and to Robert Goldwin and William Schambra for editorial assistance.

1. "Constitutional Convention Speech on a Plan of Government," in Harold Syrett, ed., *The Papers of Alexander Hamilton* (New York: Columbia University Press, 1962), vol. 4, pp. 178–207 (in particular, pp. 192, 200); "Plan for Government," pp. 207–211.

2. Broadus Mitchell, *Alexander Hamilton* (New York: Macmillan, 1957), vol. 1, pp. 391–392.

3. Douglass Adair, "Experience Must Be Our Only Guide: History, Democratic Theory, and the United States Constitution," in Trevor Colbourn, ed., *Fame and the Founding Fathers: Essays by Douglass Adair* (New York: Norton, 1974), p. 117.

4. G. Morris to John Penn, May 20, 1774, in U.S. Congress, *American Archives*, Peter Force, comp., Washington, D.C., 1837–1853, vol. 1, pp. 342–343. For recent scholarship on popular movements, see Alfred F. Young, ed., *The American Revolution: Explorations in the History of American Radicalism* (DeKalb: Northern Illinois University Press, 1976); for the reflections of two leading scholars of the subject, see Merrill Jensen, "The American People and the American Revolution," *Journal of American History*, vol. 57 (1970), pp. 3–35, and *The Revolution within America* (New York: New York University Press, 1974); and Richard B. Morris, "'We the People of the United States': The Bicentennial of a People's Revolution," *American Historical Review*, vol. 82 (1977), pp. 1–19.

5. "The Respectful Address of the Mechanics in Union," *New York Gazette*, June 17, 1776; Richard Ryerson, *The Revolution Is Now Begun: The Radical Committees of Philadelphia, 1765–1776* (Philadelphia: University of Pennsylvania Press, 1978); Edward Countryman, "Consolidating Power in Revolutionary America: The Case of New York, 1775–1783," *Journal of Interdisciplinary History*, vol. 6 (1976), pp. 545–678.

6. Thomas Paine, *Common Sense*, in Philip Foner, ed., *The Complete Writings of Thomas Paine* (New York: Citadel Press, 1945), vol. 1, pp. 3–46; Eric Foner, *Tom*

Paine and Revolutionary America (New York: Oxford University Press, 1976), pp. 81ff., 120ff.

7. John Adams, "Thoughts on Government," in Charles F. Adams, ed., *The Works of John Adams* (Boston: Little, Brown, 1854), vol. 4, pp. 193–200.

8. Paine, *Common Sense*, pp. 5–6.

9. Ibid., pp. 27–29.

10. *The Federal and State Constitutions, and Other Organic Laws*, ed. Francis N. Thorpe, 7 vols. (Washington, D.C.: U.S. Government Printing Office, 1909), vol. 7, pp. 3815–3819.

11. Pennsylvania Archives, 3rd ser., vol. 10, p. 762, cited in Foner, *Tom Paine*, p. 133.

12. Cited in Alfred F. Young, *The Democratic Republicans of New York: The Origins, 1763–1797* (Chapel Hill: University of North Carolina Press, 1967), p. 18. For the state constitutions in comparative perspective, see Jackson Turner Main, *The Sovereign States, 1775–1783* (New York: Franklin Watts, 1973); Elisha Douglass, *Rebels and Democrats: The Struggle for Equal Political Rights and Majority Rule during the American Revolution* (Chapel Hill: University of North Carolina Press, 1955); and Robert R. Palmer, *The Age of the Democratic Revolution*, 2 vols. (Princeton, N.J.: Princeton University Press, 1959), vol. 1, pp. 217–238.

13. David Ramsay, *The History of the American Revolution* (Philadelphia: R. Aitken & Son, 1789), vol. 1, pp. 315–316.

14. Staughton Lynd, "The Mechanics in New York Politics, 1774–1778," *Labor History*, vol. 5 (1964), pp. 215–246; Alfred F. Young, "The Mechanics and the Jeffersonians: New York, 1789–1801," ibid., pp. 247–276; for the general process, Gordon Wood, "The Democratization of Mind in the American Revolution," in U.S. Library of Congress, *Leadership in the American Revolution*, Washington, D.C., 1974, pp. 63–88.

15. Young, *Democratic Republicans*, p. 27.

16. Jackson Turner Main, *The Upper House in Revolutionary America, 1763–1788* (Madison: University of Wisconsin Press, 1967), and "Government by the People: The American Revolution and the Democratization of the Legislature," *William and Mary Quarterly*, 3rd ser., vol. 22 (1966), pp. 319–407.

17. Pauline Maier, *From Resistance to Revolution: Colonial Radicals and the Development of American Opposition to Britain, 1765–1776* (New York: Knopf, 1972), and "Coming to Terms with Sam Adams," *American Historical Review*, vol. 81 (1976), pp. 12–37; Elbridge Gerry, cited in Jensen, "The American People and the American Revolution," p. 31; Dirk Hoerder, *Crowd Action in Revolutionary Massachusetts, 1765–1780* (New York: Academic Press, 1977).

18. Main, *Sovereign States*, chap. 8.

19. Robert R. Livingston to William Duer, June 12, 1777, R. R. Livingston Papers, New-York Historical Society; Staughton Lynd, "A Governing Class on the Defensive: The Case of New York," in Lynd, *Class Conflict, Slavery, and the United States Constitution* (Indianapolis: Bobbs-Merrill, 1967).

20. Robert Troup to John Jay, May 15, 1777, in Richard Morris, ed., *John Jay, The Making of a Revolutionary: Unpublished Papers, 1745–1780* (New York: Harper & Row, 1975), p. 403, and p. 394 for Jay's comment; for the New York constitution, Bernard Mason, *The Road to Independence: The Revolutionary Movement in New York, 1773–1777* (Lexington: University of Kentucky Press, 1966).

21. Young, *Democratic Republicans*, chaps. 1–3; Schuyler cited at p. 2, Livingston at p. 291.

22. Main, *Sovereign States*, pp. 144, 185.

23. Ronald Hoffman, "The 'Disaffected' in the Revolutionary South," in Young, ed., *American Revolution*, p. 280.

24. Ronald Hoffman, "Popularizing the Revolution: Internal Conflict and Economic Sacrifice in Maryland, 1774–1780," *Maryland Historical Magazine* (1974), pp. 129–130.

25. Cited in Hoffman, "The 'Disaffected,'" pp. 306–307.

26. Ibid.

27. Washington to Henry Knox, December 26, 1786, in John C. Fitzpatrick, ed., *The Writings of George Washington*, 39 vols. (Washington, D.C.: U.S. Government Printing Office, 1931–1949); Robert Becker, *Revolution, Reform and the Policies of American Taxation, 1763–1783* (Baton Rouge: University of Louisiana Press, 1980).

28. Madison to Jefferson, April 23, 1787, in Julian Boyd, ed., *The Jefferson Papers* (Princeton, N.J.: Princeton University Press, 1958), vol. 11, p. 307.

29. Madison, "Vices of the Political System," April 1787, in William T. Hutchinson et al., eds., *The Papers of James Madison* (Chicago: University of Chicago Press, 1962), vol. 9, pp. 345–358; for convention versions, see Max Farrand, ed., *The Records of the Federal Convention of 1787*, 4 vols. (New Haven: Yale University Press, 1937), vol. 1, pp. 135–336, 421–423. The quotation is from the convention version, p. 136.

30. Madison to Jefferson, October 24, 1787, in *Papers of Madison*, vol. 1, pp. 205–220; Gordon Wood, *The Creation of the American Republic, 1776–1787* (Chapel Hill: University of North Carolina Press, 1969), especially chap. 9, part 4.

31. Hamilton, "Conjectures about the New Constitution," probably September 17–30, in Syrett, ed., *Papers of Hamilton*, vol. 4, pp. 275–276.

32. Madison, "Vices," in *Papers of Madison*, vol. 9, pp. 345–358, also conveniently available in Marvin Meyers, ed., *The Mind of the Founder: Sources of the Political Thought of James Madison* (Indianapolis: Bobbs-Merrill, 1973), pp. 82–92.

33. Most clearly explained in Madison to Jefferson, October 24, 1787, in *Papers of Madison*, vol. 10, pp. 205–220.

34. Charles A. Beard, *An Economic Interpretation of the Constitution of the United States* (New York: Macmillan, 1913), chap. 7; Jackson Turner Main, *Political Parties before the Constitution* (Chapel Hill: University of North Carolina Press, 1973); Forest McDonald, *We the People: The Economic Origins of the Constitution* (Chicago: University of Chicago Press, 1958); Robert L. Brunhouse, *The Counter-Revolution in*

Pennsylvania, 1776–1790 (Harrisburg: Pennsylvania Historical Commission, 1942); Young, *Democratic Republicans,* chaps. 1–5.

35. Cited in Adair, "Experience Must Be Our Only Guide," p. 119; see also Max Mintz, *Gouverneur Morris and the American Revolution* (Norman: University of Oklahoma Press, 1970), chap. 9; and for an array of extreme conservative proposals, Jane Butzner, comp., *Constitutional Chaff: Rejected Suggestions at the Constitutional Convention of 1787* (New York: Columbia University Press, 1941).

36. Robert G. McCloskey, ed., *The Works of James Wilson* (Cambridge, Mass.: Harvard University Press, 1967), vol. 1, p. 5 and introduction.

37. Farrand, ed., *Records,* vol. 1, pp. 47–53 for the quotations that follow.

38. Ibid., pp. 48, 50 (Gerry), p. 431 (Madison), p. 153 (Wilson), p. 101 (Mason). See also ibid., p. 406 (Gorham).

39. Ibid., pp. 135–136.

40. Ibid., p. 125.

41. Clinton Rossiter, "The Political Theory of Benjamin Franklin," *Pennsylvania Magazine of History and Biography* (July 1952), pp. 259–293.

42. Cf. George Billias, *Elbridge Gerry: Founding Father and Republican Statesman* (New York: McGraw-Hill, 1976), chaps. 11–13, and, in general, Jensen, *The Revolution within America,* chap. 4.

43. Farrand, ed., *Records,* vol. 2, pp. 643–644.

44. Ibid., vol. 2, pp. 201–206 and p. 225 for Gorham.

45. Ibid., vol. 2, pp. 202–204; Irving Brant, *James Madison: Father of the Constitution, 1787–1800* (Indianapolis: Bobbs-Merrill, 1950), pp. 118–119; Ralph Ketcham, *James Madison: A Biography* (New York: Macmillan, 1971), pp. 220–221; for Madison's later thoughts on the suffrage, see Hutchinson et al., eds., *Papers of Madison,* vol. 10, pp. 140–141, and Farrand, ed., *Records,* vol. 3, pp. 450–455.

46. Farrand, ed., *Records,* vol. 2, p. 249; for a summary of the convention on suffrage, see Clinton Williamson, *American Suffrage from Property to Democracy, 1760–1860* (Princeton, N.J.: Princeton University Press, 1960), chap. 7.

47. Madison to Jefferson, October 24, 1787, in Hutchinson et al., eds., *Papers of Madison,* vol. 10, pp. 205–220; and Charles F. Hobson, "The Negative on State Laws: James Madison, the Constitution and the Crisis of Republican Government," *William and Mary Quarterly,* 3rd ser., vol. 36 (April 1979), pp. 215–235, an important article challenging the notion that Madison's thoughts in *The Federalist* were identical with his private reactions to the Constitution.

48. Cecilia Kenyon, ed., *The Antifederalists* (Indianapolis: Bobbs-Merrill, 1966), introduction, and Kenyon, "Men of Little Faith: The Anti-Federalists on the Nature of Representative Government," *William and Mary Quarterly,* 3rd ser., vol. 12 (1955), pp. 3–43; J. Allen Smith, *The Spirit of American Government* (New York, 1907; reprinted Cambridge, Mass.: Harvard University Press, 1965, Cushing Strout, ed.). For Antifederalist democratic thought, see Jackson Turner Main, *The Anti-Federalists: Critics of the Constitution, 1781–88* (Chapel Hill: University of North

Carolina Press, 1961), chaps. 6–8. I have also profited from reading the manuscript of the late Herbert Storing, "What the Anti-Federalists Were For," published as the introduction to Storing, ed., *The Complete Anti-Federalist* 7 vols. (Chicago: University of Chicago Press, 1981).

49. Young, *Democratic Republicans*, chap. 2, citation at p. 22. Brunhouse, *Counter-Revolution in Pennsylvania*, chap. 7.

50. King to Madison, cited in Samuel B. Harding, *The Contest over the Ratification of the Federal Constitution in the State of Massachusetts* (New York: Longmans, Green, 1896), pp. 78–79.

51. Jonathan Elliot, comp., *The Debates in the Several State Conventions on the Adoption of the Federal Constitution*, 2d ed. (New York: Lippincott, 1888), vol. 2, pp. 101–102; Harding, *Contest over the Ratification*, p. 77n.

52. Young, *Democratic Republicans*, pp. 48–49 and chap. 5; Robin Brooks, "Melancton Smith, New York Anti-Federalist" (Ph.D. diss., University of Rochester, 1964), and Brooks, "Alexander Hamilton, Melancton Smith, and the Ratification of the Constitution in New York," *William and Mary Quarterly*, vol. 22 (1963), pp. 339–358.

53. Elliot, ed., *Debates*, vol. 2, pp. 243–251, 259–260.

54. Ibid., pp. 310–311, 407–411; see Theophilius Parsons Jr., "The Old Convictions and the New Realities: New York Anti-federalists and the Radical Whig Tradition" (Ph.D. diss., Columbia University, 1974).

55. Elliot, ed., *Debates*, vol. 2, pp. 327–331 for the amendments; Abraham Yates, Rough Hewer Notebooks, March 15, 22, 1790, Yates Papers, New York Public Library, reprinted in Young, ed., *The Debate over the Constitution, 1787–1789* (Chicago: Rand McNally, 1965), pp. 44–46.

56. Leonard Levy, *Jefferson and Civil Liberties: The Darker Side* (Cambridge, Mass.: Harvard University Press, 1963); Winthrop Jordan, *White over Black: American Attitudes towards the Negro, 1550–1812* (Chapel Hill: University of North Carolina Press, 1968), chap. 12; Merrill Peterson, *Thomas Jefferson and the New Nation: A Biography* (New York: Oxford University Press, 1970).

57. Jefferson to John Adams, November 13, 1787, to William S. Smith, November 13, 1787, to Edward Carrington, December 21, 1787, in Boyd, ed., *Papers of Jefferson*, vol. 12, pp. 349–351, 355–357, 445–447; Lafayette cited in Louis Gottschalk, *Lafayette between the American and French Revolution, 1783–1789* (Chicago: University of Chicago Press, 1950), p. 374.

58. Jefferson to Madison, December 20, 1787, in Boyd, ed., *Papers of Jefferson*, vol. 12, pp. 439–442.

59. Jefferson to David Humphreys, March 18, 1789, cited in Dumas Malone, *Jefferson and the Rights of Man* (Boston: Little, Brown, 1951), p. 178 and see chap. 9; Jefferson to Madison, 1788 (on *The Federalist*), cited in Richard Hofstadter, *The American Political Tradition and the Men Who Made It* (New York: Knopf, 1948), p. 30.

60. Staughton Lynd, "The Mechanics in New York Politics, 1774–1788," *Labor History*, vol. 5 (1968), pp. 225–246; Charles Olton, *Artisans for Independence: Philadelphia Mechanics and the American Revolution* (Syracuse: Syracuse University Press, 1975), chap. 9.

61. E. Foner, *Tom Paine*, chap. 6; for the political shifts in Philadelphia, see Owen Ireland, "Partisanship and the Constitution: Pennsylvania, 1787," *Pennsylvania History*, vol. 45 (1978), pp. 328–332, and George Bryan, "An Account of the Adoption of the Constitution of 1787," George Bryan Papers, Historical Society of Pennsylvania (brought to my attention by Steven Rosswurm).

62. Paine, "A Letter to George Washington, July 30, 1796," in P. Foner, ed., *Complete Writings of Paine*, vol. 2, pp. 691–693.

63. Ibid., p. 691.

64. See essay 1 in this volume.

65. For Paine, see essay 6 in this volume.

66. Hamilton, "To the New York Evening Post," February 24, 1802, in Syrett, ed., *Papers of Hamilton*, vol. 26, pp. 536–539 (brought to my attention by Morton Frisch); see also Mitchell, *Hamilton*, vol. 1, pp. 394–395.

67. Ibid., p. 399, and "Draft of a Constitution," in Syrett, ed., *Papers of Hamilton*, vol. 4, pp. 253–274; "Remarks on Signing," ibid., p. 253.

68. Young, *Democratic Republicans*, chap. 5, citation at p. 113.

69. Elliot, ed., *Debates*, vol. 2, p. 237.

5

How Radical Was the American Revolution?

How radical was the American Revolution? A growing body of recent scholarship contributes to an understanding of two major unresolved issues in the study of the radicalism of the revolutionary era: the sources of radicalism and the impact of radicalism on the results of the Revolution. I would like to explore both with a view, not to answering, but to establishing a framework within which to address the larger question.

This recent scholarship suggests sharply variant alternatives to the long-standing trickle-down or spillover interpretations of radicalism, in which the movements for internal change are viewed as a by-product of the political revolution against Great Britain. In 1926, J. Franklin Jameson spoke of "the stream of revolution once started [which] could not be confined within thin narrow banks but [which] spread abroad upon the land." And in 1967 Bernard Bailyn saw in the Revolution "a movement of thought, rapid, irreversible and irresistible" which "swept past boundaries few had set out to cross, into regions few had wished to enter." In the "contagion of liberty" "a spark" jumped from Whig political ideology to ignite sentiment for antislavery, religious liberty, and the rejection of deference. All historians use metaphors, and Jameson and Bailyn provided evocative physical analogies which, as they often do, allowed little room for human agency. If Jameson was vague in identifying the dynamic source of change, Bailyn, as David B. Davis has written, "tend[ed] to exaggerate the autonomous power of ideas" to effect change.[1] Who broke the banks of the river? Which people carried the sparks from one tree of liberty to another?

This scholarship leads me to posit four propositions that might restore agency to this process and move us toward a synthesis of the origins of radicalism without, however, suggesting a single paradigm:

First, there were deep roots of radicalism in ideas, values, traditions, and customs held by common people long before the Revolution.

"Cornwallis Turned Nurse, and His Mistress a Soldier" was adapted from an illustration for a set of Anglo-American nursery rhymes called "The World Turned Upside Down," depicting reversals of all sorts. "The World Turned Upside Down" was also a song an English military band is said to have played at the surrender of Lord Cornwallis at Yorktown in 1781. To Americans it epitomized their victory over the greatest military power of the eighteenth century. This cartoon appeared in a Philadelphia almanac after the American victory. From *The Continental Almanac for 1782*, Library of Congress.

Second, as groups played an active role in the Revolution and became aware of their own interests, they invoked their own traditions in addition to appropriating Whig rhetoric.

Third, experiences over an unusually long revolutionary era contributed to radical impulses, not only in the now well-known decade of resistance before 1775, but during the protracted war from 1775 to 1783 and even more from the mid-1780s on, especially through the 1790s, when the impulses of the French Revolution and the successful black revolution in Saint-Domingue rekindled American radicalisms.

Fourth, as antagonisms increased, many groups of common people acquired a heightened consciousness of themselves and their distinct interests which enabled them to become a presence in American life.

Sources of Radicalism

"That each of us may sit down under his own fig-tree and enjoy the fruits of his own labour"

The first proposition, that there were deep roots of radicalism in ideas, values, traditions, and customs held by common people which they brought to the era of the Revolution, has been analyzed by historians within various frameworks: moral economy, *mentalité*, class ideology, political culture, or "customs in common," in Edward Thompson's apt phrase for the culture shared by English "plebeians" in the eighteenth century.[2] Take, for example, yeoman farmers. A common assumption among early American farmers was that they were entitled to "the fruits of their labor," attained by the "sweat of their brow." William Manning's aphorism "labor is the soul [sole] parrant of all property" was to them a given. Farmers who plowed a furrow, sowed seeds, and reaped a harvest, or farm women who spun thread from flax or wool and saw weavers turn it into cloth, which they then made into clothing, did not need a political economist to instruct them in the labor theory of value. This is what informed the long-standing fear, among New England yeomen in particular, of being reduced to "vassals" under "lordships," a fear that Richard Bushman has established was part of their "vernacular culture." This is what made yeoman farmers so quick to respond to any threat to the security of their title to land, especially to taxes that threatened to reduce them to the status of debtors, which could lead to the loss of their land. Political leaders like John and

Samuel Adams were successful because they were attuned to such fears. This was the social nexus of the agrarian response to Whig political and constitutional rhetoric.[3]

Historians can now pull this red thread through the skein of collective agrarian responses from the late seventeenth century through the prewar Regulator movements, the political conflicts of the 1770s with England, and the Shaysism of the 1780s, to the agrarian rebellions and agrarian politics of the 1790s and early 1800s. This was the radicalism of farmers who were property holders or would-be property holders and believed they had a right to land, tools, and other productive property. These were not necessarily marginal farmers, although many were landowners with uncertain title to their land, tenants with insecure leases, or backcountry squatters. Nor did farmers have to be poverty-stricken to become radical. As often as not, they were landholders with families who worried about becoming impoverished—a fear of falling—or the sons of landholders who feared they would be unable to acquire land and duplicate the success of their fathers. Their goal was personal independence through secure landholding, a goal that merged with the political aspiration for national independence in some regions, making yeoman patriots, and which in other regions decidedly did not, leaving a large number of farmers Tory, neutral, or "disaffected" during the war.

Artisans were imbued with similar values. Also property holders or would-be property holders, they were men (and sometimes women) who practiced a productive trade as masters ("a man on his own") or as journeymen, working for others and aspiring to be masters. They were heirs to the ancient traditions of their trades as well as to a belief in property-right tenets long articulated by their forebears among English artisans of the seventeenth and eighteenth centuries.[4] In Philadelphia in 1773 "A Mechanic," writing to his fellow mechanics, argued that the Tea Act was oppressive "whether we have property of our own or not." Here was the "breach" by which the British ministry would "enter the Bulwark of our sacred liberties." At stake was "whether our property, and the dear earned fruits of our own labor are at our own disposal."[5] Artisans believed that their skill was a form of property. "Labour at that time," argued a petition signed by twelve hundred Connecticut mechanics in 1792, referring to the years before the Revolution, "was the principal property the citizen possessed."[6] Artisans in the port cities, even more than country folk, lived in fear of becoming dependent. Journeymen worried that they might remain wage earners and not rise to the ranks of the independent. Apprentices who ran away had little confidence they could ever climb the ladder into this artisan world.[7]

What values might we expect to find among the free, propertyless wage earners at the bottom? Among merchant seamen, for instance—the largest single group of wage earners in early America? As Admiral Peter Warren testified in 1745 after they fiercely resisted impressment into His Majesty's navy, seamen "have the highest notion of the rights and liberties of Englishmen, and indeed are almost Levellers." Sailors prized their freedom. Jesse Lemisch has established that impressment was a leading cause of their participation in the mob actions of the era of resistance. Marcus Rediker, looking at sailors at sea, concluded that "seamen often brought to the ports a militant attitude towards arbitrary and excessive authority, and a willingness to empathize with the grievances of others, to cooperate for the sake of self defense, and to use direct action, violent if necessary, to accomplish collectively defined goals."[8]

Throughout the colonial era, those in servitude, whether African American slaves, immigrant indentured servants from Great Britain, or native-born apprentices, demonstrated what in 1721 the Reverend Cotton Mather of Boston called a "fondness for freedom."[9] Fifty years later a slave in the same city, the African-born Phillis Wheatley, wrote, "In every human Breast, God has implanted a Principle, which we call Love of Freedom. It is impatient of Oppression, and pants for Deliverance; and by the Leave of our modern Egyptians I will assert, that the same Principle lives in us."[10] Slaves did not need the example of the Sons of Liberty to inspire them to seek their own freedom.

Slaves of the last half of the eighteenth century warrant being identified as African American. African culture contributed to their consciousness. Most slaves were native-born children, grandchildren, or great-grandchildren of men and women who had been wrenched from Africa; a large number were recent forced migrants from Africa. Tens of thousands of slaves were imported in the decades before the war, and many more from 1783 to 1808. A host of scholars have rediscovered the retentions and survivals from African culture, ranging from marriage and burial customs to folk medicine to house styles and religious systems. Moreover, slaves formed families which served as a channel to pass on their identity to successive generations—the theme of Herbert Gutman's pathbreaking research on the history of the black family. When they adopted Anglo-American religions, they blended evangelical Protestantism with African religious practices.[11]

What did slaves aspire to after emancipation? Their lives as workers were a constant reminder that their daily labor was being stolen from them, just as they or their ancestors had been stolen from Africa. The evidence of the revolutionary era, the time of the first emancipation, suggests that no less than white Anglo-American yeomen and artisans they sought the means to secure personal independence. Massachusetts slaves began a 1773 petition with the premise that "they have in common with other men, a natural right to be free, and without molestation, to enjoy such property, as they may accumulate by their industry," moved to a plea that "they may be liberated and made free-men," and ended with the request that they be granted "some part of the unimproved land, belong to this province, for a settlement, that each of us may there quietly sit down under his own fig-tree, and enjoy the fruits of his own labour." Tens of thousands of slaves fled during the war; many were transported by the British to Nova Scotia in 1783, sought land there, and when they fared poorly made their way back to Africa to the British colony of Sierra Leone in quest of land. In the 1790s, when Robert Carter began to free the five hundred slaves on his Virginia plantation by individual acts of manumission, they sought from him land or the means to pursue a trade they assumed was their right.[12]

This set of beliefs among both free farmers and artisans and unfree slaves, as their language alone suggests, was often rooted in religion, especially in the evangelical dissenting faiths. Evangelical religion surfaces in protest. Peter Wood notes that before the war there were a number of black preachers like Philip John, who preached "that there should be no more white King's Governor or great men, but the Negroes should live happily and have laws of their own." Alan Taylor finds that, after the war, "in every agrarian resistance or rebellion, anti-authoritarian evangelical preachers encouraged, clarified and invested with divine meaning their settlers' agrarian notions. They were Baptists, New Light Congregationalists, ultra-evangelical Antinomians who sought to bypass a learned clergy in pursuit of direct spiritual encounters." William Manning, although an orthodox Calvinist Congregationalist, envisioned the battle of "the Many" against "the Few" as a war in the imagery of the Old Testament.[13]

Religious awakenings reverberated through the revolutionary era. While historians continue to explore the links between the Great Awakening (1739–45) and the Revolution, far more attention is being paid to the waves of enthusiastic religions during and especially after the war.[14] Millennialism, it is now clear, took many forms—charging, for example, the radical protest of an intercolonial backcountry rebel like Herman Husband with his vision of a New Jerusalem in the West as a yeoman's utopia. By the early 1800s the evangelical Baptists and Methodists, on the way to becoming the most numerous of American denominations, contributed not only to what Nathan Hatch has called "the democratization of American Christianity," but to the democratization of American political life.[15]

Belief systems such as these—a labor theory of value, an evangelical Christian equalitarianism, plebeian notions of the rights and liberties of Englishmen—can be thought of as resources common people drew upon at times of crisis.

Appropriations of Liberty

"Who can have a better right to the land than we who have fought for it?"

If this commitment to prior sources of radical values is valid, it is not hard to argue the second proposition, namely that in the era of the Revolution, as groups of ordinary people played an active role in the Revolution and became aware of their own interests, they invoked their own traditions as well as the Whig rhetoric of lawyers, ministers, planters, and merchants. There was a synthesis of traditional veins of radical thought with newer currents forged in the experiences of the Revolution that scholars are only now analyzing.

Language reveals the synthesis. The postwar protest by New England farmers who in Alan Taylor's account settled illegally on frontier land in Maine and resisted by force the efforts of the great proprietors to oust them is a rich example of such a synthesis. They held an underlying assumption of a right to land drawn from radical Christian traditions ("God gave the earth to the children") and a sense of a moral economy ("Wild lands ought to be as free as the common air"). But their military service in the war fortified this claim ("Who can have a better right to the land then we who have fought for it?"). And the fact that the land in dispute was confiscated from England made it all the more common property ("These lands once belonged to King George. He lost them by the American Revolution & they became the property of the people who defended and won them.").

Other language showed an intricate appropriation of Whig rhetoric. The unfree people living in the centers of patriot movements were extraordinarily quick to seize on Whig ideas, especially when patriots shifted the meaning of liberty from traditional English constitutional rights to natural rights, the first transition in the meaning of this keyword that Edward Countryman analyzes. Thus, in Massachusetts, the first petition of slaves for freedom in January 1773 was a plaintive Christian humanitarian plea: "We have no Property! We have no Wives! No Children! We have no City! No Country! But we have a Father in Heaven." The second, in July, spoke of a "natural right to be free" but dwelt on a person's right to his own labor. Even their 1774 petition, in which they spoke of themselves as "a freeborn Pepel [who] have never forfeited this Blessing by aney compact or agreement whatever," continued to blend this Whig theme with Christian values. Not until a 1777 petition, which referred to their patience in presenting "Petition after Petition," did they pick up on their "natural & unalienable right" to freedom. This appropriation was so opportunistic one is tempted to argue that Whig rhetoric was more the occasion than a cause for asserting a claim to liberty.[16]

As individuals picked up ideas that were in the air, they often pushed them far beyond anything intended by patriot leaders. Years later Ebenezer Fox, a Boston-area apprentice who shipped out on a privateering vessel, wrote in his memoirs, "I thought I was doing myself a great injustice by remaining in bondage when I ought to be free; that the time was come, when I should liberate myself from the thraldom of others and set up a government of my own; or in other words, do what was right in the sight of my own eyes." His words reveal the kind of personal Declaration of Independence from all authority that Henry Thoreau would have appreciated, and that would have made John Adams shudder.

The unequals had to make a leap in their thinking to turn the talk of liberty into a demand for equality for themselves; and the leap is better explained by experience than by any logic inherent in the idea. For George Robert Twelves Hewes, a Boston shoemaker who survives in two as-told-to biographies, the experience of participating in the Boston Massacre, the Boston Tea Party, and countless other events of resistance enabled him to cast off deference. He vividly recalled the trembling he felt as an apprentice shoemaker when he called on John Hancock, one of the wealthiest mechants in Boston, and then, a decade later, the sense of equality he felt when (as he remembered it) he worked side by side with Hancock throwing the tea overboard in the Tea Party. It is unlikely that Hancock would have risked arrest at so illegal an event, but Hewes could have mistaken another gentleman for him. For the rest of his life Hewes would remember the Revolution's moments of equality—when he was as good a man as his "betters," whether John Hancock, the customs official Hewes defied, or the ship's officer for whom he refused to take his hat off.[17]

We know enough about Abigail Adams to gain insight into what led one woman to make the leap and therefore to speculate about others. In her "remember the Ladies" letter to John in March 1776, she seemed to be raising the demand to end the tyranny of husbands over their wives for the first time. For more than a decade she had been reading or hearing her husband's rhetoric of "tyranny" and "slavery" and "lords and vassals," but it does not seem that she, John, or anyone else in Massachusetts had publicly applied the principle to the status of women.

What were her experiences? Over the decade she had followed the active participation of the women of Boston and the surrounding country-side in the making of the Revolution and referred to herself as a "politician." She may well have drawn inspiration from the black petitioners and alleged conspirators of 1773–74 who, she felt, "have as good a right to freedom as we have." In 1776, only the month before her letter to John, she had read *Common Sense*, with its message to begin the world over again. But perhaps most decisive, for almost two years while her husband was intermittently away in Philadelphia, she had taken on new responsibilities outside the traditional "female sphere": she managed the family farm, boasting she had become "quite a farmeriss," and she had become "school mistress" to her three young children. Thus she had a growing consciousness both of her own capacities and her own inadequacies—how ill-educated she was for the task. It was in the context of such experiences that she lifted her voice to John to "remember the Ladies." Similar wartime experiences would lead other women to make such a leap and verbalize a new consciousness.[18]

Sources of Radicalism: Promises Unfulfilled

The third proposition, that experiences shaped radical impulses over a very long revolutionary era that extended through the 1780s, the 1790s, and beyond, is becoming more of a commonplace among historians as they think through the life histories of the revolutionary generation. The Revolution did not end in 1776, in 1783, in 1787, or even in 1801. In writing about the great leaders—Washington, Adams, Hamilton, Jefferson, Madison—historians have no problem dealing with their entire political lives, which often stretched over half a century and more. Why not think the same way of the common people who lived out their lives over the same years? For many, their radicalism was the product of their *cumulative* experience over the entire era.

"In Every Revolution," wrote Herman Husband in 1793, "the People at Large are called upon to assist true Liberty," but when "the foreign oppressor is thrown off, learned and designing men" assume power to the detriment of the "laboring people." Husband was a leader of the backcountry rebellion of the Regulators of North Carolina defeated in 1771, the Antifederalists defeated in 1788, and the Pennsylvania Whiskey Rebellion on the defensive when he wrote.[19] If early in the Revolution there was a radicalism of hope expressed by Thomas Paine's plea in *Common Sense* to "begin the world over again," late in the era there was a radicalism of promises not fulfilled or of expectations raised but dashed, often expressed with anger or bitterness.

The experiences of a long war—the longest in American history—generated a variety of radical impulses. If the war is ever "restored to the central position that it had for the Revolutionary generation," as the military historian John Shy urged, some of these experiences may be appreciated.[20] Roughly two hundred thousand men served in the military, about half in the militia, half in the regular army. The Philadelphia militia, whose artisans, journeymen, and laborers were the base of the movement that pushed Pennsylvania to independence and enacted the most radical constitution of any state, "carried their egalitarianism with them into the field" and carried it back to the streets of Philadelphia in the campaign for price controls in 1779–80.[21] The militias elsewhere, even when a cross section of their communities, were too democratic in the eyes of elitist officers. Soldiers of the regular army, who after 1776 were drawn from "the very poorest and most repressed persons in Revolutionary society," scholars now agree were no less patriotic for having their aspirations for a better life tied to the promises of land. Tension between enlisted men and officers was endemic, and Baron Von Steuben was astute enough to recognize that he had to teach American officers to adapt to the "genius" of individualistic American enlistees and win their "love and respect." "Continentals," who early in the war often expressed their bitterness at the inequities of army life in drunkenness, desertion, and bounty jumping, as they became more disciplined and cohesive, expressed their protest collectively, climaxing in the mutinies of the New Jersey and Pennsylvania lines in 1781.[22] "After eight years [of war] in which about 200,000 of the masses watched perhaps 20,000 of the so-called elite perform more or less incompetently" as officers, John Shy observes wryly, "the post-war voter had lost much of his habitual deference to men allegedly better than he was."[23]

At sea the rage for privateering gave some sixty thousand men (as opposed to a few thousand who served in the navy) a chance to "make their fortunes and serve their country," as the recruiters beguiled them. It also gave them a taste of legalized piracy, in which captains, like pirate commanders, courted the consent of their crews. And thousands of seamen who were captured, if they survived the horrors of British prisons, had the experience of collective self-government.[24]

In the countryside the Revolution took the character of a civil war for tens of thousands of ordinary Americans—or in Ronald Hoffman's apt phrase, "an uncivil war," especially in parts of the southern backcountry, where it "took on the appearance of a social convulsion." Wherever there was a prior history of intense conflict between colonial elites and common folk—especially in the two Carolinas—patriot elites encountered intense opposition. In Maryland, where there was more cohesion, there was still active opposition to large planter leadership by the "disaffected"—poor farmers and tenants. The pattern was similar in New York, where tenants opposed patriot landlords. Even in relatively tranquil Virginia there was opposition, only partially overcome when old elites embraced Patrick Henry. While alignments in the South often produced a patchwork of social classes, the principal experience for many southerners was confronting and thwarting their betters, tidewater or low-country elites.[25]

For slaves the "turbulence of the war," in Sylvia Frey's words, "rocked the slave system to its foundations." The British army was a magnet to slaves, North and South, with General Clinton repeating in 1780 in South Carolina Lord Dunmore's offer of 1775 in Virginia, although the British never risked a generalized appeal that would alarm their slave-owning supporters. In the North the urgencies of recruiting quotas forced patriots to reverse their ban on slaves, but in the end probably more slaves wielded arms for the British than against them, and even more simply took flight. Wherever the fighting was, to use Frey's term, *triagonal*—Whigs-Tories-slaves—and wherever the British army was a presence, slaves seized their chance. And in the southern low country, Philip Morgan points out, "wartime anarchy created a power vacuum in the countryside that allowed slaves to expand their liberty" or autonomy within the system.[26]

In civilian life the war created inequities, as inflation soared and profiteers flourished. Food riots were common in the North, often by crowds composed of women, pitting advocates of a moral economy in support of official governmental efforts at price control against advocates of a political economy of free trade.[27] But if the war was in so many ways a hothouse of antagonisms, it also created new vistas for ordinary people. As David Ramsay, South Carolina's participant historian, wrote in 1789, it set people "to thinking, speaking and acting in a line far beyond that to which they were accustomed.... It not only required but created talents."[28] The war circulated soldiers and seamen, bringing them into new worlds. The war thus gave tens of thousands of men and women, slave and free, an enlarged sense of American space and the potential for a new way of life. Radical action requires hope and the knowledge of alternatives, not merely desperation.

For women the war offered experiences out of the "domestic sphere." Several thousand women attached themselves to the army as cooks, laundresses, and nurses, usually following family members. And when men went off to war, women were called upon to clothe them—a traditional role—but they also assumed male roles, managing the farm or trade, repeating Abigail Adams's experience of 1775–76. Although the role of "deputy husband" was time-honored, never had so many women assumed it as a patriotic duty.[29]

The experiences of postwar society spawned a radicalism of disappointment. For those who had served in the army, the inequities of the settlement left a long-simmering resentment. Officers received pensions, and soldiers who were wounded received some recompense. But ordinary soldiers rarely received the bounty lands promised them on enlistment. The government did not enact a pension for enlisted men until 1818, and then only for those "in reduced circumstances," which produced forty thousand claims, a Domesday Book of American poverty. And not until 1832 was this means test eliminated and an unrestricted pension law enacted for those who could give "a very full account" of their service. Twenty thousand applied. Historians have only begun to take the measure of the pain, pride, and outrage in the pension applications of these survivors of the Revolution.[30]

The hard times of the Confederation era forged a radicalism of desperation: of farmers imprisoned for debt and faced with the loss of their land and property; of mechanics swamped by the flood of British-manufactured imports or ruined in the collapse of American shipbuilding; of migrants into the backcountry frustrated in their quest for land. Petitions rained on the state legislatures demanding "access to land, debtor relief, and remedies to the burden of heavy and regressive taxes." Shaysism was not confined to one state. Among elites, as Gordon Wood has made clear, there was an even greater fear that the radicalism of the "people-out-of-doors" would come "indoors," to dominate state legislatures.[31]

Thus by 1787 this fear of legal shaysism mobilized the substantial commercial interests as never before in support of the Constitution. The conflict over ratification mobilized a broader array of interests in opposition, inspiring a populist Antifederalism on a scale that is only now being recognized by scholars.[32]

The Hamiltonian economic program of the 1790s, coming on top of the new Constitution, widened the popular perception of a national ruling class that Gary Kornblith and John Murrin posit as rule by the few at the expense of the many. In this context, what David Brion Davis calls "the astonishing American enthusiasm for the French Revolution" is understandable. Once the French Revolution entered domestic politics in the guise of foreign policy issues—the war between revolutionary republican France and monarchist Britain, the Paineite effort to revolutionize Great Britain, the Federalist accomodation with Britain in 1795 and the half-war with France—it inspired new levels of equalitarianism and millennialism. Thomas Paine's *Rights of Man* seemed to pose the same issues that *Common Sense* had in 1776. The impulses to radicalism soared. As Davis writes, "sometimes foreign revolutions have reinvigorated Americans' faith in a better world, expanding and redefining the meaning of equality and exposing the hollowness of our own pretensions to social justice."[33]

Popular Consciousness: "Class," "Plebeian," or "Democratic"?

The fourth proposition about the sources of radicalism—namely, that as the antagonisms of the revolutionary era increased, many groups of common people acquired a heightened consciousness of themselves which enabled them to establish a presence in American life—is the the most problematic, not to prove, but to formulate. Historians seem to agree that a new kind of popular consciousness—a sense of "we" and "they"—came into being over the revolutionary era. They do not agree how to conceptualize it.

There is a temptation to think of it as a class-consciousness. Edward Thompson's brief formulation of class in the preface to *The Making of the English Working Class* (1963)—very likely the most quoted passage in modern scholarly discourse about class—has been enormously influential among American scholars. "Class happens," wrote Thompson, "when some men, as a result of common experience (inherited or shared), feel and articulate the identity of their interests as between themselves, and as against other men whose interests are different from (and usually opposed to) theirs." After immersing himself in explorations of popular culture in the British eighteenth century, Thompson drew nuanced distinctions about how classes come into being:

> To put it bluntly, classes do not exist as separate entities, look around, find an enemy class, and then start to struggle. On the contrary, people find themselves in society structured in determined ways (crucially but not exclusively, in productive relations), they experience exploitation (or the need to maintain power over those they exploit), they identify points of antagonistic interest, they commence to struggle around those issues and in the process of struggling they discover themselves as classes, they come to know this discovery as class-consciousness. Class and class-consciousness are always the last, not the first, stage in the real historical process.[34]

Thompson's concept of class continues to provoke controversy which need not be resolved here.[35] Historians writing about class have differing conceptions of class, yet they share Thompson's emphasis on classes' coming-into-being. They write of the "formation" of the yeomanry as a class or of the yeomanry "reinventing itself as a class" in successive backcountries, of the "making" and "unmaking" of a ruling class or of "bourgeois class formation" affecting changing conceptions of liberty. Scholars from many different vantage points are also identifying "points of antagonistic interest" in the revolutionary era around which Americans "commenced to struggle" and "discovered themselves." The points of struggle, if my analysis of this scholarship is valid, were more extensive and more intense later than earlier in the revolutionary era.

Whether self-discovery led to class-consciousness is open to debate. Thompson, in returning to the study of popular struggles in eighteenth-century England, continued to write of "the patricians and the plebs" and of "a plebeian culture" within a "patrician" society. Others use this vocabulary. Michael Merrill and Sean Wilentz characterize William Manning as a "plebeian democrat," and Wilentz has described the artisans of New York as holding to a "plebeian artisan republicanism." Gordon Wood sees a dichotomy between plebeian and patrician in America. While I, too, have fallen back on *plebeian*, on reflection, the term seems anachronistic because the vocabulary of "plebeian" and "patrician" drew on a classical tradition that was fast passing out of fashion by 1800. So much discovery in the United States occurred as groups struggled for a voice in the political process that the terms *republican, democratic,* and *citizen consciousness* have been more compelling to historians than class-consciousness.[36]

American scholars have only begun to explore the language of identities among nonelite groups.[37] My impression is that the older vocabulary that drew distinctions in the society of sorts, ranks, conditions, and estates was fading late in the eighteenth century; certainly the value-laden "better sort," "middling sort," and "meaner sort" were becoming passé, but "class" probably did not come into common usage—"working class," "middle class"—until well into the second quarter of the nineteenth century.

In the wake of the Revolution the common language of class among nonelites often expressed a polarity of two major divisions in the society. In the debate over ratifying the Constitution, Amos Singletary, a Massachusetts farmer of little formal education, feared that "lawyers, and men of learning, and moneyed men" will "swallow up us little folks." In New York, Melancton Smith, the chief Antifederalist spokesman, a self-made merchant, thought that the proposed new government would fall into the hands of "the few and the great," while excluding "those of the middling class of life."[38] In the debates of the 1790s the language of radicals suggests they drew the dividing line between the productive and nonproductive classes: "those that labour for a living and those who get one without" or "the Many" and "the Few" (William Manning); "the laboring people" against "learned and designing men" or the "idle rich" (Herman Husband); "the people" versus "the aristocracy" (Thomas Paine in *Rights of Man*). In newspapers and pamphlets the pseudonyms suggest similar identities: "A Laborer" (William Manning), "A Plebeian" (Melancton Smith), "Rough Hewer" (Abraham Yates Jr.), "A Ploughjogger" (Jedediah Peck, indeed a farmer and a sometime Baptist preacher), and "A Farmer," "A Mechanic," ad infinitum.[39]

Clearly, some nonelite groups "discovered themselves" more than others, moving toward a more interest-specific if not class-specific consciousness. The obvious candidate is the most self-conscious urban group of the era, the mechanics (analyzed in essay 1 in this volume). Mechanics unquestionably became an influence in political life; they knew it, and political leaders knew it. One hesitates to speak of a mechanic class because mechanics were so heterogeneous. Perhaps historians can agree they had a "mechanic consciousness" and that there was a "mechanic presence," and move on from there.[40]

If such groups "discovered themselves" in conflict, it does not necessarily follow that they remained in constant antagonism with their opponents. On the contrary, because the Revolution was also a war for national liberation, nascent classes formed coalitions with other classes against a common outside enemy. Indeed, the era led to a constant reforming of coalitions, especially in face of a foreign danger that persisted in major crises throughout the era. But entering into coalitions did not necessarily diminish awareness of separate identities. In 1788, the fact that in every major city mechanics as a body joined merchants and professionals to parade in political celebration of the new Constitution was a sign of mechanic consciousness; they marched en masse as mechanics, usually grouped trade by trade with emblems, symbols, or tools of their craft, displaying a consciousness of themselves as craftsmen, mechanics, and citizens.[41]

Furthermore, nascent classes divided internally. In the countryside, with the expansion of a market economy, the distinction Allan Kulikoff draws between market-embedded commercial farmers and non-market-oriented yeomen helps explain political divisions among farmers, for example, over ratifying the commercially oriented Constitution of 1787. In the cities the mechanic trades also divided according to market orientation. By the late eighteenth century free wage labor was becoming the norm in northern cities: imported indentured servitude was drying up, slavery was fading, and apprenticeship was being transformed into a form of cheap labor. As the market system made its inroads on artisan production the conflict between masters and apprentices and masters and journeymen rent the fabric of mechanic cohesion.[42]

While there undoubtedly was a growing sense of commonality among "the laboring classes" embracing town and countryside, urban mechanics usually failed to support agrarians in insurrections, whether it was the tenant uprising in New York in 1766 or Shays's Rebellion in 1786. There was a change in 1794, when the urban Democratic Societies condemned the excise tax more than they condemned the whiskey rebels. The laboring classes in countryside and city were female as well as male, but radicals who embraced Paine's *Rights of Man* (1791–92) showed no comparable interest in Mary Wollstonecraft's *Vindication of the Rights of Women* (1791). The laboring classes included blacks—in a greater proportion than at any other time in American history—yet neither agrarian nor mechanic radicals welcomed Gabriel's abortive insurrection in Virginia in 1800 or the efforts of free blacks in northern cities to forge their own community institutions. And the free blacks of Boston volunteered to put down Shays's Rebellion. Thus the multiple radicalisms of the revolutionary era remained separate.

Taken together, the argument advanced in these four propositions suggests new ways of thinking about the sources of radicalism in the revolutionary era. It posits not a single radicalism but multiple radicalisms. It does not see them stemming from one all-pervasive idea or ideology. It assumes a prior array of radical value systems which came into play at that time. The Revolution was itself an incalculable stimulus to radicalism. But if anything, scholars might pursue not a "trickle-down" theory of radicalism but rather one of "bubbling up" from below. Radicalism flourished not only in the era of political resistance (1765–1775) but during the war (1775–1783) and especially the postwar era (1783–1801) when a radicalism of frustration replaced a radicalism of hope. The multiple radicalisms of the era were often at odds with each other. These propositions provide a framework for an inquiry into the successes and failures of the radical agendas in the results of the Revolution.

Results of the Revolution: A Framework for Analysis

If recent scholarship has, as Linda Kerber writes, increased our "appreciation" of the many radical movements of the Revolution, it leaves open the question of their success. And if the recovery of the groups previously neglected by historians makes the Revolution seem more radical, there is a temptation to say our understanding of the results—especially if we focus on the peoples Kerber called "marginal" and I originally called "outsiders"—makes it seem more conservative. The retention and expansion of slavery, the maintenance of a patriarchal subordination of women, the destructive inroads of a market economy on the laboring classes in the cities, to say nothing of the devastating impact of national expansion on American Indians, were developments central to postrevolutionary society.

Scholars contrasting such results with the democratization of American politics, the opening of economic opportunity, and the surges of equalitarianism—all gains benefiting principally yeomen and mechanics and then women—often end up using words like "contradiction" or "paradox," which still leave us hanging for an explanation. Other historians, by claiming, as does Gordon Wood, for example, that however much the Revolution failed "to abolish slavery and change fundamentally the lot of women,

[it] made possible the anti-slavery and women's rights movements of the nineteenth century and in fact all our current egalitarian thinking," essentially evade their responsibility for historical analysis.[43]

In the afterword to *The American Revolution* (1976) I suggested that there were several ways to measure the success of popular radical movements, short of their achieving power: by their capacity to articulate a distinct ideology, to endure as movements, and especially to influence those in power and shape events. A compelling case could be made for the impact of radical movements on the elites, creating a sophisticated kind of American conservatism that learned how to accommodate popular pressures. But the same process of accommodation, I thought, did not work for the "outsiders" to the political system—women, blacks, Indians. The scholarship since then has convinced me I was not bold enough in asserting the impact of popular movements on the elites and that I was wrong in claiming that women and blacks had little impact on the Revolution, or the Revolution on them.

As I now see the results of the Revolution, my reflections run as follows:

First, in response to the upsurges of radicalism, elites attempting to make themselves into a national ruling class divided as to how to confront these threats. In the political sphere their responses ranged on a spectrum from the traditional methods of the English ruling class—force, deference, and influence—to negotiation leading to accommodation.

Second, the processes of negotiation were most successful with the middling classes—yeomen and mechanics—who had pushed their way into the political system, establishing a continuing presence that elites could not ignore if they wished to govern successfully.

Third, negotiation was pervasive throughout the society, offering accommodations to groups excluded from the political system—women and slaves—without destroying the subordination on which the social and economic system rested. American Indians, the real outsiders, were powerful enough in certain places and times to force a kind of accommodation on Anglo-Americans that delayed expansion.

And finally, as a result of the process of accommodation which made the political system more democratic, radical popular movements divided as to the means to effect change on a spectrum that ranged from the traditional time-honored, effective, extralegal forms of opposition to working within the new political system.

Framing the analysis of results in this way—as a process of confrontation, negotiation, and accommodation occurring in a range of separate spheres—offers the possibility of resolving the so-called contradictions in the outcome of the Revolution. It also leaves room in the analysis for the integration of the complex ways in which the transformations leading the United States toward a capitalist society both stimulated and frustrated radical impulses.[44]

Elites Divide: Accommodation in the Public Sphere

That the would-be ruling classes divided in response to the popular upheavals in the revolutionary era has been established by scholars, state by state, for some time; Kornblith and Murrin are the first to take the risk of generalizing about American ruling classes nationally for this era since William A. Williams. In the colonial era elites varied in their cohesiveness. In many colonies, elite families were ever at each other's throats, often appealing demagogically in elections to artisans or farmers with the vote, uniting only to assert their hegemony over the subordinate classes. The merchant classes were usually fragmented; so were large slaveholders or landlords in the Hudson River Valley. But, in general, elites contained the sporadic threats from below. What was new, from the 1770s on, was a persistent popular democratic presence in politics. How to handle it could divide great aristocratic families within (as with the Carrolls of Maryland) or from their neighbors and kin (as in New York), or divide even the confident ruling gentry (as in Virginia).[45]

The Revolution produced a crisis of confidence among old elites in their capacity to take their chances with democracy (to them, "the rabble" or "the mob") and with the new men responsible to popular constituencies with whom elites now had to compete for power (to them, "upstarts" and "demagogues"). Confidence of this sort was something of a dividing line within elites over the entire revolutionary era: between Whigs and Loyalists over separating from Great Britain, among Whigs in state making and constitution making, in the 1790s between Democratic Republicans and Federalists, and after their defeat in 1800, between "old school" and "new school" Federalists.

The metaphors elites used for the threats from below are telling tokens of their different outlooks. Panic-stricken conservatives referred to the people as a beast that had to be driven or as a reptile that would bite, some invoking the classical imagery of "the many-headed Hydra."[46] By contrast, Robert R. Livingston, a landlord potentate in New York typical of more risk-taking conservatives, in 1777 used the metaphor of a stream: rulers had to "learn the propriety of Swimming with a Stream which it is impossible to stem"; they should "yield to the torrent if they hoped to direct its course." Thirty years later, Noah Webster scolded his fellow Federalists who had fallen from power because they "attempted to resist the current popular opinion instead of falling into the current with a view to direct it." The since-famous lexicographer was a conciliatory conservative, who in his best-selling speller and dictionary presided over nothing less than the Americanization of the English language.[47]

What was new was that the Revolution nationalized the threat of radicalism which earlier was localized. Neither Shaysism nor the Whiskey Rebellion was confined to one state.[48] The creation of a national government created a national arena for conflicts. And the increase in the number and frequency of newspapers permitted a more rapid dissemination of opinion. Master mechanics communicated from one city to another. Some fifty Democratic Societies came into being in the backcountry as well as eastern cities. One consequence of this minor revolution in communications was that outside events could have a fairly rapid national influence. Successive events in the French Revolution produced common reactions all over the United States; the news of successful black revolutionaries in the Caribbean invigorated African American resistance North and South, alarming slaveholders as well as antislavery advocates.[49]

The torrents of national radicalism required extraordinary skill of the nation's pilots. In the postwar crisis that culminated in the Constitutional Convention of 1787, the elite leaders best able to assume national leadership were men like James Madison, who recognized it as a crisis of "the political system," itself a revealing phrase. Madison was able to negotiate on two fronts: with the conflicting substantial propertied "interests" so well represented in the convention (the haves) and with the radical democratic movements that were a "presence" at the convention, even if they were not present (the have-nots and the have-littles). The framers more or less agreed with Madison that if the Constitution was to last "for the ages," it had to conform to "the genius of the people."[50]

Bold, sophisticated conservatives had learned a lesson from the Revolution—they had to accommodate democratic-minded constituencies in advance. The Federalists of 1787–88 made two grand accommodations usually missing from civics lessons: the first, in the concessions to democratic rule they built into the Constitution itself; the second, during the process of ratification, when they divided the powerful popular opposition who wanted a less centralized and more democratic structure by promising amendments which they later reduced to the Bill of Rights, which left the essential framework intact. The result was a constitution a nationalist-minded radical like Thomas Paine and a localist plebeian democrat like William Manning could fault but accept. It was "a good one prinsapaly, but I have no doubt but that the Convention who made it intended to destroy our free governments by it," Manning wrote. It left the future open; it was, he said, "made like a Fiddle, with but few Strings, but so the ruling Majority could play any tune upon it they please."

The elites who gained power but had the least long-run success were the Hamiltonian Federalists of the 1790s, who adopted England as a model. Hamilton, after getting nowhere in the Constitutional Convention with a proposal for a government of King, Lords, and Commons, and state governors appointed by the national president with a veto power over the states, tried to consolidate a government in the 1790s based on the English system of deference, influence, and force. But deference was on the wane, and any attempt to impose it led to the charge of "aristocracy." Building influence through a funding system and bank produced a backlash against corruption. And force—whether military to put down extralegal opposition like the Whiskey Rebellion or Fries's Rebellion, or political repression like the Sedition Law of 1798 to imprison legal opposition—misjudged the "genius of the people," ushering the Federalists out of power.

The elites with the greatest capacity for survival coalesced as the Democratic Republicans, under the leadership of Madison and Jefferson. The Virginia leaders had mastered the process in their native state by building alliances with the dissenting religions in a ten-year battle to disestablish the Anglican church. They learned how to accommodate nationally: to build a coalition of southern slave-owning planters, yeomen, northern merchants in search of markets to make them independent of Britain, and mechanics and would-be manufacturers. It is not surprising that their principal northern allies were politicians from New York and Pennsylvania like Robert R. Livingston, who once again was ready to swim with the stream. The interests thus brought together could share a common aim of expanding overseas commercial markets for agricultural produce, expanding to the West, and developing American manufactures.[51]

Democratic Republicans shifted to accommodate radical agrarians to their left. In 1786 Madison sought federal power to contain Shays's Rebellion, while Jefferson was prepared for "a little rebellion now and then," as a warning to rulers. But in 1794 Madison and Jefferson fought the Federalist effort to "censure" the "self created societies" as responsible for the Whiskey Rebellion. Both were more concerned with eliminating grievances than putting down agrarian rebels. And with the vast public domain as a resource they were prepared to accommodate insistent settler demands for land. Both fought the repressive Sedition Law. They also recognized the importance of the mechanics—"the yeomanry of the city" to Jefferson. However, they could not accommodate African Americans in slavery, or American Indians, and were indifferent to the new voices among American women.

Negotiations in the Private Sphere: African Americans

All this negotiation was in the public sphere. The work of historians in a variety of fields of social history suggests that negotiation also was under way within private spheres (a distinction from the public sphere that was often dissolving). This seems true among many segments of the laboring classes, especially in the 1790s. Masters and apprentices literally signed a contract expressing reciprocal obligations for living and working under the same roof. As apprentice deference eroded, the master had to mend his ways. The stock form of the printed indenture may have read the same, but apprentices forced renegotiation of the unwritten contract. At the same time, journeymen in many trades organized on their own to deal with masters, leading to the first pattern of American strikes by journeymen ("turnouts") and lockouts by masters; in most trades unstated collective bargaining continued to affirm custom.[52] Merchant seamen confronting the masters of their vessels traditionally "used a many-sided process of negotiation and resistance to defend themselves and to protect and expand their privileges and rights," and their hand was very likely strengthened in the revolutionary ferment of the Atlantic world.[53]

In rural areas the armed confrontations between settlers and great proprietors could end in negotiations. In Maine, once the proprietors conceded the right of squatters to acquire land, the conflict could boil down to haggling over the price of land. Leading men in frontier communities often served as middlemen. And on the state level, in Massachusetts (which then included Maine) and in Pennsylvania, Democratic Republicans proved adept at drafting legislation which accommodated both sides, passing in Pennsylvania literally a "Compromise Act." Here politicians brokered a social conflict, an innovation that in time became a cliché in American politics.[54]

The war enhanced the capacity of slaves to negotiate with their masters. The new scholarship on slavery in the revolutionary era has identified the processes by which slaves won "space" for themselves within an oppressive system. In 1775–76 southern planters clearly were in no position to accommodate the massive upsurge for freedom. Yet during the war they often had no choice; slaves expanded their autonomy within the system, or made good their flight from it. And after the war the low-country blacks, for example, did not readily surrender their wartime gains, and "many continued to flaunt their increased autonomy." In the upper South, Maryland and Virginia passed laws that made it easier for individual slaveholders to free their own slaves through manumission, creating the first sizable free black population in the Chesapeake. In subsequent decades, even as slavery grew and expanded over the entire South, "continued renegotiations of the terms under which slaves worked for their masters,"[55] Ira Berlin argues, were central to the system.

In the North, where there were fifty thousand slaves on the eve of the Revolution, emancipation on a state-by-state basis was, in Berlin's apt words, "a slow, torturous process" that often dragged out for years. The thrust of recent scholarship is that the insistent black pressures for freedom did as much as white antislavery benevolence to bring about this first emancipation. During and after the war northern slaves seized freedom, by fighting with the British or the patriots or by running away; or they purchased their own freedom and that of their families. In the five northern states with the largest slave populations, the legislatures provided only gradual emancipation for children born of slaves after they reached their twenties, which explains why in 1810 there were still twenty-seven thousand slaves in the North compared to fifty thousand free blacks. Once free, blacks in the northern states faced a continuing struggle against racism for access to schools, the ballot, and civil rights. It was a grudging emancipation.[56]

By 1820 in the country as a whole the number of freed blacks approached 250,000, while the number of slaves had grown to 1.5 million. Thus, as Berlin sums it up, the Revolution "was not only a stride forward in the expansion of black liberty, [but it] strengthened the plantation regime and slavery grew as never before, spreading across a continent. Thus if the Revolution marked a new birth of freedom, it also launched a great expansion of slavery."[57]

How was this possible? The question is crucial to understanding the Revolution. The argument David Brion Davis first advanced in 1975 remains compelling. "The American colonists were not trapped in an accidental contradiction between slavery and freedom." On the contrary, as they emerged from the Revolution, "slavery was of central importance to both the southern and national economies, and thus to the viability of the 'American system.'" Moreover, "a free society was by no means incompatible with dependent classes of workers. Its central prerequisite was a large class of freeholders, unencumbered by feudal, military or political obligations. Liberty required independence, and independence required freehold property." Chattel slaves provided the property which defined independence, the long-cherished goal of southern farmers.[58] What accounts for the northern acquiescence to southern slavery? Economic interest, the high priority placed on national union, the devotion to private property in Whig ideology, and the growth of racism as the indispensable justification for continuing slavery in a land of liberty—all these contributed to what was perhaps the most fateful accommodation of the revolutionary era.[59]

Accommodations in the "Domestic Sphere": Women

This pattern of accommodation within a system of subordination assumed a different shape for women. "We are ready to ask," Linda Kerber writes, "whether and how the social relations of the sexes were renegotiated in the crucible of the Revolution." As a result of women's participation in the prewar resistance and in the war, "how much more inclusive American citizenship should be was under negotiation."[60]

Thought about this way, the oft-cited exchange of letters between Abigail and John Adams in 1776 can be viewed as the opening round of a quintessential negotiation. He would hear nothing of equality of rights but was receptive to her continuing demands for educational opportunities for women. Out of such exchanges—which we can assume were repeated without written record in countless families of the middling sort—came the accommodation Kerber has called "Republican motherhood," in which mothers were endowed with the patriotic responsibility of raising their sons and daughters as virtuous citizens for the new republic and therefore required a better education. The "role of Republican motherhood," as Kerber recently reflected, "was a conservative stabilizing one, deflecting the radical potential of the revolutionary experience"; at the same time, it contributed to the expansion of education for women, the principal gain of the decades after 1790.[61]

Thus the literate young women able to read the first American novels were the beneficiaries of the first negotiation. They in turn won another:

they defied authority and read the novels. In the long struggle by women for equal rights this may not seem very subversive, but as long as marriage was the chief option open to women, Cathy Davidson argues, a woman had "an opportunity to work out in the safe context of her imagination just what she wanted from men and from marriage." This in turn very likely contributed to "matrimonial republicanism," another product of the negotiation between the sexes. How widespread were these changes, how far they extended beyond educated middling women is not clear. Laurel Thatcher Ulrich's skillful recovery of the life of a midwife on the Maine frontier is evidence of a woman who remained "more a colonial goodwife than a Republican Mother"; the recovery of other lives suggests new patterns. Scholars have found it easier to measure the absence of change in laws and institutions; they are only beginning to tap sources that measure changes in women's consciousness.[62]

That some women should articulate independence as a goal is not surprising in an era in which personal independence was the heightened goal of every Tom, Dick, and Harry. Mary Wollstonecraft's *Vindication of the Rights of Women* found a receptive readership among educated American women. "In very many of her sentiments," the Philadelphia Quaker Elizabeth Drinker confided to her diary, "she, as some of our friends say, *speaks my mind.* In some others, I do not always coincide with her. I am not for quite so much independence." John Adams thought Abigail was "a perfect disciple of Wollstonecraft."[63] Through the 1790s Judith Sargent Murray, the most vocal American theorist of women's rights, argued for an independence that pushed at the boundaries of republican motherhood. Her daughters, she wrote, "should be enabled to procure for themselves the necessaries of life; independence should be placed within their grasp." This was partly to protect women from the vicissitudes of widowhood. "The term *helpless widow* might be rendered as unfrequent and inapplicable as that of *helpless widower.*" But Murray was also critical of raising "our girls ... with one monopolizing consideration ... an establishment by marriage ... *An old maid* they are from infancy taught, at least indirectly to consider as a contemptible being." On the contrary, she argued, "marriage should not be presented as the *summum bonum,* or as a certain, or even necessary, event; they should learn to respect a single life, and even regard it as the *most eligible,* except a warm, mutual and judicious attachment has gained the ascendancy in the bosom." But she pushed women no further to break through the barriers of the "domestic sphere."[64]

In an era when most white men had access to the means to achieve independence, most women did not; and most men were not prepared to surrender "our masculine systems," as John Adams put it. Why not? Just as the independence of the slaveholder was defined by the dependence of his slaves, or the independence of the artisan defined by the dependence of his apprentices and journeymen, so the independence of a white male, whatever his occupation, was defined by the dependence of his wife and children. Independence, as Joan Gunderson puts it, "was a condition arrived at by exclusion, by *not* being dependent or enslaved." Personal independence, the life goal of ordinary male Americans, required heading a family, being a property holder, and possessing "a requisite set of mental/moral and/or martial capacities." "All these meanings of independence," Nancy Fraser and Linda Gordon argue, "simultaneously defined contrasting senses of dependence which excluded women, slaves and children."[65]

In "a new narrative" of the Revolution which fully integrates gender, Kerber foresees that the Revolution "will be understood to be more deeply radical than we have heretofore perceived it because its shock reached into the deepest and most private human relations." But it will also be understood to be "more deeply conservative … purchasing political stability at the price of backing away from the implications of the sexual politics implied in its own manifestos, just as it backed away from the implications of its principles for changed race relations."[66]

Accommodations: American Indians, Elites, and Frontiersmen

The revolutionary era was a time of unprecedented landed expansion. The new country that emerged from the Revolution expanded with breathtaking speed over a vast geographic area. This expansion produced a triangular confrontation of American Indians, eastern national elites, and western settlers that led to alternating national policies of accommodation and warfare and to deep divisions within Native American societies.

The range of accommodation with Native Americans was limited by an ethnocentrism that made the most well-meaning Anglo-Americans incapable of coexisting with Indians as they were. During and after the war, in which most Indians fought on the side of the British, their traditional protectors, the dominant attitude among whites was encapsulated in such toasts and slogans as "Civilization or death to all American Savages" or "Civilization or extinction." But Anglo-American leaders had not calculated on the Indians' will for independence or their capacity to defend it.[67]

In the decades before and after the war, Native American societies had experienced movements of spiritual revitalization—in David Dowd's words, "Great Awakenings"—that reinforced political and military resistance. For example, behind Pontiac, the secular leader of the Indian confederacy of the 1760s, lay Neolin, the Delaware prophet. The Revolutionary war which produced "a near unanimity of the trans-Appalachian struggle against the United States" enhanced pan-Indianism. The tactics of Revolutionary war leaders such as the scorched-earth decimation of Iroquois villages (which earned George Washington the reputation among the Iroquois as "town destroyer") put Native Americans in no mood to accommodate the victorious United States.[68]

In the peace treaty, the British, as Francis Jennings puts it, "passed the card called sovereignty" over Indian land, "a legal fiction," to the new nation. But spokesmen for the Iroquois Confederacy in the North said they were "a free People subject to no Power upon earth," while the southern tribes insisted they had done nothing "to forfeit our Independence and natural Rights." Confronted with Indian power, national political leaders rapidly shifted, recognizing Indian claims to sovereignty, literally negotiating treaties, and promising, in the Northwest Ordinance of 1787, that "the utmost good faith shall always be observed towards the Indians; their land and property shall never be taken from them without their consent."[69]

The corollary of this accommodation was to bring the "blessings of civilization" to American Indians. This meant, as James Merrell writes, that "Indian men would adopt plow agriculture, women would abandon the field for the home, and all would give up their heathen ways for Christ." The symbol was engraved on the silver peace medal U.S. presidents bestowed on cooperating chieftains: a Native American male throws a broken arrow to the ground before President Washington, who is in his general's uniform, sword at his side; and in the background, a man, perhaps the same Indian, guides a plough pulled by two oxen, tilling a field.[70]

The pressures of western agrarians forced a change on national policymakers. An aggressive policy toward Indians had been a persistent demand of the most radical backcountry movements from Bacon's Rebellion in Virginia in 1676 to the Paxton Boys of Pennsylvania in 1764 to the Whiskey Rebels of 1794. In fact the radical philosophy by which settlers justified their claim to vacant land against absentee proprietors with legal title was applied to Indians. The tillers of the soil, whose labor gave it value, were alone entitled to the land. Indians, in the eyes of farmers, did nothing to improve the "howling wilderness." The same class antagonism informed the backcountryman's attitude toward absentee land proprietors and eastern opponents of an aggressive policy toward the Indians. The Tennessee territorial legislature in 1794 reminded Congress that "citizens who live in poverty on the extreme frontiers were as entitled to be protected in their lives, their families and little property, as those who were in luxury, ease and affluence in the great and opulent eastern cities." In the 1790s eastern elites, with their own agendas for expansion, bent to these pressures, sanctioning war on a massive scale.[71]

Among radical agrarians there were some muted voices of protest. William Manning was not the only agrarian who objected to the cost of the wars against the Indians: from 1791 to 1796 the five million dollars spent on the western wars were five-sixths of the total American budget. Herman Husband, a radical Bible-reading millennialist, wanted peaceful negotiations with Indians, who in his eyes were among the lost tribes of Israel. The settlers on the Maine frontier in their guerrilla war against the proprietors sometimes assumed Indian disguises, identifying themselves with the liberty-loving (sometimes terrifying) first inhabitants of the soil. Euro-Americans who practiced accommodation with Indians, living in what Richard White has called a "middle ground"—fur traders, captives who became converts, and other migrants in multiethnic villages—were few in number. Thus there were no effective voices challenging the alternatives of "civilization or extinction" that in reality were "alternative routes to obliteration."[72]

Anglo-American pressures forced Indians into their own internal processes of accommodation. The names historians have attached to the divisions—accommodationists versus nativists, progressives versus conservatives—varied but the patterns were similar. Tribal societies were divided among those who would accommodate by negotiating away land rights and moving on, those who were willing to adopt the white man's ways, including Christianity and plow agriculture, and those who rejected them or sought selective adaptation of Anglo-American ways. New waves of spiritual revival led by prophets and visionaries fed the movements for militant resistance and the revitalization of Indian societies. In the early 1800s, the Shawnee prophet Tenskwatawa made it possible for his brother, Tecumseh, to renew a confederacy and mount a powerful but unsuccessful military offensive against the United States. Where military resistance was no longer feasible, as among the Senecas, the prophet Handsome Lake laid the basis for collective action that led to moral and social reform. In this context the divisions within Indian societies confronting imperial expansion bear some resemblance to the divisions within the Anglo-American society of the same era.[73]

The Democratic Republicans, once in national power, offered their own mixture of benevolence and belligerence, paving the way for the next step, physical removal from the eastern United States. In 1783, 150,000 Indians lived east of the Mississippi; by 1844, less than one-fourth remained. That the Mashpees, faced with removal from Cape Cod, Massachusetts, appealed to the Constitution—"We as a tribe will rule ourselves, and have a right to do so; for all men are born free and equal, says the Constitution of the country"—was a token of the continuing appropriation of revolutionary ideals but not of their vitality.[74]

Radical Divisions

The processes of accommodation in the political system contributed to a division within radical popular movements as to the best means for effecting change. The norm inherited from colonial times was extralegal action: mob actions in the cities and Regulator movements in the countryside. The period of political resistance (1765–75) expanded the frequency, size, and leadership of crowds and the repetoire of popular rituals. There were more self-led crowds, more spontaneous actions, and more class-specific crowds. Colonial crowds did not fit a single model of the consensual expression of the will of the community. The crowds of the revolutionary era were even more diverse.[75]

In the eyes of the common people the success of the Revolution legitimized extralegal action, and the war sanctioned violence, endowing both with the aura of patriotism. After the war popular rituals were transmitted to new protesters by oral tradition: symbolic actions such as effigy burnings and the erection of liberty poles, acts of physical intimidation such as tar-and-feathering and warnings by apocryphal avenging figures, and "rough music" to punish offenders of community norms. If any single act became symbolic of the Revolution as a whole, it may have been the Boston Tea Party.[76]

The democratization of the political culture, the accommodations by elites, combined with a quasi-revolution in communications, undoubtedly had an effect in channeling protest into a now more open political system.

Petitioning to state legislatures, which very likely was on a greater scale than in the colonial era, lost the tone of supplication.[77] Yet extralegal action was hardly abandoned; it seemed to run parallel to the legal. In the 1790s in western Pennsylvania, farmers formed democratic societies, passed resolutions, and sent petitions to the federal government. Simultaneously, they resorted to tar-and-feathering tax collectors, erecting liberty poles, and parading thousands-strong through Pittsburgh to intimidate local elites. They were prepared for military resistance, but confronted by a massive federal mobilization of force, the rebels debated strategy and withdrew.[78]

Resorting to force produced a crisis in confidence within popular movements over achieving their ends within the system, the mirror image of the crisis in confidence among elites over taking their chances with democracy. Clearly, a kind of constitutional democratic radicalism came into being. William Manning, the plebeian democrat who had opposed Shays's Rebellion, would have members of his proposed national laboring society take an oath to support the government against insurrections. The aim of the society was to educate "the Many" to make use of their electoral power to oust "the Few." Other yeomen, who had no reason for confidence in legislative or judicial systems, continued to resort to force.

Among the mechanic classes in the cities there was more of a break with traditional modes of mob action. It was said of John Jay in 1795, after the news of his treaty arrived in the United States, that he could have traveled from Maine to Georgia by the light of his burning effigies. And in Baltimore in 1807 journeymen shoemakers debated whether tarring and feathering their anglophile Federalist foreman was not a legitimate extension of republican principles.[79] But respectable mechanics and tradesmen fashioned new, affirmative, nonviolent rituals: they paraded in civic festivals, attended Fourth of July ceremonies, and celebrated the victories of the French Revolution at dinners. They also took part in politics, and those qualified to vote—a large proportion of the total—cast ballots in increasing numbers. The ballot box was not the coffin of a plebeian citizen consciousness. The assembly election of 1796 in New York City, Hamilton reported with anguish, "in the eyes of the common people was a question between the rich and the poor."[80]

This division as to means was a persisting issue in the subsequent history of American radicalism: whether to use physical force or nonviolent persuasion, whether to take part in politics, and if so, whether to work within existing parties or to form new ones. Merely to list the alternatives is to summon up images of the splits within abolitionism, the leading radical movement of the pre–Civil War era, and later within socialism, one of the leading radical movements of the industrial era.

If by the end of the eighteenth century, African American slaves in the South had fewer legal paths to freedom, it might be argued they had enlarged their range of illegal options. The war and the rise of free black communities made flight more possible and more successful than ever before. But collective insurrection was now a possibility, inspired variously by the example of successful rebellion in Saint-Domingue, a new wave of evangelical religion, the emergence of an artisan class among slaves, and the example of the first viable free black communities. There is a temptation to speak of a new cycle of insurrection after the turn of the century.

Gabriel Prosser's failed conspiracy in Richmond, Virginia, in the summer of 1800, which to Governor James Monroe was "unquestionably the most serious and formidable conspiracy we have ever known of that kind," was led by black artisans. St. George Tucker, an antislavery Virginian, measured how far black people had come in the quarter of a century since 1775. In response to Lord Dunmore's plea, slaves had acted individually by running away; in 1800 they showed they were capable of "acting in concert"—to a degree Tucker found "astonishing." In 1775 they "fought for freedom merely as a good; now they also claim it as a right." At his trial one rebel said, "I have nothing more to offer than what George Washington would have had to offer, had he been taken by the British and put on trial by them. I have ventured my life in endeavoring to obtain the liberty of my countryman, and am a willing sacrifice in their cause."[81] On the Virginia–North Carolina border a threat of insurrection followed in 1801–2. While conspiracies would dot the subsequent landscape of southern slavery, for most slaves opposition meant everyday resistance in the work process—the quintessential negotiation to force accommodation—running away, or the cultural resistance implicit in sustaining the family and the invisible church.[82]

Among advocates of women's rights, by contrast, it is difficult to detect a split as to means. There clearly were differences among articulate women. Women who read Mary Wollstonecraft or Judith Sargent Murray divided as to how much "independence" they should claim. Women disagreed over how much and what kind of education they should have. Some women actively supported Federalists; others, the Democratic Republicans. The novels written by and for women ranged widely in their "feminism." However, the fact that women aired their differences in newspapers, magazines, and novels or privately in correspondence, diaries, and conversations suggests the boundaries of women's activities. Compared to women in the French Revolution, women in America had only begun to act collectively in public. In the 1790s women became active in church societies and benevolent organizations. Yet by 1800 it is not quite possible to speak of a women's movement much less a women's rights movement.[83]

Women who expressed their opinions may have divided between optimists and pessimists. In his 1798 feminist novel *Alcuin* Charles Brockden Brown captured a mood of disillusionment in the words he put in the mouth of Mrs. Carter, an educated Philadelphia widow, in response to the question "Are you a Federalist?" "What have I as a woman to do with politics?" she answers brusquely. The law which "annihilates the political existence of at least half of the community [treats women] as if we were pigs or sheep." On the other hand, Murray, writing in the same year, saw "young women ... at the dawn of a new era in female history," and many of the first female graduates of the schools and academies echoed her. It would be several decades before hope would combine with bitterness to inspire the radicalism of collective action.[84]

1776: Twenty-five Years Later

How successful were the multiple radicalisms that emerged in 1775–76 and flourished in the 1780s and 1790s? I have argued that over the long revolutionary era one of the best tests of the success of radical movements is their impact on the elites. In 1801 the Democratic Republicans, led by the more accommodating of the two national elites, won power. How far did they then carry the processes of accommodation in the different spheres of American life?

Some of the players are the same. Thomas Jefferson characterized his election victory over John Adams as "the revolution of 1800" and "as real a revolution in the principles of our government as that of 1776 was in its form." The country had rejected Federalist rule by coercion; the "reign of terror" was over. Adams had been less able in 1800 than in 1776 to navigate the democratic torrent. He confronted far less "veneration for persons in authority" in 1800 than in 1776. The "people-out-of-doors" had come indoors to vote, to elect new men of their own kind to Congress as well as the state legislatures. Adams had to confront the likes of Irish-born Matthew Lyon in the House of Representatives. Lyon had come to the colonies an indentured servant, made his way to wealth as a manufacturer in frontier Vermont, was elected to Congress on his fourth try as a Democratic Republican, was sentenced to jail under the Sedition Act for criticizing President Adams, and was returned to Congress by his constituents with an even greater majority.[85]

All of the demons Adams feared in 1776 were more of a menace at the turn of the century. Yeoman farmers who in 1775 had closed the courts in western Massachusetts were likely in 1800 to be waging guerrilla war against their great proprietors in Maine. As one of them said, "We once defended this land at the point of a bayonet & if drove to the necessity are now equally united, ready & zealous to defend it again the same way." Apprentices were "disobedient" enough to threaten the system of apprenticeship. The "insolence" of individual slaves had escalated to collective conspiracy for rebellion. And while in 1776 Abigail Adams had raised the issue of women's rights privately in a letter to her husband, Murray publicly urged women to cultivate "a noble ardour of independence" in her newspaper essays, subsequently published in three volumes (to which the Adamses subscribed).

In power the Jeffersonian elite would accommodate only some of these popular movements. Would-be yeoman farmers hungry for land could anticipate revisions in federal land laws making the public domain available in smaller parcels at lower prices. And when an expansionist president acquired the Louisiana Territory, he could claim to have fulfilled the expectation of his inaugural address of land "for the thousandth generation to come." Mechanics could be optimistic when they submitted to Congress in 1801 a petition for protection for American manufactures with the same wording they had submitted in 1789.

Others had less reason for optimism. The journeymen shoemakers of Philadelphia, a hundred of whom began a long strike in 1799, the first of half a dozen such strikes that would take place in as many cities in the next decade or so, would be tried and convicted for conspiracy. They drew more opposition than support from local Democratic Republicans. William Manning still tried after 1801 to get his proposal for a national society of laboring men published. Vigilance of the Many against the Few apparently was necessary, no matter who was in power. Reformers with a host of causes were in motion in the states and cities, hoping to expand the suffrage and the number of elective offices, to curb the common law or restrict lawyers, and to expand public schools. Some were native-born, inspired by the new evangelical religions; others were "Jacobin" émigrés from Great Britain anxious to fulfill the promise of Thomas Paine's *Rights*

of Man or *Age of Reason.* All these reformers composed, in effect, a left
wing among local Democratic Republicans, although they were not necessarily Jeffersonians.[86]

Nationally Jeffersonians wanted to contain, not accommodate, the radical thrusts for freedom from southern slaves. Jefferson had not published
a word of public criticism of slavery since *Notes on Virginia* in the 1780s.
His antislavery sentiment, already withering on the vine of his racism, froze
with the news of rebellions in Saint-Dominique, even before Gabriel's conspiracy at home. Jefferson differed with Governor James Monroe only in
how far Virginia had to go to deter future rebellions; in 1800 after twenty-
six conspirators had been executed, he told Monroe that "there had been
hanging enough." Confronted as president with the Napoleonic effort to
overthrow the successful slave revolutionaries in their West Indies colony,
Jefferson consistently "pressed for the devastation and destruction of the
black Jacobins."[87]

Women could expect less support from Jefferson than from Adams.
"Our good ladies," Jefferson rejoiced to Anne Willing Bingham of Philadelphia, after reporting the activities of women in France, "have been too
wise to wrinkle their foreheads with politics. They are contented to soothe
and calm the minds of their husbands returning ruffled from political
debate." Bingham disagreed, but only here and there a few maverick
Republicans—Benjamin Rush, James Sullivan, Charles Brockden Brown—
took a public stand on women's issues.[88]

The limits of Jeffersonian accommodation were soon made clear to the
American Indians. To a visiting delegation, the philosopher-scientist
expressed the hope that "we shall see your people become disposed to cultivate the earth, to raise herds of the useful animals, and to spin and weave
for their food and clothing." To the territorial governor of Ohio, Jefferson
revealed his underlying rationale: "Our settlements will gradually circum-
scribe and approach the Indians & they will in time either incorporate
with us as citizens of the U.S. or remove beyond the Mississippi." Inside a
velvet glove he kept a mailed fist. "We presume our strength and their
weakness is now so visible," he remarked in 1803, "that they must see we
have only to shut our hand to crush them." The "empire for liberty" Jefferson envisioned was for white male yeoman farmers and their families.[89]

How radical was the American Revolution? Or, if you prefer, how much
transformation was there as a result of the Revolution? The central concept I have advanced of a negotiation among contending groups, "classes,"

and individuals offers a number of advantages as an analytical tool or as a heuristic principle of investigation. It differs from the old progressive and conflict interpretations, which focused primarily on the political and saw outright victory for one side and defeat for the other (the Constitution as Thermidor). It differs from the old consensus interpretation in analyzing results as the product of conflict. It avoids the weakness of intellectual or ideological interpretations that posit a single cluster of ideas from which all change emanates. It acknowledges the systems or structures that framed what people did, but assigns priority to the agency of people in effecting change and renewing their struggles even in the face of defeat.

It enables us to encompass more of the multiple dimensions of the Revolution: as a colonial struggle for liberation from imperial rule, in which there were coalitions of nascent "classes" in both cooperative and antagonistic relationships, and as a series of internal struggles in separate but often overlapping spheres. It allows us to measure the results of these struggles, not at one stopping point, but as an ongoing process, in which negotiations were often renewed and sometimes faded. It further permits us to measure results in many different spheres of life, private as well as public. And it enables us to recognize that while the Revolution was indeed radical, there is no single answer to the question, How radical was the American Revolution?

NOTES

This essay appeared originally as the Afterword to Alfred F. Young, ed., *Beyond the American Revolution: Explorations in the History of American Radicalism* (DeKalb: Northern Illinois University Press, 1993), a collection of essays by other scholars, cited in notes, and is reprinted with the permission of Northern Illinois University Press. Early versions were presented at the seminar in early American history at the University of Maryland and at the Philadelphia Center for Early American Studies.

I am very much indebted to scholars who patiently went through several drafts of this essay—Ira Berlin, Linda Kerber, and Gary Nash—as I am to scholars who read sections of early drafts or responded to my queries: Edward Countryman, Emory Evans, Ronald Hoffman, Frederick Hoxie, Allan Kulikoff, Jesse Lemisch, Michael Merrill, Philip Morgan, Marcus Rediker, and Sean Wilentz.

1. J. Franklin Jameson, *The American Revolution Considered as a Social Movement* (Princeton, N.J., 1926), 9; Bernard Bailyn, *The Ideological Origins of the American Revolution* (Cambridge, Mass., 1967), chap. 6; David Brion Davis, *The Problem of Slavery in the Age of Revolution, 1770–1823* (Ithaca, N.Y., 1975), 274n.

2. E. P. Thompson, "The Moral Economy of the English Crowd in the Eighteenth Century," *Past and Present* 50 (1971): 76–136, reprinted in Thompson, *Customs in Common: Studies in Traditional Popular Culture* (New York, 1992), chap. 4, with a reply to his critics, "The Moral Economy Reviewed," chap. 5; James Henretta, "Families and Farms: *Mentalité* in Pre-Industrial America," *William and Mary Quarterly*, 3d series (hereafter cited as *WMQ*), 35 (1978): 3–22.

3. Richard L. Bushman, "Massachusetts Farmers and the Revolution," in Richard M. Jellison, ed., *Society, Freedom, and Conscience* (New York, 1976), 77–124; Bushman, *King and People in Provincial Massachusetts* (Chapel Hill, N.C., 1985), chap. 5.

4. See John Rule, "The Property of Skill in the Period of Manufacture," in Patrick Joyce, ed., *The Historical Meaning of Work* (New York, 1987), 99–118; Ronald Schultz, "The Small-Producer Tradition and the Moral Origins of Artisan Radicalism in Philadelphia, 1720–1810," *Past and Present* 127 (1990): 84–116; and Peter Linebaugh, *The London Hanged: Crime and Civil Society in the Eighteenth Century* (New York, 1992), for artisan customs.

5. "To the Tradesmen, Mechanics &c. of Pennsylvania" (Philadelphia, 4 December 1773), broadside.

6. James P. Walsh, "'Mechanics and Citizens': The Connecticut Artisan Protest of 1792," *WMQ* 42 (1985): 66–89.

7. See essay 1 in this volume; Gary B. Nash, "Artisans and Politics in Eighteenth-Century Philadelphia," in Margaret C. Jacob and James R. Jacob, eds., *The Origins of Anglo-American Radicalism* (London, 1984), 258–78; Nash, *The Urban Crucible: Social Change, Political Consciousness, and the Origins of the American Revolution* (Cambridge, Mass., 1979).

8. Jesse Lemisch, "Jack Tar in the Streets: Merchant Seamen in the Politics of Revolutionary America," *WMQ* 25 (1968): 371–407; Lemisch, *Jack Tar us. John Bull: The Role of New York's Seamen in Precipitating the Revolution* (New York, 1997); Admiral Warren to the Duke of Newcastle, 18 June 1745, cited in Marcus Rediker, "A Motley Crew of Rebels: Sailors, Slaves, and the Coming of the American Revolution," in Ronald Hoffman and Peter J. Albert, eds., *"The Transforming Hand of Revolution": Reconsidering the American Revolution as a Social Movement* (Charlottesville, Va., 1995); Rediker, *Between the Devil and the Deep Blue Sea: Merchant Seamen, Pirates, and the Anglo-American Maritime World, 1700–1750* (Cambridge, V.K., 1987); Rediker, "'Good Hands, Stout Heart and Fast Feet': The History and Culture of Working People in Early America," in Geoff Ely and William Hunt, eds., *Reviving the English Revolution: Reflection and Elaborations on the Work of Christopher Hill* (London, 1988), 221–49.

9. Lawrence W. Towner, "'A Fondness for Freedom': Servant Protest in Puritan Society," *WMQ* 19 (1962), 201–19; Bernard Bailyn, "Voyagers in Flight: A Sketchbook of Runaway Servants, 1774–1775," in Bailyn, *Voyagers to the West: A Passage in the Peopling of America on the Eve of the Revolution* (New York, 1986), 352ff.;

Jonathan Prude, "To Look upon the 'Lower Sort': Runaway Ads and the Appearance of Unfree Laborers in America, 1750–1800," *Journal of American History* 78 (1991): 124–59.

10. Phillis Wheatley to Samson Occom, 11 February 1774, in *Massachusetts Gazette*, 21 March 1774, reprinted in Julian D. Mason Jr., ed., *The Poems of Phillis Wheatley*, revised and enlarged ed. (Chapel Hill, N.C., 1989), 203–4. Peter H. Wood, "'Liberty Is Sweet': African–American Freedom Struggles in the Years before Independence," in Alfred Young, ed., *Beyond the American Revolution: Explorations in the History of American Radicalism* (DeKalb, Ill., 1993), 149–83.

11. Ira Berlin, "Time, Space, and the Evolution of Afro-American Society on British Mainland North America," *American Historical Review* 85 (1980): 47–78; Melville Herskovits, *The Myth of the Negro Past* (New York, 1941); Gerald W. Mullin, *Flight and Rebellion: Slave Resistance in Eighteenth-Century Virginia* (New York, 1972); Peter H. Wood, *Black Majority: Negroes in Colonial South Carolina from 1670 through the Stono Rebellion* (New York, 1974); Herbert G. Gutman, *The Black Family in Slavery and Freedom, 1750–1825* (New York, 1976); John Michael Vlach, *The Afro-American Tradition in Decorative Arts* (Cleveland, 1978); Mechal Sobel, *Trabelin' On: The Slave Journey to an Afro-Baptist Faith* (Westport, Conn., 1979); Allan Kulikoff, *Tobacco and Slaves: The Development of Southern Cultures in the Chesapeake, 1660–1800* (Chapel Hill, N.C., 1986); Mechal Sobel, *The World They Made Together: Black and White Values in Eighteenth-Century Virginia* (Princeton, N.J., 1987); William D. Piersen, *Black Yankees: The Development of an Afro-American Subculture in Eighteenth-Century New England* (Amherst, Mass., 1988); Jon Butler, *Awash in a Sea of Faith: Christianizing the American People* (Cambridge, Mass., 1990), chap. 5.

12. A Petition to His Excellency Thomas Hutchinson, Esq., *Massachusetts Spy*, 29 July 1773; Gary Nash, "Thomas Peters: Millwright and Deliverer," in Gary Nash and David Sweet, eds., *Struggle and Survival in Colonial America* (Berkeley, Calif., 1981), 69–85; James St. G. Walker, *The Black Loyalists: The Search for a Promised Land in Nova Scotia and Sierra Leone* (New York, 1976); Hannah [Harris, a weaver] to Robert Carter, 5 April 1792, in Alfred F. Young and Terry Fife with Mary Janzen, *We the People: Voices and Images of the New Nation* (Philadelphia, 1993), chap. 6.

13. See in Young, ed. *Beyond the American Revolution*: Peter Wood, "Liberty Is Sweet," 149–84; Alan Taylor, "Agrarian Independence: Northern Land Rioters after the Revolution," 221–45; Michael Merrill and Sean Wilentz, "'The Key of Libberty': William Manning and Plebeian Democracy," 246–82.

14. David Lovejoy, "'Desperate Enthusiasm': Early Signs of American Radicalism," Patrica Bonomi, "'A Just Opposition': The Great Awakening as a Radical Model," and Rhys Isaac, "Radicalised Religion and Changing Life Styles: Virginia in the Period of the American Revolution," all in Jacob and Jacob, eds., *Origins of Radicalism*, 214–55; Gregory H. Nobles, *Divisions throughout the Whole: Politics and Society in Hampshire County, Massachusetts, 1740–1775* (New York, 1983);

Richard Beeman, *The Evolution of the Southern Backcounty: A Case Study of Lunenberg County, Virginia, 1746–1832* (Philadelphia, 1984); David Lovejoy, *Religious Enthusiasm in the New World: Heresy to Revolution* (Cambridge, Mass., 1985); Patricia Bonomi, *Under the Cope of Heaven: Religion, Society, and Politics in Colonial America* (New York, 1986); Harry S. Stout, *The New England Soul: Preaching and Religious Culture in Colonial New England* (New York, 1986); Butler, *Awash in a Sea of Faith*; John Brooke, *The Heart of the Commonwealth: Society and Political Culture in Worcester County, Massachusetts, 1713–1861* (Cambridge, U.K., 1989); Ronald Hoffman and Peter Albert, eds., *Religion in a Revolutionary Age* (Charlottesville, Va., 1994).

15. Ruth H. Bloch, *Visionary Republic: Millennial Themes in American Thought, 1765–1800* (Cambridge, V.K., 1985); Mark H. Jones, "Herman Husband: Millenarian, Carolina Regulator, and Whiskey Rebel" (Ph.D. diss., Northern Illinois University, 1982). Stephen A. Marini, *Radical Sects of Revolutionary New England* (Cambridge, Mass., 1982); Nathan O. Hatch, *The Democratization of American Christianity* (New Haven, Conn., 1989).

16. Edward Countryman, "'To Secure the Blessings of Liberty': Language, the Revolution and American Capitalism," in Young, ed., *Beyond the Revolution,* 123–48. Various petitions are reprinted in Herbert Aptheker, ed., *Documentary History of the Negro People in the United States,* 2 vols. (New York, 1951), 1:5–9; and Robert Twombley, "Black Resistance to Slavery in Massachusetts," in William L. O'Neill, ed., *Insights and Parallels* (Minneapolis, 1973), 41–52; Thomas J. Davis, "Emancipation Rhetoric, Natural Rights and Revolutionary New England: A Note on Four Black Petitions in Massachusetts, 1773–1777," *New England Quarterly* 62 (1989): 248–63.

17. Ebenezer Fox, cited in W. J. Rorarbaugh, "'I Thought I Should Liberate Myself from the Thraldom of Others': Apprentices, Masters, and the Revolution," in Young, ed., *Beyond the Revolution,* 185–220. Alfred F. Young, "George Robert Twelves Hewes (1742–1840): A Boston Shoemaker and the Memory of the American Revolution," *WMQ* 38 (1981): 561–623.

18. See essay 2 in this volume; for variant interpretations, Edith B. Gelles, "The Abigail Industry," *WMQ* 45 (1988): 656–83.

19. Herman Husband, "Manuscript Sermons," 48–49, cited in Mark H. Jones, "The Western 'New Jerusalem': Herman Husband's Utopian Vision" (unpub. ms.).

20. John Shy, "The American Revolution: The Military Conflict Considered as a Revolutionary War," in Stephen G. Kurtz and James H. Hutson, eds., *Essays on the American Revolution* (Chapel Hill, N.C., and New York, 1973), 124.

21. Stephen Rosswurm, *Arms, Country, and Class: The Philadelphia Militia and the "Lower Sort" during the American Revolution* (New Brunswick, N.J., 1987), 111; Rosswurm, "The Philadelphia Militia, 1775–1783: Active Duty and Active Radicalism," in Ronald Hoffman and Peter J. Albert, eds., *Arms and Independence: The Military Character of the American Revolution* (Charlottesville, Va., 1984), 75–118.

22. Don C. Higginbotham, "The Early American Way of War: Reconaissance and Appraisal," *WMQ* 44 (1987): 230–73; James Kirby Martin, "A 'Most Undisciplined, Profligate Crew': Protest and Defiance in the Continental Ranks," in Hoffman and Albert, eds., *Arms and Independence*, 119–40; James Kirby Martin and Mark E. Lender, *A Respectable Army: The Military Origins of the Republic, 1763–1789* (Arlington Heights, Ill., 1982); Charles Royster, *A Revolutionary People at War: The Continental Army and American Character, 1775–1783* (Chapel Hill, N.C., 1979).

23. John Shy "The Legacy of the American Revolutionary War," in Larry Gerlach, comp., *Legacies of the American Revolution* (Logan, Utah, 1978), 43–60.

24. Jesse Lemisch, "Listening to the 'Inarticulate': William Widger's Dream and the Loyalties of American Revolutionary Seamen in British Prisons," *Journal of Social History* 3 (1969): 1–29.

25. Rachel N. Klein, "Frontier Planters and the American Revolution: The South Carolina Backcountry, 1775–1782," Jeffrey J. Crow, "Liberty Men and Loyalists: Disorder and Disaffection in the North Carolina Backcountry," Emory G. Evans, "Trouble in the Backcountry: Disaffection in Southwest Virginia during the American Revolution," and Richard R. Beeman "The Political Response to Social Conflict in the Southern Backcountry: A Comparative View of Virginia and the Carolinas during the Revolution," all in Ronald Hoffman, Thad Tate, and Peter J. Albert, eds., *An Uncivil War: The Southern Backcountry during the American Revolution* (Charlottesville, Va., 1985), 37–69, 125–78, 179–212, 213–39; Jeffrey J. Crow and Larry E. Tise, eds., *The Southern Experience in the American Revolution* (Chapel Hill, N.C., 1978); Ronald Hoffman, *A Spirit of Dissension: Economics, Politics, and the Revolution in Maryland* (Baltimore, 1973); Richard R. Beeman, *Patrick Henry: A Biography* (New York, 1974).

26. Sylvia R. Frey, *Water from the Rock: Black Resistance in a Revolutionary Age* (Princeton, N.J., 1991), chaps. 3–5, quotation 326; Benjamin Quarles, *The Negro in the American Revolution* (Chapel Hill, N.C., 1961), chaps. 7–9; Philip D. Morgan, "Black Society in the Lowcountry, 1760–1810," in Ira Berlin and Ronald Hoffman, eds., *Slavery and Freedom in the Age of the American Revolution* (Charlottesville, Va., 1983), 49–82; Graham Hodges, "Black Revolt in New York City and the Neutral Zone: 1775–1783," in Paul Gilje and William Pencak, eds., *New York City in the Age of the Constitution* (New York, 1992), 20–48.

27. Barbara Clark Smith, "Food Rioters and the American Revolution," *WMQ* 51 (1997): 3–38; Smith, *After the Revolution: The Smithsonian History of Everyday Life in the Eighteenth Century* (New York, 1985), chap. 1; Rosswurm, *Arms, Country, Class*, chap. 7.

28. David Ramsay, *The History of the American Revolution*, 2 vols. (Philadelphia, 1789), 2:315.

29. Mary Beth Norton, *Liberty's Daughters: The Revolutionary Experiences of American Women, 1750–1800* (Boston, 1980); Linda K. Kerber, "'I Have Don … Much to Carrey on the War': Women and the Shaping of Republican Ideology after the

American Revolution," in Harriet Applewhite and Darlene G. Levy, eds., *Women and Politics in the Age of the Democratic Revolution* (Ann Arbor, Mich., 1999), 227–57; compare Laurel Thatcher Ulrich, *Good Wives: Image and Reality in the Lives of Women in Northern New England, 1650–1750* (New York, 1980).

30. John Resch, *Suffering Soldiers: Revolutionary War Veterans, Moral Sentiment, and Political Culture in the Early Republic* (Amherst, Mass., 2000); John C. Dann, ed., *The Revolution Remembered: Eyewitness Accounts of the War for Independence* (Chicago, 1990), introduction; Jesse Lemisch, "The American Revolution and the American Dream: A Life of Andrew Sherburne, A Pensioner of the Navy of the Revolution" (unpub. ms.).

31. Ruth Bogin, "Petitioning and the New Moral Economy of Post-Revolutionary America," *WMQ* 45 (1988): 391–425; Gregory H. Nobles, "Breaking into the Backcountry: New Approaches to the Early American Frontier, 1750–1800," *WMQ* 46 (1989): 641–70; Gordon Wood, *The Creation of the American Republic, 1776–1787* (Chapel Hill, N.C., 1969), chaps. 7–11; Robert A. Gross, ed., *In Debt to Daniel Shays: The Bicentennial of an Agrarian Rebellion* (Charlottesville, Va., 1993).

32. James Madison, *The Federalist*, 2 vols. (New York, 1788, available in many editions), no. 10; compare to an earlier memorandum, Madison "Vices of the Political System," April 1987, in William T. Hutchinson et al., eds., *The Papers of James Madison*, 16 vols. (Chicago, 1962), 9:345–58; Merrill Jensen, John Kaminski, Gaspare J. Saladino, and Richard Lefler, eds., *The Documentary History of the Ratification of the Constitution*, 9 vols. of 20 planned (Madison, Wis., 1976–); Herbert J. Storing, ed., *The Complete Anti-Federalist*, 7 vols. (Chicago, 1981); Saul Cornell, "Aristocracy Assailed: The Ideology of Backcountry Anti-Federalism," *Journal of American History* 76 (1990): 1148–72.

33. Gary J. Kornblith and John M. Murrin, "The Making and Unmaking of an American Ruling Class," in Young, ed., *Beyond the Revolution*, 27–79; David Brion Davis, "American Equality and Foreign Revolutions," *Journal of American History* 76 (1989): 729–52; Davis, *Revolutions: Reflections on American Equality and Foreign Liberations* (Cambridge, Mass., 1990).

34. E. P. Thompson, *The Making of the English Working Class* (London, 1963); Thompson, "Eighteenth-Century English Society: Class Struggle without Class," *Social History* 3 (1978): 133–65, quotation at 149.

35. For discussion of class in Thompson, see William H. Sewell Jr., "How Classes Are Made: Critical Reflections on E. P. Thompson's Theory of Working-Class Formation," in Harvey J. Kaye and Keith McClelland, eds., *E. P. Thompson: Critical Perspectives* (Philadelphia, 1990), 50–77; Kaye, *The British Marxist Historians: An Introductory Analysis* (Cambridge, U.K., 1984); Bryan D. Palmer, *Descent into Discourse: The Reification of Language and the Writing of Social History* (Philadelphia, 1990), chap. 4; for related discussion of class consciousness in American history: Alan Dawley, "E. P. Thompson and the Peculiarities of the Americans," *Radical History Review* 10 (1978–79): 33–59; "Interview with Herbert

Gutman," in Gutman, *Power and Culture: Essays on the American Working Class*, ed. Ira Berlin (New York, 1987), 329–56; Sean Wilentz, "Against Exceptionalism: Class Consciousness and the American Labor Movement, 1790–1920," *International Labor and Working-Class History* 26 (1984): 1–24.

36. E. P. Thompson, "Patrician Society, Plebeian Culture," *Journal of Social History* 7 (1974): 382–405; Thompson, *Customs in Common*, 87–96; Michael Merrill and Sean Wilentz, *The Key of Liberty: The Life and Democratic Writings of William Manning, "A Laborer," 1747–1814* (Cambridge, Mass., 1993), introduction; Sean Wilentz, *Chants Democratic: New York City and the Rise of the American Working Class, 1788–1850* (New York, 1984); Gordon Wood, *The Radicalism of the American Revolution* (New York, 1992), chap. 2.

37. For recent analysis: Stuart M. Blumin, *The Emergence of the Middle Class: Social Experience in the American City, 1760–1900* (Cambridge, U.K., 1989); Allan Kulikoff, "The Languages of Class in Rural America," in Kulikoff, *The Agrarian Origins of American Capitalism* (Charlottesville, Va., 1992), chap. 4; Gregory Kaster, "'Not for a Class?' The Nineteenth-Century American Labor Jeremiad," *Mid-America: An Historical Review* 70 (1988): 125–39; for the pathbreaking English scholarship, Asa Briggs, "The Language of 'Class' in Early Nineteenth-Century England," in Briggs and John Saville, eds., *Essays in Labor History* (London, 1967), 43–73; and Gareth Stedman Jones, *Languages of Class: Studies in English Working-Class History, 1832–1982* (Cambridge, U.K., 1983).

38. Jonathan Elliot, ed. *The Debates in the Several State Conventions, on the Adoption of the Constitution*, 5 vols. (Philadelphia, 1836), 1:100–102; (Amos Singletary); 2:245–48 (Melancton Smith).

39. I have drawn my impressions from reading the newspapers. For two works that lean heavily on newspapers, see Donald H. Stewart, *The Opposition Press of the Federalist Period* (Albany, N.Y., 1969); and Alfred F. Young, *The Democratic Republicans of New York: The Origins, 1763–1797* (Chapel Hill, N.C., 1967).

40. See essay 1 in this volume In addition to the works cited in note 7, for bibliography on recent artisan studies, see Sean Wilentz, "The Rise of the American Working Class, 1776–1877," in J. Carroll Moody and Alice Kessler-Harris, eds., *Perspectives on American Labor History: The Problem of Synthesis* (DeKalb, Ill., 1989), 83–90; Gary J. Kornblith, "The Artisanal Response to Capitalist Transformation," *Journal of the Early Republic* 10 (1990): 315–21.

41. See essay 1 in this volume; Sean Wilentz, "Artisan Republican Festivals and the Rise of Class Conflict in New York City, 1788–1837," in Michael H. Frisch and Daniel J. Walkowitz, eds., *Working-Class America* (Urbana, Ill., 1983), 37–77.

42. Allan Kulikoff, "The American Revolution, Capitalism and the Formation of the Yeoman Classes," in Young, ed., *Beyond the Revolution*, 80–119 Sharon V. Salinger, *"To Serve Well and Faithfully": Labor and Indentured Servants in Pennsylvania, 1682–1800* (Cambridge, U.K., 1987); Billy G. Smith, *The "Lower Sort": Philadelphia's Laboring People, 1750–1800* (Ithaca, N.Y., 1990).

43. G. Wood, *Radicalism of Revolution*, 7; Bernard Bailyn, "The Central Themes of the American Revolution," in Kurtz and Hutson, eds., *Essays on the Revolution*, 30–31.

44. For recent work on this theme: Joyce Appleby, *Liberalism and Republicanism in the Historical Imagination* (Cambridge, Mass., 1992); James Henretta, *The Origins of American Capitalism: Collected Essays* (Boston, 1992); Kulikoff, *Agrarian Origins of American Capitalism*.

45. Kornblith and Murrin, "Making and Unmaking of an American Ruling Class"; William A. Williams, *The Contours of American History* (Cleveland and New York, 1961, 1988); Hoffman, *Spirit of Dissension*; Edward Countryman, *A People in Revolution: The American Revolution and Political Society in New York, 1760–1790* (Baltimore, 1981); Staughton Lynd, "A Ruling Class on the Defensive," in Lynd, *Class Conflict, Slavery, and the United States Constitution: Ten Essays* (Indianapolis, 1968); Rhys Isaac, *The Transformation of Virginia, 1740–1790* (Chapel Hill, N.C., 1982).

46. Peter Linebaugh and Marcus Rediker, "The Many-Headed Hydra: Sailors, Slaves, and the Atlantic Working Class in the Eighteenth Century," in Colin Howell and Richard J. Twomey, eds., *Jack Tar in History: Essays in the History of Maritime Life and Labour* (Fredericton, New Brunswick, 1991), 11–36.

47. Livingston cited in Young, *Democratic Republicans*, 15; Webster cited in Joseph J. Ellis, *After the Revolution: Profiles of Early American Culture* (New York, 1979), chap. 6, 203.

48. Barbara Karsky, "Agrarian Radicalism in the Late Revolutionary Period (1780–1795)," in Erich Angermann et al., eds., *New Wine in Old Skins: A Comparative View of Socio-Political Structures and Values Affecting the American Revolution* (Stuttgart, 1976), 87–114; David P. Szatmary, *Shays' Rebellion: The Making of an Agrarian Insurrection* (Amherst, Mass., 1980); Thomas P. Slaughter, *The Whiskey Rebellion: Frontier Epilogue to the American Revolution* (New York, 1986); Stephen R. Boyd, ed., *The Whiskey Rebellion: Past and Present Perspectives* (Westport, Conn., 1985); Jeffrey J. Crow, "The Whiskey Rebellion in North Carolina," *North Carolina Historical Review* 66 (1989): 1–28.

49. Richard D. Brown, *Knowledge Is Power: The Diffusion of Information in Early America, 1770–1865* (New York, 1989); Philip S. Foner, ed., *The Democratic-Republican Societies, 1790–1800: A Documentary Sourcebook of Constitutions, Declarations, Addresses, Resolutions, and Toasts* (Westport, Conn., 1976); Winthrop D. Jordan, *White over Black: American Attitudes toward the Negro, 1550–1812* (Chapel Hill, N.C., 1968), chap. 10.

50. The argument in this and the succeeding paragraph is developed in essay 4 in this volume and in revised form in Young, "The Framers of the Constitution and the 'Genius of the People,'" *Radical History Review* 42 (1988), with commentary by Barbara Clark Smith, Linda K. Kerber, Michael Merrill, Peter Dimock, William Forbath, and James Henretta, 7–47.

51. Williams, *Contours of American History*, 149–223; John R. Nelson Jr., *Liberty and Property: Political Economy and Policymaking in the New Nation, 1789–1812* (Baltimore, 1987); Joyce Appleby, *Capitalism and a New Social Order: The Republican Vision of the 1790s* (New York, 1984); Steven Watts, *The Republic Reborn: War and the Making of Liberal America, 1790–1820* (Baltimore, 1987).

52. Howard B. Rock, *Artisans of the New Republic: The Tradesmen of New York City in the Age of Jefferson* (New York, 1979); Rock, ed., *The New York City Artisan, 1789–1825: A Documentary History* (Albany, N.Y., 1989); Wilentz, *Chants Democratic*, chaps. 1, 2.

53. Rediker, *Between the Devil and the Deep Blue Sea* 291.

54. Alan Taylor, *Liberty Men and Great Proprietors: The Revolutionary Settlement in the Maine Frontier, 1760–1820* (Chapel Hill, N.C., 1990), chaps. 8, 9.

55. Frey, *Water from the Rock*, chaps. 7–9; Phillip D. Morgan, "Black Society in the Low Country, 1760–1810," in Berlin and Hoffman, eds., *Slavery and Freedom*, 83–142; Richard Dunn, "Black Society in the Chesapeake 1776–1810," in ibid., 49–82.

56. Ira Berlin, *Many Thousands Gone: The First Two Centuries of Slavery in North America* (Cambridge, Mass., 1998), part 3; Gary B. Nash, *Race and Revolution* (Madison, Wis., 1990); Nash, *Forging Freedom: The Formation of Philadelphia's Black Community, 1720–1840* (Cambridge, Mass., 1988); Nash and Jean R. Soderland, *Freedom by Degrees: Emancipation and Its Aftermath in Pennsylvania* (New York, 1990); Shane White, *Somewhat More Independent: The End of Slavery in New York City, 1770–1810* (Athens, Ga., 1991).

57. Berlin and Hoffman, eds., *Slavery and Freedom*, xv.

58. Davis, *Problem of Slavery*, chap. 6, quotations at 256, 259, 262; Edmund S. Morgan, *American Slavery, American Freedom: The Ordeal of Colonial Virginia* (New York, 1975).

59. Nash, *Race and Revolution*, chap. 2; Jordan, *White over Black*, pts. 4, 5; Paul Finkelman, "Slavery and the Constitutional Convention: Making a Covenant with Death," in Richard Beeman, Stephen Botein, and Edward C. Carter II, eds., *Beyond Confederation: Origins of the Constitution and American National Identity* (Chapel Hill, N.C., 1987), 188–225; Staughton Lynd, "The Compromise of 1787," *Political Science Quarterly* 81 (1966): 225–50.

60. Linda K. Kerber, "'History Can Do It No Justice': Women and the Reinterpretation of the American Revolution," in Ronald Hoffman and Peter J. Albert, eds., *Women in the Age of the American Revolution* (Charlottesville, Va., 1989), 3–42, quotation at 10.

61. Linda K. Kerber, "The Republican Mother: Women and the Enlightenment—An American Perspective," *American Quarterly* 28 (1976): 187–205; Kerber, "'I Have Don ... Much,'" 227–57; Jan Lewis, "The Republican Wife: Virtue and Seduction in the Early Republic," *WMQ* 44 (1987): 689–721.

62. Cathy N. Davidson, "The Novel as Subversive Activity: Women Reading, Women Writing," in Young, ed., *Beyond the Revolution*, 283–316; Davidson,

Revolution and the Word: The Rise of the Novel in America (New York, 1986); Laurel Thatcher Ulrich, *A Midwife's Tale: The Life of Martha Ballard, Based on Her Diary, 1785–1812* (New York, 1990); for scholarship emphasizing the limitations of reform: Joan Hoff Wilson, "The Illusion of Change: Women and the American Revolution," in Alfred F. Young, ed., *The American Revolution: Explorations in the History of American Radicalism* (DeKalb, Ill., 1976), 383–445; Christine Stansell, *City of Women: Sex and Class in New York, 1789–1860* (New York, 1986); Elaine F. Crane, "Dependence in the Era of Independence: The Role of Women in a Republican Society," in Jack P. Greene, ed., *The American Revolution: Its Character and Limits* (New York, 1987), 253–75; Marylynn Salmon, *Women and the Law of Property in Early America* (Chapel Hill, N.C., 1986); for scholarship registering changes in consciousness, Mary Beth Norton, "The Evolution of White Women's Experience in Early America," *American Historical Review* 89 (1984): 593–619; Joan Jensen, *Loosening the Bonds: Mid-Atlantic Farm Women, 1750–1850* (New Haven, Conn., 1986); Lee Chambers-Schiller, Schiller, *Liberty a Better Husband: Single Women in America, the Generations of 1740–1820* (New Haven, Conn., 1989); William J. Gilmore, *Reading Becomes a Necessity of Life: Material and Cultural Life in Rural New England, 1780–1835* (Knoxville, Tenn., 1989).

63. Elaine F. Crane, ed., *The Diary of Elizabeth Drinker*, 3 vols. (Boston, 1991), 22 April 1796; Charles W. Akers, *Abigail Adams: An American Woman* (Boston, 1980), 116.

64. Judith Sargent Murray, *The Gleaner*, 3 vols. (Boston, 1798), 1:167, 168, 193; 3:219; for the fullest analysis of Murray, see Kerber, "'I Have Don ... Much,'" 238–44.

65. Joan R. Gunderson, "Independence, Citizenship, and the American Revolution," *Signs* 13 (1987): 59–77; Ruth H. Bloch, "The Gendered Meanings of Virtue in Revolutionary America," ibid., 37–58; Nancy Fraser and Linda Gordon, "Contract versus Charity: Participation and Provision: A Reconsideration of 'Social Citizenship'" (paper presented at Newberry Library Family and Community History Center Seminar, 1992).

66. Kerber, "'History Can Do It No Justice,'" 41.

67. James H. Merrell, "Declarations of Independence: Indian-White Relations in the New Nation," in Greene, ed., *American Revolution*, 197–223.

68. Gregory Evans Dowd, *A Spirited Resistance: The North American Indian Struggle for Unity, 1745–1815* (Baltimore, 1992).

69. Merrell, "Declarations of Independence," 197; Francis Jennings, "The Indians' Revolution," in Young, ed., *American Revolution*, 341.

70. Merrell, "Declarations of Independence," 204; for the peace medal, Young and Fife, *We the People*, chap. 7.

71. Cited in Reginald Horsman, "The Image of the Indian in the Age of the American Revolution," *Newberry Library Center for the History of the American Indian Occasional Papers Series*, No. 6 (1983), 5; Alan Taylor, "Land and Liberty on

the Post-Revolutionary Frontier," in David T. Konig, ed., *Devising Liberty: Preserving and Creating Freedom in the New American Republic* (Stanford, Calif., 1995).

72. James P. Whittenberg, "Herman Husband's Plan for Peace between the United States and the Indians, 1792," *WMQ* 34 (1977): 647–50; Taylor, *Liberty Men and Great Proprietors*, chap. 7, "White Indians"; Richard White, *The Middle Ground: Indians, Empires, and Republicans in the Great Lakes Region, 1650–1815* (Cambridge, U.K., 1991).

73. Dowd, *Spirited Resistance*; R. David Edmunds, ed., *American Indian Leaders: Studies in Diversity* (Lincoln, Neb., 1980); Edmunds, *The Shawnee Prophet* (Lincoln, Neb., 1983); Edmunds, *Tecumseh and the Quest for Indian Leadership* (Boston, 1984); Anthony F. C. Wallace, *The Death and Rebirth of the Seneca* (New York, 1969); Joel W. Martin, *Sacred Revolt: The Muskogees' Struggle for a New World* (Boston, 1991); James H. Merrell, *The Indians' New World: Catawbas and Their Neighbors from European Contact through the Era of Removal* (Chapel Hill, N.C., 1989); for the continuing failure of scholars to integrate Indian history, Merrell, "Some Thoughts on Colonial Historians and American Indians," *WMQ* 41 (1989): 94–119. The pathbreaking synthesis for the colonial era is Gary B. Nash, *Red, White, and Black: The Peoples of Early America* (Englewood Cliffs, N.J., 1974; 3d. ed, 1991); the most recent synthesis is Francis Jennings, *The Founders of America* (New York, 1992); the new history is collected in Frederick Hoxie, Ronald Hoffman, and Peter Albert, eds., *Native Americans and the Early Republic* (Charlottesville, Va., 1999).

74. Bernard W. Sheehan, *Seeds of Extinction: Jeffersonian Philanthropy and the American Indian* (Chapel Hill, N.C., 1973); the Mashpees cited in Merrell, "Declarations of Independence," 217; Richard Drinnon, *Facing West: The Metaphysics of Indian-Hating and Empire-Building* (New York, 1980), part 2.

75. Thomas P. Slaughter, "Crowds in Eighteenth-Century America: Reflections and New Directions," *Pennsylvania Magazine of History and Biography* 115 (1991): 3–34; Paul A. Gilje, *The Road to Mobocracy: Popular Disorder in New York City, 1763–1834* (Chapel Hill, N.C., 1987).

76. Bryan D. Palmer, "Discordant Music: Charivari and Whitecapping in North America," *Labour/Le Travailleur* 1 (1978): 5–62; Susan G. Davis, *Parades and Power: Street Theater in Nineteenth-Century Philadelphia* (Berkeley, Calif., 1986); Samuel Kinser, *Carnival, American Style: Mardi Gras at New Orleans and Mobile* (Chicago, 1990).

77. Bogin, "Petitioning"; Edmund S. Morgan, *Inventing the People: The Rise of Popular Sovereignty in England and America* (New York, 1988), chap. 9.

78. Dorothy Fennell, "From Rebelliousness to Insurrection: A Social History of the Whiskey Rebellion, 1765–1802" (Ph.D. diss., University of Pittsburgh, 1981).

79. Charles G. Steffen, *The Mechanics of Baltimore: Workers and Politics in the Age of Revolution, 1763–1812* (Urbana, Ill., 1984), 217–21.

80. Simon P. Newman, *Parades and the Politics of the Street: Festive Culture in*

the Early American Republic (Philadelphia, 1997); Young, Democratic Republicans, chap. 22.

81. Frey, Water from the Rock, 257, 320; Douglas R. Egerton, "Gabriel's Conspiracy and the Election of 1800," Journal of Southern History 56 (1990): 191–214; Mullin, Flight and Rebellion, chap. 5, Tucker cited at 157; Eugene Genovese, From Rebellion to Revolution: Afro-American Slave Revolts in the Making of the Modern World (Baton Rouge, La., 1979); Jeffrey J. Crow, "Slave Rebelliousness and Social Conflict in North Carolina, 1775–1802," WMQ 37 (1980): 79–102.

82. Frey, Water from the Rock, chaps. 7–9; Mary Beth Norton, Herbert G. Gutman, and Ira Berlin, "The Afro-American Family in the Age of Revolution," and Albert J. Roboteau, "The Slave Church in the Era of the American Revolution," both in Berlin and Hoffman, eds., Slavery and Freedom, 175–213; Jacqueline Jones, "Race, Sex, and Self-Evident Truths: The Status of Slave Women during the Era of the American Revolution," in Hoffman and Albert, eds., Women in the Age of the Revolution, 293–337.

83. Paula Baker, "The Domestication of Politics: Women and American Political Society, 1780–1920," American Historical Review 89 (1984): 620–47; Anne M. Boylan, "Women and Politics in the Era before Seneca Falls," Journal of the Early Republic 10 (1990): 363–82; Susan Branson. These Fiery Frenchified Dames: Women and Political Culture in Early National Philadelphia (Philadelphia, 2001).

84. Charles Brockden Brown, Alcuin: A Dialogue (New York, 1798); Murray, The Gleaner, 3:188–89.

85. Thomas Jefferson to Spencer Roane, 6 September 1819, cited in Dumas Malone, Jefferson the President: First Term, 1801–1805 (Boston, 1970), 26; Aleine Austin, Matthew Lyon: "New Man" of the Democratic Revolution, 1749–1822 (University Park, Pa., 1981).

86. Richard J. Twomey, Jacobins and Jeffersonians: Anglo-American Radicalism in the United States 1790–1820 (New York, 1989); Hatch, Democratization of Christianity, chap. 2; Richard E. Ellis, The Jeffersonian Crisis: Courts and Politics in the Young Republic (New York, 1971); Michael Durey, "Thomas Paine's Apostles: Radical Émigrés and the Triumph of Jeffersonian Republicanism," WMQ 44 (1987): 661–88.

87. Thomas Jefferson to James Monroe, 20 September 1800, cited in Egerton, "Gabriel's Conspiracy," 214; Michael Zuckerman, "The Color of Counter-Revolution: Thomas Jefferson and the Rebellion in San Domingo," in Loretta Valtz Mannucci, ed., The Languages of Revolution (Milan Group in Early American History Quaderno 2, University of Milan, 1989), 83–107; Jordan, White over Black, chap. 12.

88. Thomas Jefferson cited in Norton, Liberty's Daughters, 190–91. Compare to the equalitarianism of the Massachusetts Republican James Sullivan, in Linda K. Kerber, "The Paradox of Women's Citizenship in the Early Republic: The Case of Martin versus Massachusetts, 1805," American Historical Review 97 (1992): 349–78.

89. Thomas Jefferson, "Address," 7 January 1802, and Jefferson to Gov. William

Henry Harrison, 27 February 1803, cited in Malone, *Jefferson the President*, 273–75; Sheehan, *Seeds of Extinction*, chaps. 5–9. For Jefferson's radicalism, compare Richard Matthews, *The Radical Politics of Thomas Jefferson: A Revisionist View* (Lawrence, Kan., 1984), to Leonard Levy, *Jefferson and Civil Liberties: The Darker Side* (Cambridge, Mass., 1963); Leonard Levy, *Emergence of a Free Press* (New York, 1985), and the works cited above by David Brion Davis, Winthrop Jordan, and Bernard Sheehan.

Part III

Memory: Lost and Found

6

The Celebration and Damnation of
Thomas Paine

On June 10, 1809, when Thomas Paine was buried on his own farm in New Rochelle, in Westchester County, New York, there were less than a dozen people at his funeral: Willett Hicks, a Quaker who had been unsuccessful in getting the Society of Friends to accept Paine's request that he be laid to rest in their burial grounds in New York City; Thomas Addis Emmett, a Paineite political émigré who had been imprisoned in Ireland, now a rising lawyer in the city; Walter Morton, a friend; two African American men, one perhaps the gravedigger; Margaret de Bonneville and her two young sons, Benjamin and Thomas, Paine's godson, all refugees from Napoleonic France who Paine had sustained in the United States in gratitude for the support she and her husband, Nicholas, had given Paine in France before and after his imprisonment. All these had made the twenty-five-mile journey from Greenwich Village, then on the outskirts of New York City, where Paine had died. They may have been joined by a few neighbors from New Rochelle, where he had lived intermittently since his return from France in 1802. No political leaders attended; no one, it seems, gave a eulogy. Years later Madame de Bonneville recollected the poignant moment:

> The interment was a scene to affect and wound any sensible heart. Contemplating who it was, what man it was, that we were committing him to an obscure grave on an open and disregarded bit of land, I could not help feeling most acutely. Before the earth was thrown down around the coffin, I placing myself at the east end of the grave, said to my son Benjamin, "stand you there, at the other end, as a witness for grateful America." Looking round me, and beholding the small group of spectators, I exclaimed, as the earth was tumbled into the grave, "Oh! Mr Paine! My son stands here as testimony of the gratitude of America, and I, for France!"[1]

A few others may have paid their last respects to Paine in the city in response to a paragraph the day before in the *Public Advertiser* by Jacob

At the height of his fame in England in 1792, Thomas Paine was depicted sympathetically by the English painter George Romney in a painting Paine's friends considered a good likeness. This engraving, made by William Sharp in the 1790s, was adapted from the portrait. Paine is decently dressed, healthy, and has piercing eyes. On the desk are manuscripts of his two widely read pamphlets, *Common Sense* and *Rights of Man*, the writer's quill beside them. Library of Congress.

Frank, its editor, inviting friends "to attend the funeral from [Paine's] late residence," but if so, it was not enough to write about in the papers. There was no memorial service in New York or any other city. A few tributes appeared in newspapers edited by Jacobin refugees from British persecution, now successful Jeffersonians. New York politicians who had known Paine and his record, Vice President George Clinton and his nephew, Dewitt Clinton, the mayor of the city, were silent, as were the national leaders who had been his co-workers: Thomas Jefferson, who had played host to him in 1803 at the White House on his return from France; James Monroe, the U.S. minister who had intervened to free him from a French prison in 1794; Benjamin Rush, who in 1776 had given the title to *Common Sense*—all were silent. And later in 1809, when James Cheetham, the renegade Paineite editor, brought out a scurrilous biography of Paine in New York, the source of much of the scandalous misinformation over the decades, it went unchallenged. Philip Freneau, alone among American writers of his day, paid tribute to Paine in poetry.[2]

What had happened? Thomas Paine was the author of the three most widely read and influential pamphlets in the English language in the last quarter of the eighteenth century: *Common Sense* (1776), *Rights of Man* (1791–92), and *Age of Reason* (1795). In 1776 *Common Sense*, Paine claimed with only slight exaggeration, "awaked America to a declaration of Independence."[3] It was published anonymously, so he did not reap the full fruits of authorship. But during the war, the *Crisis* papers, written by Thomas Paine, "author of *Common Sense*," which began with "These are the times that try men's souls," confirmed his reputation as a leading patriot. Washington had them read to his troops. Paine was known to all the leaders of the Revolution. Congress appointed him secretary to its Committee on Foreign Affairs. Pennsylvania made him clerk to its assembly. Robert R. Livingston, in effect the Secretary of State, and Robert Morris, the Secretary of the Treasury, issued government funds to sustain him as a pamphleteer. After the war, when Paine petitioned Congress to pay him for expenses in the public service he calculated at $6,000, Congress recognized that he was "entitled to a liberal gratification from the United States," but met only half of his claim.[4] In the Virginia legislature, a bill to reward him with land, strongly endorsed by George Washington, failed by one vote. But Pennsylvania awarded him £500 for his "many very eminent services." And New York granted him a 250-acre farm in New Rochelle, confiscated from a Loyalist, for his "eminent services" and "distinguished merit" in the Revolution.[5] The *Rights of Man*, which circulated widely in the 1790s, renewed this popular reputation.

What explains Paine's fall from grace? The most commonly offered explanation lies in the response to the *Age of Reason*, the third of his best-selling works, which followed on the heels of *Rights of Man* and circulated through the late 1790s. His attack on organized religion as the historical handmaiden of political oppression and his rational critique of the miraculous side of the Bible as superstition brought deism out of gentlemen's drawing rooms to the village tavern and the artisan's hearth as no other work before or since. It probably eclipsed *Rights of Man* in the breadth and intensity of the reaction it provoked.[6]

The religious explanation is appealing. The orthodox clergy in the United States attacked Paine with an unprecedented fury. Federalist leaders exploited the religious issue. And many Jeffersonian politicians, even if closet deists, found Paine's irreligion politically embarrassing, especially because so many of their supporters were evangelical Baptists and Methodists. The second Great Awakening of the early 1800s sank roots among poorer farmers in the countryside and artisans and journeymen in the cities, the natural constituents of the Democratic Republicans. And it may be that in the last analysis Paine's deism sealed his fate.

But was it so simple? Why was the attack on Paine's religious views so effective? I would like to explore three additional hypotheses for the eclipse of Thomas Paine.[7] First, from the outset of his American career, Paine was under attack for his democratic political radicalism. From 1776 through 1794, long before the *Age of Reason* made its appearance, Paine was the target of one wing of the American conservative elite, and he remained so throughout his life. Second, the failure of Paine to retain the popular reputation he won during the Revolution from 1776 to 1783 is part of a persistent problem in American history of passing on the history of one generation to another. And third, Paine might be considered a "victim of the Rights of Man," a felicitous phrase Robert R. Palmer used some forty years ago.[8] The election of Jefferson in 1801 and certainly his re-election in 1805 guaranteed the triumph of the core principles Paine advocated. Paine, the person, thus was a victim of the success of his political ideas.

To probe this seeming puzzle of the rejection of Paine in the first decade of the nineteenth century, we should try to unlock the secrets of his success. I will turn first to an exploration of the reception of *Common Sense* in 1776, second to the reception of *Rights of Man* in the 1790s in the United States and England, and then return to the American scene in Paine's last years from 1802 to 1809.

I

One needs *Common Sense* to understand the *Rights of Man*. It was the basis of his subsequent reputation. On the title page of the *Rights of Man* Paine identified himself as the author of *Common Sense*. More important, as Paine had no hesitation in admitting, the principles in *Rights of Man* "were the same as those in *Common Sense*.... The only difference between the two works was, that one was adapted to the local circumstances of England and the other to those in America."⁹ Indeed the very structure of the argument of Part II of *Rights of Man* and much of the language follow *Common Sense*.

Common Sense has come down in history oversimply as an argument for American independence. Actually, the message to Americans was triple-barreled: independence, republicanism, and confidence in the common people. Abandon the goal of reconciliation with the mother country, he told his readers, and adopt the goal of independence; reject not only King George III but the principle of monarchy, and put in its place republican government based on broad popular participation; and third, in a message implicit in the style addressed to ordinary people in the plainest of language, rely not on learned authorities but on your own reason, your own common sense.

The tone of the writing was warmly egalitarian. "Male and female are the distinctions of nature, good and bad the distinctions of heaven; but how a race of men came into the world so exalted above the rest ... is worth inquiring into." "Of more worth is one honest man to society, and in the sight of God than all the crowned ruffians that ever lived."¹⁰ The language was irreverent, often coarse. The first king was "nothing better than the principal ruffian of some restless gang." The claim of William the Conqueror, "a French bastard landing with an armed banditti and establishing himself king of England against the consent of the natives, is in plain terms a very paltry rascally original. It certainly hath no divinity in it."¹¹ And the appeal was suffused with a millennialist idealism: "We have it in our power to begin the world over again. A situation similar to the present, hath not happened since the days of Noah until now. The birthday of a new world is at hand."¹²

The popularity of the pamphlet was extraordinary by any measure. If its success was not quite as Paine proclaimed—"beyond anything since the invention of printing"—it very likely was read by or read to a large share of the adult white male population in the colonies and a good many women.[13] Paine, who could observe the printing history from the vantage point of Philadelphia (in effect the capital where the Continental Congress was sitting), claimed 120,000 copies by April 1776, four months after its initial printing there in mid-January, which he later raised to 150,000 and then reduced (not necessarily accurately) in 1792 to 100,000 in a footnote in *Rights of Man*.[14] Scholars have generally accepted a circulation of 100,000 to 150,000 copies (although none of them make clear how they reached their conclusions). This was in a country of about 3,000,000 (500,000 of whom were African Americans, almost all slaves), which means about 350,000 Anglo-American families. Some 200,000 men served in the militia or regular army over seven years of war. The pamphlet was cheap, one shilling, which put it in the category not of the lowest price chapbooks and almanacs but well below the cost of most books. And it was relatively short, forty-seven pages in its first edition, usually less than sixty pages in other printings, and arranged in four systematic chapters, written in a plain style which made it accessible.[15]

Between January and June 1776, the pamphlet went through some thirty-five separate printings (counting the several editions), fifteen in Philadelphia, where it first appeared and from which it was distributed to the South, sixteen in New England.[16] There was no copyright law: printers simply reprinted whatever version arrived at their shop. Paine said he never made a penny from the work. Vain and boastful as Paine was, there was something to his claim in April 1776 about the speed of its circulation: there was "never a pamphlet since the use of letters ... of which so great a number went off in so short a time."[17] Pamphlets were one of the principal forms of expression in the revolutionary decade; Bernard Bailyn has analyzed some four hundred which appeared in the decade before 1776 but prior to Paine. The best seller among them may have been John Dickinson's with a circulation of about 15,000 copies.[18] A sale of 2,000 was more common for a pamphlet. A speller might sell 20,000 copies, a psalm book 30,000, the annual printing of Benjamin Franklin's *Poor Richard's Almanack* 20,000, and an unusually popular almanac like Nathanial Ames's 60,000, but these were all steady sellers with a very broad audience.[19]

A wealth of anecdotal evidence from sources high and low attest to the enormous popularity of *Common Sense* in the first six months of 1776. A Philadelphian who sent a copy to a friend in England reported that it "is read to all ranks; and as many as read, so many become converted; though perhaps the hour before were most violent against the least idea of independence." By March, General Washington wrote, "I find *Common Sense* is working a powerful change in the minds of men." Punitive British military actions, "added to the sound doctrine and unanswerable reasoning ... was winning people to the propriety of a separation."[20]

It was successful because it came at precisely the time when people were ready for its message. After a decade of intense political controversy, war had broken out at Lexington and Concord in April 1775. Tens of thousands of men were in arms in the militia or the new regular army authorized by Congress with Washington as commander in chief. Committees were forming everywhere, setting up, in effect, a dual government, as British government collapsed. A war was on, but what were Americans fighting for? The prospect of reconciliation with Britain was fading and to more and more people was no longer desirable.

In weighing influence of a tract, the active role of the reader is often unappreciated. Reading is an act of volition. A person had to buy the pamphlet; one shilling was cheap as pamphlets went but costly to a common carpenter who might make three shillings a day or to a shoemaker who made even less and out of the question for a common laborer who earned one-eighth of a shilling a day.[21] Or a person had to borrow the pamphlet, seeking out an owner, or respond to someone's blandishments to read it. When it was read aloud, as it was in taverns and other public places, a person had to make a decision to come to listen or stay to hear it out. Alfred Owen Aldridge points out that *Common Sense* had a "high multiple readership," that handwritten copies and summaries circulated, and newspapers reprinted excerpts. Brissot de Warville, a French observer, thought the pamphlet "had such a prodigious effect only because it was a hundred times cited and reproduced in those gazettes devoured with avidity by the artisan, the farmer, and the man of all classes."[22]

As some political leaders interpreted the process, Paine's pamphlet "converted" people or "awaked" them to independence, as Paine put it. *Common Sense,* one army officer wrote to another, "has made many proselytes, and I believe will open the eyes of the common people."[23] David Ramsay, the South Carolina physician who wrote one of the first histories of the Revolution, thought it "produced surprising effects. Many thousands were convinced by it and were led to approve and long for a separation from the Mother Country." But others, perhaps more immersed in the popular upsurge, thought of Paine as expressing opinions they already held. Joseph Hawley, a leader in western Massachusetts, wrote, "every sentiment has sunk into my well prepared heart." As Ashbel Green, then a sixteen-year-old in New Jersey, remembered it more than sixty years later,

Common Sense "struck a string which required but a touch to make it vibrate. The country was ripe for independence and only needed somebody to tell the people so, with decision, boldness and plausibility."[24] Thus John Adams was not entirely wrong in claiming years later, even if he was putting down Paine, that "the idea of independence was familiar, even among the common people, much earlier than some persons pretend" and that the first idea of independence was not "suggested to them by the pamphlet Common Sense."[25]

Thus Paine, it could be argued, crystallized an inchoate or unexpressed sentiment for independence. His special contribution—which Adams could not abide—was to link independence to republicanism and give the common people (a term obviously in popular usage) a sense of their own capacity to shape events. As Adams well knew, Paine's pamphlet precipitated a three-cornered debate. The first, between the opponents and advocates of independence—between Paine and some since forgotten Loyalist pamphleteers—was easily won and after the Declaration of Independence, July 4, 1776, was irrelevant. The second was among patriots as to what kind of a republic should replace British rule, and this debate continued through the revolutionary era and into the 1790s. Here the debate was explicitly between Paine and a host of radical democratic republicans on the one hand and conservative republican patriots like Adams and ultraconservatives like Carter Braxton of Virginia on the other.

From the outset, Adams was ambivalent about Paine's multiple messages. Years later, he vividly remembered his mood in 1776:

> The arguments in favor of Independence I liked very well [but] the part relative to a form of government I considered as flowing from simple ignorance, and a mere desire to please the Democratic party in Philadelphia.... I dreaded the effect so popular a pamphlet might have.... His plan was so democratical without any restraint or even an attempt at any equilibrium or counterpoise.[26]

Very soon Adams was in the thick of this internal debate. He circulated his manuscript "Thoughts on Government," which he rapidly put into print to instruct patriot leaders in drafting safe constitutions for the newly independent states. Paine's ideals led to the Pennsylvania constitution, the most democratic of any: a one-house legislature elected annually by a broad taxpayer suffrage with no property qualifications for officeholding, a weak executive, and laws passed only after the legislature allowed them to circulate among the people. Adams's ideals were embodied in the

Massachusetts constitution of 1780 he helped draft: a two-branch legislature with graduated property qualifications for officeholding and voting; a governor with a high property qualification; and an independent judiciary. The two houses would check and balance each other, and the governor could veto their laws. Adams's plan made numerous concessions to the town-meeting democracy of New England, but a fundamental principle was respect for "persons in authority"—the antithesis of Paine's egalitarianism.[27]

Adams feared as well the spillover of this political radicalism into a "levelling spirit" or a general "impudence." He had a taste of it in his own family. In March 1776, out of the blue, Adams's wife, Abigail, wrote to him to "remember the ladies" in recasting a code of laws for America. "Do not put such unlimited power into the hands of the Husbands. Remember all men would be tyrants if they could." Adams put her down playfully, expressing shock. Everyone was casting off deference.

> We have been told that our struggle has loosened the bonds of government everywhere. That children and Apprentices were disobedient—that schools and colleges were grown turbulent—that Indians slighted their Guardians and Negroes grew insolent to their masters.... Depend upon it, we know better than to repeal our masculine systems.

It could not have been lost upon John Adams that Abigail had read the copy of *Common Sense* he had sent her the month before and was "charmed by its sentiments." Abigail Adams did not "foment a female rebellion" as she threatened, but she continued to press the issue on her husband. And everywhere elites had to contend with rebelliousness of all sorts among subordinate classes, including a wave of near insurrection and flight among slaves.[28]

In 1819, forty years later, smoke still came out of his ears as John Adams fumed about the pamphlet. "What a poor, ignorant, Malicious, short-sighted Crapulous Mass is Tom Paine's Common Sense."[29]

II

In the 1790s the *Rights of Man* appeared in the thick of a renewed conflict between the two types of republicanism epitomized by Paine and Adams in 1776. Paine's name now appeared on the title page, variously identified as the author of *Common Sense* and *The Crisis*. To understand the celebration and damnation of *Rights of Man* two contexts are needed: the history of the fifteen years gone by since 1776 and the history of Federalist policies of the 1790s, which again "struck a string which required but a touch to make it vibrate." Without these, it is a puzzle why *Rights of Man* should have been popular at all in the United States. Paine left for a trip to England in 1787; he wrote both parts I and II of the pamphlet in England for an English audience. Part I in 1791 was a lengthy, discursive defense of the French Revolution in response to an attack on it by an English politician, Edmund Burke. It had neither the immediacy nor style of *Common Sense*. In 1792, Part II (with the exception of chapter 5) was a restatement of *Common Sense*, demanding reform of the English political system and setting up the United States as a model for England to follow. Why should such a work have become popular in the United States?[30]

In the United States between 1776 and 1789 there was a struggle between the two kinds of republicanism. During the Revolution patriot elites—would-be ruling classes—divided in their strategy as to how to contain the democratic tides that overflowed all banks. Some were advocates of accommodation, others of coercion or repression. The metaphors of two New York landed aristocrats epitomize the difference. Robert R. Livingston Jr. was convinced "of the propriety of Swimming with a stream which it is impossible to stem," But Gouverneur Morris used the metaphor of a snake to describe the popular movement.

A snake had to be scotched; it could hardly be tamed. Others compared the people to a horse which had to be whipped. John Adams, with a constituency ranging from Yankee yeoman and assertive mechanics to opulent merchant princes, leaned sometimes towards accommodation, sometimes towards coercion. In 1799, Gouverneur Morris sniffed at Thomas Paine with aristocratic snobbery: he was "a mere adventurer from England, without fortune, without family or connexions, ignorant even of grammar." And as minister to France in the 1790s he was willing to let Paine rot in a French prison. Robert R. Livingston, by contrast, put Paine on the government payroll.[31]

In 1787, Morris was among the framers who were intrigued by the extremist proposal of Alexander Hamilton for a president elected for life, a senate elected for life, a house for two-year terms, and a president with the power to appoint the state governors and veto state laws. Morris, understandably, was enthusiastic. But the framers, as a group, knew that a government of King, Lords, and Commons was not suited to America. And so they adopted a more accommodating middle-of-the road plan which pleased John Adams to no end but left Paine dissatisfied. In 1788 Paine was in Paris, where he ardently debated the new constitution with Jefferson and Lafayette "in a convention of our own." Paine swallowed his objections because for him any national government was better than the weak confederation as long as it provided the means for future amendment. In 1787–88 the Federalists under the leadership of Madison made their first accommodation. In 1789–91, they made a second accommodation of the democratic opponents of the Constitution by adding a Bill of Rights.[32]

III

In the 1790s, *Rights of Man* won an audience because, once in power, the Federalists moved away from accommodation towards coercion. Federalists strung new "strings" which *Rights of Man* could vibrate. First, they attempted to give the national government what they called a "high tone," raising the seemingly dead issues of aristocracy and monarchy. Federalists toyed with the idea of titles. Vice President John Adams asked the Senate whether he should address President Washington as "His most benign highness" or "His elective highness." Some irreverent senators suggested Adams might be called the "Duke of Braintree" (his home town) or "His Rotundity." But the cat was out of the bag, and Adams, undismayed, was soon in print with a series of articles justifying titles to create an aura of dignity around officials in order to command the respect of the common people.[33]

Second, Alexander Hamilton, by his financial policies—funding the national debt, assuming the state debts, and chartering a Bank of the United States—by a wave of the Secretary of the Treasury's wand, created a monied interest to support the national government. Consciously modeled after the British system, the Hamiltonian program raised questions as to whether the United States was adopting the corruption it had abandoned. Moreover, the taxes to raise this grand Hamiltonian edifice seemed to fall heavily on the backs of farmers.[34]

Federalist foreign policies provided a third string to vibrate. In 1789–90, the French Revolution was not a partisan issue; France had been America's indispensable ally in the Revolution and a formal Franco-American alliance was still in place. But the Revolution moved to the left, establishing a republic, the republic practiced the regicide Americans had done only symbolically in '76, and a radical reform movement threatened revolution in Great Britain. As France and Britain went to war, two contrasting philosophies of government seemed to be at stake. The Federalists, by pursuing a policy of economic and ideological alliance with Britain, brought the French Revolution and the French alliance into American politics. By 1791–92 the coalition that Washington held together was fracturing on the national level as Jefferson and Madison parted company with Hamilton. From 1792 to 1794 popular opposition to the internal excise taxes on the farmer's production of whiskey was in full bloom. In 1793 policy to France and the French Revolution moved to center stage, and in 1795, with Jay's Treaty, policy to Great Britain was central. By 1795 more than forty Democratic Republican Societies were meeting. Electoral battles for Congress, under way in 1794, were in full swing in 1796 as Jefferson challenged Adams for the presidency.[35]

Federalist policy veered from accommodation to repression. In 1794–95, they sent an army to put down the Whiskey Rebellion in western Pennsylvania, attempted in Congress to "censure" the Democratic Societies as "self created," and condemned the crowds demonstrating against Jay's Treaty as "the swinish multitude." In 1798, with Adams as president, Congress ended up passing the Alien and Sedition Laws, under which Federalists prosecuted criticism of the government as sedition—a "reign of terror" Jefferson called it.[36]

Thus the *Rights of Man*, while directed at the British system of government, unintentionally could vibrate some of the same American strings that *Common Sense* had plucked. Once again, Paine blasted away at monarchy: "If I ask the farmer, the manufacturer, the merchant, the tradesman and down through all the occupations of life to the common laborer, what service is monarchy to him? He can give me no answer."[37] Adams and Hamilton had defended the system of King, Lords, and Commons as appropriate for Great Britain with enough rigor to create an American resonance to Paine's attack.

Paine went after what he called the "farce of titles" which Adams had advocated. "Titles are like circles drawn by the magician's wand," wrote Paine, "to contract the sphere of man's felicity. He lives immured within the Bastille of a word, and surveys at a distance the envied life of man."[38] Paine was merciless to the hereditary principle, in language appealing to Americans who sought recognition on the basis of achievement. "Hereditary succession is a burlesque upon monarchy.... It requires some talents to be a common mechanic, but to be a king, requires only the animal figure of a man—a sort of breathing automaton."[39]

Paine had harsh words for the English funding system, which his American readers could construe against its Hamiltonian imitation. Most important, Paine returned again and again to the theme of the "excess and inequality of taxation." His target was always Britain; in America, he contended, "their taxes are few because their government is just. There the poor are not oppressed, the rich are not privileged."[40] But to farmers in western Pennsylvania and Kentucky ready to tar and feather excise-tax collectors, such lines may have been more an incitement than a comfort.

Paine linked the cost of monarchy and aristocracy to taxation. The issue for the individual was "whether the fruits of his labor shall be enjoyed by himself, or consumed by the profligacy of governments," and in so framing the issue, he touched a deep nerve among American farmers which, when rubbed raw, had contributed to the Revolution and agrarian rebellions before and after. It is also entirely likely that Paine's remarkable chapter 5 in Part II, addressing the "mass of wretchedness" in civilized countries ("We see age going to the work-house and youth to the gallows") also resonated in America. In the United States one might not be "shocked by ragged and hungry children and persons of seventy and eighty years of age begging for bread" as was Paine in England. But in the seaboard cities the poor houses were often overcrowded, and hard-put journeymen printers and shoemakers, who lived on the edge of poverty, conducted the first strikes against master artisans. Unquestionably there were, as Paine wrote, "a considerable number of middling tradesmen who having lived decently in the former part of life, begin, as age approaches to lose their business and at last fall into decay."[41] In 1818, when Congress finally got around to pensions for veterans of the Revolution, restricting them to those "in the lowest grade of poverty," thirty thousand men applied. Such men and women might well have responded to Paine's plan for a system of old-age pensions, education, and child subsidies—the lineaments of the welfare state.[42]

In the 1790s, no less than in 1776, Paine appealed to the millennialist streak among Americans. "It is an age of revolutions in which everything may be looked for." And everything was not confined to governments.

> When it shall be said in any country in the world, my poor are happy; neither ignorance nor distress is to be found among them; my jails are empty of prisoners, my streets of beggars; the aged are not in want, the taxes are not oppressive; the rational world is my friend because I am a friend of its happiness—when these things can be said then may that country boast of its constitution and its government.[43]

Rights of Man thus had the potential to reach a wide audience in the United States. Exactly how wide was it? There is no study of the publishing history of the pamphlet in the United States, as there is for *Common Sense*. It clearly was one of the most widely circulated titles of the 1790s, but how many copies is difficult to say. This time Paine—who was in England until 1792 and then in France until 1802—was not in a position to make a claim for the total sales in the United States, as he had in 1776 for *Common Sense*. The frequency and location of printings offers the best clue. There were more printers than in 1776, and they were in more places. There may have been more partisan printers. But printers were in business to make money. Whatever their politics, they could not afford to bring out nonsellers.[44]

Using the standard bibliographic guides, I count for the 1790s about twenty-six printings of *Rights of Man*, twelve of Part I in seven different cities and nine of Part II in six cities, plus several combined printings of parts I and II.[45] If the circulation statistics are beyond recovery, there are several clues as to its popularity. First, there were multiple editions in the large coastal cities, New York, Philadelphia, and Boston. There were also editions in small towns where printers had distribution networks into the countryside (Bennington, Vt.; Carlisle, Pa.; Albany, N.Y.; and New London, Conn.). Knowledgeable, successful printers like Isaiah Thomas, Hugh Gaine, and Matthew Carey brought out *Rights of Man*. Second, printers were willing to risk bringing out the collected "works" or "writings" of Paine in two or more volumes, something which could probably not be said at this time for many other leaders of the Revolution. The Albany printers, for example, published his writings, acting for a consortium of printers in the Hudson Valley at Lansingburgh, Hudson, Poughkeepsie, and New York. Third, printers brought out cheap editions. In Boston, Thomas and John Fleet, whose stock in trade was broadside ballads and chap books, advertised a "cheap edition in two parts stitched together at only 3 shillings" (still cheap allowing for inflation since the one-shilling price of *Common Sense* in 1776). American booksellers and book peddlers also sold cheap copies imported from England. My guess, taking into account all of these sources, is that *Rights of Man* had a total sale of from fifty thousand to one hundred thousand copies. And this would not measure its full readership. It was doubtless stocked by circulating libraries, of which there were more than 250 by 1800. And passages were frequently reprinted in newspapers, which had grown in number from about 44 in 1776 to 100 in 1790 to 201 in 1800.[46] It may be that, all told, as many people in the United States read *Rights of Man* as read *Common Sense;* certainly as many knew about it.

The *Age of Reason*, by way of comparison, followed from 1794 to 1796 with eighteen American printings in five cities, seven of them in New York sponsored by John Fellows, an active deist. Isaiah Thomas, ever attuned to what would sell, whether it was *Mother Goose* or *Fanny Hill*, brought out two printings in Worcester, in central Massachusetts, perhaps not as solidly Congregational and Baptist as we have thought. In the 1790s, *Age of Reason* probably did not match *Rights of Man* in number of copies, although, if the number of titles published in opposition is any measure, it stirred up more passionate responses, pro and con.[47]

Measuring the impact of *Rights of Man* is difficult. The population was larger than in 1776–four million people in 1790, five million in 1800. Unlike *Common Sense*, *Rights of Man* was not focused on a single goal like independence, and it circulated over a longer period of time, from 1791 to the late 1790s. It therefore lacked the immediacy of the 1776 publication. It began as a cause célèbre as a result of the brouhaha over the first printing of Part I in Philadelphia. Madison had sent Jefferson his copy, one of the first to arrive from England; Jefferson by agreement sent it to Samuel Harrison Smith, a Philadelphia printer, with a note he claimed he did not intend for publication which Smith ran as a preface: "I am extremely pleased to find it will be reprinted here, and that something is at length to be publicly said against the political heresies which have sprung up among us. I have no doubt our citizens will rally a second time round the standard of Common Sense."[48] Jefferson of course had John Adams in mind. Adams obligingly put the shoe on. "I detest that book and its tendency from the bottom of my heart," he wrote privately in 1791. Staying his pen, the vice president allowed his son, John Quincy Adams, to take on Paine, writing as "Publicola" (which everyone took to be John Adams anyway).[49] Republican writers took up the gauntlet, and the controversy was hot and heavy in the newspapers in 1791–92. It was as if all the characters in the political play had taken their assigned parts, dramatizing the issues Paine was discussing. In 1791, shortly after Part I appeared, Jefferson, the Secretary of State, wrote enthusiasticly to Paine that it was "much read here with avidity and pleasure," but his frame of reference was Philadelphia, the capital.[50] Moreover, it is not possible to match this with similar anecdotal comment for the rest of the decade. *Rights of Man* did not produce an epiphany in readers, as had *Common Sense* and as would *Age of Reason*.

There are, however, several measures of its impact. One lies in the toasts that became a common feature of political celebrations of independence on July 4 or of victories of the French Revolution. Toasts in New York City may well be representative. The Tammany Society—a fraternal order with an aura of liberalism, not yet a party appendage—toasted "The Clarion of Freedom—Thomas Paine" in mid-July 1792, and in December, "The Citizen of the World, Thomas Paine." The General Society of Mechanics and Tradesmen lifted a glass to "The mechanic, Thomas Paine." On July 4, 1795, the mechanics, Tammany, and the Democratic societies in a joint celebration sang a song, "The Rights of Man," which dwelled on Paine's theme, the nexus of aristocracy to taxes:

> Luxurious pomp, which brings taxes and woes
> No more we'll maintain with the sweat of our brows.

It ended with:

> To conclude—Here's success to Honest TOM PAINE
> May he live to enjoy what he well does explain.

After 1795, the toasts to Paine faded. A toast from the Patriotic Junior Association in 1797—"Thomas Paine: May his Rights of Man be handed down to our latest posterity but may his Age of Reason never live to see the rising generation"—suggests that among Republicans, a process of disassociation from deism was under way.[51]

A second measure of the influence of the pamphlet is the use of the phrase "the rights of man." On July Fourth celebrations, which were rapidly becoming Democratic Republican festivals, invariably there was a toast to the "The Rights of Man," but the reference, I think, was less to Paine's book than to the concept which Paine's title unquestionably had popularized. In the 1760s and 1770s Americans defended their "liberties" or their "rights as Englishmen," and in the Declaration of Independence their natural rights. The phrase "rights of man" does not seem to have entered the American political vocabulary until the 1790s, a change which has eluded a generation of scholars preoccupied with the language of republicanism.[52]

Finally, the rhetoric of the Democratic Republican societies, which lasted to about 1797, is a token of Paine's influence. The largest and most influential clubs were in the cities, where their membership was drawn overwhelmingly from mechanics and tradesmen but included merchants, doctors, and lawyers. But they were also in country towns, some four in Vermont, several in New York State, two on the Pennsylvania frontier, three in Kentucky, five in South Carolina. They did not owe their founding, as Federalists charged, to Paine or Citizen Genet, the French minister.

Yet as one reads through their numerous manifestoes and resolutions, it is impossible not to feel that these were the work of writers who had read Paine, their "lodestar" in the eyes of a modern historian of the societies. And one can say as much for the more numerous Independence Day orations given under Republican auspices.[53]

A comparison of the response to *Rights of Man* in the United States to Great Britain sets off the limits of the American reception. The pamphlet almost did for the British what *Common Sense* had done for Americans in 1776. In the 1790s, we have it on the commanding authority of E. P. Thompson, "something like an 'English Revolution' took place," in which Paine's works played a decisive role. Edmund Burke's *Reflections on the French Revolution* (1790) sold an estimated thirty thousand copies over two years. *Rights of Man*, Part I, sold fifty thousand copies in 1791, and by 1793 parts I and II together, Thompson is convinced, sold two hundred thousand copies in England, Wales, and Scotland. In a population of ten million, this was "in a true sense phenomenal." Part I was priced at three shillings, but Part II was six pence, making it unusually cheap. Thompson is not alone among scholars in these claims. By 1802 Paine claimed a circulation of four to five hundred thousand copies.[54]

The pamphlet reached deep into the laboring classes. One could not write for the United States a paragraph comparable to Thompson's summary for England:

> In Sheffield it was said that "every cutler" had a copy. At Newcastle, Paine's publications were said to be "in a almost every hand" and in particular those of the journeymen potters: "more than two thirds of this populous neighborhood are ripe for revolt, especially the lower class inhabitants." Paine's book was found in Cornish tin-mines, in Mendip villages, in the Scottish highlands, and a little later in most parts of Ireland.... The book, wrote an English correspondent, "is now made as much a standard book in this country as Robinson Crusoe & the Pilgrim's Progress."

Small wonder, then, that a frightened government indicted Paine for sedition and after he fled to France tried him in absentia and found him guilty. The movement for radical reform was suppressed, but in the nineteenth century the book became, in Thompson's words, "a foundation-text of the British working-class movement."[55]

Thus by comparison, the influence of *Rights of Man* in America, it could be argued, was neither as widespread nor as intense as in the British Isles. Nor, insofar as we can tell, did it sink roots as deeply among the laboring classes and the poor. Rather it percolated over a period of years through a democratic movement largely of the middling sort, helping to set its tone. It also won readers among women who found that Mary Wollstonecraft's *Vindication of the Rights of Women* (1791) "speaks my mind," as Elizabeth Drinker confided to her diary. In the 1790s, Paine was simply not as much of a hero in America as he was in Britain or as he had been in America in the Revolution. Moreover, in Britain he was the target of vicious attacks—scurrilous biographies, countertracts (historians have counted some four hundred to five hundred titles), and cartoon caricatures—which made their way to the United States and were replenished by poison-pen journalists like William Cobbett, then in his arch-Tory phase in Philadelphia. In fact, Tom Paine was on the way to becoming an antihero. From the mid-1790s on, his enemies tarred him with the excesses of the French Revolution, even though as a member of the French Convention he had opposed the execution of the king and had been imprisoned for almost a year under the Reign of Terror. In 1796, he had made the political blunder of writing a pamphlet blaming the heroic Washington for his long incarceration (when in reality Gouverneur Morris, the American minister to France was to blame). And a barrage of tracts answering the *Age of Reason* branded him as an "atheist" and an "infidel." Taken together, all of this helps to explain why, despite the success of *Rights of Man*, he failed to consolidate his earlier reputation.[56]

IV

Let me return now to the hypotheses I suggested to explain the eclipse of Paine in the United States between 1802 and 1809.

First, the question of Paine's deism. When Paine, at age sixty-five, returned to the United States in 1802 after a fifteen-year absence, he was greeted with a wave of abuse in which the dominant theme was religious blended with an attack on his private moral character. He was, to take the epithets only from the most genteel Federalist papers, "a lying, drunken, brutal infidel," "the loathsome Thomas Paine, a drunken atheist," "an obscene old sinner"; he was "godless," "impious," "a blasphemer."[57]

This attack on Paine caught on among ordinary people. In Washington, D.C., inn keepers refused to put Paine up, and he finally entered a hotel under an assumed name. At Trenton, one stagecoach driver refused to carry him to New York: "I'll be damned if he shall go on my stage." And

Pull away Pull away my Son dont fear I'll give you all my assistance
Oh! I fear it is stronger than I expected but rooted with the assistance of my old Friend & a little more Brandy I will bring it down
FED^L
GOVR^NT
G.WAS
J.ADA
Letters to the Citizens of
Brandy

MAD TOM in A RAGE

In this hostile cartoon, "Mad Tom in a Rage," Thomas Paine is depicted as trying to pull down the federal government built by Presidents George Washington and John Adams. The eagle screams at him while the devil offers him "all my assistance." Paine avows that with "a little more brandy I will bring it down," a bottle marked "Brandy" at his feet. The cartoon probably appeared around 1800, when the conservative Federalist depiction of Paine as a drunkard and disorganizer was under way. Courtesy of the American Philosophical Society.

another refused, saying, "My stage and horses were once struck by lightning, and I don't want them to suffer again." A preacher who visited Paine in New York was disciplined by his church. In New Rochelle mothers warned their children to stay away from Paine—he was a bad man. Paine, in short, was demonized. In New York City he was at first honored by a small testimonial dinner and Republican papers ran his articles, but over the years he had a dwindling circle of admirers confined to deists, "old Jacks" (Jacobins) from the British Isles, and mechanics.[58]

Given the long history of political opposition to Paine, the *Age of Reason* was a godsend to his enemies, to use a phrase that would not have found favor with Paine. There is much to the Republican claim that the attack on him was political. Paine got the nub of it in a letter to Samuel Adams in 1803. "All this war whoop of the pulpit has some concealed object. Religion is not the cause but is the stalking horse. They put it forward to conceal themselves behind it."[59] As William Duane, the Paineite editor of the *Philadelphia Aurora*, put it, "It is not Thomas Paine's want of *religion* but his *want of faith* in kings and priests that has made him the object of Tory detestation" (1801). "His religious sentiments have been denounced for political purposes and nothing else" (1803). John Adams offered a backhanded confirmation. "His political writings," he wrote in 1810, "I am singular to believe, have done more harm than his irreligious ones. He understands neither government nor religion."[60]

While the antagonism of orthodox religion to deism was widespread and intense, we should not exaggerate it. In the making of the American Revolution, at key moments there had been an alliance of evangelicals and deists. The Philadelphia radical democrats drew from both groups. Even in Boston, Samuel Adams, the Puritan politician, protected his deist lieutenant, Dr. Thomas Young, from the wrath of church deacons. Earlier, Young had been tried for blasphemy in New York; his book *Reason the Only Oracle of Man*, written in collaboration with Ethan Allen, would be published under Allen's name in 1784. Allen himself was the leader of a movement of Congregationalist and Baptist settlers of Vermont, the Green Mountain Boys, who shared with him a common hatred of New York's land-engrossing aristocrats.[61] And in Virginia, Jefferson, the gentleman deist, and Madison formed an alliance with the state's dissenting Protestant denominations in their common cause of separating church and state, which led in 1786 to Virginia's famous Statute for Religious Liberty. Baptists elsewhere remembered this when they voted for Jefferson. After 1801, Baptist farmers in Cheshire, Massachusetts, paid homage to their benefactor by sending a mammoth four-hundred-pound cheese to him at the White House.[62]

Paine was aware of the common stake of deists and evangelicals in religious liberty. In the election campaign for Jefferson in the fall of 1804, in the sleepy fishing village of Stonington, Connecticut, Paine was visited by a group of Baptists who included three ministers. As he reported the conversation to Jefferson, one of them said,

> They cry out against Mr Jefferson because they say he is a Deist. Well a Deist may be a good man, and if he think it right it is right to him. For my own part, [said he] I had rather vote for a Deist than a blue-skin presbyterian [a reference to the rigid Connecticut blue laws].[63]
>
> You judge right, [said I] for a man that is not of any of the sectaries will hold the balance between all; but give power to a bigot of any sectary and he will use it to the oppression of the rest, as the blue skins do in Connecticut.

Equally important, there was a species of evangelicals, unappreciated by scholars, who blended the Bible with Paine. Thompson has called attention to them: in Wales, for example, there were "itinerant Methodist preachers who descant on the Rights of Man and attack Kingly government." Nathan Hatch has found them to be prominent in the United States. Lorenzo Dow, the Methodist circuit rider who, according to Hatch, "preached to more people, travelled more miles, and consistently attracted larger audiences to camp meetings than any preacher in his day ... could begin a sermon by quoting Tom Paine." Dow wrote a pamphlet, *Analects upon the Rights of Man*, which breathed Paine's egalitarianism. The two shared a "deep-seated aversion to traditional inquiry."[64]

But despite these cracks in the orthodox world, the religious issue functioned to silence the Jeffersonians on Paine. True believers among them, like Samuel Adams, were hostile. Unitarian Jeffersonians, like Joseph Priestly, wanted to disassociate their religious liberalism from radical deism. Others were unwilling either to come out of the closet with their deism or to take a stand on the principle that religion was a matter of private opinion. Jeffersonian politicians, fearful of losing their constituents, were scared off.[65]

Second among the hypotheses is the role played by the loss of historical memory. The fading of Paine's achievements in the Revolution in the public mind made possible the success of the attack that isolated him. This was part of the larger difficulty of passing on the historical experience of one generation to another, a problem which shocked the aging leaders of the revolutionary generation early in the nineteenth century no less than succeeding generations. Paine put his finger on it in 1806 after he suffered the humiliation of the election inspectors in New Rochelle denying him the right to vote on the grounds (inspired by Gouverneur Morris, his old nemesis) that he was no longer an American citizen because he had served in the French legislature. From New York City Paine beseeched Vice President George Clinton for support.

> As it is a new generation that has risen up since the declaration of independence, they know nothing of what the political state of the country was at the time the pamphlet Common Sense appeared; and besides this there are but few of the old standers left and known that I know of in this city.[66]

There were as yet few historians of the Revolution, and they were not widely read. Even the Republican Mercy Otis Warren, whose three-volume history of the Revolution appeared in 1806, found no room for Paine (or the efforts of Abigail Adams or other women). In 1784 Congress had dangled the job of "Historiographer of the American Revolution" before Paine in lieu of settling his claims, but when Paine rejected the idea, it made no effort to find someone else for the job. The institutions that pass on official heritage, historical societies and museums, were in their infancy, and those in the making were under the auspices of conservative gentlemen. Fourth of July orators who celebrated the Revolution passed on historical abstractions.[67] The tens of thousands of war veterans passed on largely their personal military experiences by oral transmission.[68]

The problem was not confined to radical democrats. In 1809, the year Paine died, a conservative republican like John Adams complained bitterly of "a very extraordinary and unaccountable inattention in our countrymen to the History of their own country." The "original historians" of colonial times were "very much neglected," patriots like Samuel Adams and John Hancock were "almost buried in oblivion," and the newspapers were full of "falsehoods."[69] Adams, of course, was especially jealous of his own place in history, overshadowed as he had always been by such great men as Washington and Franklin, and defeated in public opinion by men like Jefferson and Paine. In general, most of the men whose chief claim to fame lay in the making of the Revolution before 1776—Samuel Adams, Patrick Henry, even John Adams (to Jefferson "the Atlas of American independence")—were being cast aside in favor of George Washington, the father of his country who filled a need for a symbol of nationalism. Parson Weems's life of Washington, replete with its numerous fabricated cherry-tree stories, was on the way to becoming the best selling historical work of the nineteenth century.[70]

Finally, Paine, it could be argued, as have Robert R. Palmer and others, was the victim of the success of his political ideas. Paine's ideological targets had been defeated. There was never a serious prospect of monarchy in America. As Paine put it, "If I ask a man in America if he wants a king, he retorts, and asks me if I take him for an idiot."[71] The idea of a hereditary aristocracy never took root; witness the fate of the Society of Cincinnati. In 1799, Matthew Lyon, the Vermont Republican congressman, was found guilty under the Sedition Law for assailing John Adams for "his unbounded thirst for ridiculous pomp," but his constituents reelected him to Congress from jail while Adams was retired to private life.[72] In 1801 the coercive school of American conservatism was defeated, and Jefferson, and Madison, the accommodators, took over. Out of power, Hamilton reflected ruefully to Gouverneur Morris, "This American world was not made for me." And Morris could have said the same. They had learned neither to swim with the tide nor scotch the snake of democratic opinion.[73]

It was not that the principles of *Rights of Man* were irrelevant. The Jacobin refugees from British persecution who established themselves as Jeffersonian editors and politicians in American cities took up a variety of causes: expanding suffrage, making more offices elective, democratizing state constitutions, reforming the judicial system, eliminating English common law, and expanding education. Paine dabbled in these issues in his last years, but they did not sustain his attention.[74] Nor did the issue of slavery, which he had found compelling when he first came to the country. He wrote against retaining slavery in the Louisiana territory and wanted Jefferson to abandon his fearful policy of refusing admission to fugitives from Saint-Domingue, but he was silent on slavery in the South. Nor did he return to the "rights of women," which he spoke for in his first year in America in 1775. Had not the core of his ideas triumphed?[75]

In the United states, neither Paine nor the middle-class bearers of his eighteenth-century radicalism were prepared to extend the principles of chapter 5 of the second part of the *Rights of Man* or of *Agrarian Justice* (1797) to do battle with poverty. The cause of poverty to Paine lay in corrupt governments' redistributing the "fruits of labor" of the common people via unjust taxes. In the first decade of the nineteenth century, neither Paine nor the Jeffersonians were willing to take up the cause of journeymen shoemakers as they went out on strike in one city after another against a poverty created by master artisans, much less the cause of women workers in city sweatshops or of women and children in the first textile mills of New England. There was a mote of utopian optimism in Paine's aging eyes that seems to have blinded him to the harshest realities of American life. Very soon, others would take up these causes, many of them inspired by Paine's republicanism.[76]

For all of Paine's fading from public favor in his last years, there is a truth to an observation by John Adams about his *long-term* influence. Adams, Paine's lifelong foe, is at first blush an unlikely witness to testify about Thomas Paine. Paine was Adams's nemesis in 1776, in 1791, and again in 1801, his ideas contributing to Adams's defeat by Jefferson. Adams's judgment was not always reliable; he often resorted to hyperbole and he clearly could be vitriolic, but over the decades he had calibrated Paine's influence the way a seismograph tracks an earthquake.

In 1805, a friend had written Adams using the phrase "the Age of Reason" to refer to the era of the American and French Revolutions. Adams was besides himself: "Call it the Age of Folly, Vice, Frenzy, Fury, Brutality ... or the age of the burning brand from the bottomless Pitt ... anything but the age of Reason." Then he made a quick leap.

> I know not whether any man in the world has had more influence on its inhabitants or affairs for the last thirty years [1776–1805] than Tom Paine. There can be no severer satyr [satire?] on the age. For such a mongrel between pigs and puppy, begotten by a wild boar on a bitch wolf, never before in any age of the world was suffered by the Poltroonery of Mankind to run through such a career of mischief. Call it then the Age of Paine.[77]

NOTES

This essay appeared in a festschrift for Robert S. Cohen, Professor of Physics and Philosophy at Boston University, edited by Kostas Gavroglu, John Stachel, and Marx W. Wartofsky, *Science, Mind, and Art*, 2 vols. (Dordrecht, the Netherlands: Kluwer Academic Publishers, 1995). It is reprinted with permission of Kluwer Academic Publishers.

An earlier version was given in New Rochelle, New York, in 1991 at a conference sponsored by the Thomas Paine National Historical Association on the two hundredth anniversary of the publication of the *Rights of Man*. For valuable criticisms, my thanks go to Marcus Daniel, Simon Newman, Richard Twomey, and David Wilson. For suggestions, I am indebted to librarians John Aubrey and James Green and to David Henly, Elizabeth Reilly, and Sean Wilentz.

1. Cited in Alfred Owen Aldridge, *Man of Reason: The Life of Thomas Paine* (Philadelphia, 1959), 316.

2. For the funeral and response to Paine's death, Moncure Daniel Conway, *The Life of Thomas Paine*, 2 vols. (New York, 1892; 1 vol. ed, New York, 1969), 322–324; David Freeman Hawke, *Paine* (New York, 1974), 399–401.

3. "The Will of Thomas Paine," in Philip S. Foner (ed.), *The Complete Writings of Thomas Paine*, 2 vols. (New York, 1945), 1498, paged continuously.

4. For Paine's account of his services, "Petition to a Committee of the Continental Congress [October, 1783]," in Foner (ed.), *Complete Writings*, 1226–1242, and Paine to Robert Morris, May 19, 1783, in Elizabeth Nuxoll and Mary Gallagher (eds.), *The Papers of Robert Morris*, 9 vols. (Pittsburgh, 1973–99), 8:95–102.

5. For summaries: John Bach McMaster, *A History of the People of the United States* (New York, 1896), 1:75, 153–154; Hawke, *Paine*, 138–140, 142–148; Conway, *Life of Paine*, 80–86; Aldridge, *Man of Reason*, 97–98, 101–104; for contemporary recognition of Paine's services to the Revolution, Eric Foner, "The Preeminent Historical and Lasting Significance of Thomas Paine to the Nation" (Washington, D.C., April 11, 1994, ms. testimony before National Capitol Memorial Commission, for which I provided research); for later recognition, see Joseph N. Moreau (comp.), *Testimonials to the Merit of Thomas Paine* (Boston, 1874).

6. For the attack on Paine, see sec. IV; for deism: G. Adolf Koch, *Republican Religion: The American Revolution and the Cult of Reason* (New York, 1933); Herbert M. Morais, *Deism in Eighteenth-Century America* (New York, 1934).

7. For various interpretations of the problem of Paine's reputation: Dixon Wecter, "Hero in Reverse," *Virginia Quarterly Review* 28 (1942), 234–259; Aldridge, *Man of Reason*, 317–322; Conway, *Life of Paine*, 279–317; Eric Foner, *Tom Paine and Revolutionary American* (New York, 1976), 261–270; Gregory Claeys, *Thomas Paine: Social and Political Thought* (Boston, 1989), 209–217.

8. Robert R. Palmer, "Tom Paine, Victim of the Rights of Man," *Pennsylvania Magazine of History and Biography* 66 (1942), 161–175.

9. "To the Citizens of the United States," Letter 1, November 15, 1802, in P. Foner (ed.), *Complete Writings*, 910.

10. Paine, *Common Sense*, in P. Foner (ed.), *Complete Writings*, 16.

11. Ibid., 14.

12. Ibid., 45; for analysis of the rhetorical qualities of *Common Sense*: E. Foner, *Tom Paine*, 74–87; Harry Hayden Clark (ed.), *Thomas Paine: Representative Writings* (New York, 1961, rev. ed.), introduction, part 6; David A. Wilson, *Paine and Cobbett: The Transatlantic Connection* (Kingston, Can., 1988), 48–56.

13. Paine to Henry Laurens, January 14, 1779, in P. Foner (ed.), *Complete Writings*, 1160–1165, gives the printing history and his claim, "not short of 150,000." For women readers, see n. 28.

14. For his 1792 claim of "not less than one hundred thousand copies," P. Foner (ed.), *Complete Writings*, 406, n. 29. In Philadelphia Paine had supervised a printing

of six thousand copies with two printers; he may have projected his total from estimates of the size of runs multiplied by the number of printings in other cities he heard about.

15. For a recent discussion of circulation, Alfred Owen Aldridge, *Thomas Paine's American Ideology* (Newark, N.J., 1984), 45; for comparative data on length and costs of books, Elizabeth Reilly, "Common and Learned Readers: Shared and Separate Spheres in Mid-Eighteenth-Century New England" (Ph.D. diss., Boston University, 1994), ch.4.

16. Richard Gimbel, *A Bibliographic Checklist of Common Sense* (New Haven, 1956); Thomas R. Adams, *American Independence, the Growth of an Idea: A Bibliographical Study of the American Political Pamphlets between 1764 and 1776 Dealing with the Dispute between Great Britain and Her Colonies* (Providence, 1965), with a supplement, *Papers of the American Bibliographical Society of America* 69 (1975), 398–402. Adams lists twenty-five "editions" of *Common Sense*; I prefer "printing." Paine added to the original work, allowing us to speak of three editions, but each printing was not a new "edition."

17. Paine, "The Forester's Letters," in P. Foner (ed.), *Complete Writings*, 67.

18. Bernard Bailyn, *Ideological Origins of the American Revolution* (Cambridge, Mass., 1964). Bailyn considered *Common Sense* "a superbly rhetorical and iconoclastic pamphlet," citing Harold Laski that Paine "with the exception of Marx was 'the most influential pamphleteer of all time'"; for Bailyn's later interpretation, Bailyn, "Common Sense," *American Heritage* 25 (1973), reprinted in Bailyn, *Faces of Revolution: Personalities and Themes in the Struggle for American Independence* (New York, 1990).

19. For the context of printers: G. Thomas Tanselle, "Some Statistics on American Printing, 1764–1783," in Bernard Bailyn and John B. Hench (eds.), *The Press and the American Revolution* (Boston, 1981), 315–372; for colonial book distribution and readership, Reilly, "Common and Learned Readers," ch. 4.

20. Letter from Philadelphia, April 4, 1776, in Margaret W. Willard (ed.), *Letters on the American Revolution, 1774–1776* (Boston, 1925), 390–391; Washington cited in Hawke, *Paine*, 47; for other contemporary opinion, Merrill Jensen, *The Founding of a Nation: A History of the American Revolution, 1763–1776* (New York, 1968), 669. For the fullest summary of contemporary responses, see Arnold King, "Thomas Paine in America, 1774–1787" (Ph.D. diss., University of Chicago, 1951), 72–86.

21. Reilly, "Common and Learned Readers," ch. 4; Jackson Turner Main, *The Social Structure of Revolutionary America* (Princeton, N.J., 1965), ch. 8; Billy Smith, *"The Lower Sort": Philadelphia's Laboring People, 1750–1800* (Ithaca, N.Y., 1990).

22. Aldridge, *Paine's American Ideology*, 45, citing Brissot de Warville, *Memoires* (Paris, 1830–1832) 3: 65.

23. James Cogswell to Joseph Ward, March 5, 1776, Ward Papers, Chicago Historical Society, reprinted in Alfred Young, Terry Fife, and Mary Janzen, *We the*

People: Voices and Images of the New Nation (Philadelphia, 1993), 51; Extracts of a Letter from New York City, April 12, 1776, in Willard, (ed.), *Letters on the American Revolution*, 306; for the outmoded historical interpretation of Paine as a "propagandist" and "manipulator of opinion," Philip Davidson, *Propaganda and the American Revolution, 1763–1783* (Chapel Hill, N.C., 1941), 13–14, 349.

24. David Ramsay, *History of the American Revolution*, 2 vols. (Philadelphia, 1789), 1:338–339; Joseph Hawley cited in E. Foner, *Tom Paine*, 86; *The Life of Ashbel Green* (New York, 1849), 46. In the 1840s, Green, a Presbyterian minister and no friend of Paine's writings, wrote, "I think this pamphlet had a greater run than any other ever published in our country." He remembered it advertised for eighteen pence.

25. John Adams to Benjamin Rush, May 21, 1807, in John Schutz and Douglass Adair (eds.), *The Spur of Fame: Dialogues of John Adams and Benjamin Rush, 1805–1813* (San Marino, Calif., 1966), 88; Page Smith, *John Adams*, 2 vols. (Garden City, N.Y., 1962), 1:239–240.

26. L. H. Butterfield (ed.), *Diary and Autobiography of John Adams*, 4 vols. (Cambridge, Mass., 1961), 3:330–341.

27. Smith, *John Adams* 1:243–249; Elisha Douglass, *Rebels and Democrats: The Struggle for Equal Political Rights and Majority Rule during the American Revolution* (Chapel Hill, N.C., 1955), chs. 9–11 (Massachusetts) and chs. 12–14 (Pennsylvania); Merrill Jensen, *The American Revolution within America* (New York, 1974), ch. 2.

28. Abigail Adams to John Adams, March 31, 1776; John Adams to Abigail Adams, April 17, 1776; Abigail Adams to Mercy Otis Warren, April 27, 1776, all in L. H. Butterfield (ed.), *Adams Family Correspondence* (Cambridge, Mass., 1963), 369–371, 381–383, 396–398; Peter Wood, "'Liberty Is Sweet': African-American Freedom Struggles in the Years before White Independence," in Alfred Young (ed.), *Beyond the American Revolution: Explorations in the History of American Radicalism* (DeKalb, Ill., 1994), 149–184; W. J. Rorabaugh, "'I Thought I Should Liberate Myself from the Thraldom of Others': Apprentices, Masters and the Revolution," ibid., 185–217.

29. John Adams to Thomas Jefferson, June 22, 1819, in Lester J. Cappon (ed.), *The Adams-Jefferson Letters*, 2 vols. (Chapel Hill, N.C., 1959), 2:542.

30. Paine, *Rights of Man* and *Rights of Man, Part Second*, in P. Foner (ed.), *Complete Writings*, 243–344, 345–462; for an accessible modern reprint, Michael Foot and Isaac Kramnick (eds.), *Thomas Paine Reader* (New York, 1987), and Eric Foner (ed.), *Thomas Paine: Collected Writings* (New York, 1995), in the Library of America.

31. Robert R. Livingston to William Duer, June 12, 1777, and Governeur Morris to John Penn May 20, 1774, both cited in Alfred F. Young, *The Democratic Republicans of New York, 1763–1797* (Chapel Hill, N.C., 1967), 12, 15; Gouverneur Morris cited in P. Foner (ed.), introduction to *Complete Writings*, xviii.

32. I have elaborated this interpretation in essay 4 in this volume and in "The

Framers of the Constitution and the 'Genius of the People,'" *Radical History Review* 42 (1988), with commentary by others, 7–47.

33. Smith, *John Adams* 2:749–760; Kenneth R. Bowling and Helen Veit (eds.), *The Diary of William Maclay* (Baltimore, 1988).

34. John R. Nelson, *Liberty and Property: Political Economy and Policymaking in the New Nation, 1789–1812* (Baltimore, 1987), chs. 2–4; Michael Merrill and Sean Wilentz (eds.), *The Key of Liberty: The Life and Democratic Writings of William Manning, "A Laborer"* (Cambridge, Mass., 1993).

35. Young, *Democratic Republicans*, chs. 16–20; Eugene Perry Link, *Democratic-Republican Societies, 1790–1800* (New York, 1942); Joyce Appleby, *Capitalism and a New Social Order: The Republican Vision of the 1790s* (New York, 1984).

36. Thomas Slaughter, *The Whiskey Rebellion: Frontier Epilogue to the American Revolution* (New York, 1986); James Morton Smith, *Freedom's Fetters: The Alien and Sedition Laws and American Civil Liberties* (Ithaca, N.Y., 1966); Leonard W. Levy, *The Emergence of a Free Press* (New York, 1985).

37. Paine, *Rights of Man*, in P. Foner, (ed.), *Complete Writings*, 1:326–327.

38. Ibid., 287.

39. Ibid., 366.

40. Ibid., 360.

41. Ibid., Part II, ch. 5, quotations at 404, 405; see also 431.

42. On American poverty, Lee Soltow, *The Distribution of Wealth and Income in the United States in 1798* (Pittsburgh, 1989); John Resch, *Suffering Soldiers: Revolutionary War Veterans, Moral Sentiment, and Political Culture in the Early Republic* (Amherst, Mass., 1999).

43. Paine, *Rights of Man*, in P. Foner (ed.), *Complete Writings*, 344, 446.

44. Stephen Botein, "'Meer Mechanics' and an Open Press: The Business and Political Strategies of Colonial American Printers," *Perspectives in American History* 9 (1975), 127–225; Isaiah Thomas, *The History of Printing in America* (Albany, N.Y., 1874, 2nd ed.; reprint, New York, 1970).

45. Charles Evans (comp.), *American Bibliography: A Chronological Dictionary of All Books, Pamphlets, and Periodical Publications Printed in the United States of America ... 1630 ... to ... 1820*, reprint, ed., 12 vols. (New York, 1941–42); vol. 13 by Clifford Shipton; vol. 14, *Index*, by Roger P. Bristol (Worcester, Mass., 1959); Clifford K. Shipton and James E. Mooney, *National Index of Early American Imprints through 1800: The Short-Title Evans*, 2 vols. (Worcester, Mass., 1969). With the assistance of John Aubrey, reference librarian at the Newberry Library, I conducted a search for *Rights of Man* in several recently available electronic catalogs, comparing these entries to the standard printed guides. This search has not located any significant number of additional printings to alter the pattern I have outlined.

46. For the circulation of printed material in the new nation: Cathy Davidson, *Revolution and the Word: The Rise of the Novel in America* (New York, 1986), ch. 2;

William J. Gilmore, *Reading Becomes a Necessity of Life: Material and Cultural Life in Rural New England, 1780–1835* (Knoxville, Tenn., 1989), chs. 5, 6; for newspapers, Donald H. Stewart, *The Opposition Press of the Federalist Period* (Albany, N.Y., 1969), and Michael Durey, "Thomas Paine's Apostles: Radical Émigrés and the Triumph of Jeffersonian Republicanism," *William and Mary Quarterly*, 3d ser., 44 (1987), 661–688. James Green, curator of the Library Company of Philadelphia, estimates a run of one thousand for each American printing, two thousand for the collected edition, and that British booksellers "flooded" the American market after 1793 with copies banned in the British Isles (letter to author, March 6, 11, 1992).

47. I have used the finding aids listed in note 45; for *Age of Reason*, P. Foner (ed.), *Complete Writings*, 463–604, available in many modern printings; Conway, *Life of Paine*, ch. 35; Claeys, *Thomas Paine*, ch. 7.

48. Thomas Jefferson to George Washington, May 8, 1791; Jefferson to James Madison, May 4, 1791; Jefferson to James Monroe, July 10, 1791, 911 in Paul L. Ford (ed.), *The Works of Thomas Jefferson* (New York, 1904), 6:254–256, 257–258, 280–281; Jefferson, preface to *Rights of Man*, ibid., 283.

49. Smith, *John Adams* 2:815–825.

50. Dumas Malone, *Jefferson and the Rights of Man* (Boston, 1951), ch. 21.

51. Young, *Democratic Republicans*, part 4, passim; Simon Newman has provided additional toasts from other cities which thus far support the pattern I have suggested.

52. Edward Countryman, "'To Secure the Blessings of Liberty': Language, the Revolution and American Capitalism," in Young (ed.), *Beyond the American Revolution*, 123–148; Gordon Wood, *The Creation of the Republic, 1776–1787* (Chapel Hill, N.C., 1969).

53. Philip S. Foner (ed.), *The Democratic Republican Societies, 1790–1800: A Documentary Sourcebook of Constitutions, Declarations, Addresses, Resolutions and Toasts* (Westport, Conn., 1976), passim; Link, *Democratic-Republican Societies*, 104, 109.

54. E. P. Thompson, *The Making of the English Working Class* (London, 1963; New York, 1966), 107–108. According to Thompson, in 1802, Paine claimed four hundred thousand to five hundred thousand copies for the British Isles, including Ireland, and in 1809, 1.5 million "was claimed" (by whom is not clear). R. R. Palmer, *Age of the Democratic Revolution*, 2 vols. (New York, 1959–1964) 2:476, accepts two hundred thousand and mentions 1.5 million as "unbelievable." For the impact, see, among others, Albert Goodwin, *The Friends of Liberty: The English Democratic Movement in the Age of the French Revolution* (London, 1979), 208–258; and Claeys, *Thomas Paine*, ch. 5.

55. Thompson, *Making*, 108, 90 (foundation-text).

56. Elizabeth Drinker cited in Linda Kerber, *Women of the Republic: Intellect and Ideology in Revolutionary America* (Chapel Hill, N.C., 1980), 223–224; Drinker

read Paine and disliked him. For the campaign against Paine in the 1790s: Hawke, *Paine*, chs. 18–23; Aldrige, *Man of Reason*, chs. 14–22; Wilson, *Paine and Cobbett*, 129–135; Claeys, *Thomas Paine*, ch. 6.

57. For the abusive epithets: Jerry W. Knudson, "The Rage around Tom Paine: Newspaper Reaction of His Homecoming in 1802," *New-York Historical Society Quarterly* 53 (1969), 34–63, and Hawke, *Paine*, ch. 25; for details on Paine's personal life over the course of his life, see the numerous entries in the index to Hawke, *Paine*, under "Paine, personal life," for appearance, drinking, health, and living habits; Conway, *Life of Paine*, ch. 43, "Personal Traits." Paine drank on social occasions; he drank to prime himself when writing; he drank when he was sick and in pain, as he was after his imprisonment in France; he drank to excess when he was isolated, rejected, and lonely, as he was frequently in his last few years in New York. But he was hardly a drunkard. And his drinking was not a subject of public discussion until the political attacks of the 1790s.

58. Cited in Hawke, *Paine*, 366; Mark Lause, "The 'Unwashed Infideltiy': Thomas Paine and Early New York City Labor History," *Labor History* 27 (1986), 385–409.

59. Paine to Samuel Adams, January 1, 1803, in P. Foner (ed.), *Complete Writings*, 1436.

60. *Philadelphia Aurora*, August 3, 1801, January 11, 1803, cited in Aldridge, *Man of Reason*, 277; John Adams to Benjamin Rush, January 21, 1810, in Schutz and Adair (eds.), *Spur of Fame*, 160.

61. For Young, Pauline Maier, *The Old Revolutionaries: Political Lives in the Age of Samuel Adams* (New York, 1980), ch. 3; Michael Bellesiles, *Revolutionary Outlaws: Ethan Allen and the Struggle for Independence on the Early American Frontier* (Charlottesville, Va., 1993).

62. Dumas Malone, *Jefferson the President: First Term, 1801–1805* (Boston, 1970), 106–108.

63. Paine to Jefferson, January 25, 1805, in P. Foner (ed.), *Complete Writings*, 1459–1460.

64. Thompson, *Making*, 108; Nathan Hatch, *The Democratization of American Christianity* (New Haven, Conn., 1989), 36–37.

65. For analysis of the controversy in England, Marcus Daniel, "Reason and Revelation: Morality, Politics and Reform in the Debate on Thomas Paine's *Age of Reason*" (unpublished ms., Princeton, 1990); Claeys, *Thomas Paine*, ch. 7.

66. Paine to Vice President George Clinton, May 4, 1807, in P. Foner (ed.), *Complete Writings*, 2:1487–1488; see also Paine to Madison, May 3, 1807, and Paine to Joel Barlow, May 4, 1807, ibid., 1486–1487, 1488–1489.

67. Mercy Warren, *History of the Rise, Progress and Termination of the American Revolution*, 2 vols. (Boston, 1805); for changing popular perceptions of the Revolution, see especially Michael Kammen, *A Season of Youth: The American Revolution and the Historical Imagination* (New York, 1978); Kammen, *Mystic Chords of Memory: The Transformation of Tradition in American Culture* (New York, 1991), part 1.

68. Alfred F. Young, "George Robert Twelves Hewes (1742–1840): A Boston Shoemaker and the Memory of the American Revolution," *William and Mary Quarterly*, 3d ser., 38 (1981), 561–623; John C. Dann (ed.), *The Revolution Remembered: Eyewitness Accounts of the War for Independence* (Chicago, 1980).

69. John Adams to Joseph Ward, June 6, 1809, Ward Papers, Chicago Historical Society, reprinted in Young, Fife, and Janzen, *We the People*, 191.

70. Garry Wills, *Cincinattus: George Washington and the Enlightenment* (Garden City, N.Y., 1984).

71. Paine, *Rights of Man*, in P. Foner (ed.), *Complete Writings*, 1:326–327.

72. Aleine Austin, *Matthew Lyon: "New Man" of the Democratic Revolution, 1749–1822* (University Park, Pa., 1981), chs. 8–10.

73. Hamilton to Gouverneur Morris, February 29, 1802, in Harold C. Syrett et al. (eds.), *The Papers of Alexander Hamilton*, 27 vols. (New York, 1961–1987), 25:544–545.

74. Richard Twomey, *Jacobins and Jeffersonians: Anglo-American Radicalism in the United States, 1790–1820* (Westport, Conn., 1990); Durey, "Thomas Paine's Apostles."

75. For Paine's early writings on these themes: P. Foner (ed.), *Complete Writings*, "African Slavery in America," "A Serious Thought," and "Emancipation of Slaves," 15–22, "An Occasional Letter on the Female Sex," 134–138.

76. For the revival of Paine in the labor movement, Sean Wilentz, *Chants Democratic: New York City and the Rise of the American Working Class, 1788–1850* (New York, 1984), passim; for the boundaries of Paine's liberalism: E. Foner, *Tom Paine*, chs. 5, 6; Isaac Kramnick, *Republicanism and Bourgeois Radicalism: Political Ideology in Late Eighteenth-Century England and America* (Ithaca, N.Y., 1990), ch. 5; Harvey Kaye, *Thomas Paine and the Promise of American Life* (New York, 2005), is the fullest study of Paine's later reputation.

77. John Adams to Benjamin Waterhouse, October 29, 1805, in Adrienne Koch and William Peden (eds.), *The Selected Writings of John and John Quincy Adams* (New York, 1946), 147–148; for other letters on Paine, Adams to Benjamin Rush, April 12, 1809, and January 21, 1810, ibid., 153–157.

7

The Freedom Trail

Walking the Revolution in Boston

Given the reinterpretation of the American Revolution produced by a generation of scholars, a reassessment of the public presentation of history on Boston's venerable Freedom Trail, formed in the 1950s, is long overdue. Indeed, in 1995 a team of outside consultants commissioned by the Boston National Historical Park (BNHP), after a searching review of all facets of its operation, concluded that "the Freedom Trail as an entity has not kept pace with the richer and more inclusive stories unveiled at many of the Sites." It warned that the trail needed "to tell this more complex story [of the Revolution] or risk losing relevance." The 1995 report, with a 1996 follow-up by a set of task forces which laid out an agenda for "reinvigorating" and "revitalizing" the trail, gathers dust, and in 2000, at a conference sponsored by the National Park Service (NPS) on the occasion of the 225th anniversary of the Revolution attended by a wide range of historians associated with the new history of the Revolution and a host of Boston's keepers of the past, not a soul mentioned the report.[1]

The Freedom Trail, it needs to be said at the outset, is not a single entity under a central administration like Colonial Williamsburg or Sturbridge Village. It is in fact merely a name, adopted in 1951 to link what are now sixteen sites spread over a two-and-a-half-mile route (marked in red on the streets and sidewalks) that wends from downtown Boston in the heart of the business district, through the North End, across the Charles River to Charlestown, sites of the United States Navy Yard, the naval vessel USS *Constitution*, and the Battle of Bunker Hill monument (see map). Each site is managed by either a private association or a government agency, chief among which is BNHP, created in 1974, a unit of the NPS. About half of the sites have interpretive programs; the Park Service operates two small visitor centers and provides park rangers as guides for the minority of tourists who choose to go on guided tours. There is "minimal coordination"

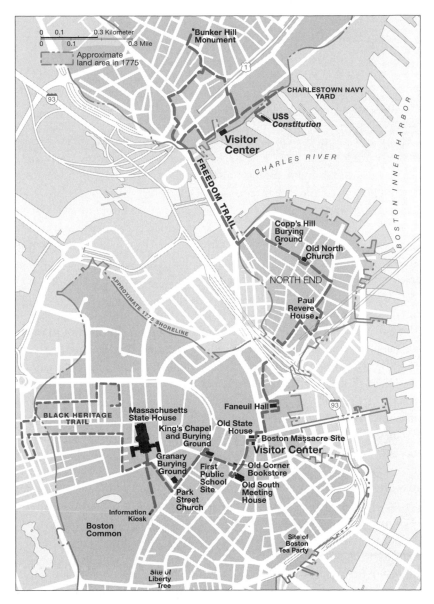

This map traces the Freedom Trail from the Boston Common (lower left), through the heart of downtown Boston, into the North End, and over the Charles River to the sites surrounding the Charlestown Navy Yard (upper right). It was prepared by a cartographer of the National Park Service, who by request of the author included the sites of the liberty tree and the tea ships, neither of which is on official maps of the trail. Reprinted from *The Public Historian* 25, no. 2, by permission of the University of California Press, © 2003 by The Regents of the University of California.

of the sites, to use the diplomatic language of the 1995 report: a Council of Sites in existence at the time is no more; the Freedom Trail Commission, a city agency, deals, in effect, with traffic on the trail and admitting new sites; and the Freedom Trail Foundation has functioned primarily as a marketing agency.[2]

This is not to imply that there is inactivity on the Freedom Trail—quite the opposite. Between 1992 and 1997, large-scale restorations were completed at the three major public buildings on the trail: Faneuil Hall, the Old State House, and, most recently, Old South Meeting House—all thanks to massive federal funding. There are new exhibits in old spaces: Voices of Protest in Old South (which includes a segment on the Tea Party) and a display on the early African American community at the restored Abiel Smith school (on the Black Heritage Trail). The Bostonian Society mounted an adventurous temporary exhibit on the Boston Massacre. Revisions of other exhibits are in progress: at the USS *Constitution* museum, depicting life at sea; at the Battle of Bunker Hill monument; and at the Boston Tea Party museum (recently the victim of a fire). Proposals have been put forth (and languish) for developing the site at the liberty tree.[3] A new trail guidebook published by NPS includes a lucid essay distilling the scholarly history of the Revolution in Boston by the historian Barbara Clark Smith, as well as a guide to the sites by Susan Wilson. NPS initiatives have produced both an eye-opening research project on people of color at the Battle of Bunker Hill and the Lexington-Concord battle road and an artists-in-residence program at Freedom Trail sites in conjunction with the Institute of Contemporary Art.[4] Meanwhile, the privately managed sites with active programs—Old South, the Bostonian Society, and the Paul Revere Memorial Association—conduct ongoing programs aimed both at general audiences and schoolchildren. There are annual reenactments of the Massacre and the Tea Party.[5]

Since the late 1990s, there has been an unprecedented ferment in public history for Boston as a whole. New "trails" have been laid out. The Black Heritage Trail (initiated in 1968) has been joined by a Boston Women's Heritage Trail; a Literary Trail of Greater Boston; a maritime trail, "Boston by Sea," a boat tour dramatizing the historic sites of Boston's harbor; and "Innovation Odyssey," a trail highlighting Boston inventions—the latter three under the aegis of the Boston History Collaborative (BHC), formed in 1996. There are guidebooks to help visitors find their way on these new trails, which, in effect, exist only on a map and in a guidebook.[6] The Collaborative, under creative leadership, has been able to tap the energies of academic historians and writers, while mobilizing business and civic support.[7] An ethnic museum has opened, and new ones are in the offing. It may be a sign of the times that it is hard to keep abreast of all that is going on in public history in Boston.

Meanwhile, there is a prospect of new public spaces for history as a result of the land reclaimed by the city's "Big Dig" operation, placing a major highway underground. There may be open land equal in size to 50 percent of the city's current parkland. This has rekindled a demand for a much-needed expanded visitor-orientation center, and for some it has raised the possibility of a major new museum with perhaps 150,000 to 200,000 square feet, which might be devoted to the three-hundred-year history of Boston as a whole. To an outsider, this ferment in Boston about telling many histories suggests an atmosphere of creative possibilities in confronting old problems with the Freedom Trail.[8]

Boston, I have discovered only recently, has not always been as committed to preserving and presenting its history. Some years ago, when I was combing the attics and archives of the Chicago Historical Society for artifacts for an exhibit on the American Revolution, I stumbled across an unpublished letter John Adams wrote in 1809 lamenting "the extraordinary and unaccountable Inattention in our countrymen to the History of their own country." Only twenty-five years after the Revolution, the former president was convinced that "our own original Historians are very much neglected" and that Samuel Adams and John Hancock were "almost buried in oblivion." He was prescient. Samuel Adams's wood-frame house disappeared in the 1820s, and the city did not get around to honoring him with a statue until 1873. In 1863, the city allowed John Hancock's magnificent stone mansion on Beacon Street to be torn down. Paul Revere's house in the North End was not rescued until 1906, despite the fame Longfellow's poem brought him.

This indifference extended to Boston's leading public buildings. In 1876, Old South Meeting House was auctioned off and was literally about to be sold for scrap when a last-ditch effort saved it. And the city was so indifferent to the Old State House that it was prepared to tear it down to improve the flow of traffic—Chicago even made an offer to move it there. These were the leading men and places of the Revolution proper. In 1888, when, after a campaign of many decades, a monument finally went up on the Common to Crispus Attucks and the other victims of the Boston Massacre, it was over the opposition of leaders of the Massachusetts Historical Society, who condemned them as a "riotous mob," the "aggressors," and "vulgar ruffians."[9]

This was part of a very old process of selective remembering and willful forgetting of the history of the Revolution in Boston. Over the past two hundred years, there has been an ongoing contest to appropriate the public memory of the American Revolution. We often assume that what is iconic today has always been so, forgetting the historian Eric Hobsbawm's provocative concept, "the invention of tradition." The destruction of the tea in 1773, for example, was virtually lost in the sixty years after the Revolution as the elites who established their cultural domination chose to erase the radical or "popular" side of the Revolution: the "mob" actions, the farmers' rebellions, the quest for equality. When the event was recovered in the 1830s, it returned as "The Boston Tea Party," a name that reduced an act of civil disobedience to a comic, frivolous, and safe event. Today, the more that keepers of the past are aware that Bostonians throughout their history have made choices as to what to remember and what to erase, the more they have a critical perspective on making their own choices.[10]

My reflections on the state of history on the Freedom Trail are made from the perspective of someone who has taken part in the emergence of the new history of the Revolution, has been in and out of the city over the past thirty years doing research on Boston, and who in recent years has had the pleasure of working with several institutions on the trail. In effect, I am an attentive outsider who has been only an occasional insider. I can still remember my first visit to a poorly marked Freedom Trail in the early 1960s, when I got lost and a gentleman in a bowler hat who saw my confusion guided me to the Revere House in the North End. I offer these reflections in a series of propositions, a term suggesting that they are tentative and therefore open for debate.[11]

PROPOSITION 1. *The new analytical framework for the history of the American Revolution has brought into sharp focus a two-way conflict: the struggle for liberty from Great Britain and the multisided struggle for liberty within America.* In the "old" history, patriotic colonists faced only one way: towards Great Britain and their Loyalist allies within America. In the new narratives, Americans more commonly face two ways: confronting Great Britain but also confronting each other. This new history has clarified the character of the Revolution for the country as a whole in three important ways. It has broadened the cast of characters who participated in the shaping of well-known events, making for a more complex version of resistance in the decade from 1765 to 1775. Because its emphasis is on ordinary people, who were often at odds with their betters, on "the people out of doors" (as opposed to people within doors in places of power), it has also "restored rebellion to the history of the Revolution," as historian Linda Kerber puts it. And in its outcome, although this more inclusive Revolution is in many ways more democratic and more radical, it is also darker. Thus the new history helps us in striking a balance between achievements and the failure to achieve the ideals of the Revolution. The Revolution fits into a long-range vision of Americans constantly enlarging and redefining freedom as an ongoing process.[12]

The picture that emerges from this scholarship is of a Revolution that lasted longer than the period of its making from 1765 to 1775 (with which a majority of sites on the Freedom Trail are associated) or with the war from 1775 to 1783 and of a Revolution that played out in the shaping of the new nation into the early nineteenth century. It is a Revolution in which the promise of the Declaration of Independence, "all men are created equal," was partly fulfilled for the majority of white men (artisans and yeoman farmers) but remained unfulfilled for women, and one in which promises were never made to African Americans or Native Americans. Although the new history presents a fractured vision of a many-sided, incomplete Revolution, in some ways it is easier to make sense of and is more consistent with our understanding of the history that followed.

When the Freedom Trail "was first set up," as the 1995 consultants report phrased it, "the nation of 1950 emerging from World War II sought consensus and saw the American Revolution through its heroes and great events." The managers of individual sites on the trail just picked their way through whatever traditional scholarship was in the air. Although the creation of BNHP in 1974 and the bicentennial celebrations kindled some rethinking, it was not until the massive restoration projects of the major buildings were under way that serious attention was given to a more comprehensive interpretation.[13]

The new narratives can no longer be contained within a traditional framework, as was attempted, for example, in the Old State House exhibit called "From Colony to Commonwealth," still the only exhibit in the city that attempts an overall narrative of the Revolution. Based on a rich array of treasures of the Bostonian Society, it is organized around five "Leading Persons," John Hancock, James Otis, John Adams, and Samuel Adams, the best-known patriot leaders, who confront Thomas Hutchinson, symbol of royal authority. The exhibit was already old hat when it was curated by NPS in collaboration with the Bostonian Society in the late 1980s, insensitive to the newer history even though such artifacts on display as the lantern and flag that hung on the liberty tree would have permitted "popular" voices to be dramatized.

If, today, you were choosing five individuals who might epitomize today's two-way vision of the Revolution, who might the candidates be? Let me, for purposes of illustration, nominate five Massachusetts residents who confronted the "Leading Persons" on the patriot side while they also confronted the British, who would be appropriate for a museum located in a building that was the center of governmental decisions.

Abigail Adams faced her husband, John, in the Continental Congress, asking him "to remember the ladies" in "the new code of laws" he was writing. "Do not put such unlimited power into the hands of the husbands," she wrote. John's putdown would be part of their dialogue. "As to your extraordinary code of laws I cannot but laugh."[14]

Ebenezer Mackintosh was a shoemaker who led the united South End and North End Companies at Boston's annual Pope's Day festivity in demonstrations against the Stamp Act. He escorted Stamp Act Commissioner designate Andrew Oliver—Thomas Hutchinson's associate—to a forced resignation at the liberty tree. Known as the "Captain General of the Liberty Tree," Mackintosh was feared by John Adams as a "Masaniello," symbol of proletarian revolt in Europe, and was shunted aside by Samuel Adams as a leader of mob actions.[15]

Prince Hall, an African American leather dresser of Boston, crafted drumheads for the patriot armies and organized the first African Masonic Lodge. A free man manumitted by his master, he confronted the Massachusetts legislature in the Old State House with angry petitions: before the war, to free the slaves; after the war, to end the trade in slaves, admit black children to the town's public schools, and then to support those free blacks who might choose to return to Africa.[16]

Elder Isaac Backus, foremost leader of New England's Baptists, traveled from his home in Middleborough to the Continental Congress in Philadelphia and embarrassed delegates John and Samuel Adams by confronting them with a plea for religious liberty from the Massachusetts Congregationalist Church establishment. He advocated nonpayment of ecclesiastical taxes or civil disobedience to win "soul liberty."[17]

Daniel Shays, a leader of the farmers of western Massachusetts, rose from private to captain in the Continental Army and fought at Bunker Hill, Saratoga, and Stoney Point. In 1774–75 farmers closed the courts in western Massachusetts. After the war, Shays joined his fellow debt-ridden farmers in closing down the courts again to prevent them from foreclosing farms and imprisoning debtors. Shays confronted Samuel Adams, the rebel against Britain who denied a right to rebel against a republic.[18]

This new history does not imply that we displace "leading persons" with "ordinary persons"; rather, it is an invitation to see leaders as many-sided. If we turn, for example, to John Adams, who at last is coming into the fame that eluded him in his lifetime, we realize how much energy this revolutionary conservative poured into containing the many radicalisms of the Revolution. Adams consistently faced two ways. As a lawyer defending the British soldiers in the Boston Massacre trial, he blamed the event on "a motley rabble of saucy boys, negroes and molattoes, Irish teagues and out landish jack tarrs." In reply to his wife's plea to "remember the ladies," Adams lamented that "we have been told that our struggle has loosened the bands of government everywhere … that Children and apprentices were grown turbulent—that Indians slighted their guardians and Negroes grew insolent to their masters." In response to Thomas Paine's irreverent, democratic *Common Sense*, Adams wrote a pamphlet advising constitution-makers how "to preserve respect for persons in authority." Later, as president, he administered the Alien and Sedition Laws under which his Jeffersonian opponents were jailed for criticizing the president. In other words, history at the top can look different when viewed from the bottom up.[19]

PROPOSITION 2. *Buildings do not "speak for themselves" or the events that took place within them. There is a question whether the Freedom Trail does justice to the "popular" side of the Revolution.* While other early American restorations at outdoor museums permit the recovery of the social history of everyday life, Boston, like Philadelphia, has intact the sites of the major public events of the Revolution. The State House was the seat of colonial government, composed of the royal governor, his appointed council, and the General Court, an assembly elected by the towns, and then from 1775 to 1798, it was the seat of the independent state government. Faneuil Hall was the place where the town meeting met and voters of small property expressed the democratic will. Old South Meeting House, the largest church in Boston, was the scene of the major protests of "the whole body of the people" at which the bars of property were let down and every Tom, Dick, and Harry turned out. Legislators contested the crown inside the State House, and citizens contested British soldiers in the square outside where the Massacre took place. The Tea Party was launched from an overflow meeting at Old South; the Declaration of Independence was read from the State House balcony.

The events that took place within are not "self-evident." There are, of course, inherent difficulties today in presenting a narrative of the Revolution in the heart of a bustling city whose steel and glass buildings overshadow the eighteenth-century sites. Granted, tourists can follow (after a fashion) the red line from site to site, but there is no narrative logic to the trail; the sites cannot be arranged in a sequence of Revolutionary events. In fact, the sites of some major events of the people "out of doors" are not even on the trail. Visitors need more help than they get in linking sites to events. Although 250,000 or so tourists a year take "trolley" tours or the very popular "duck" tours with History Lite, only about 25,000 take the thousand or so tours conducted annually by NPS rangers.[20]

The institutions in charge of the buildings struggle valiantly with interpreting to visitors the history that took place within. In some ways the unintended consequences of faithful restorations pull against the history. (The Revere House, restored early in the 1900s to its seventeenth-century state, is successfully interpreted today as the house Paul Revere lived in at the time of the Revolution). From its appearance within, you would not know that the Old State House once housed legislative chambers. In Old South Meeting House, the beauty of the restoration inspires reverence and a hushed silence appropriate to a sacred place. Faneuil Hall has been restored to its state as the building the architect Charles Bulfinch later enlarged, and an incongruous, giant painting of the famous Webster-Hayne debate at the front pulls us towards the abolitionist history of the nineteenth century. NPS guides thus have a burden of pulling visitors back to the era of the Revolution. No building tells its own story, and no one (park rangers aside) assumes the burden of drawing connections between events that took place in one building and events in another.

In their programing, the major institutions on the trail assume responsibility for missions that extend beyond the Revolution: Old South as a landmark for traditions of freedom of expression in Boston; the Bostonian Society as a museum covering the sweep of the city's history. Although the Bostonian Society plays host to an annual reenactment of the Massacre, everyday passers-by have only a brass plaque outside, which does little justice to an event that is at best difficult to explain. (People know there is something wrong with Paul Revere's version of the event in his engraving but are not sure what.) Every December Old South sponsors an annual reenactment of the debate over the tea tax, from which patriots sally forth for the tea ship. Capturing such moments for the everyday visitor, however, is daunting.[21]

Meanwhile, the two sites in Boston that epitomize the Revolution "out of doors" are orphans: the liberty tree and the Boston Tea Party. The site of the Tea Party (1773) is not on the Freedom Trail, presumably because it is managed by a profit-making entity that charges tourists to visit a reenactment of the tea action on a replica of the *Beaver* tea ship and throw a cask of tea overboard. (The official map does no more than locate the site.) The site of the liberty tree, a public center of Sons of Liberty activity in the Stamp Act protests (1765–66) and thereafter a common symbol of Revolutionary ideals, is unmarked on most maps. At the site, about five blocks from the downtown sites, there is one plaque on what was later called the Liberty Tree Building and another in the pavement across the street. Presumably it is not on the official trail because it is in a neighborhood long known as "the combat zone," at which tourists might balk. Until recently a porn store next door to the site celebrated freedom of expression with a bas-relief replica of the liberty tree.[22]

If Boston ever develops the site, how will it interpret the place where effigies of detested British officials were hung and the shoemaker Mackintosh became "Captain General of the Liberty Tree"? One park ranger told me he flinched at the prospect of hanging effigies, which could be read as championing violence. In truth, historians have contributed a great deal to setting the "mob" into perspective; the crowds of revolutionary-era Boston actually were remarkable for their relative restraint and for targeting property and symbols of authority, as opposed to persons. These are among the unmet challenges on the Freedom Trail.

PROPOSITION 3. *The issue is no longer whether to include ordinary people in public presentations of history, but how to include them. We are past the point where all we want to say is "they too were there."* The multivolume *American National Biography* (1999), with an array of 17,450 entries which includes little-known and unsung Americans never admitted to the august *Dictionary of American Biography* (1928–36), registers a sea change in the attitudes of professional historical opinion to ordinary people in history.[23] This change is also reflected in college and high school textbooks, biographies, museum exhibits, television documentaries, and the National Standards for History.[24]

I may run the risk of drawing too much from my own experiences, but for the Revolution the response among Boston's keepers of the past to my scholarship about George Robert Twelves Hewes is a case in point.[25] Hewes was a shoemaker, a poor man in one of Boston's "inferior" trades, a nobody who for a moment became a somebody in the Revolution. Born in Boston in 1742 to a tanner, he became an active participant in some of the best-known events in the making of the Revolution, including the Massacre and the Tea Party. Never a success in his trade, during the war he left Boston, raised a large family in Wrentham, Massachusetts, and after the War of 1812 went west to join several of his children in central New York. He was "discovered" in 1834, when he was in his nineties and thought to be one of the last survivors of the Tea Party, and became the subject of an "as told to" memoir. When he returned to Boston in 1835, he became the hero for the day on the Fourth of July, the subject of a portrait and of a second memoir. He died in 1840.

We know of him only because he lived so long and had an excellent memory and because he surfaced in the 1830s at a moment when the Tea Party was being rediscovered. My findings about Hewes did not fit the conventional views of the mob. He was not a member of any organization and was not particularly shaped by "propaganda" (indeed, he was not much of a reader). He was not one of the violence-prone rabble portrayed by Hutchinson or John Adams (he was opposed, for example, to a tar-and-feathering he unwittingly instigated). His memory gives a clue as to what the Revolution meant to him.

When my article about Hewes appeared in the *William and Mary Quarterly* in 1981, it was dramatized by the American Social History Project in a slide show that became a video for classroom use, but no one on the Freedom Trail rushed to find a place for Hewes.[26] In the late 1990s, after readers of the *Quarterly* voted it as one of the ten most influential articles to appear in that journal in the half century gone by, several things happened. Boston's venerable Beacon Press invited me to publish the article on Hewes and his private memory as a book and add an essay on the public memory of the Revolution. The Bostonian Society restored his portrait and returned it to a place of prominence in the Old State House; CNN televised the unveiling with Hewes's descendants in attendance; and Bryan Lamb interviewed me on *Book Notes*. The Park Service included a profile and picture of Hewes in its new handbook on the Revolution, and Old South Meeting House commissioned a sculpted mannequin of Hewes (who had been christened there) for the Tea Party segment of its new exhibit. The History Collaborative then dramatized him in a cameo for its harbor history tour. For keepers of the past in Boston, Hewes seems to fill a need for an ordinary person on whom they could hang a side of the story that they recognize has long been neglected.

The issue then became how Hewes should be portrayed. From my foray into public memory, I realized that when Hewes first appeared on the scene, the Revolution was a subject of political contention. In the 1830s, when Hewes reappeared, it was an unusually turbulent time in Boston when radicals were invoking the heritage of the Revolution. A journeymen trade union movement paraded through the streets and heard the fiery oratory of the labor leader, Seth Luther, claiming that "the mechanics of Boston" threw the tea in Boston Harbor. William Lloyd Garrison opened his campaign for an uncompromising abolition of slavery by citing the Declaration of Independence, for which a white-collar mob came close to lynching him. Meanwhile, with Andrew Jackson elected to a second term as president, in part with the votes of workers, Boston's merchants and mill owners formed the Whig political party, its name an effort to appropriate the patriot tradition of the Revolution. Whigs were learning to parade as the party of the common man. In 1834, Abbott Lawrence, Boston's Whig congressman, had squired Davey Crockett, the Whig frontiersman, around his own textile mill in Lowell. In the presidential election of 1840, Whigs would masquerade in a "log cabin and hard cider" campaign.[27]

In 1835, Hewes was taken over by such conservatives, not by the labor movement. On the Fourth of July he was celebrated not for what he did in the Revolution, but as one of the last survivors of the tea action "on the verge of eternity." The portrait, entitled *The Centenarian*, depicted him not as a shoemaker or the poor man that he was, but in his Sunday-best clothes leaning on his cane. Hung in the fashionable gallery of the Boston Athenaeum, it was reassuring to the genteel: he was a kindly old codger nearly one hundred years old. In the second biography, the Whig author treated Hewes, a member of defiant mobs, as one of "the humble classes," a prankish boy and a jolly old man. In sum, Hewes's sponsors tamed him, sanitizing him and the audacious popular movement he had been part of.

In Boston's second discovery of Hewes in the late 1990s, the question of how to depict Hewes came up in a very literal way. How should he be sculpted for the mannequin in Old South's new exhibit? In the portrait he was in his nineties. A series of decisions had to be made: at what age should he be depicted? What should he be doing? Should he be a shoemaker at his bench? No, we agreed we should portray the man who in his thirties became an active citizen in the Revolution. If in action, then at what event, because he was in so many: at the Massacre, where a man shot by a soldier dropped wounded into his arms? On a tea ship where he insisted he worked alongside John Hancock breaking open chests and throwing them overboard? In the streets, we decide, as if on the verge of some unnamed action. In what clothing? Obviously, not his Sunday best, but in his work clothes, as if he were coming from his shop. But doing what? He was an angry man, riled up, but not violent. What should he look like? Can we morph the man in the portrait back sixty years? He was about five foot two—heroes are supposed to be tall and commanding.

And so, there he is in the exhibit at the back of the church, a very short man in his midthirties, a leather apron tied around his waist (so much a symbol of mechanics that they were often called "leather aprons"), a cobbler's hammer (molded from an authentic original) tucked in his belt. He is poised to take off to some unnamed action, a determined look on his face. Have we done justice to him as a "man in the street"? Perhaps. Have we caught what the Revolution meant to him? I think not, and I am not sure how an exhibit could have done that.

PROPOSITION 4. *We need to avoid the danger of add-on history. If we add representative characters who make for a more inclusive history, then we have to ask, Does their presence change the narrative?* Glance through the elementary and high school history textbooks for the Revolution, and some are now replete with images of Phillis Wheatley, Abigail Adams, and Paul Revere—no more than token add-ons to the conventional story. This is feel-good history which comforts democratic sensibilities for inclusion, but does it enhance our understanding of the era?[28]

Was Hewes important? Did he change the course of the Revolution? No, not as an individual; but arguably, he and others like him, acting together, made a difference. If the actions in the streets and meeting places of Boston were important, then Hewes shares in that importance. Indeed, he was one of the people "out of doors" that leaders like the two Adamses had to learn to accommodate to build a political system that would last.

He was also important for what the Revolution meant to him. In the memories he retained for over half a century, Hewes insisted that he remembered John Hancock alongside him on the tea ship. His memory was otherwise extraordinary, but it was unlikely that Hancock was present. (The leaders conspicuously remained behind in Old South.) But in this memory lay the meaning of the Revolution to him. Hewes remembered Samuel Adams and John Hancock as his "associates." In wealth and status, he could hardly have been less equal to Hancock, perhaps the wealthiest merchant in Boston, but in his memory he brought him down to his own level. He was no social leveller, but he thought himself the equal of Hancock as a citizen. What he was remembering was a moment of equality.

Others in Boston demonstrated a variant mechanic consciousness. Paul Revere, Boston's best-known artisan of the middling sort, has been swallowed by the Longfellow legend of the midnight rider that obscures his own sense of commonality with others of his class. As the Revolution unfolded in Boston, Revere identified himself as a mechanic. A silversmith, his first contribution to the cause was as an engraver of popular images for the Sons of Liberty, *The Bloody Massacre perpetrated on King Street* only the most famous among them. He was also a manager of patriot public displays and a leader trusted by his fellow Northenders. He allowed himself to be painted by John Singleton Copley as a craftsman at his bench, a piece of silver he crafted in his hand, a tool on the bench, an unusual expression of artisan pride. In the 1790s, in his own account of his famous ride, he wrote, "I was one of a group of about 30 assigned to watch the British troops in Boston." Then he paused, went back to put a caret mark after "about 30," and inserted "chiefly mechanics." In 1795, he was elected the first president of the Massachusetts Mechanics Association. He became a successful owner of a brass foundry and rolling mill. But when he died in 1818, people spoke of him as "a prosperous North End mechanic. He was a born leader of the people; and his influence was pervading, especially among the mechanics and workingmen of Boston, with whom his popularity was immense." As David Hackett Fischer points out, "In his own mind, he was an artisan, a businessman and a gentleman altogether." As a tradesman, however, Revere was never quite accepted by the new gentry on Beacon Street.[29]

In creating a vocabulary for public history from the evidence that survives, we have to learn ways of allowing one person to speak for many, which requires envisioning a person both for his or her achievements as an individual and as representative of a group.

PROPOSITION 5. *It is difficult to convey the theme of the quest of ordinary people for equality in a society of social inequality when so little survives in Boston from the material world of eighteenth-century private life.* Visit Colonial Williamsburg and its environs and there is no escaping that you are in a stratified society of well-to-do plantation owners at the top, slaves at the bottom, and middling craftsmen and women in their shops. Visit Sturbridge Village, whose buildings have been assembled from the New England countryside, and you know you are in a community of middling yeoman farmers and artisans, women and men. But what is the Boston of the revolutionary era to today's visitor?

How do you portray the inequality of that time when almost nothing survives of the private city of either George Hewes near the bottom or

John Hancock at the top, and only the house of Paul Revere is left to stand for the middling sort?[30] In present-day Boston we have almost no sense of the immense plebeian presence in the colonial era. The North End then teemed with the maritime trades: shipyards, workshops, taverns, and the houses of the men and women who worked there, merchants mixed in higgledy-piggledy among them. The houses of only two artisans remain: Revere and his neighbor and relative, Nathaniel Hitchborn, a boatbuilder. The educators of the Paul Revere Association successfully convey a sense of craft, family, and neighborhood, but the two houses cannot carry the burden of representing the diversity of the old North End.[31]

Amazing as it may seem, there is very little left of the patrician presence in early Boston. In other places homes of the colonial elite still stand, solidly built and kept up by descendants. But it is as if the Boston merchants who were indispensable for the Revolution (a minority were Loyalist, a majority were Whig patriot) have vanished. The Harrison Gray Otis House and the houses on Beacon Hill were a postwar development, the product of the architect Charles Bulfinch refashioning a neighborhood for newly risen men of wealth who did not want to mix with the hoi polloi in the North End. Thomas Hutchinson's mansion in the North End, rebuilt after it was gutted by Stamp Act rioters, lasted after he went into exile in England but then was torn down; today you need the help of a park ranger to locate a plaque on the site.[32]

In the nineteenth century, Boston Brahmins were ill at ease with the traditions of their radical forebears. A president of the then elite Massachusetts Historical Society was said to utter a string of profanities when he passed John Hancock's elegant mansion on Beacon Hill. Men of wealth were uncomfortable with a man who pledged his fortune to the cause of Revolution and chased after political popularity. Small wonder that in the 1860s no one saved the house after Hancock's heirs were unable to get either the state or city to take it over. But how much easier would it be today if we had the mansions of Hancock and Hutchinson as a vantage point from which to view the Revolution.[33] Nor do we have any sign of the sources of merchant wealth: ships, wharves, warehouses, or counting houses. "Boston by Sea," the new harbor-cruise history lesson, is so welcome because it is such a refreshing reminder of the city that was first and foremost a seaport.

Today, to find Boston's ladies and gentlemen of that era, you have to go out to the Boston Museum of Fine Arts in the Fenway, where you can stare at them in their aristocratic splendor in Copley's portraits. Copley, who painted everybody who was anybody, fashioned his sitters as they wished to be portrayed, displaying their wealth in their silks and velvets. He presented Hancock, however, in his counting house, dressed in a more subdued velvet, fingering an account book—a merchant of republican virtue. (He portrayed Samuel Adams as a tribune of the people in a simple, russet-colored wool suit, pointing to the colony's charter and "instructions" from the town meeting.) Make your way to the museum's galleries of colonial decorative arts and you can see Revere's silverware, which graced the tables and cabinets of the rich in the portraits. But how many tourists do that, or if they do, how many draw the connections to the historical actors in the buildings downtown?[34]

On the Freedom Trail, if you bring the knowledge with you, you can imagine this elite in their positions of influence: in the Old State House as members of the Governor's Council; or as worshipers in Old South, Old North, or King's Chapel, where they bought the most prestigiously placed pews. Park Service exhibit designers are fond of models laying out miniatures of the buildings of revolutionary-era Boston. (They made one for the museum in the Old State House and refurbished another for Old South.) There is something in the toy houses, churches, and wharves neatly laid out on streets that appeals to the child in all of us, especially when we can press buttons to light up famous places. But these spatial relationships cannot measure the social distances between classes or suggest what might have brought together such unequals as a Hancock, a Revere, and a Hewes in a political cause.

What can keepers of the past do to make up for such absences on Boston's social landscape? A small exhibit in an alcove of the Old State House is a poignant reminder of the Hancock house that was torn down. One little-visited building in the Charlestown Navy Yard provides a glimpse of the maritime trades that made and outfitted ships and provides a smell of rope and tar. (A long, cavernous nineteenth-century ropewalk is closed.) Should we not be re-creating the world of the working tradesmen of the pre-industrial era? And where are the taverns where events of the Revolution were hatched?[35]

If we ponder the limitations of what has survived, we may find ways to compensate for what is missing. Will it be harder for Boston to come to grips with class than it was for Colonial Williamsburg to confront race? PROPOSITION 6. *In dealing with race and gender, Boston is at risk of fragmenting the history of the Revolution, and in a sense of resegregating American history.* Boston now has, besides the Freedom Trail, a Black Heritage

Trail, a Women's Heritage Trail, an Irish Heritage Trail, and an ethnic museum. They all belong; each has a theme that sinks in only as you move through a long stretch of remnants of sites. Yet has there been an unintended consequence for the Freedom Trail?

On which trail, for example, do we put Phillis Wheatley, African American, female, poet, patriot in the Revolution? Here is a happy report: she is on all trails: Black, Women's, and Literary Heritage, and since 2000 she is on the Freedom Trail represented by a mannequin in the new exhibit at Old South Church (which she attended), a few yards from Hewes. But her very ubiquity creates another problem. In 1770, there were about seven hundred blacks in Boston in a town of about fifteen thousand, with some five thousand in Massachusetts, all but a small number slaves. Wheatley should not bear the burden of representing the many-sided roles of African Americans. The Black Heritage Trail and the museum located on the back of Beacon Hill pick up black history a few decades *after* the Revolution in the physical place where Boston's first free black community lived. In the revolutionary era, however, there were blacks scattered throughout the city who petitioned collectively for their own freedom; blacks who later fought at Bunker Hill; and black Loyalists, some of whom joined the exodus from America to settle in Nova Scotia. In the aftermath of the Revolution, free blacks in Boston had to fight for their most elementary civil rights.[36]

Phillis Wheatley cannot contain these multitudes, any more than can Crispus Attucks (the "jack-tarr" who was killed by British soldiers in the Massacre at a site marked in the square outside the Old State House and who is buried in a site marked in the Old Granary burial grounds and depicted on a brass plaque on the base of the statue on the Common memorializing the victims of the Massacre). But we are in a trap if the only two blacks Boston valorizes are patriot heroes. Has the creation of a Black Heritage Trail allowed the Freedom Trail sites and guides to evade responsibility for telling the many different stories of blacks in the revolutionary era?

On whose trail should Abigail Adams go? And Mercy Otis Warren—poet, patriot, historian? And Judith Sargent Murray, the American Mary Wollstonecraft? What about these three women, the most articulate American voices of the era for the recognition of the "equal worth" of women? Thanks to the guide to the Women's Heritage Trail, we can locate Mrs. Adams's Boston house on what was once Brattle Square and Mrs. Murray's on Franklin Place. A statue of Abigail Adams is at the family home in the

Adams National Historical Park in suburban Quincy, whose public pro-grams appropriately deal with women of the era. How do we get these women into the narrative of the Freedom Trail?[37]

Such women were "ladies." How do we recover the ordinary women who were active in the making of the Revolution: Mrs. Seider, whose eleven-year-old son, Christopher, was killed in a boycott demonstration; Anna Green Winslow, a twelve-year-old who wrote in her diary, "As I am (as we say) a daughter of liberty, I chuse to wear as much of our own man-ufactory as pocible"? Or the women who jammed the annual meetings at Old South Meeting House memorializing the young men killed in the Massacre? Women's history also runs a risk of being the story of elites.[38]

The challenge to public historians, in view of the academic specializa-tion that has fragmented social history by groups, is to integrate such his-tories into the larger narrative—or else to show the ways these histories run on separate tracks with their own timetables.

PROPOSITION 7. *If we avoid telling the dark side of the Revolution, we are at risk of falling into an exclusively celebratory history.* When keepers of the past put up a statue, make a shrine of a person's house, or guide visitors through a site, generally they are celebrating history. But we all know this is not the only way to express historical memory. In 1995, Boston dedi-cated a New England Holocaust Memorial and in 1998, an Irish Famine Memorial, both at points adjoining the Freedom Trail. Two statues on the State House lawn acknowledge the religious bigotry of seventeenth-century Massachusetts Puritans by honoring their victims: Anne Hutchin-son, the dissenter the colony exiled, and Mary Dyer, the Quaker the colony hanged. We do this to remind ourselves: we commemorate, we memorial-ize. What does Boston do to remember the dark side of the Revolution?[39]

Take slavery. Massachusetts in the eighteenth century was not a slave society built on the labor of slaves as was Virginia, but it was a society with slaves.[40] Boston has no statues honoring slaveholders (none save George Washington) that elsewhere are embarrassing. But in one sense, the statues paying tribute to Boston's own famous abolitionists, William Lloyd Garri-son and Wendell Phillips, and to Colonel Robert Shaw and the black sol-diers who fought in the 54th Massachusetts Regiment in the Civil War, displace the issue of slavery onto the South and hinder the city from acknowledging its own history of slavery.[41]

Massachusetts eliminated slavery during the Revolution, not by its con-stitution or statute but in good part through the efforts of slaves them-selves, who ran away or fought in the army. (In Stockbridge, "Mumbet" brought a legal suit under the Massachusetts Declaration of Rights of 1780, won her freedom, and changed her name to Elizabeth Freeman.) Early in the nineteenth century, as New England became a righteous opponent of the "slavocracy" and southern slavery, the region blotted out the memory of its own history as a society that once held slaves and kept free Negroes as second-class citizens.[42]

New England did something of the same thing with Indians, burying the memory of Indians who once populated New England, and turning upside down the history of their role in the Revolutionary war. By the end of the colonial era, Indians in the region were decimated by warfare, disease, and assimilation, yet tribal entities existed. In the war, historian Jill Lepore writes, "Mashpees from Cape Cod, Penobscots and Passamquoddies from lower Maine, and Pequots and Mohegans from Connecticut all fought on the colonists' side" and "all also suffered severe losses." But because many more Native Americans, including the powerful Iroquois confederation, fought on the side of the British, New Englanders created the fiction that all Indians were on the side of the British, which justified further dispossession of Indian lands. In 1788, Massachusetts repealed a 1763 ruling by which the Mashpees had been incorporated as a self-governing district. Thus, for Indians in New England, Lepore writes, "the American Revolution signalled not a gain but a loss of liberty."[43] In present-day Boston, the few surviving symbols of Indians perpetuate a mythology of racial harmony and cooperation: the Massachusetts seal of state, the state flag, the murals in the state house. The colonial artisan Shem Drowne's gilded bronze weathervane which once stood aloft on a fashionable mansion might be a more fitting symbol. It depicts an Indian warrior poised with his bow and arrow, as if in combat.

Will Massachusetts find a way to present this history it has erased? In the aftermath of King Philip's War (1675–76), the colony imprisoned some nine hundred Wampanoag Indians on Deer Island in Boston Harbor, half of whom died in what in effect was the country's first internment camp. NPS recently commissioned a scholarly report on the episode by Lepore with a view to developing the site. Here is a strong first step, but will a site on a harbor island reachable only over water do justice?[44]

There are always roadblocks to going down this path. The tug of Americans for a Norman Rockwell version of the American past is ever present, the desire to see only "the smiling side of American life," as Boston's nineteenth-century realist novelist William Dean Howells put it. These days, a good share of visitors to Boston's iconic sites come with more sophisticated expectations. Recall the experience of Colonial Williamsburg (CW), which a few years ago boldly took the plunge, dramatizing the African American history it had so long ignored. Colonial Williamsburg was restored in an era of segregation by Rockefeller philanthropy, and you would hardly know that in colonial days Williamsburg was a town half of whose residents were black, a society based on the labor of slaves. When CW's education department confronted the issue and came up with a set of public reenactments on the streets—a slave auction and the return of a runaway slave—it faced a chorus of doubters, including African Americans who felt more comfortable with a history stressing achievement rather than victimization. But there are no reports of attendance dropping off on this score. In "giving slavery a human face," as the head of the local NAACP put it, CW made for a more compelling experience. Museums of conscience are now going up all over the world.[45]

Boston's keepers of the past may have to confront dark corners of American history in unexpected places. The curator of the USS *Constitution* museum writes, "We are hoping to give the visitors the look, the feel, smells, and sounds of being aboard ship, as an ordinary seaman." Are they prepared to show the horrors of the lash that led Cambridge's Richard Henry Dana to write his since classic *Two Years before the Mast* (1840)? The Boston Academy of Music produced Gilbert and Sullivan's *HMS Pinafore* in the Boston Navy Yard. Are they ready for Benjamin Britten's opera based on *Billy Budd*, Herman Melville's searing novel of life at sea?[46]

Revising the exhibit at the Bunker Hill Monument site in Charlestown presents another sort of challenge. NPS no doubt will find ways to incorporate the new scholarship it commissioned showing African American soldiers to have been far more numerous at the battle than anyone imagined. But can they also navigate the claims of present-day Irish working-class Charlestown, which has long celebrated Bunker Hill Day as its own? And how do we give meaning to the heroism of those who fell in battle without celebrating the romance of that battle as portrayed in John Trumbull's painting?[47]

PROPOSITION 8. *The future of the Freedom Trail requires a greater coordination of responsibility for the trail as a whole with responsibility for interpreting the sites remaining with each institution.* The 1995–96 consultants report, the fruit of extensive discussions with the many "stakeholders" (and several historians), pleaded for "a richer, more evocative telling of the story [of the Revolution] which weaves the Sites and Trail together." The scores of recommendations ranged from the generally accepted need for more restroom facilities, a larger visitor-orientation center, and more skill-ful marketing, to imaginative proposals for reenactments, public art, self-guided audio tours, and more staff interpretations at sites. Who will take responsibility for change? Asserting that "the current system of minimal coordination is no longer working," the report pointed to a need for fur-ther "collaborative ventures" and "a renewed organizational structure."[48]

Perhaps only an outsider can say it, but to be blunt, there is no frame-work for implementing the report, even though leaders of the major insti-tutions identify the "lack of a unified mission" and "lack of long term and annual planning for collaboration" as their principal challenges. In a con-versation with me, one Boston businessman, highly successful in tourism, used the word "Byzantine" to describe decisionmaking for the trail. The Freedom Trail Foundation, an umbrella organization of sorts, does not seem constituted to cope with long-range issues. Whatever happened to the Council of Sites, which functioned up to about 1995? Four sites and BNHP are currently represented in the foundation, but to an outsider, the sites seem to need their own organization to deal with their common problems as well as to give them the voice they deserve in overall decisionmaking. The sites alone have the personnel with historical expertise, the experience in interacting with audiences, and an institutional memory. They need an Articles of Confederation government which would address their common needs with the urgency they demand while retaining their autonomy.[49]

Boston National Historical Park remains an indispensable player at its own sites and in formal partnerships with other institutions on particular projects. Where it is good, it is very good: receptive to the new history and responsive to initiatives. Boston owes its three skillfully restored public buildings to BNHP. It alone has the financial resources, the capacity for major research projects, and a large skilled staff, including park rangers who manage the visitor's center and conduct tours. But, though it launches initiatives, it fails to follow through, the consultants report being a prime example. BNHP is part of a national agency, the NPS, and often creaks under a layered bureaucratic culture with a fear of going out on a limb. (Typically, Park Service exhibit labels have been notorious for a museumspeak filled with straddling and the evasion of the passive voice.) Nationally, the NPS commands a growing respect among historians; locally, it is a token of its achievements that expectations for BNHP remain so high.[50]

There is no deus ex machina to rescue the Freedom Trail. In light of a lack of coherence in the history conveyed by the trail as a whole, a modern visitors' center to help tourists navigate the city's riches is long overdue. It has the potential to draw connections among sites and between trails. Keepers of the past of course may get more than they wished for. My fear is that the inevitable fast-paced film geared to the short attention span of tourists, common to visitor's centers, can end up presenting the same old stereotyped history. A museum covering three hundred years of Boston history has the potential to deal with the many strands of history now left out; it also runs the risk of squeezing the Revolution into a single gallery with a single vision.[51]

Given the unparalleled asset of the iconic sites, from the point of view of a historian, the goal of any reforms should be to get visitors to the sites and help provide a framework to understand what took place there—and what did not. This should also lead to expanding interpretation at the sites; this double chore will require all the imagination curators, guides, historians, and educators can muster. Decentralization, a weakness for the trail as a whole, is potentially a source of strength.

Each time I returned to Boston over the past few decades, my sense of wonder was rekindled. A few years ago I wrote, "as the city all around booms with one redevelopment after another, the Trail retains its historical integrity, resisting thus far the pressures of tourism to sanitize history. It is not Disneyland."[52] Was my wish father to my thought? The 1995 report also rejected "the Disney model as undesirable." If the drumbeat for a reassuring, entertaining version of the American past increases in times of national crisis, so does the interest of Americans in understanding their heritage. Is it possible that a successful alternative lies in the more multisided, more exciting version of the American Revolution that a generation of historians has uncovered?

NOTES

This essay appeared under the title "Revolution in Boston? Eight Propositions for Public History on the Freedom Trial," in *The Public Historian* 25 (spring 2003), an issue devoted to public history in Boston, and is reprinted with the permission of the University of California Press. An early version was presented at the conference "Changing Meanings of Freedom: The 225th Anniversary of the American Revolution" (Boston, 2000), sponsored by the National Park Service and other organizations.

My thanks to the many keepers of the past in Boston who provided information or responded to various drafts of this essay, to the editors of *The Public Historian* and Martin H. Blatt, editor of the special issue, and to Michael Zuckerman and two anonymous reviewers for comments.

1. David Dixon/Goody Clancy Planning and Urban Design, a Division of Goody, Clancy and Associates, "The Freedom Trail: Foundations for a Renewed Vision" (Boston, September 1995), and "The Freedom Trail: A Framework for the Future" (Boston, May 1996), reports prepared by a consulting firm for the Boston National Historical Park, quotation from the 1996 report, p. 6. The recommendations are discussed below under Proposition 8.

2. For an institutional survey of the history of the trail, see Matt Greif, "Freedom Trail Commission Report for the National Historical Park" (unpublished ms., Boston, 1995). The trail deserves a full-scale study in the context of Boston confronting the American Revolution.

3. "Voices of Protest Opens at Old South Meeting House," *Broadside* (Boston National Historical Park) 1 (2000); "USS Constitution Museum Phase III Renovation Under Way," *Broadside* 1 & 2 (1999); proposals for the liberty tree site are summarized briefly in Alfred Young, *The Shoemaker and the Tea Party: Memory and the American Revolution* (Boston: Beacon Press, 1999), 247.

4. Barbara Clark Smith, *Boston and the American Revolution* (Washington, D.C., National Park Service Handbook No. 146, 1998); George Quintal, *Patriots of Color, "A Peculiar Beauty and Merit": African Americans and Native Americans at Battle Road & Bunker Hill* (Boston: National Park Service, 2002); Chris Frost and Sheila Gallagher, "Artists in Residence" (2000), and Laura Baring-Gould and Michael Dowling, "Conspire" (2001), brochures by the Boston Institute of Contemporary Art.

5. See Nina Zannieri, "Not the Same Old Freedom Trail: A View from the Paul Revere House," *Public Historian* 25, no. 2 (spring 2003): 43–53. There is no Freedom Trail newsletter. For activities at the sites, see the following newsletters: *Bostonian Society News; Dial* (Old South Meeting House); *Revere House Gazette; Broadside* (Boston National Historical Park).

6. Polly Welts Kaufman, Bonnie Hurd Smith, Mary Howland Smoyer, and Susan Wilson, *Boston Women's Heritage Trail: Four Centuries of Boston Women* (Gloucester, Mass.: Curious Traveller Press, 1999); Susan Wilson, *Literary Trail of Greater Boston* (Boston: Houghton Mifflin, 2000); Susan Wilson, *Boston Sites and Insights: A Multicultural Guide to Historic Landmarks in and around Boston* (Boston: Beacon Press, 2003). For other guides, see Byron Rushing and staff of the Museum of Afro-American History, *Black Heritage Trail* (NPS, Boston African American National Historic Site); Charles Chauncey Wells, *Boston's Copp's Hill Burying Ground Guide* (Oak Park, Ill.: Chauncey Park Press, 1998).

7. Robert M. Krim and David Hackett Fischer, "The Boston History Collaborative" (paper presented at the Massachusetts Historical Society Seminar, April 1999). Each trail and most sites may be followed on its own website; see also www.bostonhistorycollaborative.org. For the artists, see Sarah J. Purcell,

"Commemoration, Public Art, and the Changing Meaning of the Bunker Hill Monument," *Public Historian* 25, no. 2 (spring 2003): 55–71.

8. Robert J. Allison, "Exciting Time for History in the Hub," *Boston Globe*, 1 January 2001; Anne Emerson, "Building Boston's History: Creating a Boston History Museum," and David Hackett Fischer, "Chance of a Lifetime" in *Bostonian Society News* (spring 2001): 2–3 and 1, 7. Emerson, formerly director of the Bostonian Society, is executive director of the Boston Museum Project. See also in the *Boston Globe*: Anne Emerson, Nancy Moses, and Barbara Franco, "City Museums Tell Us Much," 10 January 2000; Steve Bailey, "Telling Our Story," 17 December 1999; David Warsh, "Old Puzzle, New Pieces," 19 January 2001.

9. John Adams to Joseph Ward, 6 June 1809, Chicago Historical Society, reprinted in Alfred Young, Terry Fife, and Mary Janzen, *We the People: Voices and Images of the New Nation* (Philadelphia: Temple University Press, 1993), 190–91; *Massachusetts Historical Society Proceedings*, 2nd ser., 3 (1886–87): 313–18.

10. Michael Kammen, *Season of Youth: The American Revolution in the Historical Imagination* (New York: Knopf, 1978), remains the best overall guide; Young, *Shoemaker and the Tea Party*, part 2; Michael Holleran, *Boston's "Changeful Times" Origins of Preservation and Planning in America* (Baltimore: Johns Hopkins University Press, 1998), deals with historic preservation in Boston; Eric Hobsbawm and Terrence Ranger (eds.), *The Invention of Tradition* (New York: Cambridge University Press, 1983).

11. Full disclosure: I was a consultant for the National Park Service for *Boston and the American Revolution* (Handbook No. 146) and for the exhibit on Hewes in the Old South Meeting House, Voices of Protest; I was a consultant for the Bostonian Society on their exhibit on the Boston Massacre; I worked with the Boston History Collaborative on the dramatic segment on Hewes for *Boston by Sea*; I gave a program for several summers in the National Park Service "People and Places" Institute for elementary school teachers and have given lectures at Old South Meeting House and the Bostonian Society.

12. For a synthesis of this theme, see Eric Foner, *The Story of American Freedom* (New York: Norton, 1998); for surveys of recent scholarship on the Revolution, see Linda Kerber, *The Revolutionary Generation: Ideology, Politics, and Culture in the Early Republic* (Washington, D.C.: American Historical Association Pamphlet, 1997); for recent syntheses with bibliographic essays, see Edward Countryman, *The American Revolution* (New York: Hill and Wang, 1985; rev. ed., 2003), and Gordon Wood, *The American Revolution* (New York: Random House, 2002). I discuss twentieth-century historiography of the Revolution in "American Historians Confront the Transforming Hand of Revolution," in Ronald Hoffman and Peter Albert (eds.), *The Transforming Hand of Revolution: Reconsidering the American Revolution as a Social Movement* (Charlottesville: University of Virginia Press, 1996).

13. Dixon/Clancy, "Freedom Trail," 6.

14. The exchange between Abigail and John Adams between March and May

1776 is in L. H. Butterfield (ed.), *Adams Family Correspondence* (Cambridge, Mass.: Harvard University Press, 1963), 1:369–71, 381–83, 396–98, 401–3, and in L. H. But-terfield et al. (eds.), *The Book of Abigail and John: Selected Letters of the Adams Family, 1762–1784* (Cambridge, Mass.: Harvard University Press, 1975), 120ff.

15. George P. Anderson, "Ebenezer Mackintosh: Stamp Act Rioter and Patriot," *Colonial Society of Massachusetts Transactions* 26 (1927): 15–64, and "A Note on Ebenezer Mackintosh," ibid., 346–61. Mackintosh was also a firefighter; see Benjamin L. Carp, "Fire of Liberty: Firefighters, Urban Voluntary Culture, and the Revolutionary Movement," *William and Mary Quarterly*, 3rd ser., 58 (2001): 782–818.

16. Sidney Kaplan and Emma Nogrady Kaplan, *The Black Presence in the Amer-ican Revolution* (Washington, D.C.: Smithsonian Institution Press, 1975; rev. ed., Amherst: University of Massachusetts Press, 1989), 202–14; Charles Wesley, *Prince Hall: Life and Legacy* (Washington, D.C.: United Supreme Jurisdiction Masonic Order, 1977); Thaddeus Russell, "Prince Hall," *American National Biography* 9 (1999): 867–68.

17. William G. McLoughlin, *Isaac Backus and the American Pietistic Tradition* (Boston: Little, Brown, 1967).

18. David Szatmary, *Shays' Rebellion: The Making of an Agrarian Insurrection* (Amherst: University of Massachusetts Press, 1981); Robert A. Gross (ed.), *In Debt to Daniel Shays: The Bicentennial of an Agrarian Rebellion* (Charlottesville: Univer-sity of Virginia Press, 1993); Peter Onuf, "Daniel Shays," *American National Bio-graphy* 19 (1999): 760–61; Ronald Formisano, "Teaching Shays/The Regulation: Historiographical Problems as Tools for Learning," *Uncommon Sense* (Newsletter of the Omohundro Institute of Early American History) 106 (1998): 24–35, argues convincingly that the term "Shays' rebellion not only distorts a complex populist movement but obscures its central meaning."

19. David McCulloch, *John Adams* (New York: Simon & Schuster, 2001); Joseph Ellis, *Passionate Sage: The Character and Legacy of John Adams* (New York: Norton, 1994); for Adams's conservatism see Alfred F. Young (ed.), *Beyond the American Revolution: Explorations in the History of American Radicalism* (DeKalb: Northern Illinois University Press, 1993), intro., 3–24, and "Afterword: How Radical was the American Revolution?" 318–64.

20. For statistics on attendance at Boston sites, see Sean Hennessey, NPS Infor-mation Officer (Sean_Hennessey@nps.gov). For three fiscal years, 1996–99, NPS conducted about 1,000 tours each year with from 24,000 to 27,000 participants; for 2000–2001, a year in which tourism plummeted after September 11, there were 676 tours with 15,260 participants.

21. The account in Hiller Zobel, *The Boston Massacre* (New York: Norton, 1970), should be read in conjunction with Dirk Hoerder, *Crowd Action in Revolu-tionary Massachusetts, 1765–1780* (New York: Academic Press, 1977); Jesse Lemisch, "Radical Plot in Boston (1770): A Study in the Use of Evidence," *Harvard Law*

Review 84 (1970): 485–504; and Pauline Maier, "Revolutionary Violence and the Relevance of History," *Journal of Interdisciplinary History* 2 (1971): 119–35.

22. On August 14, 1996 and 1997 (Liberty Tree Day), the historian David Hackett Fischer spoke at a commemorative ceremony on the Boston Common sponsored by Mass ReLeaf, a division of the Massachusetts Department of Environmental Management; see Young, *Shoemaker and the Tea Party*, 247.

23. For an appreciation of the magnitude of the change, see Edmund S. Morgan and Marie Morgan, "Who's Really Who," *New York Review of Books* 47 (March 9, 2001): 38–43. For a sense of the new microhistory, see Jill Lepore, "Historians Who Love Too Much: Reflections on Microhistory and Biography," *Journal of American History* 88 (2001): 129–44.

24. For a survey organized around seven individuals, see Countryman, *American Revolution*; for a museum exhibit organized around four individuals, see Barbara Clark Smith, *After the Revolution: The Smithsonian History of Everyday Life in the Eighteenth Century* (New York: Pantheon, 1985); for the ideas of six leaders including Samuel Adams and Dr. Thomas Young of Boston, see Pauline Maier, *The Old Revolutionaries: Political Lives in the Age of Samuel Adams* (New York: Knopf, 1980); for a textbook in which each chapter begins with a sketch of a representative American, see Gary Nash et al., *The American People: Creating a Nation and a Society*, 3rd ed. (New York: Harper and Row, 1994); "National Standards for History," rev. ed. (National Center for History in the Schools, 1996), and "Causes of the American Revolution: Focus on Boston" (copublished with the Organization of American Historians), both available from www.sscnet.ucla.edu/nchs.

25. "George Robert Twelves Hewes (1742–1840): A Boston Shoemaker and the Memory of the American Revolution," *William and Mary Quarterly*, 3rd ser., 38 (October 1981): 561–623, reprinted in Young, *Shoemaker and the Tea Party*, part 1.

26. American Social History Project, "Tea Party Etiquette," video (New York: American Social History Project/Center for Media and Learning, 1984); my article was reprinted in *In Search of Early America: The William and Mary Quarterly, 1943–1993* (Williamsburg, Va.: Institute of Early American History, 1993) and in other collections.

27. For the preceding paragraphs, see Young, *Shoemaker and the Tea Party*, chaps. 6–8; for the Whig elite, see especially Harlow Sheidley, *Sectional Nationalism: Massachusetts Conservative Leaders and the Transformation of America, 1815–1836* (Boston: Northeastern University Press, 1998).

28. For the state of history textbooks, see Frances Fitzgerald, *America Revised: History Schoolbooks in the Twentieth Century* (New York: Random House, 1979), which is, alas, still valid; James W. Loewen, *Lies My Teacher Told Me: Everything Your American History Textbook Got Wrong* (New York: New Press, 1995); for the battle over national standards introducing the new history, see Gary B. Nash, Charlotte Crabtree, and Ross E. Dunn, *History on Trial: Culture Wars and the Teaching of the Past* (New York: Knopf, 1998).

29. The Revere letter of 1792 is in Edmund S. Morgan (ed.), *Paul Revere's Three Accounts of His Famous Ride* (Boston: Massachusetts Historical Society, 1968); the comment is quoted in Patrick Leehey, "Reconstructing Paul Revere: An Overview of His Ancestry, Life and Work," in *Paul Revere—Artisan, Businessman, and Patriot* (Boston: Paul Revere Memorial Association, 1989), 33; David Hackett Fischer, *Paul Revere's Ride* (New York: Oxford University Press, 1994), chap. 1, quotation at 19. For my interpretation of Revere, see my review of the exhibit by the Revere Association in *Journal of American History* 76 (1989): 852–57. Jayne Triber, *A True Republican: The Life of Paul Revere* (Amherst: University of Massachusetts Press, 1998), covers his entire life.

30. For the pathbreaking articles about inequality in Boston in the era, see James Henretta, "Economic Development and Social Structure in Colonial Boston," *William and Mary Quarterly*, 3rd ser., 22 (1965): 75–92, and Allan Kulikoff, "The Progress of Inequality in Revolutionary Boston," *William and Mary Quarterly*, 3rd ser., 28 (1971): 375–412. For a synthesis, see Gary Nash, *The Urban Crucible: Social Change, Political Consciousness, and the Origins of the American Revolution* (Cambridge, Mass.: Harvard University Press, 1979).

31. Walter Whitehill, *Boston: A Topographical History* (Cambridge, Mass.: Harvard University Press, 1959), chap. 2, is the classic description; Esther Forbes, *Paul Revere and the World He Lived In* (Boston: Houghton Mifflin, 1942), is a vivid description.

32. Harold Kirker and James Kirker, *Bulfinch's Boston, 1787–1817* (New York: Oxford University Press, 1964); Whitehill, *Boston*, chap. 3; for analysis of merchant divisions, see John W. Tyler, *Smugglers and Patriots: Boston Merchants and the Advent of the American Revolution* (Boston: Northeastern University Press, 1986).

33. William M. Fowler, *The Baron of Beacon Hill: A Biography of John Hancock* (Boston: Houghton Mifflin, 1980); Louis Leonard Tucker, *The Massachusetts Historical Society: A Bicentennial History, 1791–1991* (Boston: Massachusetts Historical Society, 1996), 55–56 (cursing Hancock); Bernard Bailyn, *The Ordeal of Thomas Hutchinson* (Cambridge, Mass.: Harvard University Press, 1974).

34. Paul Staiti, "Accounting for Copley" and "Character and Class," a revealing essay in social history, in Carrie Rebora et al. (eds.), *John Singleton Copley in America* (New York: Metropolitan Museum of Art, 1995), 25–52, 53–78; Department of American Decorative Arts and Sculpture, Museum of Fine Arts, Boston, *Paul Revere's Boston, 1735–1818* (Boston: New York Graphic Society, 1975).

35. See David Conroy, *In Public Houses: Drink and the Revolution of Authority in Colonial Massachusetts* (Chapel Hill: University of North Carolina Press, 1995).

36. For the recognition of Wheatley, see *Phillis Wheatley and the Origins of African American Literature* (Boston: Old South Meeting House, 1999); for black patriots and Loyalists, see Kaplan and Kaplan, *Black Presence*, chap. 3; for black petitions, see Herbert Aptheker (ed.), *Documentary History of the Negro People in the*

United States (New York: Citadel Press, 1951), vol. 1; on the diversity in black culture, see William D. Piersen, *Black Yankees: The Development of an African American Subculture in Eighteenth-Century New England* (Amherst: University of Massachusetts Press, 1988).

37. For teaching this history, see Sheila Cooke-Kayser, "Boston Women: The Struggle for Freedom, 1760–1850: People and Places Summer Teacher Workshop, 2002," *Broadside* (BNHP) 2 (2002): 5; for lesson plans organized around primary documents for grades 5–8, see "Women of the American Revolution," which can be ordered from http://www.sscnet.ucla.edu/nchs; for background, see Mary Beth Norton, *Liberty's Daughters: The Revolutionary Experience of American Women, 1750–1800* (Boston: Little, Brown, 1980; Ithaca, N.Y.: Cornell University Press, 1996); Rosemarie Zagarri, *A Woman's Dilemma: Mercy Otis Warren and the American Revolution* (Wheeling, Ill.: Harlan Davidson, 1995); Sheila Skemp, *Judith Sargent Murray: A Brief Biography with Documents* (Boston: Bedford Books, 1998).

38. See essay 2 in this volume.

39. Marty Carlock, *A Guide to Public Art in Greater Boston* (Boston: Harvard Common Press, 1993), identifies statues; James W. Loewen, *Lies across America: What Our Historic Sites Get Wrong* (New York: New Press, 1999).

40. For analysis, see especially Ira Berlin, *Many Thousands Gone: The First Two Centuries of Slavery in North America* (Cambridge, Mass.: Harvard University Press, 1998), chaps. 2, 7, 9.

41. For Boston's revisiting of the "Shaw memorial" monument, see Martin H. Blatt, Thomas J. Brown, and Daniel Yacovone (eds.), *Hope and Glory: Essays on the Legacy of the 54th Massachusetts Regiment* (Amherst: University of Massachusetts Press, 2001), essays in part 2.

42. For Elizabeth Freeman, see Kaplan and Kaplan, *Black Presence*, 244–48; Susan Sedgwick, *Elizabeth Freeman*, a miniature on ivory (1811), is in the collections of the Massachusetts Historical Society; for the erasure, see Joanne Pope Melish, *Disowning Slavery: Gradual Emancipation and "Race" in New England, 1780–1860* (Ithaca, N.Y.: Cornell University Press, 1999).

43. Jill Lepore, *The Name of War: King Philip's War and the Origins of American Identity* (New York: Knopf, 1998), 188–89; Lepore, "Revenge of the Wampanoags," *New York Times*, 25 November 1998, and "The Year Thanksgiving Was Canceled," *Los Angeles Times*, 27 November 1997 (both op-ed essays).

44. Jill Lepore, "No Safety for Us: The Internment of Native Americans on the Boston Harbor Islands during King Philip's War, 1675–1676" (final report, National Park Service, 1999); Lepore, "When Deer Island Was Turned into Devil's Island: A Historian's Account," *Bostonia* (Boston University) (summer 1998): 14–19.

45. For the old Colonial Williamsburg, see Mike Wallace, *Mickey Mouse History and Other Essays on American Memory* (Philadelphia: Temple University Press, 1996); for the recent turn, see Richard Handler and Eric Gamble, *The New History in an Old Museum: Creating the Past at Colonial Williamsburg* (Durham,

N.C.: Duke University Press, 1997); "Historic Sites of Conscience," *Museum* (American Association of Museums) (January–February 2001): 1.

46. Anne Grimes Rand, cited in "USS Constitution Museum Phase III Renovation Underway," *Broadside* (BNHP) 1 & 2 (1999): 4.

47. For the black soldiers, see Quintal, *Patriots of Color*; for the Irish, see Michael Musuraca, "The 'Celebration Begins at Midnight': Irish Immigrants and the Celebration of Bunker Hill Day," *Labor's Heritage* (July 1990): 48–61; for art, see Sarah J. Purcell, "Commemoration, Public Art, and the Changing Meaning of the Bunker Hill Monument," *Public Historian* 25 (2003): 55–71, and Purcell, *Sealed with Blood: War, Sacrifice, and Memory in Revolutionary America* (Philadelphia: University of Pennsylvania Press, 2002).

48. Dixon/Clancy, "Freedom Trail," 33.

49. See minutes of "Partners Meeting," Boston National Historical Park, 30 May 2001 (typescript), reporting a poll of senior staff members of the park and directors of the major partners; for the foundation, see "The Freedom Trail Foundation: A Thousand Days of Progress, January 1998 through August 2000," a looseleaf collection of newspaper clippings assembled by the foundation.

50. It remains to be seen what BNHP will do with "An Action Agenda for the National Park Service: 225th Anniversary of the American Revolution Commemoration Initiative" (Boston: National Park Service, 2002).

51. See the warning by James Green, "A City of Multiple Memories," *Boston Globe*, 9 December 1999; James Green, a Massachusetts historian steeped in the city's labor history, is the author of *Taking History to Heart: The Power of the Past in Building Social Movements* (Amherst: University of Massachusetts Press, 2000).

52. Young, *Shoemaker and the Tea Party*, 202.

8

Liberty Tree
Made in America, Lost in America

Originally, it was known in Boston as the Great Elm or the Great Tree. After it became a site of patriot resistance to Britain from 1765 to 1775, it was commonly called "the liberty tree" or simply "liberty tree," but those who wanted a name with more resonance and dignity might refer to it as "the tree of liberty." It was a little like the difference between calling Boston's patriot leader Sam or Samuel Adams. "Liberty tree" was a claim to familiarity. By both names liberty trees were dedicated and liberty poles were erected throughout the colonies in the decade before independence was declared. The tree became the major symbol of the American Revolution.[1]

This essay is an exploration of the liberty tree, together with the liberty pole—its naked brother, often a mast or a flagstaff made from a tree—as sites of resistance and as a symbol and metaphor. It also takes up the liberty cap mounted on the staff of liberty, cousin to tree and pole. It focuses first on Boston, a city in which the liberty tree was central. It then moves to the other colonies in search of patterns in the role of trees and poles. Here the focus is on events at these sites. After attempting to track the symbolic use to which the tree was put in the Revolutionary war from 1775 to 1783 and after, I turn to the question of origins: how were customs, rituals, and symbols that appeared in the American Revolution transmitted from the "old world" to the "new world"? What role and function did tree and pole have in the popular politics of the Revolution? The exploration then moves forward to the 1790s, when the liberty tree and liberty cap became the principal icons of the French Revolution and when the pole and cap were revived in the United States as a symbol of political protest against the Federalist Party in power for betraying the Revolution. I close with an exploration of the public memory of these symbols: why did they fade in the nineteenth century and pass into a virtual eclipse in twentieth-century America?

Boston's liberty tree as depicted by Paul Revere late in 1765 in one of two drawings of the tree by a contemporary present on the scene. The effigy, hung on the tree November 1, 1765, is John Huske, an American member of the British Parliament said to favor the Stamp Act. The monstrous dragon represents the Stamp Act clutching Magna Charta, symbol of the "Rights of Englishmen." Revere's engraving, only part of which is shown here, was an adaptation of an English print to which he added the liberty tree. "A View of the Year 1765." Courtesy of the American Antiquarian Society.

The process of recovering this history is complicated by loss. Few trees survived into the twentieth century; the poles decayed; and the sites of the numerous trees and poles generally went unmarked or were little remembered. In Boston, one of several hundred lanterns which once hung on the tree and most of the flag hoisted above it survive at the museum of the Old State House. But as a subject, the tree has also been lost to historians, myself among them. In the renaissance of scholarship about the American Revolution in the second half of the twentieth century, there was one article on the subject by a scholar who considered the tree as part of the Whig campaign of propaganda, an interpretation that did not inspire further exploration. In the 1950s, in the miasma of the Cold War setting parameters for American historical scholarship, the radical side of the Revolution was going out of fashion. Symbols were low in the priorities of historians, who were trying to establish intellectual history as a distinct field, who treated the ideas expressed in pamphlets, sermons, and newspapers of the Revolution as ideology, and to whom propaganda was an invidious concept. The historians of English, French, and American history intent on rescuing the "crowd" from the pejorative label of "mob" were attentive to the composition and actions of crowds, but at first inattentive to customs, rituals, and symbols. The result was that the study of such radical symbols as the liberty tree fell into a gap.[2]

I offer several hypotheses about the liberty tree and pole. First, they were important and in some places central in shaping events, and the process reveals the double character of the Revolution: the upsurge of popular resistance from below and the efforts of the self-appointed leaders of the Sons of Liberty to direct the people "out of doors" into safe channels. Second, the liberty tree and liberty pole were essentially "made in America"; they were American inventions. And third, the liberty tree, a major icon at the time, has since been lost to the dominant public memory of Revolution at great expense to the comprehension of the double theme it encapsulated.

1. *Boston: Liberty Tree and "Liberty Hall"*

In Boston, site of the first and most influential liberty tree, the political protest against the Stamp Act at the tree came first; a month later the tree got its name. The elm was located in the south end of town on the grounds of "Deacon Elliot's house" at the intersection of Essex and Newbury streets (today Essex and Washington), well known since early in the century as "Deacon Elliot's corner." Boston was on a peninsula, and the tree was a half-mile into town on the only roadway that led from the narrow neck of land from the mainland into the heart of the city. It was a few blocks from the common, where there was a grove of great elms, and five or six blocks from the political center of the colony, where the Town House (today the Old State House) was the site of the provincial government of Massachusetts. It housed the chambers of the royal-appointed governor and his appointed council, the supreme court of the province, and the General Court, composed of delegates elected by each town.[3]

The Stamp Act could hardly have been more obnoxious to American colonists. It was an act of taxation passed by Parliament in which the colonists were unrepresented. The incidence of the tax could not have been broader. The law required stamped paper of a specified amount to be affixed to legal documents, land transactions, lawyers' licenses, ship clearances, appointments, liquor licenses, articles of apprenticeship, newspapers and printed matter (including almanacs), college diplomas, even playing cards and dice. And it came in the midst of hard times for the seaport cities when cash was scarce. In the summer of 1765 the stamps were on the high seas on the way to each colony, along with commissions to the Americans appointed as Stamp Act distributors.

As dawn broke on August 14, 1765, two effigies were found hanging from a branch of the tree, one stuffed with straw labeled "A.O." identifying Andrew Oliver, Secretary to the Province, the Bostonian commissioned as distributor of the Stamp Act paper; the other a large boot with a devil peeping out holding the Stamp Act, meant to symbolize the Earl of Bute, considered the éminence grise behind King George III. Oliver was the brother of Peter Oliver, justice and later chief justice of the Supreme Court of Massachusetts; the Olivers were in-laws to Thomas Hutchinson, the lieutenant governor. The boot was a pun on Bute, and the green-painted bottom—"a green-vile sole"—was a reference to George Grenville, the minister responsible for the act, a pun so arch it had to be explained to passers-by. Boots and shoes, by the common lore of New England, were used to ward off or trap an evil spirit that attempted to enter a dwelling.[4]

It was the beginning of a day of mockery, at first hilarious then grim. As farmers drove their carts into town delivering produce, the patriot organizers stopped each cart and did a mock "stamping" of the goods, a piece of street theater worthy of the Marx brothers. The news spread fast. Over the course of the day, "a vast number of spectators" or "many thousands" showed up at the tree, including women, apprentices, two or three hundred schoolboys who paraded with a flag, and African Americans, slave and free. A good part of the town of about fifteen thousand turned out. It was not that effigies were new to Boston: for several decades every November 5—Guy Fawkes Day in England, Pope's Day in New England—North End and South End "companies" organized by neighborhood paraded giant effigies of the devil, the Pope, and the Stuart pretender to the British throne through town on carts and at nightfall fought a bone-breaking battle royal, the victor burning the loser's effigies on a high hill. But burlesquing living political figures, one of them in their midst, was uncommon. The governor ordered that the effigies be taken down, but the sheriff would not risk a confrontation. The hanging effigies were a mock execution.[5]

At 5:00 p.m., a mock funeral began, following the common practice in Boston of carrying the coffin of the deceased through the streets on the way to a burial ground. The effigies were cut down, laid on a bier carried by six men, and a cortege of several thousand marched behind them in solemn procession to the town center. They passed the State House, where they shouted the slogans "Liberty, Property, and No Stamps," gave three huzzahs for the governor and his council, and after some disagreement as to the route, proceeded to Andrew Oliver's office on Oliver's Dock, assumed to have been built to house the stamps. Using a battering ram, they leveled the building in half an hour. Pulling down buildings whose owners were in defiance of some public purpose was another time-honored crowd custom in Boston.[6]

A smaller contingent then made its way to Oliver's nearby mansion to demand that he publicly resign his commission, but he had already left. The street theater now reached a climax. The crowd cut off the head of the effigy of Oliver and threw it into a giant bonfire on nearby Fort Hill (a traditional site for public bonfires), pulled down Oliver's fence and the doors to his coach house, ceremoniously stamping each piece of timber before throwing it in the fire. Meanwhile, part of the crowd entered the mansion, destroying such tokens of Oliver's wealth as his huge mirrors, glass windows, and fine furniture and helping themselves to his liquor. Lieutenant Governor Hutchinson and the sheriff appeared but beat a hasty retreat. The next morning Oliver sent word via friends: he would resign.

All these rituals of mockery, as the historian E. P. Thompson has said of the rites of rough music in England, were "like a keyboard that can be played lightly, satirically, or struck brutally." On August 26, twelve days later, a smaller mob of another sort struck Hutchinson's elegant mansion brutally, virtually gutting it, a subject to which we will return.[7]

Two weeks after this, on September 11, 1765, after news arrived that the detested Grenville might be succeeded by William Pitt, considered a friend of America, the tree was dedicated. A copper plaque with the words "The Tree of Liberty stamped thereon in Golden Letters," according to the newspaper, was nailed to the trunk with "large deck nails," and a British flag was hoisted high in the tree with the motto "Pitt the Supporter of Liberty and the Terror of Tyrants." The dedication of the tree and the action of August 14 was planned by the Loyal Nine, about whom more in a moment.[8]

For a good part of the decade that followed, until the tree was cut down by British troops in August 1775, it was the principal site of popular resistance in Boston by the people "out of doors." It was the place where effigies were hung, warnings and calls to political action were posted, and where a flag was hoisted on a flagstaff, called the liberty pole (which, the governor observed, "went through the tree and a good deal above"), as a signal for people to assemble. The flag was huge: the surviving piece is twelve by seven feet, with vertical red stripes on a white background. The tree was a place for street theater, deliberations, and celebrations. In March 1766, at the (false) news of the repeal of the Stamp Act, the tree was "decorated in a splendid manner" with "lanthorns," and at noon there was music, followed by a choral singing of the "Song of Liberty." In May 1766, at the news of the actual repeal, 45 lanterns were hung the first night (in honor of John Wilkes), 108 the second night (in honor of the "glorious majority" in Parliament), augmented with so many more that "the boughs could hold no more." An "obelisk" on the common, designed by Paul Revere, featured the liberty tree as a central symbol of the successful struggle. Fireworks, rockets, and serpents burst into the air, and the obelisk, alas, went up in flames before it could be moved under the liberty tree.[9]

The tree was also a place at which martyrs to the cause were consecrated. In 1770, Christopher Seider, an eleven-year-old boy was killed in the aftermath of a mass picketing by boys of a merchant who refused to comply with the patriot boycott of British imports. A coffin with his corpse was set down under the tree and a biblical warning to the murderer posted on it. The funeral procession of several thousand began at the tree. A month later, the massive cortege for the first four victims of British troops in the Boston Massacre began downtown, wended its way past the tree, and made its way back to the burial grounds in the center.

Above all, the tree was a site for rituals of popular justice. In the words of Justice Oliver in his history of "the late horrid rebellion," written in exile, his pen dipped in bile: "This tree stood in the Town and was consecrated for an Idol for the Mob to worship; it was properly the *Tree ordeal* where those, whom the Rioters pitched upon as state delinquents, were carried to for a trial, or brought to as the test for political Orthodoxy." In December 1765, his brother Andrew was summoned to "appear under liberty tree" for a formal public resignation of his commission. In February 1766, a mock trial of a chained "Stamp Act" was conducted on a stage erected under the tree before a crowd of two thousand in which a jury found the prisoner guilty of a "breach of Magna Charta" and a "Design to subvert the British Constitution." In 1768, the customs commissioners and, in 1773, the agents for the sale of East India Company tea were summoned to the tree for their resignations—all of whom refused to appear.[10]

The area under and around the tree became known as "Liberty Hall," a public space where white male Bostonians without regard to property could take part in public life. For the moment such assemblages replaced the official town meeting, the most democratic institution in the city, for which there was a property requirement for voting which excluded a large segment of the laboring classes. They also usurped the judicial function where a small number of men might sit on a jury—a prized right of Englishmen—but where the people at large were expected only to ratify the decisions of the court by attending executions en masse.

The actions around the tree in 1765–66 brought into play the social classes that contended with each other in the resistance to Britain in the decade that followed: the "better sort" (some 150 to 200 export-import merchants at the apex of Boston's economy and society); the "middling sort" (master artisans, shopkeepers, and professionals); and the "lower sort" (artisans in the "inferior" trades, journeymen, apprentices, day-laborers, seaman, and sometimes Negroes). The Loyal Nine, who coordinated the initial activities, were a small social circle of the middling sort, for the most part prosperous artisans in the higher trades: a jeweler, a painter, two braziers, two distillers, a printer, and a sea captain. Several members had connections to other groups: Benjamin Edes was co-printer of the patriot newspaper, the *Boston Gazette*; John Avery Jr., the only Harvard graduate among them (baited by a Tory as "mob secretary"), was the son of a principal merchant.

The Loyal Nine made the arrangements for August 14 with Ebenezer Mackintosh, the head of the South End Pope's Day company who alone

This broadside was posted around Boston by the Loyal Nine, a patriot group, in December 1765. It summoned "The True-born Sons of Liberty" to "meet under Liberty Tree" to witness the resignation of the Stamp Act Commissioner. Ebenezer Mackintosh and a company of his men escorted Andrew Oliver to the site, where he resigned in the presence of about two thousand Bostonians. Broadside. Courtesy of the Massachusetts Historical Society.

had the experience and network to mobilize the lower sort and negotiate a "union" with the North End company, led by a shipwright, Henry Swift. The group met in the office of a member's distillery close to the site from which they could keep track of activities at the tree. When they named the elm the Tree of Liberty, they took to calling themselves the Sons of Liberty, the phrase Isaac Barre used to identify the colonists in a speech to Parliament. Before long, patriot leaders of Boston took it over as a generic name for themselves, but it did not became the name of a specific organization as it did in some other towns.[11]

Lieutenant Governor Hutchinson was very conscious of the class divisions among patriots as he explained this new "model of government" in Boston to his superiors in London. It had three "branches" (a play on the word *tree*?): "the lowest branch," composed of "the rabble headed by one Mackintosh" who act "when there is an occasion to hang or burn effigies or pull down houses." They were "*somewhat* controuled [his emphasis] by the master masons, carpenters &c," in effect the middle branch. But "when anything of more importance" was to be determined such as "any matters of trade," these first two groups "are under the direction of a committee of merchants," presumably the upper branch. Matters of "a general nature" might be submitted to the town meeting. Hutchinson's analysis was not off the mark: merchants had recently formed their own chamber of commerce; the North End caucus which more or less managed the town meetings included major town officials; master artisans had no overall organization but were accustomed to taking action by trades or meeting in social groups. And the Pope's Day companies were the only ad hoc organizations among the "lower sort," bonded by years of the rituals of a day in which they took over the town.[12]

From the very first, merchants and master artisans practiced crowd control of "the rabble." At the head of the anti–Stamp Act procession on August 14 were "40 or 50 tradesmen decently dressed" (Hutchinson's phrase), taken by Governor Bernard to be "gentlemen disguised as tradesmen." Earlier that day, when the label blew off the effigy of Oliver, the man who climbed up a ladder to replace it ("an handchif over his Face"), according to a gentleman observer, wore trousers (artisan clothing) over his breeches (gentlemen's clothing). But when a leg of his trousers slid up, it was clear he was wearing "a silke Stokinge and breeches," a garment "not of the lowest Class," he wryly observed. This man very likely was one of the Loyal Nine. The day after the August 26 action, prominent town leaders (the "third branch" in action) demanded Mackintosh's release from jail and got it.[13]

In October 1765, the better sort swallowed their class pride and cemented this cross-class alliance at a dinner. John Hancock and several other "gentlemen of fashion" wined and dined the officers and a good many members of the two Pope's Day companies at an affair attended by about two hundred. Hancock, who had inherited the largest fortune in New England the year before, also paid for the handsome uniforms in which the Pope's Day leaders soon appeared. At the November 1 procession, Colonel William Brattle, commander of the province's militia (and a member of the governor's council), marched "arm in arm" with the newly regaled Mackintosh, treating him as an officer of government. In short, merchants and the middling sort in the Loyal Nine did their best to flatter, steer, and fence in Mackintosh and his colleagues, who could bask in a respectability they had never known before. For seven years (1765 until 1773), the annual Pope's Day celebrations became harmonious peaceful spectacles, targeting the current enemy of the day detested by patriots of all classes. But after 1766, the Sons of Liberty leaders shunted Mackintosh aside, substituting one of their own inner circle whenever they wanted to "raise a mob" they could control.

Historians have found it unusually difficult to document the inner workings of the several patriot circles in Boston and only in recent years have shed the stereotype of Samuel Adams as the puppeteer who pulled all the strings in Boston. Leadership flowed from different centers which had to be coordinated, but central control under a single person or group was not likely. In the only letter which spills the beans for 1765–66, Henry Bass, a member of the Loyal Nine, reported shortly after the forced resignation of Oliver on December 17 that "the whole affair" was "transacted by the Loyal Nine." He spelled out their actions: "writing the Letter [demanding Oliver's resignation], getting the advertisements Printed" (broadsides calling people to the event), and having the notices "Pasted up to the amount of a hundred," a chore done the night before between nine o'clock and three in the morning. This became the modus operandi of actions sponsored by the Sons of Liberty: planning, formal printed notices calling a meeting at a designated place, action decided upon in advance. Bass asked his correspondent "to keep this a profound Secret.... We do everything in order to keep this and the first affair private; and are not a little pleased to hear that McIntosh has the Credit of the whole Affair." "We" was the Loyal Nine, and the "first affair" was the event of August 14.[14]

The "first affair" was definitely not the destruction of Hutchinson's mansion on August 26, which was formally disavowed by the town meeting and by Samuel Adams as the work of "a lawless unknown rabble" and which to this day remains something of a mystery. Hutchinson attributed it to the "private resentments" of a handful of merchants who wanted to destroy public records in his keeping, most likely about smuggling, possibly about land claims. Governor Bernard thought it stemmed from "popular resentments" to Hutchinson's public policies that reached back two decades. Both resentments were likely. Hutchinson was so despised—for example, for his efforts to do away with the town meeting form of government—that years before, when his house caught fire, the assembled crowd yelled, "Let it burn." Hutchinson was also the epitome of wealth, his three-story neo-Palladian mansion in the North End a stark contrast to the modest dwellings of artisans or the hovels of the poor. The action which left his house a shell and destroyed his handsome furnishings and manuscripts was in a very old tradition of house attacks expressing pent-up class antagonisms. The day after, Governor Bernard breathlessly reported that fifteen more houses had been targeted and "that it was now becoming a War of Plunder, of general leveling & taking away the distinction of rich and poor."[15]

Such "general leveling" never came off—the primary target of Boston crowds remained the homes of upper-class royal officials and Tory collaborators—but the underlying class resentments often surfaced. Two weeks later, in 1765, Bernard was telling London that unless "persons of property" united, "necessity will soon oblige and justify an insurrection of the poor against the rich, those that want the necessities of life against those that have them." From midcentury on, Bostonians suffered from a near Biblical succession of woes intensifying hard times.[16]

In the context of the timing of the events of the summer of 1765—the more or less controlled violence of August 14, the destructive "mob" violence of August 26 against Hutchinson's house—the dedication of the liberty tree on September 12 suggests that the tree was intended by the Sons of Liberty leaders to assert their authority and to disassociate themselves from the event of August 26. Over the decade, they pursued the pattern of 1765: disavow August 26 and celebrate August 14. Consecrating the tree in the South End and celebrating August 14 each year thereafter as the birthday of the tree was part of this strategy. "No violence or you will hurt the cause" and "no mobs—no confusions—no tumults" became their mottoes. A crowd action the leaders disapproved of might be condemned as "not the true Sons of Liberty which acted without authority" or dismissed as made up of boys, Negroes, strangers, and seamen—people outside the formal body politic of the town meeting. John Adams was in this tradition at the Boston Massacre trial when he characterized the crowd that harassed the British soldiers he was defending as "a motley rabble of saucy boys, negroes and molattoes, Irish teagues and out landish jack tarrs." It was a half-truth.[17]

As the "unauthorized" used the liberty tree to legitimate actions they initiated without the approval of the self-appointed managers of the tree, the tree became a contested site. This is transparent in the escalation of protest in 1767–68, when the customs commissioners arrived in Boston to enforce the new Townsend duties passed by Parliament. At their landing on November 5, 1767, they were greeted by peaceful Pope's Day marchers carrying effigies of them with the motto "Liberty, Property and No Commissioners." Two weeks later, when notices were posted on the liberty tree and elsewhere calling for direct action against the commissioners, the town meeting immediately condemned the proposal. In March 1768, two commissioners were harassed by parades of "lads" and "lusty fellows," "blowing horns, beating drums and making hideous noises." On the anniversary of the repeal of the Stamp Act on March 18, 1768, two effigies put up on the tree were immediately taken down by three members of the Loyal Nine. The parade of the dissidents that followed, reported as "a considerable mob of young fellows & Negroes," paid their respects to the liberty tree.[18]

This tense tug of war over the tree peaked in June 1768 in the *Liberty* ship riot, which blended opposition to the customs laws with furious opposition to impressments. In May, the man-of-war HMS *Romney* arrived in Boston Harbor with a double objective: to crack down on merchants in violation of the laws and to impress men into the navy. Naval officers accompanied the customs commissioners to seize John Hancock's ship *Liberty*. The seizure, as the contemporary historian Reverend William Gordon observed, took place "between the hours of six and seven [in the evening] when the lower class of people were returning from their day labor." A crowd of one thousand to two thousand soon collected. "They had before been irritated by the captain of the man of war pressing some seamen belonging to the town," Wrote Gordon. ("*Only* eighteen seamen had been impressed," the obtuse captain of the *Romney* exclaimed.) An enraged crowd (minimized by both Samuel Adams and Hutchinson as "chiefly sturdy boys and Negroes") pelted the naval crew and beat up two more-accessible customs commissioners on shore. Then, as customs commissioner Joseph Harrison reported the event, the crowd hauled his own elegant pleasure boat out of the water "and dragged her thro' the streets to Liberty Tree (as it is called) [where] she was formally condemned [i.e., after a trial] and from thence dragged up into the Common and there burned to Ashes." The crowd then took a formal vote to disperse. Royal authorities considered it the largest crowd yet assembled in Boston.

This took place late Saturday night. On Monday Whig leaders posted handbills calling a meeting the next day at Liberty Hall to "promote the Peace, Good-Order, and Security of the Town." On a rainy Tuesday "thousands of the lower class" (Gordon's phrase) assembled under the tree but adjourned to Faneuil Hall, where a motion passed to issue a formal call for a legal town meeting later in the day at Old South Meeting House. There, resolutions condemning both impressments and the ship seizure were passed and a respectable committee of twenty-one dispatched to deliver them to the governor. The Sons of Liberty leaders weathered a storm raised by the "lower class" in which both sides sought the sanction of the liberty tree.

Other crowds taking spontaneous, spur-of-the-moment action also sought out the tree as a symbol of justice. This was especially true of tar-and-feathering crowds, which in Boston were initiated by and drawn mostly from the laboring classes. Early in 1774, the crowd that gave a "New England jacket" to the customs informer John Malcolm (after he caned the patriot shoemaker George Robert Twelves Hewes) "hied him away to liberty-tree," as a newspaper put it, as if this had become the obvious thing to do. "Gentlemen" argued with the crowd to leave Malcolm to the law, but to no avail with people who had lost faith in the official system of justice. Sons of Liberty leaders seemed beside themselves to control events: they imperiously announced a fictitious "Committee on Tarring and Feathering" headed by "Joyce, jun."—the Cromwellian soldier who had captured King Charles I—which alone would authorize such actions. When British soldiers tarred and feathered one Thomas Ditson for buying a gun from a soldier, they paraded him past the liberty tree—a mockery that confirmed its status as a symbol of popular justice.[19]

Leaders seemed constantly aware of the need to head off potentially explosive activity at the tree. Typically, for their annual dinner on August 14 commemorating the birthday of the liberty tree, the Sons of Liberty assembled at the tree but rode out in carriages to a Boston suburb (350 people in 137 carriages in 1769) to enjoy a festive meal at the Liberty Tree tavern, free from the hoi polloi (who could not afford the tab anyway). The diners who can be tracked on tax lists were mostly of the better and middling sort. In general, as popular protest escalated, leaders shifted the venue indoors, where formal procedures and oratory might contain the energy of audiences. In 1770, when public anger was at white heat after the Massacre, they called meetings of "the whole body of the people" within Old South, and for the next five years Boston observed the anniversary in this packed church with formal orations on the danger of a standing army. A newspaper blatantly hoped that this observance might replace Pope's Day.

In November 1773, in the opening response to the tea tax, patriot hand-bills signed "O.C." (for Oliver Cromwell) summoned citizens to the liberty tree to hear the resignation of the tea consignees (who did not appear), but in mid-December, leaders called meetings indoors at Old South. The boarding parties for the tea ships on the night of December 16 collected at different places—among them the liberty tree—but proceeded to a variety of indoor sites where men could blacken their faces or don Indian disguises to minimize detection. Then in 1774, when the Sons of Liberty had to win over the merchants regarding how the town should respond to Britain's acts punishing Boston, they held their deliberations at an official town meeting in Faneuil Hall limited to legal voters.[20]

In sum, the liberty tree had served to delegitimize British authority and to mobilize plebeians, but to maintain their own authority, leaders literally had to bring the people "out of doors" indoors. As a site of patriotic resistance, "Liberty Hall," the public space at the liberty tree, thus has as much a claim on the public memory of the American Revolution in Boston as the celebrated Faneuil Hall and Old South Meeting House.[21]

2. *Ebenezer Mackintosh: "Captain General of the Liberty Tree"*

Clearly, the liberty tree empowered people who were either outside the political system or only at its edges. Many ordinary people felt they "owned" the tree. The carpenters who pruned the tree refused payment for their services. The copper nameplate tacked to the tree as well as the numerous lanterns hung on its branches were made by metal workers. The giant flag hoisted high above on the liberty pole was made of wool spun by women, woven by weavers (who could have been men or women) and sewn by seamstresses. Strong artisans most likely from the shipbuilding trades helped raise the pole. The tree became something ordinary people felt they had to defend. In March 1770 on the night of the Massacre, the rumor that enraged soldiers intended to cut it down brought a crowd of

150 to the tree who then marched to the center of town, joining the fateful confrontation with soldiers. The men who died were a ropewalk worker, a sailor, a second mate on a ship, an apprentice to a leather-breeches maker, and an apprentice to an ivory turner.[22]

Some sense of the mobilization of the "lower sort" over the decade is suggested by the size of the turnout at different venues. In the decade before 1775 the official town meeting with a property qualification drew from five hundred to seven hundred voters, while a contested election might bring out as many as one thousand. Faneuil Hall, site of the town meeting (then much smaller than the present building) could hold about twelve hundred, the number of tickets the selectmen printed. Attendance at the outdoor events at Liberty Hall varied from a few hundred to several thousand. And when meetings were called of the "whole body of the people," at which property bars were dropped, they were held in Old South, the largest meeting house in town. The reports of attendance at the Massacre protest in 1770 ran to several thousand, and at the crucial deliberations on tea in December 1773, the claims were from five thousand to seven thousand jamming the church and overflowing into the streets.

In the first year of resistance, the liberty tree became identified with the only plebeian in Boston to emerge from the mechanic classes from 1765 to 1775 as a popular leader. Ebenezer Mackintosh, a shoemaker, was called "Captain" or the "First Captain General of the Liberty Tree," a title that mocked the royal governor's official title. Indeed, the resistance was built on the scaffolding and leadership of the annual Pope's Day festival, the "red-letter day" of the year for apprentices, artisans in the lower trades, boys of all classes, and sometimes African Americans. Mackintosh's only prior claim to fame was as captain of the South End company. In 1765 he was twenty-seven, a single man who in 1758–59 had served in the British army recruited in New England in the French and Indian War. On his return he became a member of a volunteer fire company and by 1764 the captain of the South End company, whose officers, like the militia's, were elected. Together, the two companies had perhaps 150 members; in November 1765, Mackintosh led processions of two thousand and more Bostonians.[23]

Mackintosh was a major presence in the five principal crowd actions against the Stamp Act in 1765–66, four of which were associated with the liberty tree. In the August 14 action against Andrew Oliver, Governor Bernard considered Mackintosh "the principal leader of the mob." In the August 26 action, which had no link at all to the tree, Hutchinson considered him "among the most active" in demolishing his house, and he and others were arrested the next morning and let go by the sheriff at the insistence of prominent citizens. On November 1, the day set for the Stamp Act to go into effect, Mackintosh led the mass procession of two thousand which took down the effigies from the tree and carted them to a ritual execution at Boston's gallows. On November 5, Pope's Day, he was a conspicuous leader of the ceremonious "union" of the two companies who paused for refreshments "under the shadow" of "the Tree of Liberty" before they jointly burnt effigies of the devil, Pope and "stamp men." At noon on December 17, in a cold rain, Mackintosh escorted Andrew Oliver through the streets to his formal resignation at a window in a house facing the liberty tree. In sum, in the first half-year of resistance to the Stamp Act, Mackintosh and his following were indispensable in mobilizing the mass movement that created an alternative source of authority, for which the liberty tree was a symbol of legitimacy. The two massive peaceful demonstrations that Mackintosh led on November 1 and 5 were decisive in enabling Boston merchants to adopt the radical tactic of conducting trade without stamps, in effect nullifying the law.[24]

Should it surprise us that to Massachusetts's principal crown-appointed officials—all gentlemen of wealth and education—the activity at the liberty tree with Mackintosh conjured up terrifying images of centuries-old English and European plebeian rebellions? Governor Bernard, English born and Oxford educated, said it put him "in mind of Jack Cade's oak of reformation," conflating the leader of the uprising of 1450 that stormed London with another led by Robert Kett in Norfolk in 1549. Kett had indeed dispensed popular justice under an oak tree on Mousehold Heath near Norwich. The events also evoked Wat Tyler, leader of England's peasant rebellion of 1381. In 1765 a newspaper reprinted the couplet associated with Tyler: "When Adam delved and Eve span / Who was then the gentleman?"

But above all Mackintosh invoked Masaniello, the name given Tomas Anielo, the fisherman who in 1649 led a bloody proletarian insurrection in Naples. To Peter Oliver, the leaders had "hired a shoemaker who was the antitype of Masaniello"; to Hutchinson, Mackintosh was "as likely for a Masaniello as you can well conceive." Mackintosh was so frightening because the parallels with Masaniello's revolt, as it came down in books that were likely known to Boston elites, were so striking. In Naples the target also was imperial rule (by Spain); the provocative issue was a tax (on fruit); the fisherman had been a leader of Naples's ritual celebrations of victory over the Turks in which there were mock battles; and Masaniello was elected Captain General of all Naples. What must have terrified the better sort was that in his nine days of rule, according to the stories passed down, Masaniello executed some 250 enemies before he himself was assassinated. For the British governing classes and colonial elites, Masaniello took a place alongside Tyler, Cade, and Kett as a symbol of popular rebellions that they could only conceive of as anarchical, destructive, and leveling.[25] No wonder then that in 1775, when the British army occupying Boston had the liberty tree chopped down, the Tory newspaper ran a "Soliloquy" (spoken as if by the tree) that equated Boston's resistance with all the classic images of rebellion:

> Trample rebellion under foot,
> And crush the monster, branch and root;
> Quell Tylers, Cades and Massaniellos,
> Who sweat at puffing treason's bellows.
> From giving shades to mobs, I go,
> Their future shades are shades below.[26]

Patriot elites shared this fear of the shoemaker as a popular leader. John Adams was interrogated whether Mackintosh would "rise" and whether he was "a man of abilities." After all, no less an authority for Whigs than John Locke had warned them of the danger of a Masaniello. If Thomas Paine, who had such a good ear for the political imagery of his readers, warned in *Common Sense* in 1776 that unless the colonists declared independence and set up their own government, "some Masanello" may "collect together the desperate and the discontented" and "sweep away the liberties of the continent like a deluge," would he not have assumed that such a figure would be common knowledge?[27]

But if Mackintosh terrified his upper-class contemporaries who could see him only as a tool of his alleged employers, should we share their class prejudices? It is easy to make a case that Whig patriot leaders sought to control Mackintosh in crass ways, using both a carrot and a club. In February 1765, when he and others were indicted by a grand jury for the accidental death of a child in the Pope's Day battles of the previous November, members of the Loyal Nine stood surety for several of the indicted men, and later the charges were dropped. In March 1765, the town meeting, whose appointments were vetted in Boston's "Caucus Club," appointed the shoemaker as "a sealer of leather," a minor position. Mackintosh was in arrears in his taxes, and on August 12, 1765 (two days before the first Stamp

Act demonstration), Samuel Adams, one of the town's four tax collectors, asked the sheriff to serve him with a warrant for back taxes, but the warrant was returned unexecuted. In 1766 Mackintosh married, and he and his wife soon began to raise a family, having two children. Through 1768 each year the town renewed Mackintosh's position, the fees from which might have rescued him and his family from dire poverty.

However Mackintosh began, the image of him as a puppet does not fit well with the dramatic scenes that followed. It does not allow for either the sources of his authority or his ideas. In November 1765, he "paraded the town with a mob of 2000 Men in two files," Peter Oliver wrote. "If a whisper was heard among his followers, the holding up of his finger hushed it in a moment." The Pope's Day companies were not even 5 percent of the marchers. The procession showed the discipline of the militia; in fact, most of the members of the town's militia would have been in the parade, taking orders from the shoemaker.[28]

Mackintosh was hardly the "extraordinarily unsavory, brutal, boastful bully" that one otherwise sensitive historian has called him. Indeed, Judge Oliver, for all his upper-class bias, called him "sensible and manly.... he dressed genteelly." Brutal? In his later years he was described as "slight of build, of sandy complexion and a nervous temperament." Unsavory? Mackintosh had a reputation for reciting poetry from memory and was fond of Edward Young's romantic, melancholy epic, *Night Thoughts on Life, Death, and Immortality* (1742–45). He named his son Paschal Paoli Mackintosh, after the man widely toasted by American patriots as a leader of the "Sons of Liberty of Corsica" who liberated the island from Genoese rule (and was no Masaniello). May he not have shared a love of liberty with his betters? "Boastful" he undoubtedly was, but for good reason. When he appeared at the head of the November 1765 procession, Governor Bernard described him as "dresst in blue & red, in a gold lace Hat & a gilt Gorget on his breast, with a Rattan Cane hanging at his wrist, & a speaking Trumpet in his hand, to proclaim his orders." May not the respectability in which he was cloaked by his betters and the willing support given him by rank-and-file Bostonians have given him a sense of his own potential?[29]

What was the fate of Boston's plebeian leader? As Oliver wrote down the story later in England, "by neglecting his Business, [Mackintosh] was reduced to part with his Last & all, took to hard drinking, was thrown into a jail and died." The first part of this account could have been true; in 1770 he landed in debtors' prison (as did another poor shoemaker, George

R. T. Hewes), but a death in prison squares not at all with what we know. A customs informer reporting on the Sons of Liberty—granted not the most reliable source—claimed in 1769 that Mackintosh "was one that attended their night meetings" (which suggests collaboration) and knew so much that he "had already been threatened with Death in case he should inform." If true, he may have stayed mum because he believed in the cause and did not want to betray his associates: informers were not heroes in Revolutionary America; in Boston they were tarred and feathered. He may also have retained his old following. On November 5, 1773, amidst the rising tension over the Tea Act, the truce between the two Pope's Day companies, that was negotiated in 1765 collapsed, and their warfare broke out with all its old fury—whether with or without Mackintosh's sanction we do not know. Five weeks later, on the night of the destruction of the tea, Mackintosh may or may not have been a member of the boarding party, but in later years he was said to have boasted, "it was my chickens that did the job," a reasonable claim.

The cordwainer's reputation as a radical threat lingered. In 1774 a Boston correspondent considered him "a leading man," and a patriot paper reported the rumor that the British troops on their way to occupy Boston would seize and return four Bostonians to Great Britain "in irons": Samuel Adams, John Hancock, John Rowe (another prominent merchant), and Ebenezer Mackintosh, explaining that "the latter has been very active among the lower order of people, and the other [three] among the higher," a remarkable claim in view of the fact that since 1766 the Sons of Liberty had replaced the shoemaker in street actions. Mackintosh took the threat seriously. After British troops turned Boston into a garrison town in 1774 he fled, by lore walking to Haverhill, New Hampshire, with his two young children, Paschal and Elizabeth. In the war he served two stints as a soldier and then lived out his life in North Haverhill, a shoemaker, sometimes a sealer of leather for the village, and as far as we can tell, poor and landless, his early deeds unsung. Later generations could not even get his name straight for a marker.[30]

"The Year 1765," John Adams confided to his diary in December of that year of Mackintosh and the liberty tree, "has been the most Remarkable year of my Life," a remark that any number of people in Boston could have made. "The People, even to the lowest Ranks," Adams observed, "have become more attentive to their Liberties." The young lawyer, a resident of nearby Braintree who was in and out of Boston, had written a tract on the ancient origins of American liberties that made his political reputation as a learned patriot. For Samuel Adams, already a leader of Boston's town meeting, the year marked his emergence as a colonywide leader, as Boston's representative to the General Court. For young, newly rich John Hancock, his lavish patronage of Mackintosh et al. marked the beginning of a lifelong political career of public theater and courting public opinion. In the decade that followed, these three men each stood for a different response to the new world of popular democratic politics that the Stamp Act explosion set off: Samuel Adams as a tribune of the people; John Hancock as the master of an aristocratic paternalism; John Adams now radical, now conservative, as the deviser of constitutions to balance the democratic with the aristocratic. Ebenezer Mackintosh owed his meteoric rise as well as his rapid fall to the liberty tree. The Sons of Liberty leaders owed more to Mackintosh and the popular movement that he had helped bring into being than it was politic for them to admit. Late in 1765, the two slogans that the Loyal Nine pinned to effigies on the tree epitomized the double theme of the liberty tree: "Vox populi est Vox Dei" ("The voice of the people is the voice of God") and "Good order and steady." The year was a prelude to the decade that followed.[31]

3. *"The spirit of liberty spread where it was not intended"*

In the decade that followed, the "spirit of liberty spread where it was not intended," a comment Thomas Hutchinson made about the rebellion of students in 1767 at Harvard College, across the river from Boston, which easily could have been made about a range of insurgencies. The students, he wrote, "met in a body, under, and about a great tree [in Cambridge], to which they gave the name the tree of liberty!" The exclamation point in Hutchinson's history, written years later in exile, speaks to his sense of amazement at their action that still lingered. Tutors had cracked down on the college's lax policy of allowing students to be excused from required "prayers and college exercises." Students declared the college action "*unconstitutional*," a word Hutchinson considered so audacious that he put it in italics, as if to say: Here is where the talk of rights under the British constitution and Magna Charta led—what next? Students broke the windows of the tutors' residence; three or four "rioters were discovered and expelled"; the freshman, sophomore, and junior classes resigned; Harvard's overseers confirmed the expulsions, and the students gave in. Hutchinson got the events right, leaving out only that the whole affair was sparked by a protest over the rancid butter served in the dining hall, perhaps because he did not want to trivialize an episode he took so seriously.[32]

The extent to which Boston's tree per se inspired other appropriations of liberty is hard to disentangle from the many inspiring events of the decade. The tree clearly sanctioned women entering politicized space: they were welcomed as spectators at events at the tree or looking out from "the windows of the neighboring houses" as a sign that the entire community endorsed the protest. At the mock trial of the Stamp Act, the act was labeled "For the oppression of the widows and the fatherless," a blatant appeal to the large number of impoverished widows in Boston. Women were numerous as mourners in the two huge funeral processions of 1770: for the boy Seider and for the victims of the Massacre. Broadside engravings depicted women at both events. The Sons of Liberty dubbed them Daughters of Liberty, which was an effort to co-opt women in the many new roles they had taken.[33]

There is little question that the tree also politicized boys. In 1765, more than half the town's white male population was under sixteen—which means that about eighteen hundred were of school age, of whom only nine hundred were enrolled in public schools. "Boys," the term used to denigrate crowds, could refer to schoolboys, but it also might designate apprentices, who usually served from fourteen or younger through twenty-one. A strapping eighteen-year-old apprentice might still be called a "boy." These probably were the "sturdy" boys in the dismissive accounts of the crowd actions of 1768. If Pope's Day—an irreverent, noisy spectacle—was a day that belonged to boys of all ages and ranks (and to girls as spectators and daytime participants), the defiant, boisterous events at the tree were natural draws for them. And of course the very name Sons of Liberty might have had special meaning to boys, whose primary status was still as sons, a good many of whom were without fathers.[34]

Can we not assume that political consciousness among such youth expanded? The schoolboys who walked en masse with their teachers to see the effigies hanging on the tree in August 1765 may have marched in the boycott picketing in 1770 in which Christopher Seider was killed and then in funeral procession that began at the tree. Apprentices turned out on the night of the Massacre (two of the victims were seventeen), attended the tea protest meetings in December 1773, and were among those who boarded the tea ships. It was the sort of politicization that Ebenezer Fox, indentured first to a farmer and then to a Boston barber and wig-maker, may have had in mind when he wrote years later, "I and other boys situated similarly to myself ... made a direct application of the doctrines we daily heard, in relation to the oppression of the mother country, to our own circumstances." In his memoir Fox recalled that he felt "the time was come when I should liberate myself from the thralldom of others, and set up a government of my own."[35]

How much the tree inspired the political awakening of African Americans is more problematic. In 1765 they numbered seven hundred, about a tenth of the population, most of them enslaved. One has only to read between the lines of patriot statements disavowing crowds of "Negroes and boys" or excluding Negroes from their processions to recognize that they were a presence. But years of being banned and put down had its alienating effects. One charge that white leaders leveled against the British troops who arrived in 1768 was that they inspired Boston's Negroes to say, "now that the soldiers are come, the Negroes shall be free, and the Liberty Boys slaves." Indeed in 1774, when a British army occupied the town, we should not be surprised at Abigail Adams's frantic report of a "conspiracy" by blacks to join with the British in return for their freedom. Such actions were consistent with the response of slaves in the Chesapeake area on the approach of British armies. The first anguished petitions that Boston blacks sent to the legislature in 1773 and 1774 demanding emancipation do not suggest that they were inspired by the rhetoric of liberty; on the contrary, they may have been more sensitive to the hypocrisy of patriot rhetoric. Later they changed.[36]

Boston's liberty tree might have aroused in Negroes echoes of African traditions associated with trees. In West Africa a tree was planted on the grave of a loved one as a sign of everlasting life. The lanterns hung on the liberty tree might have evoked African "bottle trees," which were "trees garlanded with bottles, vessels, and other objects for protecting the household, through invocation of the dead." And patriot funeral processions past the tree could have had special meaning for Boston Negroes, whose own funeral processions through the streets were so intensely emotional that the town regulated them. We are still sorting out the ways in which such cultural traditions entered into a many-sided quest for liberty in the era of the Revolution.[37]

4. Liberty Poles: *"It is now common here to Assemble at the Liberty Pole"*

Did the "spirit of liberty spread where it was not intended" in other colonies, inspired by other liberty trees or liberty poles? Were there other

Ebenezer Mackintoshes? Did sites of the tree or pole serve elsewhere as a focus for patriots contending with each other?

Just how many trees were consecrated and poles raised in the colonies as a whole awaits a full tallying. Half a century ago, Arthur Schlesinger Sr., relying for the most part on newspapers, found eight trees and twenty-two poles from 1765 through 1776. A modern researcher, J. L. Bell, found others by searching for key words in the digitized version of Philadelphia's *Pennsylvania Gazette*, a paper published at the center of the colonies, and in the computerized index to the *Virginia Gazette*, published in Williamsburg, Virginia's capital. David Hackett Fischer, using Google to search the Internet (where historical societies and patriotic organizations often report on historical events), found a good many more. The newly digitized *American Archives* produced others. Add to these sites indexed in the *Hartford Courant* or found in a miscellany of local sources, and we can announce (roll of militia drums and flourish of fifes!) a grand total of thirteen trees and fifty-five poles, or half as many more trees and two and a half times as many poles.[38]

Most of the liberty trees were in New England, very likely inspired by the example of Boston, the "mother" tree. They were in Massachusetts (Boston, Cambridge, Dorchester, Deerfield, Great Barrington, Plymouth, Roxbury); in Connecticut (Bloomfield, Norwich); and in Rhode Island (Newport, Providence). We know of none in the middle colonies and only two in the South, in Annapolis, Maryland, and Charlestown, South Carolina. The first and most famous pole was raised in New York City, and most of the other poles—in southeastern New England, the Hudson Valley, Long Island, and East Jersey—appear to have been diffused from its example, while other poles in western and northern New England may have been based on eastern examples. There was one pole, it seems, in Pennsylvania and one in Maryland, none in Delaware, and only two in Virginia. Of the four largest coastal cites, Philadelphia alone was bereft of either tree or pole—or so it appears. And in the five states of the South, there were in all two trees and five poles. Or at least this is the pattern that emerges from using newspapers as a major source. I suspect that all the trees made it into the historical record but that the poles are underreported. Local newspapers—the chief means of spreading political news—might reveal more, as might private letters by people in the patriot communication network. Then again, not all the Sons of Liberty organizations and not all the other popular movements of the day resorted to liberty poles—an intriguing subject to which we will return at the end of this section.[39]

A full history of trees and poles would require revisiting the history of resistance movements place by place, focusing especially on the interplay between the leaders and the rank and file and between moderates and radicals, which in the cities meant especially between merchants and middling mechanics and the lower sort, and in the countryside, between the gentry and yeomanry. It would also require being attentive to groups outside the political system—women, boys, seamen, and African Americans.[40]

If, for example, we turn to Charleston, the major southern city with a tree (and pole), which had a population of twelve thousand in 1775, half of whom were African American slaves, we sense at once the tensions of a seaport and a slave society intruding on politics. Charleston patriots weathered the turbulence of the Stamp Act crisis of 1765–66 without a tree. (They erected a gallows from which an effigy of a stamp collector was hung.) Henry Laurens, a wealthy merchant and slaveholder suspected of being appointed Stamp Act commissioner, was visited in his mansion by sixty to eighty sailors, their faces blackened, "who handled me pretty uncouthly," Laurens wrote, chanting "Liberty, Liberty & Stampd Paper." A few days later a huge crowd paraded to celebrate the resignation of the stamp officials, carrying a British flag inscribed with a single word: "Liberty." In December 1765, a large number of sailors, out of work because customs officials would not clear ships attempting to sail with unstamped papers, "formed a Mob to collect Money of the People in the Streets," the governor wrote, "but these Sons of Liberty suppressed them instantly, and committed the Ring-leaders to Gaol." In January 1766, in the wake of all these appeals for "Liberty," "some negroes … mimick'd their betters in crying out *Liberty*," as they paraded through the streets, Laurens wrote. "Here in town *all* were soldiers in arms for more than a week." After this, the lieutenant governor was relieved that "apprehensions of a Negro insurrection … happily proved abortive."[41]

White mechanics initiated a liberty tree in the spring of 1766 in celebration of the repeal of the Stamp Act—one of them listed twenty-three tradesmen among the twenty-six men present at the event. Mechanics were already organized in a Fellowship Society and now formed the John Wilkes Club. But the tree does not seem to have been put to use until 1768 in the enforcement of the nonimportation agreements. "The principal mechanics" according to a newspaper, initiated meetings under the "most noble live oak" in "Mr. Mazyck's pasture" near the waterfront, at which Christopher Gadsden, a merchant leader of the Sons of Liberty, usually presided. A committee of thirty-nine that was chosen to enforce the boycott measured the kind of political balance struck in this southern city: thirteen places each for mechanics, merchants, and planters (who had mansions in the city and plantations in the countryside).

Charleston's tree became a place of deliberation, intimidation, and celebration, revealing class tensions among patriots. By 1775, as the mechanics showed their staying power, the royal governor reported that "The Men of Property begin at length to see that the many headed power of the People who ... have Discovered their own strength & importance, and will not be so easily governed by their former Leaders." By 1778, Gadsden, who had lost favor with mechanics, wondered out loud whether "we have too many amongst us who want again to be running upon every Fancy to the Meetings of liberty tree. ... It was a Disease." A wartime occupying British army cut down the tree and burned out its roots.[42]

In general, liberty poles seem to have been much more of a vehicle for expressing popular opinion than liberty trees. Poles were more numerous, more a site of contention between Whig patriots and Loyalists and in New York between patriots and soldiers. Raising a pole was a very willful act. There did not have to be a community consensus, but there had to be a collective effort by a body of workers. On the eastern seaboard, the poles usually were masts of enormous height, reported in the newspapers as forty-five, seventy-five, eighty-five, and one hundred feet high and more. Inland they might have been smaller, stripped-down trees that farmers could put up. While some saw poles as a surrogate for a liberty tree, more commonly they were referred to as flag staffs, flag poles, or masts and had somewhat different functions than the tree. Four towns with trees also had poles (Boston, Newport, Plymouth, Charleston). If you wanted people to assemble, even if you had a tree, you needed a pole to raise a flag high enough to get the message out. In the first wave (1766 and the following years) poles celebrated the repeal of the Stamp Act and loyalty to Britain, flying the Union Jack. In the second major wave (1774–76), when poles became common in small towns, they were acts of defiance associated with military preparations against Britain and the intimidation of Tories.[43]

New York City's experience illustrates how much the liberty pole itself became a lightning rod for events. The city, as the headquarters for the British army in North America, by 1767 had two regiments of troops, which according to the Quartering Act had to be paid for by the New York Assembly, another goad to colonists who did not believe in taxation without representation. New York City also had the largest proportion of Loyalists of any major city, led by a segment of the colony's landed and merchant aristocracy.

New York City's liberty pole, in the only known drawing by a contemporary, is enmeshed in iron to keep British soldiers from destroying it, as they did the short pole in the background. The man in jail (to the left) is Alexander McDougall, who was jailed by the colonial assembly. The number "45" at the top of the pole links him to England's imprisoned reformer John Wilkes. The female admirers of the Sons of Liberty leader peer from a window (to the right). P. E. DuSimitiere, "Raising the Liberty Pole in New York City," c.1770. Courtesy of the Library Company of Philadelphia.

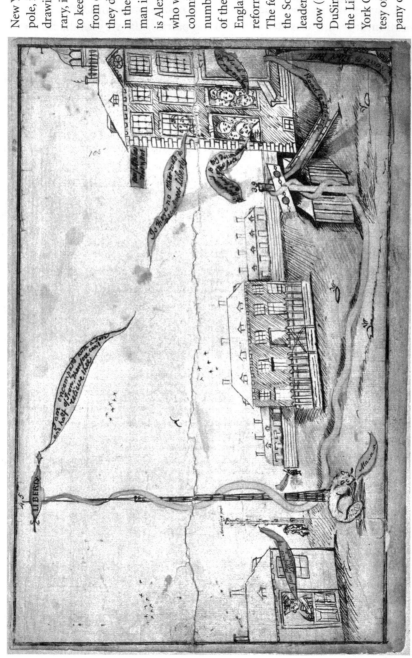

A pole (actually two) went up in the spring of 1766 to celebrate the Stamp Act repeal. A British flag was hoisted with an image of King George and of Pitt. Located in "the fields," New York's common, close to a soldiers' barracks and parade ground, it was a provocation. Soldiers cut down the pole four times, and civilians restored it no less than five times. Soldiers sawed the pole, mined it, and blew it up. Some sixty-eight feet tall and topped by a smaller pole of twenty-two feet, it was a ship's mast, which means it was crafted by mast makers, hauled by teamsters, raised by crews of shipyard workers and sailors, and eventually fortified by blacksmiths with protective iron hoops. The laboring classes clearly were invested in the pole.[44]

In no city did seamen play a greater role in street politics. The Stamp Act "insurrection" of 1765, according to General Gage, was "composed of great numbers of Sailors headed by Captains of Privateers." In the 1766 riots, the two "general officers," according to Captain John Montressor, "were Tony and Dale two ship carpenters, who it seems ... can either raise or suppress a Mob instantly." The leaders with staying power were a small group of middling radicals of humble origins who called themselves the Sons of Liberty and were sometimes referred to as the Sons of Neptune. They championed the economic grievances of sailors and laborers, who were suffering unemployment and poverty because off-duty soldiers were hired at half their wages.

The liberty pole was at the center of events. In 1769–70, when the radical leader Alexander MacDougall was jailed by the Assembly, the Sons of Liberty mounted the symbol "45" on the pole to link their hero with John Wilkes, jailed by the English Parliament. After the fifth pole was erected in 1770, General Gage reported, "It is now common here to Assemble on all Occasions of Public Concern at the Liberty Pole and Coffee House, as for the Antient Romans to repair to the Forum. And the Orators harangue on all sides." In 1770, sailors and laboring men engaged with soldiers in two days of hand-to-hand combat, which began with a defense of the pole—the "Battle of Golden Hill." In 1774, the day after a small number of New Yorkers destroyed the cargo of a tea ship, thousands gathered at the pole to affirm the action. In 1775, radical leaders were "calling out the People almost every Day to the Liberty Pole." What began in 1766 as a celebratory pole ended as a staging place for military resistance. In the final crisis, 1774–76, when mechanics formed their own committees to vie with merchants for a place on revolutionary committees, they met in a building of their own that they christened "Mechanics Hall." The pole survived until the British army occupied the city in 1776 and took it down.[45]

A representation of one of many skirmishes at New York's liberty pole, in which the artist left no doubt that it was leather-aproned artisans confronting British soldiers, who are using bayonets and firing at them. Such an armed confrontation led to the "Battle of Golden Hill" in the city in February 1770. This mid-nineteenth-century drawing is by Felix Darley, book illustrator. Library of Congress.

Liberty trees and poles were clearly important and could be central, as they were in Boston and New York, but I am also struck by their relative absence in one place after another. Explaining absences in history, while treacherous, can be revealing. Take three areas where historians have explored strong movements from below that shaped the response to imperial issues: Philadelphia, Virginia, and western Massachusetts. The absence of tree and pole in Philadelphia has already been mentioned: the city was the center of a well-articulated artisan radical movement that in 1774–76 triumphed over a ruling class that had withdrawn to a neutrality vis-à-vis Great Britain. Regarding Virginia, where I came up with only two poles, the author of a now classic study of symbolic action in the colony encountered neither liberty trees nor poles, and the author of a recent study that weaves the complex interplay of poor farmers, slaves, and Indians and large planters and merchants similarly turned up none. In this slave society, in which in some areas slaves might be 40 to 50 percent of the population, large planters and yeoman farmers alike had cause to be fearful of inciting them. When the British army appeared in Chesapeake Bay, slaves deserted plantations in droves. In western Massachusetts, where there also were only a very few liberty poles and one tree, it may be that the yeoman majority felt they did not need them: they could mass several thousand men to shut down county courts and intimidate judges and sheriffs. Indeed, to such radicals the liberty trees and poles in the East may have seemed too tame a tactic.[46]

Nor does the liberty tree or pole seem to have been adopted in areas where desperate farmers were consumed with internal grievances with their own gentry which overshadowed imperial issues. This appears to be true of the "Regulators" in the North Carolina backcountry who in 1770 were defeated in a pitched battle with troops mustered by the royal governor; of the foes of the large land proprietors in New Jersey; and of tenant farmers in the Hudson Valley who fought for secure leases from their aristocratic landlords, some Whig, some Loyalist. New York's tenants began and ended the pre-Revolutionary decade with localized uprisings against their manor lords. All such farmers fighting to hold on to or acquire title to land may simply have been of no mind to raise a symbol they might with good cause have identified with their class enemy.

Urban radicals did not join hands with agrarian radicals. The Sons of Liberty in New York City were "great opposers to these riots" by tenants, Captain Montressor reported: "They are of opinion that no one is entitled to riot but themselves." And in North Carolina, the backcountry Regulator leader Herman Husband warned that "while the Sons of Liberty withstand the Lords of Parliament, in behalf of true Liberty, Let not Officers under them carry out unjust Oppression in our own Province." Such mutual distancing by agrarian radicals and the Sons of Liberty helps us in defining the role played by liberty trees and poles. They flourished in communities where there was conflict *within* the patriot movement: they expressed both resistance from below and the efforts of the Sons of Liberty leaders and the "better sort" to control the radical impulses from below.[47]

5. Icon: "The Tree of Liberty must be refreshed by the blood of patriots and tyrants"

In the revolutionary era, the liberty tree became an icon, even where it was not a physical presence, with a speed that suggests it filled some deep unmet need for symbolic representation of the American cause. In Boston the patriot engraver Paul Revere portrayed the tree (or liberty cap) in his cartoon drawings and on his famous silver bowl. The tree was celebrated in song in John Dickinson's very popular "Liberty Song" (1768), in which singers hailed "the TREE their own hands to LIBERTY rear'd," and in Thomas Paine's poem "The Liberty Tree" (1775), which was also set to music. By 1774–75, London's political caricaturists invariably depicted each new Boston event against the background of a tree labeled "Liberty Tree."[48]

During the war the symbol of the tree became part of the visual vocabulary of armed resistance. More than one New England soldier carved a crude image of the tree on his powderhorn. James Pike, for example, placed a pine tree labeled "Liberty Tree" in the center of a tableau, on one side of which was a line of six soldiers labeled "British Regulars Aggressors, April 19, 1775," and on the other, a line of six colonials labeled "Provincials Defending." The scene encapsulated the patriot version not only of the Battle of Lexington, but of the entire war. The tree was painted on drums. A tree, usually a pine, sometimes an elm, was the central emblem on flags adopted by military units; one such was at the Battle of Bunker Hill. A common motif was a flag with the motto "Appeal to Heaven," shorthand for John Locke's justification of the right of a people to revolt when they had exhausted all other means of redressing their grievances. One flag had an elm in the center, identified above it as "Liberty Tree," with "Appeal to God" below. Another combined an elm with the immensely popular coiled rattlesnake at its base and the motto "Don't Tread on Me."[49]

Soldiers put green boughs in their hats, long a token of the forest "as a seat of greenwood liberty" among English rebels. Early in the war, Washington ordered his diversely clad, ragged soldiers to "adorn their Hats with *Green-Boughs*" to provide a token of uniformity on parade. In 1783, at the tail end of the war, in the mutiny of the Pennsylvania line, soldiers demanding a settlement for back pay marched down Market Street in Philadelphia, "bayonets fixed, drums beating and green boughs in their hats." So did farmer rebels in 1786 in western Massachusetts led by Captain Daniel Shays; the green boughs in their hats were understood by an observer to be "the badge of rebellion." In Vermont, a man could declare himself a member of Ethan Allen's defiant "Green Mountain Boys" simply by putting a fir twig in his hat.[50]

As a metaphor, "The Tree of Liberty" entered the American political vocabulary. A keyword search by Eric Slauter in the recently digitized version of Evans's *Early American Imprints* suggests that the tree caught on quickly.[51] Witness the imprints for Philadelphia alone (a city with neither tree nor pole). At the commencement exercises of the College of Philadelphia in 1766, a graduating orator asked that the "streams of learning" be directed "to water the goodly TREE OF LIBERTY." By 1774 John Leacock, Philadelphia's patriot satirist of New England's biblical ways, made fun of a Boston leader as "Jeremiah, the son of the prophet" who "gat himself up on high and climbed on the top of Liberty Tree," from which he spoke to the multitude. There was also a poem by Philip Freneau in 1775 mourning the cutting down of Boston's liberty tree as "fair freedom's shrine" and a meditation by the composer Joseph Hopkinson on colonists replacing an old tree planted by the king with "another tree, young and vigorous; and we will water it and it shall grow." The liberty pole enjoyed no such encomiums. Conservative writers portrayed it as a symbol of the anarchy of the Revolution. In a mock epic poem, *M'Fingal* (1775–76), by the Connecticut wit John Trumbull, a Tory village squire who calls the pole "the maypole of sedition" ends up carted by patriots, tarred and feathered, and hoisted halfway up a liberty pole.[52]

After the war, New England ministers and orators invoked "the tree of liberty" as a metaphor for liberties that had been won: "the fair fruits of the tree of liberty" (Hartford, Conn.); "the last seed of the tree of liberty" (Newburyport, Mass.); science "flourishing under the shade of the tree of liberty" (New Hampshire). At Boston's Independence Day celebration in 1783, Dr. John Warren, whose famous brother, Joseph, was martyred at Bunker Hill, asked his audience to remember that the roots of "*the stately Tree of Liberty* ... were watered with your blood."[53]

Thus, in 1787, when Thomas Jefferson penned the since famous lines, "the Tree of Liberty must be refreshed from time to time with the blood of patriots and tyrants. It is its natural manure," the metaphor had some currency. Jefferson may well have gotten it from Viscount Bolingbroke (1678–1751), whose numerous aphorisms he copied into his student notebook. It was probably known to men with a classical education. In 1793 in the debate in the French national convention over sentencing King Louis XVI to death, deputy Bertrand Barere invoked it, remarking to his fellow deputy Thomas Paine that it stemmed from "a classical author."[54]

At the time, however, Jefferson's comment was neither public nor famous. In Paris as American minister to France, he made it late in 1787 in a letter to a political friend criticizing the newly drafted federal constitution. He thought that the framers had placed too much power in government, overreacting to Shays's Rebellion. Calculating that one rebellion for thirteen states in the eleven years since independence "comes to one rebellion in a century and a half, for each State," he asked, "What country ever existed a century and a half without a rebellion? And what country can preserve its liberties, if its rulers are not warned from time to time, that this people preserve the spirit of resistance?" Jefferson issued not a call to rebellion but a warning against the consequences of repressing one. He expressed the same sentiment to James Madison when we wrote, "I hold it, that a little rebellion now and then, is a good thing, and as necessary in the political world as storms in the physical."[55]

How widely the thinking behind Jefferson's "tree of liberty" phrase was shared by the founders is hard to say; I suspect not very widely. Would-be rulers in 1787 were divided, as they had been since 1765. The remark would place Jefferson among leaders willing and anxious to accommodate democratic movements; many more leaders leaned towards curtailing or repressing them. The division was in the constitutional convention and would reappear in the 1790s and shape a new wave of liberty poles and the attempt to repress them.

6. *Roots: Of Royal Oaks, Village Maypoles, and Liberty Caps*

To probe how far the liberty tree sank roots in American soil, we have jumped ahead of ourselves. Where did the liberty tree come from? And what about its brother the liberty pole? And the liberty cap perched atop a staff, possibly an ancestor of the pole? In America, tree and pole flourished, as we have seen, from 1765 to about 1776, and the symbol and metaphor of the tree was rampant during the war, from 1775 to 1783. The pole, but not the tree, returned from 1793 to 1801. The *image* of the cap of liberty on a staff was ubiquitous in the revolutionary era, and in the 1790s the cap itself emerged.

We have to widen our scope. Our search takes us racing breathlessly back and forth across the Atlantic: from early modern England to the colonies; from revolutionary era America to revolutionary era France and near-revolutionary England in the 1790s; and then back again to the United States. At this stage of our knowledge this much can be sorted out:

1. *Several generalized traditions of trees in Britain would have flowed into the American liberty tree.* Trees could indeed have been part of the lore attached to some popular rebellions. Legendary outlaws and rebels made the forest their domain (like Robin Hood in Sherwood Forest). The garbled memory of Kett's rebellion included an "Oak of Reformation." In the calendar of British holidays, however, the only day valorizing a tree was an unlikely inspiration to Americans: May 29, Royal Oak Day, celebrating the triumphal entry of King Charles II to London in 1660, by legend after hiding from his Cromwellian pursuers in a hollow oak. This day was "for a long time an extremely popular holiday" in England.[56]

In New England, where Stuart monarchs were honored in the breach as enemies of their Puritan ancestors, the royal oak was not the stuff of celebrations. But Boston had a way of appropriating English traditions and turning them upside down. Guy Fawkes Day, "the fifth of November," which in England marked the deliverance of a Stuart king from a Popish plot, in New England became Pope's Day, celebrating the Hanoverian succession which delivered Anglo-America from the Stuart pretenders to the throne allegedly in league with the pope. Effigies of the devil and the pope prompting the Stuart pretender were often central to Pope's Day. In Massachusetts, minister and magistrate sanctioned the day, banning only its excesses, because it kept alive the historical Puritan hatred of the Stuarts and popery.

The same process was at work for January 30, a day set by English authority to mourn the execution of Charles I. A century earlier, however, New England had provided a refuge for the regicides Goffe and Whalley, the memory of whom was still alive. Royal governors dutifully marked the day, but services were held only in the small number of Anglican churches, Congregationalists honoring it in the breach. In 1750, Reverend Jonathan Mayhew took the occasion to preach *A Discourse Concerning Unlimited*

Submission and Non-Resistance to Higher Powers, in which he justified regicide—"the most famous sermon preached in pre-Revolutionary America." So it is not farfetched that there was an element of reversal in Boston's adopting an elm as its symbol of liberty as opposed to the royal oak.[57]

In England the elm, while well known, was not especially an object on veneration. Colonists were probably drawing on the larger tradition of the oak as a national symbol. "In countless eighteenth-century broadsides, pamphlets, ballads, inn signs, and allegorical engravings," Simon Schama informs us, "the Heart of Oak became the bulwark of liberty, all that stood between freeborn Englishmen and Catholic slavery and idolatry." The heart of the oak was the "core of the tree ... the most defiantly resistant." Thus the oak, while royal, was also national; it was not contradictory that Dickinson's "Liberty Song" not only took the tune of the British drinking song "Hearts of Oak," but adapted its lyrics as well. In consecrating trees as a symbol of liberty (whether elm, oak, or poplar), Americans would have been echoing the British sacralization of the oak. And perhaps they were also mocking it, which may account for the zeal of British soldiers in taking down liberty trees and poles.[58]

2. In the thirteen American colonies, where traditions tended to be highly localized, there were only faint traces of specific sacred trees. The legend of the "charter oak" in Connecticut—that in 1687 Hartford residents hid their colony's charter in a hollow oak to keep it from royal officials—did not appear until *after* the American Revolution. In Pennsylvania, the legend of the Quaker William Penn signing a humane treaty with the Lenni Lenape Indians under the "treaty elm" was cultivated in the 1770s by the Penn family interest for political purposes. In Maryland, the claim that the ancient poplar that became Annapolis's liberty tree was the site of an Indian treaty has also been discredited. In other words, these legends of a local tradition appear to be post-Revolution inventions, not known at the time liberty trees were initiated.[59]

Although there were no special trees with political associations, trees in general were much venerated by the colonists. After all, they came to a leafy green continent where trees were the prime source of their shelter, warmth, and livelihood. Probably half of all artisans worked in wood. New England towns would not experience a craze for elms lining village streets until the early nineteenth century, but in the colonial era, rural families often planted elms on their own land: "homestead" elms, "dooryard" elms, "bridal" elms, which became landmarks in family history. And Massachusetts clearly valorized the pine tree, which the colonial government put on the "pine tree shilling," paper money, and military flags. This may explain why the liberty tree on James Pike's powderhorn was a pine (aside from the fact that a pine was a lot easier to carve on an ox's horn than a leafy elm).[60]

3. *What of the intriguing maypole?* In Britain as in Europe, the maypole was the cynosure of May Day, the first of May, "the great rural festival of our fathers," as a correspondent told William Hone, the indefatigable compiler of British popular lore, as late as 1825. A custom that was many centuries old and suppressed by Puritans under Cromwell, it came back with the Stuart restoration and thrived in the eighteenth century as "one of the principal holidays of the Spring for young people." The maypole was either a small tree or a tree stripped down to a pole. On May Day, young men and women went into the woods "amaying" to bring back a fresh tree or gather green boughs and flowers to decorate an existing maypole; it was a day of song, dance, drink, and especially sexual license associated with ancient spring fertility rites, a day young people lived for. The "phallic maypole," observes the historian Christopher Hill, was "for the rural lower class, almost a symbol of independence of their betters." In the seventeenth century, after Puritans made the maypole an object of reformation, it became a Royalist symbol. In the eighteenth century, while it was not generally put to political uses, if some reforming magistrate interfered with maypole festivities, he might provoke a riot or run the risk of having his own property damaged.[61]

What happened to the maypole in the colonies is a small mystery that awaits a squad of historical detectives. It made its way to New England early in the seventeenth century but did not survive the harsh Puritan moral climate, that much we know. In 1627 authority squelched Thomas Morton's setting up an eighty-foot maypole at his trading post at Merry Mount (modern-day Quincy near Boston). His sin was not only "inviting the indian women for their consorts, dancing and frisking together like so many fairies or furies," as Governor William Bradford of the Plymouth colony blustered, but as the ever class-conscious Thomas Hutchinson grasped, Morton's worst sin was to "set all the servants free," allowing them to join the revelry on a par with their masters. This single event seems lost to the public memory of New Englanders, however, until Hutchinson recounted it in his history of the colony published in 1764. While mid-eighteenth-century Massachusetts saw a revival of a cluster of traditional English customs—rough music, Guy Fawkes Day, Christmas mumming—frolicking around a maypole was not one of them.[62]

What about the other colonies? In New York City, May 1 was the traditional moving day and no more, more chaotic than festive. In Pennsylvania, on the other hand, first of May festivities were common, perhaps because it was settled in the eighteenth century by migrants from Germany, Wales, Scotland, and Ireland, still fresh with village folkways. At midcentury a German traveler reported the custom of "merrymaking" in eastern Pennsylvania on May 1 and 2, especially among "unmarried" young men and women who took part in "games, dancing, shooting and the like"—but he made no mention of a maypole. In Philadelphia by midcentury, the folklorist Roger A. Abraham tells us, the Schuylkill Fishing Club began its sporting season ceremoniously on May 1, and by the 1760s and 1770s the fraternal group that became the Sons of St. Tammany had appropriated the day for its celebration of a mythological Indian King Tammany. But folklorists and antiquarian historians have uncovered no maypoles in Pennsylvania, either in the city or countryside. Elsewhere, the only report of a maypole I know of is for Annapolis c. 1771 as part of a Tammany May Day festivity.[63]

We may be closer, however, to precedents for a striking, little-noted celebration on May 1, 1778, by soldiers in Washington's army at Valley Forge in eastern Pennsylvania, at which poles abounded. Fortunately, we have a soldier's description of the event. "I was woke by three cheers in honor of King Tammany," Private George Ewing of New Jersey recorded in his journal. The whole day was spent in "mirth & Jollity." (There was good reason to celebrate the recently arrived news of a Treaty of Alliance between the United States and France that held out such promise.) The night before, each regiment had raised its own maypole; then on May 1 a sergeant in the costume of King Tammany was escorted by thirteen sergeants, each carrying a bow and arrow, followed by thirteen drummers and fife players, with privates in thirteen platoons bringing up the rear. The soldiers, "their hats adorned with white blossoms," paraded through camp "huzzaing at every Pole they pass'd." Officers later dispensed whiskey. Save for the absence of women and sexual play (as far as we know), it was a May Day. The ceremony blended "playing Indian" and playing patriot.[64]

Knowing that the army of some thirteen thousand men (and several hundred women) at Valley Forge was drawn disproportionately from the "lower sort" from all parts of the country, we can speculate that how soldiers experienced this spectacular event depended on what they brought to it: those familiar with May 1 in Philadelphia might have thought they were at a Tammany festival; recent immigrants may have taken it for a traditional May Day of the old country and interpreted the poles as maypoles; but for the numerous New Englanders and New Yorkers in the army, the day would have echoed rallying round a liberty pole or liberty tree.

Unless folklorists correct us and excavate some more maypoles in the right places, we can rule out maypoles as the source of liberty poles. It may be that it was the other way around: liberty poles came first, maypoles second—if at all. The liberty pole flourished in New England, where there was no continuous tradition of either May Day or maypoles and the few areas we know of where the day was observed as a Tammany festival (with one known exception, Annapolis) did not produce either liberty poles or liberty trees. The flagpole was a more likely source for liberty poles than maypoles.

4. *What about the liberty cap atop a staff?* The common lore for centuries was that the Phrygian cap of liberty, a soft, floppy, conical cap, also called the pileus, originated in ancient Rome as part of the ritual in which a slave became a free man. He was touched with a wand and the cap bestowed upon him. How well diffused this lore was geographically or socially is unclear.[65]

As scholars trace transmissions, the cap atop a staff (sometimes depicted by artists as a spear or a pike but more commonly as a short pole about the height of a person) became a symbol of liberty in the Netherlands and migrated to England in the "Glorious Revolution" of 1688 that brought William of Holland to the English throne as a constitutional monarch. In the eighteenth century, artists personified Britain as "Britannia," a female in classical garb holding a staff topped by a liberty cap, and the continent "America" as a near-naked Indian princess often holding a spear with a cap. By the 1760s, when London crowds chanting "Wilkes and Liberty" carried the cap on a pole above their heads and a caricaturist depicted John Wilkes wearing a cap that resembled a chamber pot, it was clearly part of the visual vocabulary of protest.[66]

In the Stamp Act crisis, the *image* of the cap on a staff circulated in America. It appeared on a medal and on a commemorative silver bowl made and engraved by Paul Revere for the Sons of Liberty; in 1770 Revere put the image on the masthead of Boston's two major patriot newspapers. Meanwhile a processional pole made its appearance. In the New Hampshire protest, a crowd carried an effigy of a stamp commissioner mounted on a tall pole. And in the boycott of stamped paper early in 1766, in at least six New England towns patriots carried poles through the streets in angry processions. Patriots tacked any stamped paper they uncovered, like a ship's manifest, to a pole, parading it through town and burning it at the town gallows or stocks. These processional poles were all without a cap. There were still other "pole" traditions. In the seventeenth century Boston artisans tried to carry an interloper out of town on a pole, a time-honored form of rough music in England. In 1770, in the Boston boycott of merchants in violation of the nonimportation agreements, the boys picketing T. Lillie's store carried the image of a head tacked to a pole, a grim reminder of the custom of authority beheading someone for treason and mounting the severed head on a pole.

The first liberty pole, raised in New York in the spring of 1766, thus may have had several sources: the inspiration of Boston's liberty tree; the Netherlands' tradition of the cap of liberty on a staff known to Dutch New Yorkers; the recent processional poles and probably the flagpole. But the feeling of the huge overawing masts, it must be said, is very different from either the short staffs or the thin portable processional poles. Moreover, the New Yorkers never seem to have adorned any of their five successive poles with the cap of liberty, although two poles—one in New Jersey and one in connecticut—seem to have been.

The image of the liberty cap, either by itself or atop a staff, was pervasive. British cartoonists ridiculed ragged "Yankee Doodle" soldiers as wearing a Phrygian cap marked "Death or Liberty" and carrying a flag with the liberty tree. The symbol of cap and staff was adopted by several military units, by the Continental Congress for the title page of its journal, and by the *Pennsylvania Magazine*. Over time it made its way onto seals adopted by several states. Thus by 1790, when Benjamin Franklin bequeathed to George Washington his walking stick with a gold head shaped in the form of a cap of liberty, it had become a very American symbol.[67]

After all this breathless influence-chasing, we are still left with a yawning gap to account for the origins of the liberty tree and liberty pole on American soil. For the tree, colonists did not reach back to recover the tradition of a specific tree associated with liberty in the mother country or in their own colonies because such traditions were scant. To a generalized tradition of the oak, a national British symbol, they likely did reach. For the liberty pole, colonists did not draw on the maypole, because where liberty poles appeared, there was no popular tradition of maypoles, and where the day was observed (as in Pennsylvania), there were no (detectable) poles until the array of thirteen poles in the army at Valley Forge on May 1, 1778. For the poles, Americans would have been drawing on the other uses of poles.

One could argue that because liberty trees and poles sprang up so rapidly in so many places, communities were drawing on some deep-buried memory of May Day. Perhaps, but certainly not in New England, chief spawner of trees and poles. This may be an example of a newly felt political need impelling colonials to reach back into the past of the old country. It was hardly a custom that was long frozen in early America which then thawed. Rather, trees and poles were diffused by the examples of the celebrated first tree in Boston and first pole in New York City, both widely reported in the newspapers. Trees moreover very likely inspired poles. The liberty tree, I have argued, was made in America—an invented tradition—and so was the liberty pole.

7. *Uses: "Some convenient tree will afford them a state house"*

Given the relative absence of a tradition, to account for the popularity of the liberty tree we have to return to the attributes of the tree itself and the functions it performed, and do the same for the pole. As we have the fullest record of Boston's elm, let us take it as our prototype for the liberty tree.

Boston's elm did not so much refer to a tradition as possess the qualities for the creation of one. Liberty was a concept in eighteenth-century America that was "ubiquitous and protean," as the historian Eric Foner puts it and as everyone who has puzzled over the subject has pointed out. The word meant some things that all would hold in common and also meant different things to different people. The tree easily could have inspired devotion. It was "one of the trees for which so many have a veneration," wrote the *Boston Gazette*, referring to a cluster of great elms within sight of each other. First, by its very size the tree was imposing. In 1825, when the "Great Elm" on the nearby common was measured, it was sixty-five feet high, twenty-two feet in girth, and eighty-six feet in spread. We don't know the size of the liberty tree elm, but contemporaries spoke of it as "a stately elm … whose lofty branches seem'd to touch the skies," or as "This glorious tree, tho' big and tall." Second, the tree was old. It was said to have been planted in 1646 (a date that would have put descendants of the Puritan admirers of Cromwell in mind of the capture of Charles I in 1647 and his execution in 1649). To Americans in a young country such a tree was ancient and deeply rooted, like "the rights of Englishmen," the Magna Charta, and the rights to self-government granted in colonial charters. Third, the tree was a gift of nature. As a deciduous tree which became green again each spring, it was a symbol of the renewal of nature and of life everlasting, easily associated with the natural rights of man. Fourth, it could easily have put a people steeped in the Bible in mind of the tree of knowledge and the tree of life in the holy book as well as of the many biblical parables in which trees figured. The Bible was a book the devout in New England read from beginning to end and then started over again. To Congregationalists the tree could have stood for the religious liberty their forefathers came to the new world to protect (which in their eyes faced renewed Anglican and papist threats). And to dissenters from the Congregational establishment, like the Baptists, the tree could have stood for "soul liberty." What the liberty tree might have meant to those "unequals" who believed that they were being denied liberty I have suggested earlier. The meaning of the liberty for which the tree stood thus was in the eyes of the beholder and could have changed over time, even in the span of the decade from 1765 to 1775.[68]

In Boston the tree filled several explicit political functions. Its branches were the right height for hanging effigies, a reminder of the official gallows less than a half-mile away, where thousands usually turned out for the ritual execution of a criminal. (In Newport and Charleston in 1765 they had to build a gallows to hang effigies before they adopted the tree.) In Britain, of course, the gallows was known as "the hanging tree." Located at a crossroads, Boston's elm was a capacious tree whose branches provided a canopy for people assembling on the ground, making for the naturally demarcated public space called Liberty Hall.[69]

The tree was very well situated politically. At "Deacon Elliot's corner," it was already familiar as a landmark in an age when Bostonians located houses and shops not by street numbers but by their proximity to well-known sites. Everything in Boston was in walking distance of everything else, but the older North End was densely populated with the houses, workshops, and shipyards of the maritime economy; the South End was "a relatively open area of fields, pastures, gardens and ropewalks," a newer and more prosperous part of town. Aside from the likelihood that no such tall trees were left in the North End, the site was in the part of town most in need of political cultivation. North End artisans, apprentices, seamen, and boys—the core constituency for street actions—would answer a call to a site some distance away but South–Enders might have been less responsive to a plea to rally in the North End. What's more, the tree was on the road that country folk had to take coming into town on market days.[70]

Liberty poles elsewhere fulfilled some of the same functions as the trees: they provided sites for celebration, deliberation, and confrontation. Intentionally erected, they seem to be much more of an "in your face" provocation. They bore little resemblance to the maypole, even if Tories dubbed them "the maypole of sedition." In England and Europe, maypoles were seasonal, observing the rebirth of spring; American liberty poles went up and saw action at all times of the year. Maypoles were usually small trees of a human dimension; the giant liberty poles were meant to be overawing, like the tall ship masts they were: at sea, symbols of the authority of the ship's officers, and on shore, of the would-be authority of the Sons of Liberty. American liberty poles, as far as we can tell, were not garlanded with flowers, and there was no dancing around them. They were a place for grim political business, not for a "frolic." The ceremonies at Valley Forge would have been an exception.

Perhaps the proof of my hypothesis that the liberty tree was an American invention is negative: despite all the patriot rhetoric about Britain as the source of their liberties, no one seems to have claimed descent from a British ancestry for the liberty tree. Thomas Hutchinson, who was knowledgeable about the English precedents for the numerous political rituals he witnessed in Boston, drew no such connection for the tree. And in the only surviving oration dedicating a liberty tree, a Sons of Liberty leader in Newport claimed no more than that deliberations under the tree would guard "that liberty which our forefathers sought out and found under trees and in the wilderness" in America.[71]

Nor did Thomas Paine make a claim for a British lineage in his poem "The Liberty Tree." Paine, who had arrived in Philadelphia from England in 1774 at age thirty-seven, was steeped in English political traditions and sopped up American political culture rapidly. His poem appeared in July 1775, only a few months before he started to compose *Common Sense*, the pamphlet so attuned to the sensibilities of a mass audience which appeared in January 1776.[72]

In "The Liberty Tree" (note that he used its familiar name rather than the more elevated "Tree of Liberty" as did Jefferson), Paine celebrated not so much a tree as America's embodiment of the principles of the tree. He offered no image at all of the tree passing from Britain to America. Rather, the "Goddess of Liberty," guided by "ten thousand celestials," brought "a far budding branch from the gardens above," planted it in America, and named it "Liberty Tree." Here it flourished and

> The fame of its fruit drew the nations around,
> To seek out this peaceful shore.
> Unmindful of names or distinctions they came,
> For freemen like brothers agree;
> With one spirit endued, they one friendship pursued,
> And their temple was Liberty Tree.

Granted that on this issue Paine may not be the best witness: after all, in *Common Sense* he was trying to wean Americans away from their affection for Britain as "the parent country." Yet Paine's silence should not be dismissed; had there been an English tradition for the tree, would he not have invoked it in the poem?[73]

If anything, the American liberty tree was one of Paine's inspirations for *Common Sense*. In the very opening paragraphs Paine posits a tree as a site at which a people exercising their natural rights formed a government. Imagining "a small number of persons settled in some sequestered part of the earth" who felt the "necessity of establishing some form of government," Paine held that "some convenient tree will afford them a State House, under the branches of which the whole colony may assemble to deliberate on public matters." Here was the idealized image of the liberty tree as a site of direct democracy. The passage was intended to help Americans envision themselves in a state of nature transforming their existing colonial governments into states governed by new constitutions—an indispensable step if they were to imagine themselves becoming independent from Britain. And this may be precisely what alarmed conservatives: returning to a state of nature. As if in response to Paine, a crude woodcut on a broadside verse in New Haven in 1776 that celebrated "the difficulties our fore-fathers endured in planting Religious and civil-liberty in this western world" depicted men and women gathering under an elm-like tree to form either their government or their church.[74]

8. *Atlantic Crossings: L'arbre de la Liberté and le Bonnet Rouge*

What happened to the cluster of symbols of liberty we have been puzzling out—tree, pole, and cap—in the last quarter of the eighteenth century? Wherever British armies occupied American coastal cities they cut down trees and poles. But let's face it: after the war, conservative patriot leaders, and not only former Loyalists, would have said, "good riddance" to liberty trees, liberty poles, hanging effigies, pulling down houses, tar-and-feathering, Indian disguises—the whole kit and caboodle of popular revolutionary rituals. Much to the consternation of conservatives, in the 1790s the symbols reappeared in the French Revolution and then in the United States. The entwined political history of the United States, France, and Great Britain in the 1790s suggests the following processes at work with these symbols:

1. In the United States there was an erasure in the "official" or dominant public memory. As elites attempted to put the genie of radicalism back in the bottle, they either wiped out the tree and pole from public memory or converted the tree from Jefferson's symbol of defiant resistance to unjust authority into a harmless metaphor celebrating liberties already won.

The process stands out starkly in Boston only because the city had more radicalism to erase. It is apparent, for example, in the changes in the holiday calendar eliminating commemoration of all the popular events of the Revolution. The celebration of the "good" mob of August 14, 1765, previously marked as the birthday of the liberty tree by the Sons of Liberty to wipe out the memory of the "bad" mob of August 26, disappeared. So did the annual observance of the Massacre of March 5, 1770, as a day to warn against the danger of standing armies and December 16, 1773, the date of the destruction of the tea, which had never been observed. Pope's Day, November 5, was banned, first by Boston leaders in 1774, then among soldiers by General Washington in 1775. July 4 rolled all these holidays into one, observed in a safe, formal, indoor space as marking American independence but not the American Revolution.

The erasure is epitomized in a stone monument erected atop Beacon Hill in 1790 in Boston's newly fashionable West End. Its fifty-seven-foot height faintly echoed the liberty pole, but the plaque's recounting of events wiped out all human agency by using the passive tense. It read, "Stamp Act Passed 1765 / Stamp Act Repealed 1766 / Tea Act Passed 1773 / Tea Destroyed in Boston, Decem. 16." The city's new Brahmin elite did not want to celebrate crowd actions, organized or spontaneous, nonviolent or violent.[75]

2. In France in the 1790s the liberty tree and the liberty cap became nothing less than the principal icons of the French Revolution. An older popular culture came into play in France, leading to even more of a conflict over symbols than in America. The tradition of observing the first of May with a maypole, "le mai," was deeply rooted in French village culture, so much so that when peasants rioted in 1790 after discovering that rents to their landlords would not be abolished by the Revolution as rumored, they planted the wild maypole, "le mai sauvage." Revolutionary authority attempted to suppress these maypoles and, that failing, appropriated them. In 1792, the National Convention decreed the planting of "arbres de la liberté" as the central feature of official civic festivals, and by May 1792 it was said that sixty thousand such trees had been planted in town centers. Whereas American trees and poles represented the defiance of government, which revolutionary leaders attempted to control, in France the revolutionary government regulated and tamed the symbols of popular resistance. In the civic tree-planting, the trees were saplings, small enough to be planted by a handful of men, but the ceremony was enveloped by formal processions and official pomp. Artists sometimes portrayed men and women dancing joyously around the tree singing "La Carmagnole"— a remnant of le mai absorbed by the Revolution.[76]

Enter the pileus as "le bonnet rouge," a soft cloth cap with a flipped-over top. French artists already associated the liberty cap on a staff with the American Revolution. In 1792 the government adopted this image as the official seal of the Revolution: the cap on a staff held by a classically garbed woman, her hair flowing wildly. But even before that, the cap had figuratively jumped off the staff to adorn the top of the French liberty tree or liberty pole. The cap was also worn. Resembling a workman's stocking cap, it was adopted by the radical sans-culottes men of Paris as well as by women. The Parisian women who confronted Louis XVI at his palace in Versailles literally forced a bonnet rouge on the king. "Marianne," a French woman wearing the cap, became the visual symbol of the Revolution. The news of all this symbolism reached American reading publics in vivid newspaper reports. Le bonnet rouge came to epitomize France's popular revolution.[77]

3. *In England the liberty tree and cap became so identified with the French Revolution as to make them symbols of sedition and regicide.* In the early 1790s, an emergent movement for republican reform, rooted in the societies of respectable London artisans, acquired a mass national following after Thomas Paine's pamphlet *Rights of Man* (1791–92) circulated in the hundreds of thousands. (Paine had returned to England in the late 1780s.) English republicans embraced the French Revolution, but the historian E. P. Thompson in calling it a time of "Planting the Tree of Liberty" was speaking metaphorically. Reformers, who "faced constant harassment and the threat of prosecution," as the historian James Epstein writes, "were constantly denied the use of both formal and informal public space." The banner which the Sheffield republicans carried in a procession of five

thousand people in 1792 was a fit symbol of this repression: "the pole of liberty lying broken on the ground inscribed 'Truth is Libel.'" (Paine now fled to France to avoid prosecution.) Republicans might circulate Thomas Spence's token coins showing Englishmen dancing around a liberty pole topped by the liberty cap, and a republican martyr might march to his trial bearing a small liberty tree, but as the London Corresponding Society put it, the government's ministers "have lopped the tree of liberty to a stump, but have not killed it." The tree flourished somewhat more openly among republicans in Scotland and Ireland.[78]

4. *The symbols were revived in the United States in the 1790s by popular movements opposing the dominant Federalist regime.* This occurred first in 1793 in celebration of the French Revolution, then in 1794 in an agrarian rebellion in Pennsylvania, and again in 1798–1800 in nationwide protest against the repressive Alien and Sedition Laws.

To Democratic Republicans—a name now taken by the party emerging in opposition to the ruling Federalists—the French Revolution was carrying out the ideals of the American Revolution they considered betrayed by the Federalists. In Albany, New York, for example, French revolutionaries were hailed as "The Liberty Boys of France"; in Poughkeepsie, a bower of entwined French and American flags was marked "In Honor of the Tree of Liberty in France." Republicans paid homage to the American liberty tree wherever a relic kept its memory alive, for example in Boston, where a huge celebratory procession in 1793 stopped at the stump of the tree. In Philadelphia at the dinner receiving "Citizen" Genet, the new French minister placed a miniature tree of liberty on his head and then passed it around the table.[79]

Symbolic precedence in celebrating the French Revolution, however, went especially to articles of dress. Enter the liberty cap as a physical presence in America. Before and during the American Revolution, it will be recalled, the cap on a staff was well known in print culture. The cap per se without the staff now made a public appearance. It might be mounted tauntingly in some public place, like a merchants' coffee house, or it might be carved in wood and placed on a liberty pole. It was also worn, but how commonly is not clear. In Philadelphia, some women donned the cap or a French turban. More commonly, supporters of the French Revolution wore a tricolor cockade—a rosette of red, white, and blue ribbons—men on their hats, women on their garments, prompting their Federalist opponents to wear a black cockade. The cap, associated with a symbolic woman, became a ubiquitous image. The new female personification of America, replacing the Indian maiden, was a classically garbed woman called "Liberty," "Miss Liberty," "The Goddess of Liberty," or "Columbia," who was usually depicted with a cap on a staff in the background. Coins issued by the U.S. mint with "Liberty" as the motto bore the image of a woman with a cap over her flowing hair or with the cap atop a liberty pole. Seamen had themselves tattooed with a female "Liberty," the liberty cap, or the liberty tree.[80]

If the liberty cap emerged in a celebratory mood, the liberty pole returned defiantly. Farmers in western Pennsylvania protesting an excise tax in the misnamed "Whiskey Rebellion" revived a gamut of rituals of the American Revolution: they blackened their faces, tarred and feathered excise men, and put up liberty poles. "It was said by the whole of the people, that liberty poles were raised [in the] last war," a tavern keeper testified in a trial of rebels, "and they ought to be raised now." In the town of Dears, Northumberland County, two to three hundred inhabitants gathered, as a modern historian describes the event, "and voted on whether to raise a pole, on what slogan the flag attached to the pole should carry (they agreed on 'Liberty, Equality of Rights, a Change of Ministry and No Excise'), on who should go into the woodland to cut down a tree," and "who would go door to door to get people to sign a petition." In Franklin County five hundred militia marched through the county with a wagon loaded with lumber to set up liberty poles. This democratic insurgency was put down with the might of the U.S. army, but its symbolism survived: In 1801 in Pittsburgh, a center of the defeated insurrection, a newspaper took the name *The Tree of Liberty*.[81]

The uprising in Pennsylvania took place outside the political system. In 1798–1800, Democratic Republicans, members of the first opposition party within the system, raised liberty poles to defy the Alien and Sedition Laws aimed at suppressing them. Poles were in profusion in New England, New York, Pennsylvania, and New Jersey, as well as in the South and on the frontier, and were far more numerous than in the 1770s. They again were sites of contention: Federalist bands cut them down or burned them. The poles became avowedly partisan. In Dedham, Massachusetts, home of a liberty "pillar" in the Revolution, David Brown, an itinerant agitator, helped townspeople set up a pole with the fiery inscription, "No Stamp Act / No Sedition Act / No Alien Bills / No Land Tax / Downfall to the Tyrants of America / Peace and Retirement to the President [Adams] / Long Live the Vice President [Jefferson]." For this, Federalists had Brown indicted for sedition (one charge was inciting people to set up a liberty pole), fined $480, and jailed for eighteen months. In New York City, one charge against Ann Greenleaf, publisher of the city's leading Republican newspaper, was advocating the right to set up liberty poles.

As the election of 1800 approached, Republicans put the poles to electoral use. In Bridgehampton, Long Island, for example, they raised a liberty pole seventy-six feet high, sang "the celebrated song of the Liberty Tree," and toasted "The Tree of Liberty" and Vice President Thomas Jefferson. On Jefferson's victory in 1801, his Republican supporters in Philadelphia paraded, carrying a "Liberty Pole" and wearing liberty caps; they also planted "Liberty Trees." From Charleston, Republicans sent President Jefferson the head of a cane carved from the root of the liberty tree the British had cut down.[82]

The result of a decade of revived liberty poles was to restore them to their original meaning in the American Revolution as symbols of the defiance of unjust laws. But to Federalists, as to elites everywhere, the French Revolution now replaced the localized rebellions of Masaniello, Kett, and Cade as a symbol of the horrors of mass revolution. In the long run, this association of the American symbols with the French Revolution may have contributed to their displacement.

9. *Invented Histories: The Lost Phallus*

If the liberty tree was invented in the American Revolution, and if the tree and cap became the icons of a second revolution in France, should it surprise us that that there were competing invented histories of their origins? In the United States, to Federalists, the adoption of the symbols by the Democratic Republicans was proof that they were a "Frenchified" and "Jacobinical" party; to them the tree, pole, and cap were Gallic. In 1798, as Federalist war hawks whooped up a hysteria over a nonexistent threat of a French invasion of the United States, they called the poles "sedition poles" or "maypoles of sedition." In contrast, "An Old Fashioned Republican" who knew some history defended "the wholesome practice of erecting Liberty Poles" which bore "the classical and long established emblem of Liberty, the LIBERTY CAP."[83]

In the British Isles, republicans had a sense of the historical passing of liberty from the new world to the old: Thomas Paine was a living exemplar of this, and the success of republicanism in the United States was a theme of his *Rights of Man*. English conservatives were well aware that the "contagion" of liberty came from America but chose to tar Paine's followers with the brush of the more easily demonized French Revolution. They branded the three symbols—tree, pole, and cap—as French. In Ireland, on the other hand, where the radical United Irishmen were avowedly francophile, a catechism summed up a different version of the transatlantic crossing:

> What have you got in your hand?
> A green bough.
> Where did it first grow?
> in America.
> Where did it bud?
> in France.
> Where are you going to plant it?
> In the crown of Great Britain.[84]

In France, where the government had transformed the tree from the symbol of peasant revolt to the centerpiece of a ceremony pledging allegiance to the Revolution, Henri Grégoire, a deputy to the National Convention, trimmed his official history accordingly. He played down the roots of the tree in village maypoles. The French maypole, by his lights, had a new birth when it passed "from England to the banks of the Delaware, where it rediscovered its original dignity" and "became, once again in each commune a sign for citizens to gather together"—in other words, he made the American liberty tree the progenitor of the official French civic festival.[85]

To Joel Barlow (1754–1812), the Connecticut Yankee honored by France as "Citizen Barlow" for his passionate antimonarchical pamphlets and poetry, the origin of the tree was not Gallic but phallic. A witness to two revolutions and a friend of Jefferson, Grégoire, and Paine in France in the 1790s, Barlow found the origins of the tree in ancient mythology.[86] While American consul in Algiers, Barlow discovered the myths of Egypt, which became the basis for his short manuscript "Genealogy of the Liberty Tree." He traced the origin of the tree to the Egyptian fable of Osiris, the Sun, who was hacked to death by Typhon, the power of darkness, and whose genitals were cast into the Nile to become the source of the fertility of the river valley. To celebrate this fecundity, "a solemn feast was instituted in which the Phallus in a posture of strong erection was carried in a procession." Later, in Rome, this god became known as "*Liber (Free)* so that the Phallus became the emblem of *Libertas*" (celebrated in a festival at the vernal equinox, which in time became the first of May).[87]

Over the ages, wrote Barlow, "Men forgot the original object of the institution, the *Phallus* [which] has lost its *testicles* and has been for many centuries been reduced to a simple pole." In England, this May frolic "has acquired the name of May-pole or liberty-pole." When "the Liberty Pole passed over to America it assumed a more venerable appearance; it grew to an *enormous mast* and without regard to any particular day it was planted in the ground as a solid emblem of *political* liberty." Then, wrote Barlow, it "recrossed the Atlantic" to take the form of the liberty tree planted in France. In a postscript, Barlow suggested that the liberty cap in Rome, used to recognize the freeing of a slave, had the same origin: it was "the head of the Penis, an emblem of liberty."

Was Barlow's "priapic radicalism" serious, or a pornographic joke? the historian Simon Schama asks. As far as we know, Barlow never published his phallic interpretation (nor did he work it into his epic poetry about America). Had it appeared in print, he might have found a sympathetic reception both in the libertine high culture of Enlightenment intellectuals as well as in bawdy plebeian culture. Christopher Hill, as we have noted, called the English village maypole the "phallic maypole," and May Day, a time of sexual freedom. The "Genealogy" would not have been any more shocking than the political pornography that helped bring about the downfall of the royal family in France or the satire widely circulated in the American political debate of 1787 comparing the proposed Constitution to a tight pair of new breeches that "conspired against the liberty of my thighs, knees and loins." Barlow's "Genealogy," Eric Slauter argues, was "a learned manifestation of a common connection between liberty and the phallus." Barlow, writes Schama, answering his own question, "wanted to root the most important emblem of freedom in both the American and French revolutions in a cult of nature," which would make "the urge to liberty not just a modern notion but an ancient irresistible instinct, a truly *natural* right."[88]

10. *Lost in America: "The world should never forget"*

Mapping the transformation of American memory over two centuries, the historian Michael Kammen posits two kinds of public memory: "dominant memories (or mainstream collective consciousness)" and "alternative (usually subordinate memories)." The first corresponds more or less to "official," the second to "popular" memory, although there is often no "sharp dichotomy" between the two. In nineteenth-century America, in official memory, as an emblem of America "the liberty tree withered," as the cultural historian John Higham put it. The tree was unable to compete with the eagle as a "more dynamic" symbol of the nation, yet in popular memory the symbols of the liberty tree, pole, and cap retained vitality.[89]

Of the original trees, only the one in Annapolis, located on a college campus, seems to have survived into the twentieth century and to have been celebrated. The stately elms which spread across New England and the Midwest in the nineteenth century did not revive a public memory of their famous ancestor in Boston. As the more numerous poles decayed, some were replaced or had their site marked. New Englanders who migrated from Liberty Pole, Vermont, called their new town in Wisconsin Liberty Pole. There are other Liberty place-names on the map. Political parties exploited the liberty pole in festive election campaigns. Mark Twain could say of a character in *Huckleberry Finn* that "he drew himself up as straight as a liberty pole." The liberty cap also held on: in early cartoons of "Uncle Sam," emerging as a new symbol of the nation, he wears a liberty cap. But the only tree of the revolutionary era to acquire mythic fame was the cherry tree that the boy George Washington chopped down in "Parson" Mason Weems's fictitious biography.[90]

As a metaphor, the tree of liberty took on a new life chiefly among those who were denied its promise. When Toussaint L'Ouverture, the leader of Saint-Domingue's successful slave revolution of the 1790s, was imprisoned by the French, his parting words in 1802 were, "In overthrowing me, you have cut down in San Domingo only the trunk of the tree of liberty. It will spring up again by the roots for they are numerous and deep." The phrase was common coinage in American free black communities: in toasts at association events, poems, and in letters and articles in African American newspapers, Frederick Douglass's paper among them.

The liberty cap also reappeared as a symbol of freedom for slaves, its original classical meaning. In *The Genius of America*, a huge oil painting hung in the Library Company of Philadelphia (1792), a classically garbed woman holding a staff topped by a white cap of liberty welcomes the emancipation of a band of slaves in the background who dance around a liberty pole.[91] The city of Charleston, which required slaves to wear a metal badge marked "Servant," adopted a liberty cap mounted on a staff as a badge for free blacks, with the word "Free" above it. Slaveholders had no doubt that the cap of liberty resonated among slaves. In 1855, when the U.S. government commissioned sculptor Thomas Crawford to erect a female "Statue of Freedom" on top of the new capitol dome, Secretary of War Jefferson Davis (the future president of the Confederacy) intervened to prevent him from giving her a liberty cap. (Instead she wears a helmet with an Indian headdress.) In the Civil War era, the liberty cap was associated with the Union cause. Charlotte Perkins Gilman, the feminist leader, recalled that as a child in 1868, while watching a torchlight election parade of ex-soldiers for General Ulysses S. Grant, she was dressed as the "goddess of Liberty—eight years old! A white dress, a liberty cap, a liberty pole."[92]

In the first half of the nineteenth century, Boston continued to pay homage to the liberty tree site. On his tour of the United States in 1824, the Marquis de Lafayette "the hero of two Revolutions," stopped at the site to pay the tree a moving tribute before cheering throngs: "The world should never forget the spot where once stood Liberty Tree, so famous in your annals." But Bostonians did forget. The name was taken by successive buildings on the site, and a wooden bas-relief of the elm made by two ship carvers in the 1850s adorns its façade to this day. But this was not enough to preserve memory in a city whose Brahmin elite fostered a willful forgetting of the radical side of the Revolution. The literary keepers of New England's past did the tree no justice. Nathaniel Hawthorne in one of his "grandfather's tales" for children disassociated his narrator from the "young and hot headed people" active at the tree. In his brooding tales he retrieved the maypole at Merry Mount, needling his Puritan ancestors for their bigotry. But in his well-known short story "My Kinsman, Major Molineux," Hawthorne offered a nightmarish vision of a tar-and-feathering in Boston, in which he took no notice of the liberty tree, a customary stop for such events. The poet Longfellow, venerated only "the spreading chestnut tree" under which "the village smithy stands."[93]

Boston artists did no better: in histories of the city, illustrators either reduced the great elm to a small tree with only a few passers-by or put the tree on a landscape totally devoid of people—the ultimate conservative erasure of the "mob" of the Revolution. New York artists, by contrast, Recovered their city's liberty pole: one portrayed brawny mechanics raising a giant mast as aristocratic ladies and gentlemen stand aghast; another captured the warfare at the pole between soldiers and "leather aprons."[94]

In the class warfare of the late nineteenth century, symbols associated with the French Revolution did not survive. To conservatives, Marianne wearing the cap of liberty in Eugene Delacroix's painting of "Liberty" standing on the barricades in Paris in the 1830 uprising, her breast exposed, a cap of liberty on her head, became a frightening icon of revolution. Thus in the 1870s, when Frederic Bartholdi was constructing the Statue of Liberty in Paris as France's gift to the United States, he knew better than to put "the red cap of liberty" on her head. (Instead she wears a classical diadem.) As president, the historian Theodore Roosevelt, who loathed the French Revolution, vetoed the cap of liberty for American coins as an object "never worn [and which] never had been worn by any free people in the world," betraying only his ignorance. For that matter, the American labor movement, which in the 1880s chose the first of May as "Labor Day," seems to have had little awareness of the historic traditions of that day.[95]

In the twentieth century, in "dominant" or "official" public memory, visual representations of the liberty tree and liberty pole were rare, and of the liberty cap they were nonexistent. Thomas Hart Benton, for example, a painter who incorporated so many historical scenes of the common people in his murals, painted no liberty trees. In 1933 it was left to Diego Rivera, the famous Mexican muralist, and a communist at that, to put the Stamp Act protest at the liberty tree in a panel of a mural of American history, alongside images of tar-and-feathering, Thomas Paine, Shays's Rebellion, and the words of Jefferson's 1787 letter writ large. But the mural, a fresco whose panels were mounted on movable frames, was lost, just as Rivera's more famous mural in Rockefeller Center, on which he painted an image of Lenin, was ordered torn down by the Rockefellers.[96]

In the mid-1970s, amidst the hoopla of the mainstream celebration of the bicentennial of the American Revolution, the plea of a prominent historian that "the time has come to reclaim our noble tree" struck few sparks. John Higham argued that "as a symbol of the potential harmony between nature and society," the tree "speaks for an ecologically responsible patriotism," while "the relation between branches and the trunk suggests the joining of unity with diversity, which is the genius of America." The government put the tree on a thirteen-cent stamp (and more recently on a quarter). But a six hundred-page compendium of sites could list only one liberty pole (in New Jersey) and one tree (at Annapolis). Once again, as before the Civil War, the symbol was revived primarily in "subordinate" memory. A New Left student group supported a Massachusetts factory strike with a vivid poster depicting the tree with the caption "Old Roots, New Roots in Rebellion." In Grafton, Vermont, on July 4, 1976, the internationally famous Bread and Puppet Circus created a festival of giant puppets wearing liberty caps and dancing around liberty poles (and the following year the troupe dramatized the tale of Masaniello). Since the 1980s, after the development of a disease-resistant elm, environmentalists have sponsored the planting of several hundred thousand American Liberty elms.[97]

In Boston it is not only that the site of the tree, as mentioned at the outset, is not on Boston's famed Freedom Trail, initiated in the 1950s, but maps of the trail do not even locate it. A bronze plaque on the sidewalk marks where it once stood, and if you look closely at the second story of the government building across the street, the bas-relief carving of the tree is still there. In the 1970s the city actually doomed the site for tourism when it rezoned the area to permit porn shops and strip joints. Ironically, the owner of the "Liberty Tree II Adult Entertainment Complex" (now gone) put up a replica of the liberty tree above his door (should we say, an unknowing echo of Joel Barlow's vision of its phallic origins?). In recent years a small band has tried to keep the memory of the tree alive. And the city promises a minipark on a sliver of land close to the site which would feature a living elm and a replica of Paul Revere's obelisk of 1766. I have seen the architect's drawings for the park and hope that my grandchildren will walk in it some day.[98]

If the keepers of the past in history-conscious Boston have thus far failed the liberty tree, can the rest of the country be blamed? If you Google "liberty tree" or "tree of liberty," you find tens of thousands of entries yet can only wonder as you browse, Is this what the icon of two revolutions has come to? You can buy merchandise marketed under its name. In the Magic Kingdom at Disney World, you can visit a tree adorned with thirteen lighted lanterns outside the Liberty Tree Tavern, where at a lunch of New England dishes you might be entertained by Minnie Mouse, Goofy, or Pluto. And you can visit numerous right-wing websites and bookstores. If you like, you can buy a T-shirt from one of them imprinted with Jefferson's words, "The Tree of Liberty must be watered from time to time with the blood of patriots and tyrants"—that is, if you don't mind wearing a copy of the T-shirt Timothy McVeigh wore the day he blew up the Oklahoma City federal building.[99] Commercialization, trivialization, and the misreading of the American Revolution to justify an act of terrorism—what a price the country pays for its failure to come to grips with the liberty tree, which inspired so many diverse movers and shakers of the American Revolution. Ebenezer Mackintosh, the Loyal Nine, the Sons of Liberty, Samuel Adams, John Adams, John Hancock, Thomas Paine, Thomas Jefferson, Lafayette—where are you now that we need you?

NOTES

1. This essay was presented originally at the Newberry Library Seminar in Early American History and Culture, September 2003, and then presented as the E. P. Thompson Lecture, University of Pittsburgh, October 2004, and at a seminar of the Charles Warren Center, Harvard University, March 2005. I am indebted to participants on those occasions for their comments. I would not have been able to expand my knowledge of liberty trees and liberty poles within and outside of Boston without the research in modern digitized sources by J. L. Bell and Eric Slauter, to both of whom I am deeply grateful. After I completed the 2004 draft of this essay I benefited from David Hackett Fischer's *Liberty and Freedom: A Visual History of America's Founding Ideals* (New York, 2005), which assembles a treasure trove of images from U.S. history. The first two chapters are devoted to the liberty tree and liberty pole of the revolutionary era. David Fischer generously shared his documentation with me and engaged in a dialogue over our differences of interpretation.

For incisive criticisms of drafts of this paper I am indebted to J. L. Bell, Samuel Kinser, Greg Nobles, Eric Slauter, David Waldstreicher, and Walter H. Wallace. I am very grateful to the following individuals who shared their knowledge of subjects or who answered my queries: Roger D. Abrahams, John K. Alexander, Michael Bellesiles, Ira Berlin, Marty Blatt, Terry Bouton, Douglas Bradburn, Bruno Cartosio, David Corrigan, Seth Cotlar, Edward Countryman, S. Max Edelson, James A. Epstein, Matthew Greif, Tobie Higbie, the late John Higham, Wythe W. Holt Jr., Woody Holton, Thomas Humphrey, Benjamin Irvin, Rhys Isaac, Mark Jones, Mitch Kachun, Harvey Kaye, Kevin Kelly, Eric Kimball, Bruce Laurie, Staughton Lynd, Brendan McConville, Mikal Muharrar, Carla Mulford, Bruce Nelson, Simon P. Newman, George Quintal, Ray Raphael, Marcus Rediker, Rainey Tisdale, Richard Twomey, Susan Wilson, Andy Wood, Elizabeth Young, and Michael Zuckerman.

2. Arthur M. Schlesinger Sr., "Liberty Tree: A Genealogy," *New England Quarterly* 25 (1952): 435–58; Schlesinger, *The Colonial Merchants and the American Revolution* (New York, 1918), and *New Viewpoints in American History* (New York, 1926), chap. 7; compare Schlesinger, *Prelude to Independence: The Newspaper War on Britain, 1764–1776* (New York, 1957). For an analysis of historiography, see Alfred F. Young, "American Historians Confront 'The Transforming Hand of Revolution,'" in Ronald Hoffman and Peter J. Albert, eds., *The Transforming Hand of Revolution: Reconsidering the American Revolution as a Social Movement* (Charlottesville, Va., 1995), 346–492.

3. "Boston c. 1775," in Lester J. Cappon, ed., *Atlas of Early American History: The Revolutionary Era, 1760–1790* (Princeton, N.J., 1976), 9. John Rowe, *Letters and Diary of John Rowe, Boston Merchant, 1759–1762, 1764–1779*, ed. Anne Rowe Cunningham (Boston, 1903), 88. For the area and a detailed map, see Anne H. Thwing,

The Crooked and Narrow Streets of the Town of Boston, 1630–1822 (Boston, 1929), sec. 3; Walter Whitehill, *Boston: A Topographical History* (Cambridge, Mass., 1959), 22.

4. Edmund S. Morgan and Helen Morgan, *The Stamp Act Crisis: Prelude to Revolution* (New York, 1963), chap. 5. In the first three sections of this essay I draw on my scholarship documented in Young, *The Shoemaker and the Tea Party: Memory and the American Revolution* (Boston, 1999), and in essays 2 and 3 in this volume. The most authoritative account of street politics in Boston is in Dirk Hoerder, *Crowd Action in Revolutionary Massachusetts, 1765–1780* (New York, 1977), and in his essay, "Boston Leaders and Boston Crowds, 1765–1776," in Young, ed., *The American Revolution: Explorations in the History of American Radicalism* (DeKalb, Ill., 1976), 233–71. For the larger context, I draw especially on Gary Nash, *The Urban Crucible: Social Change, Political Consciousness, and the Origins of the American Revolution* (Cambridge, Mass., 1979). Robert Blair St. George, *Conversing by Signs: Poetics of Implication in Colonial New England Culture* (Chapel Hill, N.C., 1998), 192 (boots).

5. For Pope's Day, I draw on my own "Pope's Day, Tar and Feathers and Cornet George Joyce, Jr.: From Ritual to Rebellion in Boston" (Paper presented at the Anglo-American Labor Historians Conference, Rutgers University, 1973); see also Peter Benes, "Night Processions: Celebrating the Gunpowder Plot in England and New England," in Peter Benes and Jane M. Benes, eds., *New England Celebrates: Spectacle, Commemoration, and Festivity* (The Dublin Seminar for New England Folklife Annual Proceedings, 2000), 9–28; Francis D. Cogliano, *No King, No Popery: Anti-Catholicism in Revolutionary New England* (Westport, Conn., 1996); Brendan McConville, "Pope's Day Revisited, Popular Culture Reconsidered," *Explorations in Early American History* 3 (2000): 258–80; Wojciech Dadk, "Pope's Day in New England," *Revere House Gazette* 73 (2003): 1–3. For depictions by a contemporary artist, hitherto unused by scholars, see J. L. Bell, "Du Simitiere's Sketches of Pope Day in Boston, 1767," in Peter Benes, ed., *The Worlds of Children* (The Dublin Seminar, 2004), 207–15.

6. For the events of August 14, 1765: Francis Bernard to Earl of Halifax, August 15, 16, 1765, Sparks Mss. IV, Letterbooks 137–41, 141–43, Houghton Library, Harvard University; Malcolm Freiberg, ed., "An Unknown Stamp Act Letter," August 15, 1765, *Proceedings of the Massachusetts Historical Society* 78 (1967): 138–42; Cyrus Baldwin to his brother, August 15, August 19, 1765, Misc. Bound Mss., Massachusetts Historical Society; Peter Oliver, *Peter Oliver's Origin & Progress of the American Revolution: A Tory View* ed. Douglass Adair and John A. Schutz (Stanford, Calif., 1961), 50–55. The standard accounts are Morgan and Morgan, *The Stamp Act Crisis*, chap. 8, and Merrill Jensen, *The Founding of a Nation: A History of the American Revolution* (New York, 1968), part 1; Hoerder, *Crowd Action*, chap. 3.

7. Edward P. Thompson, "Rough Music," in Thompson, *Customs in Common* (London, 1991), 514–15; see also William Pencak, "Play as Prelude to Revolution: Boston, 1765–1776," in William Pencak, Matthew Dennis, and Simon P. Newman,

eds., *Riot and Revelry in Early America* (University Park, Pa., 2003), 125–55, a rich essay. For a perspective on American celebrations, see David Waldstreicher, *In the Midst of Perpetual Fetes: The Making of American Nationalism, 1776–1820* (Chapel Hill, N.C., 1997), chap. 1.

8. *Boston Gazette*, September 26, 1765.

9. For these events, see Hoerder, *Crowd Action*, chaps. 2, 3; *Boston Gazette*, May 25, 1766 (celebration), March 5, 1770 (Seider funeral). For the flag, see "Everything We Know about the Liberty Tree Flag," by Rainey Tisdale, Collections Manager, Bostonian Society, where the flag is on display. I am also indebted to Tisdale for providing information from the Society's files on the lanterns hung on the tree. See also Richard H. Gideon, "The Flags of the Sons of Liberty," http://www.americanvexillum.com/flags (January 2003).

10. Oliver, *Origin & Progress*, 54; Hoerder, *Crowd Action*, 130 (trial); for "Liberty Hall," see Rowe, *Letters and Diary*, 172, and Thomas Hutchinson, *History of the Colony and Province of Massachusetts-Bay*, ed. Lawrence Mayo, 3 vols. (Cambridge, Mass., 1938), 3:138.

11. For the social composition of Sons of Liberty leaders, see Pauline Maier, *From Resistance to Rebellion: Colonial Radicals and the Development of American Opposition to Britain, 1765–1776* (New York, 1972), 297–312; and William Pencak, *War, Politics, & Revolution in Provincial Massachusetts* (Boston, 1981), chaps. 8, 9. For the underappreciated role of merchants, see John W. Tyler, *Smugglers and Patriots: Boston Merchants and the Advent of the American Revolution* (Boston, 1986); Charles W. Akers, *The Divine Politician: Samuel Cooper and the American Revolution in Boston* (Boston, 1982), a study of the minister of Boston's wealthiest congregation.

12. Thomas Hutchinson to Thomas Pownall, March 8, 1766, Hutchinson Mss. Massachusetts Archives, vol. 26, which I read in typescript in several drafts at the Massachusetts Historical Society. For the Hutchinson papers, see Bernard Bailyn, *The Ordeal of Thomas Hutchinson* (Cambridge, Mass., 1974), 409–12.

13. For the August 14 and August 26 events in this paragraph and the following one, see the sources cited in notes 6 and 15. Freiberg, ed., "An Unknown Stamp Act Letter," reprints an unknown source on repairing the effigy on the tree; for wining and dining Mackintosh, see especially the letters of Governor Francis Bernard, fall 1765, cited in notes 15 and 16.

14. Henry Bass to Samuel P. Savage, December 19, 1765, *Proceedings of the Massachusetts Historical Society* 14 (1910–11): 688–89; for Samuel Adams, see Pauline Maier, *The Old Revolutionaries: Political Lives in the Age of Samuel Adams* (New York, 1980), chap. 1, and John K. Alexander, *Samuel Adams: America's Revolutionary Politician* (Lanham, Md., 2002). For patriot organizations in Boston, see Richard D. Brown, *Revolutionary Politics in Massachusetts: The Boston Committee of Correspondence and the Towns, 1772–1774* (New York, 1970).

15. For the August 26 event: Thomas Hutchinson to Richard Jackson, August

30, 1765, Massachusetts Archives, vol. 26: 146–47, reprinted in Edmund S. Morgan, ed., *Prologue to Revolution: Sources and Documents of the Stamp Act Crisis, 1764–1766* (Chapel Hill, N.C., 1959), 108–09; Hutchinson, *History of Massachusetts-Bay*, 3:89–93; Hutchinson to Henry Seymour, October 1, 1765, Conway Ms., Massachusetts Historical Society; Governor Francis Bernard to the Earl of Halifax, August 31, 1765 (British Public Record Office, C.O. 5/755), reprinted in Merrill Jensen, ed., *English Historical Documents: American Colonial Documents to 1776* (New York, 1955); Bailyn, *Ordeal of Thomas Hutchinson*, chap. 2; St. George, *Conversing by Signs*, chap. 3, "Attacking Houses"; Tyler, *Smugglers & Patriots*, 60–63.

16. Francis Bernard to Earl of Halifax, September 7, 1765, Bernard Papers, IV, 158ff., cited in Bailyn, *Ordeal of Thomas Hutchinson*, 37n. For the social context, see Nash, *Urban Crucible*, chaps. 7, 9, 12; James Henretta, "Economic Development and Social Structure in Colonial Boston," *William and Mary Quarterly*, 3rd ser., 22 (1965): 75–92; and Alan Kulikoff, "The Progress of Inequality in Revolutionary Boston," *William and Mary Quarterly*, 3rd ser., 28 (1971): 375–412. For seamen, see Jesse Lemisch, "Jack Tar in the Streets: Merchant Seamen in the Politics of Revolutionary America," *William and Mary Quarterly*, 3rd ser., 25 (1968): 371–407; and Marcus Rediker and Peter Linebaugh, *The Many-Headed Hydra: Sailors, Slaves, Commoners, and the Hidden History of the Revolutionary Atlantic* (Boston, 2000), chap. 7.

17. For radical Whig tactics and slogans, see Maier, *From Resistance to Rebellion*, 123–24 and passim; John Adams "Case No. 64 Rex v. Weems," December 4, 1770, in L. H. Butterfield, ed., *The Legal Papers of John Adams*, 3 vols. (Cambridge, Mass., 1965), 3:266. "Teague" was a derogatory term for an Irishman.

18. For this and the following two paragraphs: William Gordon, *The History of the Rise, Progress, and Independence of the United States*, 4 vols. (London, 1788), 1:230–35; Hoerder, *Crowd Action*, 158–59, 164–70, 170–76; D. H. Watson, ed., "Joseph Harrison and the Liberty Incident," *William and Mary Quarterly*, 3rd ser., 20 (1963): 589–94; George G. Wolkins, "The Seizure of John Hancock's Ship 'Liberty,'" *Proceedings of the Massachusetts Historical Society* 55 (1921–22): 239ff.

19. See essay 1 in this volume and Young, *Shoemaker and the Tea Party*, 42–51.

20. See Hoerder, *Crowd Actions*, 138–40, for an analysis of the 345 diners on the 1769 list. He calls the Sons of Liberty "a middle-class dining club after 1768." For the tea action, see Young, *Shoemaker and the Tea Party*, 40–45, 99–107; Benjamin W. Labaree, *The Boston Tea Party* (New York, 1964), chap. 7.

21. Young, *Shoemaker and the Tea Party*, 92–98.

22. For artisans and the tree, see Young, *Shoemaker and the Tea Party*, 54; for action at the tree the night of the Massacre, see Edward Payne, "Affidavit No. 56," in *A Short Narrative of the Horrid Massacre ...* (Boston, 1770); for the victims, see Hiller B. Zobel, *The Boston Massacre* (New York, 1970), 191–92; for the flag and lanterns, see research files, Bostonian Society. The lantern was donated to the Society by a descendant of Shubael Hewes, a butcher and the brother of George R. T. Hewes, the shoemaker.

23. My research draws on my paper, "The Rapid Rise and Decline of Ebenezer McIntosh in the Stamp Act Resistance" (Shelby Cullum Davis Center, Princeton University, 1976). I am indebted to Walter F. Wallace for tracking Mackintosh in New Hampshire, as well as for his analysis of the parallels between him and Masaniello. The basic authority on the subject remains George P. Anderson, "Ebenezer Mackintosh: Stamp Act Rioter and Patriot," *Publications of the Colonial Society of Massachusetts* 26 (1927): 15–64, and Anderson, "A Note on Ebenezer Mackintosh," ibid., 348–61. For a summary, see William Pencak, "Ebenezer Mackintosh," *American National Biography* (New York, 1999), 14:261–62. For the importance of fire companies, see Benjamin L. Carp, "Fire of Liberty: Firefighters, Urban Voluntary Culture, and the Revolutionary Movement," *William and Mary Quarterly*, 3rd ser., 58 (2001): 781–818. I have followed the common spelling "Mackintosh" because it was used in North Haverhill, N.H., where he lived from 1774 to 1816.

24. For the actions of November 1 and 5, 1765: Francis Bernard to John Pownall, November 1, 5, 25, 1765, Sparks Mss. Harvard, Letterbook 5: 16–23, 43–46; Oliver, *Origin & Progress*, 54; Thomas Hutchinson, *The Diary and Letters of Thomas Hutchinson*, ed. Peter Orlando Hutchinson, 2 vols. (Boston, 1884–86), 2:71.

25. For the political image: Walter Wallace, "'A Lion with Nails and Fangs': Masaniello of Naples and the Folklore of Political Violence" (Paper presented at the Milan Group in Early United States History Symposium, 1990), a superb essay published as "Masaniello e il folklore della violenza politica," *Communita: Rivista di Informazione Culturale Fondata Da Adriano Olivetti* 193–194 (1992): 191–218; Oliver, *Origin & Progress*, 54; Francis Bernard to John Pownall, November 1, 5, 26, 1765, Sparks Mss. Harvard, Letterbook 5: 18–23, 43–45. For American usage in the late seventeenth century, see David Lovejoy, *The Glorious Revolution in America* (New York, 1972), chap. 16. For England, see Andy Wood, *The 1549 Rebellions and the Making of Early Modern England* (Cambridge, U.K., forthcoming), chap. 8, a masterful account.

26. "Soliloquy of the Boston Liberty Tree …," *(Boston) Massachusetts Gazette*, February 22, 1776; "Masanello from the Shades Below …," *Boston Evening Post*, June 23, 1766; *(Boston) Massachusetts Gazette*, February 22, 1776; "A New York Free-holder," ibid., October 27, 1774 (Wat Tyler couplet).

27. Thomas Paine, *Common Sense*, in Philip Foner, ed., *The Complete Writings of Thomas Paine*, 2 vols. (New York, 1945), 1:29–30; John Adams, *Diary and Autobiography*, ed. L. H. Butterfield, 4 vols. (Cambridge, Mass., 1961), 1:300 (January 20, 1766).

28. For Mackintosh's personal life, see George P. Anderson, essays cited in note 23.

29. The negative comment is by Esther Forbes, *Paul Revere and the World He Lived In* (Boston, 1942), 96, who also misnamed him "Andrew or Alexander"; Oliver, *Origin & Progress*, 54–55. Oliver seems reliable only for what he observed of Mackintosh in street actions and for his demeanor. For the November events, see Francis Bernard to John Pownall, cited in note 25.

30. For the informer in 1769, see Bailyn, *Ordeal of Thomas Hutchinson*, 127–28; Mackintosh's comment on the Tea Party is attributed by Anderson, "Ebenezer Mackintosh," to a man in Haverhill, N.H., who as a boy of ten heard it from the aged Mackintosh. Whether Mackintosh was at the tea action is problematical; he did not boast of it. The first known list of alleged participants, which appeared as an appendix to Benjamin Bussey Thatcher, *Traits of the Tea Party ...* (New York, 1835), lists a "——McIntosh" (i.e., without a first name) who has not been further identified. George Quintal, who has made a Meticulous study of two hundred or so men with claims to have been at the tea action, finds no corroborating evidence for Ebenezer Mackintosh. For the threat of a trial, see *Massachusetts Spy*, April 7, 1774; for the claim in 1774 that Mackintosh "has ever since [the Stamp Act actions] continued a leading man among us," see "Extract of a Letter from Boston, November 24, 1774," in Margaret Willard, ed., *Letters on the American Revolution, 1774–1776* (Boston, 1925), 31.

31. John Adams, *Diary of John Adams*, 1:263; Alexander, *Samuel Adams*, chap. 2; for Hancock, see William Fowler, *The Baron of Beacon Hill: A Biography of John Hancock* (Boston, 1979), and Akers, *Divine Politician*, chaps. 5, 6; Gregory Nobles, "'Yet the Old Republicans Still Persevere': Samuel Adams, John Hancock, and the Crisis of Popular Leadership in Revolutionary Massachusetts, 1775–1790," in Hoffman and Albert, eds., *Transforming Hand of Revolution*, 258–85.

32. Hutchinson, *History of Massachusetts-Bay*, 3:135–36; William C Lane, ed., "The Rebellion of 1766 in Harvard College," *Publications of the Colonial Society of Massachusetts* 10 (1907): 33–59, a collection of sources. The tree could have been the "Washington Elm" on the Cambridge Common, where, according to popular myth, George Washington assumed command of the army in 1775. See Thomas J. Campanella, *Republic of Shade: New England and the American Elm* (New Haven, Conn., 2003), 60–68.

33. See essay 3 in this volume.

34. J. L. Bell, "'Latin School Gentlemen' in Revolutionary Times: The Culture of Boston's South Latin School under the Lovells" (unpublished ms., 2003), about the politics of schoolboys. For interpretations of the role of boys, see Pencak, "Play as Prelude to Revolution," 125–55; and Peter Shaw, *American Patriots and the Rituals of Revolution* (Cambridge, Mass., 1981), chap. 8.

35. Ebenezer Fox, *The Adventures of Ebenezer Fox* (Boston, 1847), 47. For rebellious apprentices, see W. J. Rorabaugh, *The Craft Apprentice from Franklin to the Machine Age in America* (New York, 1986), chaps. 1, 2.

36. Oliver Dickerson, ed., *Boston under Military Rule, 1768–1769, as Revealed in a Journal of the Times* (Boston, 1936), 16, 18; Thomas J. Davis, "Emancipation Rhetoric, Natural Rights and Revolutionary New England: A Note on Four Black Petitions in Massachusetts, 1773–1777," *New England Quarterly* 62 (1989): 248–63.

37. Robert Farris Thompson, *Flash of the Spirit: African and Afro-American Art and Philosophy* (New York, 1983), 139–45 (burial trees and bottle trees); William

D. Piersen, *Black Yankees: The Development of an Afro-American Subculture in Eighteenth-Century New England* (Amherst, Mass., 1988), chap. 7, at 77–78 (funeral processions).

38. Schlesinger, "Liberty Tree." J. L. Bell searched the *Pennsylvania Gazette* archives online (accessible.com) and the *Virginia Gazette* archives online (pastportal.com), as well as his personal collection of sources on Massachusetts. David Corrigan, of the Museum of Connecticut History, searched the index to the *Hartford Courant.* A few of the newly found poles may be past the 1776 cutoff date in Schlesinger. Fischer, *Liberty and Freedom*, chap. 1 (trees), chap. 2 (poles).

39. These are the towns for which there is evidence of liberty poles from 1765 to 1776: *Massachusetts*: Barnstable, Boston, Braintree, Bridgewater, Concord, Dedham, Deerfield, Granville, Hadley, Hanover, Machias, Middleborough, Milton, Nantucket, Petersham, Plymouth, Sandwich, Shutesbury, Taunton, Vineyard Haven, Williamsburg, Worcester; *Connecticut*: East Hartford, Farmingdale, Farmington, New Haven, Northford, Norwich; *Rhode Island*: Newport, Providence, South Kingston; *New Hampshire*: Greenland, Kingston, Portsmouth, Westmoreland; *Vermont*: Bennington, Springfield, Wheelock; *New York*: Brooklyn, East Hampton, German Flatts, Hampton, Hempstead, Huntington, New York City, Poughkeepsie, Shawangunk, Tappan Zee; *New Jersey*: Elizabethtown; *Pennsylvania*: Carlisle; *Maryland*: Hagerstown; *South Carolina*: Charlestown; *Georgia*: Savannah; *Virginia*: Accomack County, Williamsburg.

My list includes liberty poles identified by David Fischer, *Liberty and Freedom*, 47, 753 n. 80, on the basis of his Google search, December 2001. The fact that the index to the *Hartford Courant* revealed six poles in New England not reported in the *Pennsylvania Gazette* suggests that a search of other local newspapers might show other poles. The fact that a search of Vermont sources—[Esther Swift, *Vermont Place Names: Footprints in History* (Brattleboro, Vt., 1977), and Abie Hemenway, *The Vermont Historical Gazetteer*, 3 vols. (Burlington, Vt., 1867)]—yielded three other poles suggests the value of local history sources. Unfortunately, some of the present-day claims by local groups found on the Internet are not time specific and may refer to the more numerous poles raised in the late 1790s. My thanks to Kevin Kelly of Colonial Williamsburg, Inc., who identifies Charles Steuart to James Parker, November 17, 1774, Charles Steuart Papers, National Library of Scotland, as the source for a pole outside Raleigh Tavern, Williamsburg, Va. For the digitized *American Archives*, ed. Peter Force, see http://dig.lib.niu.edu.

40. For scholarship on this theme, see essay 5 in this volume. For a guide to recent scholarship on popular movements, see Edward Countryman, *The American Revolution*, 2nd ed. (New York, 2003), appendix; and Alan Kulikoff, *The Agrarian Origins of American Capitalism* (Charlottesville, Va., 1992), bibliography, 275–329.

41. In Philip M. Hamer et al., eds., *The Papers of Henry Laurens*, 16 vols. (Columbia, S.C., 1968–2003): Laurens to John Lewis Gervais, January 29, 1766

(5:53); *Charlestown Gazette*, October 3, 1768 (6:123); fn. May 14, 1770 (7:226); "Meeting under the Liberty Tree," August 22, 1770 (7:322–23); note December 13, 1770 (7:411). For these references my thanks to S. Max Edelson. George Flagg, "A List of Those Persons Who First Met at Liberty Tree, in Charleston in the Fall of the Year 1766 ...," Christopher Gadsden Mss, South Carolina Historical Society, www.SC History-org website.

42. Richard Walsh, *Charleston's Sons of Liberty: A Study of the Artisans* (Columbia, S.C., 1959), 87 (citation of Gadsden, 1778); Pauline Maier, "The Charleston Mob and the Evolution of Popular Politics in Revolutionary South Carolina, 1765–1784," *Perspectives in American History* 4 (1970): 173–96; Peter H. Wood, "'Liberty Is Sweet': African-American Freedom Struggles in the Years before White Independence," in Alfred F. Young, ed., *Beyond the American Revolution: Explorations in the History of American Radicalism* (DeKalb, Ill., 1993), 156–59 (Lieutenant Governor Bull at 159).

43. My analysis of the functions of the poles owes much to J. L. Bell, who watched events as they unfolded year by year in the *Pennsylvania Gazette*, digitized edition.

44. For this and the following paragraph: Jesse Lemisch, *Jack Tar versus John Bull: The Role of Merchant Seamen in Precipitating the Revolution* (New York, 1997); Paul Gilje, *The Road to Mobocracy: Popular Disorder in New York City, 1763–1834* (Chapel Hill, N.C., 1987), chap. 2; Edward Countryman, *A People in Revolution: The American Revolution and Political Society in New York, 1760–1790* (Baltimore, 1981), chap. 2; Lee R. Boyer, "Lobster Backs, Liberty Boys, and Laborers in the Streets: New York's Gold Hill and Nassau Street Riots," *New-York Historical Society Quarterly Bulletin* 57 (1973): 280–308.

45. Countryman, *People in Revolution*, chaps. 2, 4, p. 64 (Captain Montressor); Maier, *Old Revolutionaries*, 68ff.; Roger J. Champagne, *Alexander McDougall and the American Revolution in New York* (Schenectady, N.Y., 1975), chap. 1; General Thomas Gage to Lt. Col. William Dalrymple, January 8, 1770, Gage Mss., American Series, 89, brought to my attention by Mikal Muharrar.

46. Steven Rosswurm, *Arms, Country, and Class: The Philadelphia Militia and the "Lower Sort" during the American Revolution* (New Brunswick, N.J., 1988). For Virginia, see Rhys Isaac, *The Transformation of Virginia, 1740–1790* (Chapel Hill, N.C., 1982); and Woody Holton, *Forced Founders: Indians, Debtors, Slaves, and the Making of the American Revolution in Virginia* (Chapel Hill, N.C., 1999). For western Massachusetts, see Ray Raphael, *The First American Revolution: Before Lexington and Concord* (New York, 2002); and Gregory Nobles, *Divisions throughout the Whole: Politics and Society in Hampshire County, Massachusetts, 1740–1775* (Cambridge, U.K., 1983). Raphael finds poles at Hadley and Worcester. Nobles finds liberty poles only in Williamsburg and Deerfield.

47. Marjoline Kars, *Breaking Loose Together: The Regulator Rebellion in Pre-Revolutionary North Carolina* (Chapel Hill, N.C., 2002); Brendan McConville,

Those Daring Disturbers of the Public Peace: The Struggle for Property and Power in Early New Jersey (Ithaca, N.Y., 1999); Staughton Lynd, *Class Conflict: Slavery and the United States Constitution* (Indianapolis, 1967), essays 2, 3; Thomas Humphrey, *Land and Liberty: Hudson Valley Rioting in the Age of Revolution* (DeKalb, Ill., 2004), citing Captain John Montresor, chap. 2; Herman Husband cited in Mark Jones, "The Western 'New Jerusalem': Herman Husband's Utopian Vision" (unpublished ms.).

48. Clarence S. Brigham, *Paul Revere's Engravings* (New York, 1969), plates 5, 6; Gillian Anderson, comp., *Freedom's Voice in Poetry and Song* (Wilmington, Del., 1977), no. 475, "Liberty-Tree" (1775), and the index for newspaper reprints; Kenneth Silverman, *A Cultural History of the American Revolution* (New York, 1976), 110–18; Lester C. Olson, *Emblems of American Community in the Revolutionary Era* (Washington, D.C., 1991), tracks both tree and pole. Donald H. Cresswell, comp., *The American Revolution in Drawings and Prints: A Checklist of 1765–1790 Graphics in the Library of Congress* (Washington, D.C., 1975) (caricatures).

49. Alfred F. Young and Terry J. Fife, with Mary E. Janzen, *We the People: Voices and Images of the New Nation* (Philadelphia, 1993), 64–65 (James Pike's powderhorn) and 62–63 (Nathan Plummer's powderhorn). For the flags, see Fischer, *Liberty and Freedom*, 32–36, 77, 152–65; and William Furlong and Byron Candles, *So Proudly We Hail: The History of the United States Flag* (Washington, D.C., 1981) chaps. 2–6. Liberty Tree flags with the mottoes "Appeal to God" and "Appeal to Heaven" can be seen at http://www.history.villanova.edu/centennial/js1g.htm. For the "Bucks of America" flag, with a pine tree, presented to blacks in Boston, see Sidney Kaplan, *The Black Presence in the Era of the American Revolution, 1770–1800* (Washington, D.C., 1973), 57–58.

50. Washington cited in Charles Royster, *A Revolutionary People at War: The Continental Army and American Character, 1775–1783* (Chapel Hill, N.C., 1979), 236; for the mutiny, see *(Philadelphia) Freeman's Journal*, July 2, 1783; for Shays, see William Pencak, "'The Fine Theoretic Government of Massachusetts Is Prostrated to the Earth': The Response to Shays's Rebellion Reconsidered," 128, and Gregory Nobles, "Shays's Neighbors: The Context for Rebellion in Pelham, Massachusetts," 201, both in Robert Gross, ed., *In Debt to Daniel Shays: The Bicentennial of an Agrarian Rebellion* (Charlottesville, Va., 1993); for Vermont, see Michael Bellesiles, *Revolutionary Outlaws: Ethan Allen and the Struggle for Independence on the Early American Frontier* (Charlottesville, Va., 1993), 83.

51. Eric Slauter searched the "page text" in the digital edition of Evans, *Early American Imprints*, using the form "Liberty NEAR3tree," which, he explains, "should locate all documents where the term 'liberty' and 'tree' appear within three words of each other in any order." This search found sixty-three documents, including some that did not fit. At the time of this search (May 2003) the digital edition went only through 1785 and had only the original Evans entries (about nineteen thousand). Given these limitations, the findings should be

considered suggestive of a larger body of materials. Even so, this search engine is remarkable.

52. *Four Dissertations ... at the Public Commencement in the College of Philadelphia, May 20th, 1766* (Philadelphia, 1766); John Leacock, *The First Book of the American Chronicles of the Times* (Philadelphia, 1774); Philip Freneau *A Voyage to Boston: A Poem* (New York, 1775); Francis Hopkinson, *The Miscellaneous Essays and Occasional Writings of Francis Hopkinson, Esq.*, 3 vols. (Philadelphia, 1792), 1:92–97, cited in Winthrop Jordan, "Familial Politics: Thomas Paine and the Killing of the King, 1776," *Journal of American History* 60 (1973–74): 306; John Trumbull, *M'Fingal: A Modern Epic Poem* (Philadelphia, 1776), with an engraving of the action at a liberty pole.

53. John Devotion, *The Duty and Interest of a People ...* (Hartford, Conn., 1777); John Murray, *Jerubbaal, or Tyranny's Grove Destroyed ...* (Newburyport, Mass., 1784); Samuel MacClintock, *A Sermon Delivered before [the New Hampshire officers of government] ... June 3, 1784* (New Hampshire, 1784); John Gardiner, *An Oration Delivered July 4, 1785* (Boston, 1785); John Warren, *An Oration Delivered July 4th, 1783 ...* (Boston, 1783).

54. Staughton Lynd, *Slavery, Class Conflict, and the United States Constitution*, 260–61, traced the phrase to Bolingbroke, "A Dissertation upon Parties," in Viscount Henry St. John Bolingbrook, *Works*, 3 vols. (repr., London, 1809), 3:254–55; Barere cited in John Keane, *Tom Paine: A Political Life* (New York, 1995), 367.

55. Thomas Jefferson to William Stephens Smith, November 13, 1787, in Julian Boyd, ed., *The Papers of Thomas Jefferson* (Princeton, N.J., 1975), 12:355–57; Jefferson to James Madison, January 30, 1787, in Merrill Peterson, ed., *The Portable Thomas Jefferson* (New York, 1975), 417. It would be useful to track the occurrence of this phrase. I do not find Jefferson using it on other occasions, nor have I encountered it in public or private writings by others at the time. Merrill Peterson, *The Jefferson Image in the American Mind* (New York, 1960), does not take it up. For the context, see Dumas Malone, *Jefferson and the Rights of Man* (Boston, 1951), chap. 9.

56. Simon Schama, *Landscape and Memory* (New York, 1995), 139–52; Christina Hole, *A Dictionary of British Folk Customs* (London, 1978), 221–22.

57. Mayhew's sermon is in Bernard Bailyn, ed., *Pamphlets of the American Revolution, 1750–1776* (Cambridge, Mass., 1965), 213–48, and Bailyn's generalization is at 204.

58. For the elm, see Campanella, *Republic of Shade*, 33; for the oak, see Schama, *Landscape and Memory*, 163–64.

59. For Connecticut, see Roger F. Trent, "The Charter Oak Artifacts," *Connecticut Historical Society Bulletin* 49 (1984), unpaged; for Pennsylvania, see Robert C. Alberts, *Benjamin West: A Biography* (Boston, 1978), 110–11, for West's painting *William Penn's Treaty with the Indians* (1772); for Maryland, see Edward C. Papenfuse, "What's in a Name? Why Should We Remember? *The Liberty Tree* on St. John's

College Campus, Annapolis, Maryland," http://www.mdarchives.state.md/us/msa/educ/htm/liberty.html.

60. Campanella, *Republic of Shade*, chap. 2.

61. William Hone, *The Every-day Book; or Everlasting Calendar of Popular Amusements, Sports, Pastimes …*, 2 vols. (London, 1826), 1:538–99; Robert W. Malcolmson, *Popular Recreations in English Society, 1700–1850* (Cambridge, U.K., 1973), 30; David Underdown, *Revel, Riot, and Rebellion: Popular Politics and Culture in England 1603–1660* (Oxford, U.K., 1985), 86–88, 274–75; Christopher Hill, *Society and Puritanism in Pre-Revolutionary England* (New York, 1964), 184.

62. William Bradford, *Of Plymouth Plantation, 1620–1647*, ed. Samuel Eliot Morison (New York, 1952), 204–10; Hutchinson, *History of Massachusetts-Bay*, 1:8–9; Michael Zuckerman, "Pilgrims in the Wilderness: Community, Modernity, and the Maypole at Merry Mount," *New England Quarterly* 50 (1977): 255–77. The only other maypole that has come to light was in Charleston, Mass., in 1687. Mary Beth Norton, Richard Godbeer, and Michael Zuckerman each reassure me on the basis of their research that there was no continuity of May Day observances in colonial New England. I am indebted to the late John Higham for earlier exchanges on this subject.

63. For this and the preceding paragraph, see Roger D. Abrahams, "White Indians in Penn's City: The Loyal Sons of St. Tammany," in Pencak, Dennis, and Newman, eds., *Riot and Revelry*, 179–204, and Abrahams, "Making Faces in the Mirror: Playing Indian in Early America," *Southern Folklore* 52 (1995): 121–36; Philip J. Deloria, *Playing Indian* (New Haven, Conn., 1998), chap. 1; Edwin P. Kilroe, *Saint Tammany and the Origins of the Society of Tammany or Columbian Order in New York City* (New York, 1917), 33–39, 85–87, 108–9; Gottfried Mittelberger, *Journey to Pennsylvania in the Year 1750 …*, trans. Carl Theo Eben (Philadelphia, 1898), 112; William Eddis, *Letters from America*, ed. Aubrey K. Land (Cambridge, Mass., 1969), 58–59, 123.

64. *The Military Journal of George Ewing, 1754–1824, a Soldier at Valley Forge* (Yonkers, N.Y., 1928), 44–46; George Washington, General Orders, May 1, 1778, takes no note of the event. See John C. Fitzpatrick, ed., *The Writings of George Washington*, 39 vols. (Washington, D.C., 1931–44), 11:342.

65. James A. Epstein, "Understanding the Cap of Liberty: Symbolic Practice in Early Nineteenth-Century England," *Past and Present* 122 (1989): 75–118, at 86–87 for earlier usage; J. David Harden, "Liberty Caps and Liberty Trees," *Past and Present* 146 (1995): 66–102.

66. For this and the following paragraph: for medallions struck in 1688 and the following years, see E. Hawkins, *Medallic Illustrations of the History of Great Britain and Ireland to the Death of George II* (London, 1978), nos. 35, 58, 63, brought to my attention by Simon Newman; for the cap and Wilkes, see John Brewer, *Party, Ideology, and Popular Politics at the Accession of George III* (Cambridge, U.K., 1976), chap. 9; for cartoons, see M. Dorothy George and P. G. Stephens, *Catalogue of*

Prints and Drawings in the British Museum ..., 11 vols. (London 1870–1954), 4: nos. 4029, 4050, 4130; for Wilkes in America, see Maier, *From Resistance to Revolution*, esp. 162–69, 172–78; for the personification of America, see John Higham, "Indian Princess and Roman Goddess: The First Female Symbols of America," *Proceedings of the American Antiquarian Society* 100 (1990): 45–79.

67. For a survey, see Yvonne Korshak, "The Liberty Cap as a Revolutionary Symbol in America and France," *Smithsonian Studies in American Art* 1 (1987): 53–89; Brigham, *Paul Revere's Engravings*, plates 67, 70; for the Revere medal and bowl, see Fischer, *Liberty and Freedom*, 101–3; see also the numerous entries to "liberty cap" indexed in Cresswell, comp., *American Revolution in Drawings and Prints*. J. L. Bell found processional poles in articles in the *Pennsylvania Gazette* for 1766 in the following towns: Boston, Salem, Marblehead, Falmouth (Massachusetts), and Milford and New London (Connecticut). An artist placed a liberty cap atop a pillar in an emblem on the title page to *Journal of the Proceedings of Congress ... September 5, 1774* (Philadelphia, 1774). For the use of a pole in rough music, see essay 2 in this volume, and for the pole mounted with a head, see the engraving in essay 3.

68. Eric Foner, *The Story of American Freedom* (New York, 1998), chap. 1, quotation at 7; Edward Countryman, "'To Secure the Blessings of Liberty': Language, the Revolution and American Capitalism," in Young, ed., *Beyond the American Revolution*, 123–48; "Liberty, Property and No Excise: A Poem ...," August 1765, in Mason L. Lowance Jr. and Georgia Bumgardner, eds., *Broadsides of the American Revolution* (Amherst, Mass., 1976), 19; Justin Winsor, ed., *The Memorial History of Boston*, 4 vols. (Boston, 1881), 1:21n. 1 ("Great Elm" on the Common); *Boston Gazette*, September 16, November 4, 1765.

69. For traditions, see Peter Linebaugh, *The London Hanged: Crime and Civil Society in the Eighteenth Century* (London, 1991). For the majesty of elms, see the photographs in Campanella, *Republic of Shade*, passim. As may be apparent, I am at odds with the interpretation of universal "tree-spirits" in James George Frazer, *The Golden Bough: A Study in Magic and Religion* (New York, 1922), chap. 10, and with Peter Shaw, *American Patriots and the Rituals of Revolution* (Cambridge, Mass., 1981), for his loose standards for the evidence of customs in America, as well as for his interpretation of patriot rituals as regressive infantile behavior.

70. Walter Whitehill, *Boston: A Topographical History*, 2nd ed. (Cambridge, Mass., 1968), 32.

71. Silas Downer, *A Discourse ... July 25, 1768 at the Dedication of the Tree of Liberty ... by a Son of Liberty* (Providence, R.I., 1768), 15.

72. For the personal context, see Keane, *Tom Paine*, chaps. 1–4; for the political context, see Eric Foner, *Tom Paine and Revolutionary America* (New York, 1976), chaps. 1–2.

73. Thomas Paine, "Liberty Tree," in P. Foner, ed., *Complete Writings*, 2:1091–92.

It was widely reprinted in contemporary newspapers and separately as a song. Paine, *Common Sense*, in P. Foner, ed., *Complete Writings*, 1:19.

74. Paine, *Common Sense*, quotation at 5. Eric Slauter pointed out to me that Paine also used the analogy of a tree when he wrote, "Now is the seed-time of continental union, faith and honor. The least fracture now will be like a name engraved with the point of a pin on the tender rind of a young oak; the wound would enlarge with the tree, and posterity read it in its full grown characters" (P. Foner, ed., *Complete Writings*, 17). "Some Poetical Thoughts on the Difficulties Our Fore-Fathers Endured …," broadside (New Haven, Conn., 1776).

75. For Boston, see Young, *Shoemaker and the Tea Party*, 108–20; for the national changes, see Waldstreicher, *In the Midst of Perpetual Fetes*, chap. 1; for oratory, see Robert P. Hay, "The Liberty Tree: A Symbol for American Patriots 1777–1876," *Quarterly Journal of Speech* 55 (1969): 414–24, based on some six hundred Fourth of July orations nationally.

76. Mona Ozouf, *Festivals and the French Revolution* (Cambridge, Mass., 1988), 232–43; Lynn Hunt, *Politics, Culture, and Class in the French Revolution* (Berkeley, Calif., 1984), chap. 2; Bryan D. Palmer, *Cultures of Darkness: Night Travels in the Histories of Transgression* (New York, 2000), 306–8. For visual representations of the French Revolution I have relied on my notes from visits in 1984 to exhibitions in Paris of engravings in the Musée Carnavalet and of symbolic trees in Le Musée National des Arts et Traditions Populaires (e.g., reference cases 241.6, 242.03). I have not examined the microform "French Revolution Research Collection/Images of the French Revolution," sec. 4, "Commemorations and Celebrations," which would repay study. For other visual sources, see Jack Censer and Lynn Hunt, "Imaging the French Revolution: Depictions of the French Revolutionary Crowd: An Online Collaboration," *American Historical Review* 110 (2003): 38–45.

77. Harden, "Liberty Caps and Liberty Trees," 66–102; Maurice Agulhon, *Marianne into Battle: Republican Imagery and Symbolism in France, 1789–1880* (Cambridge, U.K., 1981), chap. 1. Neil Hertz, "Medusa's Head: Male Hysteria under Political Pressure," *Representations* 4 (1983): 27–54, points out the distinction art specialists draw between the Phrygian cap and the pileus.

78. Edward P. Thompson, *The Making of the English Working Class* (London, 1963; New York, 1964), part 1; Epstein, "Understanding the Cap of Liberty," 86–91; James A. Epstein, *Radical Expression, Political Language, Ritual, and Symbol in England, 1790–1850* (New York, 1994), 150–51. For the marginalization of the tree, see James A. Epstein, *In Practice: Studies in the Language and Culture of Popular Politics in Modern Britain* (Stanford, Calif., 2003), 88, 73; and Saree Makdisi, *William Blake and the Impossible History of the 1790s* (Chicago, 2003), 24, 58, 306–9 (Citizen Lee). Marcus Rediker called my attention to images of Spence's tokens, copies of which he sent me from English eBay. Seth Cotlar gave me a copy of the London Corresponding Society letter, 1795 ("liberty tree stump").

79. Alfred F. Young, *The Democratic Republicans of New York: The Origins,*

1765–1797 (Chapel Hill, N.C., 1968), chap. 16, citations at 353; Simon P. Newman, *Parades and the Politics of the Street: Festive Culture in the Early Republic* (Philadelphia, 1997), chap. 4 at 122–26; Roland Baumann, "The Democratic Republicans of Philadelphia: The Origins, 1776–1797" (Ph.D. diss., Pennsylvania State University, 1970), 427–29.

80. Korshak, "Liberty Cap as a Revolutionary Symbol," esp. 61–69; Newman, *Parades and Politics*, chap. 5; Susan Branson, *These Fiery Frenchified Dames: Women and Political Culture in Early National Philadelphia* (Philadelphia, 2001), chap. 2; Simon P. Newman and Susan Branson, "American Women and the French Revolution," in Pencak, Dennis, and Newman, eds., *Riot and Revelry*, 229–54; Simon P. Newman, *Embodied History: Reading the Bodies of Philadelphia's Lower Sort, 1780–1830* (Philadelphia, 2003); Higham, "Indian Princess and Roman Goddess"; Fischer, *Liberty and Freedom*, 233–42.

81. Dorothy Fennell, "From Rebelliousness to Insurrection: A Social History of the Whiskey Rebellion, 1765–1802" (Ph.D. diss., University of Pittsburgh, 1981), 116–21; Wythe Holt, "'Coercion by Law': The Federal Whiskey Rebellion Cases Take Working-Class Insurrection to Court, 1794," *Australian Journal of Law and Society* (forthcoming); citations for liberty poles in Northumberland and Franklin counties from Terry Bouton, "Taming Democracy: Pennsylvania Farmers and the Betrayal of the American Revolution" (unpublished ms.), chap. 10.

82. Newman, *Parades and Politics*, 174–76; for Dedham, see James Smith, *Freedom's Fetters: The Alien and Sedition Laws and American Civil Liberties* (Ithaca, N.Y., 1955), 257–70; for upstate New York, see ibid., 398–99. My thanks to Douglas Bradburn for a memorandum, "Liberty Poles in the 1790s," expanding on his "Revolutionary Politics, Nationhood, and the Problem of American Citizenship, 1783–1800" (Ph.D. diss., University of Chicago, 2003), chap. 6. Albrecht Koschnik, "Political Conflict and Public Contest: Rituals of National Celebration in Philadelphia, 1788–1815," *Pennsylvania Magazine of History and Biography* 118 (1994): 242–44.

83. Alfred F. Young, "The Federalist Attack on Civil Liberties," *Science and Society* 17 (1953): 59–64; "An Old Fashioned Republican," *Philadelphia Aurora*, May 3, 1799, reprinted in Richard N. Rosenfeld, *American Aurora: A Democratic-Republican Returns* (New York, 1997), 627, a compilation of excerpts charting battles over liberty poles in 1790–99.

84. Cited in David Wilson, *United Irishmen, United States: Immigrant Radicals in the Early Republic* (Ithaca, N.Y., 1998), 14.

85. Hunt, *Politics, Culture, and Class*, 59–60, 90; Henry Grégoire, *Essai Historique et Patriotique sur les Arbres de la Liberté* (Paris, 1794), 20–21. I have read the Grégoire in the original but use here the translation by Harden, "Liberty Caps and Liberty Trees," 90. For Grégoire, see also Ozouf, *Festivals and the French Revolution*, 243–56.

86. For Barlow's intellectual sources, see Schama, *Landscape and Memory*, 17,

246–54; and David B. Davis, prefatory note to Joel Barlow, *Advice to the Privileged Orders in the Several States of Europe* (1792, 1795; repr., Ithaca, N.Y., 1956).

87. Joel Barlow, "Genealogy of the Tree of Liberty," Notebook (c. 1796–97), pp. 10–13, bMS Am 1448 (vol. 13), Houghton Library, Harvard University. Carla Mulford generously shared her transcript of this manuscript with me as well as her understanding of it. See Carla Mulford, "Radicalism in Joel Barlow's *The Conspiracy of Kings* (1792)," in J. A. Leo Lemay, ed., *Deism, Masonry, and the Enlightenment: Essays Honoring Alfred Owen Aldridge* (Newark, Del., 1987), 137–57.

88. Hill, *Society and Puritanism*, 184; Eric Slauter, "Being Alone in the Age of the Social Contract," *William and Mary Quarterly*, 3rd ser., 62 (2005): 56–58, citing Peter Prejudice, "The New Breeches," *(Philadelphia) Federal Gazette*, April 15, 1788; Schama, *Landscape and Memory*, 252 and 17.

89. Michael Kammen, *Mystic Chords of Memory: The Transforming of Tradition in American Culture* (New York, 1991), 9–10; John Higham, "Symbolizing the U.S.," *New York Times*, December 18, 1975 (op-ed page); see also E. P. Thompson, "C is for Country, A is for Anniversary, S is for Solitude, H is for History," *New York Times*, April 27, 1976 (op-ed page); Hay, "The Liberty Tree," 416–24 (orations).

90. Campanella, *Republic of Shade*, esp. chaps. 6, 7 (spread of trees); Robert P. Turner, ed., *Lewis Miller: Sketches and Chronicles* (York, Pa., 1966), 82; Schlesinger, "Liberty Tree," 456–58 (electioneering poles); Fischer, *Liberty and Freedom*, 208–11 (electioneering), 228–32 (Uncle Sam); Jean Baker, *Affairs of Party: The Political Culture of Northern Democrats in the Mid-Nineteenth Century* (Ithaca, N.Y., 1983), 297–98. For twentieth-century survivals, see "What's in a Name? ... Annapolis, Maryland," www.archives.state.md; "Liberty Pole, Portsmouth, NH," www.goseacoast.com; "The Mystic Liberty Pole," *Historical Footnotes: Bulletin of the Stonington Historical Society* (1986). For New York City's plaque "The Liberty Pole on the Commons," *New-York Historical Society Quarterly Bulletin* (1919): 109–30. For Brooklyn and Rochester, where poles are still a landmark, see Fischer, *Liberty and Freedom*, 46. A search of *Omni Gazetteer* for American place-names reveals one town named Liberty Pole (Wisconsin), a Liberty Pole Road, and a Liberty Pole Hill.

91. C. L. R. James, *The Black Jacobins: Toussaint L'Ouverture and the San Domingo Revolution* (New York, 1963), 334. In seven African American papers published between 1827 and 1870, listed on "Accessible Archives," Mitch Kachun identified twenty-eight separate uses of "the tree of liberty," which he generously shared. William Nell, *The Colored Patriots of the American Revolution* (Boston, 1855), 38. For a Native American appropriation: William Apess, *A Son of the Forest and Other Writings by William Apess, a Pequot*, ed. Barry O'Donnell (Amherst, Mass., 1992), 31.

92. Eric Foner, *The Story of American Freedom* (New York, 1998), 93–94 (capitol dome statue); Fischer, *Liberty and Freedom*, 298–300 (statue); and for the Statue of Liberty, see Marina Walker, *Monuments and Maidens: The Allegory of the Female*

Form (London, 1985), 3–17, 270–77, and Fischer, *Liberty and Freedom*, 368–74. A search of the Library of Congress Prints and Photographs Division on-line catalog revealed a number of cartoons of the pre– and post–Civil War eras that assume blacks associated the tree of liberty with freedom. For Gilman, see Fischer, *Liberty and Freedom*, 362–63.

93. For the Boston site, see "The Old Liberty Tree," *Boston Daily Evening Transcript*, February 19, 1850; "Report of the Boston Landmarks Commission on the Potential Designation of the Liberty Tree Building as a Landmark under Chapter 772 of the Acts of 1975" (Boston, 1985), typescript; Lafayette quoted in Samuel Adams Drake, *Old Landmarks and Historic Personages of Boston* (Boston, 1873), 396–99. My thanks to Matthew Greif for searching for nineteenth-century sources. Nathaniel Hawthorne, *Liberty Tree: With the Last Words of Grandfather's Chair* (Boston, 1841, 1842, 1851), reprinted in Hawthorne, *True Stories from History and Biography* (Athens, Ohio, 1972), 143–214. Hawthorne's "My Kinsman, Major Molineux," first published in 1831–32, is widely anthologized.

94. Winsor, ed., *Memorial History of Boston*, 3:159. An earlier depiction of the tree, with no people at all, is in Caleb Snow, *A History of Boston* (Boston, 1825), 266. For the New York art, see F. A. Chapman, "Raising the Liberty Pole" (c. 1876), and Felix Darling, "Defense of the Liberty Pole in New York City," in Benjamin Lossing, *Our Country* (1879), both in Library of Congress Prints and Photographs Division.

95. In pursuit of the origins of May 1 as Labor Day and possible connections with the maypole and/or liberty tree, I have consulted David Montgomery, "Labor Day and May Day," H-Net, Labor History Discussion List (September 6, 1995); *International Labor and Working-Class History* 29 (spring 1986); Eric Hobsbawm, "Mass Producing Traditions: Europe, 1870–1914," in Eric Hobsbawm and Terence Ranger, eds., *The Invention of Tradition* (Cambridge, U.K., 1983), 284–86; James Green, *Taking History to Heart: The Power of the Past in Building Social Movements* (Amherst, Mass., 2000), 105–7; Bruce Nelson, *Beyond the Martyrs: A Social History of the Chicago Anarchists, 1870–1900* (New Brunswick, N.J., 1988). My thanks to Bruce Nelson, James Green, Joshua Freeman, Bruno Cartosio, and Bruce Laurie for answering my queries.

96. For the absence of these symbols in twentieth-century iconography, I rely on Michael Kammen, *A Season of Youth: The American Revolution and the Historical Imagination* (New York, 1978), confirmed by Fischer, *Liberty and Freedom*, passim. A full search of murals painted by WPA artists might reveal depictions of the tree or pole. For the mural, see Diego Rivera, *Portrait of America*, with an explanatory text by Bertram D. Wolfe (New York, 1934), 90–96, panel 2. Wolfe reprints black-and-white photos. See also Laurance P. Hurlburt, *The Mexican Muralists in the United States* (Albuquerque, N.M., 1989), 175–93. The murals were exhibited by the International Ladies Garment Workers Union at its summer camp, after which several panels were bought by private collectors and the others disappeared.

97. Higham, "Symbolizing the U.S."; Mark Boatner III, *Landmarks of the American Revolution* (Harrisburg, Pa., 1973); Fischer, *Liberty and Freedom,* 629–31 (New Left); for Bread and Puppet theater, I am indebted to Walter Wallace, a participant (conversation with the author, August 2005); for elms, see Campanella, *Republic of Shade,* epilogue, and Fischer, *Liberty and Freedom,* 686–87.

98. For recent efforts to commemorate the liberty tree in Boston, see Young, *Shoemaker and the Tea Party,* 247 n.3. In 1964 the Massachusetts legislature established August 14 as "Liberty Tree Day." For enlightening me in 2004 about plans for Liberty Tree Park my thanks to Tai Lim, Ralph Cole, and Michael Taylor.

99. Lou Michael and Dan Herbeck, *American Terrorist: Timothy McVeigh and the Oklahoma City Bombing* (New York, 2001), 137, 154, 226, 244.

Index

Page numbers in italics signify an illustration or caption on the page.

"Abigail Trust" (pseudonym), 121

Abraham, Roger A., 360

Academic Bill of Rights for Historians, 18

Accommodation: of African Americans, 236–238, 348; of boys, 348; of democracy, 195–202, 208, 232–243; by Democratic Republicans, 246–247; by Federalists, 234–235, 274, 276; of Indians, 240–243, 248; by Jefferson, 356; by Jeffersonians, 247–248; radicalism of American Revolution, 232–243; republicanism, 274; of sailors, 348; of slaves, 237–238; of women, 238–240, 348

Adair, Douglass, 183

Adams, Abigail Smith: Adams (Elizabeth) and, 130–131; Adams (John) and, 100–101, 130, 131, 132, 223, 238, 239, 273, 302, 303; African Americans, 346; articulate women, 16; Boston, knowledge of, 102; Boston's trails, 312–313; *Common Sense,* 131–132, 223, 273; education of women, 131; List of Female Grievances, 101, 130; Macaulay and, 128; male roles, 226; Paine and, 286; "Portia," 128; public discourse, 134; rebellion among women, 100, 102, 130; statue of, 312–313; textbooks, 308; titles for women, 131; Warren (Mercy Otis) and, 129, 131; women's inequality, 100–102, 130–131, 247

Adams, Elizabeth, 130–131

Adams, John: Adams (Abigail Smith) and, 100–101, 130, 131, 132, 223, 238, 239, 273, 302, 303; Adams (Samuel) and, 189, 286, 299; *Adulateur,* 129; African Americans, 100; on aspirations of mechanics, 36–37; Backus and, 302; balancing democratic and aristocratic forces, 9; Boston Massacre, 336; on Brattle Street meetinghouse, 109; on commemoration of Boston Massacre, 120; *Common Sense,* 186, 272, 273, 303; constituency, 274; constitutions, 189; criticism of, 247, 287; Cromwell and, 158, 159, 161; Declaration of Independence, 10;

decline in deference, 132; democracy, 344; dependence of the poor on the rich, 35–36; distinctive New England institutions, 107; fears experienced by yeoman farmers, 217–218; Freedom Trail, 301; Hancock and, 50, 286, 299; Henry and, 189; historical memory, 286, 299; independence, 272; Indians, 100; Jefferson and, 205, 276, 279, 286; Mackintosh (Ebenezer) and, 302, 341; Massachusetts constitution, 273; overshadowing of, 286; Paine and, *283, 284,* 286, 288; "the people," 7; personal declarations of independence, 222; political life, 223; popular activity, 102; presidential election (1796), 276; presidential election (1800), 246–247; radicalism, 189; republicanism, 274; Seider's funeral, 119; in "Signing of the Declaration of Independence," 9; on skimmingtons, 151, 152; Stamp Act, 8; tar-and-feathering, 156; *Thoughts on Government* (book), 186; "Thoughts on Government" (manuscript), 272–273; Warren (Mercy Otis) and, 129; Washington and, 275; women, 100, 240, 248; on year 1765, 343–344

Adams, John Quincy, 279

Adams, Samuel: Adams (Elizabeth) and, 130; Adams (John) and, 189, 299; Backus and, 302; "Baubles of Britain," 47; biography of, 8; British plans to seize, 343; as colonywide leader, 344; Committee on Donations, 123; Copley and, 311; Cromwell and, 158, 164; crowd control by, 336; destruction of Hutchinson's mansion, 335; fears experienced by yeoman farmers, 218; Freedom Trail, 301, 302; General Court, 344; Gerry and, 189; Hewes and, 308; historical memory, 286, 299; Loyal Nine, 118; Mackintosh (Ebenezer) and, 342; mechanics, 49, 62; Molineaux and, 117; Paine and, 284, 285; "the people," 9; Shays and, 303; Sons of Liberty, 189; spinning wheels, 117; Stamp Act, 8; stereotype of, 334; wife, 130; Young (Thomas) and, 117

"Address of John Humble" (anonymous), 61–62

Adulateur (Warren), 129

African American history, 15

African Americans: Abiel Smith school (Boston), 298; accommodation of, 236–238, 348; Adams (Abigail Smith) and, 346; Adams (John) and, 100; Afro-American culture, 148; American Revolution, 237–238; annual holiday, 68; Boston, 312; British army, 346; cities, 31; collective action, 245; Colonial Williamsburg, 17, 315; Declaration of Independence, 301; demonstrations by, 348; free blacks, 231, 312; Freedom Trail, 312; Jefferson and, 236; liberty poles, 348; liberty trees, 7, 346, 374; Madison and, 236; mechanics, 73; "Negro election day," 148; population, 31; progressive historians, 14; radicalism of American Revolution, 230–231; Shays's Rebellion, 231; skilled trades, 73; Washington and, 245. *See also* Black Heritage Trail

Age of Reason (Paine): influence, 267; Jefferson and, 268; Paine's enemies, 284; Paine's fall from grace, 268, 282; promise of, 247–248; public readings, 70; reaction to, 268; response to, 279; *Rights of Man*, 279

Agrarian Justice (Paine), 77, 287

Albany (New York State), 59, 61

Alcuin (Brown), 246

Aldridge, Alfred Owen, 271

Alien and Sedition Laws (1798), 276, 369, 370

Allen, Ethan, 15, 284, 355

Allen, Richard, 16

Allen, Stephen, 70

American Archives, 347

American Chronicle of the Times (pamphlet), 146, 164

American Federation of Labor, 79

American Indians. *See* Indians

American National Biography (1999), 305

American Political Society, 122

American Revolution (1775-1815), 217–261; African Americans, 237–238; anthem of, 16; anti-slavery movement, 232; artisans, 6; class-based interpretations, 12–13; communications revolution, 234; conservatism of, 240; Constitution, 16; control of, 121; dark side of, 313–315; double character, 327; evangelism, 220–221; farmers, 15; historical memory, 300; human agency, 217, 249; Indians, 6, 231, 314; interpretations of, 12–16, 300–302; landed expansion, 240; liberty from Great Britain, 300; liberty

within America, 300; mechanics, 15; 29; multisidedness/multicoloredness, 16; National Standards for History, 15; new history of, 300–303; nineteen seventies, 13–14; nineteen sixties, 13; ordinary people, 3–12; "the people," 7; plebeian currents, 12; popular consciousness, 227; popular movements, 4; popular revolutionary rituals, 367; "popular" side of, 303–305; post-World War II historians, 13; progressive historians, 12–13, 14; public memory, 6; to radical right, 18–19; radicalism (*see* Radicalism of American Revolution); rebellion in, 301; relations between the sexes, 238; results of, 232–233; runaway slaves, 11; sanitization of, 13; slavery, 15, 17, 237–238; symbol of, 243, 325; television, 17; temporal extent, 27–29, 223–224, 301; textbooks, 17, 308; as two-way conflict, 300; women, 6; women's rights movement, 232; would-be rulers, 6; yeoman farmers, 6

American Revolution (Young), 232

"American Scholar" (Emerson), 12

American Social History Project, 306

Ames, Levi, 111

Analects upon the Rights of Man (Dow), 285

Anielo, Thomas, 117. *See also* Masaniello

Annapolis (Maryland): Carroll (Charles) and, 192; liberty tree, 347, 358, 374, 376; maypole, 360

Anti-slavery movement, 232

Antifederalists: Constitution, 203–206; Husband and, 224; mechanics, 61; New York City, 62; Philadelphia, 62; Smith (Melancton) and, 61; yeoman farmers, 61

Apprentices: boys, 345–346; decline of, 75; deference, 236; definition, 32; fondness for freedom, 41; hazing customs, 42; love of freedom, 219; male patriot movement, 113; master artisans, 32–33, 35, 41, 236; mechanics, 66; mechanics parades, 63, 65; Pope's Day, 111; runaways, 41; social mobility, 218–219; transformation of, 230

Aprons, leather, *28*, 30, 308

Artisan republicanism: elements of, 165; mechanics, 29, 68–74

Artisans: American Revolution, 6; Baltimore, 165; Boston, 33, 34; class, 31–32; collective identity/pride, 39; colonial cities, 30; Constitution, 206–207, 208; dependencies among, 35–36; English plebeian culture, 5, 150, 164–167; erosion of artisan system, 29; ethnicity of, 32; Franklin and, 30, 37–39, 77, 80; genders, 32; guilds, 164; ideals of, *184*; institutions

of, 148; labor movement, 80; leather aprons, 28, 30; literacy, 70; male patriot movement, 113; marching en masse in parades, 5; merchants, 37; occupational hierarchy, 32–33; Paine and, 69–70, 206; "petty bourgeois," 31; Philadelphia, 33; property rights, 218; religious affiliation, 32; *Rights of Man* (Paine), 69, 73; skills of, 218; social mobility, 33–34; social status, 34–35; tariff protection, 207; trade emblems, 166; *Vindication of the Rights of Women,* 73; wealth, 33–34. *See also* Mechanics; Tradesmen; *individual trades such as "Bakers" or "Blacksmiths"*
"Aspatia" (pseudonym), 126
Association of Tradesmen and Manufacturers (Boston), 58
Attucks, Crispus: actions against British, 50; Boston Massacre, 299, 312; funeral, 119–120
Autobiography (Franklin), 29–30
Avery, John, Jr., 331
Awl (newspaper), 79

Backus, Isaac, 16, 158, 302
Bacon's Rebellion (1676), 241
Bailyn, Bernard, 147, 215, 270
Bakers, 35, 63, 165
Baltimore: artisans, 165; Democratic-Republican societies, 69; mechanics, 61, 68, 70; population, 31
Bamford, Samuel, 160
Bank of Pennsylvania, 78
Banks, John, 159
Barclay, Jannette Day, 105–106
Barere, Bertrand, 356
Barlow, Joel, 16, 372–373, 377
Barre, Isaac, 333
Bartholdi, Frederic, 376
Bass, Henry, 334
"Battle of Golden Hill," 351, 352
Beard, Charles, 13, 18, 203
Becker, Carl, 13
Beekman family, 188
Beggar's Opera (Gay), 116
"Belinda" (pseudonym), 126
Bell, J. L., 347
Benton, Thomas Hart, 376
Berlin, Ira, 3, 237
Bernard, Francis: on crowd action, 118; destruction of Hutchinson's mansion, 335; Mackintosh (Ebenezer) and, 339, 340, 342; Stamp Act protesters, 333
Bigelow, Timothy, 15
Bill of Rights, 18, 205, 235

Billings, William, 109
Billy Budd (Britten), 315
Bingham, Anne Willing, 248
Black Heritage Trail (Boston), 298, 311–312
Blacksmiths: dependencies, 35; mechanics parades, 63, 64, 165; slogan, 166; social mobility, 33; status, 53
Blackstone, William, 130
Bloody Massacre perpetrated on King Street (Revere), 309
Bloomfield (Connecticut), 347
BNHP (Boston National Historical Park), 296, 301, 316
Boat builders, 63
Bolingbroke, Henry St. John, 1st Viscount, 356
Bonneville, Benjamin de, 265
Bonneville, Margaret de, 265
Bonneville, Nicholas de, 265
Bonneville, Thomas de, 265
Boston: 1830s, 307; Abiel Smith school, 298; adult white females, 103–104; African Americans, 312; artisans, 33, 34; "better sort" in, 331; Black Heritage Trail, 298, 311–313; bookstores, 108; Brahmin elite, 375; Brattle Street meetinghouse, 109; British occupation, 47, 49, 54, 118–119, 122–123, 341, 346; Bunker Hill Monument, 315; Charles River bridge, 67; Charlestown Navy Yard, 311; class divisions, 34, 335; craftswomen, 104; crowd action, 48, 49, 107, 112, 118, 155; crown action, 114; cultural hero, 110; "Deacon Elliot's corner," 364; "Deacon Elliot's house," 327–328; Democratic-Republican societies, 69; economic depression, 34; elections, 107; Faneuil Hall, 43, 107, 298, 303, 304, 338, 339; Federalists, 62, 72; female-headed households, 103–104, 106; Fort Hill, 329; free blacks, 312; Freedom Trail (*see* Freedom Trail); gap between rich and poor, 34; General Court representative, 344; Great Awakening, 110; "Great Elm," 363; hangings, 111; Harrison Gray Otis House, 310; historical memory, 299; inequality, 309–310; Irish Heritage Trail, 312; journeymen, 33; "Joyce, Jun.," 168; King's Chapel, 311; "Liberty Hall," 331, 339; liberty pole, 346–349; *Liberty* ship riot (1768), 336–337; liberty tree, 7, 297, 305, 325, 326, 327–338, 346, 363–366, 375; Liberty Tree Building, 305; linen manufacturing, 107; Literary Trail of Greater Boston, 298, 312; "lower sort" in, 331; Loyalists, 50, 113, 123, 189; male patriot movement, 113; Massachusetts state constitution, 54; master artisans, 33, 44; mechanics, 30, 49, 51, 53–54, 58–59, 60, 61, 62–63, 70, 72;

Boston (*Continued*)
  mechanics parades, 65; merchants, 113, 115, 121, 123, 310, 333, 362; Museum of Fine Arts, 310–311; nonimportation of British goods, 115, 118, 121, 362; North End, 310, 364; Old North Church, 311; Old South Meeting House, 43, 298, 299, 304, 306, 311, 312, 338; Old State House, 298, 299, 303, 311, 327, 328; persons per household, 105; political conflict, 34; political institutions, 107–108; poor relief, 106–107; Pope's Day, 42, 48, 111, 117, 336, 357; population, 31, 103; port closure, 122; public bonfires, 329; public history, 298–299; public schools, 108; pulling down buildings, 329; reputation, 42; Revere House, 304, 310; riding the wooden horse, 151; *Rights of Man*, 278; riots in, 42, 111–112, 336–337; "she-merchants," 105; siege of, 112–113, 123–124, 161; slaves, 31, 66; social structure, 103; Sons of Liberty, 48, 51, 128; South End, 364; Stamp Act, 8, 48, 50, 113–114; tar-and-feathering, 118, 154, 155–156, 343, 375; town meetings, 43, 107–108, 333, 339; voting, 43; Washington and, 166; Whitfield and, 40, 110, 133; widows, 103–104, 105, 124; women, 100–143; Women's Heritage Trail, 298, 312; work relief, 122
Boston Academy of Music, 315
Boston Committee of Correspondence, 121
Boston Evening Post (newspaper), 115
Boston Gazette (newspaper): Cromwell as savior, 163; crowd action, 115; Edes and, 331; female pride, 126–127; "Great Elm," 363; printer, 331
Boston History Collaborative (BHC), 298, 306
Boston Massacre (1770): Adams (John) and, 336; Attucks and, 299, 312; catalyst, 118–119; commemoration of, 120, 133; exhibit on, 298; fame, 112–113; Hewes and, 5, 222, 306, 307; liberty tree, 330, 338–339; Old State House, 303; reenactments, 298, 304; Revere and, 120, 304; trial, 336; women, 345
Boston National Historical Park (BNHP), 296, 301, 316
Boston Navy Yard, 315
Boston News-Letter (newspaper), 115
Boston Tea Party (1773): fame, 112–113; Freedom Trail, 305; Hewes and, 5, 222, 306, 307–308; museum about, 298; Old State House, 303; rediscovery of, 300, 306; reenactments, 298, 304; response to, 121; symbolism of, 243; tar-and-feathering, *145*; women, 120–121
Bostonian Society: Freedom Trail, 298, 301; Hewes and, 306; as a museum, 304

Boys, 345–346, 348
Brackenridge, Hugh Henry, 73
Brackett, Joshua, 161, 164
Bradford, William, 359
Braintree (Massachusetts), 102
Brant, Joseph, 16
Brattle, William, 334
Braxton, Carter, 272
Bremer, Francis, 158
Brewster, William, 70
Bridgehampton (Long Island, New York), 371
Briggs, Katherine, 159
Brimmer, Herman, 164
Bristol (England), 167
British army: African Americans, 346; liberty poles, 366; liberty trees, 366; occupation of Boston, 47, 49, 54, 118–119, 122–123, 341, 346; occupation of Charleston, 54; occupation of New York City, 47, 54, 124, 349; occupation of Philadelphia, 54, 124; slaves, 225
Britten, Benjamin, 315
Brown, Charles Brockden, 246, 248
Brown, David, 70, 370
Brown, William Hill, 73
Bryan, Samuel, 62
Bulfinch, Charles, 304, 310
Burke, Edmund, 153, 274, 281
Burke, Peter, 148, 149
Burns, Ken, 18
Burr, Esther Edwards, 109
Bushman, Richard, 217
Butchers, 67
Bute, John Stuart, 3rd Earl of, 328
Butler, Pierce, 198–199

Cabinet makers, 63
Cade, Jack, 340, 341, 371
Cambridge (Massachusetts): Harvard commencements, 110; liberty pole, 347; liberty tree, 344; rumor of British attack, 123
Cannon, James, 15, 50
Capitalism, 233
Carey, Matthew, 278
Carlyle, Thomas, 160
Carpenters, 53, 56, 165
Carpenters Company of Philadelphia, 41
Carroll, Charles (of Annapolis), 192
Carroll, Charles (of Carrollton), 192, 196
Carroll, Daniel, 196
Carroll family (Maryland), 233
Carrollton (Maryland), 192
Carter, Robert, 220

Cathcart, Susanne, 119
Catskill (New York State), 59
"Caucus Club" (Boston), 341
Centenarian (portrait of Hewes), 307
Chairmakers, 56, 64
Chappel, William, 73
Charles I, King of Great Britain and Ireland: beheading of, *157*; call for execution of, 158; capture and execution, 363; commemorations of execution of, 162; "Joyce, Jun.," 156, 163–164, 337; mourning for, 357
Charles II, King of Great Britain and Ireland, 160, 357
Charleston Mechanic Society, 49, 59, 348
Charleston (South Carolina): British occupation, 54; deference, 45; Democratic-Republican societies, 69; Fellowship Society, 49, 59; gallows, 364; John Wilkes Club, 49; liberty pole, 348; liberty trees, 347, 348–349; Loyalists, 50; mechanics, 45, 49, 50, 51, 53, 61, 348; mechanics societies, 60; population, 31; slave owners, 31; slaves, 31, 66, 374; Stamp Act protests, 348
"Charter Oak" legend, 358
Chauncy, Charles, 110
Cheetham, James, 267
Chicago Historical Society, 17
Chimney sweeps, 66
Chronicles (Holinshed), 155
Civil War (film), 18
Clark, Abraham, 16
Class: artisans, 31–32; Boston, 34, 335; cities, 148; class-based interpretations of American Revolution, 12–13; class divisions, 34, 52, 71, 148, 225–226, 229, 244, 333, 335; class feeling, 71; class representation, 53, 185; deference, 132; in European revolutions, 169; house attacks, 335; language of, 229; Maryland, 225; "middle class," 229; New York City, 244; New York State, 225; Thompson on, 227–228; uprisings against landlords, 353; Virginia, 225; "working class," 229; yeoman farmers, 228
"Class," 31, 229
Cleary, Patricia, 105
Clergy, 65
Clinton, Dewitt, 267
Clinton, George: Livingston (Robert R.) and, 191; New York State constitution, 203; Paine and, 267, 286
Clinton, Henry, 225
Coach makers, 35
Cobbett, William, 282
Collins, James, 16

Colonial era: artisans, 30–31; banks, 35, 74; "class," 31; class feeling, 71; crowds, 243; deference, 44; elites, 44; literacy, 147–148; localization of tradition, 358; "manufacturer," 30; "mechanic," 27, 30; nonimportation of British goods, 47, 115, 118, 121, 362; occupational hierarchy, 31; "people out of doors," 5, 198; "people within doors," 5, 199; politics in, 44; population statistics, 30–31; seaports, 32, 34; "shopkeeper," 30; skimmingtons, 150–151; "sorts," 31; "tradesman," 30; urban population, 31; urban poverty, 37; veneration of trees, 358–359
Colonial Williamsburg: African Americans, 17, 315; depiction of artisan world, 30; slaves, 315; social stratification, 309
Columbian Centinel (newspaper), 72
Commentaries on the Laws of England (Blackstone), 130
Committee for Tar-and-Feathering (Boston), 156
Committee of Privates (Philadelphia), 49, 50, 51, 53
Committee of Tradesmen (Boston), 63
Committee on Donations (Boston), 122–123
Committees of Correspondence, 4, 49, 121
Committees of Inspection, 4
Committees of Mechanics (New York City), 185–186
Committees of Safety, 4
"Common people," 7. *See also* Ordinary people
Common Sense (Paine): Adams (Abigail Smith) and, 131–132, 223, 273; Adams (John) and, 186, 272, 273, 303; central government, 60; composition of, 365; constitutional recommendations, 54; contribution made by, 272; and Declaration of Independence, 272; democratic ideology, 186–187, 206–208; George III, 269; hope, 224; influence, 51–52, 267, 271–272; liberty trees, 366; Masaniello and, 341; message, 269, 271; ordinary people, 272; popularity, 270–271; in portrait of Paine, *266*; price, 278; printings, 270; purpose, 366; radicalism of the American Revolution, 227; readership, 10, 269–270, 271; reception in America, 269–273, 281; and *Rights of Man*, 269, 270, 276, 278, 279, 281; Rush and, 267; sales, 270; state constitutions, 187; three-cornered debate precipitated by, 272; title page, 269; Washington and, 270–271; writing style/tone, 269, 270
Commons, John R., 41
Compromise. *See* Accommodation
Connecticut: Bloomfield, 347; "Charter Oak" legend, 358; Cromwell and, 161; Hartford, 355,

Connecticut (*Continued*)
　358; liberty trees, 347; New Haven (*see* New
　Haven); Norwalk, 69; Norwich, 161; Saybrook,
　161; Stonington, 285
Conservatives, 183–214; accommodation of
　democratic movement, 195–202, 208, 232–236;
　conservative patriots, 190; Constitution, 6,
　183–214; democracy, 185–195, 196; elites, 66,
　233, 268; enlargement of the sphere of gov-
　ernment, 195, 198; landlord estate holders,
　190; liberty trees, 355; Maryland, 191–192;
　mechanics, 66; merchants, 190; metaphors
　for threats from below, 233–234; minority
　rights, 194–195; mobs, 185; national govern-
　ment, 194–195; national veto of state legisla-
　tion, 195, 198, 202; New York State, 190–191;
　"people out of doors," 198; "people within
　doors," 199; property requirements for vot-
　ing, 200, 202; Shays's Rebellion, 193; slave-
　holders, 190; state governments, 194–195; state
　legislatures, 188
"Constance Trueman" (pseudonym), 45
Constitution (U.S.), 183–214; accommodation
　of democratic movement, 195–202, 208;
　agrarian majority, 6; amendments, 207;
　American Revolution, 16; Antifederalists,
　203–206; artisans, 206–207, 208; Bill of Rights,
　18, 206, 235; breeches compared to, 373; checks
　and balances, 203; chief architects, 195, 199,
　202; conservatives, 6, 183–214; democracy, 6,
　170, 205–208; direct election of Representa-
　tives, 196–202; farmers, 230; framers, 6;
　Hamilton and, 208; Jefferson and, 205–206,
　207; legal Shayism, 227; mechanics, 54, 60, 61,
　62; mechanics parades, 146, 165, 170, 208; mid-
　dle of the road, 202, 203; Morris (Gou-
　verneur) and, 195; Paine and, 207, 275; radical
　right, 18; ratification, 62–67; runaway slaves,
　11; as sacred text, 18; slavery, 67; spirit of 1776,
　208; Wilson (James) and, 195, 202
Constitution, USS, 298
Constitutional Convention (1787): accommo-
　dation of democratic movement, 195–202,
　208, 234; delegates to, 11, 195; direct election of
　Representatives, 196–202; diversity, 199–200,
　202; Gerry and, 199; ghosts of popular move-
　ments, 11; Hamilton's proposal, 183–185, 196,
　202, 208, 235; Jay and, 196; Livingston (Robert
　R.) and, 196; Mason and, 199; mechanics, 61;
　Morris (Gouverneur) and, 196; Paine and, 11;
　property requirements for voting, 200, 202;
　Shays and, 11; Washington and, 199; Wilson
　(James) and, 196, 202

Continental Army: green boughs, 355; liberty
　poles, 360; memoirs by veterans, 1, 3–4; pen-
　sions for veterans, 2–3, 226, 277; Pope's Day
　celebrations, 367; promises of land, 1–2, 224,
　226; size, 3; soldiers' dress, 355; Valley Forge,
　360, 365; women in, 5
Continental Congress (1774-1776), 9, 51, 362
Cook, Edward, 161
Coopers, 56, 164, 165
Coopers Society (New York City), 56
Copley, John Singleton: Adams (Samuel) and,
　311; on clients' view of painters, 35; Hancock
　and, 50, 311; Murray (Elizabeth) and, 105; por-
　traits by, 310–311; Revere and, 29, 56–58, 309
Cordwainers: craft consciousness, 56; Democ-
　ratic Republicans, 71; mechanics parades, 63;
　petition by, 36; restraint of trade, 76; strikes,
　76. *See also* Shoemakers
"Corinna" (pseudonym), 126
Cornplanter, 16
Cornwallis, Charles, 1st Marquis, *216*
Cotton, John, 158
Council of Appointment (New York State), 190
Council of Censors (Pennsylvania), 187
Council of Revision (New York State), 190
Countryman, Edward, 222
Cox, James, 15
Crawford, Thomas, 374–375
Crisis (Paine), 267, 273
"Crispin Heeltap" (pseudonym), 45
Crockett, Davey, 307
Cromwell, Oliver: Adams (John) and, 158, 159,
　161; Adams (Samuel) and, 158, 164; admirers
　of, 158, 363; in *American Chronicle of the
　Times*, 146, 164; as avenging savior, 159, 160,
　162–164; biographies of, 159; Connecticut, 161;
　English folklore, 159–160; evangelism, 159;
　Hutchinson (Thomas) and, 161; Macaulay
　and, 158; Mather and, 161; maypoles, 359; New
　England, 156, 158, 161–162, 164; nineteenth-
　century crusaders, 168; "O. C.," 338; ordinary
　people, 169–170; Otis and, 158; pamphlets
　about, 148, 156; in popular politics, 156–164;
　popularity with leaders of the Revolution,
　146; Puritan line on, 158; Revere and, *157*, 161;
　Sons of Liberty, 163; summoning the ghost of,
　5; Whigs, 158–159; zeal, 159
Cromwell's Head Tavern (Boston), *157*, 161
Crowd action: Bernard (Francis) on, 118;
　Boston, 48, 49, 107, 112, 118, 155; *Boston
　Gazette*, 115; mechanics, 52, 71; New York City,
　48; Philadelphia, 49; public meetings, 185;
　Sons of Liberty, 335–336; tar-and-feathering,

155; types, 118; Whigs, 155–156; Whitfield and, 48; women, 118
Cummings, Ann, 105
Cummings, Betsy, 105, 115–116
Curriers, 36

Dana, Richard Henry, 315
Darley, Felix, 352
Daughters of Liberty: exhortations by, 121; roles played by, 5; Sons of Liberty, 133, 345; spinning, 116; Stamp Act protests, 114
Davidson, Cathy, 239
Davis, David Brion, 215, 227, 237–238
Davis, Jefferson, 375
Dawes, William, 49
Declaration of Independence: Adams (John) and, 10; adoption of, 9; African Americans, 301; *Common Sense,* 272; "convulsions within," 51; Hancock's signature, 9; Indians, 301; journeymen, 77; Old State House, 303; "the people," 7–8; popular support for, 10; promise of, 301; reprints, 79; as sacred text, 18; signing of, 9–10; slavery, 12; women, 301
Declaration of Rights (Pennsylvania), 187
Deerfield (Massachusetts), 347
Defeat (Warren), 129
Deference: Adams (John) and, 132; apprentices, 236; Charleston, 45; class 132, 45; colonial era, 44; decline in, 132; Maryland, 43; master artisans, 76; mechanics, 43–45, 76, 185; Thompson on, 45
Delacroix, Eugene, 375
Delancy family, 44, 188
Delaware: New Castle, 69; Newark, 69; Wilmington, 68
Deming, John, 127
Deming, Sarah, 127
Democracy: accommodation of, 195–202, 208, 232–243; Adams (John) and, 9, 344; Antifederalists, 203–206; *Common Sense,* 186–187, 206–208; conservatives, 185–195, 196; Constitution, 6, 170, 205–208; domestic violence, 194; evangelism, 221; Loyalists, 189; mechanics, 170, 208; Whigs, 191; Wilson (James) and, 196, 197
Democratic Republicans: accommodation, 246–247; Federalists, 371; Fourth of July celebrations, 280; French Revolution, 369; Indians, 243; journeymen, 247; Kentucky, 280; left wing of, 247–248; liberty poles, 370–371; lower trades, 71; manufacturing, 74; Massachusetts, 236; mechanics, 61, 68–74; New York State, 280; newspapers, 69; Paine and, 280; Pennsylvania, 236, 280; Revere and, 72; seaport cities,

68; societies of, 69, 234, 280; South Carolina, 280; strikes by journeymen, 76; Vermont, 280; women, 248
Democratic Societies, 234
Dickinson, John, 270, 354, 358
Dictionary of American Biography (1928-1936), 305
Discourse Concerning Unlimited Submission and Non-Resistance to Higher Powers (Mayhew), 357–358
Ditson, Thomas, 337
Dixwell, John (1607-1689), 161, 162
Dixwell, John (1680-1725), 162
Dock workers, 66
Doctors, 65
Dorchester (Massachusetts), 347
Douglass, Frederick, 374
Dow, Lorenzo, 285
Dowd, David, 241
Down-Renters, 3
Dragging Canoe, 16
Drinker, Elizabeth, 239, 282
Drowne, Shem, 314
Duane, James, 196
Duane, John, 190
Duane, William, 284
Dunmore, John Murray, Earl of, 225, 245
Dyer, Mary, 313

Early American Imprints (Evans), 355
Edes, Benjamin, 331–333
Edwards, Jonathan, 159
Effigies: of Jay, 244; liberty trees, 305, 328; of Oliver (Andrew), 328; Pope's Day, 329; popularity, 367
Ellsworth, Oliver, 200
Ely, Samuel, 15
Emerson, Ralph Waldo, 12
Emmett, Thomas Addis, 265
English plebeian culture, 144–179; amalgamation, 150; artisan culture, 5, 150, 164–167; carryover, 150; choice, 149; degree of retention, 148–149; delayed adoption, 150; eighteenth-century American radicalism, 169; innovation, 150; mechanics parades, 164; ordinary people, 170; parades by English workers, 166–167; popular politics, 149–150, 156–164; popular punishment, 149–156, 167; proof of influence, 149; recovery, 150; retention, 150; revolution and, 170; riding the stang (1675), 144, 150–152; skimmingtons, 150–151; "storing" and "thawing" of, 150; tar-and-feathering, 5, 144–146, 150, 155; Thompson on, 170, 217;

English plebeian culture (*Continued*)
transmission to America, 144, 147–148; usage, 150
Epstein, James, 368
Equalitarianism: French Revolution, 227; Hewes and, 222–223; mechanics, 73; Whitfield and, 110
Essex Gazette (newspaper), 144–146
Evangelism: American Revolution, 220–221; Cromwell and, 159; deism, 284; democracy, 221; mechanics, 40; millennialism, 220–221; orthodox ministers, 40; Paine and, 285; protest, 220
Ewing, George, 360

Farmers: American Revolution, 15; Constitution, 230; divisions among, 230; goal, 218; imprisonment for debt, 226; labor theory of value, 217; liberty poles, 353; liberty trees, 353; Massachusetts, 355; New England, 221; Paine and, 69–70. *See also* Yeoman farmers
Farmers and Mechanics Bank (Philadelphia), 74
Farriers, 166
Federalist Papers (Hamilton, Madison, Jay): bread-and-butter realities, 62; Hamilton and, 208; mechanics, 71–72; No. 10, 194–195
Federalists: accommodation of democratic movement, 234–235, 274, 276; Alien and Sedition Laws, 276; Boston, 62, 72; coercive republicanism, 274, 275, 276; Democratic Republicans, 371; divisions among, 233; foreign policies, 275–276; French Revolution, 275–276, 371; indictments for sedition, 370–371; liberty caps, 325; liberty trees, 325; Livingston (Robert R.) and, 191; Madison and, 275; manufactures, 72; mechanics, 61, 62, 68–69, 71–72; merchants, 72; national coalition, 276; New England, 69; Paine and, 268, 283; populism, 72; *Rights of Man*, 274; titles, 275; Whiskey Rebellion, 276
Fekes, Robert, 56
Fellows, John, 279
Fellowship Society (Charleston), 49, 59
Feltmakers, 166
Findley, William, 16
Firemen, 73
Fischer, David Hackett, 309, 347
Fishermen, 66
Fleet, John, 278
Fleet, Thomas, 278
Foner, Eric, 363
Fourth of July, 280

Fox, Ebenezer, 222, 345–346
Frank, Jacob, 265–267
Franklin, Benjamin: Adams (Samuel) and, 286; artisans, 30, 37–39, 77, 80; autobiography, 77; *Autobiography*, 29–30; as cultural icon, 40; death, 67, 77; direct election of Representatives, 200–202; Fekes and, 56; individualism, 39; as inspiration, 78; inventions, 39; "Leather Apron," 30; maxims, 30, 37–39; mechanics, 53; *Poor Richard's Almanac*, 37, 38, 270; popularity, 199; portrait of, 56, 64; renown, 39; reputation, 29–30; self-portrayal, 35; in "Signing of the Declaration of Independence," 9; stereotypes of, 80; success of, 33; time and money, 42; virtues advocated by, 37–39; Washington and, 362; "Way to Wealth," 39; work ethic, 42
Fraser, Nancy, 240
Frazier, E. Franklin, 148
Freedom Trail (Boston), 296–324; 1995 report, 296–298, 301, 316, 317; add-on history, 308–309; African Americans, 312; bicentennial celebrations, 301; Boston Tea Party, 305; Bostonian Society, 298, 301; celebratory history, 313–315; Council of Sites, 298, 316; dark side of the American Revolution, 313–315; exhibits, 298, 301–302; Freedom Trail Commission, 298; Freedom Trail Foundation, 298, 316; future of, 315–317; Guidebook, 298; Hewes and, 306, 312; large-scale restorations, 298; length, 296; liberty tree, 297, 298, 305; map of, 297; narrative logic, 304; new history of the American Revolution, 300–303; ordinary people, 7; "popular" side of the American Revolution, 303–305; privately-managed sites, 298; proposed two-way vision of the American Revolution, 302–303; public memory, 6–7; relevance, 296; resegregating American history, 311–313; sites along, 296–298; slavery, 313; tourists per year, 304; women, 312–313
Freeman, Elizabeth "Mumbet," 16, 313–314
French Revolution: American enthusiasm for, 227; celebrations of, 369; Democratic Republicans, 369; English republicans, 368; equalitarianism, 227; Federalists, 275–276, 371; liberty caps, 325, 367–368, 371–372; liberty poles, 371–372; liberty trees, 325, 367–368, 371–372; maypoles, 372; millennialism, 227; Paine and, 282; reactions to, 234; Thompson on, 368; women, 246
Freneau, Philip, 16, 267, 355
Frey, Sylvia, 225
Fries, John, 15
Fries's Rebellion (1799), 235

Gabriel (Gabriel Prosser), 230–231, 245
Gadsden, Christopher, 50, 348, 349
Gage, Thomas, 122, 146, 351
Gaine, Hugh, 278
Gallatin, Albert, 74
Gannett, Deborah Sampson, 5, 16
Garrison, William Lloyd, 307, 313
"Genealogy of the Liberty Tree" (Barlow), 372
General Society of Mechanics and Tradesmen of New York: elected office holders, 70; Franklin and, 77; membership certificate, 55, 56, 75–76, 166; motto, 55; Paine and, 280
Genius of America (painting), 374
"Genius of the people," 11, 198
Genovese, Eugene, 149
George III, King of Great Britain and Ireland: bosses compared to, 79; *Common Sense*, 186, 269; éminence grise behind, 328; lands lost by, 221; Stamp Act repeal, 351
Georgia: legislature, 188; Savannah, 53, 59, 61
Gerry, Elbridge: Adams (Samuel) and, 189; Constitutional Convention, 199; direct election of Representatives, 197–198; Shays's Rebellion, 196–197
Gibson, Mel, 17
Gilman, Charlotte Perkins, 375
Gloucester (Massachusetts), 154
Glovers, 104
Goffe, William, 161, 357
Gordon, Linda, 240
Gordon, William, 336
Gorham, Nathaniel, 199, 201
Gorman, John, 167
Grafton (Vermont), 376
Grant, Ulysses S., 375
"Gray Champion" (Hawthorne), 162
Great Barrington (Massachusetts), 347
"Great men," 8–9, 18–19
Green, Ashbel, 271–272
Green, Nat, 36
Green Mountain Boys, 3, 284
Greenleaf, Ann, 371
Greenman, Jeremiah, 16
Grégoire, Henri, 372
Grenville, George, 328, 330
Group (Warren), 129
Gunderson, Joan, 240
Gunmakers, 63
Gutman, Herbert, 148–149, 219

Hadley (Massachusetts), 161, 162
Hakluyt, Richard, 155

Hall, Prince, 16, 66–67
Hamilton, Alexander: British constitution, 183; Constitution, 208; Constitutional Convention proposal, 183–185, 196, 202, 208, 235, 274; domestic violence, 194; economic program, 227; elective monarchy, 183; financial policies, 275; ideal American government, 183–185, 208; Jefferson and, 276; Madison and, 208, 276; manufactures, 72, 74; mechanics, 71–72; Morris (Gouverneur) and, 183, 196, 274, 287; on New Yorkers, 244; political life, 223; Schuyler and, 196; Washington and, 183; Yates (Abraham) on, 11
Hammond, Rezin, 16
Hampden, John, 161
Hancock, John: Adams (John) and, 50, 286, 299; aristocratic paternalism, 9, 344; British plans to seize, 343; Copley and, 50, 311; Freedom Trail, 301; Hewes and, 222–223, 307–308; historical memory, 286, 299; house (mansion), 299, 310; *Liberty* (ship), 118, 336–337; Mackintosh (Ebenezer) and, 344; mechanics, 50, 62; Pope's Day, 50, 334; signature, 9; Stamp Act, 8; wealth, 308
Handsome Lake (Seneca Indian), 242–243
"Hannah Hopeful" (pseudonym), 120–121
Hartford (Connecticut), 355, 358
Hartford Courant (newspaper), 347
Harvard College, 110, 344–345
Hatch, Nathan, 221, 285
Hatters, 33, 56
Hawley, Joseph, 271
Hawthorne, Nathaniel, 161–162, 375
Heimert, Alan, 159
Henry, Patrick, 189, 225, 286
"Henry Flynt" (pseudonym), 126, 127
Heritage trails, 298, 311–312. *See also* Freedom Trail
Herskovits, Melville, 148–149, 164
Hewes, George Robert Twelves: activist artisans, 15; Adams (Samuel) and, 308; Boston Massacre, 5, 222, 306, 307; Boston Tea Party, 5, 222, 306, 307–308; Bostonian Society, 306, debtors' prison, 342–343; equalitarianism, 222–223; Freedom Trail, 306, 312; Hancock and, 222–223, 307–308; importance, 308; Malcolm and, 337; memory of the Revolution, 5; "people out of doors," 308; portrait, 306; sanitizing of, 307; scholarship about, 305–308; tar-and-feathering, 306
Hicks, Willett, 265
Higham, John, 374, 376
Hill, Christopher, 159, 359, 373

Historians: Academic Bill of Rights for Historians, 18; progressive historians, 12–13, 14, 249; public historians, 313; training of, 16–17
Historical memory: Adams (John) and, 286, 299; Adams (Samuel) and, 286, 299; American Revolution, 300; Boston, 299; Hancock and, 286, 299; Paine and, 268, 285–286. *See also* Public memory
History: add-on history, 308–309; African American history, 15; buildings, 303; celebratory history, 313–315; heritage trails, 298, 311–312 (*see also* Freedom Trail); National Standards for History, 15, 17–18, 305; new history of the American Revolution, 300–303; oral history, 162; ordinary people, 305–308; resegregating American history, 311–313; revisions, 19; women's history, 15
History of Massachusetts (Hutchinson), 161
History of the Three Judges of Charles I (Stiles), 162, 168
Hitchborn, Nathaniel, 310
HMS Pinafore (Gilbert and Sullivan), 315
Hobsbawm, Eric: classes in European revolutions, 169; invention of tradition, 149, 300; pre-industrial urban mobs, 111
Hoffman, Roland, 192, 225
Hogarth, William, 152
Holinshed, Raphael, 155
Hollis, Thomas, 36
Hone, William, 359
Hopkinson, Joseph, 355
Housewrights, 73
Howells, William Dean, 314
Huckleberry Finn (Twain), 374
Hudibras series (Hogarth), 152
Hudson (New York State), 59
Hudson Valley landlords: conservative patriots, 190; divisions among, 233; influence, 54; uprisings against, 353
Husband, Herman: agrarian movements, 15; Antifederalism, 224; class divisions, 229; Indians, 242; millennialism, 220–221; rebellions led by, 3; Regulators, 224, 353–354; Whiskey Rebellion, 224
Huske, John, 326
Hutchinson, Anne, 313
Hutchinson, Thomas: *Adulateur,* 129; class divisions among patriots, 333; Cromwell and, 161; crowd control by, 336; Dixwell (John, 1680-1725), 162; Freedom Trail, 301; Harvard College student rebellion, 344–345; *History of Massachusetts,* 161; liberty trees, 365; Mackintosh (Ebenezer) and, 8, 339–340; mansion,

114, 310, 330, 334–335; Morton and, 359; Oliver (Andrew) and, 129, 302, 328, 329; Oliver (Peter) and, 125, 129, 328; satires of, 129; servants and masters, 359

Impressment, 47, 336–337
Indentured servants: drying up of, 230; fondness for freedom, 41, 219; runaways, 41
Indians: accommodation of, 240–243, 248; Adams (John) and, 100; American Revolution, 6, 231, 314; backcountry movements, 241–242; Brant, Joseph, 16; chieftains, 16, 241; claims to sovereignty, 241; Cornplanter, 16; Declaration of Independence, 301; Democratic Republicans, 243; divisions among, 242–243; Dragging Canoe, 16; Handsome Lake, 242–243; imprisonment/internment of, 314; Indian disguises, 367; Iroquois Confederacy, 241, 314; Jefferson and, 236; Jeffersonians, 248; Lenni Lenape, 358; Madison and, 236; Mashpees, 243, 314; Massachusetts, 314; McGillivray, Alexander, 16; military resistance, 242; Mohegans, 314; Neolin, 241; New England, 314; Nimham, Daniel, 16; pan-Indianism, 241; Passamquoddies, 314; peace medal given chieftains, 241; Pennsylvania, 358; Penobscots, 314; Pequots, 314; power, 232; progressive historians, 14; Red Jacket, 16; removal from eastern United States, 243; Revolutionary War, 240; Senecas, 242–243; spiritual revitalization, 241; Tecumseh, 242; Tenskwatawa, 242; Wampanoags, 314; wars against, 242
Institute of Early American History, 17
Invention of tradition, 5, 149
Irish Famine Memorial (Boston), 313
Irish Heritage Trail (Boston), 312
Iroquois Confederacy, 241, 314

Jackson, Andrew, 307
Jackson, William, 115
Jameson, J. Franklin, 12–13, 215
Jay, John: Constitutional Convention, 196; effigies of, 244; New York State constitution, 191; on politicians, 188; swimming with the stream, 190
Jefferson, Thomas: accommodation, 356; Adams (John) and, 205, 276, 279, 286; African Americans, 236; *Age of Reason,* 268; chosen people, 68; Constitution, 205–206, 207; deism, 285; on *Federalist,* 206; Gallatin and, 74; Grégoire and, 372; Hamilton and, 276; Indians, 236; Lafayette and, 205, 275; liberalism of, 205; liberty trees, 356, 365, 371, 377; Louisiana Pur-

chase, 247; Madison and, 194, 202, 205–206, 279, 356; manufacturing, 68, 74–75; mechanics, 68; Monroe and, 248; *Notes on the State of Virginia,* 68, 248; Paine and, 205, 267, 275, 279, 285, 288; political life, 223; popular majorities, 205; presidential election (1796), 276; presidential election (1800), 246–247, 268, 287; rebellion, 356; *Rights of Man,* 279; Saint-Dominique, 248; seaport cities, 68; Sedition Act (1798), 235–236; separation of church and state, 284; Shays's Rebellion, 206, 356; in "Signing of the Declaration of Independence," 9; slave rebellions, 248; Smith (Samuel Harrison) and, 279; Whiskey Rebellion, 235–236; women, 236, 248; yeoman farmers, 29

Jeffersonians: accommodation, 247–248; editors, 287; Indians, 248; Paine and, 268; poverty issue, 287–288. *See also* Democratic Republicans

Jennings, Francis, 241
John, Philip, 220
John Wilkes Club (Charleston), 49, 348
Johnson, Samuel, 34, 73
Johnson, William Samuel, 183
Jones, Absalom, 16
Journeymen: Boston, 33; collective action, 41, 166; Declaration of Independence, 77; decline of, 75; definition, 33; Democratic Republicans, 247; fears experienced by, 218; hazing customs, 42; male patriot movement, 113; master artisans, 29, 33, 35, 41, 236; mechanics, 66; mechanics parades, 63, 65, 68; Paine and, 77; Philadelphia, 33; Pope's Day, 111; property in skill, 46; strikes, 68, 76–77, 166, 236, 247, 287
Joyce, George ("Joyce, Jun."): Boston, 168; Charles I and, 156, 163–164, 337
July Fourth, 280

Kammen, Michael, 373–374
Karsten, Peter, 159, 161, 164
Kentucky, 280
Kenyon, Cecilia, 203
Kerber, Linda: depth of the Revolution, 240; on histories of the American Revolution, 14; radical movements, 231; rebellion in the American Revolution, 301; "Republican Motherhood," 131, 238
Keteltas, William, 71
Kett, Robert: Federalists, 371; London uprising (1450), 340; memory of, 357; as a symbol, 341
Kimber, Isaac, 159
King, Boston, 16

King, Rufus, 203
King Philip's War (1675-1676), 161, 314
Kings County (New York State), 59
Knowles riot (1747), 112
Knox, Henry, 2
Kornblith, Gary, 227, 233
Krimmel, John Lewis, 73–74
Kulikoff, Allan, 230

Labor movement: 1820s and 1830s, 78–79; artisans, 80; market economy, 231; May Day, 376; wage workers' strike (1827), 41
Labor theory of value: farmers, 217; master artisans, 46–47; mechanics, 36; Whigs, 46–47
Laborers: male patriot movement, 113; mechanics parades, 66; poverty, 351; Sons of Liberty, 351; status, 34
Lafayette, Marquis de: Jefferson and, 205, 275; liberty trees, 375; Paine and, 205, 275; parade honoring, 168
Lamb, Bryan, 306
Lansing, John, 196, 199
Lansingburgh (New York State), 59
Laurens, Henry, 348
Lawrence, Abbott, 307
Lawyers, 65
Leacock, John, 355
"Leather Apron Club" (Philadelphia), 44
Leather aprons, 28, 30, 308
Leather trades, 36, 64
Lemisch, Jesse, 219
Lenin, V. I., 376
Lenni Lenape Indians, 358
Lepore, Jill, 314
Lexington, Battle of, 2
Lexington (Massachusetts), 123
Liberty: within America, 300; from Great Britain, 300; impressment, 47; master artisans, 46–47
Liberty caps: an American invention, 327; Federalists, 325; French Revolution, 325, 367–368, 371–372; images of, 357; and liberty poles, 361–363; and liberty trees, 325; public memory, 325; Revere and, 361; slaves, 374–375; Stamp Act protests, 361; as a symbol, 369, 374–375; Uncle Sam, 374; Wilkes and, 361; women, 369–370
"Liberty Hall" (Boston), 331, 339
Liberty Pole (Vermont), 374
Liberty Pole (Wisconsin), 374
Liberty poles, 346–354; absence of, 353–354; African Americans, 348; Alien and Sedition Laws, 370; American invention, 363; Boston,

Liberty poles (*Continued*)
346–349; British army, 366; Charleston, 348; Continental Army, 360; Democratic Republicans, 370–371; in England, 368–369; farmers, 353; flags atop, 330; French Revolution, 371–372; functions/roles, 349, 365; height, 349; and liberty caps, 361–363; and liberty trees, 325, 349, 363; locations, 347, 349, 354, 371, 376; May Day, 363; maypoles, 362, 365; New England, 363; New York City, 347, 349–354, 350, 362, 375; Newport, 347, 349; origins, 362–363; Pennsylvania, 370; phallic interpretation, 371–373; popularity, 367; post-Revolutionary era, 357; public memory, 367; Sons of Liberty, 347, 354, 365; Valley Forge, 360, 365; Whiskey Rebellion, 370

Liberty (ship), 118, 336–337

"Liberty Song" (Dickinson), 354, 358

"The Liberty Tree" (Paine), 354, 365

Liberty trees, 325–394; absence of, 353–354; African Americans, 7, 346, 374; American invention, 327, 363; Boston, 7, 297, 305, 325, 326, 327–338, 346, 363–366, 375; Boston Massacre, 330, 338–339; boys, 345–346; British army, 366; calls to public action, 330, 336; Cambridge (Massachusetts), 344; "Captain General of the Liberty Tree," 8, 338–344; Charleston, 347, 348–349; commemoration of martyrs, 330; *Common Sense*, 366; Connecticut, 347; conservatives, 355; cutting down of, 330; effigies hung from, 305, 328; in England, 368–369; extant trees, 374; farmers, 353; Federalists, 325; first appearance, 8; Freedom Trail (Boston), 297, 298, 305; French Revolution, 325, 367–368, 371–372; functions/roles, 325, 330–331, 349, 363–366; "Genealogy of the Liberty Tree" (Barlow), 372; "Great Elm," 363; Hutchinson (Thomas) and, 365; as icons, 354–356; influence abroad, 366–371; Jefferson and, 356, 365, 371, 377; Lafayette and, 375; liberty caps, 325; "Liberty Hall," 331; liberty poles, 325, 349, 363; "The Liberty Tree," 354; locations, 347, 349, 354, 374; Loyal Nine, 330, 331, 333, 336; Mackintosh (Ebenezer) and, 305; Maryland, 358; Massachusetts, 347, 353; May Day, 359–361, 363; maypoles, 359–361; McVeigh (Timothy) and, 377; New England, 347, 363; Oliver (Andrew) and, 331, 339; Oliver (Peter) and, 331; ordinary people, 338–339; origin, 325, 356–363, 372–373; Pennsylvania, 358; Philadelphia, 353; politicization, 345–346; popularity, 367; public memory, 325, 327, 338, 367, 373–377; public resistance, 7; radicalism of American

Revolution, 327; resistance to British, 339; Revere and, 326, 354; Rhode Island, 347; Sons of Liberty, 7, 305, 335, 337–338, 354, 365; the South, 347; Stamp Act protests, 305, 327–330, 331, 333; surviving trees, 374; as a symbol, 7, 8, 327, 337, 354–356, 357, 363–364, 369; tea tax, 338; trees in Britain, 357–357; veneration of trees, 358–359; Virginia, 353; Whigs, 327; women, 345

Lillie, T., *101*, 119, 362

Lillie-Richardson affair (1770), 118

Lincoln, Hannah, 129

Linebaugh, Peter, 153

Literacy, 70, 147–148

Literary Trail of Greater Boston, 298, 312

Livingston, Edward, 70

Livingston, Robert R.: Clinton (George) and, 191; Constitutional Convention, 196; father-in-law, 196; Federalists, 191; Paine and, 207, 267, 274; Pennsylvania state constitution, 54; Schuyler and, 196; in "Signing of the Declaration of Independence," 9; swimming with the stream, 8–9, 51, 190, 233–234, 235, 274

Livingston family, 44, 188, 191

Locke, John, 46, 341, 354

Lockridge, Kenneth, 147

London Corresponding Society, 369

Longfellow, Henry Wadsworth, 29, 309, 375

Longworthy, John, 144

Louis XVI, King of France, 356, 368

Louisbourg, Nova Scotia, 151

Louisiana Purchase (1803), 247

Loyal Nine (Boston): Adams (Samuel) and, 118; broadside by, 332; liberty tree, 330, 331, 333, 336; Mackintosh (Ebenezer) and, 334; mechanics, 49; membership, 331; patriot movement, 113; Pope's Day, 341

Loyalists: Anglican priests, 109; Boston, 50, 113, 123, 189; Charleston, 50; democracy, 189; divisions among, 233; Maryland, 192; Massachusetts, 189; mechanics, 50–51; mobs, 189; New York City, 50, 349; Philadelphia, 50; slavery, 189; stereotypes of, 189; Virginia, 189

Ludlow, Edmund, 158

Luther, Seth, 79, 307

Lynn (Massachusetts), 79

Lyon, Matthew, 16, 246–247, 287

Lyon, Patrick, *28*, 78

Macaulay, Catherine, 128, 158

Mackintosh, Ebenezer: activist artisans, 15; Adams (John) and, 302, 341; Adams (Samuel) and, 342; Bernard (Francis) and, 339, 340, 342;

British plans to seize, 343; "Captain General of the Liberty Tree," 8, 338–344; children, 342, 343; debtors' prison, 342; fear of, 341–342; Hancock and, 344; Hutchinson (Thomas) and, 8, 339–340; images conjured up by, 340; Liberty Tree, 305; Loyal Nine, 334; marriage, 342; as Masaniello, 117, 302, 340–341; Oliver (Andrew) and, *332*, 340; Oliver (Peter) and, 340, 342; Pope's Day, 8, 117, 302, 331–333; Sons of Liberty, 8, 334, 339, 343, 344; Stamp Act, 8

Mackintosh, Elizabeth, 343

Mackintosh, Paschal, 343

Madison, James: African Americans, 236; cities, 200, 201; direct election of Representatives, 197–198, 200–202; enlargement of the sphere of government, 195, 198; *Federalist* No. 10, 194–195; Federalists, 275; Gallatin and, 74; Hamilton and, 208, 276; Indians, 236; Jefferson and, 194, 202, 205–206, 279, 356; judicial review, 202; legal Shayism, 193; manufacturing, 74; minority rights, 194–195; national veto of state legislation, 195, 198, 202; ordinary people, 11; "the people," 7; political life, 223; "political system," 6, 234; presidential election (1800), 287; *Rights of Man,* 279; Sedition Act, 235–236; separation of church and state, 284; Shays's Rebellion, 235–236; state constitutions, 193; Whiskey Rebellion, 235–236; women, 236

Magna Charta, *326*, 344

Maier, Pauline, 189

Main, Jackson Turner, 188, 191

Maine: Portland, 59, 69; squatters, 236; war against absentee proprietors, 242

Making of the English Working Class (Thompson), 227–228

Malcolm, John, *145,* 156, 169, 337

Manning, William: battle of the Many against the Few, 220, 229, 244; cost of wars against Indians, 242; on labor, 217; national laboring society, 244, 247; opposition to insurrections, 244; as plebeian democrat, 228, 235; radicals, 16; Shays's Rebellion, 244; "To the Republicans, Farmers, Mechanics and Laborers in America," 70

Mantua makers, 104

"Manufacturer," 30

Manufacturers and Mechanics Bank (Boston), 74

Manufactures/manufacturing: American manufactures, 47–48, 58, 247; Association of Tradesmen and Manufacturers, 58; Boston, 107; British manufactures, 47, 55, 58, 62, 226; Democratic Republicans, 74; Federalists, 72;

Hamilton, 72, 74; linen manufacturing, 107; mechanics, 47–48, 55, 58, 62, 226; Monroe and, 74; "Report on Manufactures," 74

Manufacturing Society (Philadelphia), 65

Maritime trades, 58

Martin, Joseph Plumb: on great and little men, 8, 19; *Narrative of the Adventures, Dangers and Sufferings of a Revolutionary Soldier,* 1; Revolutionary War veterans, 16; war memoirs of, 1–3

Martin, Luther, 199

Marx, Karl, 31–32, 75

"Mary Truth" (pseudonym), 120–121

Maryland: Annapolis (*see* Annapolis); Carrollton, 192; class divisions, 225; conservatives, 191–192; deference, 43; distribution of wealth, 191; liberty trees, 358; Loyalists, 192; manumission, 237; state constitutions, 191–192

Masaniello (Tomas Anielo): Bread and Puppet Circus, 376; *Common Sense,* 341; Mackintosh (Ebenezer) and, 117, 302, 340–341; as a symbol, 341

Mashpee Indians, 243, 314

Mason, George: Constitutional Convention, 199; direct election of Representatives, 197–198, 200; "genius of the people," 11

Mason, Susanna, 158

Massachusetts: adultery in, 152; Boston (*see* Boston); Braintree, 102; Cambridge (*see* Cambridge); Deerfield, 347; Democratic Republicans, 236; Dorchester, 347; farmers, 355; Gloucester, 154; Great Barrington, 347; Hadley, 161, 162; Indians, 314; liberty trees, 347, 353; Loyalists, 189; Lynn, 79; Newburyport (*see* Newburyport); pine trees, 358; Plymouth, 347, 349; politics in colonial era, 44; protective tariffs, 58; Quincy, 313; rough music, 359; Salem (*see* Salem); slavery, 312, 313–314; slaves, 220, 222; state constitution, 54, 132, 273; traditional English customs, 359; wife beating in, 152; Worcester, 59, 122, 279

Massachusetts Centinel (newspaper), 134

Massachusetts Historical Society, 299, 310

Massachusetts Mechanics Association (Boston), 27, 59, 309

Massachusetts Provincial Congress (1774), 47–48

Massachusetts Spy (newspaper), 69, 120–121

Master artisans: apprentices, 32–33, 35, 41, 236; Boston, 33, 44; city-to-city communication, 234; collective action, 41; controlling "the rabble," 333; decline of, 75, 76; deference due, 76; electoral politics, 44; journeymen, 29, 33, 35,

Master artisans (*Continued*)
  41, 236; labor theory of value, 46–47; liberty, 46–47; life style, 39; lockouts by, 236; Marx on, 31–32; mechanics parades, 63, 65; merchants, 35; organizations of, 41; petitions by, 41; Philadelphia, 33, 76; property in skill, 46; skills of, 46; slaves, 31; typical master, 32–33. *See also* Artisans; Mechanics
Mather, Cotton: on apprentices and indentured servants, 41, 219; Cromwell and, 161; on a veteran of Cromwell's army, 158
Matlack, Timothy, 50
Matrimonial republicanism, 239
May Day: American labor movement, 376; France, 367–368; liberty poles, 363; liberty trees, 359–361, 363; New York City, 360; Pennsylvania, 360; Philadelphia, 360
Mayhew, Jonathan, 158–159, 357–358
Maypoles: Cromwell and, 359; French Revolution, 372; liberty poles, 362, 365; liberty trees, 359–361; New England, 359
McCloskey, Robert, 196
McDougall, Alexander: jailing of, *350,* 351; privateering, 49–50; urban radicalism, 15
McGillivray, Alexander, 16
McVeigh, Timothy, 377
"Mechanic," 27, 30
Mechanic Society (Charleston), 49, 59, 348
"Mechanick on Taxation" (Brewster), 70
Mechanics, 27–99, 308; Adams (Samuel) and, 49, 62; African Americans, 73; American manufactures, 47–48, 58, 247; American Revolution, 15; 29; Antifederalists, 61; apprentices, 66; artisan republicanism, 29, 68–74, 165; aspirations, 29, 36–40, 47–48; Baltimore, 61, 68, 70; banners, 167, *184;* Boston, 30, 49, 51, 53–54, 58–59, 60, 61, 62–63, 70, 72; British manufactures, 47, 55, 58, 62, 226; British occupation of Boston, 118; certificates of societies, *55,* 56, 59–60, 75–76, 166; Charleston, 45, 49, 50, 51, 53, 61, 348; citizen consciousness, 61–68, 72–73, 165; citywide associations, 58; committees/organizations of, 49, 58–60, 72–73, 165–166; "competency" as goal, 36; condescension toward, 35, 52–53; consciousness of themselves, 29, 55–68, 164; conservative elites, 66; Constitution, 54, 60, 61, 62; Constitutional Convention (1787), 61; craft consciousness, 56–58, 165; crowd action, 52, 71; customs and traditions, 41–43; deference, 43–45, 76, 185; definition, 34; democracy, 208; democratic government, 170; Democratic Republicans, 61, 68–74; depiction by novelists and artists,

73–74; direct class representation, 53, 185; divisions among, 230; drink breaks, 42; elected office holders, 70; entrepreneurial spirit, 75; equalitarianism, 73; erosion of artisan system, 29; evangelism, 40; Federalists, 61, 62, 68–69, 71–72; Franklin and, 53; Gadsden and, 349; Hamilton and, 71–72; Hancock and, 50, 62; horizontal solidarities, 42; humanitarianism, 73; influence within patriot coalition, 51–52; Jefferson and, 68; Johnson (Samuel) on, 34, 73; journeymen, 66; labor theory of value, 36; leaders, 49–50; leather aprons, 308; legacy, 75–80; Loyal Nine, 49; Loyalists, 50–51; merchants, 47, 51, 60, 66, 71, 72, 348; mob action, 244; moral economy, 36; national government, 60; national independence, 60; New England, 43, 72; New York City, 49, 50, 51, 53, 58–60, 61, 68, 70; Paine and, 50, 53; parades, 61–68, 75, 78, 146, 164, 165, 166, 168, 170, 208; Philadelphia, 49, 50, 53, 58, 61, 68, 70; political life, 29, 43–55, 68–75, 232; portraits of, 56; poverty, 37; producer and mechanic interest consciousness, 58–60, 165, 229–230; property rights, 46; reciprocal obligations among, 41; respect, 73–74; Revere and, 27, 30, 49, 62, 80, 309; Revolutionary War (1775-1783), 54–55; Rush and, 50; "Saint Monday," 42; Shays's Rebellion, 60, 230; slogans, 64; Sons of Liberty, 49; Stamp Act protests, 50, 51; state constitutions, 54; symbols of, 166, 308; tariff protection, 74; Tea Act, 46, 51, 218; vacant lands, 75; Washington and, 49, 165; wealth, 36–37, 50; Whitfield and, 53; work week patterns, 42; workplace rituals, 42; writings by, 70; yeoman farmers, 29, 60; Young (Thomas) and, 49, 51. *See also* Apprentices; Artisans; Journeymen; Master artisans; Tradesmen
Mechanics Bank (New York City), 74, 75–76
Mechanics Institute (San Francisco), 78
Mechanics Society (New York City), 59. *See also* General Society of Mechanics and Tradesmen of New York
Melville, Herman, 315
Memory. *See* Historical memory; Public memory
Merchants: artisans, 37; Boston, 113, 115, 121, 123, 310, 333, 362; conservatives, 190; controlling "the rabble," 333; divisions among, 233; Federalists, 72; master artisans, 35; mechanics, 47, 51, 60, 66, 71, 72, 348; mechanics parades, 65; New York City, 351; "she-merchants," 105; war profiteering, 55
Merrell, James, 241

Merrill, Michael, 228
M'Fingal (Trumbull), 154, 355
"Middle class," 229
"Midnight Ride of Paul Revere" (Longfellow), 29
Miller, Perry, 147
Milliners, 104
Minority rights, 194–195
Mintz, Sidney, 149
Mitchell, Samuel L., 70
Modern Chivalry (Brackenridge), 73
Mohegans, 314
Molineaux, William, 117, 128
Monroe, James: Gabriel (Gabriel Prosser) and, 245; Jefferson and, 248; manufacturing, 74; Paine and, 267
Montressor, John, 351
Moral economy: farmers, 221; free trade, 225–226; mechanics, 36; relief as a right, 123; women, 107
Morgan, Edmund S., 147
Morgan, Philip, 225
Morris, Gouverneur: class divisions, 52; Constitution, 195; Constitutional Convention, 196; direct election of Representatives, 200; Hamilton and, 183, 196, 274, 287; mobs, 185, 189, 190, 196; Morrisania, 185; Paine and, 207, 274, 282, 286; Pennsylvania state constitution, 54; property requirements for voting, 200, 202
Morris, Robert, 196, 207, 267
Morton, Thomas, 359
Morton, Walter, 265
Murray, Elizabeth, 105–106, 115–116
Murray, Judith Sargent: articulate women, 16; Boston's trails, 312; new era for women, 246; "On the Inequality of the Sexes," 134; readership, 245; women's independence, 239, 247
Murrin, John, 227, 233
"My Kinsman, Major Molineaux" (Hawthorne), 375

Nailers, 64
Narrative of the Adventures, Dangers and Sufferings of a Revolutionary Soldier (Martin), 1
Nash, Gary B.: class polarities in cities, 148; colonial seaports, 34; female-headed households in Boston, 103–104; Great Awakening in Boston, 110; on histories of the American Revolution, 14; linen manufacturing in Boston, 107; social structure of Boston, 103, 105
National Endowment for the Humanities (NEH), 17–18

National Park Service (NPS): Boston National Historical Park (BNHP), 296, 316; "From Colony to Commonwealth" exhibit, 301; handbook on the Revolution, 306; imprisonment of Wampanoag Indians, 314; interpretations of its sites, 17; tours sponsored by, 304
National Standards for History, 15, 17–18, 305
Native Americans. *See* Indians
Neagle, John: *Pat Lyon at the Forge, 28,* 78
Negotiation. *See* Accommodation
NEH (National Endowment for the Humanities), 17–18
Neolin, 241
New Castle (Delaware), 69
New England: Cromwell and, 156, 158, 161–162, 164; distinctive institutions, 107; farmers, 221; Federalists, 69; Indians, 314; liberty poles, 363; liberty trees, 347, 363; maypoles, 359; mechanics, 43, 72; public executions, 153; Puritans in, 156–158; rescue riots, 153; rough music, 42, 111, 152; skimmingtons, 111, 152–153; Stamp Act protests, 361–362; tar-and-feathering, 146, 149, 154; voting, 43
New England Holocaust Memorial, 313
New Hampshire, Portsmouth in, 59, 61, 154
New Haven (Connecticut): Democratic-Republican societies, 69; liberty trees, 366; mechanics parades, 61; regicides in, 161–162
New history of the American Revolution, 300–303
New Jersey: charivari, 152; liberty pole, 376; Trenton, 61; uprisings against landlords, 353
New York City: *Age of Reason,* 279; Antifederalists, 62; artisan mayor, 70; "Battle of Golden Hill," 351, 352; British occupation, 47, 54, 124, 349; class divisions, 244; crowd action, 48; Democratic-Republican societies, 69; indentured servants, 31; Labor Day parade, first, 79; liberty pole, 347, 349–354, *350,* 362, 375; Loyalists, 50, 349; May Day, 360; mechanics, 49, 50, 51, 53, 58–60, 61, 68, 70; mechanics parades, 63, 64, 65, 67, 168; merchants, 351; persons per household, 105; Pope's Day, 42; population, 31; *Rights of Man,* 278; riots in, 153; seamen, 351; slave owners, 31; slaves, 31, 66; Sons of Liberty, 49, 351, 353–354; Stamp Act, 50; voting, 43
New York Historical Society, 65
New York Journeymen House Carpenters, 77
New York Society of Pewterers, 65
New York State: Albany, 59, 61; Bridgehampton, Long Island, 371; Catskill, 59; class divisions, 225; conservatives, 190–191; Council of Appointment, 190; Council of Revision, 190;

New York State (*Continued*)
Democratic Republican societies, 280; Erie Canal, 67; Hudson Valley landlords (*see* Hudson Valley landlords); Kings County, 59; Lansingburgh, 59; legislature, 188; New York City (*see* New York City); Paine and, 267; politics in colonial era, 44; protective tariffs, 58; Sons of Liberty, 190; state constitution, 54, 190–191, 203
Newark (Delaware), 69
Newburyport (Massachusetts): liberty trees invoked, 355; mechanics societies, 59; tar-and-feathering, 154; Whitfield and, 40, 110
Newport (Rhode Island): Democratic Republicans, 68; gallows, 364; liberty pole, 347, 349; liberty tree, 349; tar-and-feathering, 154
Night Thoughts on Life, Death, and Immortality (Young), 342
Nimham, Daniel, 16
Norfolk (Virginia): Democratic-Republican societies, 69; Democratic Republicans, 68; mechanics societies, 59; tar-and-feathering, 154
North Carolina, Regulators in, 224, 353
North End Caucus (Boston), 49
Northwest Ordinance (1787), 241
Norwalk (Connecticut), 69
Norwich (Connecticut), 347
Notes on the State of Virginia (Jefferson), 68, 248
Novick, Peter, 13
NPS. *See* National Park Service

Old Sturbridge Village, 30, 309
Oliver, Andrew: *Adulateur*, 129; effigy of, 333; Hutchinson (Thomas) and, 129, 302, 328, 329; liberty trees, 331, 339; Mackintosh (Ebenezer) and, 332, 340; office, 329; resignation of commission, 329, 331, 334; Secretary of the Province, 328; Stamp Act, 114, 125
Oliver, Peter: *Adulateur*, 129; on Congregationalist ministers, 109, 125–126; Hutchinson (Thomas) and, 125, 129, 328; liberty trees, 331; Mackintosh (Ebenezer) and, 340, 342; New Englanders as Cromwellians, 164; *Origin and Progress of the American Rebellion*, 125; on tar-and-feathering, 155; on women in Boston, 124–125
Oliver Cromwell's Ghost, or Old Noll Revived (pamphlet), 160
Oliver Cromwell's Ghost Dropt from the Clouds (pamphlet), 160
"On the Inequality of the Sexes" (Murray), 134
Oral history, 162

Ordinary people: American Revolution, 3–12; "common people," 7; *Common Sense*, 272; Cromwell and, 169–170; definition, 7; English plebeian culture, 170; extralegal action, 243; Freedom Trail, 7; genius of, 198; "genius of the people," 11, 198; great men, 8–9; history, 305–308; influence, 9–12; liberty trees, 338–339; Madison and, 11; Martin (Joseph Plumb) on, 19; Mason and, 11; National Standards for History, 305; new history of the American Revolution, 303; "the people," 7–8, 9; Revolutionary War, 226; Sons of Liberty, 4; Wilson (James) and, 11
Origin and Progress of the American Rebellion (Oliver), 125
Osborn, Sarah, 105
Otis, James: *Adulateur*, 129; black regiment, 125; Cromwell and, 158; Freedom Trail, 301; sister, 128–129
Overseers of the Poor (Boston), 106, 108

Paine, Thomas, 265–295; Adams (Abigail Smith) and, 286; Adams (John) and, *283*, 284, 286, 288; Adams (Samuel) and, 284, 285; admirers, 284; "Age of Paine," 288; *Age of Reason* (*see* Age of Reason); *Agrarian Justice*, 77, 287; artisans, 69–70, 206; attacks on, 282–284; Barere and, 356; biography of, 267; Bonneville family and, 265; Cheetham and, 267; Clinton (George) and, 286; co-workers, 267; Committee on Foreign Affairs, 267; *Common Sense* (see *Common Sense*); conservative elites, 268; Constitution, 207, 275; Constitutional Convention, 11; *Crisis*, 267, 273; death, 265; deism, 268, 282–285; Democratic Republicans, 280; eclipse in United States, 268, 282–288; enemies of, 284; in England, 278, 281; evangelism, 285; as exemplar, 371–372; farm, 265, 267; farmers, 69–70; Federalists, 268, *283*; in France, 265, 267, 278, 281, 282, 286, 369; French Revolution, 282; funeral, 265–267; godson, 265; as hero, 282; historical memory, 268, 285–286; indictment for sedition, 281; influence, 7, 288; Jefferson and, 205, 267, 275, 279, 285, 288; Jeffersonians, 268; journeymen, 77; journeymen shoemakers, 287; Lafayette and, 205, 275; "The Liberty Tree," 354, 365; Livingston (Robert R.) and, 207, 267, 274; mechanics, 50, 53; on monarchy, 287; Monroe and, 267; Morris (Gouverneur) and, 207, 274, 282, 286; Morris (Robert) and, 267; nationalism, 235; New Rochelle, 265, 267; New York State, 267;

Pennsylvania, 267; Pennsylvania state constitution, 54, 206, 207; popularity, 11; portrait, 266; poverty issue, 287–288; public memory, 6–7; republicanism of, 288; reputation, 282; *Rights of Man* (see *Rights of Man*); Rivera and, 376; separation of church and state, 284; slavery, 287; Smith (Melancton) and, 204; success of his political ideas, 268, 287–288; taxation, 287; Thompson on, 281; toasts to, 279–280; urban radicals, 15; Warren (Mercy Otis) and, 286; Washington and, 267, 282, 283; Wilkesite political culture, 147; women's rights, 287

Palmer, Bryan, 150, 168
Palmer, Robert R., 268, 287
Passamquoddies, 314
Pat Lyon at the Forge (Neagle), *28, 78*
Patriot (film), 17
Patriotic Junior Association (New York City), 280
Paul Revere Memorial Association, 298, 310
Pavoirs (street-pavers), 166
Paxton Boys Uprising (1763-1764), 241
Peale, Charles Willson, 165
Peck, Jedidiah, 16, 229
Penn, William, 358
Pennsylvania: agrarian rebellion, 369; Council of Censors, 187; Declaration of Rights, 187; Democratic Republican societies, 280; Democratic Republicans, 236; Indians, 358; legislature, 188; liberty poles, 370; liberty trees, 358; May Day, 360; Paine and, 267, 272; Philadelphia (*see* Philadelphia); politics in colonial era, 44; protective tariffs, 58; state constitution, 54, 187–188, 203, 206, 207, 272; Supreme Court, 187; Valley Forge, 360, 365
Pennsylvania Gazette (newspaper), 347
Pennsylvania Magazine, 362
Penobscots, 314
"The people," 7–8, 9. *See also* "Great men"; Ordinary people
"People out of doors": connotation, 5; conservatives, 198; Hewes and, 308; new history of the American Revolution, 300–301; presidential election (1800), 246; radicalism of, 227; Sons of Liberty, 327; state legislatures, 227
"People within doors," 5, 199
Pequots, 314
Peter, Hugh, 158, 164
Peters, Thomas, 16
"Petty bourgeois" as analytical category, 31
Peveril of the Peak (Scott), 161
Pewterers, 56, 65, 166

Philadelphia: Antifederalists, 62; artisans, 33; British occupation, 54, 124; crowd action, 49; Democratic-Republican societies, 69; general strike, 79; indentured servants, 31; journeymen, 33; liberty tree, 353; Loyalists, 50; master artisans, 33, 76; May Day, 360; mechanics, 49, 50, 51, 53, 58, 61, 68, 70; mechanics parades, 63–64, 65, 66, 67–68, 78; militia, 224; persons per household, 105; population, 31; price controls, 224; push for independence, 51; *Rights of Man,* 278; slave owners, 31; slaves, 31, 66; voting, 43; widows, 104
Philadelphia Aurora (newspaper), 284
"Philagius" (pseudonym), 115
Phillips, Wendell, 168, 313
Phyfe, Duncan, 30, 58, 76
Pike, James, *2,* 354, 359
Pitt, William (Pitt the Elder), 330, 351
"Plebeian" (pseudonym), 61
Plymouth (Massachusetts), 347, 349
Politicization, 127–129, 345–346
Pontiac (Ottawa Indian chief), 241
Poor Richard's Almanac (Franklin), 37, *38,* 270
Pope's Day (Guy Fawkes Day in England): apprentices, 111; banning of, 367; Boston, 42, 48, 111, 117, 336, 357; boys, 345; celebrants, 166; companies, 50, 333, 343; Continental Army, 367; effigies, 329; Hancock and, 50, 334; journeymen, 111; Loyal Nine, 341; Mackintosh (Ebenezer) and, 8, 117, 302, 331–333; New York City, 42; patriot movement, 113; seaports, 162; Stamp Act, 48, 113–114; tar-and-feathering, 155; uniforms for companies, 50; Washington and, 367
Port Act (1774), 122
"Portia" (pseudonym), 128
Portland (Maine), 59, 69
Portsmouth (New Hampshire), 59, 61, 154
Potters, 63
Powderhorns, 2
Power of Sympathy (Brown), 73
Prendergast, William, 15
Priestly, Joseph, 285
Prince, Sarah, 109
Printers: craft consciousness, 56; mechanics parades, 63, 64, 165; status, 35
Proctor, Edward, 164
Progressive historians, 12–13, 14, 249
Property rights, 46, 218
Prosser, Gabriel (Gabriel), 230–231, 245
Providence (Rhode Island): Jefferson and, 68; liberty pole, 347; mechanics societies, 59, 60
Public Advertiser (Frank), 265–267

Public memory: American Revolution, 6; Freedom Trail, 6–7; liberty caps, 325; liberty poles, 367; liberty trees, 325, 327, 338, 367, 373–377; Paine and, 6–7; radicalism of American Revolution, 367; Revere and, 77–78. *See also* Historical memory

"Publicola" (pseudonym), 279

Puritans in New England, 156–158

Putnam, Israel, 1

Pym, John, 161

Queen Anne's War (1702-1713), 112

Quincy, Josiah "Wilkes," 158

Quincy (Massachusetts), 313

Radical right, 18

Radicalism of American Revolution, 215–261; abolitionism, 244; accommodation, 232–243; Adams (John) and, 189; African Americans, 230–231; American radicalism, 244–245; American Revolution, 6, 12, 14–15, 169; Boston Brahmins, 375; "bubbling up" of, 231; capitalism, 233; channeling protest into political system, 243–244; Cold War, 327; *Common Sense,* 227; consensus interpretation, 249; customs of common people, 217–221; desperation and disappointment, 226–227; eighteenth century, 169; English plebeian culture, 169; extralegal action, 243; frustration, 231; Henry and, 189; hope, 224, 231; Jeffersonians, 247–248; liberty trees, 327; long gestation, 223–227; multiplicity of, 231, 246; nationalization of the threat of radicalism, 234; negotiation among contending groups, 248–249; origins of, 215–231; "people out of doors," 227, 246; progressive historians, 249; promises not fulfilled, 224–227; propertyless wage earners, 219; public memory, 367; *Rights of Man,* 227, 230; socialism, 245; success of, 246–249; symbols of, 327; as a synthesis of traditional and newer currents, 221–223; *Vindication of the Rights of Women,* 230; Whig rhetoric, 221–223; willful forgetfulness of, 375

Ramsay, David, 3, 188, 226, 271

Randolph, Edmund, 199

Reason the Only Oracle of Man (Young and Allen), 284

Red Jacket, 16

Rediker, Marcus, 219

Reflections on the French Revolution (Burke), 281

Regulators, 224, 353–354

"Report on Manufactures" (Gallatin), 74

"Republican Motherhood," 131, 238

Republicanism: accommodation, 274; Adams (John) and, 274; artisan republicanism, 29, 68–74, 165; coercion, 274; English republicans, 368; independence, 272; kinds of, struggle between, 274; matrimonial republicanism, 239; Paine's, 288; *Rights of Man,* 371

Republicans. *See* Democratic Republicans

Revere, Paul: activist artisans, 15; Boston Massacre, 120, 304; Committee of Tradesmen, 63; Committees of Correspondence, 49; condescension toward, 35; Copley and, 29, 56–58, 309; Cromwell and, *157*, 161; death, 77; Democratic Republicans, 72; dress, 77; house of, 299, 304, 310; liberty caps, 361; liberty trees, *326*, 354; Longfellow legend of, 309; Massachusetts Mechanics Association, 27, 309; mechanics, 27, 30, 49, 62, 80, 309; metallurgy, 39; museums, 30; obelisk, 330, 377; Paul Revere Memorial Association, 298, 310; popularity, 309; portrait, 58; prosperity of, 33; public memory, 77–78; renown, 39; reputation, 29–30; ride, 27, 309; silverware, 311; Sons of Liberty, 49, 309, 361; stereotypes of, 80; surname, 32; textbooks, 308; tradesmen, 27

Revolutionary War (1775-1783): as a civil war, 225; class divisions, 225–226; Continental Army (*see* Continental Army); food riots, 225; Indians, 240; mechanics, 54–55; militias, 224; mutinies, 224; ordinary people, 226; participation in the political process, 188; privateering, 225; veterans' memoirs, 1, 3–4; women, 226. *See also* American Revolution (1775-1815)

Rhode Island: liberty trees, 347; Newport (*see* Newport); Providence (*see* Providence)

Richard I, King of England, 155

Richardson, Ann, 154

Richardson, Ebenezer, 119, 169

Richardson, John, 154

Riding the stang, 144, 150–152

Rights of Man (Paine): and *Age of Reason,* 279; artisans, 69, 73; circulation in England, 368; class divisions, 229; coastal cities, 278; and *Common Sense,* 269, 270, 276, 278, 279, 281; Federalist policies, 274; impact, 279–282; influence, 267; Methodists, 285; monarchy, 276–277, 287; Part I, 278, 281; Part II, 278, 281, 287; pensions for veterans, 277; in portrait of Paine, *266*; poverty, 277; price, 278, 281; principles of, 287; printings, 278; promise of, 247–248; radicalism of the American Revolution, 227, 230; reaction to, 268; readership, 278; reception in America, 273–282; reception

in Britain, 281; republicanism, 371; sales, 278; taxation, 277; title page, 273; titles, 276; toasts to, 279–280; writing style/tone, 274
Rivera, Diego, 376
Robin Hood, 357
Rockwell, Norman, 314
Rogers, Nicholas, 167
Romney, George, *266*
Roosevelt, Theodore, 376
Ropemakers, 165
Rossiter, Clinton, 199
Rough music: definition, 42, 150; enforcement of sexual morality, 167; Massachusetts, 359; New England, 42, 111, 152; skimmingtons, 111; tar-and-feathering, 48; Thompson and, 150, 329; women, 111
Rowe, John, 154, 343
Roxbury (Massachusetts), 347
Runaways: apprentices, 41; indentured servants, 41; slavery, 245; slaves, 11, 41, 225, 237, 313, 353
Rush, Benjamin: *Common Sense,* 267; mechanics, 50; on mechanics parades, 66; women's issues, 248
Russian Revolution, 13

Saddlers, 63
Sailmakers, 56
Sailors: accommodation of, 348; customs, 42; male patriot movement, 113; New York City, 351; panhandling by, 348; poverty, 351; Sons of Liberty, 351; status, 34
Saint-Dominique, 245, 248
"Saint Monday," 42
Salem (Massachusetts): mechanics, 59, 70; Saint Catherine's day celebrations, 42; tar-and-feathering, 144–145, 150, 154, 155
"Sarah Faithful" (pseudonym), 120–121
Savannah (Georgia), 53, 59, 61
Schama, Simon, 358, 373
Schlesinger, Arthur, Sr., 347
Schuykill Fishing Club, 360
Schuyler, Philip, 190, 191, 196
Schuyler family, 188
Scott, Walter, 161
Sears, Isaac, 15, 49–50
Sedition Act (1798), 70, 235–236, 247
Seider, Christopher: broadsides about, 133; killing of, *101*, 119–120, 169, 313, 330, 345
Seneca Indians, 242–243
Servants, 66
Sewall, Samuel, 151, 152
Sharp, William, *266*

Shattuck, Job, *193*
Shaw, Robert, 313
Shayism, 193, 226–227, 234
Shays, Daniel: Adams (Samuel) and, 303; agrarian movements, 15; Constitutional Convention, 11; depiction of, *193*; Freedom Trail, 302–303; green boughs, 355; rebellion in western Massachusetts, 3
Shays's Rebellion (1786-1787): conservatives, 193; free blacks, 231; Gerry and, 196–197; Jefferson and, 206, 356; leaders, *193*; Madison and, 235–236; Manning and, 244; mechanics, 60, 230; rescue riots, 153; Rivera and, 376
Sherburne, Andrew, 16
Sherman, Roger, 9
Ship joiners, 64
Shipbuilders, 164
Shipwrights, 56, 165
Shirley, William, 168
Shoemakers: dependencies, 35; mechanics parades, 64, 164; motto about, 53; patron saint, 42, 167; social mobility, 34, 35; status, 53; strikes, 76, 247. *See also* Cordwainers
"Shopkeeper," 30
Shopkeepers, 113
Shy, John, 224–225
Siege of Boston (1775-1776), 112–113, 123–124, 161
"Signing of the Declaration of Independence" (Trumbull), 9–10
Simpson, Samuel, 15
Singletary, Amos, 203, 229
Skimmingtons: Adams (John) on, 151, 152; adulterers, 151–152; English plebeian culture, 150–151; New England, 111, 152–153; widespread usage, 168; wife beating, 151–152. *See also* Rough music
Slauter, Eric, 355
Slavery: American Revolution, 15, 17, 237–238; anti-slavery movement, 232; black rebellions/revolutionaries, 234, 245, 248; Constitution, 67; continuance, 238; Declaration of Independence, 12; expansion of, 231; Freedom Trail, 313; Loyalists, 189; Massachusetts, 312, 313–314; the North, 237; Paine and, 287; racism, 238; retentions/survivals from African culture, 219; runaways, 245; Sons of Liberty, 219; Whigs, 238
Slaves: accommodation of, 237–238; Baptist religion, 149; Boston, 31, 66; British appeal to, 12; British army, 225; Charleston, 31, 66, 374; Colonial Williamsburg, 315; everyday resistance, 245; legal suits brought by, 313–314; liberty caps, 374–375; love of freedom, 219;

manumission, 220, 237; Massachusetts, 220, 222; master artisans, 31; negotiations with masters, 237; New York City, 31, 66; petition for freedom, 222; Philadelphia, 31, 66; power, 232; rebellions/revolutions, 234, 245, 248; runaways, 11, 41, 225, 237, 313, 353; "space" for themselves, 237

Smith, Alan, 159, 160

Smith, Barbara Clark, 298

Smith, Billy, 34

Smith, J. Allen, 203

Smith, Melancton: Antifederalists, 61; class divisions, 229; origins, 16; "Plebeian," 61; on representation, 204–205

Smith, Samuel Harrison, 279

Social class. *See* Class

Social mobility, 33–34, 218–219

Society of Cincinnati, 287

Society of Master Sailmakers of the City of New York, 56, *57*

Society of Pewterers (New York City), *184*

Solemn League and Covenant (Boston, 1774), 121–122, 133

Solemn League and Covenant (England, 1643), 122

Sons of Liberty: Adams (Samuel) and, 189; Barre and, 333; Boston, 48, 51, 128; boys, 345; Brackett and, 161; Cromwell and, 163; crowd action, 335–336; Daughters of Liberty, 133, 345; female admirers, *350*; Gadsden and, 348; leaders, 185; liberty poles, 347, 354, 365; liberty trees, 7, 305, 335, 337–338, 354, 365; Macaulay and, 128; Mackintosh (Ebenezer) and, 8, 334, 339, 343, 344; mechanics, 49; name, 333; New York City, 49, 351, 353–354; New York State, 190; ordinary people, 4; "people out of doors," 327; Revere and, 49, 309, 361; slavery, 219; slogan, 48; South End company, 339; tea tax, 338

Sons of Neptune, 351

Sons of Saint Tammany, 69, 360

"Sorts," 31

South, the, liberty trees in, 347

South Carolina: Charleston (*see* Charleston); Democratic Republican societies, 280; state constitution, 54

Spence, Thomas, 369

Spirit of '76 (Willard), 79

"Squibo" (pseudonym), 126, 127

Stamp Act (1765): Adams (John) and, 8; Adams (Samuel) and, 8; Boston, 8, 48, 50, 113–114; Charleston, 348; Commissioner, 114, 125; fame, 112–113; Hancock and, 8; implementers of, 46; liberty caps, 361; liberty trees, 305, 327–330, 331, 333; Mackintosh (Ebenezer) and, 8; Magna Charta, *326*; mechanics, 50, 51; mock trial of, 345; New York City, 351; nullification of, 340; Oliver (Andrew) and, 114, 125; Pope's Day, 48, 113–114; repeal, 330, 336, 349, 351; resistance to/protests against, 8, 48, 50, 51, 113–114, 305, 327–330, 331, 333, 348, 351, 361–362; widows, 114

Stanton, Elizabeth Cady, 130

State constitutions: *Common Sense*, 187; Madison on, 193; Maryland, 191–192; Massachusetts, 54, 132, 273; New York State, 54, 190–191, 203; Pennsylvania, 54, 187–188, 203, 206, 207, 272; South Carolina, 54

Steuben, Baron von, 224

Stewart, Steven, 150

Stiles, Ezra, 162, 168

Stonington (Connecticut), 285

Stout, Harry, 158

Street pavers (pavoirs), 166

Street peddlers, 66

Students, 65

Succession Crisis, 160

Sullivan, James, 248

Supreme Court (Pennsylvania), 187

Swift, Henry, 333

Sylvester, Richard, 163

Syncretism, 148

Tailors: mechanics parades, 165; social mobility, 33; status, 34, 35

Tallow chandlers, 64, 71

Tammany: King Tammany's day, 42; Sons of Saint Tammany, 69, 360; Tammany Society (New York City), 280

Tanners, 36

Tar-and-feathering: Adams (John) and, 156; as an American invention, 156; Boston, 118, 154, 155–156, 343, 375; Boston Tea Party, *145*; Committee for Tar-and-Feathering, 156; crowd action, 155; customs informers, 118; enforcement of sexual morality, 167; English plebeian culture, 5, 144–146, 150, 155; first of the revolutionary era, 146, 149; Hewes and, 306; informers, 343; of Malcolm, *145*; "My Kinsman, Major Molineaux" (Hawthorne), 375; New England, 146, 149, 154; official punishment, 153, 154; Pope's Day, 155; popularity, 367; rough music, 48; Salem, 144–145, 150, 154, 155; seaports, 154; Whiskey Rebellion, 168; women, 118, 126

Tariffs, 58, 74, 207

Taylor, Alan, 220, 221
Tea Act (1773): defiance of, 122; mechanics, 46, 51, 218; oppressiveness, 218; tension over, 343
Teachers, 65
Tecumseh, 242
Television, 17
Tenskwatawa, 242
Textbooks, 17
Thomas, Isaiah: *Age of Reason,* 279; *Massachusetts Spy,* 69; *Rights of Man,* 278; Seider killing, 120
Thompson, E. P. (Edward): "agency of working people," 14; class, 227–228; culture formation, 149; on deference, 45; English plebeian culture, 170, 217; evangelicals and Paine, 285; French Revolution, 368; Paine and, 281; *Rights of Man,* 281; rough music, 150, 329; work week patterns, 42
Thoreau, Henry, 222
Thoughts on Government (Adams; book format), 186
"Thoughts on Government" (Adams; manuscript), 272–273
Tilly, Charles, 149
Tinmen, 33
"To the Republicans, Farmers, Mechanics and Laborers in America" (Manning), 70
Toussaint L'Ouverture, 374
Towner, Lawrence W., 153
Trades Union (Boston), 79
"Tradesman," 30
Tradesmen: Association of Tradesmen and Manufacturers, 58; branches of, 32; Committee of Tradesmen, 63; "competency," 36; definition, 30; leather trades, 36; luxury tradesmen, 35; maritime trades, 58; "respectable" tradesmen, 39; Revere and, 27; skilled trades, 66; social status, 34–35; "substantial" *vs.* "inferior," 33–34, 39–40. *See also* Artisans; General Society of Mechanics and Tradesmen of New York; Mechanics
Tree of Liberty. *See* Liberty trees
Tree of Liberty (newspaper), 370
Trenton (New Jersey), 61
"True Assistant Society" (New York City), 56
"True Confessions and Dying Warning" (pamphlets), 153
Trumbull, John: depiction of Bunker Hill battle, 315; *M'Fingal,* 154, 355; "Signing of the Declaration of Independence," 9–10
Tucker, St. George, 245
Twain, Mark, 374
Two Years before the Mast (Dana), 315

Tyburn (London, England), 153
Tyler, Wat, 340, 341

Ulrich, Laurel Thatcher, 116–117, 239
Upholsterers, 64, 165
Urban laborers, 42–43
Urban mobs, 111
Urban population, 31
Urban poverty, 37
Urban radicals, 15

Valley Forge (Pennsylvania), 360, 365
Van Rensselaer family, 188
Vermont: Democratic Republican societies, 280; Grafton, 376; legislature, 188; Liberty Pole, 374
Vietnam War, 13–14
Vindication of the Rights of Women (Wollstonecraft): artisans, 73; radicalism of the American Revolution, 230; readership, 239, 282
Virginia: class divisions, 225; liberty trees, 353; Loyalists, 189; manumission, 237; Norfolk (*see* Norfolk); *Notes on the State of Virginia,* 68, 248; Williamsburg (*see* Colonial Williamsburg)
Virginia Gazette (newspaper), 347
Voyages (Hakluyt), 155

Wampanoag Indians, 314
Warner, George James, 15, 72
Warren, James, 129
Warren, John, 355
Warren, Joseph, 355
Warren, Mercy Otis: Adams (Abigail Smith) and, 100, 131; articulate women, 16; Boston's trails, 312–313; correspondents, 129; female patriotism, 128–129; Paine and, 286; patriotic writings, 100–101; writings, 129
Warren, Peter, 219
Warville, Brissot de, 271
Washington, George: Adams (John) and, 275; Adams (Samuel) and, 286; African Americans, 245; Boston, 166; cherry tree, 374; combustibles in states, 193; *Common Sense,* 270–271; Constitutional Convention, 199; death, 67; fame, 1; Franklin and, 362; Hamilton and, 183; Iroquois, 241; mechanics, 49, 165; National Standards for History, 18; Paine and, 267, 282, *283*; political life, 223; Pope's Day celebrations, 367; popularity, 199; runaway slaves, 11; soldiers' dress, 355; as symbol of nationalism, 286–287; title for, 275

"Way to Wealth" (Franklin), 39

Wayne, Anthony, 1

Weavers, 33

Weber, John, 50

Webster, Noah, 73, 234

Weems, Parson (Mason Locke Weems), 286, 374

Wells, Charles, 70

Wendover, Peter Hercules, 70

Whalley, Edward, 161, 357

Wheatley, Phillis: articulate women, 16; Boston's trails, 312; love of freedom, 219; textbooks, 308; Whitfield and, 40

Wheelwrights, 33, 63, 166

Whigs: Cromwell and, 158–159; crowd action, 155–156; democracy, 191; divisions among, 233; labor theory of value, 46–47; liberty trees, 327; presidential election (1840), 307; private property, 238; radicalism of American Revolution, 221–223; slavery, 238; slogan, 46

Whiskey Rebellion (1794): extent of, 234; Federalists, 276; Husband and, 224; Indians, 241; liberty poles, 370; military force, 235; name, 370; responsibility for, 236; tar-and-feathering, 168

White, Richard, 242

Whitfield, George: Boston, 40, 110, 133; crowd action, 48; as cultural icon, 40; death, 40, 110; equalitarianism, 110; eulogies for, 40; mechanics, 53; tours of the colonies, 40, 147; Wheatley and, 40; women, 110; zeal, 159

Whitman, Walt, 12

Widger, William, 16

Wilentz, Sean, 168, 228

Wilkes, John: clubs honoring, 49; depiction, 350; jailing of, 351; liberty caps, 361; lights honoring, 330; Paine and, 147

Wilkinson, Jemima, 16

Willard, Archibald, 79

Willard, Daniel, 36–37

William III, King of Great Britain and Ireland, 361

William the Conqueror, 269

Williams, William A., 233

Williamsburg (Virginia). *See* Colonial Williamsburg

Wilmington (Delaware), 68

Wilson, James: Constitution, 195; Constitutional Convention, 196, 202; democracy, 196, 197; direct election of Representatives, 197–198, 201; ordinary people, 11

Wilson, Susan, 298

Winslow, Anna Green, 127–128, 313

Winthrop, Hannah, 129

Winthrop, John, Jr., 164

Wollstonecraft, Mary: Boston's trails, 312–313; readership, 245; women factory workers, 79. See also *Vindication of the Rights of Women*

Women, 100–143; accommodation of, 238–240, 348; Adams (Abigail Smith) and, 100–102; Adams (John) and, 100, 240, 248; American Revolution, 6; bees, 116–117; Bible reading, 109; bookstores, 108; Boston, 100–143; Boston Massacre, 345; Boston Tea Party, 120–121; as boycotters, 115–116; British occupation, 118–119; churches, 107, 108–110; collective action, 246; in Continental Army, 5; crowd action, 118; "dame" schools, 108; Declaration of Independence, 301; Democratic Republicans, 248; divisions among, 245–246; domestic sphere, 112; education, 108, 131, 134; as exhorters of men to patriotism, 112, 120–121, 133; female pride, 126–127; Freedom Trail, 312–313; French Revolution, 246; goal, 239–240; holiday rituals, 110; impact of, 124–125; independence, 107, 239–240, 247; inequality, 100–102, 130–131; informal networks, 109; Jefferson and, 236, 248; legal protections, 152–153; liberty caps, 369–370; liberty trees, 345; literate young women, 238–239; Madison and, 236; male networks, 108; male roles, 226; as manufacturers, 116–117; matrimonial republicanism, 239; mechanics parades, 66; as military supporters, 122–123; moral economy, 107; as mourners, 119–120, 125; new era for, 246; occupations, 104–105, 124; optimism, 132; Paine and, 287; participation in patriotic activities, 126–127; patriotism, 128–129, 132–134; political will, 122; politicization, 127–129; post-Revolutionary War decade, 134; power, 232; prenuptial agreements, 105; public punishment, rituals of, 111; rebellion among, 100, 102, 130; as refugees, 123–124; "Republican Motherhood," 131, 238; Revolutionary War, 226; as rioters, 117–119; rituals of the life cycle, 107; roles, 107, 113, 122, 132–133; rough music, 111; as shamers of cowardly soldiers, 112; "she-merchants," 105; skilled trades, 66; as spectators, 113–114; spinning, 116–117, 125–126, 128, 133; Stamp Act protests, 114; subordination of, 231; tar-and-feathering, 118, 126; titles for, 131; tyranny of husbands, 134; Whitfield and, 110; widows, 103–104, 105, 114, 124; wife beating, 151–152; Women's

Heritage Trail, 298; women's rights movement, 232
Women's Heritage Trail (Boston), 298, 312
Women's history, 15
Wood, Gordon: assessments of the American Revolution, 231–232; plebeian *vs.* patrician America, 228; radicalism of "people out of doors," 227; vices of state governments, 194
Wood, Peter, 220
Woolen drapers, 35
Woolman, John, 16
Worcester (Massachusetts), 59, 122, 279
"Working class," 229
Wortman, Tunis, 16

Yates, Abraham: Antifederalism, 205; on Hamilton, 11; origins, 15–16; popular movements, 11; pseudonym, 229
Yates, Robert, 196, 199
Yeoman farmers: American Revolution, 6; Antifederalists, 61; as a class, 228; fears experienced by, 217–218; Jefferson and, 29; mechanics, 29, 60; political life, 232. *See also* Farmers
Young, Edward, 342
Young, Thomas: Adams (Samuel) and, 117; Allen (Ethan) and, 284; mechanics, 49, 51; *Reason the Only Oracle of Man,* 284; urban radicals, 15
"Young American" (pseudonym), 126–127

About the Author

A historian of the American Revolution for more than forty years, Alfred F. Young is the author of, most recently, *The Shoemaker and the Tea Party* (1999) and *Masquerade: The Life and Times of Deborah Samson, Continental Soldier* (2004). He is also the author of *The Democratic Republicans of New York, 1763–1797*, winner of the Jamestown Award, and the editor of *The American Revolution: Explorations in the History of American Radicalism* (1976) and its sequel, *Beyond the American Revolution* (1993). He is coauthor of *We the People: Voices and Images of the New Nation* (1993), based on an exhibit at the Chicago Historical Society for which he was cocurator. He has received Guggenheim and NEH fellowships and was recognized in 2004 by the Organization of American Historians for Distinguished Service to the Historical Profession. He is Emeritus Professor of History at Northern Illinois University and, since 1990, Senior Research Fellow at the Newberry Library in Chicago.